Douglas Hyde:
A Maker of Modern Ireland

Douglas Hyde by John Butler Yeats, painted ca. 1903.
(Courtesy the National Gallery of Ireland)

Douglas Hyde

A Maker of Modern Ireland

Janet Egleson Dunleavy
&
Gareth W. Dunleavy

UNIVERSITY OF CALIFORNIA PRESS

Berkeley / Los Angeles / Oxford

University of California Press
Berkeley and Los Angeles, California

University of California Press
Oxford, England

Copyright © 1991 by The Regents of the University of California

Printed in the United States of America

1 2 3 4 5 6 7 8 9

Library of Congress Cataloging-in-Publication Data
Dunleavy, Janet Egleson.
   Douglas Hyde: a maker of modern Ireland / J. E. Dunleavy and
G. W. Dunleavy.
      p.   cm.
   Includes bibliographical references and index.
   ISBN 0–520–06684–7 (alk. paper)
   1. Hyde, Douglas, 1860–1949. 2. Presidents—Ireland—
Biography. 3. Nationalists—Ireland—Biography. 4. Scholars—
Ireland—Biography. 5. Ireland—History—20th century.
I. Dunleavy, Gareth W. II. Title.
DA965.H9D88 1991
941.5082′2′092—dc20
[B]   90–40120
                                                                 CIP

For Henry J. Dunleavy
In Memoriam

Contents

Acknowledgments

For assistance with this study of the public and private life of Douglas Hyde, we are indebted first of all to Sean O'Luing, biographer, translator, poet, and friend, who one August day in 1978 stopped us on the steps of the National Library of Ireland and urged that we undertake this task. The following day, on these same steps, he placed in our hands two shopping bags full of Hyde materials—letters, interviews, cuttings, manuscripts, notes—that he had patiently gathered over the years. At every turn, this book bears witness to his invaluable gift and continuing encouragement and advice.

To the executors of the Douglas Hyde estate, to his late daughter, Una Hyde Sealy, and to all his living heirs, we owe a special debt, not only for their generosity in providing access to family holdings, answering hundreds of inquiries, and permitting us to quote from Hyde materials, but also for their friendship.

We are deeply grateful for the support we have had from the American Council of Learned Societies, American Irish Foundation, American Philosophical Society, Camargo Foundation, John Simon Guggenheim Foundation, and College of Letters and Science and Graduate School of the University of Wisconsin—Milwaukee which has made our work possible. We wish also to thank Bernard Benstock, Shari Benstock, John Halperin, Eric Hamp, Fred Harvey Harrington, Ann Saddlemyer, David H. Greene, Alf MacLochlainn, T. Kevin Mallen, William Roselle, and William V. Shannon, whose confidence, expressed at critical junctures in this project, guaranteed its completion.

We sincerely appreciate the help we have received from scholars, archivists, and others in England, Ireland, Canada, and the United States whose special knowledge of or access to much-needed information was often crucial to us. Among those who patiently answered our many questions on aspects of written and spoken Irish and Hiberno-English, on the nuances of Irish culture, and on lesser-known facts of local and national Irish history were Bo Almquist, Dan Binchy, Richard J. Byrne, James Carney, Tomás de Bhaldraithe, Pádraig de Brun, Bernard Finan, Dorothy Fox, David Greene, Thomas Hachey, Maura Harmon, Maurice Harmon, Patrick Henchy, Michael Hewson, Richard M. Kain, Mary Lavin, James Liddy, Gerard Long, John Lyons, M.D., Eoin MacKiernan, Fionnuala MacLochlainn, Deirdre McMahon, Maureen Murphy, Breandán Ó Conaire, Tomás Ó Concannon, Betty O'Connell, Maurice O'Connell, Daithi Ó hÓgain, D.S.O Luanaigh, Tomás Ó Maille, Nessa ní Sheaghdha, T. P. O'Neill, Brid O'Siadhail, Micheal O'Siadhail, Bruce Rosenberg, Michael MacDonald Scott, Colin Smythe, and Christopher Townely.

Our thanks are due also to those who facilitated our research in special subjects and assisted us in other areas of professional expertise, especially Jeanne Aber, Lance J. Bauer, Alan M. Cohn, Pierre Deflaux, John P. Ferré, James Ford, Patrick Ford, Howard Gotlieb, Herbert Kenny, Helen Landreth, Judith Livingston, Ciaran McGonigle, William Moritz, Catherine Murphy, Michael Pretina, Henry Siaud, Lola Szladits, Raymond Teichman, Alan Ward, and Russell Young.

From 1978 to 1989, as we steadily expanded the combined collection of notes and documents presented to us by Sean O'Luing and previously accumulated by us in connection with earlier projects, we were fortunate to have the help of scores of men and women acquainted with Hyde himself, his life and times, and his achievements. Among those who shared with us their personal recollections, correspondence, and memorabilia were Colonel Thomas Manning and Colonel Eamon de Buitléar, aides-de-camp to Douglas Hyde, and their families; Desmond McDunphy, Eileen Monahan, and Brenda Warran-Smith, whose father, Michael McDunphy, held the office of secretary to the president during and after Hyde's presidential term; Erskine Childers, former president of Ireland; members of the family of the O'Conors of Clonalis, especially the Reverend Charles O'Conor Don, S.J., Josephine O'Conor, Eva Staunton, Captain Maurice Staunton, Gertrude Nash, and Group Captain Rupert Nash; The Macdermot, Madame Macdermot, and other members of the family of the Macdermots of Coolavin; Thomas

Kilgallen, M.D., of Boyle, physician to Lucy Hyde; members of Hyde's household staff at Ratra, including Carrie and Tom Mahon, Annie Mahon, and Peter Morrisroe; Bob Connolly, sexton, Church of Portahard; Hyde's American friend Ben Greenwald; and a number of Hyde's former students, including Dan Bryan, Eileen Gannon, Christine Keating, and Liam MacMeanman. President Erskine Childers showed us through the state rooms of Áras an Uachtaráin and described their appearance when Hyde was in residence; President Patrick Hillery authorized a second visit that enabled us to recheck specific details; Ambassador William V. Shannon and his wife, Elizabeth Shannon, answered our questions about the presidency, American-Irish relations, and the history of the official residences in Phoenix Park.

In north Roscommon and Sligo we talked extensively with men and women whose local memories of people, places, and events were significant to the life of Douglas Hyde. Kate Martin and the late Bertie MacMaster of Kilmactranny shared with us facts about Hyde's birthplace and local recollections of members of the family of the Reverend Arthur Hyde, Jr., who once made their home there. Pa Burke, for many years the oldest living resident of Castlerea, recalled for us his first Irish lessons in the early days of the Gaelic League. Michael Cooney reminisced about the Frenchpark in which he had lived as a boy at the turn of the century. Tommy and Mary Bruen, Kevin and Margaret Dockery, and Mick and Peggy Ward shared their knowledge of the oral tradition of north Roscommon as it pertained to local families and to local geography, including place-names. The Reverend Robert Holtby and Mrs. Maud Holtby searched Church of Ireland records for both Kilkeevan and Portahard for details concerning dates and events. And dozens of other current and former residents of Roscommon, Sligo, Leitrim, Galway, and Mayo whom we met informally in the course of our research— in shops, in pubs, walking along country roads—contributed family memories, anecdotes, tales of local interest, and little-known facts of local history to our store.

Among private collectors of Hyde's books and papers, we are indebted to the late Captain Tadgh MacGlinchey, Ciaran MacGlinchey, Aidan Heavey, the Trustees of the O'Conor Papers at Clonalis House, and others who prefer to remain anonymous. Hyde figured largely of course in other private collections as well. Maeve Morris gave us copies of Hyde items in the Henry Morris Papers. Francis Barrett supplied information about the Trinity College Historical Society. C. Joseph Neusse, Provost Emeritus, Catholic University, contributed information concerning Hyde's visits to Washington, D.C. Geraldine Willis searched the archives of the Representative Church Body. William Flynn, Beverly Goldner, Desmond MacNamara, Frank Martin, and John Woolsey tapped other sources, including their own experiences and memories, to provide a range of perspectives on Hyde himself, his life and times, and his family background. Among representatives of the media in Ireland and Irish booksellers who frequently extended themselves on our behalf, we thank particularly Andrew Hamilton, Caroline Walsh, and Conor Brady of the *Irish Times*; the late Micheal O'Callaghan of the *Roscommon Herald*; Padraig O'Reilly and James Fahy of Radio Teilifís Éireann; and the Kenny family of Kenny's Book Shop in Galway.

For permission to consult holdings and for assistance in using research materials and facilities we are indebted to administrators and staff members of the following libraries and archives:

In the United States: the Boston Public Library; Bapst Library of Boston College; Mugar Library of Boston University; Franklin D. Roosevelt Memorial Library; Houghton Library of Harvard University; Milwaukee Public Library; National Archives of the United States; Berg Collection and Special Collections of the New York Public Library; Providence (Rhode Island) Public Library; Morris Library of Southern Illinois University; McFarlin Library of the University of Tulsa; University of Wisconsin—Madison library; and Golda Meir Library of the University of Wisconsin—Milwaukee.

In Canada: the Harriet Irving Library of the University of New Brunswick.

In France: the University of Haut-Bretagne at Rennes and the regional libraries of Aix-en-Provence, Avignon, Cassis, and Marseilles.

In England: the British Museum Library, Public Records Office, and Postal Archives.

In Ireland: the National Library of Ireland; the libraries of the Royal Irish Academy and the Dublin Institute for Advanced Studies; the University College, Dublin, library; the Trinity College, Dublin, library; and the University College, Galway, library; the Archives of the Trinity College, Dublin, College Historical Society and the Department of Folklore, University College, Dublin; the State Papers Office; and the Public Record Office.

In Ireland we profited also from the generous assistance of Peter Beirne of the Kilrush branch of the County Clare Library, Helen Maher and Helen Kilcline of the Roscommon County Library, Nora Niland of the Sligo County Library and Museum, and the staff of the Sweeney Memorial Library in Kilkee.

In developing our composite portrait of Douglas Hyde we have depended primarily on Hyde's own diaries, letters, mementos, manuscript drafts, and memorabilia and the oral and written testimony of his family, friends, associates, acquaintances, and their heirs. Among the published sources we have consulted for confirmation of dates, facts, and events, for other images of both the private and the public man, and for background, historical context, and multiple perspectives, none has been more useful than Dominic Daly's *The Young Douglas Hyde* (1974). We recognize that even in our occasional differences we owe much to Daly's pioneer effort; we deeply regret that his untimely death cut short our conversations on subjects of mutual interest in the early stages of our work. Many others named above—including those personally acquainted with Hyde—also have died in the years since 1978. We mourn their passing and regret that they are not alive to see the fruits of their contributions, but we feel privileged to be able to preserve here their memories, observations, and opinions.

In the penultimate stages of our work, Sal Healy of Dublin, Priscilla Diaz-Dorr of Tulsa, and Margaret Kendellan of Milwaukee provided cheerful and thoughtful research assistance. Francey Oscherwitz's queries encouraged sensible revisions.

Finally—for his wisdom, patience, and understanding without which we might never have reached this point—we are deeply indebted to our editor, Scott Mahler.

April 1990   Janet Egleson Dunleavy
                                                      Gareth W. Dunleavy

1

Douglas Hyde and the Generational Imperative

In an introductory tale to the *Táin Bó Cuailnge,* or "Cattle Raid of Cooley," Senchán Torpéist, an Irish laureate of the seventh century, convenes the poets of Ireland for the purpose of reconstructing this most famous of Irish epics, the centerpiece of ancient Ireland's mythic and cultural traditions. The poets are unsuccessful. As a last hope one of their number is sent to Gaul to recover what he can from a "certain sage" there. On the way he stops in Connacht, at the grave of Fergus mac Roich, a major figure of the *Táin* and the last man known to have had the entire narrative in his head. Fergus himself appears; the lost epic is recovered; the tradition is preserved intact.

The concept of a generational link among Irish poets, scholars, heroes, leaders—of the responsibility of each, during his or her lifetime, to assure the future by preserving the past—has continued to bind successors to Fergus mac Roich and Senchán Torpéist, even to the twentieth century. "When Pearse summoned Cuchulain to his side, what stalked through the Post Office?" asked W. B. Yeats, whose poetic vision of modern Ireland etched ancient traditions on the events of 1913–1923. An image from the *Táin,* Oliver Sheppard's *Death of Cuchulain,* was the nation's answer. Today, guarding the entrance to the Dublin General Post Office, it commemorates not only the martyred leaders of 1916 but all of Ireland's champions, past, passing, and to come. Bound by their generational imperative, poets and historians continue to fuse future, past, and present as the years make and remake modern Ireland. Visible in the changing pattern—now prominent in the foreground,

1

now unnoticed in the background, by turns in and out of focus—is the figure of Douglas Hyde.

One bright, beautiful day in May 1968 in Frenchpark, county Roscommon—uncharacteristic weather for the small west-central Irish village nestled among hill and bog where rains fall generously in the spring of the year—a large official vehicle maneuvered confidently along narrow twisting roads and through crossroads, attracting the attention of pedestrians and bicyclists engaged in daily errands. Beyond the village center, on the road to Ballaghaderreen, it stopped at a churchyard nearly within sight of historic Rathcroghan, the plain pregnant with prehistoric monuments where legend has it that the *Táin* began. The familiar-looking stranger who stepped from the car was tall and thin, with the military manner befitting a man called "the Chief." Eamon de Valera had come to kneel at the grave of Douglas Hyde. With him were his grandchildren. Bob Connolly, the sexton, was the only other person present. After a few moments de Valera entered the empty church where the Reverend Arthur Hyde, Jr., rector of Frenchpark, had presided from 1867 to his death in 1905. In that church, as a boy, Douglas, fourth son of the Reverend Arthur Hyde (third to survive infancy), had listened unwillingly to his father's sermons, silently formulating conflicting opinions based on a broader vision of the world. There during his adolescent years he had obediently but reluctantly conducted Sunday school classes for children of the Big House landlords and local squirearchy who comprised his father's flock, and had assisted with other church duties. Manhood had taken him to Dublin, to London, to the Continent, and to North America, where his own ideas had flourished. Yet throughout his long life he had returned often to this same cemetery of the Church of Ireland in the parish of Tibohine in the village of Frenchpark to kneel at the graves of mother, father, daughter, brother-in-law, wife. Here, before Vatican II, in predominantly Catholic Ireland, with hundreds crowding near to bid him farewell and thousands more paying tribute along the route of the funeral procession from Dublin to Frenchpark, he himself had been buried in 1949.

Far more than an ecumenical gesture, de Valera's 1968 visit to the grave of Douglas Hyde was the personal tribute of a younger maker of modern Ireland to his mentor and predecessor; of one old friend, old comrade, to another; of modern Ireland's third *uachtarán*, or president, to its first. It was also an affirmation of the generational link forged by Senchán Torpéist centuries before, of the obligation each

Irish leader has to Ireland's past and future. Others had come the preceding day to mark the seventy-fifth anniversary of the Gaelic League, the organization Hyde had helped to found and had led during a long and significant chapter of his life. Churchyard and church had echoed with familiar oratory. But this personal pilgrimage Eamon de Valera had chosen to make alone, with only his grandchildren to accompany him. He had not come to shout speeches to the crowd, calling out, "People of Ireland! People of Ireland!" with the note of urgency characteristic of his public addresses, but to whisper softly to the man who, like Fergus mac Roich, had made of himself a link in a great chain of national being, creating a commodious vicus of recirculation more accessible than that of James Joyce through which the old-new nation, modern Ireland, might be sustained.

Whispering at the grave of Douglas Hyde in the May sunshine of 1968, de Valera might have recalled the mission of the seventh-century poet to the grave of Fergus mac Roich. More likely his memories were of his own late-night visits to Áras an Uachtaráin when Hyde was president. The purpose of their nightly meetings had not been to reconstruct the past but to consider the present and develop strategies for the future. Hyde had been de Valera's personal choice for the presidency established under the Constitution of 1937. Few had understood why. Even after Hyde's unanimous election in 1938, newspapers and gossip mongers had talked of de Valera's "sop" to the Protestant Ascendancy, to the Gaelic revivalists, to the Trinity intellectuals, and to the Church of Ireland, as if ever in his political career this stern man had given weight to such considerations. No, de Valera had chosen Hyde for himself—for his experience, his judgment, and his political skills, honed over a period of nearly half a century; for his ability to move easily and smoothly in circles of which de Valera had never been part; for his shrewd understanding of Americans, Canadians, the British, the French, and the Germans at a crucial time in modern history when an independent Ireland was about to take its place on the world stage.

By 1938 de Valera, born in 1882, had been a schoolteacher, a mathematician, a soldier, a leader of the republican insurrectionists, and an architect of the Free State. His political strengths had been his determination, singleness of purpose, and endurance, his ability to inspire others to degrees of patience, fortitude, loyalty, and courage of which they might not have thought themselves capable. Hyde, born in 1860, had been a poet, a folklorist, a playwright, a philologist, a literary historian, a university professor, an antiquarian, a leader of the Gaelic Revival, a pioneer of the Irish Literary Renaissance, and an Irish Free State senator. Cosmopolitan, politically sophisticated, and an easy conversationalist comfortable within a wide range of social contacts, during fifty years of public life he had proved adept at probing the thoughts and feelings of others while revealing little of himself, at signaling from offstage and providing onstage support to others who assumed major roles, and at concealing his own confrontational intentions behind a benign exterior. On the question of Ireland, the two men had long shared ideals and goals. De Valera was better understood, a strong and forceful leader whose life was like an arrow shot through the air. Hyde was an enigma, a man whose career, by 1938, had given rise to a myth, an internally inconsistent accretion of half-truth, misunderstanding, presumption, expectation, rumor, and opinion that until now has not been challenged by evidence. Clues to Hyde's motivation, goals, character, and personality lead through public and private records and personal memories to extraordinary conclusions. As in all good detective stories, investigation must begin with a review of documented and objective facts, with the public scaffolding of the private life.

2

A Smiling Public Man

Douglas Hyde had lived a long and controversial life when, at the age of seventy-eight, he was unanimously elected first president of modern Ireland. His seven-year term (1938–1945) coincided with that crucial period in modern history when the war that swept Europe and Asia and buffeted the Americas not only threatened Ireland's very existence but compounded the social, economic, political, and cultural pressures already at work in the self-proclaimed new nation.

Born in Castlerea, a market town in county Roscommon seven miles west of the village of Frenchpark where he now lies buried, Hyde spent the first six years of his life approximately thirty miles to the north in the modest glebe house of Kilmactranny, where his father was rector until 1867. Although still remote by modern standards, the county Sligo village already had won the small place in Irish history that later fascinated Hyde, for it was here in the early eighteenth century that Donnacha Liath (Denis O'Conor), although impoverished during the wholesale confiscations of 1692–1700, had maintained his position as descendant of Connacht kings and Irish high kings. In O'Conor's modest cottage Blind O'Carolan had played on his celebrated harp the musical compositions for which he was known throughout Europe. This same cottage, a refuge for hedge schoolmasters and unregistered priests during Penal times, often had sheltered O'Conor's banished brother-in-law, the daring Bishop O'Rourke, who traveled the country disguised as "Mr. Fitzgerald" under the nose of English soldiers.

"The Hill," the handsome Georgian mansion in Castlerea where

5

Douglas Hyde was born (since altered by later owners), was not his own family home but the glebe house of Kilkeevan parish, home of his maternal grandparents, the Venerable John Orson Oldfield, archdeacon of Elphin and vicar of Kilkeevan, and Maria Meade Oldfield, daughter of Frank Meade, Q.C., of Dublin. Elevated by the hill that gave the house its name, in 1860 it looked across Main Street and over the walls and gardens of the Sandford demesne, now Castlerea town park, on the banks of the river Suck. A few hundred yards along the same street was the more modest birthplace of Sir William Wilde, a distinguished eye surgeon and antiquarian, son of the town doctor and father of Oscar Wilde. Although Oscar himself was born in Dublin in 1854, long after his father had left Castlerea, local memory continued to associate the house with the Wilde family. Prevalent in Hyde's boyhood were rumors, persistent even today, of a mysterious message scratched on a back window. When its street-level rooms were converted to a pub, the name given it was the Oscar Bar. At the time of Hyde's birth historic Clonalis—the walled estate at the edge of town on the Castlebar road that is still held by the O'Conors of Connacht—was the home of Charles Owen O'Conor Don, M.P., great-great-great-grandson of Donnacha Liath of Kilmactranny. Preserved and expanded by O'Conor Don, its extensive library and manuscript archive reflected then as today the interests of Donnacha Liath's son and grandson, Charles O'Conor ("the Historian") of Bellanagare and Dr. Charles O'Conor, scholar, translator, and librarian to the Duke of Buckingham at Stowe. Distinguished visitors included not only well-known political figures but scholars from England and abroad. As a young man invited to visit the forty-four-room mansion with its halls and dining room lined with portraits of O'Conor ancestors, Hyde had examined there such ancient Gaelic manuscripts as the fourteenth-century Book of the Magauran (now in the National Library) and the earliest known fragment of Brehon law. At Clonalis also he had stood wondering before the harp that O'Carolan had played in Kilmactranny.

Hyde's paternal grandfather was the Reverend Arthur Hyde, Sr., vicar of Mohill, a town near Drumsna, where Anthony Trollope, then a post office inspector, had found the germ of his first novel, *The Macdermots of Ballycloran*. As a lineal descendant of Sir Arthur Hyde, whose reward for service to Elizabeth I had been a knighthood and letters patent to 11,766 acres of county Cork, he belonged, however—through a junior line—to the Cork Hydes of Castle Hyde, a celebrated estate on the Blackwater that had remained the family seat until 1851. Father, grandfather, and great-grandfather before him had served the Church of Ireland since the seventeenth century. Regarded before disestablishment as more social and economic than religious in nature, the respectable career the church provided—as Lady Melbourne had advised her son William—was particularly suited to younger sons. Indeed, had William's elder brother not died, clearing the way for him to become Lord Melbourne, he would have had neither the means nor the social position to rise as he did to prime minister and so earn his place in English political history.

No providential death having intervened to raise the eighteenth-century family of Douglas Hyde from junior-branch status, son followed father: the heir of the Reverend Arthur Hyde of Hyde Park, county Cork, became the Reverend Arthur Hyde, vicar of Killarney. His marriage to a daughter of George French of Innfield established a connection with the Frenches, the family of Lord de Freyne, proprietary landlord of Frenchpark. So it was that in 1867, when he was appointed rector of the parish of Tibohine, the Reverend Arthur Hyde, Jr., son of the Reverend Arthur Hyde of Mohill and father of Douglas Hyde, moved his family to Frenchpark, to live among country squires and landed gentry in a social environment more favorable than that offered by Kilmactranny. Neighboring kinsmen in Frenchpark included not only Lord de Freyne but his brother, John French, whose Roscommon estate, Ratra, was later to become, in 1893, the home of Dr. Douglas Hyde.

Such a pedigree was not the kind from which controversy ordinarily might be expected, nor was there anything apparent in Hyde's childhood or youth that pointed to the many and various careers that were later to engage him. When he grew old enough to handle fishing rod and gun, he was included in the sporting activities his father organized with his sons. But as Douglas's two brothers, Arthur and Oldfield, were in general too old to be his companions and his sister, Annette, who was five years his junior, was too young, most of Hyde's days were spent alone with his dog, Diver, or tagging along behind amiable workmen, or with the sons of neighboring cottagers from the glebe lands and nearby estates. Crossing meadow and bog on these daily rambles, he often stopped for a cup of tea and a biscuit in the thatched cabins that dotted the countryside. His welcome was warmest in those in which Irish was the primary language, where it was a matter of some amusement that the master's boy had an ear for the language and liked to try his few phrases on willing listeners. Douglas's interest in Irish won attention at home, too, where until he and his brothers were old enough to assert different aspirations both the Reverend and Mrs. Hyde assumed that all three of their sons would follow the family tradition and enter the ministry. The church, advised the Reverend Hyde, when young Arthur and Oldfield mocked Douglas for making a serious study of what they considered a language of servants, was particularly interested in young men who might qualify for a living in one of the areas to the west where Irish was still dominant. But Douglas—who was educated at home, as were his brothers and sister, in his father's well-stocked library—also was given to understand that history, natural science, mathematics, the classics, and Continental languages and literature were more important subjects, in which one day he would be required to pass entrance examinations for admission to Trinity College.

Before his sixteenth birthday Douglas had acquired the informal elementary education in the Irish language and Irish history and the interest in Irish folktale and song which he then began to pursue through self-directed study of texts bought in secondhand bookstores on rare boyhood trips to Dublin. It was in a Dublin bookstore when he was not yet eighteen that he first met members of the Society for the Preservation of the Irish Language, an organization of which O'Conor Don of Clonalis was a founding member and officer. Through the society he was introduced to the old manuscripts and rare books of the Irish-language collection of the Royal Irish Academy and to new friends who encouraged his attempts at translating and writing original verse in modern Irish. Before he was twenty-one his Irish poems and translations had appeared in periodicals published on either side of the Atlantic, and he had been accepted as a cultural nationalist by fellow members of both the sedate and literary society and its splinter organization, the more activist Gaelic Union.

Meanwhile there was Trinity to be concerned about. Admitted in 1880 to the divinity program through which, from the sixteenth century, sons of the Ascendancy (including his own father and grandfathers) had received their university education, Hyde quickly won a reputation as an outstanding scholar. To his father it seemed that for Douglas a career in the church and a living in Irish-speaking Mayo was assured. Hyde himself was ambivalent, especially when he discovered that Trinity circles equated an interest in modern Irish with nationalism and regarded nationalists as anathema. Despite the disapproval of influential faculty, he not only continued his membership in the society and the Gaelic Union but joined the beautiful and radical Maud Gonne, the flamboyant young Yeats, and other women and men of their age and class in a circle called "the Young Irelanders" (after the revolutionary Young Ireland movement of the 1840s) that clustered around John O'Leary, an old Fenian leader returned from exile. Yet to most people Hyde seemed harmless enough, for between 1886 and 1890, having earned B.A., M.A., and LL.D. degrees, he appeared intent on becoming nothing more dangerous than a Dublin man-about-town: a gentleman scholar who spent his days in the library of the Royal Irish Academy and his evenings at theaters, concerts, and dinner parties; a convivial member of proper clubs; a familiar and socially adept figure at teas and tennis parties who talked easily about his travels to English watering holes and the fashionable and scenic gathering spots he had visited on the Continent; an aspiring candidate for a respectable university post in literature and language.

This appearance of indolence and indifference was misleading. By the time Hyde was thirty, his scholarly publications (at which he had been working in fact very seriously) were attracting as much attention as his published poems and translations; his growing international reputation as an authority on Irish folklore and as a theorist and methodologist in the new field of folklore scholarship was bringing him respectful inquiries and requests for assistance from eminent scholars abroad. Had he not been opposed (because he advocated educational support for modern Irish) by such powerful political academicians as John Pentland Mahaffy, later provost of Trinity College, he might have had the Irish university post he coveted. But on this issue Hyde was as implacable as his enemies. Alternatives were few until an invitation to Canada to serve a one-year term as interim professor of modern languages at the University of New Brunswick offered an opportunity beyond Mahaffy's sphere of influence.

In Fredericton, where life was both pleasant and comfortable, Hyde soon began to weigh the possibility of emigrating permanently to Canada or the United States. His duties, which he enjoyed, included teaching French and German; he quickly acquired a circle of congenial friends; he became fascinated with the language and culture of nearby native American tribes; and he set for himself such compatible scholarly tasks as that of comparing native American folklore with the folklore of Gaelic Ireland. Yet at the same time, in what seemed a strange departure to acquaintances who knew of such activities, he sought contacts with such men as O'Donovan Rossa and Patrick Ford, known Fenians and Irish compatriots who were unwelcome in Ireland because of their political activities. And in his diaries and in notes that he sent home he attempted to gauge Irish-American reactions to contemporary events in Lord Salisbury's England and Parnell's Ireland. Although Hyde's letters from Canada cite his father's illness as the deciding factor in his return home at the end of his New Brunswick year, they also reflect his strong support of Charles Stewart Parnell and his interest in the trials and scandals that had weakened Parnell's position and divided public opinion on the question of his reelection.

By October 1891 Parnell was dead, and with him the energy, excitement, and hope he had generated. The Parnellite nationalists were in rout; the entire Home Rule party was in disarray; the populace was too discouraged to respond to political attempts to rally them. Back in Ireland, Hyde had returned to his usual circles, where his reputation was enhanced by the success of *Beside the Fire*, published in 1890 and the first of his books to establish his work as an important source for the young writers of what was soon being called "the Irish Literary Renaissance." Word from abroad was that his poems and translations, reprinted in Paris and Rennes, were being enthusiastically received on the Continent, especially in Paris and Brittany where Celtic studies had become a growing area of scholarly investigation and a pan-Celtic movement was gathering popular strength. He was receiving letters soliciting his new work from both popular and scholarly publications.

Elected president of the newly organized National Literary Society in 1892, Hyde boldly chose as both title and theme of his inaugural speech "The Necessity for De-Anglicizing Ireland." Its call for cultural revolution raised few alarms among English authorities, apparently because they could not conceive of an effete literary circle that was seditious, or of folktales, folk songs, and traditional games that could pose a clear and present danger to the state. Nor did the government take notice a year later, in 1893, when Hyde was chosen first president of another new organization, the Gaelic League. Officially its policy was to avoid conflict with the British government by steadfastly maintaining a nonpolitical stance. Unofficially it engaged in activities expressly designed and publicly proclaimed to have as their purpose the fulfillment of the goals Hyde had set forth in his speech on deanglicization. But the prime reason why Hyde's tentative plans for a return to Canada were dropped was that his friendship with Lucy Cometina Kurtz, an attractive, intelligent, and intellectually independent young heiress to whom he had been introduced by his Oldfield aunts, had ripened into engagement. By 1893 they were married. As the turn of the century and his fortieth birthday approached, Hyde's professional and private life were by all appearances both promising and satisfying.

During the next twelve years Hyde continued composing, collecting, and translating the Irish stories and poems that provided, according to Yeats, the "entire imaginative tradition" that stirred the writers of the Irish literary revival. His scholarly studies—expanded to include philology and literary history—drew inquiries from such eminent academicians as Harvard's Fred Norris Robinson and Georges Dottin of the University of Rennes. His circle of friends grew to include the distinguished German Celticist, Kuno Meyer. By 1899 Hyde had published *A Literary History of Ireland,* a full-length pioneer study still regarded as authoritative. Persuaded by Lady Gregory and W. B. Yeats to join their newly formed Irish Literary Theatre, forerunner of Dublin's famous Abbey, he successfully tried his hand at writing original plays in Irish for its repertoire. By 1905 he had composed a corpus of Irish plays performed throughout the country and available in print, and he had preserved hundreds of poems and stories from the oral tradition in such collections as *Beside the Fire* (1890), *Love Songs of Connacht* (1893), *The Three Sorrows of Storytelling* (1895), and *Songs Ascribed to Raftery* (1903). Extracts of his work that appeared in translation in France and in English-language periodicals in the United States and Ireland had attracted enthusiastic readers who, writing to editors, were requesting more. So varied and prolific were Hyde's activities in the years between 1893 and 1905 that Yeats publicly compared him to Frederic Mistral, the Provençal poet and founder of the Félibrige who won the Nobel Prize in literature in 1904.

During these years the Gaelic League, still led by Hyde, also was gathering strength, abroad as well as in Ireland, and political and revolutionary pressures for Home Rule were increasing. Despite the clearly political implications of many of his activities, Hyde continued to maintain a nonpolitical stance and to insist that his own and the league's efforts were confined within a purely cultural framework. In 1899, with testimony from eminent scholars from abroad to support him, he defeated the governors of the British education system in Ireland on the question of the validity of formal study of the Irish language. In 1900 he took on the British Post Office in an epic battle that ended in a Pyrrhic victory for Goliath, so numerous were those who came to the aid of David. Word of these successes traveled, winning new supporters for Hyde and the Gaelic League not only in Ireland but also in England, on the Continent, in Canada, the United States, Mexico, Argentina, and even in the Phillipines and far-off Australia.

As through branches and affiliate organizations the influence of the league spread, Hyde's personal popularity increased correspondingly. In persuasive letters urging Hyde to present a series of lectures in the United States, John Quinn of New York, a wealthy Irish-American philanthropist and lawyer, declared that academic and community groups in fifty-two American cities were eager to sponsor an eight-month tour, if he would but agree. Among prominent Americans who showered Hyde with invitations in 1905–1906, as he crossed and re-crossed the United States and Canada by rail, carriage, and boat, were the presidents of Harvard, Yale, Catholic University, the University of Wisconsin, and the University of California; the daughters of Ralph Waldo Emerson and Henry Wadsworth Longfellow; Andrew Carnegie; Finley Peter Dunne (Chicago's famous "Mr. Dooley"); and President Theodore Roosevelt. All San Francisco seemed to embrace him: its citizens responded generously to his request for financial contributions to continue the league's efforts on behalf of Irish culture and the Irish language.

The year before his fiftieth birthday Douglas Hyde began a new career as professor of modern Irish at University College, Dublin. Among his students were women and men who later taught Irish in this and other Irish universities. Some were appointed to the distinguished faculty of the Dublin Institute of Advanced Studies. Two months after Hyde's fifty-sixth birthday a small host of brilliant young men whom he had inspired and taught went to their deaths in the Easter Rising of 1916. He had opposed their action not, as is often stated, because he was against physical force as a means of gaining national independence but because he feared that their brave vulnerability would result in just such a blood sacrifice at a time when he believed that all alternatives had not yet been exhausted. Armistice in 1918 provided relief for neither Douglas Hyde nor Ireland. Physically ill, emotionally depressed, and beset by personal and family troubles and tragedies, he struggled to regain his equilibrium as Ireland struggled through the war of independence (1918–1921) and the civil war (1921–1923) that hampered efforts to build the limited self-government permitted under the divisive Treaty of 1921. Called upon to serve in the Free State Senate in 1925, Hyde readily assented, hoping to find relief from the sorrows of his personal life in renewed political activity and his continuing commitment to scholarship, writing, and teaching. What he found instead was a factionalism that forced him to expend most of his energies on defending himself from personal attack in a climate in which old alliances were often abandoned and new ones were quickly repudiated. At the end of his senate term Hyde nevertheless made a bid for reelection—and lost.

During the next seven years, at an age when most men contemplate retirement, Hyde continued to devote long hours of every day to his teaching and scholarship and to *Lia Fáil,* a new literary journal in Irish studies that he had launched. Meanwhile anti-Treaty republicans who had been boycotting the Free State government reentered politics with the purpose of winning by election what they had been unable to gain by guerrilla warfare. Eamon de Valera, American-born survivor of the Easter rebellion, war of independence, and civil war, a committed nationalist who had been one of Hyde's young Gaelic Leaguers, soon emerged as the dominant political leader. His success was greeted by some as a sign of a new political optimism. To many dispirited citizens of the Free State it seemed that Thomas Davis's promise of a nation once again might yet be fulfilled. On de Valera's agenda was the writing of a new Constitution that would eliminate the provisions of the treaty he had opposed and establish the framework of the republic he had long envisioned.

In 1937 de Valera persuaded Hyde—then seventy-seven, retired from the university, but still actively engaged in scholarship at home in Roscommon—to return to Dublin to serve a second term in the Free State Senate. On December 29, 1937, the new Constitution was ratified. In the spring of 1938, at de Valera's insistence, Hyde agreed to stand for the office of *uachtarán,* or president, that had been created by the new Constitution. The same document silently abolished the Irish Free State, establishing by fiat the independent modern Irish nation called Ireland, or Éire. In May all political factions united to elect Douglas Hyde first president of an independent Ireland. For himself de Valera had reserved the post of *taoiseach,* or prime minister.

Seven years later, in 1945, at the end of a first full presidential term that had spanned the difficult war years, Hyde was asked if he would stand for a second term. He was eighty-five years old and he had suffered a stroke that had left him unable to walk, but his mind was as young and curious, his wit as active, and his commitment to the Irish nation as firm as ever. Nevertheless, he declined: the character of the office of president had been shaped under his aegis; it was time, he believed, for someone else to take a hand in its future development. This time, however, instead of returning to his native Roscommon, he wanted to remain in Dublin, characteristically close to the action. "Little Ratra," a home in Phoenix Park near Áras an Uachtaráin, was made available to him. There he died, modern Ireland's first elder statesman.

Energetic, amiable, eminently approachable, an easy conversationalist and a charismatic speaker in several languages, Hyde was the kind of man whom people liked to refer to by nickname. In the Big House milieu in which he had been brought up, he was "Dougie." To the millions who knew him best through his work on behalf of the Irish language, he was "An Craoibhin," (from An Craoibhín Aoibhinn, "the delightful little branch," an Irish pen name he had adopted as a young poet). His sister, Annette, called him "Humpy," a name she had given him in childhood, when to her it seemed that whenever she wanted his company outdoors, he was bent over book or notebook. To his daughters he was their affectionate, prank-loving "Tweet." Yet he was also, contemporaries avow, an enigmatic figure, a strange and complex man with a private self kept well hidden from others and a goal-oriented capacity for callousness and thoughtlessness that shocked his most intimate co-workers whenever it emerged. Remembered by the people of northwest Roscommon as among the kindest and friendliest of the local gentry, he was also capable, they admitted, of a petty stinginess. In social circles he was regarded as a devoted husband and father, yet to this day private recollections and rumors of both serious and short-term romantic attachments persistently circulate. Widely perceived as a man dedicated to a cause, he was a puzzle to many who openly wondered at a commitment that, given his class, birth, and social status, cost him so much and held so little personal promise. On occasion his emotional involvement became so intense as to lead him to betray a friend. At the same time he was amused rather than annoyed by associations drawn between his name and that of the protagonist of Robert Louis Stevenson's *Dr. Jekyll and Mr. Hyde*. After his death conflicting statements by others concerning the date and place of his birth raised questions about his parentage. Unchecked by formal investigation and published evidence, over the years anecdote, rumor, recollection, and opinion have been quoted as fact.

Known thus to everyone and no one, Douglas Hyde, a maker of modern Ireland, died in 1949, leaving behind him no easy explanations of his life story but diaries, letters, copybooks, and journals, written mostly in Irish but also in English, French, German, and occasionally Latin and Greek, to be sifted and winnowed in search of truths. His published writings include not only his own work, translated and published in many different countries, but his collaborations with Lady Gregory and W. B. Yeats. Among hundreds of correspondents from all over the world whose letters he answered, usually within twenty-four hours of receipt, were such disparate figures as Theodore Roosevelt, president of the United States; Katharine Tynan, distinguished poet; and Eoin O'Cahill, a native Irishman who had left Ireland as a young man but who returned to it in spirit at the end of his life when, living in Michigan, he refashioned figures from Irish mythology to create stories in Irish of the American Wild West. Hyde touched the lives of thousands; hundreds preserved recollections of specific incidents that reveal aspects of his character and personality. His wide circle of close friends was as varied as the range of his correspondents. To the end of his days it included Maud Gonne, whom he had once tried to teach Irish; Sinéad de Valera, who had played the Fairy to his Tinker in his play *The Tinker and the Fairy*; the O'Conors of Clonalis in Castlerea; An Seabhac (Pádraig Ó Siochfhradha), folklorist of Dingle; Thomas Lavin, a former Frenchpark neighbor and a contemporary, father of the Irish writer Mary Lavin; old comrades from the Gaelic League; and the Mahons and Morrisroes of the cottages just outside the gates of Ratra, the home two miles from the center of the village of Frenchpark in county Roscommon that had been purchased for him from the estate of John French by the Gaelic League.

Today an afternoon's ramble that takes as its starting point the remains of the foundation of the now ruined Ratra passes over nearby meadow, along bog roads, through farmyards, and by stone cabins, many also in ruins, where 128 years ago a clergyman's son learned his first Irish words and the transformation from Douglas Hyde to An Craoibhin and *an t-uachtarán* began. Not far from the cottages outside the gates, in which there are still Mahons and Morrisroes who remember Douglas Hyde, is the cemetery in which he lies buried, next to the church in which the Reverend Hyde served as rector from 1867 to 1905.

Behind these public facts there was a private life.

3

The Budding Branch

February 28, 1940, was brisk and cold. A chill wind swept through Phoenix Park, rattling the great windows of its three stately homes, former residences of British government officials. From the chimneys of Áras an Uachtaráin, official residence since 1938 of the president of Ireland, smoke from turf fires rose and quickly dispersed, its unmistakable scent evoking warm recollections of distant cottages in hearty Dubliners walking or cycling nearby. During the hard winter months past, to relieve distress caused by wartime shortages, the president had ordered that the mansion's coal stores be distributed among the people of Dublin. A turf fire was in any case what he himself preferred, nor did he mind giving up dusty bins of shiny black coal for the velvet-brown stacks from midland bogs that he now had the pleasure of seeing when he took an occasional turn outdoors, striding along purposefully or stopping to banter with a workman, his long woolen muffler and the smoke from his pipe both curling around and behind the collar of his tweed jacket.

Built as an eighteenth-century ranger's lodge, Áras an Uachtaráin had been enlarged in 1816 to create a proper viceregal residence for the British lords lieutenant who then governed Ireland. It was at that time that the wings and portico that give the mansion its neoclassical appearance had been added. Hastily and not yet completely renovated in 1938 to serve as the home of the first Irish president, it needed just such touches as a turf fire, in its new occupant's opinion, to give it a proper Irish flavor. Similar patriotic sentiments, he sometimes explained to visitors, his eyes wide and shining with feigned innocence, led him to keep a small flask of poteen in the presidential study. Michael McDunphy, secretary to the president, frankly disapproved of the poteen—and had not been so sure of the turf. An efficient, conscientious, and serious man favored by de Valera for the newly established government position to which he had been appointed even before Hyde's election, McDunphy worked hard at the job of hiring and heading the presidential staff, assuring its efficient operation, establishing protocol, maintaining liaison between Áras an Uachtaráin and other branches of the government, and communicating through diplomatic channels and the media with the world at large. Stacking turf outside the presidential mansion was just one of many things he had to be concerned about, for fear of what the newspapers might make of it. McDunphy was right, of course—from previous experience Hyde knew that political cartoonists, like cats, should never be overfed—but in this case wartime exigencies allowed the president to have his turf and the people of Dublin to have their coal, yet left the caricaturists, good hunting cats all, still lean and hungry.

Caricaturists and cats both figure in Irish history—probably because, as a monk with an ironic bent observed some eleven centuries ago, they employ similar skills:

I and Pangur Ban my cat,
'Tis a like task we are at:
Hunting mice is his delight,
Hunting words I sit all night.

The original of that old Irish poem—found in Austria, in the margins of a manuscript of a codex of St. Paul—was well known to Hyde. As a young man he had made oblique and playful allusion to it in a mock lament he had written in modern Irish, about the loss of a kitten, companion of his study, on which a portly friend had sat. Himself a Gaelic scholar, translator, and poet, Hyde admired the way in which Robin Flower had hunted and caught the flavor of the poem in a singsong English different from Kuno Meyer's earlier and more literal verse translation. The German Celticist, an old friend, had struck a nice balance beween scholarly integrity and poetic sensibility, but Flower's greater concern for the spirit of the original was more consistent with Hyde's own translation ethic.

Better far than praise of men
'Tis to sit with book and pen;

Pangur bears me no ill will,
He too plies his simple skill.

On this February day in 1940, that was Hyde's task: to ply his simple
skill with words. Warmed by the turf fire in his study, he sat at his writing desk, his sturdy figure hunched over three sheets of blue four-by-six-
inch notepaper, his rounded back to the door.

'Tis a merry thing to see
At our tasks how glad are we,
When at home we sit and find
Entertainment to our mind.

Less able to find time to entertain his imagination since taking office
as president, Hyde delighted in opportunities such as the one before
him that combined duty with pleasure. His task was to make a rough
draft of what he planned to say to an audience of schoolchildren on
the subject of studying Irish.

Oftentimes a mouse will stray
In the hero Pangur's way;
Oftentimes my keen thought set
Takes a meaning in its net.

Seeking meanings that he might catch in his nets, Hyde looked up
from his work to glance through French windows, past formal gardens,
at the high, white sky beyond. It was an old habit of his, resting his
eyes on the sky while he was thinking, learned when he was a boy of
twelve or thirteen and had begun to have the soreness of his eyelids
that had plagued him off and on ever since. A nuisance, that soreness
of the eyes. Fortunately it had never completely disabled him, nor had
he ever let it interfere seriously with either his reading or his writing,
not even at home in Roscommon, where it always seemed worse. If
some days through habit he found himself looking up at the sky
more often than usual, it was not always to rest his eyes but to search
for—what?

'Gainst the wall he sets his eye
Full and fierce and sharp and sly;
'Gainst the wall of knowledge I
All my little wisdom try.

In his presidential study in Áras an Uachtaráin, whenever his glance
strayed first round the room and then through the French windows to

the sky above the garden, the sky was full of wheeling gulls. A great country for birds, Ireland. Even in the center of the city, in the reading rooms of the National Library, they could be heard scuffling on the roof and screaming overhead. In Roscommon, in that same sky continually covered and uncovered by scudding gray clouds, a teal might be dropping back to the sheltered ledge bordering the lake near Caoile from which the entire flock had arisen, moments before, at the sound of a hunter's first shot. At Ratra, if the turlough in the far field were larger today, a lapwing reflected in its shallow waters would be an easier target. If not, for the hunter's gun there were always the omnipresent crows silhouetted in the leafless trees of late winter.

Though miles away in Dublin, any Roscommon man would know from the look of the sky how the air smelled west of the Shannon, how the wind felt on a reddened cheek. Days toward the end of February often were fine there: brisk and cold, with perhaps a light dusting of new snow to limn the prints of a saucy hare after a week's thaw. In the early, frosty morning on just such a day as this when he was a boy Hyde used to walk down to Cloigionín-a-naosc's in snow that squeaked underfoot; flush a snipe at the flash; return home slowly, sometimes stepping in his own earlier footprints, grown large since he had left them. On such a day, as a boy, he often went out again after supper, sending Diver to retrieve a jackdaw shot close by the house or running along well-worn paths, the dog at his heels, to enjoy for a while in the lengthening twilight the comfort of Seamas Hart's turf fire and the warmth of his companionship.

Such thoughts of the past inevitably crowd out the present when a writer faces the kind of task Hyde had before him on that last Wednesday in February at the start of his eighty-first year, a winter's day with a promise of spring in the air. To think what would draw a response from children requires remembering what it is like to be a child.

When a mouse darts from its den
O how glad is Pangur then!
O what gladness do I prove
When I solve the doubts I love!

Hyde wrote and crossed out and wrote again. Sixty-five, seventy years had passed since he was a boy. Curious turns and twists of fate separate youth and age. A memory that would bridge the distance between himself and the children he soon would meet, that was what he needed: something that would persuade them that near the end of the journey of life the old must look to the young for assurance of that continuity of effort that is their last earthly reward. Would the children respond to such a memory? How would they regard him? Would they listen to what he had to say? Or would they squirm, suppressing giggles and yawns, wishing the event over, the old man gone? If Hyde could have met each youngster separately, coaxed from the eyes of each the mirror of his own, surely they would have become friends. Protocol, however, required that the president of Ireland address schoolchildren in groups.

Hyde always had had an easy rapport with children. Summers in Roscommon in the years before his wife became ill, while she chatted with other ladies in the drawing room at Clonalis, he used to play hide-and-seek with the six O'Conor girls, up and down stairs, behind chairs, under beds, and through the forty-odd rooms of the "new" house (so-called to distinguish it from the old one, down by the river, abandoned in 1872 after the first wife of Charles Owen O'Conor Don died there of the tuberculosis that also had killed his mother). Hyde liked visiting Clonalis with Lucy, even when none of the O'Conor men was about, not only for enjoyment of the children but for the pleasure of past associations. Castlerea was a familiar seven-mile drive from Frenchpark village; it was just nine miles from Ratra, the old John French estate forever associated with Seamas Hart where he expected that one day he would end his days. The road through the top of the town passed the nine-hole Clonalis golf course where he still sometimes played when he was home, then curved along high stone walls past the great iron gates of the estate on its way to Castlebar. When he and Lucy had business to transact in Castlerea they would turn left onto Main Street before reaching Clonalis, cross the bridge over the river Suck, and pass the post office on the left, to the market square. The road entering from the right a few yards beyond ran down to the railroad station. On one side of this road, at the junction of Main Street, was Kilkeevan Church, where he had been baptized; on the other was the Hill, then the glebe house of Kilkeevan parish, home of his grandparents, where he had been born. His grandfather Oldfield had died later that year. Sometime after, his grandmother and unmarried aunts, Maria and Cecily, had moved to Blackrock, in county Dublin. In addition to Maria, Cecily, and his own mother (her name was Elizabeth, but everyone called her Bessie), the Oldfield daughters included Ann, wife of Dr. William Cuppaidge, the physician who was always called to treat his chronic soreness of the eyes and other family ailments.

Charles Owen O'Conor Don, whose first wife had died at Clonalis,

had known the Oldfield family. He had been a young man serving his
third year in Parliament when Douglas Hyde was born. The O'Conors
also had known the Wildes, Oscar Wilde's father and grandfather. Sir
William, who had received his early education at the Elphin Diocesan
School, had left Roscommon for Dublin long before Oscar was born,
so Oscar and Douglas had not been acquainted as children. George
Moore, however, who had grown up at Moore Hall near Partry in
Mayo, used to tell of summertime boating and picnicking, himself and
his brother Maurice, with the Wilde boys, Oscar and Willie, on Lough
Carra. As a young man Hyde had been fascinated by stories of the boys'
mother, Lady Wilde, who called herself "Speranza" and who had written poetry for the *Nation*.

February 28, 1940: more than seventy-nine years had elapsed since
the Venerable John Orson Oldfield had been laid to rest behind the
iron gates of the overgrown Church of Ireland cemetery on Castlerea's
Main Street, across from Kilkeevan Church; almost thirty-six since
Charles Owen O'Conor Don had taken his place in the family plot of
the Roman Catholic cemetery adjacent to Clonalis, his ancient title passing to first one nephew and then another. Oscar Wilde had died in
1900. George Moore was dead, too; it was seven years since his ashes
had been buried on an island in his silver-green lake. Where were the
O'Conor girls on this crisp winter morning? Married, some of them—Jo
working in London for the British Foreign Office. On a postscript to
a letter, Hyde had written that he could not send her his love as long
as she held *that* job.

But on this February day Hyde had no time to reflect either on the
curious convergence of personalities associated with Castlerea or on the
whereabouts of the six O'Conor sisters. The work at hand had nothing
to do with Frenchpark or Castlerea or any other part of his native
county. The children for whom he was planning his brief talk were not
those he had known as Roscommon neighbors and friends. Who was
he to these young citizens of a new and different Ireland? A symbol—
their first constitutional president? How old he must seem to them, how
distant his memories of the past. Would they understand that once upon
a time *an t-uachtarán* had been a child like each of them? Could he talk
to them perhaps not as their president but as An Craoibhin Aoibhinn,
the poet, playwright, and folklorist whose work they had read or recited? If he had taught their parents or teachers, some might have heard
of him as the Dr. Hyde who had been professor of modern Irish at
University College. He was often photographed for the newspapers,

greeting visiting scholars and other dignitaries from abroad. But what do children care about scholars and dignitaries? What *do* they care about? Wars, heroes, history? What had he cared about when he was a boy?

Against the high, white sky over Phoenix Park there rose in the mind of Douglas Hyde the image of a small boy, not more than ten years of age, who had been taken from his native Connacht bog and mountain across the troubled Irish Sea to England. A crowd of other boys surrounded him, mocking him because (the written words leaned forward as Hyde wrote, straining to outdistance his pen as they raced uphill across the page) "nach raibh mé cosamhail leo féin" (I was not like them). One boy—Hyde recalled wryly that he was "in the same situation as myself" (that is, another Irish boy in England)—led the attack, calling Hyde an "Irish Paddy." Hyde wrote out the scene in Irish, that he might reconstruct it for the children he was to address: "Never say that again," he had threatened the boy, raising his fists. "You're nothing but a lazy loafer; I can beat you any day. I speak your language as well as you, and can you say a single word of mine? You had better realize that I'm twice the man—the double and better of yourself. And you, you grinning half-brain, *you* make fun of *me* and call *me* names."

"I was young then, and hot-tempered." Hunched over as Annette always remembered him, Hyde continued his recollection, contracting the size of his letters in his haste to finish before his remembered emotions cooled, excusing the fury of the embattled child he had been as he became again the elderly president of Ireland. But a blaze is not easily extinguished, even after seventy years, especially when it has been kindled by thoughts of injustice; firm and clear were the letters of the words with which he ended his account: "I still think I was right."

He had it then, three full sheets of notes and phrases from which to develop what he would say to the children.

> So in peace our tasks we ply,
> Pangur Ban, my cat and I;
> In our arts we find our bliss,
> I have mine and he has his.

All he needed to finish his task were a few final words in Irish to encourage the children to continue their study of the national language.

Each of you, every boy or girl among you . . . you can say as courageously and truly as I did that *you* are the better person, twice over! But you can't say it without your own language, so don't lose a bit of your Irish, because if you do it is history that you lose. Speak Irish among yourselves, for fear of losing it. And don't be timid—it won't be long before Irish spreads all over the world.

As he worked the little drama into his speech, for a short while Hyde was no longer, as he sometimes complained, a bird in a gilded cage. He had rummaged through memories of his childhood to find his characters; he had turned the clock back to set them moving and talking. He was a guest again at Coole Park, working on the script of a new play that he would read out to Lady Gregory and Yeats after dinner. At Coole, when he finished the scene he was working on, he used to walk down to the lake to watch the swans before dinner. At Áras an Uachtaráin, he might take a turn around the house to enjoy the turf-fragrant air.

> Practice every day has made
> Pangur perfect in his trade;
> I get wisdom day and night
> Turning darkness into light.

Had such an event as Hyde described occurred when he was ten? Did it take place in England? Were the circumstances as he related them? In the diary of his eighteenth year he had recorded in retrospect a few facts about his brief and only school experience, apparently the kernel of his story. It had taken place when he was thirteen: "My brother Arthur went to college in the year 1871 and my other brother Oldfield did the same in 1875. I stayed all the time safe at home except in 1873 I hurt my left thigh." The leg injury had set him back in his studies. He was sent in consequence to a "thieving school in Dublin" where he remained about three weeks and "learned nothing." Dissatisfied with the quality of the school, his father soon had withdrawn him.

Hyde's later accounts of this experience, separately retold by his daughter, Una Hyde Sealy, and his first biographer, Diarmid Coffey, suggest other reasons for his withdrawal: on the one hand, a case of measles; on the other, the Reverend Arthur Hyde's unwillingness to shoulder the cost of Douglas's tuition. Between these two sources there are discrepancies also in just how long Douglas remained at the school before he was taken home. The school is not named, but Una Sealy was sure that it was in Kingstown, now Dún Laoghaire, a suburb south of Dublin, rather than in Dublin proper. Coffey agreed, adding that only the shortness of Hyde's enrollment "prevented his becoming as Anglicised as most Dublin schoolboys," for such Irish schools, catering as they did to upper-class families, were modeled on English boys' schools. Recreating the experience in 1940, Hyde seems to have mirrored reality not as it was but as it might have been. Creating a scene reminiscent of *The Lord of the Flies,* he increased the tension between boy and setting by repositioning his remembered self in England rather than Dublin, then enhanced the potential for conflict by providing his boyhood persona with the verbal ability to defend a principle he but half understood against a half-felt wrong.

The truth is that in 1873, when Douglas Hyde was thirteen, he could not have made any honest claim to being an Irish speaker. His excercise books indicate that what he then knew of the language probably was limited to at most twenty or thirty common phrases. These he had but recently begun to record as part of a newly serious effort to learn Irish, which until then he had simply parroted. His new method was to listen carefully to the Irish speakers who lived and worked on the glebe lands, at nearby Ratra, or at the edge of the bog; to repeat the sounds he thought he had heard; then like a magpie to take them home and store them in his exercise book, together with their meanings, using a phonetic system he had devised for himself. Such a primitive program of study was possible because, contrary to the conclusions of 1851 census takers who had identified northwest Roscommon (a sparsely settled midland area west of the Shannon, bordering Leitrim, Sligo, and Mayo) as largely English-speaking, when Hyde was a boy many men and women of hill, hollow, and bog (including those employed by Hyde's father and other local landlords) still spoke Irish among themselves or used a mixture of Irish and English in their daily lives. In the cottages of Frenchpark, Fairymount, and Ballaghaderreen, even in some of the houses in Castlerea, Irish was therefore the first language of countless very young children and the only language of most *ould wans*—women and men in their seventies, eighties, and beyond who spoke the local north Roscommon dialect that has now long since died out and who were revered for their wisdom and memory and respected as guardians of cultural lore and traditions. Contemporary scholars suggest that their dialect probably was close to the Irish still spoken today in Menlo, in east Galway.

The content of Hyde's beginning Irish vocabulary was restricted, of course, by the context in which it was learned. The first expressions he reconstructed in his exercise book involved shooting, drinking, agricultural chores, marketing, and the weather. Sometimes in the shop in Ballaghaderreen or at the fair in Bellanagare, he would eavesdrop on other Irish speakers, testing his comprehension. Although Hyde's brothers shared his environment, neither took the trouble to learn to communicate in Irish, nor apparently did their father. It is almost certain that Hyde's upper-class schoolfellows in Kingstown would have known no Irish either. These were the boys whom Hyde apparently set out to impress with his *blas* (fluency), going so far as to pretend not only that he was bilingual, but that Irish was his native tongue. With twenty or thirty phrases at the ready to hurl into the contest he set up, there is no doubt that he would have had the advantage, *if* he had found anyone who considered a knowledge of Irish worthy of the challenge. Naive as he was at thirteen, with so little experience outside his native Roscommon (was this the reason why, in retrospect, he thought the incident in the schoolyard had occurred when he was only ten?), possibly he expected that his arcane knowledge would confer upon him the status a new boy always needs. His ability to rattle off an expression in Irish had won indulgent attention at home. Even his father, a Trinity graduate for whom education meant fluency in Latin and Greek, had shown interest in the increasing number of Irish words he was able to use, and Douglas's brother Arthur had told him that at Trinity College, Irish speakers were eligible to compete for a sizarship. "*Maith an buachaill*" (good boy) and "Good on you, boy," the country people of Tibohine would say, smiling and shaking their heads as if in amazement, whenever he mastered a new phrase.

Reactions in Kingstown were predictably different. To be sure, scholars did study Irish at Trinity College, then a bastion of Ascendancy attitudes and culture in the center of Dublin, but by "Irish" Trinity scholars meant the old language of Continental scribes that had been deciphered by European philologists, the classical language of bardic poets, or the literary language of chroniclers and historians artfully inscribed on parchment or vellum. Regarded not as the heritage of modern Ireland but as artifacts of a lost civilization, such manuscripts, many of them collected a century earlier for the Duke of Buckingham by Dr. Charles O'Conor, the duke's librarian, were accessible only to those who could qualify for admission to the libraries and manuscript rooms of Trinity, Oxford, the Royal Irish Academy, or the British Museum Library, or to such private holdings as the family archive of the O'Conors of Clonalis. But the unrecorded daily language of thatched hut and bog cabin? To suggest that such Irish had any relation to the language of the manuscript tradition was, to most nineteenth-century scholars, to equate the cries of Italian street vendors with the poems of Catullus and Horace or the superstitions of Greek seamen with Homer's *Iliad* and *Odyssey*. No wonder the Kingstown schoolboys laughed and jeered.

By the time Douglas realized that, contrary to his expectations, native fluency (real or pretended) in modern Irish would not enhance his stature in the Kingstown school—that, on the contrary, it would actually diminish him in the eyes of the other boys—apparently he had gone too far to reverse himself. His spirited defense, if delivered at all (the words remembered in 1940 for delivery to Irish schoolchildren may represent only what Hyde wished he had said) no doubt seemed in retrospect the right answer to their jeers. In 1873, in a school for Ascendancy boys, it could not have been more than a brave front, after which Douglas returned to Roscommon and to a life that went on much as it had before.

To Dominic Daly, author of *The Young Douglas Hyde,* Hyde's Roscommon childhood seemed idyllic. Free from school routine, with a boat and a horse at his disposal, a dog for companionship, and unencumbered hours to spend rambling the countryside, boxing with local youths in the glebe house farmyard, playing cards in the kitchen with gamekeepers, stewards, and farm laborers, or listening to Irish stories before cottage fires, it had a Huck Finn quality. These were indeed pleasant days when together the rector of Frenchpark and his three sons constructed targets for rifle practice, checked the turlough in the meadow for waterfowl, hunted birds and rabbits, and rowed, sailed, and swam in Lough Gara. But Douglas's diaries also document tension and unhappiness, especially between sons and father; illnesses that eroded family relationships; and an angry resentment of the tyrannical and unpredictable behavior of the Reverend Arthur Hyde.

A microcosm of all that Trollope had portrayed of western Ireland, especially in *The Macdermots of Ballycloran*—its complexities misunderstood by Englishman and Dubliner alike, its way of life alien to the anglicized eastern establishment, its attitudes and values rooted in crosscurrents of written and unwritten history—the town of Mohill in county Leitrim where the Reverend Arthur Hyde, Jr., grew up in the half century before disestablishment had defined for him the choices available to the son of a clergyman born in Leitrim in 1820 into the junior branch of an Ascendancy family. By heritage he was thoroughly Ascendancy, by social and educational background he was thoroughly Anglo-Irish. To continue in the family tradition, to become the fourth Reverend Arthur Hyde of the Church of Ireland, was for him an appropriate choice at a time when the social fabric and economic and political mores of the west of Ireland could be counted on to support his taste for security on the one hand and independence on the other.

At Trinity College the Reverend Arthur Hyde distinguished himself as an excellent classicist. In the churches to which he was assigned he served as a man of the cloth on Sunday; the rest of the week he divided between his library, where he enjoyed the role of gentleman scholar, and the fairs, fields, and bogs where he was known as a handsome, devil-may-care country squire and sportsman. For his sons he wished no more than that they, too, should become country vicars, learn to shoot accurately and drink lustily, carry out their responsibilities civilly, and devote themselves, as behooved Hydes of their birth and breeding, to a gentlemanly kind of scholarship.

Scholarship was important to the Reverend Arthur Hyde: Trollopian in many respects, he was a dignified man, not a Somerville-and-Ross Church of Ireland minister. Proud of his achievements at Trinity (he had been awarded the bachelor of arts in 1839, when he was but nineteen, and a second-class divinity testimonium a year later), at home he quoted Greek and spoke Latin to his sons, insisting that they develop a similar fluency, especially before servants. (It was this practice, carried over by his sons Arthur and Douglas in their diaries, that resulted in entries in which "*nova ancilla*" signaled the arrival of the new housemaid, to be followed shortly by "*ancilla expulsa est.*") In Kilmactranny he was remembered as a man who eagerly studied the natural world, especially the medicinal properties of local plants and the habits of birds and animals. No subject was too esoteric to warrant his attention. Additions to the library of the glebe house were made regularly. Douglas notes in his diary that invariably the packages his father brought home from his frequent trips to Dublin included new books for the library shelves.

But the Reverend Arthur Hyde was neither so patient nor so reflective as his love of reading and scholarship might suggest. "Passionate" was the adjective employed by old Bertie McMaster of Kilmactranny when he recalled stories that the elders of his generation used to tell, of how the vicar bullied the young men of the parish into joining his cricket team, then raged at them during practice sessions for their unskilled performance; how he pilloried boys and girls who had not learned their Sunday school lesson; how he stopped in the middle of a Sunday sermon to scourge latecomers; how he was known for miles around as an exemplary shot—a man who, drunk or sober, could knock a magpie off a pig's back with a single bullet or catch a plover in flight.

In Frenchpark, in the pubs along the road between the village and Tibohine, local people who remembered the rector would say of him with a smile and a wink, "He was a playboy, he was."

Unorthodox, impetuous, strong-willed, scarcely the reticent and reserved Christian clergyman portrayed in some biographical sketches of Douglas Hyde, the Reverend Arthur Hyde, Jr., was not a man to accept disappointment or disobedience from his sons nor to encourage meekness by example. Inevitably there were clashes. His disagreements with young Arthur, although heated, were usually intellectual. His more frequent quarrels with Oldfield at times ended in violence. To the Reverend Hyde a thigh injury would not have been an acceptable excuse for Douglas's falling behind in his studies. Capricious as well as contentious, he was clearly capable of one day, without warning, packing the boy off to the hated Kingstown school—and then withdrawing him just as quickly the next, especially if the school failed to meet his exacting standards. Chronic attacks of gout (brought on by chronic drinking) did not improve his normally irascible nature. If he had no patience with the shortcomings of others, he had less with his own: his illnesses were perceived by him to be both a deficiency and a curse. Yet he was also a man of boundless energy and ingenuity who could tackle drains and the souls of the damned with similar enthusiasm, devise and construct mechanisms for moving rocks, labor alongside the hardiest workmen during haying or harvest season, encourage his sons to match and surpass his own ability at sports, and in a dozen other ways present himself as a father to admire and emulate. About money he was at times miserly, at times generous. Although in private he mouthed a narrow bigotry particularly upsetting to Douglas, his behavior toward Catholic tenants, workmen, and neighbors was above reproach. Frequently unreasonable, in general (except for one lengthy feud with Oldfield) he did not hold a grudge. Frequently penitent, his resolutions to change his ways did not last either. A mercurial man capable of softness, understanding, high good humor, pigheadedness, irrational anger, and boorishness, all within the space of minutes or hours, he was neither easy to love nor easy to despise, although by turns he inspired these and other strong emotions in all three of his sons.

Following his return from the school to which he had been briefly banished, Douglas appears to have coped with his unpredictable father by assiduously meeting his obligations and concealing feelings that would not meet with parental approval, meanwhile subtly distancing himself. Yet to most people he seemed a typical adolescent, wandering off on his own with his gun and his dog; seizing opportunities to ride into town or to a local fair with Connolly, his father's steward; helping Dockry, a workman, with minor repairs; matching his strength and skill in boxing and broad-jumping against that of cottage boys near his own age. But in the notebooks in which he faithfully wrote out the academic exercises that were assigned but rarely reviewed by his father, he also allowed himself opportunities to exercise his imagination in ways that provide early clues to the character, personality, and attitudes beneath his untroubled mask.

Most striking in Hyde's boyhood exercise books is his playful delight in words—whether in English, French, or Irish—and his aptitude for using them to set mood and create character. His earliest constructions are easily recognized projections of himself introduced in roles devised for his own ironic amusement. Complaining, for example, of chronic soreness of his eyelids, adolescent Douglas chose a mock-heroic stance, a popular verse form, and third-person narrative in French to make light of his discomfort:

J'ai grand mal aux mes yeux,
Dit le brave D.H.
J'ai grand mal aux mes yeux,
Dit le brave D.H.

J'ai grand mal aux mes yeux,
Aux mes yeux si beaux et bleus,
Mais enfin je suis au bout,
Dit le brave D.H.

Very different although of approximately the same date is the limited diction, wavering tone, uncertain rhythm, and unmusical meter of his rhymed composition extolling the pleasures of alcohol, written in un-punctuated schoolboy English:

What drink is so nice
    As a tumbler of punch
Hot with lemon and spice
    Just after one's lunch.

Lordpunch is the loveliest beverage can be
    Tis the wholesomest sweetest and nicest of all
And the greatest restorer I ever did see
    After weakness or illness a shake or a fall.

Punch must not be made carelessly or badly
    If you would wish to thoroughly enjoy it
The water must be boiling fierce and madly
    For if it is not so you will destroy it.

Give me punch both hot and strong
    And I'd ask for nothing more
I would drink all evening long
    Till I fell upon the floor

Now I feel my head is going
    Round and round the room doth spin
One glass more to overflowing
    And I think I'll turn in.

Different again is the melodramatic diction and swashbuckling, declamatory style of the voice of his rebel patriot:

Let each son of Erin unsheath his bright blade
Let the ruthless oppressor insult us no more
We'll avenge our houses in ruin low laid
We'll avenge the injustice they've done us of yore.

Because the Reverend Hyde's educational method was to assign lessons, establish the levels of achievement he expected, make books available, and then leave his sons to arrange their own study schedule in the tradition of the English tutorial system, Douglas was free to play his verbal games whenever he pleased, without fear of a schoolmasterly reprimand. From time to time, apparently at Douglas's own request, his brother Arthur would review his work, especially his English essays and his translations from Latin; Cecilly Hyde, his favorite aunt, helped him with his French. Irish was a language he had to learn viva voce, from such tutors as Seamas Hart, Mrs. Connolly, and Biddy Crummy, for although many native speakers learned to write English in school, Irish remained for them the oral language of cottage and field. Using symbols and spellings from French, Greek, English, and (later, when he was introduced to it) German, Douglas devised for himself as a study aid a phonetic system through which he could record in writing the useful phrases, wise sayings, and snatches of poetry and song that he was then acquiring daily. *"Noreya ve dhoul rotin,"* Douglas's phonetic rendering of *nuair bhí an diabhal ró-tinn* (when the devil was very sick), a case in point, begins one of many Irish-language stories he transcribed in his exercise book, using the system he had developed. A similar system was devised by Jeremiah Curtin, the American-born folklorist and linguist (at his death he reportedly commanded sixty languages) who in 1887, 1891–1893, and 1899 collected and recorded Irish folktales using symbols and spellings from German, French, and Polish.

With young Douglas thus occupied to his own and his father's satisfaction, life in the glebe house of Tibohine parish settled for a time into a reasonably pleasant routine. Sundays everyone in the family went to church where (unless crippled by gout or otherwise "not well") the Reverend Arthur Hyde preached temperance, gentleness of spirit, moderation of behavior, verbal restraint, and other virtues he did not practice at home. Sometimes Lord de Freyne attended the service, after which Lady de Freyne often invited Mrs. Hyde to Frenchpark for luncheon or tea. Annette usually accompanied her mother and helped entertain Lady de Freyne and other visitors invited in turn to the glebe house, but Douglas rarely joined them. In his early adolescence he was particularly wary of social situations that required him to be cordial to girls of his own age, especially Lady de Freyne's daughter, whose mother seemed intent on their becoming friends. More to his liking were invitations to Ratra, then the estate of John French, Lord de Freyne's brother, where open fields that sloped down to Lough Gara offered good shooting almost any time of the year.

Among frequent visitors to the glebe house there were always aunts, uncles, cousins, and friends, chiefly from Mohill, Galway, Cork, and Dublin, whom singly and together Douglas's family visited in return, often for days and weeks at a time. Again, as much as possible, Douglas avoided such visits, preferring his rambles at home, alone or with Seamas Hart, Lord de Freyne's gamekeeper. Drumkilla, the home of the Mohill Hydes, was an exception. Although modest in size by Ascendancy standards, to Douglas it was spacious and charming. Neat, comfortable, and attractively furnished, built high on a hill overlooking a wooded pond, on a fine day it offered a view of four counties from its large and graceful windows. By contrast, the glebe house of Tibohine stood in a grove of trees that obscured distant views, even as it provided shade and shelter from the wind. When Douglas returned from Drumkilla his own house always seemed to be unpleasantly small, dark, and cluttered, with books, papers, clothing, guns, rackets, balls, and other items—all the paraphernalia associated with the multiple daily activities of its occupants—scattered about. At Drumkilla, moreover, where servants were not new and inexperienced and no one had to endure the Reverend Arthur Hyde's quick temper, household affairs ran smoothly under Frances, eldest of the Reverend Arthur Hyde's five sisters, with the help of Douglas's unmarried Drumkilla aunts, Cecilly and Emily. Frances's husband, FitzMaurice Hunt, archdeacon of Armagh, encouraged Douglas's Irish interests, sometimes bringing him books from Dublin. Nearby lived Anne, who was married to John Kane of Mohill

Castle. And in Mohill, in addition to Drumkilla and the Castle, there were other Big Houses, estates of family friends and distant relatives, where Douglas was always welcome at luncheons, tennis parties, teas, and dinners.

At home, although Douglas's time was neither scheduled nor supervised, he was surprisingly organized. Weekdays he devoted to reading, study, and daily chores, relieved by occasional trips with William Connolly to Frenchpark, Ballaghaderreen, or Ballina to buy shot, whiskey, ale, stout, and other provisions or to attend local fairs. Late afternoons he often boxed with Michael Lavin. In summer he spent the long Irish daylight hours at the lake, swimming, boating, and fishing. For sheer pleasure and sport, shooting—at targets, birds, wild rabbits, whatever the season could offer—was the glebe house passion.

In season the Reverend Arthur Hyde and his sons seem to have nearly decimated the Roscommon bird population. Hundreds of teal, partridge, lapwing, redwing, snipe, rook, grouse, curlew, and duck fell regularly to their guns, according to the family's monthly bird-kill statistics, charted by both gunman and species of bird, with additional notes on the number of hares that had been shot. Keeping these records was initially Arthur's responsibility. In the fall of 1873, with Arthur preoccupied by his studies at Trinity, Douglas was appointed to this task. That same year the Hydes acquired Diver, an excellent retriever that was always at Douglas's heels. In late autumn and winter the spirited dog added to the daily excitement focused on the rise and fall of the turlough that lured migrating waterfowl to nearby meadows.

Externally at least, except for Douglas's brief enrollment in the school in Kingstown, little disturbed or disrupted Hyde family life in the years 1873 and 1874. Aside from Douglas's measles and thigh injury, his father's chronic complaints, his mother's asthma, and such minor ailments as colds and unspecified aches and pains, family health remained reasonably good. The comings and goings of neighbors, parishioners, friends, uncles, aunts, and cousins provided occasional diversion (in season, when there were enough to play, cricket and tennis were favorite games) as well as opportunities to enjoy the company of others. Father and sons enjoyed—or so it seemed—an easy companionship.

II

In March 1874, Douglas Hyde began another journey. This time it was no voyage out, nor did it require that he board the

train from Ballaghaderreen to Dublin as he had when he had been taken
to school in Kingstown. Instead, by means of a simple diary whose field
of exploration was his own consciousness, he traveled inward. His
vehicle, neither elegant nor new, was an old cash book covered in
mottled paper that had been used by his mother for household accounts.
Along with scratched-out sums and abbreviated notes, its inside cover
was inscribed twice with her name ("Bessy Hyde," and then "Bessie
Hyde"), twice with his own ("D. Hyde," partly obscured by a large
inkblot, then "Douglas Hyde," with flourishing capitals). Douglas
added also a drawing of a snub-nosed witch or dunce with unruly hair.
In this first of many diaries Hyde was to keep throughout much of his
long life, he set out to discover worlds not yet imagined, even in his
fourteen-year-old fancy: external worlds that he helped to create; worlds
within him that developed gradually as, traveling silently and alone
through his inner universe, his more daring leaps of dream and imagination undetected, he was assured protection from the kind of misstep
or misjudgment that in 1873 had made him the butt of schoolmate
jokes and jibes.

Among educated Victorians, diaries were, of course, commonplace.
The nineteenth century, R. L. Stevenson had once declared, was the
age of the optic nerve in literature. Letters and journals of the period
typically contain visual observations and descriptions that provide a
continuing source of information about Victorian society. But the
nineteenth century also prized subjectivity: it was an era of confession,
reflection, and self-examination. In its private and public writings,
documentary as well as fictional, what appear to be external truths often
mask inner responses to outer realities. Toward the end of the century
psychological novels and tales were increasingly in vogue; even short
fictions serialized in newspapers as "letters," "journals," or "true accounts" reveal the trend toward subjectivity.

Books and newspapers were numerous in the Hyde household, yet
at first Douglas's boyhood diary, unaffected by popular fashion, seems
much like that of any country-bred fourteen-year-old:

Got new boots from Narry on Feb 21
Had two new lambs on March 2
Snow on March 9. Heavy on March 10
Pa made a double shot at snipe at the flash on March 9
I shot a jackdaw Pa shot two snipe on March 10
Pa shot a jackdaw
Snow & frost on March 11
Pa shot a jackdaw on March 12

Thaw on March 12
Began thathing [sic] the cowhouse
Out shooting shot a partridge & field hare on Mar 13
Took a ride on the pony
Pa went to French park fine day 14
Sunday Fine day 15
Wet day 16
Fine day 17
Fine day. Shot a seagull, took a ride
Pa out shooting. Shot 2 snipe 18
Finished thaching [sic] the cowhouse 18
Hart gave me a black-thorn 18
Connolly began harrowing 18
Rough day. Pa out shooting shot a snipe. Ma's sheep had two lambs 19
Fine day. Ma's sheep had a lamb. 20
Arthur came home from Dublin. Wet day. O went to London on the 21
Sunday 22
Arthur out shooting and shot a snipe, fine day took a ride on the pony 23
Hart gave Arthur a black-thorn on the 23
Very fine day. Pa and Arthur went to Cornwall [the Irish town, not the English
    district] Connolly harrowing. I sowed some oats 24
Connolly branded the lambs. Pa shot a couple of rooks for the oats. Fine day.
Connolly bought 2 calves at Ballagh a derreen [sic] for ᶠ12ˢ10 25
Connolly harrowing, pretty fine day. Pa went to Slievroe [sic] & gave cigars to
a man who had astma [sic] on 26th
Had a third lamb. Very wet day. Harrowed a little 27

Although the voice of these entries—matter-of-fact, noncommittal, emotionally remote from events observed—strongly resembles the diary voice of Douglas's older brother Arthur at the same age, Arthur was far neater than Douglas and wrote with a businesslike dispatch. The diary of his adolescent years was also more efficiently circumscribed in terms of purpose: with few exceptions he confined his terse accounts to the arrival and departure of housemaids, the daily bird kill, and lessons completed. Typical of Arthur's diary entries, "7 November 1866. Shot 2 redwings, did 30 lines of Salust" provides, characteristically, few clues to anything beyond his immediate concerns.

Unfocused and unhurried, Douglas's very different chronicle meanders like the river Suck, washing impersonally over a broader range of observations: the weather, the activities of others, changes in flora and fauna, anything that happened into his stream of consciousness at the moment of writing. At times the stream narrowed to a trickle, leaving wide margins and interlinear spaces to be filled with sketches and doodles. Some sketches are caricatures. One labeled "owner of this book" shows a male figure holding a bouquet. Others—detailed drawings of guns, flintlocks, pistols, tumblers, and pitchers on tables—display a draftsmanlike skill. Words wind between and around these illustrations, their letters difficult to contain within narrowly ruled lines. Wherever Douglas's pen paused, ink formed pools that obliterated what he had written, sometimes obscuring half a page or more. When the stream moved on he did not bother to rescue what had been lost. At times his pen moved hastily, uncertainly, impatiently scratching out letters that had not been formed as intended. Occasionally he lingered over a page, embroidering his firm, round, open letters, double-inking and thickening lines, shading spaces, and enhancing capitals with elaborate flourishes and curlicues. The leisure he devoted to these graphics contrasts with the short shrift he gave to the syntax, diction, and punctuation of his elliptical sentences and phrases.

Despite similarities in diary voice, Douglas at fourteen was in fact the opposite of his brother Arthur in almost every respect. Nor was he much like Oldfield or even Annette, although with his sister he always had a strong bond of affection and understanding not evident in his relations with his brothers. As in many families, these differences in personality seem related in part to sequence of birth. Arthur, born November 10, 1853, had been named not only for his own father and the three earlier Reverend Arthur Hydes who had preceded the rector of Tibohine into the ministry but also for the Arthur Hyde who had been knighted by Elizabeth I and had established the Irish branch of the family in Cork. The burden of family tradition and expectation fell heavily upon him. Oldfield, born almost a year to the day after Arthur, was so close in age as to be constantly paired with him, as if the two were twins, creating a situation that Oldfield often vehemently rejected. Douglas, the fourth son, born January 17, 1860, was separated from his elder brothers not only by an expanse of years but by the intervening birth of Hugh, who did not survive infancy. Fifth and last born May 19, 1865, was Annette, younger than Douglas by five years (therefore much younger than Oldfield and Arthur), and the only daughter. Her brothers were understood to be the care and responsibility of their father; different attitudes and expectations shaped her future and placed her, during childhood and adolescence, under her mother's supervision.

More removed than his brothers and sister from his father's passions and his mother's concerns, Douglas had in some respects the easiest childhood. Less closely supervised, he was freer to come and go unquestioned, to let his imagination wander, to speculate on aspects of his own nature and the nature of others, and to sketch and doodle and experiment with ways of putting his thoughts and feelings on paper in the poems, prose pieces, and drawings of 1873–1876 found in his exercise books and diaries.

It was in a diary entry of March 28, 1874, that Douglas tested a new voice, different from any he ever had used before—his own voice in Irish: "Wet day *Thoine moisther war shane a l'oure ulk de Arthure oge* [italics ours]. Had a fight with the gloves with Michael Lavin. Pa made a double shot at rooks for the oats." He had previously used his phonetic system to copy into his exercise book Irish words and phrases that he had heard, but this was his first recorded attempt to put his own thoughts and observations into a form of written Irish.

Among Hyde scholars, Dominic Daly has devoted the most time and effort to analyzing Hyde's phonetic script and suggesting readings for key passages. "*Thoine moisther*," he notes, a recurrent phrase in Hyde's boyhood-diary Irish, and the two words with which the March 18, 1874, Irish entry begins, is easily identified as *tá an máistir* (the master is); "*shane*" is surely *sé féin* (himself), with the *f* aspirated as it usually is in conversation. Less convincing is Daly's suggestion that "*a l'oure ulk de Arthure oge*" may be transliterated as *a labhair olc de Arthure óg*, which Daly translates as "who spoke badly of young Arthur." A major problem is "*war*," for which Daly tentatively offers *i bhfeirg* (angry), admitting that it does not provide the link necessary to make sense out of the whole.

An alternate reading, based on identifying "*war*" as "*bhfuair*" and "*l'oure*" as *leabhar*, provides *Tá an máistir, an bhfuair sé féin an leabhar olc de Arthure óg?* (ungrammatical Irish for "The master, did he himself get/take the bad book from young Arthur?"). This not only makes sense but has the virtue of credibility, given the Reverend Arthur Hyde's relationship with his eldest son. Omission of the *an* before *bhfuair* is easily explained by the fact that it is scarcely audible if not dropped altogether in conversation; for similar reasons *an* before *leabhar* would be reduced to "*a*." As for the question mark, even in English, Douglas was careless about punctuation, so its omission cannot be considered significant. A parlor game, however, easily could be made of other possible readings.

More significant than a literal translation of this uncertain line is the way in which Douglas's new voice introduced in his diary entry of March 28, 1874, drops the purely objective, matter-of-fact, and noncommittal stance imitative of Arthur to express, if only obliquely, perceptions concerning his relationships with those around him. This new persona changes figure and ground: it presents him as an observer rather than a participant within the family circle. Its diction is that of Seamas Hart, William Connolly, Mrs. Connolly, the Lavins, and Dockry, the Irish country people with whom his unsupervised days were spent. It interposes distance between himself and selected others. Although Daly regards *"Thoine moisther"* (the master), *"Arthure oge"* (young Arthur), and (in later entries) *"Thoine moisthuress"* or *"moistrass"* (the mistress) as merely a result of Douglas's "having picked up his Irish from listening to the servants and the local people who had dealings with the Rectory," the effect of these terms is to emphasize separation. The Irish equivalents of "Pa" and "Ma," the English terms Douglas normally used to refer to his father and mother, are *"Da"* and *"Mam,"* not *"thoine moisther"* and *"thoine moistrass"*—and as he never, in English or Irish, referred to his father by his first name, he had no reason of course, to add *"oge"* (Irish *óg,* young) to *"Arthure"* to distinguish brother from father.

That Douglas's shift in figure and ground is intentional and specific is evident in its selectivity: although names of other family members (e.g., "Fiach" for Hunt; "Sisilla" for Cecilly) are Irished, the people themselves are not distanced but rather drawn along with Douglas into his new milieu. As Douglas developed greater fluency in Irish, his Irish persona (which he later referred to as "Dubhglas de h-Íde") used language with an even greater sophistication that reflected on the one hand ambivalence toward felt social and psychological relationships within each of the two worlds to which he belonged, and on the other hand acceptance of the duality of his own attitudes and emotions. Clearly he did not want to discard his English persona but to maintain distinctions between the English and Irish selves he had identified within him. His treatment of his relationship with James, or Seamas, Hart, is a case in point: In English entries the voice of the narrative *I* is that of the son of the Reverend Arthur Hyde, kinsman of Lord de Freyne; the gamekeeper, called simply "Hart," is presented as a minor figure. In Irish entries, the narrative *I* is a country boy; the gamekeeper, called "Shamus," is a major presence, a loved and respected friend, companion, and father figure.

As Douglas's use of Irish improved and increased, examples of his hidden persona proliferated, revealing emotional qualities of hitherto unrecognized perspectives and relationships. Eventually his visible and invisible selves were reintegrated in the public figure known to the world as An Craoibhin, but in 1874 and for some years after, only his diaries held evidence of how different young Douglas was from the boy his family and friends thought that they knew.

In the months that followed March 28, 1874, Douglas introduced French in addition to Irish into his diary entries. When his vocabulary in one or the other did not provide the words he needed, he sometimes combined the two languages in a single hodgepodge expedient. At first he advanced faster in French, but as a small but steady stream of new Irish words were added to his phonetically written Irish, he found new opportunities to use what he called "Gaeliclish." On April 19 he completed in Irish a sentence begun in Greek. These verbal experiments signaled not only his future linguistic interests and ability but also the extent to which language was for him what paint is to the artist or sound to the composer: a means of self-expression, a medium for interpreting life.

For Douglas, progress in Irish did not come easily. It required repeated modification of the simplest phrases as his ear detected new aspects of non-English sounds. Alert to differences in pronunciation and intonation patterns among individual speakers, he constantly varied the form in which he recorded common expressions. Before he wrote he tried each phrase himself, twisting his tongue around strange-sounding phonemes as best he could, searching for English-language sounds that could be combined to indicate them. If Irish lines in his diary are sometimes undecipherable, it is because this form of mimicry, based on what he thought his ear had heard as well as what his tongue had tried to reproduce, at times resulted in strange constructions.

Like most students of Irish as a second language, Douglas struggled also with syntax. However much he tried to guard against intrusions from English, in the process of weaving simple Irish sentences into short descriptive passages he inevitably mangled constructions. Some nonstandard expressions that he continued to use long after he achieved fluency were not, however, the result of his own linguistic errors or misunderstandings but adoptions from the changing idiom of north Roscommon which became a bogus currency when that dialect vanished.

By spring of 1875 Douglas was able to sustain a short written narrative in both French and Irish. But while French diary entries revealed an acquaintance with literature as well as language, Irish entries—which he continued to write phonetically—reflected only the oral culture. For the moment there was no remedy for this situation, for he was without either tutors literate in Irish or Irish books from which he might learn to read and write on his own. Then in August, Hyde found in a storage cupboard of the glebe house an Irish-language Church of Ireland catechism left behind by one of his father's predecessors. With the English version readily available as a trot, he immediately set himself the task of learning to form Irish letters, spell Irish words, and understand Irish grammar.

As a result of Douglas's experiments linking voice and language, three personae began to take shape in his diary entries during 1874–1876. Chief among them was of course his English persona, expressed in the public voice so much like that of his brother Arthur. Very much that of a squire in the making, it presents him as prosaic, proper, restrained in his expression of feelings, uncritical in his acceptance of his own social and economic position, confident, and satisfied. The idiom of upper-class English is evident in its diction (e.g., "fetched capitally" to describe Diver's performance in retrieving a duck downed by his gun). Its interest in the environment is focused on sports and on the practical aspects of estate management. It is the voice of privilege and plenty, of the writer of the drinking songs recorded in his exercise book, of an Ascendancy lad who regards ample supplies of porter, whiskey, and tobacco as perquisites of a young squire's life.

With this English persona filtering out any hint of unpleasantness, Hyde's diary in English shows little evidence of family tension, incompatibility, anger, resentment, or even mere disagreement: it paints a family portrait in which brothers, sister, mother ("Ma"), and father ("Pa," or "Governor") enjoy a genial, stress-free relationship in a benign world. Unmentioned is the agrarian unrest that threatened the Irish social order of the 1870s. Awareness of the violent character of nearby confrontations is evident only in the report that at the Sligo races four landlords, "Harman King & 3 others," were "stabbed by a man of the name of Clancy." Little else suggests concern with contemporary political or intellectual issues or an interest in world events. Shooting is the major interest, the goal of Douglas's English persona being always to increase the number of "things" killed. No empathy for bird or animal, no awareness of one as a living creature, is ever expressed. The "things" themselves are regarded as no more than targets. A list at the end of the 1875 diary names the books Douglas has been reading, but their texts are not discussed, nor is there any mention of daily lessons or recitations. The general impression (accepted by Dominic Daly and Diarmid Coffey) is that as a boy Douglas Hyde was "no bookworm." If it were not for his exercise book of 1873–1876 and a later, more detailed diary account of his reading and study during this period, it would be easy to assume that, scholastically, Douglas was the unidentified dunce who sometimes shows up in his drawings.

The persona presented in Douglas's diary entries in French is strikingly different. It expresses a reverence for life and ambivalent feelings toward the killing of a hare in an account of an incident in which he is the boy with the gun: "I tried to take a shot at one of the rabbits, but the gun failed me because the powder was wet," begins the French text. Subsequent shots also fail as the rabbit crouches, trembling, before him. Finally, "the fourth time I killed him. The poor rabbit was so filled with fear that he could not move." Other French entries reveal a persona that is less lusty, more sophisticated than Douglas's English persona. Boastful accounts of drinking sessions are reduced to wry references to a brief "*malade*" both caused and remedied by drinking "*l'eau de vie.*" Response to the natural beauty of the world is poetically if inaccurately and ungrammatically expressed in such lines as "Ils avait beaucoup de astres dans le soir." The French persona celebrates a capacity for tenderness and sensitivity that he repressed—for a time at least—in English. It demonstrates also a greater interest in "*un livre.*"

Douglas's Irish persona seems shier and less sophisticated. It immediately retreats to sidelined observer in situations involving members of his own immediate family but is foregrounded when, alone and conscious of the natural world on a frosty morning, it expresses a sense of being at one with the universe. In the company of Hart, Lavin, Mrs. Connolly, and other Irish speakers (all referred to by their names in Irish), it is described as socially engaged, sitting before the fire, drinking, smoking, and talking. Its gregariousness in this company contrasts with the reserve of the solitary persona of English entries whose encounters with local people (referred to by English names) occur for the most part by accident, when he is out walking with his brother Arthur or alone with his dog. The cumulative effect does not come quite to the point of casting Douglas's Irish persona in the role of local country lad, but it does present the narrative *I* of Irish entries as more at home among country people than with the Anglo-Irish of manor and glebe house.

As Douglas improved his ability to communicate in Irish, his diary entries began to show distinctions between subjects chosen for treatment in English and those recorded in Irish. English becomes the language of facts and events related to his Anglo-Irish milieu (his home, his father's library, the church in Tibohine, its parishioners, family friends and relations, and Ascendancy-class neighbors). Roscommon weather, flora, and fauna are (to the extent that vocabulary was available) noted in Irish, as are facts and anecdotes from Irish history, and stories learned from Hart, Connolly, and Dockry.

On March 23, 1875, less than six months after he had successfully written his first short, simple narrative in Irish, Douglas tackled a complex account of a curious incident in which a *pooka,* or ghostly apparition, resembling his brother Arthur (at that time in Dublin) suddenly opened the door of a room in which he and other family members were entertaining visitors, the Lloyds, and then just as suddenly disappeared. Annette was close to the apparition; so was Hyde's mother. The account is given verisimilitude by the report that this was not the ghost's first visit: it had been seen before by his aunt Emily and his mother; by Jane Drury, a former local schoolteacher who had become a member of the Hyde household (she is buried with the Hydes in the Tibohine churchyard); and by a painter working about the house whom it had so frightened when it appeared on the stone stairs that he nearly had collapsed from fright. Although still dependent on his phonetic system, Douglas imbues this story with a sense of wonder and suspense. He skillfully arranges details so that he first captures reader attention with the announcement that something extraordinary has happened; second, he states his facts simply and matter-of-factly, to answer the immediate question of what has happened; third, he names unimpeachable eyewitnesses (Annette and Hyde's mother, who were even closer to the apparition than the Lloyds) to silence the incredulous; and he concludes with testimony designed to remove any question of error or conspiracy (the same thing, observed by a workman, had happened here before). Interestingly, Hyde does not call on himself as witness, although he is among those reported to have been present. Instead, he presents the entire story (Daly identifies it as possibly one told to Douglas by Seamas Hart) through the reports of others. In an interview late in his life Hyde stated that his lifelong interest in the art of storytelling had begun when he was a boy. The art of this narrative suggests that by 1875 this interest was well developed—and that he already had decided that his storyteller would be his Irish persona.

III

Three months after his fourteenth birthday, on April 22, 1874, Douglas reported in his diary that he weighed nine stone six pounds and was growing rapidly: not a bad record for a boy his age. By the end of October the new boots he had bought at Narry's on February 21 had to be replaced because they were too small. Such evidence of his physical growth and development delighted him. He also liked to test his muscular strength and agility. "I jumped about 15 feet on one of the grass walks on pretty level ground," he noted proudly two months after he turned fifteen, in his diary entry for March 30, 1875.

Year by year, Douglas indeed was changing, but life in Roscommon retained the same predictable rhythms. In the spring—an exciting time for Douglas, as he was the owner of several sheep—the lambs were born. One or two of the new lambs usually belonged to him. May was the month when all the sheep were washed and sheared. In May 1874 he dutifully recorded that Connolly had sold his wool for £13 and his new lambs for £3.16. After sheepshearing there were cricket games with Arthur and Oldfield, home from Trinity by the third week of May. May was the month also, according to the Reverend Arthur Hyde (who had made a particular study of folk medicine), for giving Diver sulphur in his dinner and making sure that the dog was "rub'd . . . well with sulphur & unsalted butter" in accordance with his prescription.

Day-to-day chores were a fact of life throughout the year, but especially during the drier months between spring and fall, for the glebe lands of the Tibohine church were energetically and efficiently worked by the Reverend Arthur Hyde, assisted by his three sons, his steward, and several farm workers. The Reverend Arthur Hyde also attended to whatever farm or household objects needed mending or fixing, from flower boxes to drains, and together with his sons planned and executed remodeling and construction projects, some essential, some associated with one or another of the sporting activities that were a regular feature of Frenchpark life. Douglas's diary records one afternoon in June 1875 when brothers and father designed and set up a target for gun practice:

After tea we raised the large stone out of the little yard with ropes and rollers for which we cut down a tree. And with great difficulty we placed it in the garden. . . . [The next day we] painted the target & fired at it.

Pleased with their success, they began their next task, the building of a summer house, two weeks later; they completed it in three days.

Experienced in handling tools and confident of his skills, Douglas also had his own separate building and mending projects. One year he made a swing for his sister, Annette, and painstakingly assembled cartridges only to discover, when he went to use them, that they had been torn apart by mice. In his diary he noted how he had planed a bow that had splintered and mended a torn stirrup with a piece of hemp. A prized possession was a "lucky briar" that he had cut for himself. It was, he declared, "nearly 7 feet long & very straight."

Boxing was a popular pastime whenever the weather permitted. Usually Douglas's opponent was Michael Lavin, with whom he was fairly evenly matched, but sometimes he liked to challenge others. One afternoon in 1875 he discovered that putting on the gloves with another neighbor, MacDermotroe, was more than he could handle. He fared better on Corpus Christi Day when the Tibohine church sponsored an outing attended by about eighty people who "came for cricket & box'd with the gloves & a little with naked fists."

After Corpus Christi, to Douglas's delight, the weather usually turned warm enough for the Hyde boys to bathe in the lake. Summer nights, mostly clear, were filled with the fascination of stars. On one clear night, the fourteenth of July, 1875, Hyde was awed by the sight of a comet, plainly visible in the northwest sky. As August approached, he added his voice to the general concern that the good weather continue through the next two months of haying and harvest time, for the crops would be spoiled if they could not be brought in because of a period of prolonged rain. Between August and December shooting fever increased, especially when water birds were spotted along the borders of the lake or near the turlough. Douglas filled his diaries of these fall months with details of ammunition purchased, birds killed, and the rise and fall of the turlough. In accordance with the ritual he and his brothers had been taught by their father, he regularly took apart, cleaned, and reassembled his guns. In this way he tracked the seasons of the year.

Next to the Reverend Arthur Hyde, William Connolly bore chief responsibility for managing the glebe estate, washing and shearing the sheep, sowing the oats, looking after sick cows, buying and selling the Hyde family's livestock at local fairs, and dealing with local suppliers of equipment and provisions. Douglas and Annette—either or both—frequently accompanied him on his trips to Ballaghaderreen, Frenchpark, and Castlerea. A staple item always included in the glebe house shopping list was whiskey. One day Connolly bought a barrel of porter and a gallon of *uisce beatha* (whiskey) in Castlerea, then went to Boyle for a canister of powder, a potted ham, Worcestershire sauce, pickles—and another gallon of whiskey. Arthur, moreover, who had accompanied Connolly to Boyle ostensibly to help with the purchase of provisions, had come home with a separate bottle of whiskey for himself as well.

Strong drink was consumed in considerable quantities by everyone associated with the glebe house. All the Hyde boys were introduced early to porter, hot punch, whiskey, and poteen; all developed a taste while still children for these "national" drinks, as Hyde used to call them. Only for Oldfield was the habit to become, as for the Reverend Arthur Hyde, a serious problem.

Neighboring farmers and workmen came and went informally in the Hyde kitchen, sometimes stopping for a cup of tea or glass of ale during the day or a game of cards and tumbler of whiskey in the evening. Douglas and his brothers came and went just as informally in the cottages along the lanes that crisscrossed meadow and bog. When Dockry's son was short of powder and caps, he came up to the glebe house to borrow some from Douglas. Douglas regularly went down to the Lavins to box with Michael. Sometimes he rode his pony to Hanly's in the village. Among these local companions, especially during the summers of 1874 and 1875, Hyde's Irish persona was strengthened. His brother Arthur, aloof and serious, very much the Trinity man, no longer could be counted on to fish with him from the iron bridge or ramble around the countryside: he was continually arriving from or leaving for Dublin with an air of great importance. Oldfield was in London during much of the summer of 1874. Annette, who had just turned nine, was too young to join Douglas in his excursions on foot over meadow and bog or by boat on the river, and in any case she was often in Mohill or Dublin or Galway with their mother. Douglas did not mind; he preferred his independent life. He could choose if he pleased to accompany the men and boys from along the road and from the back of the meadow to see the "great race" in Bellanagare or, as on one very wet day, he could stay warm and comfortable, chatting with old men and old women by a cottage fire. Even on a pleasant morning that might have lured him away from his usual haunts, he declined an invitation from a crowd bound for the Sligo races to remain with Seamas Hart, helping clear the meadow of sticks and stones. His favorite hours were those he spent with Hart in the meadow and on the bogs or sitting before a fire in the gamekeeper's cottage, listening to his stories.

When in 1875 a series of family illnesses disrupted life in the glebe house, Douglas was especially glad of Hart's company and the friendship of neighbors. During the Reverend Arthur Hyde's attacks of gout he took refuge with them. When Bessie Hyde, weakened by asthma, was too ill to attend church services, when both Arthur and Oldfield were incapacitated by unspecified complaints that required the attention of Dr. Cuppaidge, and when the glebe house was silent and gloomy, they provided a comforting place in which to spend Sunday afternoons. During this period Douglas complained vaguely to his diary in phonetic Irish of his own health: "I am not well" and "I am not well at all." He was in fact fine, but he tended to make such complaints when illness focused attention on others, leaving him lonely and alone. The only physical problem that repeatedly troubled him was a recurrent muscle pain, unpleasant but not incapacitating, in his right leg; at fifteen he was prone to "growing pains." Other than that, except for a bruised arm suffered when his gun kicked, a thumb sprain from boxing, a single bout with a queasy stomach, and an occasional sore throat, he was a sturdy adolescent, with consistently fewer illnesses, accidents, and injuries than anyone else in his family, except possibly his sister, Annette.

Seamas Hart, with his fluent Irish, his talent for reciting poem and story, his rich store of Irish historical and cultural tradition, his knowledge of the natural world of Frenchpark and environs, his Fenian sympathies, his calm strength, and his capacity for warmth and affection, was not only a central figure in Douglas's daily life but a major influence on his development. Brief notes—that Seamas was here or was not here or was ill or had begun to improve; that Douglas had walked down to Hart's or was with him at Ratra; that Douglas, Arthur, and Oldfield had gone together to Hart's in the evening—recur throughout his 1875 diary. From time to time Hart even stayed overnight at the glebe house, helping out in times of illness or other kinds of trouble that required his patience and wisdom. Between May and September when Bessie Hyde was seriously and recurrently ill, Douglas's days began to take their character from these diary notes, recorded in his phonetic Irish: "Ve Shamus in sho" (Seamas was here); "Neil Shamus gummoich" (Seamas is not well); "Shool mae iga tyoch Shamus"; (I walked down to Seamas's house); "Ve Shamus liom" (Seamas was with me). After August, when he began studying the Irish catechism he had found, his spelling gradually changed. First he introduced the long stroke, or *fada,* over vowels that he had been writing as *oa, ah, ee,* and *oo.* He did not always employ the mark consistently or correctly, but it was a step in the direction of conventional spelling.

In May, when Douglas's mother suffered several long and severe asthma attacks, "Ne ve a Moistrass gummoich" (The mistress was not well) and "Thoine Moistrass besuch" (The mistress is improving) joined "Ve Shamus in sho" as alternating refrains. Illness struck the farm animals also. "Mo cuira foor shee baus" wrote Douglas, after one of his sheep died. Seamas was there, too. Three cows became so sick with a common infection called "red water" that the doctor had to be called; one cow almost died. Seamas was again present.

Although dependent on the daily presence of Hart, more and more during the troubled May of 1875, Douglas wandered on his own through the fields and bogs of Frenchpark and Tibohine to the countryside beyond, often staying out very late at night. He also began keeping enough money in his pocket to purchase whiskey and porter in Ballaghaderreen. In July there was great excitement at the glebe house, during a period when Bessie Hyde seemed to be improving, over a sailboat that the Reverend Arthur Hyde had bought in Carrick-on-Shannon. For a time Douglas, his brothers, his sister, and his father grew close again, spending entire days together as, pairing up in various combinations, together they learned to manage the craft. Sailing briefly replaced shooting as the family sport. When the newness wore off, relations returned to normal; Douglas again went his separate way.

The year progressed: as the voice in which Douglas recorded his day-to-day activities and experiences in Irish became more personal, his diary began to reflect not just actions and ideas but fears, disappointments, pleasures, interests. The rector's son remains present in entries written in English; no ripple disturbed the surface calm of his carefully managed existence. Lines written in Irish, however, though briefer and less polished, tell a fuller story. On August 10, Douglas employed both English and Irish to describe a boat race on Lough Gara. Oldfield had been appointed sole judge of the event, a sensitive situation, since the Hyde boat, with Arthur as steersman, was among the competitors. All went well until the last race, which Arthur won by a quarter length. Oldfield's judgment was challenged by members of the crowd. "There was near being a faction fight on account of it," wrote Douglas in English, distancing himself from the situation by characterizing the protest as a kind of brawl among the country people rather than as the howl of indignation it actually was. His apprehension, however, was clear from his Irish: The crowd did not regard the Hyde boys as merely Ascendancy onlookers. Many of the men who participated in the race were joined by supporters from the crowd in what became an increasingly heated protest. A particularly hot-tempered man by the name of Mark was loudest; he was to be feared the most. Dockry warned that the situation was dangerous. "If one man stoops to pick up a stone, others will also," he warned Douglas; "if one man is struck, two hundred will be at it." Cool heads prevailed in the end, and the crowd dispersed without incident. Douglas's English persona replaced his Irish persona after the danger was past.

In September Douglas's mother was again seriously ill. Hart was at the glebe house almost daily, often sleeping there. These facts, plus the monthly register by species and number of birds killed, were recorded, as usual, in Irish. One day, while shooting the "wild bog," Douglas noticed "a very curious sort of ring around the sun such as is round the moon late at night"; it mystified him. In the swamp he spotted a strange-looking duck: "his bill was very large and broad and his wings were a kind of greyish blue." Diver proved himself an extraordinary dog once again by catching and killing a bat in the kitchen. These incidents were noted in English, probably because Douglas's Irish vocabulary was inadequate to their content.

Fine weather had prevailed during September; in contrast, October was often dark, windy, and cold. A few berries remained on the bushes in the garden, but all other natural signs indicated that the harvest season was over. The appearance of large numbers of water birds tempted Douglas outdoors with his gun early each morning and late each night. His success was chronicled in a three-page account that began under a profile sketch of an unidentified bald, smiling man. The receding forehead, which takes its angle from the receding chin, gives the figure a vaguely imbecilic appearance. A sequence of round collars, each larger than the one above it, encircles his neck and shoulders. On the facing page there is a wine glass and a bottle. Were the round collars intended to signify that the man was a cleric? Was this a caricature of the Reverend Arthur Hyde? (His drinking during Bessie Hyde's illness had been troubling Douglas; he had figured less and less in his youngest son's life as the father-son relationship between Douglas and Seamas Hart had intensified.) Or is this Everyman as Douglas—who himself had been experimenting with ale, porter, whiskey, and even poteen, usually in the company of one or both of his brothers—then saw him? An incongruous note on an adjacent page provides the only evidence that academic studies also had been occupying portions of Douglas's time—that he had been reading and rehearsing Horatian odes.

Toward the end of October, Hart became ill. Douglas took a small bottle down to him. In November, Hart was no better. Hyde's diary entries became less detailed, briefer, sometimes containing no information beyond the fact that day after day and sometimes several times a day, he visited Hart's house. A marked decrease in the proportion of Irish to English restores Douglas's impersonal, public persona to control of this portion of his diary, perhaps because he could not take the time to write in Irish, perhaps because he could not cope with his feelings. Irish regained ground as Hart improved at the beginning of December. On December 9, out walking with Arthur, Douglas had a frightening experience that he recounted entirely in Irish, in the first long passage written in months: They had been in the potato field near Hart's cottage when Arthur suddenly fell to the ground, suffered convulsions, and lapsed into unconsciousness. Certain that Arthur was dead, Douglas did not know what to do. Fortunately the incident was witnessed by Thomas Higgins, who quickly obtained from Beirne, a nearby cottager, a door that could be used as a stretcher, then called others to help carry Arthur home. Arthur recovered, but ironically by the twenty-seventh of the month Higgins himself was dead. "*Drimma mudya ig a suchreca*" (I went to his funeral), wrote Douglas in his phonetic Irish, the first such event to be noted in his diary. Soon, however, there was another.

On December 20 Hart was, as usual, at the glebe house. On December 21 he slept there. On December 22 "ní bhí Semuis go maith," wrote Douglas in an entry in Irish in which everything but Hart's first name is spelled correctly: once again, Hart was ill. On December 28 Hart was dead. It was the most devastating loss Hyde ever had suffered—a loss he remembered throughout his life. He expressed his sorrow in a simple, direct, and moving passage written partly in phonetic Irish, partly in conventional Irish script in his diary for December 29:

> Seamas died yesterday. A man so decent and generous, alas, so true and honest, alas, so friendly, alas, never will I see again. He was sick about a week and today he is gone. Poor Seamas, I learned Irish from you. A man so good with the Irish, never will there be another like you. I can see no one at all from now on whom I would love as well as you. May seven angels be with you and may your blessed soul be in heaven now.

4

The Voices of the Fathers

Although years passed before Douglas Hyde again wrote of Seamas Hart, their relationship did not end at Hart's grave but continued in Hyde's consciousness throughout his long life, even into Áras an Uachtaráin. Hart had introduced Douglas to Irish history, folklore, myth, and legend; had shared with him his own store of poems and stories; had passed on to him, as if he were a son, the *seanfhocail*—fragments of ancient wisdom and folk belief—that he had received from his elders. It was from Hart—"the best reciter I ever knew," Hyde later declared—that he had heard his first tales of the Irish spirit world: of ghosts and banshees and the *alp luachra* (newt) which had so afflicted a wealthy Connacht farmer that only "the best doctor in the five provinces," The MacDermot, prince of Coolavin, could save him. From Hart he had learned love songs, religious songs, drinking songs, and laments. Hart had schooled him in histories not found in books but written across the face of the land. Caves, cairns, sacred wells, old temples, ancient forts, dolmens, standing stones, a rippled path across a winter lake—all, Hart had assured him, could be read; all told of Irish heroes, kings, queens, and celebrated events, of powerful poets and enchanters, of a nation that was and a time when Ireland would be a nation once again.

Douglas loved words: their sounds, the look of them on paper, the different qualities they assumed on his tongue, in his exercise book, in the handwriting of another, and on a printed page. Woven in words, the combined riches of antiquity and folk imagination to which Hart had introduced him had fired his desire to see if he himself could fashion stories spun from them. Encouraged by Hart, he had struggled to acquire the Irish language that was the key to these treasures: in his daily diary entries he had laboriously practiced the alchemy of its diction and syntax; on the pages of his exercise books and the blank back leaves of his diary he had cultivated its wordsong. The miscellany he thus accumulated in text and translation included such varied items as "Socraidh na gClein" (Clinton's burial), a song for singer and chorus in five verses of five lines each; a thresher's motto of four lines; a five-line charm for exorcising crickets; and three verses of "Róisin Dubh" (Dark Rosaleen). In his diary and exercise book he had pasted word inventories cut from printed sources, among them a table comparing the botanical, Irish, and English names of common flowers. Experimenting with Irish dialogue, he had created short scenes in strophe and antistrophe and tested his descriptive, comic, and narrative powers in simple prose and imitative verse. One of the last items he had written before Hart's death was a short narrative describing a few hours in which, slowly and pleasantly, warmed by whiskey, a turf fire, and the evening's camaraderie, he, his father and brothers, and the gamekeeper had quietly slipped together into a mellow drunkenness.

In prefaces and introductions to the works he published throughout his long career, Douglas Hyde faithfuly acknowledged Seamas Hart's contributions to his poetry and prose, his folklore studies, and his literary and historical scholarship. In his diary he recorded his more personal debt to Hart during a difficult period of his life when on the one hand he was struggling free of the constraints of the Kiplingesque world of nineteenth-century Anglo-Ireland, while on the other hand he was attempting to make of the hyphen between the two cultures that claimed him a mark of connection rather than division.

In Áras an Uachtaráin, when journalists asked Hyde where and how he had acquired his knowledge of Irish, he used to respond by reciting, in the north Roscommon dialect long vanished by the time he became president, a quatrain that Hart had taught him—"the first verse of Gaelic I ever learned," he would avow. He never spelled the words conventionally but always wrote them out for the inquisitive in his own peculiar phonetic Irish, just as he had recorded them in his schoolboy copybook when, imitating the voice of the gamekeeper, he had hurried home, repeating the sounds to himself so that he would not lose them before he had the chance to capture them on paper:

Ballagh-a-derreen a chran
Bolla gon aggus gurtugh,
Munna will thu st'yeeh in om
Yucee thu woll' a trussgo.

Beneath these lines he would write the English translation that Hart
had given him:

Ballaghaderreen of the tree,
A town scanty and famine stricken,
Unless you are there in time,
You will come home fasting.

Scanty and famine stricken: that was how Tibohine seemed to Douglas Hyde when in January 1876 he faced the new year without Hart.
For more than a month he wrote no more than a half dozen phrases
and a few sentences in Irish, taking refuge from the emotions he
could not express in the aloof, remote, English-speaking persona of
his early 1874 diary entries—a persona so like his brother Arthur's, despite marked differences in their personalities. Terse and noncommittal,
avoiding the people whose sympathy might have renewed his pain and
the cottages in which talk would have turned, inevitably, to Hart's unexpected death, he focused once again on insignificant external events.
More than a month went by without a single reference to Connolly,
Dockry, or the Lavins. His own birthday passed without mention. He
was a son bereaved; he had lost his Irish father.

Douglas's actual father, the dominating, mercurial, and passionate
Ascendancy rector of Frenchpark, was lonely too. Arthur was in his fifth
year at Trinity; Oldfield was in his first. Since their childhood he and
his two elder sons had been almost constant companions. In their absence in the early months of 1876 he turned for company to his third
son, Douglas. Before long, at his urging, Douglas had begun to join
him in activities, indoors and out, that in former days he had been accustomed to sharing only with Arthur and Oldfield. They went shooting together almost daily. When the two elder boys returned home for
brief holidays, Douglas was not excluded; father and sons formed a
foursome. For a time his father and brothers were very nearly the only
companions with whom Douglas broke his solitary rambles. In rain,
heavy dew, and an occasional wet, gray snowfall that quickly turned
to ice and mud, through a long, damp, chill January as gloomy and
overcast as Douglas's spirits, they tramped, all four together or two or

three at a time, across bog, field, and meadow, along river path and edge of lake, in search of game.

Shooting was the Reverend Arthur Hyde's favorite sport; his sons had caught the fever from him. Normally it was a sport they easily enjoyed together, for the observation, concentration, and action it required allowed little opportunity for discussion of subjects on which they disagreed. And all four were superb marksmen, skilled in predicting the movements of birds and small animals. In January of 1876, however, birds were scarce. One day father and sons came home with but a single snipe among them. Another day, alone with Diver, having been disappointed at Ballinphuil, Douglas wandered along the Lung River near the Crinaun bridge, straying inadvertently beyond the bounds of de Freyne territory until he was confronted by an angry gamekeeper of alien fields. A shilling sent the man home grumbling. It was more than Douglas himself got for his time and trouble.

What the month did offer Hyde, in addition to companionship in a time of need, was a kind of schooling in the manners and mores of the Anglo-Irish squirearchy that he had not had before, partly because he had been a third and much younger son, until now excluded for the most part from the social activities of father and older brothers, partly because his own temperament had led him to make a separate life for himself with Hart, Dockry, Connolly, the Lavins, and other local men and boys rather than tag along where he had not felt wanted. Contrasts did not escape him: His father's anecdotes about the races in Roscommon and Galway presented a different side to stories he had heard from gamekeeper and tenant farmer. Watching his father and his father's peers at a cattle fair, he noted that the talk and techniques used by a country gentleman to strike a bargain were not the same as those he had witnessed in the company of Connolly and Dockry. Information obtained from readings in natural history provided the basis of the Reverend Arthur Hyde's lectures on the habits of birds and other game; Hart's traditional lore had been drawn from practical experience, his own and that of the men who had taught him. Focusing on time past, the Reverend Arthur Hyde reminisced about cricket fields, his playing companions at Trinity, and the team he had organized as a young minister in Kilmactranny. Hart's nostalgic recollections, although local in setting, had included stories of wondrous events for which he used to cite for authority eyewitnesses who had preceded him to the grave.

There were similarities, too, between the gamekeeper and the minister. Hart had been a strong-minded man. Sometimes Douglas had been afraid to question assertions that he did not fully understand, for fear of trying Hart's patience. Equally strong-minded, the Reverend Arthur Hyde had unshakable opinions on such subjects as the best method for building turf ricks, the best recipe for making whiskey punch, and the best strategies to use when playing cards or chess. Telling a story or singing a song, Hart could be soft and nostalgic. Remembering the classical scholar he was in his youth, the Reverend Arthur Hyde intoned Homer in a voice not at all like that in which he delivered Sunday sermons, barked instructions to his sons, or ordered workmen about. Hart had given Douglas lines of Irish poetry to memorize. The Reverend Arthur Hyde lectured Douglas on the need for applying himself more diligently to the study of Horatian odes. Evenings in the gamekeeper's cottage or at a neighboring hearth Douglas and Hart used to listen to old men's tales of past events: the monster meetings of fifty years ago through which O'Connell had demonstrated public support for repeal of the laws that had barred Catholics from serving in Parliament; the daily tragedies encountered on western roads during the Famine; the land clearances of the 1850s. Since Hart's death Douglas often spent evenings at home in the glebe house, hunched over a game of chess or backgammon with his father. Intent on the strategies the game required, the Reverend Hyde was less expansive in this setting than he was out-of-doors or sitting idly before the fire, telling stories of his youth, a glass of whiskey in his hand: to his son's questions and comments he replied monosyllabically if at all. That was a lesson, too. Douglas learned that for an Anglo-Irish gentleman social games were serious business.

Between the winter and early spring of 1876 father and son developed a mutual tolerance and respect previously not evident in their relationship. Perhaps it was the memory of these months that sustained them through less companionable, more difficult times ahead. For the moment, for Douglas, they helped dull the pain of Seamas Hart's death.

Otherwise unbountiful, nature also provided helpful diversions during these trying months. On February 9 an unusually heavy snowfall blanketed the ground. Whipped by strong winds it piled itself into drifts of a size and depth seldom seen in northwest Roscommon. From the middle of December there had been no mention of Connolly's or Dockry's name in his diary, but on this day, rolling huge snowballs into the yard with Annette and Connolly, Douglas discovered that he could still enjoy the older man's companionship. Soon Dockry's name reappeared also, in an entry describing an afternoon's shooting in which he had joined Douglas and Arthur. On the night of February 19, at the end of a day spent outdoors cutting wood, a spectacular display of northern lights lured everyone out again into field and meadow. In awe and astonishment Hyde watched great, glowing curtains of eerie blue and green and dark red, the color of drying blood, sweep across the sky. Old men, their eyes bright and fixed on the ancient world they seemed to see in their turf fires, told stories about such skies, which in ancient legend usually portended death and destruction. If Douglas, remembering those traditional tales, shivered as he watched, it was perhaps only partly from the cold; partly from some instinct he shared with Diver, for on such nights dogs seek dark places in which to hide; and partly from a memory of the shining eyes of old men.

Birds, meanwhile, remained as scarce throughout February as the Irish in Douglas's diary. On the fifth of the month, in one of but eleven entries between January 1 and March 1 in which he used any Irish at all, he complained that, devil a thing, not even a crow or a hare, was to be found. More frustrating was the night of the seventh: he had gone out at ten; he had returned empty-handed at two-thirty in the morning, unable to bring down a single bird, although the float river had been full of wild geese. On the seventeenth, again in Irish, he recorded the killing of a grouse rat in the haggard. In meadow and bog and along the riverbank, his luck had been poor, but this incident at least provided comforting evidence that his marksmanship was still good. The twenty-fourth brought better sport at last: he bagged a snipe and a "very curious bird," a "dipper," that had no tail and was unable to fly. It was a new "thing" to be noted on March 12, the next date set by family custom for totaling and recording the monthly kill of birds and small animals.

Meanwhile, "Bhí Shán an so" (John [Sean] was here), Douglas wrote on February 15, echoing "Vee Shamus an so" of happier days in the still partly phonetic but increasingly conventional Irish script that he had begun to develop just before Hart's death. Seamas Hart had not been replaced, but Johnny Lavin with his fluent Irish and Fenian sympathies was gradually becoming a new and needed friend. With the end of winter came a physical complaint, the first recorded since December, an aching cheekbone. It flared up during the last days of February when changing temperatures and humidity inflamed Douglas's sinuses even as they were harbingers of spring. Unpleasant as it was, the pain was homey, familiar, the kind of thing that besets only the living. It separated him from the dead.

In the weeks that followed, Lavin was often mentioned, as "John" or "Johnny" in English, "Eóin" or "Seán" in Irish, the uncertainty of his Irish name indicating that he was better known to all but Douglas by his name in English. For a time "Bhí Dockry annso" (Dockry—sometimes written "Coiducruidh" or "Colducruidh"—was here) was a competing refrain. Employed, like Connolly, by the Reverend Hyde, therefore a frequent companion in work and sport, Dockry was a Frenchpark Irish speaker with strong Fenian sympathies. Douglas liked him but sometimes became impatient with his dogmatism. Johnny Lavin, to be sure, could often be argumentative, especially when he had "a drop too much taken" of the whiskey that flowed freely in cottage and glebe house, but he, like Hart, brought to political questions a cultural and historical perspective. Dockry, when determined to make a point, had no perspective at all. For him there were never two sides to a political question, only his own.

Douglas had been schooled by both his fathers, Seamas Hart and the Reverend Arthur Hyde, Jr., to value cultural and historical perspective. From the stories of each he had learned that in appearance the west of Ireland in which he was growing up had not changed significantly since the sixteenth or seventeenth century. Before then there had been great forests and enormous game animals. Elizabethan axes had cut down most of the forests, leaving little beyond the wooded acres of Big House estates spared for the benefit of English and Anglo-Irish lords who were their owners. The enormous game animals had disappeared completely. Only the great antlered heads mounted in the entrance halls of castle and Big House bore witness to the size of the extinct red deer.

Cramped, crude stone cottages, many either unroofed and derelict or, their thatch gone to seed, given over to sheltering animals, also had their place in the history Douglas learned, chiefly from Hart and his Irish-speaking neighbors. In the folk imagination such cottages provided the setting for many traditional tales. It was behind a half-door the like of that, or before just such a hearth, the storyteller, or *seanachie,* would declare, that our kings and queens of old reigned in splendor; it was in a cottage much like the one beyond that the king of Ireland's son encountered a visitor from the Celtic otherworld. Both the folk memory drawn upon by Hart and the written history on which the Reverend Arthur Hyde relied preserved tales of nearby castles in northwest Roscommon, former homes of provincial monarchs more powerful than local kings and queens. Douglas knew that Ballintober, just outside Roscommon town, had been the seat of the O'Conors; Moygara, near Ballaghaderreen, had been the home of the O'Garas. Ballintober was the more impressive of the two. Covering as much ground as a small village, it had thick, turreted walls surrounded by a moat, a spacious courtyard, and a keep so large and well-built that part of it was still being used as a residence by descendants of Rory and Turlough O'Conor and Cathal of the Red Hand. Moygara, by contrast, was in ruins, for the O'Garas had been forced to abandon their castle in 1690, following the Battle of the Boyne in which King Billy had routed the leaderless Irish soldiers of the renegade James II.

Douglas learned, not only from his father but also from the lavishly illustrated books written by antiquarians that he found in his father's library, that the smaller but thick-walled rectangular fortified houses popularly known as "ten-pound castles" had not been built by the Irish. Constructed in the fourteenth and fifteenth centuries with ten-pound subsidies from the Crown, they were the former strongholds of Saxon knights who had crossed the Irish Sea with commissions from English kings to establish English order in rebellious Ireland. In Frenchpark as throughout the country, the wide-windowed Big Houses surrounded by lavish gardens that were hidden behind high stone walls also were called castles by their cottage neighbors. These, however, were more recent additions to the landscape, most going back no further than the early eighteenth century, when rebel Irish chieftains having been subdued or exiled, a siege mentality no longer dictated Ascendancy architectural fashions. The home of Lord de Freyne in Frenchpark and that of Sandford in Castlerea were such Big Houses, Douglas knew. So was Castle Hyde, the Hyde family seat on the Blackwater near Cork. A frequent focus of illustrated newspaper and journal essays on famous Irish residences, it no longer belonged to the senior Hyde line (having been sold in 1851 under the Encumbered Estates Act), yet young Douglas was fascinated by pictures of the mansion and demesne as well as by "Sweet Castle Hyde," a composition by a poetaster often called "probably the worst ballad ever written." Douglas had memorized it as a boy; as professor of Irish at University College, Dublin, and even later, as president of Ireland, he would sometimes amuse himself and guests with off-key renditions of such verses as:

> 'Tis there you'd hear the thrushes warbling,
>   The dove and partridge I now describe,
> And lambkins sporting every morning,
>   All to adorn sweet Castle Hyde.

To the Reverend Arthur Hyde, who read history as a record of English kingships and calculated years by the passing of an estate from one owner to another, castles and Big Houses were not a source of amusement but symbols of order and hierarchy. Castle Hyde was a case in point. Built on the portion of the earl of Desmond's Cork estates that had been granted to Hyde's ancestor, Sir Arthur Hyde, in 1599, in 1851 it had been purchased by John D. Sadleir, M.P. Sadleir had sold it to Sir Henry Becher in 1862. As Sir Henry was a descendant of Fane Becher, who had been granted the neighboring portion of Desmond's Cork estates in 1599, the Desmond lands that had been divided were thus recombined in ways that reinforced for men of the Reverend Arthur Hyde's background the concept that aristocratic order and history were philosophically related. In 1876 this concept was being challenged by Charles Stewart Parnell, M.P., a young Protestant land-owner who had aligned himself politically with Joe Biggar and Isaac Butt. A believer in aristocratic order, the Reverend Hyde was uncom-promising in his opposition to Parnell.

While absorbing his father's frequent dinner-table pronouncements, Douglas had acquired from Hart and Lavin and the talk of others in Frenchpark cottages a different historical perspective on land, its uses, and its ownership. Folk history treated time as space, depicting the great pre-Elizabethan forests as standing both physically and chronologically between anglicized Ireland and the ancient world of story and saga. It compacted centuries to create a measured sequence of myth and historic event. Recent history was no exception: eleven years had passed since the arrest, trial, imprisonment, and exile of the Fenians, yet stories told around cottage fires gave to Fenian exploits, in Ireland and America, the immediacy of yesterday. Nor were other events of Irish Ireland's history more remote. Before the Fenians, there had been the Bold Men of 1848, their survivors still active in Boston and New York. The Great Famine of 1846–1848 had driven abroad sisters and brothers of Frenchpark neighbors and had sent countless souls to quicklime graves through the dreaded "Black Gable" of the Castlerea workhouse (which stood but twelve years and a few hundred yards from the house where, in 1860, Douglas had been born). In 1829 Daniel O'Connell had led to victory the struggle for Catholic emancipation.

Like *leachta cuimne,* the memory stones that line Irish country roads, vivid accounts of such events evoked the past, creating narrative markers that led, one beyond the other, back through time: to Robert Emmet's defiant speech from the dock following the rebellion of 1803; to the rising of 1798, coordinated by Wolfe Tone, founder and leader of the United Irishmen; to the hedge schoolteachers who risked their lives resisting laws that threatened to reduce the native population to hewers of wood and drawers of water; to the broken Treaty of Limerick and Flight of the Wild Geese in 1691; to the Irish soldiery left leaderless by James II at the Battle of the Boyne in 1690; to the Cromwellian invasions and "plantations" of the mid-seventeenth century; to the turbulent reigns of Charles I, James I, and Elizabeth I. Cutting down trees, building ships, creating the empire on which for nearly three hundred years the sun would never set, the Elizabethans had been the first to bring in "planters": English subjects loyal to the Crown who were deeded homesteads from which the native Irish had been driven in order to "pacify" the land.

In cottage history, Gaelic Ireland, shrouded in Celtic myth, flourished on the far side of this space/time continuum, its distant shores preserved for succeeding generations in an oral tradition older than England. There where wild boar and great stag roamed, land belonged not to those who bought and sold it but to those who used it; justice prevailed under Brehon law. Similar ideas, it was said in the cottages, were now being proclaimed even by the son of a landlord, the new young Protestant M.P., Charles Stewart Parnell. To men like Hart, Lavin, and Dockry who dreamed of an Irish Ireland in which Irish women and men would once more till their own fields and no more labor fruitlessly on acres rented from English landlords, these ideas were lawful and just; they reflected an historical imperative. Stirred by their romance and rhetoric, Douglas embraced them. Only Dockry, in Douglas's opinion, lacked a vision of the future. Greedy, short-sighted, and embittered, he regarded all landlords with the same disdain. Yet, Douglas noted, he, too, supported Parnell.

With April came the first swallow of 1876, the first butterfly, and—for Douglas—more progress in written Irish. In early May from his uncle in Drumkilla he received a present of an Irish dictionary that gave impetus to his reading and composition. Such items as "Lá Bealtine," a poem of four alternating verses of Irish and English celebrating the first day of May, were added to the miscellany preserved in the back pages of his diary. From daily entries in Irish he constructed a continuing discourse that lasted almost four weeks. Among the ominous notes of this period was one that recorded the death of Terence Carty, a local man who had been killed on May 1, the day of the Ballaghaderreen fair.

June and July 1876 brought a succession of visitors to the glebe house, among them an unidentified man with whom Douglas had several conversations in Irish. Douglas lunched with the visitors, joined their boating and swimming parties, and even went sightseeing with them and accompanied them on visits to fairs, although at first with no great show of enthusiasm. They interrupted his studies, he complained to his diary; they opposed Parnell; they talked excitedly of the "agrarian crime" reported in newspapers and repeated what they had heard of murders and deaths and injuries caused by weakened bridge supports and blocked roads in other localities. Some blamed damage to crops on maliciously opened sluice gates and vandalized drainage devices; some muttered darkly about the maiming of cattle. Distancing himself from such topics, Douglas confined his concerns to the drought, so severe that it was thought to have caused the observable decline in the grouse population. When he did join in the conversation, it was usually to echo the general sentiment that rain was badly wanted. It was the thing to say, of course, but to his diary he confessed that he did not really mean it, despite the grouse problem. He had begun to enjoy the continuing fair skies and the diversions—long walks, tennis, cricket, croquet, swimming, boating—that fine weather made possible.

On July 7, 1876, Douglas went with his father to the bishop for a long talk about his future. Together the older men outlined a program of home study that would lead to his admission to Trinity, a degree in theology, and a career as a clergyman. Douglas listened without agreeing or protesting, but to himself he acknowledged that the prospect was not to his liking. Yet there seemed no alternative. His father's willingness to support his education was clearly dependent upon his choosing a career in the church. Both Arthur and Oldfield had refused to follow in the footsteps of father, grandfather, and great-grandfather: the Reverend Hyde was determined to have a successor. The onus of avoiding a break in tradition was now on Douglas. He could do worse, he told himself; he would consider it, he promised himself, in the fall. Meanwhile, so filled were his days with social engagements that for the moment there was no possibility of his giving any thought to the schedule of reading and study that he would have to adhere to in order to prepare himself properly for entrance examinations to Trinity. He could not put off these matters for long, however. He was devilishly weak, he reminded himself, in several important curricular areas. Arthur, to whom he sometimes sent his exercises, had identified the subjects in which he was deficient and noted those which he had not yet begun to study. Yet summer activities were so distracting that he did not even fulfill his promise to himself to keep up his work in Irish.

On July 8, the day after Douglas's talk with his father and the bishop, young Lord de Freyne attained his majority. Frenchpark House festivities were the talk of provincial Big House society. They included dinner under a marquee, music, dancing, and fireworks in which Frenchpark servants and tenants were invited to participate. As neighbors and kinsmen, the Hydes of course attended. It was difficult to feel threatened by agrarian crime on such an occasion; it was even more difficult to think that such a pleasant summer would end and that soon autumn days would be filled with lessons and exercises. Throughout the remainder of the month new guests arrived daily for luncheon, dinner, or tea. Some stayed on. Lawn tennis, cricket, and boating occupied the young people; everyone played croquet.

On July 29 Douglas and Oldfield went to Drumkilla for a similar round of social activities. Although heavy rains at the beginning of August briefly broke the dry spell, another unusually long stretch of exceptionally fine weather followed. Enjoying himself, Douglas remained at Drumkilla even after Oldfield left for Dublin. Perfunctory notes in his diary, mostly in English, record only where he had been and whom he had seen, but to Oldfield he wrote long, chatty letters full of enthusiasm for the pleasures of Anglo-Irish society. For a time it appeared as if the voice of Seamas Hart had been stilled, not by a persuasive bishop and a determined father but by the self-indulgent ease of Ascendancy life against which bishop and father fared no better.

As fine weather meant a good harvest, Douglas was needed at the glebe house in late August to help with the haying and with bringing in the oats. Another death had occurred in his absence: Diver, the dog that had been his almost constant companion since 1873, was gone. Even this fact was recorded unemotionally, in the diary to which Douglas no longer confided feelings but only, like his brother Arthur, facts and events. The only exception was an invitation from his two favorite Hyde aunts to accompany them on a sightseeing trip through the west of Ireland, which—as his diary reveals—he obviously anticipated with pleasure.

The timing of the trip arranged by Douglas's aunts could not have been better for a number of reasons: Away from his father, on neutral ground, Douglas hoped that he would be able to reflect on the present and assess the prospects he soon would have to face. Turning sixteen had been a milestone: since the summer his social role had changed markedly; agreeable as he found his new position, he had not yet digested its implications. Whatever he decided about the future, he felt he must return to work on the Irish language. The trip, he told himself, would provide a ready-made subject for an Irish journal. At the same time it would give him a chance to see more of the Irish countryside. Except for occasional visits to Mohill, Galway, and Dublin, he had traveled very little outside Roscommon.

Douglas and his aunts set out from Castlerea on September 5. Their plan was to travel north and west through Mayo and Connemara, then south through Galway, Clare, and Kerry en route to Killarney; then east to Cork for the train home via Portarlington. In his new, neatly lettered Irish script modeled on examples of Irish printing that he had been studying, Douglas recorded their departure. Although he still had to rely in large part on phonetic spellings, he was pleased and relieved to find that Irish words and phrases were coming to him more easily than he had expected. His Irish persona was another matter. Occasional associations—a fragment of a story, a place-name, the look of the sky on a particular morning, the open door of a cottage—evoked involuntary memories of a gamekeeper and a young boy. In other respects, although the language in which he wrote was Irish, Douglas's Irish self seemed to be fading with his rapidly receding childhood.

Never before had Douglas visited the countryside through which he traveled with his aunts, but he did know something of its history. The route from Castlerea to Castlebar formed the first leg of the travelers' journey: in Frenchpark cottages he had heard about "the Races at Castlebar," a 1798 battle in which the British had been put to rout by outnumbered French troops that had been joined by ill-equipped, untrained but determined Irish forces. The short-lived victory—when British reinforcements arrived the rebels were defeated—had been the beginning of a strange drama, for the British reinforcements had been under the command of a Scotsman called John Moore, and among those captured by the British was John Moore of Moore Hall, leader of the Irish rebels, who had been proclaimed president of the Republic of Connaught. Louisa Browne Moore, mother of the rebel John and a cousin of the marquess of Sligo, had tried in vain to use both money and family position to secure her son's release. The man who opposed her was her own kinsman, Denis Browne, the "hanging judge" of Mayo; John Moore died a British prisoner. Rumor had it that rebel sympathies had continued for a time among the Moores: John's nephew, the late George Henry Moore, M.P., was said to have been a friend and supporter of the Fenian leader O'Donovan Rossa. George Henry Moore had died in 1870; in 1876 his eldest son, George Augustus Moore, was an art student living in Paris. Little that was said of the son suggested

that soon he would become the talk of the Dublin literary world—
or that one day he would stage Hyde's Irish play *An Tincéar agus
an t-Sidheog* (The tinker and the fairy) in his Dublin garden.

On September 6 Douglas and his aunts set out for Westport, a pretty
seaside town and popular touring center on Clew Bay in county Mayo.
Here, too, the past had its ghosts, the future its shadow of things to
come. From Westport House, on the edge of town, Lord Altamont had
joined George Henry Moore in various schemes to relieve victims of
the Famine in 1847–1848. The new Protestant church that soon would
be built would be served one day by Canon J. Hannay (the novelist
George A. Birmingham) who would become one of Hyde's close
friends and a staunch supporter within the Gaelic League. Nearby was
Sheeaun, a prehistoric mound doubly famed as the site of one of Daniel
O'Connell's "monster meetings." Six miles to the south, directly on the
bay, rose Ireland's "Holy Mountain," Croagh Patrick, its sugarloaf peak
on which St. Patrick himself was said to have fasted and prayed for forty
days dominating the landscape. The site drew thousands of pilgrims
during the last week in July. Hyde wished he could explore it. His aunts
were merely thankful that in September the area was pleasantly quiet.

On September 7 scenic roads leading south toward Connemara offered magnificent views of the coast and opportunities to study at close
range the antiquities for which west Mayo was deservedly famous: ancient churches, dolmens, prehistoric pillarstones, and an intricately
carved eleventh-century High Cross. By evening the travelers reached
Letterfrack, where Douglas met an Irish-speaking schoolmaster with
whom he carried on a brief but encouraging conversation: in his diary
he noted with pleased surprise that he had had no difficulty understanding the man or making himself understood. At Kylemore his aunts
agreed to wait while he climbed part way up a mountain less mystical
than Croagh Patrick but nevertheless worth the exertion for its spectacular full view of the Atlantic. Clifden was disappointing: to Douglas
the bustling market town was "dirty and ugly." He was glad to leave
it for the trip eastward, through the central valley of Connemara and
the Joyce country, toward Cong, where in 1198 Rory, last high king
of Ireland and an ancestor of the O'Conors of Castlerea, had died.
The route took them past picturesque lakes and stony fields still bloom-
ing with golden gorse and purple heather, a romantic picture viewed
against the backdrop of the Twelve Bens and the Maamturk Mountains.
They were not far from Moytura Castle on Lough Corrib, where Sir
William Wilde and his family spent their summers, when all romance

vanished, for Cecilly discovered that she was missing the bag that contained much of her money. Certain that the rest of the trip would have to be cancelled, Douglas was miserable. To his relief, the loss delayed them but did not change their itinerary, and his aunts' spirits were dampened only temporarily.

From Cong the travelers boarded a steamer across Lough Corrib to Galway, following a route later described in Trollope's posthumous novel, *The Landleaguers*. From Galway, where one day Hyde would play the poet Raftery in the premiere performance of another of his dramas in Irish, *An Pósadh* (The Marriage), they continued by boat across the harbor to county Clare and by carriage to Lisdoonvarna, missing Craughwell, where Raftery lay buried, and Coole Park, the estate of Lady Gregory, sites that would figure importantly in Douglas's future. On September 10, well wrapped for the day's expedition, he and his aunts stood on the Cliffs of Moher, scene of the tragedy in Trollope's *An Eye for an Eye*. Mesmerized by the force with which the wind-whipped Atlantic crashed against menacing rocks two hundred yards below, Douglas was astonished to discover that he could taste the salt spray from the impact. By contrast, the comfortable rooms in which they lodged that evening, overlooking the horseshoe bay of fashionable and sheltered Kilkee, seemed to belong to another world.

The next morning Douglas and his aunts left Kilkee for Kilrush, a few miles to the south on the Shannon estuary, to board an eastbound steamer across the Shannon to Foynes, from which they traveled by train to Limerick. After touring the historic city associated with both Brian Boru, the high king said to have defeated the Danes at Clontarf in 1014, and Patrick Sarsfield, hero of the Siege of Limerick, they caught the train for Killarney, arriving at eleven o'clock on the morning of September 12 for a week's stay. There, overwhelmed by the majesty of the Torc Cascade, the panorama of the Gap of Dunloe, the beauty of the three Lakes of Killarney (explored by boat under fine, clear skies), the picturesque ruins at every turn, Douglas's descriptive vocabulary failed him. After four days' sightseeing, "Never saw the likes of that scene ever" was all he could record of his impressions in his Irish diary. In Glengarriff on September 20 his Irish vocabulary failed him again, until the excitement of finding himself walking about on the actual ground that once had belonged to his ancestors inspired him to compose short Irish lyrics, or "ranns."

The route to Cork on September 21 had been planned to take in Gouganebarra and Macroom, two of the best-known scenic spots of the southwest, but the weather was so bad that the three travelers could see nothing but the lashing rain from their carriage. Douglas was thoroughly and uncomfortably soaked, the rain having penetrated even his heavy overcoat. Nevertheless, awaiting the afternoon train from Cork, he could not resist browsing in bookstores and shopping for souvenirs, especially as he anticipated that once Portarlington had been reached he would have a hot meal, comfortable bed, and good rest in the hotel in which Cecilly had made reservations. When they arrived in Portarlington, however, they found that the hotel had been over-booked. By the time alternative private accommodations were arranged, all three travelers were exhausted and Douglas was thoroughly chilled. The next day's journey was also long and uncomfortable—twice they were delayed for three hours at intermediate stops—but by the evening of September 23, Douglas and his aunts were again home in Drumkilla, where the opportunity to relive their trip by talking about it to others revived the excitement of their adventures. September 24 began with a new round of picnics, boatrides, tennis, croquet, long walks, and other diversions of Anglo-Irish life.

As he had promised himself, Douglas did keep a full account of his tour of western Ireland entirely in Irish, but the persona he adopted for the task was that of his English-speaking self: aloof, removed, tunnel-visioned. No notice of Irish-speaking communities was included in his written record, although in 1876 the Gaeltacht stretched along the entire coast, from Donegal to Killarney. Except for his conversation with the schoolmaster in Letterfrack, he spoke no Irish but remained physically and psychologically within the Anglo-Irish corridor of hotels and guest houses that extended the length of the land. It was a narrow, insulated world in which he and his aunts regularly encountered family friends and other tourists who, if not prior acquaintances, were known to them by name and family connection. Shielded from everyone and everything else, Douglas made no decision—he did not even attempt to make a decision—about his future.

Little changed for Douglas internally or externally during the next three months. If his intention was to follow the course that his father and the bishop had laid out for him, he did nothing toward removing deficiencies in his academic preparation. If he planned to choose a different course, he did nothing to weigh potential alternatives. His few diary entries, mostly about shooting, were written in English. The weather ranged from indifferent to harsh, with hard frost by October 10 and days of strong, biting wind. In late October one of his Hyde aunts, his father's sister Barbara, died in Dublin, where she had lived with her husband and children. The Reverend Arthur Hyde and his wife attended the funeral, after which Mrs. Hyde went on to Munster while her husband returned to the glebe house where Douglas and Annette had been left in charge. There he took to his bed almost immediately with a severe attack of gout. A few days later, at the beginning of November, while the Reverend Arthur Hyde was still bedridden, Arthur came home from Trinity with first-class honors but also with excruciating pains in his back. By the time Bessie Hyde returned to Frenchpark on November 20, Arthur's unrelieved suffering had become a cause for concern. Fortunately, Cecilly had come home with her, for Bessie was not entirely well herself and there were two patients to nurse. It was an unhappy household, very different from the one that had been the scene of summer parties, to which Emily Hyde journeyed from Mohill on November 27, nor had there been much improvement when the Lloyds arrived for luncheon on November 30.

To escape the sickroom atmosphere that permeated the glebe house, Douglas had spent most of November outdoors, shooting. On November 19 he had acquired a new companion, on loan from Narry, from whom he and Annette had bought new boots: a dog called "Shot," half brother to Diver, and just as black. Cecilly stayed on through December. The weather was mostly fine, if frequently cold. By the middle of the month Arthur was up and around at last, able to join Douglas, Annette, and Cecilly on walks down to the float river. The Reverend Arthur Hyde improved, too, but slowly, with setbacks. Meanwhile, under Douglas's careful tutelage, Shot turned out to be a fine hunter; on December 19 he retrieved six snipe that Douglas had downed in the rushy fields near Lissachurcha and three more that Douglas had caught wheeling overhead as he walked home in the dark. Three days later, "after a great stalk, behind a low ditch" near the Lung River, Douglas killed a scotch grey at sixty yards with a green cartridge of No. 1 shot. The goose, also retrieved by Shot, weighed about seven pounds, he noted proudly.

Meanwhile, spurred on perhaps by Arthur's academic successes, at last Douglas initiated a formal program of study. His diary entries, most of them written wholly or partly in conventionally spelled Irish, record his progress in translating Latin verse and conquering elementary German. But they also include short paragraphs devoted to observation and description that suggest a reawakening of Douglas's Irish persona and old love of words as well as a new conscious attention to Irish prose style. Among them the following, dated December 7, is evocative even in English translation:

Since I was born I have not seen anything like the look of the lake, nor water so quiet, nor a scene so pleasant. The water and the air were as one, and I saw every island in the water so plainly that I did not know what was an island, what was water. At the end, as we were going home, there was great fog, but we guided ourselves by the one star only. There was great danger in it.

On Christmas morning it was evident from the gifts Douglas was given (a Gaelic Bible, a history of the Church of Ireland) that, whatever Douglas had said or failed to say, his family had assumed that the question of his future had been settled. Only from Cecilly Hyde, who perhaps knew him best, did he receive a different kind of present: a *Lett's Diary or Bills Due Book and Almanac for 1877*. His mother's cast-off household account book—the makeshift journal with its inkblots, its pen-and-ink soldiers and knights on guard at top and bottom margins, and its arsenal of swords, daggers, and pistols stored along each side in which he had been keeping a record of his inner and outer life since a month past his fourteenth birthday—was stored away with other artifacts of his childhood. He was almost seventeen; he had decisions to make about his future; he had work to do before he could implement those decisions.

A new Hyde emerged in the new diary begun January 1, 1877. Serious and studious, he scheduled his time carefully, kept track of his daily accomplishments in a neat, small hand, and in businesslike fashion divided each entry so that half was written in English, half in Irish. More socially confident and congenial than in the past, he now went out of his way, returning from a walk along the lake, to speak with Marie de Freyne, whose carriage he had spotted on the road. So remarkable was the external transformation that at first it seemed as if it could not last. Week after week, however, until well into March, Douglas kept to his rigorous program, encouraged by Cecilly Hyde, who had volunteered to stay on after Christmas to tutor him in French. To his diary Douglas confessed that he was quite sure that she did not know much more of the language than he, but he gladly accepted her help for the companionship she provided. She was, he wrote in his diary, his best friend in the family; there was no one, he avowed, for whom he had more love.

Bad weather also helped keep Douglas at work indoors: in all of January there were but four fine days, none of them mild. The rest were too cold, too windy, and too wet to spend much time outside. Shooting had to be curtailed despite the fact that Douglas's guns were probably in better condition than ever before, for he cleaned them over and over in anticipation of good weather that did not come. By January 30 the turlough, the winter lake in the meadow generally agreed to be the best site for bagging waterfowl, had risen so high that nearby cottages had to be abandoned.

Staying indoors at home day after day was not easy for Douglas, especially as his father, still crippled by gout, was usually irritable; his mother was not well, either; and until they returned to Dublin, Arthur and Oldfield regularly took refuge from the situation in short visits to Drumkilla. The management of the glebe house was thus left to Douglas and Annette—a considerable responsibility as Annette was then not quite twelve years old. On January 15 Oldfield packed books and clothing sufficient for a four-month stint at Trinity: results of examinations for which he had to prepare would determine his eligibility for honors and a scholarship; therefore, he announced, he had no plans to return home before May. As Arthur, too, had returned to Dublin, it was a quiet seventeenth birthday, with just Cecilly and Annette for company, that Douglas celebrated on January 17, 1877. His present from Cecilly was a two-volume life of Bishop Peterson. She, too, had come to believe that he had reconciled himself to a career in the church. He himself was still not sure exactly what he might do.

A few days after Douglas's birthday a Tibohine parishioner, John Carty, died of natural causes. No one had told the Reverend Arthur Hyde, still housebound because he was too lame to walk, that Carty's body had been placed inside the church. When no arrangements for burial had been made by January 21, there was "great trouble" within the congregation. The incident embarrassed Douglas, increasing the old distance between himself and his father, evident in his diary since late October.

On January 27 Douglas noted in his diary "considerable talk" of his "going out for an Irish sizarship in the college." Such an appointment was attractive because of the independence it would offer him. Realistic in appraising his academic capabilities, he observed, "It is not so hard but I . . . have a lot to do." Redoubling his efforts in Greek, Irish, Latin, German, and French, he became his own strictest taskmaster. No tutor could have been more disapproving when he failed to put in the minimum number of hours he had assigned himself or did not complete the work he had scheduled within the time allotted. On a typical day his plan of study called for two hours of Latin before midday dinner;

an hour or two of Irish between dinner and supper; and an hour of Greek, another hour of Latin or German, and an hour of French between supper and bed. There were in addition books to read and poetry to memorize.

Roscommon weather continued to be cloudy and wet through February and March. Even on fine days there were sudden showers; storms and squalls were frequent. Meadows and fields in which Douglas walked regularly became so marshy from the repeated rains that a man could sink in them. Turloughs appeared where even the oldest of "ould wans" had never seen them before. Cecilly, who had delayed her departure so that she could continue to be of help not only to Douglas but to the entire household, left for Dublin and Stillorgan on February 8. The next day a dispirited Douglas, dissatisfied with himself and cranky at being confined, complained to Connolly of the way in which he had cut the laurel hedge, the ivy, and the fuchsia. The laurel would never grow again, he insisted peevishly. New plants would have to be bought at once. On February 10 he wrote petulantly in his diary in Irish, "I have nothing to do because there is no fowling, nor games, nor visiting, nor sport at all." Yet, he added, bringing himself up short: "I am well settled down now studying." On February 12, feeling tired and unhappy, he diagnosed a sore throat as the root of his problem, dosed himself with whiskey, and went to bed. In a similar frame of mind, stiff from rheumatism as well as sore from gout, unable to go out shooting or walk along the road or even take a turn in his garden, the Reverend Arthur Hyde was making regular use of the same medicine, in much larger quantities.

Lonely and depressed, Douglas began dropping into the Connolly cottage for conversations in Irish with Connolly's wife, a native speaker in her youth who had promised to try to recover her former fluency for Douglas's benefit; he also renewed ties with Johnny and Michael Lavin, Cloigionín-a-naosc, and Dockry, with whom he had spent little time for more than half a year. Under their cottage roofs he was assured of a warm fire, a glass of whiskey, and a friendly chat to counter the gloom of the glebe house. Johnny Lavin was the man whose company he now enjoyed most.

Lavin had a sharp mind, in Douglas's opinion, except when he was drinking, when he had no sense at all. Like so many other Frenchpark Irish speakers, he was fluent but illiterate in his native language, having been taught reading and writing only in English in the local school; but unlike others, he wanted to learn to read and write in Irish as well.

Douglas loaned him the Irish catechism out of which he himself had traced Irish letters and studied the spelling of simple words and phrases. Cloigionín-a-naosc, one of the few local people who not only read Irish but owned several Irish books, was a different sort. Douglas borrowed a volume of Irish ballads from him, lending him in return one of his own books, the Reverend William Neilson's *Introduction to the Irish Language* (a grammar printed in 1843 for the use of Protestant missionaries in Irish-speaking districts). The ballad book interested Douglas. He liked not only the ballad stories but their narrative modes. Storytelling was an art that enticed him. He was intrigued by connections between the narrative techniques used by the ballad makers and those of the traditional storytellers.

Mrs. Connolly was a good source of oral tradition. Visits with her always yielded interesting stories as well as a variety of Irish expressions. Whenever Douglas stopped to see her she had a few new phrases which she presented to him as happily as if they were gifts. He was quick to perceive the pleasant truth: she enjoyed their Irish conversations as much as he, for in the process of searching her memory for words forgotten in her youth she recalled forgotten incidents as well. Douglas took both words and stories home with him for phonetic inscription in his exercise book, then tried to work out their standard spellings according to the patterns he was learning to recognize and apply. Dockry alone among these old companions had become less congenial. Douglas was beginning to find him tiresome, for drunk or sober, in Irish or English, he talked of nothing but land and money.

With two glebe house neighbors, Michael Lavin and Francis O'Ruark, young Hyde sometimes put on the gloves for a round of boxing. Francis was an easy man to be with; he and Douglas sometimes planned small expeditions together. One day, taking the boat out on Lough Gara as far as Coolavin, they rowed across Doctor's Lake, beached the boat, and walked along the railroad tracks until they reached a path on their right that led up the hill to Moygara Castle. The four towers of the old castle, one at each corner, were connected by walls fifty yards long and so broad that they were easily able to walk the whole length of them as if they were on a country road. Some expeditions were spoiled by Douglas's practical jokes. One evening when they were coming home together in the dark, Douglas tried to trick Francis into thinking that they had walked in the wrong direction. Against all Francis's protests he insisted that they were approaching not Tibohine but Castlerea. By the time he acknowledged his joke, Francis was confused and upset, but Douglas was neither embarrassed nor contrite. He took his relationships with Frenchpark cottagers at face value, never wondering if his welcome was something they could not refuse because of their relative social positions, or if under their surface cordiality something akin to Dockry's resentments were stirring—not against him personally, perhaps, but against the Ascendancy world to which (like it or not, as he himself was learning) he inescapably belonged. Yet the new persona that appeared in 1877 did reveal moments of self-awareness and sensitivity. From time to time he took stock of himself and his behavior. Often he was dissatisfied. On January 17—his seventeenth birthday—he was particularly harsh: "Alas, alas, O the sorrows of Mary," he lamented in Irish to his diary, "I'm afraid I'm not what I should be." Shamefacedly he also admitted, "I have written that under the power of a bottle. . . . I got the courage to write that from whiskey."

On the positive side, Douglas was, as he himself said, "well settled down" to his studying. Certainly the evidence was encouraging: he had completed Virgil's *Georgics* on January 31; he began the *Aeneid* on February 24. He had started the New Testament in Greek and Irish during the last week in January; by February 22 he had finished the Fourth Gospel in Greek. Nor was life so joyless and solitary as he sometimes made it out to be. Cecilly, to be sure, had gone back to Drumkilla, but Arthur had come home, and even if he was not Douglas's favorite companion, he could be counted on to go shooting when the weather permitted. On one rare day when the weather was reasonably good the two brothers took their guns and went out in their boat on Lough Gara. With no particular destination but a place where they might find game, they happened upon a bog neither had seen before in which there was a little lake, perhaps a turlough, around which eighty to a hundred snipe had gathered. As they considered how best to approach the birds across the spongy ground, they were challenged by an old woman who, having identified herself as wife of the keeper of the bog, scolded them in "Béarlaige," the mixture of English and Irish increasingly found in transitional areas where the native language was dying out and English was not yet fully established. Using the same talent for caricature evident in his drawings in his diary and exercise book, Douglas parodied the incident in a lighthearted Béarlaige of his own that anticipates the writings of "Myles na gCopaleen" (i.e., Brian O'Nolan):

I shot a brace in the bog, but after a little time an old cailleach who said she was bean na keeper came up & put triobloid mor on me, blaidaircacht &

barging, refusing to take airegeod no uiscebeatha, so that in spite of my most soothing sentences in the teanga blasda milis, I had, air dheiradh, to leave the bog & let a fine gearrfiadh escape . . . & come home inglorious.

On another expedition by boat that yielded no game but gave Douglas a chance to practice his conversational Irish with visitors to Roscommon from Mayo, the brothers stopped so long at a shebeen that they did not come home until considerably after dark.

Political talk, always available at Johnny Lavin's, was another favorite diversion. Like the summer visitors to the glebe house, the cottagers were divided on the subject of Parnell, especially as in 1877 it now looked as if Biggar and Parnell were taking over Butt's Home Rule movement. There were those who, remembering the trial of the Fenians in 1865, were sympathetic to Isaac Butt, who had stood alone against Keogh. Others argued that sentiment could not be allowed to interfere: Parnell was the man for the job. Still, O'Kelly's election as M.P. from Roscommon was a surprise to everyone. Some said it was about time—the old O'Conor Don had been in the House for twenty years, and what, they asked, had he done for the tenants. Others defended O'Conor Don's record, reminding the Parnellites that the O'Conors had been the best landlords in the area for as long as anyone could remember; that it was an O'Conor who had worked with O'Connell for Catholic emancipation; that this same O'Conor had been among the first Catholics to be elected to Parliament in 1831; and that it was an O'Conor in Parliament during the Famine who had answered the skeptics with facts and figures concerning the sick and dying people of the west.

On February 21, a man who had been ten years old in 1798 when the French sailed into Killala Bay spent the evening at Johnny Lavin's. Young Hyde sat close to him, near the fire. Fascinated, he listened to the old man's vivid recollections of the event. On February 27 Douglas was again at Lavin's for an account of a Fenian meeting held in Frenchpark that all present jubilantly hailed as a success. Aware of his father's attitudes and those of the neighboring Anglo-Irish, Douglas kept what he learned about the Fenians to himself. Anything he might say almost certainly would reveal sympathies unacceptable to the Reverend Arthur Hyde. In the years since his confrontation with Dublin schoolboys Douglas had learned to be discreet in some circles. But on the question of Parnell, Douglas admitted to himself that the flamboyant new M.P. was a fascinating figure—a Protestant like himself with radical sympathies that resembled his own.

At the end of March the weather turned fine at last. Douglas had adhered to a schedule of seven and more hours of intensive study every day while the rain and cold persisted. He was doing well. By the middle of March he had finished the *Aeneid*; by the middle of April he had covered most of the lessons in Neilson's Irish grammar. He also had read *Pendennis* and several books of poetry, including a Latin-Irish text by a man from Derry. His Irish was improving dramatically. No longer did he write phonetically, using English characters: entries in his diary and exercise books showed the same talent for drawing evident in the sketches and caricatures that used to decorate his work, producing a handsome imitation of printed Irish in which most words were spelled correctly and formed grammatically, with appropriate diacritical marks, and standard abbreviations were used. His exercise books had become commonplace books into which he copied portions of texts that particularly appealed to him, sometimes with and sometimes without comment.

Toward the end of April, Douglas's pace slowed. He was drinking more than was good for him, he knew—so much, he confessed to his diary, that at times he was unable to work. Even when he had drunk nothing at all, he often felt subdued, restless, lacking in his usual vitality. In his diary *"mar a riamh"* (as always) began to replace his previous careful accounting of how his daily time was spent. There were things that were bothering him, he acknowledged, among them questions to which he did not know the answers: What if he passed the examinations for Trinity but refused to enroll as a theology student? Would his father really cut off the funds he needed to attend college?

It was not unusual for Douglas to interrupt an afternoon's shooting to explore a prehistoric site. Antiquities had fascinated him ever since he had first learned about them from Seamas Hart. Liosairgul, not far from Hart's bog, Lough Gara, the Lung River, and Ballinphuil—all favorite haunts within an easy walk of Tibohine—always had seemed to him to be "a curious place, all full of raths & holes going down perpendicularly in the ground sometimes 20 yards wide & as many deep & always round." Often a man cutting turf would find in the bog an artifact of such intricate design that there was no doubt of the sophistication of the people who would make or own such a thing. Old Irish castles—not the tower houses built by the English with a small subsidy from the Crown, but formidable structures of the kings of Ireland, such as Ballintober—fired his imagination.

Eighteen months had passed since the death of Seamas Hart when, on the morning of May 24, 1877, telling no one, Douglas silently left the glebe house before six o'clock for a strange and solitary expedition. During most of that time he had allowed himself to be carried along by shifting currents. For the last four months he had seemed to be following the course set for him by his father and the bishop, but without enthusiasm. Taking with him no food, only a candle, he walked to the float river, from which he caught the train to Kilfree, then tramped across "rugged country without roads or paths" toward Keshcorran, highest of the stony mountains near Ballymote that comprise an extended prehistoric cemetery of cairns, promontory tombs, and caves in which it is said that remains of reindeer, Irish elk, and other extinct animals have been found. Too tired to reach his objective, the cairn atop Keshcorran, Douglas entered one of the caves. Lighting his candle, he made his way along a narrow passage as far as he could go—about thirty yards. The central chamber, he reported, was "large enough for 10 couples to dance in." He says nothing more about what he did or saw although he does indicate that he lingered for a considerable time before returning to Kilfree by way of sparsely traveled roads that crisscross Keshcorran, providing a longer but easier descent. At the station he discovered that he would have a long wait for the next train back to Ballaghaderreen.

The mood or thought or doubt or conflict that had precipitated the day's behavior apparently left Douglas as he waited for the train. Boyish again, he passed the time, he wrote, amusing himself by "letting on to be Catholic" and pretending to know no English to a man whom he engaged in conversation in Irish. The man not only believed him, he gleefully confided to his diary, but took him to be a young priest or seminarian. Faced with a tired and bedraggled young stranger who spoke Irish with a pronounced Ascendancy accent while claiming to be a monolingual native Irish speaker, the Kilfree man no doubt had amused himself as well, pretending to believe Douglas's pretenses. But to what extent was the pretense which Douglas maintained as if it were just one of his practical jokes related to his behavior earlier in the day?

During the months that followed, nothing more came of either Douglas's strange psychodrama of May 24 or his father's ultimatum concerning his future, partly because other issues, public and personal, dominated glebe house conversation, partly because Douglas had made up his mind to try for the Irish sizarship. At first, public issues appeared to be the greater concern. Agrarian crime was increasing; it could no longer be denied, even by Douglas, who on the one hand feared and on the other hand was fascinated by its potential. Incidents involving threats and physical violence were no longer remote. Mysterious fires broke out on nearby estates. In Frenchpark at the beginning of May, five to six hundred angry men had confronted a bailiff, demanding the price of a heifer that had been taken from one of them. On June 2, Captain Sandford's agent, Mr. Young, was shot dead. His body was found close to his own house in Castlerea, no more than several hundred feet from town, covered by a large sheepskin.

Public outcry demanded immediate and swift justice, but local gossip expressed confidence that Young's killer would never be named or found. Dockry's behavior reflected a new militant attitude evident among some of the cottagers. A few days after Young's death he stood on the back doorstep of the glebe house, holding forth about land reform and similar measures, refusing to change the subject or simply go away, to Douglas's increasing irritation. The next day word spread that another delegation of angry tenants had presented a list of demands backed by felonious threats to Sandford.

Although never in danger themselves, the Hydes could not help but be uneasy. For Douglas, who felt himself a member of both worlds, Anglo-Irish and native Irish, there was tension in what was said as well as what was unsaid in glebe house and neighboring cottage. Ambivalent toward both, he tried to concentrate on the reading and study schedule he had set for himself in January. He wanted to keep in touch with what was happening, yet he knew that if he was going to try for a sizarship at Trinity, he could not allow himself to be distracted. It was almost the middle of June and he had begun Euclid, the next subject, following Arthur's advice, that he had to cram. Even shooting was curtailed while he bent over his writing table for hours at a time, his books and papers scattered about him on the floor. Some days his diary contained nothing more than a cryptic record in a newly devised system of symbols and abbreviations of how he had allocated his waking hours. One day, in need of a break, he walked to Buckhill—a distance of three to four miles, he estimated, possibly a bit more—to talk with Rochesfort, a man with scholarly interests, a good library, and a good command of Irish whom he had sometimes visited with his father. It was, he declared, a "successful pilgrimage" that gave him a chance to rest his eyes and stretch his legs— as well as to discover an unusual Irish poem that he took home with him to reread and analyze.

Meanwhile, Bessie Hyde's long, debilitating illness, later diagnosed as asthma, continued. Day after day she stayed in bed or dragged herself around, neither improving nor getting worse despite powders and herbal teas and other homegrown remedies. She did not feel up to a journey to Dublin, but everyone agreed that there was no alternative: she had to consult a specialist. Douglas was glad to accompany her, for her sake as well as his own. Except for an occasional respite such as the day spent at Keshcorran or the afternoon at Buckhill, he had been working hard for months. He needed a change of scene and a different pace, if only for a few days.

The trip to Dublin on June 19 was fortuitous. Douglas and his mother stayed as usual with the Oldfields in Blackrock where she could rest comfortably in her sisters' home between doctors' appointments while he was free to walk about the city and browse in its bookstores. In a shop on Anglesea Street where on previous trips he had purchased Irish books (the owner was John O'Daly, honorary secretary of the Ossianic Society, and a well-known publisher of Irish texts), he discovered that a "new society founded for keeping up the Irish language" was holding a meeting. He took a seat and listened "for a good while," looking around at the small but serious group of articulate and well-dressed women and men of different ages who had been drawn together by a subject in which he would not have expected Dubliners to be interested. When at last he got up to leave, a tall, muscular man with a small imperial beard also stood up and, walking with him to the door, invited him to tea the next afternoon.

Described by Dominic Daly as "a tireless worker for the . . . language," the man who approached Douglas was Thomas O'Neill Russell, a native of Westmeath who sailed regularly between Ireland and the United States, serving both his vocation (he was a commercial traveler for a whiskey firm, Hyde later learned) and his avocation, the promotion of Irish. He and the others at the meeting, Douglas discovered, were members of the Society for the Preservation of the Irish Language, a respectable semischolarly organization to which O'Conor Don, one of its founders, already had introduced him.

The next afternoon, after accompanying his aunt Cecily Oldfield on a visit to Dublin cousins, the Mansfields, Douglas went to Kingstown to have tea with O'Neill Russell and his wife. At first he thought that Mrs. O'Neill Russell was French, for that was the language in which the couple spoke to each other. Later, surmising that they had met in France where O'Neill Russell had lived for a time, he concluded that she was Swedish or Danish. In the hours they spent talking together about the fortunes of the Irish language, Douglas heard for the first time that there was strong interest in Irish in the United States—that indeed, there were American societies organized for the sole purpose of promoting Irish culture—and that some of those societies actually held regular classes in conversational modern Irish. O'Neill Russell also chatted familiarly about old Irish books and manuscripts that could be read in Dublin, at the Royal Irish Academy, and offered to introduce Douglas to the librarian and show him around the library there.

At eleven o'clock on June 21, Douglas stood on Dawson, a short street that runs between St. Stephen's Green and Trinity College, at the gracious entrance to the neoclassical residence that had been built for the Knox family in 1770 and acquired by the Royal Irish Academy in 1852. Itself an architectural gem, as Douglas admiringly noted, it was, he soon discovered, but the setting for such treasures as he had never dreamed existed. Hearing a friendly shout, he spied the tall figure of O'Neill Russell energetically cutting his way through dawdling pedestrians, surveying his walking stick as if it were a companion. Russell introduced Douglas to Mangan, director of the library, a kindly man who accepted a pinch of snuff and offered to provide Douglas with "every help . . . in learning Irish" if he could manage to come to the academy regularly. J. J. MacSweeney, the assistant librarian, repeatedly assured him that he was welcome to return whenever he liked. To his diary that evening Douglas confessed that the sight of so many priceless Irish artifacts—"old books eight hundred years of age, spearheads, harps, swords, the Tara brooch, the Cross of Cong, bog butter"—so dazzled him that he could not remember all that he had seen and examined. Two weeks later, back home in Roscommon, he received the very first letter ever sent to him in Irish, precursor of thousands. It was from O'Neill Russell, asking him for a contribution to help support the work of the society. Douglas's response was the first letter he had ever composed in Irish—written, he apologized, "as best he was able."

The Dublin trip with its unexpected outcome was exhilarating. For Douglas it provided a first indication that he could pursue his interest in Irish culture and the Irish language without necessarily limiting himself as his father thought to the life of a country vicar in a remote village in the west. At home there were Rochesfort three or four miles away in Buckhill and O'Conor Don about double that distance at

Clonalis. That Dublin could gather together in one room so many people of his own class and background who shared his interests in modern Irish was a revelation. His excitement, however, was short-lived, for other realities soon impinged on his mood. For one thing, despite his mother's consultations with Dublin doctors, her condition did not improve. The new carpet with which she had come home had cheered her temporarily, but within days she was again weak and dispirited. Well into July she often lacked sufficient strength even to go to church on Sunday. Nor was she the only one who had to be looked after. Johnny Lavin was sick, too. Douglas made frequent visits to his cottage to try to encourage him. And the Reverend Arthur Hyde also was spending much time in bed, although "not for a good reason," Annette confided: he had been drinking heavily again. But it was a minor matter that seemed to occupy Douglas disproportionately: during his absence the Hyde boat, which had been taken without permission, had been scraped in some mishap. As a conciliatory gesture Dockry (whom Hyde suspected of involvement in the unauthorized borrowing) had painted and caulked it. But Dockry also had inscribed on its hull a new name of his own choosing: *Home Rule*.

Within the two short years since Charles Stewart Parnell had entered Parliament, Home Rule had become, throughout Ireland, the most divisive political issue of the day. County Roscommon was no exception: it had been the rallying cry of the Parnellites who had supported O'Kelly against O'Conor Don in the last parliamentary elections. O'Conor Don's position had been regarded as unquestionably solid, but to the voters what counted more than trust and tradition was Parnell's membership in the Amnesty Association and his publicly proclaimed belief in the innocence of the Manchester Martyrs, who had been hanged in 1867 for their role in a plot to secure the release of Fenian prisoners. Moreover, there always had been radicals and political nonconformists in the Parnell family, it was said: in 1800 Sir John Parnell, Charles Stewart Parnell's great-grandfather, had opposed the Act of Union; Parnell's mother was an American; his sister, Fanny, wrote poetry for the *Irish People*. In the cottages of Frenchpark and Castlerea talk of an Irish bloc that could win parliamentary support for Irish interests evoked memories of 1850 and arguments for solidarity. If voters would give Parnell the wedge of support he needed, many were heard to declare, he could insist that the major parties negotiate with him. If the major parties refused, he could bring the government to a standstill. Parnell was not just a member of Parliament. He was a cause.

A political rather than a cultural nationalist, Charles Stewart Parnell (1846–1891) had grown up, like Douglas Hyde, hearing stories of 1898 and 1848 from his father's tenants, many of them veterans of these events. From Avondale in county Wicklow he had gone to Cambridge where (as in the Ascendancy school in Dublin briefly attended by Hyde) to identify oneself as Irish was to risk being regarded as déclassé. Little had changed in the attitudes of most nineteenth-century Englishmen, as Sarah Bradford, Disraeli's biographer, points out, since Swift complained of his loss of status when he crossed the Irish Sea. In 1877 Douglas was unaware of the particulars of Parnell's education and experience. What attracted him was the combination of nationalist sentiment and Anglo-Irish background that he saw in himself. For him Parnell was one more man to be admired and emulated in a long tradition of nineteenth-century Protestant Ascendancy leaders who had declared themselves for Ireland.

Douglas's irritation with Dockry was not caused therefore by Dockry's impudence in naming the Hyde boat *Home Rule* but by his ignorance and lack of interest in Irish history. Dockry, like Lalor and Mitchel, saw Ireland as a land divided between landlord and tenant, not unionist and nationalist. His philosophy was simple: a good landlord was preferable to a bad one; far better to have no landlord at all. If he supported Home Rule it was because Parnell and his bloc were said to be on the side of the tenants. For Douglas, Ireland was a land that conferred its unique and ancient heritage on all its people, regardless of class or background; both land and heritage were threatened by those who, careless of its cultural riches and historic identity, governed Ireland only to exploit it as a source of money, position, and power. To Douglas, Parnell was the heir of Wolfe Tone, Robert Emmet, and Thomas Davis.

Douglas was particularly stung by Dockry's wholesale condemnation of all landlords, which to him was eminently unfair. Even his own father, although thoroughly unionist and inalterably opposed to Home Rule, was scarcely a rack-renting landlord. A man of great physical energy and a genuine love for the outdoors, he often worked side by side with his tenants and his sons during planting and haying seasons. Rector of Frenchpark, he was at the same time a man of the land: he could care for his crops and livestock and mend his walls and roads as competently as Connolly and Dockry. In his role of "masther" he might refer to Connolly, Dockry, and others as "the lower orders," but he got on well with them. Douglas knew that his father was not a man who would take a family's cow or evict a tenant down on his luck. He was simply an English subject born and living in Ireland who had a one-sided view of Irish history and little or no knowledge or understanding of Irish culture. Never did it occur to him that Dockry's target was not landlords as individuals but landlords as a class.

At home in the glebe house the target was the Parnellites. When the government's position on the subject was propounded, Arthur and Oldfield could be counted on to echo the sentiments of the Reverend Arthur Hyde. Visitors entertained in the drawing-room affirmed that similar opinions were expressed in the Georgian houses of friends and relatives as far away as Dublin and Cork. Theirs were the views also of O'Conor Don and other Catholic landlords. To them the Fenians were dangerous conspirators supported by ill-advised Americans who, if unchecked, would bring violence and bloodshed to peaceful Roscommon. Parnellism, they avowed, was but another name for parliamentary Fenianism. No one seemed to notice that Douglas had little to say on the subject. Discreet among family members and friends, he gave full vent to his nationalist sympathies in fiery poems and radical essays written in English and Irish—juvenilia, riddled with clichés—that he preserved in his commonplace book and diary. Yet he also considered privately all that he had heard of the disappointment and disenchantment that had followed the rise of hopeful movements of the past. How had they been undermined? By what had they been defeated? If the United Irishmen, the Men of 1848, the Young Irelanders, the Repealers, and the Fenians all had failed, could the Parnellites succeed? In his young heart, Douglas regarded himself as a champion of the Irish people; he too wanted Ireland to achieve nationhood; he too wanted to throw off what, following the poetasters of the period, he called "the hated yoke of the Saxon." His own personal independence, however, depended not on Parnell but on the Irish sizarship.

During the next twelve months Douglas steadily increased the hours he spent studying. He added Euclid to his schedule; helped by Cecilly Hyde, he made his way through "twenty or thirty" lessons of Ollendorff, a German text. Respites were few, although from time to time he had long talks with Rochesfort at either Buckhill or the glebe house. Around him life proceeded as usual: Johnny Lavin was soon up and about again, but then Mrs. Connolly fell ill, and his mother and father, if no better, were at least no worse. Observing the embarrassing behavior of his father and his brother Oldfield, for a time he restricted his own consumption of beer and whiskey. One day when he and Annette were visiting the Hamiltons, he was concerned to find that a bottle of Hollands had left him in danger of becoming, as he said, "non compos mentis." He had been out boating with others when he began to feel foolish and light-headed. Curling up in the boat's cabin, he went to sleep. By dinner he was all right, but he drank nothing more that day.

O'Neill Russell continued to send Douglas letters in Irish, usually about the progress of the language, but sometimes on other subjects. In one letter O'Neill Russell advised Douglas to read Ruskin. It was a great pity, Douglas's new mentor declared, that such a man was not Irish. "So ignorant was I at this time," Hyde later confessed, "that I had to inquire who Ruskin was!" But even as he had begun to realize how much there was to learn, how much he did not know, he was steadily becoming more confident of his ability to quantify his academic accomplishments and to set for himself realistic intermediate and long-range goals. One intermediate goal before him at the beginning of 1878 was the schedule of work he had determined to finish by the end of June. His Drumkilla aunts, Emily and Cecilly Hyde, had invited him to join them on a summer tour of France and Switzerland, but he could not allow himself to go without first making substantial progress toward proficiency in the subjects in which he knew he would be examined when he applied to Trinity. The tour was to begin and end in London. That in itself was an exciting prospect. Never before had he been out of his own country.

5

First Flowering

On his first trip to the Continent in July 1878 Douglas continued the love affair with France begun when, as a boy of fourteen, he had first tried to compose poems and simple descriptive prose paragraphs in elementary French. Now quite competent in the language, he enjoyed reading French literature, especially romances. During the spring he had started St. Pierre's *Paul et Virginie*. He finished it in Paris, then browsed in the stalls along the Seine, looking for similar books to buy.

One disappointing purchase was Voltaire's *Lady Babylon and Other Stories,* chosen as much for its author as for its contents. Voltaire, it was said, was a son who had desired no profession but literature who had been opposed by a father who considered literature no profession at all. The parallel to Douglas's conflict with his own father was irresistible. Voltaire, moreover, had been a champion of the oppressed; in his youth, like Douglas, he had secretly written dangerous poems libeling the existing political regime and opposing its persecuting and privileged orthodoxy. A striking feature exploited by caricaturists who depicted Voltaire was the unusual brilliance of his eyes. Douglas's eyes also were unusual in their brightness and intensity. Voltaire reportedly had many mistresses. Douglas had not yet had any at all, except vicariously, through identification with the heroes of the romances he liked to read. But during the past year he had become increasingly if cautiously interested, from a safe distance, in certain women. Only recently it had struck him that Christine Wilson, sister of his friend Mackey, was very pretty, while Marie de Freyne was very plain. He particularly enjoyed attention from sophisticated older women who did not giggle or blush but showed a real interest in what he had to say. Two years ago on his trip to Kerry with Emily and Cecilly Hyde, a chance encounter with his aunts' warm and charming friend, Anna White, had left him smitten. In his diary he wrote of her as "Una Bán." It was, of course, a direct translation of her name, but it also had a romantic undertone that appealed to him.

The similarities Douglas had noted between himself and Voltaire did not extend to the ideas that the French author expressed in his fiction. Having taken his newly acquired copy of *Lady Babylon* back to his lodgings, he had opened it—and been repelled by what he read. It was nothing, he avowed, that he would ever write. Granted the story was cleverly composed. But to even an advanced thinker like himself (he was certainly advanced, he assured himself, in comparison with his father and brothers) it was clearly "atheistic, dirty, and ugly." This did not mean, however, that he should stop reading or discard the book or not buy more books by the same author: he prided himself on his agreement with Voltaire that taste must never become the basis for censorship. (Later, when he tried his pen at satire, Voltaire was one of his models.) He also shared Voltaire's belief in educating the masses. His favorite Paris landmark was the Bibliothèque Nationale. For him it epitomized France, a country "so fine," where "so many books are written that they are put out free."

After Paris, London at first seemed pedestrian. In France Douglas had observed "a greater measure of civility among people, women and men," than he had seen in England or Ireland. He noted, for example, that when Frenchmen were spoken to, they raised their hats, a custom he considered adopting. He approved of French gallantry, especially the Frenchman's habit of taking off his hat and holding it in his hand whenever a woman passed by. But London was agreeably less foreign, a relaxing change from France, once he had completed the ordeal of converting his remaining francs back into pounds and then translating his record of expenditures into the same currency. London was also fun. In the fashionable district where he and his aunts were staying, he kept running into people he had met in Ireland. One happy encounter was with none other than Anna White. To his diary he confessed, "I think I am in heaven when I am with her." Dashing about London by himself, visiting Anna White, and making impromptu appointments with others, Douglas felt that he had become very sophisticated. Alone and with groups of two or three or more, he dined out, went to the theater, and shopped for such a number of books, gifts, and souvenirs that on his last day in England he had to buy an extra portmanteau to carry them all.

On July 29 Douglas and his aunts began the long journey home, by train through Wales to Holyhead, by night ferry to Dublin. Arriving at the North Wall at six o'clock the next morning, they first checked their luggage at Broadstone, then separated briefly, his aunts to spend the day with friends, Douglas to wander about the city, seeing it with the new eyes of a young Irishman just returned from England and the Continent. Strolling about aimlessly, he stopped first for a large, leisurely breakfast, next for a warm bath, and then headed for his usual haunts, the bookstores, where he used his leftover travel money to buy several pictures of Ireland, a book of prophecies in Irish and English, a history of Ireland, a copy of the *Proceedings of the Ossianic Society,* and a first edition of Donlevy's Irish catechism, published in Paris in 1742. In one of the bookstores he encountered Father Nolan, secretary of the Society for the Preservation of the Irish Language, who told him that John O'Daly had died and that there was to be a grand auction of books from his shop. Father Nolan also announced to Douglas that, in response to a memorial on the subject of education in the Irish language that had been sent by the society to the National School Commission in June, the commissioners had agreed to grant result fees for student proficiency to secondary-school teachers of Irish on the same terms as those that applied to secondary-school teachers of Greek, French, and Latin. It was not only a major breakthrough in the struggle to preserve modern Irish, Nolan triumphantly declared, but proof of what might be accomplished, for until the society had entered the debate on the side of the language, the National School commissioners had refused to recognize modern Irish as an academic subject.

In midafternoon Douglas hurried to Broadstone to meet his aunts and catch the four o'clock train to the west. They reached Drumkilla before midnight for a happy reunion with Frances, her husband, and Douglas's brother Arthur, who had come up from Frenchpark for a visit. Despite the hour they promptly began distributing gifts and recalling excitedly everything they had seen and done. In turn they received the latest news of Mohill. As usual, it had been a whirl of activity: lunches, dinners, teas, cricket, soccer, tennis—even one enormous early-morning-to-late-night party at Drumkilla to which a hundred people had been invited. It was easy to get caught up in such an agreeable society, Douglas admitted to his diary. It would be pleasant to stay longer. But at the end of a week he faced the fact that he had been away from his studies for over a month.

On August 8 Douglas and Arthur left Drumkilla for Frenchpark. Before them, alas, was a far from happy homecoming. Arthur had warned Douglas that both their father and Oldfield had been drinking heavily. What he found was worse than he expected. Dinner was not yet over when Oldfield staggered upstairs and fell asleep, only to wake up vomiting. At ten o'clock he was back downstairs, obstreperously demanding more to drink. Meanwhile the Reverend Arthur Hyde, with a glass before him, obviously satisfied with himself for having proved his greater drinking prowess, declared that he felt as if he were a college man again. "Indeed, there is a great difference between this place and Drumkilla," Douglas wrote that night in his diary, with a wry restraint he was soon to find hard to maintain.

On August 14 Douglas received an enthusiastic report from Russell on the progress of Irish classes in America and the details of the important agreement struck with the National School commissioner about which he already had been briefed by Father Nolan. The same mail brought a list of the books and manuscripts that were to be auctioned at O'Daly's bookshop on August 19. It was a pity, he thought, that he would not be able to take advantage of such an opportunity, but his final reckoning of trip expenses confirmed that he had spent the last of his money in Dublin on his return from Europe. To his amazement— the Reverend Arthur Hyde was rarely generous with money, even only shillings and pence—his father offered him six pounds. Delighted with his good fortune, Douglas immediately made plans to return to Dublin on Saturday, August 17, for a pre-auction look at the items that would be included in the Monday sale.

Before Saturday, however, there was trouble in the glebe house. On August 15 Douglas noted that "Ma was not well and the Master was bad enough as usual for the same reason—too much of the full jug." Arthur bitterly reproached his father, but the rector, behaving as if he were a Trinity student conducting a mock debate with one of his contemporaries, answered "full of *sophistia* and a kind of slippery wisdom." Oldfield did not occupy his usual third position in the old trio; he was despondent for a different reason. Without money or prospects that would enable him to make an offer of marriage, he had been courting a young woman from Carrick-on-Shannon. Her father, who had previously made clear his disapproval, had told him never to come to the house or otherwise try to see the young woman again. Douglas was sympathetic: "I think O was hot after this girl. . . . I think she felt warmly toward him, too." Yet he recognized the hopelessness of Oldfield's position and took it as a warning to himself. If he refused to consider a career in the church, what would his own prospects be in five or six years, when he was approaching Oldfield's age? His father already had raised the question with him, sneeringly suggesting that with his interest in languages, he might consider becoming a missionary "to the black men in foreign lands." He realized that it was not just some hypothetical future desire to marry but the whole question of how and where he would live that was at stake. When he returned from Dublin, Douglas vowed, he would redouble his efforts to qualify for the Irish sizarship. At the very least it would give him a measure of independence during the next few years.

On Saturday, August 17, Douglas was up at five o'clock in the morning. Connolly drove him to Boyle, where he caught the eight o'clock train to Dublin. As soon as he arrived he went to D'Olier Street where the books to be auctioned had been set out for examination. Both their number and variety astonished him. He had determined, however, that he would buy only Irish items, so it was on these that he concentrated, moving slowly from one to another, carefully noting the contents and condition of each, through a long and tiring yet exciting day. At six o'clock in the evening he left D'Olier Street to catch the train from Westland Row Station to Blackrock, where he stayed with his Oldfield aunts and his grandmother. He could hardly wait for Monday morning. Only Sunday intervened. It was not easy for him to sit through morning services with his grandmother and aunts, then accompany Cecily Oldfield on her usual rounds of afternoon and evening sermons in the different churches of the area—especially as most of the ministers were not so eloquent as Dr. O'Gallagher, author of the collection of sermons printed in English and Irish on facing pages that had become Douglas's usual Sunday reading. In the last church they visited on Sunday evening, he had scarcely settled into his seat for the last sermon of the day when his head began to nod and, to his aunt's distress, soon he was fast asleep.

Although the O'Daly auction did not begin until one in the afternoon, Douglas was back in Dublin early Monday morning. In his diary he wrote regretfully, "There was many a book on which my heart was set but which I had to let go because I could not offer as much as others." At the same time he noted that he was lucky to get what he bought as cheaply as he did, for there was more interest in Irish items than he had expected, and more money going on them. He had bid five shillings and ninepence for Keating's *History of Ireland* "translated by O'Mahony the Fenian in America"—a good book to show Dockry, who prided himself on his Fenianism, but had so little interest in Ireland's past. What would Dockry think of his hero, John O'Mahony, a founder of the Fenian Brotherhood, undertaking such a task? Among the other eight items he purchased were O'Reilly's *Dictionary* with a supplement by John O'Donovan, published in 1864; *The Celtic Miscellany* for 1849; and *Oidche Cloinne Uisneach* (The fate of the sons of Usna) published by the Gaelic Society in 1808. Had it not been for a bookseller named Traynor, his strongest competitor throughout the day, he also would have had a copy of the *Annals of the Four Masters,* but his bidding at least had kept the bookseller from getting it for a pound.

On Tuesday morning Douglas returned to the auction, where he now felt quite at home. A good part of the excitement of each day was the chance it offered for discussion of Irish books and manuscripts with other members of the Dublin Irish-language circle to which he now felt that he belonged. He found to his pleasure that he knew a lot more than he had realized about the subject. He put in his bid for a rare Irish catechism published in Rome in 1707, acquiring it "very cheaply entirely at ninepence." He and Traynor struck a bargain that allowed Douglas to obtain a lot of ten books at a good price with the understanding that Douglas would give the bookseller three if he would stay out of the bidding. Among the items Douglas wanted were several in Scots Gaelic, which he had just begun to study seriously, and a copy of Bunyan's *Pilgrim's Progress* in Irish. The three items he gave to the bookseller were, he wrote gleefully, the least interesting of the ten.

Clearly enjoying the clublike atmosphere of the auction (many of the bidders and observers were people with whom he had become acquainted through O'Neill Russell, the Society for the Preservation of the Irish Language, or O'Daly's bookstore), Douglas returned again on Wednesday and Thursday, making additional book purchases and buying the first manuscripts to be added to his collection. Among them was a bound manuscript by John O'Donovan containing many religious poems that Douglas later published in his *Religious Songs of Connacht.* There was no doubt that he had bargained shrewdly. Remembering how his father always used to come home from Dublin with packages of books under his arm, he looked forward to telling him about his week's experiences. Yet after the auction Douglas remained in Dublin another sixteen days, visiting friends and relatives in the company of Cecily Oldfield, making the rounds of churches with her on Sunday, going to the dentist, sightseeing, shopping.

One day Douglas went to Trinity to talk about the Irish sizarship with a Mr. Millar and a Mr. Gellett. It was an intensely disappointing interview. He had set his heart on becoming a sizar, but he was told that his father was too well-off for him to be eligible. He could still try for prizes, of course. Indeed he had intended to: he had hoped he could equal Arthur's and Oldfield's record. Arthur had taken his B.A. with first honors. Oldfield had earned a university scholarship, the vice-provost's prize for composition, and the vice-chancellor's gold medal for Latin. But honors and prizes would not give him the independence he needed. Certainly they had been no help to Oldfield, who was always at odds with the Reverend Arthur Hyde now. Remembering what his father had said about his future, he asked Cecily what she thought about his becoming a missionary in some foreign land. As she seemed startled by his question, he tried to put the Trinity problem out of his head, but with little else to claim his attention beyond daily sessions with the dentist—a painful tooth required a series of office visits—that was a hard thing to do. Nor did the weather help. Most days were rainy. He caught a cold. He wondered if the weather was the same at Bundoran, where his mother had gone with Annette and Emily in the hope that the sea breezes might do her some good. He found a book he thought she might like and posted it for her.

For his mother's sake as well as his own, Douglas wished that the weather might change for the better, but it remained wet, cold, and unhappy for all the Hydes of Frenchpark not just in September but for the entire rest of the year. Repeated bouts of asthma disabled his mother. Arthur became so ill in October that he had to be sent to Drumkilla, where his aunt Frances and her husband, Hunt, could look after him. Oldfield, still disconsolate over the unhappy end of his love affair, was drinking heavily. The Reverend Arthur Hyde alternated between staying in bed with the gout and staying in bed with a hangover. Even when he was up and around and reasonably well, his mood was black, and he railed against his elder sons in whom he had invested so much of himself only to have them disappoint him. Arthur's academic record at Trinity had proved both his son's worth and the value of the preparatory education he had been given. Now Arthur ungratefully refused to enter the ministry, and Oldfield was taking the same stand. Neither would carry on the family tradition; neither cared anything about it.

The last setback, to which the Reverend Arthur Hyde responded with a burst of temper out of all proportion to its significance, was a letter from Lord de Freyne which suddenly and inexplicably ordered the Hydes to refrain from shooting partridge on his land.

Upset by the tensions and problems that afflicted the Hyde household, Douglas tried to bury himself in his studies, but every evening his schedule was interrupted by his parents' insistence that he play cards with them after supper. Hours of work were left undone if he agreed; there were arguments, recriminations, and charges of ingratitude if he refused. Sundays brought more arguments and recriminations if he objected to teaching Sunday school. Since his chance of an Irish sizarship had been ruled out, his father had again begun his old threats that he would not send to the university a third son who did not show more interest in clerical obligations and some clear intention of studying for the ministry.

One day a letter arrived for Douglas from a Dr. Welland, a professor of divinity in England, in response to a request he had received, apparently from Cecily Oldfield, for information about the proper preparation of a missionary. There was no escape: Dr. Welland's answer was that Douglas should enroll in divinity school, either in Trinity or in some English university. When Douglas tried to discuss the letter with his father, the Reverend Arthur Hyde flew into a rage. "T.C.D. be damned!" he shouted. "Look at how it made an undisciplined scoundrel of Oldfield and an agnostic of Arthur. I won't let you through any college! You can be a preacher to your own Irish-speaking countrymen." Wise enough to know that it was useless to point out that even this alternative would require a Trinity education, Douglas wrote a long letter to Cecily thanking her for her kindness and returned to his studies. Surely, he thought to himself, his father would see him through Trinity if he ranked among those who sat for the entrance examinations.

November brought snow so heavy that at times Douglas could not get out the door to shovel it away. Some days he finished shoveling only to begin again immediately, as more snow fell. If he delayed, the wet snow formed solid blocks of ice. He was continually troubled now by a soreness in his eyes so painful at times that he could not read. Yet if he stopped reading or even reduced his study schedule, he would reduce his chances of doing well on the Trinity entrance examinations. With or without a sizarship, he had set his sights on Trinity. November also brought word from Drumkilla that Arthur was no better. Twice during the month Frances had summoned Douglas, but he did not see how he could get there. One problem was the snow and ice that impeded travel; another was his reluctance to leave Annette to look after things at home, with his father half crippled from gout and his mother weak from severe attacks of asthma. In the middle of the month he sent Francis O'Ruark to be of what help he could. When his father was somewhat better—at least able to get around the house—he himself responded to his aunt's second call, on November 25.

Actually, except for Arthur's condition, which continued to be a source of worry, Drumkilla was a pleasant place to be, with its opportunities for visiting, shooting, and walking. One day on the road he met a blind piper from county Galway, a good Irish speaker and, like others of his occupation, an inveterate traveler. The piper had been in twenty-seven of the thirty-two Irish counties, he said. Douglas walked along with him for a while, asking questions, and carefully listening to his cleverly phrased answers. His favorite counties, the piper said, citing his reasons, were Mayo, Kerry, Tipperary, and Dublin. He was not too fond of Longford and Limerick. Something of the piper's personality and experiences, carefully noted in Hyde's diaries, eventually found its way into his poems, plays, and stories.

By December 12 Douglas had left Drumkilla and was again home in the glebe house. Bitter cold had continued; there was still snow on the ground. His mother was better one day, worse the next. His brother Oldfield, home for the holidays, quarreled almost constantly with his father. Everyone was concerned about Arthur. Except for a pleasant hour or two when he and Annette opened presents together—she gave him O'Curry's *Lectures on the Manuscript Materials of Ancient Irish History,* a book by Voltaire, another by Schiller; he gave her *Alice in Wonderland* and *I Promissi Sposi*—Christmas, 1878, was sober and subdued. More snow fell on St. Stephen's Day, leaving a blanket of about ten inches. Douglas tried to study, but his eyes hurt so badly that it was becoming more and more difficult for him to read.

On January 7 Douglas joined Oldfield, who was returning to Trinity, on the train to Dublin. Arrangements had been made for him to consult Fitzgerald, an eye specialist. Fitzgerald diagnosed Douglas's problem as "weak eyes," recommended eyeglasses, and advised that he not try to read without them. Douglas bought a pair of eyeglasses at Spenser's for twelve and sixpence, then caught the train to Mohill. There Arthur's appearance, so weak and thin and "quite worn away," gave Douglas "a great fright." It said more than words about the steady and continuing deterioration of Arthur's health. Most of the time now, Frances said, he was too weak to get out of bed. On even his best days he could not get downstairs without assistance. It was clear that Frances both wanted and needed not only help but emotional support—she could hardly speak of Arthur without weeping. Douglas assured her that he would stay on for a few days to do what he could to buoy up Arthur's spirits and be generally as useful as possible. To himself he noted that it would be necessary to improve his aunt's spirits as well.

Days turned into weeks, weeks into months. Everyone talked of Arthur's getting better even as he grew steadily and visibly worse. For Douglas, the winter and spring of 1879 was a strange and surrealistic time in which he discovered a number of things about himself that both surprised and confused him. At first he was genuinely concerned and solicitous, eager to do his part, and grateful for all the unselfish attention Frances and Hunt gave to Arthur. In his long talks with Frances he showed a mature understanding of Arthur's intermittent peevishness and his aunt's increasing panic as she sensed that all her efforts might well be in vain. But, as inside Drumkilla the battle against Arthur's illness took on the quality of a siege while outside everything remained unchanged, Douglas privately found himself coping with feelings he could not express. One day when, thoroughly chilled and wet from having fallen through the ice on the pond, he started to feel feverish, he realized that, preoccupied as everyone was with Arthur, there was no one to be concerned about him. Twinges of jealousy began to alternate with periods of shame and remorse. These feelings increased as he tried to cope with other physical complaints which he himself suspected of being aggravated by his state of mind. Pains in his joints kept him awake half the night; his eyes were still terribly sore, despite his eyeglasses; he was beset by a general sense of malaise.

At the beginning of February, when Douglas had been at Drumkilla about three weeks, his father arrived in response to a message from Frances. She had sent word for him to come as soon as he was able, for Arthur had grown increasingly depressed. To everyone's relief the Reverend Arthur Hyde was not drinking—in fact, having recently completed a regimen of diet and rest prescribed for a severe case of gout, he both looked and felt cheerful and well. There was no doubt that the visit revived Arthur's spirits. Douglas also was glad to see his father. He wished he could return with him to Frenchpark. With Arthur so sick, however, he said nothing, for he felt his duty was to remain and help Frances. A few days after his father's departure he had reason to regret his selflessness. In addition to pains in his joints, he had developed an ugly boil on his neck. But as both Emily and Sisilla were now in bed with flulike symptoms and Hunt had been called to Dublin to attend to his dying elderly aunt, there could be no question of Douglas's going anywhere. The only good news was that for a week or two Arthur seemed a bit better, but by the end of February he was worse again. Resigned to remaining at Drumkilla through spring if necessary, Douglas took powders morning and evening to help ease the pains in his joints and treated his boils (another had appeared on his knee) with compresses. Whenever he could he studied; he tried not to complain.

Warmer weather came at last at the beginning of March, and with it the opportunity to take long walks along a pretty country road that led to a little lake in a meadow. Hunt returned from Dublin with a thoughtful selection of Irish books that Douglas could hardly wait to read: O'Donovan's notes on Irish annals; a life of Columcille; a Latin life of Adamnam; an old Irish grammar that used Latin declensions; and Irish glosses by Whitley Stokes. But if Douglas was slowly recovering, Arthur was now rapidly declining. The doctors were agreed on their diagnosis: it was, as everyone had feared, consumption. The judgment of the doctors was harsh. They did not expect Arthur to live through the summer, perhaps not even through the month.

In a letter to Oldfield, Douglas described the situation in full detail; to his parents he wrote but a partial truth, then went out on the bogs hunting a snipe with which he hoped he might tempt Arthur's appetite. On March 8 he wrote in his diary in Irish, "I killed a wild pigeon for Arthur." His aunt Anna Kane traveled to Frenchpark by carriage to bring back Bessie Hyde, still very sick herself, but determined to visit Arthur whom she had not seen since October. A week later the Reverend Arthur Hyde returned. Awakened by noises in the middle of the night, Douglas and Hunt found the poor man crying and beating on the wall. He was a minister; he had seen enough of death and dying to know that he was losing his eldest son. Douglas gave his father half a glass of gin to help him sleep. Back in his own room he wrote in his diary, "O dear Mary, that I may be out of this place!!!"

On March 22 Douglas returned to the glebe house with his father. He was still not well; he had been at Drumkilla coping with his brother's slow and inevitable decline, his own needs and wants overlooked or forgotten, for more than two months; he was far behind in his work. Never had the glebe house seemed so welcoming. By the end of April he was feeling stronger, but the problem with his eyes had become worse. There was talk of sending him to a specialist in London.

Meanwhile, from Lavin, Dockry, and others, Douglas learned that all the misery of the world had not been divided, as he had sometimes thought during the past six months, between the glebe house and Drumkilla. The harsh winter and delayed spring of 1879 had taken a terrible toll. In some parts of the country crop failure, eviction, and hunger had reached proportions that evoked the nightmare of 1846–1848. A general shortage of dry peat had left those lucky enough to escape the bailiff without fuel to warm their bones or to cook what little food they had. The government was preparing harsher measures against the forces of "Captain Moonlight," who roamed the countryside, intimidating landlords and their agents.

Arthur died on Wednesday, May 14, at about five o'clock in the afternoon. The Reverend Arthur Hyde was at his bedside; Oldfield was in Dublin; Annette was in Frenchpark, taking care of her mother; Douglas had just arrived in London to see a specialist named Critchett. Douglas did not know of Arthur's death until May 17, the day set for the funeral at Drumkilla, when he heard the news quite by chance while paying a call on Anna White: she had just received a letter from Emily Hyde. His diary entries of the next few days record his ambivalent feelings: pity for the "poor boy," who was better off dead than suffering; awareness that, of his two brothers, he had always preferred Oldfield; sympathy for his father and the others at home; hope that Arthur's death might "improve the Master"; sadness that Arthur, who was twenty-six, had not been in good health for the last six years; admiration for the excellent academic record Arthur had achieved despite his debilitating illnesses; self-pity that the rest of the family would be together, he alone would not be present, for the family ceremony mourning Arthur's death; awareness that, as brothers, he and Oldfield shared Arthur's loss in a particular way. "I will never see him again," he wrote, in one disconnected diary entry. "I abhor lamenting him, but I think he was willing. . . . I am very sad . . . to hear that he is gone." Another, more coherent entry, concerned chiefly with details of a morning and afternoon church service, an afternoon visit with Anna White, and an evening's conversation with a low-church young Irishwoman staying at his lodging house in Bayswater, made no direct reference to Arthur's death but ended with a lament written in Irish that was obviously intended for him:

> My sorrow that there is nothing for us now
> In place of the wise man but a lament and a tear

A tear and a cry and a lament
Is all there is for us, and a breaking heart.

On Tuesday, May 20, Douglas wrote to his mother. He had had
"no idea" of Arthur's death, he said, describing how the news had
reached him; it had shocked him greatly. Strictly speaking, this was not
true, for he had known when he left Drumkilla in March that Arthur's
condition was hopeless. But as he had then softened the blow for his
mother, he could not now admit to it. He assured her that his sore eyes
seemed better already, although he was not sure whether the improvement was due to medication or rest, and he sent word through her to
Annette, whose birthday was coming, that he had bought for her "a
beautiful book of Italian poetry." The next day Douglas received a letter
from his mother that had crossed his letter in the mail. It said nothing
about him, his recent illness, his eyes, or Annette's birthday; it was full
of nothing but Arthur, his last days, and his funeral. Arthur had used
his last breath, she wrote, to effect a reconciliation between Oldfield
and his father; he had been a wonderful boy "greatly loved by all who
knew him." This last line opened at last the floodgates of pent-up resentment: "Not me," declared Douglas to his diary in Irish. "He and the
Master seemed made to be the two most opposed to my way of thinking
than anyone else on the ridge of this world."

Douglas returned to Ireland at the beginning of June. His eyes were
somewhat improved, but he was not yet free of the pains in his chest
that he had complained of during his long stay at Drumkilla. The Dublin doctors he consulted diagnosed his problem as pleurisy, recommended rest, and gave him some pills to help him sleep. Reading the
Dublin newspapers on his way back to Roscommon, Douglas learned
that Michael Davitt had succeeded in mustering support for Parnell
among all but the most radical of the Fenians. Davitt's idea, outlined
in Parnell's speech delivered in Westport on June 7, was that tenant
farmers could gain relief for themselves if they would but stand together
in a massive show of strength and commitment to unity. "A fair rent
is a rent the tenant can reasonably pay," Parnell declared. But to make
landlords see this position, tenant farmers would have to demonstrate
their determination to hold on to their homesteads and lands. "You
must not allow yourselves to be dispossessed as your fathers were dispossessed in 1847," he insisted; "you must help yourselves." It was a
message that appealed to Douglas, but for the moment he was too ill
to do more than remember it. Back in Frenchpark he told Dr. Cup-

paidge, his uncle by marriage, what the Dublin doctors had said. Cuppaidge checked his lungs, declared them clear, found no sign of pleurisy, and insisted that, despite his continuing complaints, there was nothing wrong with him. The next five weeks were a nightmare: Douglas's chest pain became more severe; he developed chronic diarrhea. Remembering that these had been Arthur's symptoms in the last months of his illness, he was badly frightened, but there was no one to turn to for help. Oldfield had gone to England, his mother was in Dublin, and Annette was in Scotland. He and his father were left alone, he declared, "in Connacht and in hell."

Belligerent often to the point of violence, the Reverend Arthur Hyde was refusing to eat but finishing a bottle and more of whiskey each day until Douglas managed to get possession of the household keys, lock up all the bottles in the house, and gradually reduce his father's drinking to four or five glasses daily. Quarrels erupted at all hours of the day and night as a tug-of-war over the keys ensued. Unable to study or rest, Douglas grew weaker and weaker until finally his father came to himself long enough to realize that something was seriously wrong. Bypassing Cuppaidge, he sought another medical opinion. Again the diagnosis was pleurisy; Dr. Cuppaidge was the only one who disagreed. Dr. O'Farrell, the man who responded, advised rest and prescribed cod liver oil and iodine, one to be taken after meals and the other at bedtime. The best medicine was that the Reverend Arthur Hyde, no doubt fearful that he was about to lose another son, managed to get hold of himself and began to moderate his drinking.

Three weeks after Dr. O'Farrell's visit, Bessie Hyde and Annette returned home. Still seriously ill, Douglas was unable to leave his bed for another week, but then slowly began to recover. It was during his convalescence, while he remained quiet and for the most part too weak to move about or to study, that "the spirit of poetry rose" in him, and he composed a number of poems, most of them in Irish, a few in English, and at least one of them inspired by Parnell's speech of June 7. His muse, he was now convinced, was Irish. It had always been so, he believed, ever since he had learned his first Irish words.

Douglas gradually recovered from the ravages of the summer; his relationship with his father did not. Throughout October, November, and December of 1879 and well into 1880, exchanges over the Reverend Arthur Hyde's drunken rampages increased in harshness and frequency. Usually these took place at night, but sometimes they broke out in the middle of the day, even with visitors present. Meanwhile,

Douglas's father and mother quarreled constantly between themselves, usually about Oldfield, whom his father had barred from the glebe house. At times these quarrels became so heated as to require Annette's intervention. Like Arthur before him, Douglas reproached his father for his brutishness, his lack of feeling for anyone in the family, and the hypocrisy of the sinful ways against which he himself preached when he was well enough to mount the pulpit. "Ugly is the sinner with us, very ugly," he wrote in his diary on October 30. By the end of December, when Douglas made his customary summary of the year past, an uneasy calm had returned to the glebe house at last: for the time being his father's animosity toward Oldfield appeared to have abated; everything seemed "civil and settled" between them. Remembering, however, the brief reconciliation that had followed the death of Arthur, Douglas did not expect the peace to last.

Of his own past year Douglas wrote, "It was harsh, harsh, my health to be attacked from the month of May until now, but glory be to God that it was short—I am becoming myself again." The truth is that by the end of 1879 Douglas was a different self than he ever had been before, not simply because he was about to begin his twenty-first year, nor even because the past year had been a crucible in many respects, but because he was now a published writer. Two of his Irish poems already had appeared in "Our Gaelic Department," a regular Irish-language feature of two English-language weeklies, The *Irishman* and the *Shamrock,* that were circulated in both Ireland and North America. These columns, edited by David Comyn, cofounder of the Society for the Preservation of the Irish Language, had been introduced in response to criticism that the weeklies served only enthusiastic supporters, not speakers, of Irish. They proved so popular that Comyn added a third column, "Fáinne an lae," to which Douglas contributed not only poems but also short prose passages. In his diaries and his correspondence with O'Neill Russell and other members of the Irish-language circle to which he now belonged, he often had Irished his name to Dubhglas de h-Íde. With the public emergence of what until now had been his private persona, he adopted a pseudonym, An Craoibhin Aoibhinn, "the delightful little branch." It was surely not a whimsical choice but a deliberate act of discretion. He intended to sit for the entrance examinations at Trinity in June 1880. To publicly identify himself by his own name (even his own name translated into Irish) with what the Ascendancy would term "Fenian sentiments" clearly would have been unwise.

Hyde's first published poem, "Shiubhal mé lá go tuirseach trom" (I walk today wearily, with heavy step)—a lament narrated by an impoverished old man, a homeless wanderer, who has lost everything, children, family, and comrades—appeared in both the *Irishman* of Saturday, October 25, 1879 and the *Shamrock* of November 1, 1879. The *Irishman* was the more serious of the two publications; the *Shamrock* was humorous and gently satirical. In the latter, Hyde's poem of eighteen stanzas—none humorous or satirical, but nevertheless to the public taste—shared space with "Mick McQuaid, Alderman," an episode in Major William F. Lynam's famous series about a rascally hero, and chapter 31 of "Wilful Pansy; or, The Bride of a Week" by Emma Garrison Jones. Four weeks later, on November 29, a second Hyde poem, "Ól-famaid sláinte na tíre" (We drink the health of the land), a spirited patriotic drinking song with a rattling rhythm, appeared in the *Irishman*. The following week, on December 6, it was reprinted in the *Shamrock*.

On New Year's Eve, 1879, the Reverend Arthur Hyde began a period of heavy drinking that lasted for two weeks. Douglas and Oldfield joined him to toast the old year out and the new year in, but they both went to bed an hour after midnight on the first day of 1880, for each had much reading and studying before him. In the weeks that followed the brothers worked on something of a schedule. Both would concentrate on their own work much of the day, with occasional rest breaks to check the turlough or to take a walk with a gun, on the chance of finding birds; after supper, often in the company of Connolly and John and Michael Lavin, they drank whiskey and poteen (Douglas called it "'rum,'") and played cards until about one o'clock in the morning.

On January 17, Douglas's twentieth birthday, there was a hard frost that continued for nearly a week. His eyes were again very sore. He did not want to abandon the schedule he had laid out for himself (actually, he did not want to abandon all but Euclid, which he had come to hate), but Oldfield advised him to give his eyes a rest lest their condition deteriorate further. Oldfield returned to Dublin on January 18; Bessie Hyde, her asthma worse, was too tired and weak to leave her bed. Annette was busy looking after her mother and overseeing the household. With no choice but to give up reading and studying for a few days, Douglas allowed himself to be tempted outdoors by the ice on the turlough, but it was so cold that he could not skate more than twelve or fifteen feet before returning to the glebe house, where he restlessly cleaned his guns. A letter from Comyn received on his birthday helped dispel the dreariness of a week's idle wait for his eyes to improve, a third poem was to be published in the *Irishman* and the *Shamrock*. Readers had responded enthusiastically to his first two poems. Furthermore, everyone—including O'Neill Russell, who was then in America—was insisting that Comyn identify An Craoibhin Aoibhinn. O'Neill Russell had declared that he was the "best new Irish poet" on the horizon.

February brought warmer weather but heavy rains. As Bessie Hyde had improved, Annette left on the twelfth for a three-month sojourn in France. Douglas accompanied her to Dublin, where he visited Oldfield, who had not been well. He also had a long and serious talk about poetry with Comyn, who had now received even more fan letters from readers, urging him to continue to publish the poems of An Craoibhin Aoibhinn and to identify him. Comyn proposed writing a brief sketch of Douglas for the March issue. It was exhilarating news, which countered his father's threats and predictions and added to his general optimism about his future. Reviewing the work he had completed in preparation for the Trinity examinations, Douglas felt sure that he was ready for college.

This was Douglas's mood on February 24, 1880, when, walking around outside the glebe house, he could not shake the impression that a ghost was following him. It was not a malevolent spirit, he assured himself—it did not make him uneasy—but he could not help but wonder why it was there.

Mixed weather in March provided days suitable for the long walks that helped Douglas rest his eyes between reading and study sessions. In the middle of the month his mother went to Castlerea for a week. She seemed better when she came back, but within two weeks of her return she began losing blood. Before long she was so weak as to seem, to Douglas, "like a stone." Worried about her repeated lapses, Douglas tried to remember how long it had been since she was well. When she began to improve again early in April, he was relieved, but he could not help thinking that it would not be long before she had another relapse. The awful thing was that no one seemed absolutely sure just what was causing her illnesses. Repressing his fears, Douglas tried to concentrate on his work. He had received an encouraging letter from O'Neill Russell who had been delighted to discover that the young poet he admired was none other than his own protégé. Praising Douglas's achievement, he had enclosed an American newspaper that contained his review of the poems of An Craoibhin Aoibhinn. Reading the review had given Douglas's spirits still another boost. Yet he could not help but notice that, in the same issue of the same newspaper, another reviewer had printed an attack on Irish writing in general and the poetry of An Craoibhin Aoibhinn in particular. Even among nationalists, Douglas observed wryly, there was no agreement on the language question.

Oldfield wrote often, encouraging Douglas to keep up with his studies. He was now in the home stretch, Oldfield reminded him; the examinations for Trinity would be held in June. Oldfield also included good news of his own. He had taken fourth place in the examination for the Royal Irish Constabulary. Mercurial as always, the Reverend Arthur Hyde was delighted, although just a few days earlier he had been abusing Oldfield in a quarrel with his wife. He went immediately to Arthur O'Conor of Mount Druid with a note for £100 to pay for Oldfield's official uniform. From Mount Druid he returned full of political talk, for Arthur O'Conor was a cousin of O'Conor Don who, along with Meopother, had just lost another election. The victors were O'Kelly and Dr. Brennan, both Home Rulers. There was to be a victory meeting at the crossroads on May 31 at which both O'Kelly and Brennan were scheduled to speak.

To the Reverend Arthur Hyde the election results were a shocking turn of events. It meant that the Parnellites were now stronger than ever. Douglas, who also had heard the election news, would have liked to attend the victory celebration, but he knew that this was impossible. If his father as much as suspected his Parnellite sympathies, there would be another uproar in the glebe house. Dockry would go, however, and he, Douglas knew, would provide a complete report.

Annette returned home in the middle of May, bringing with her a concertina. Although he had no ear at all for music, Douglas was determined to learn to play the instrument. To everyone's dismay, he spent hours practicing, although it was only a month to his examinations. As for his studies, he continued to review the subjects on which he would be tested, but he had reduced his schedule in order to save his eyes. It was a relief to be able to turn to something as relaxing and inconsequential as the concertina. He was also devoting more time to writing poetry, for he was now a regular contributor to the *Irishman* and the *Shamrock*. As Comyn had promised, a short piece about him had appeared in the March 13 issue of the *Irishman*. Comyn had not revealed his name but with some exaggeration had identified the poet who signed himself An Craoibhin Aoibhinn as "one of the founders of the Gaelic Union and of the Society for the Preservation of the Irish Language." (Douglas was indeed a member of both organizations, the first a new offshoot of the second, but he had had no founding role in either.) The item had drawn even more letters from readers.

The themes of Douglas Hyde's early poems published in the *Shamrock* and the *Irishman* were largely those he had been working and reworking in his exercise books from the time he was thirteen or fourteen: nature, love, drink, English injustice to Ireland, the evils of landlordism, the greatness of the Irish past, the glories of the Irish cultural tradition. A few items with more topical references were drawn from his 188-page, four-by-seven-inch, black-bound notebook of 1877–1880 in which he carefully and neatly copied in ink, in addition to finished examples of his own compositions, polished translations and adaptations from German, French, and Irish which he had completed both for his own pleasure and as a way of reviewing the languages and literature in which he would soon be examined. Some of these translations were as sophisticated as the use of such models would suggest. Some were as simple and naive in manner and expression as "After the Irish," which conveys in English much of the feeling of Hyde's own short Irish compositions:

> God grant our country may thrive
> God devastate England instead
> Who so does not wish us alive
> We wish that himself he was dead.
>
> God keep us from famine and ill
> And grant that we yet may be free.
> Who does not wish Ireland well
> It's ill that we wish he may be.

Other poems developed around a central narrative employ different techniques and a variety of voices. One, on the subject of hunger, an ever-present specter in nineteenth-century Ireland, presents a scene recurrent in nineteenth-century poetry and prose: Death personified appears at the door of a cabin in which mother and father lie starving, she in bed, he on the floor. Their sole wish is to depart this world swiftly so that in heaven they may join their children, who died the night before. Life has been hard and cruel. With a greater capacity for pity than Life has ever shown, Death, granting their wish, "stabs them both together that selfsame minute and day." Also in this genre is "The Famine," a long narrative poem that consists of ninety lines of rhymed couplets in which memories of a fictional survivor of 1846–1848 are presented through a voice characterized by such unsubtle devices as (in

Hyde's term) "peasant pronunciation." Yet its subtly shifting attitude, between first line and last, is both dynamic and dramatic. Most significant is the obvious debt that the entire poem owes to Parnell's Westport speech of June 7.

The speaker of "The Famine" begins in a low-key conversational tone: with the long, cold nights coming, he says, people soon will be telling tales again of such times as the Famine of Forty-eight. He poses a musing question: how account for "the quare sort of softness that we found in the great" whose sleep was untroubled by the corpses heaped in the graveyards and the "bodies that lay thrown on the roadside like stones"? Imagine, he suggests, as if with detached curiosity, people so hungry that they would eat anything, even "an ould sae-gull or a crow or a kite," for whom "an armful of nettles" would be "a blessing from God." An undertone of pity gives an unexpected vibrancy to the speaker's voice as remembered scenes come into focus: old men of eighty weeping to hear a dying child's cries; a bleak and blasted countryside in which there is "no gathering of neighbors, no wakes, no cardplaying at night, and no dancing or cakes"; a village "corpse house" filled to overflowing. Suddenly stark and real, all come to life in a scene in which even the living are dead: "The people was as quiet as an angel or saint, Och! to see them dying off there without a complaint." Resentment stirs slowly as the narrator recalls how docile everyone was, himself as well as others: why, he asks, had "we let ourselves starve off like men that were crazed" while the landlords "had lashings and lavings, enough and too much"? Fiercely angry at last, eloquent in his anger, with little trace of his "peasant pronunciation," he ends with a direct call for violence: if castastrophe strikes twice, do not die—organize and seize what you need by force to feed yourselves, your wives, your children.

An unusual series of poems, each discrete, yet together forming a suite, introduces different perspectives on the root of Ireland's problems and again suggests a topical source—in this case, the kind of running debate that in 1879 and 1880 could be read in the editorial columns and letters to the editor of Irish newspapers. In the first poem in the sequence, it is indifferent and uncaring England from which a united Ireland, it is said, must break free:

Yes strong indeed our master
The Saxon chain is strong
And bind it bind it faster

Is all the Saxon's song.
But writhe no more in pain,
Up! rend thy bloody chain,
Rise Catholic and Protestant.
We wait our opportunity
To rise and right our land.

A second poem cites the power of the landlords as the root of Ireland's problems:

And me sons, now I've told you of the bad times I saw
How the people were ejected without thrial or law.

A third deplores the greed and selfishness of the Irish people themselves:

The Catholic crawling to social position
The wrongs of his nation refuses to heal,
The Protestant sneers at his petty ambition
Regardless as he of the national weal.

A fourth laments defeatist attitudes:

Hark Liberty is calling:
But we are crushed and broken
And sore are we oppressed,
And land and laws and language
And literature are lost.

Although derivative in form and diction, these early poems reveal a capacity for tonal restraint, historical perspective, and poetic abstraction not usually found in juvenilia.

On a fine evening in the middle of June, less than a week before he was to go to Dublin to take the examinations for which he had been working intensively for more than three years, Douglas strolled down the sloping meadow to Lough Gara with a group of friends. Mrs. Dockry, whose house was near the lake, had just made poteen. The men sat about talking as usual—at times in conspiratorial whispers, at times, as political discussions grew heated, in more strident tones— while she filled and refilled their glasses. Douglas later estimated that he must have had perhaps five or six glasses before he began to feel queasy. A few others were not too well either, whether because the poteen was unusually strong or because it was a bad batch, no one could say. Everyone hoped it was the former, for it was well known what could happen to a person if the poteen were bad. Even so, an adverse reaction to even good poteen could lay up a man for a week. All through the night and the next day, Douglas was sick, but on the second day, although shaky, he was able to get up and move around. It had been a close call, but he went off to Dublin on schedule. His mother took the train with him—happily, as she was feeling quite well, not for appointments with doctors but to visit her sisters and see Christine Wilson's new baby. With a day or so to spare before he had to sit for his examinations, Douglas visited Oldfield in Phoenix Park. Oldfield looked very smart in his new uniform. He was as usual very encouraging.

On June 21, Douglas's examinations began. On the first day he wrote papers on Euclid, algebra, history, contemporary geography, ancient geography, and English poetry. For the subject of his composition in English he chose the life of Oliver Cromwell "and gave him hell for an hour." He was "dead exhausted" when he came out, but on the morning of June 22 he was back at ten o'clock to begin assignments on the odes of Horace, four books of Virgil, three books of Homer, and three books of Xenophon. In the afternoon he took an oral examination in Euclid. On the morning of June 23 his name was on the college gate. Out of 16 he had placed fifth; 158 had gone out. On June 24 he wrote three more papers, in classics and history, then returned in the afternoon for mathematics. There were sixteen questions on the examination. "The moment I saw these I knew I would do no good on them," he wrote in his diary, "so I left the hall." On the morning of June 25 his name was again on the college gate. This time—despite his obvious failure in mathematics—out of 17 he had placed seventh; 100 had gone out. He had succeeded in the required subjects. Next came electives. On June 28 he was examined in Irish. He took first place, receiving books from Hodges Figgis as a prize. He was a Trinity scholar at last. The stage was set; the next part of his life was about to begin.

6

Between Connacht and Dublin

Although formal admission to Trinity College in 1880 changed Douglas Hyde's perception of his status, outlook, and prospects with obvious implications for his sense of self, it had little immediate effect on the day-to-day pattern of his life, for like his brothers before him he was enrolled initially in a nonresident program popularly known in Trinity jargon as the "steam-packet degree." Instead of living behind high stone walls, shielded from the bustle and noise of late Victorian Dublin—instead of walking each day along tree-lined paths and across cobblestone courtyards shaped and worn by centuries of Trinity graduates, including Berkeley, Burke, Congreve, Goldsmith, Grattan, Swift, and his own ancestors—instead of sitting beside marble busts of Trinity notables in drafty, high-ceilinged lecture halls—instead of climbing tall, thin ladders to reach library books bearing centuries of thumbprints shelved under the timbered barrel-vault ceiling of the two-story Long Room—instead of dining beneath portraits of dyspeptic provosts now deceased and gathering evenings in gray stone residences for a glass of punch, a pipe of tobacco, and an impassioned debate—Douglas continued to study at home in Frenchpark on much the same schedule as he had adopted in 1877. Trinity's only requirement was that he sit at designated times for the examinations by which his progress was judged and recorded.

As Dominic Daly explains, Trinity's credit-by-examination "steam-packet" option got its unofficial name from its popularity with English students who studied at home and took the Dublin steam packet across the Irish Sea only when examinations were scheduled. Douglas and his brothers, however, were less isolated from college life than this explanation suggests. From both Ballaghaderreen and Boyle there was good railroad service to Dublin. In Blackrock, just south of the city and an easy tram ride from Trinity, their grandmother Oldfield and unmarried Oldfield aunts were always pleased to provide a warm welcome and a comfortable bed. In nearby Monkstown, Foxrock, and Stillorgan they had standing invitations to dinners, evening parties, and Sunday afternoons at the homes of cousins and family friends. Certainly Douglas was no stranger to the city, nor were his reasons for frequently spending time there—to shop, keep appointments with dentist and eye specialist, visit friends and relatives, have his photograph taken—different from what they always had been. Although often transferred from place to place, his brother Oldfield, now well established as an officer in the Royal Irish Constabulary, often met Douglas in Dublin—sometimes casually, as one day when a half hour after Douglas arrived in the city they came upon each other quite by accident. For similar casual encounters with fellow members of Dublin Irish-language circles, Dubhglas de h-Íde (as he now called himself in letters to David Comyn and O'Neill Russell) had only to make the rounds of bookstores that stocked titles in Irish or stop by the Royal Irish Academy. Once he was in town, it was easy also for him to drop in at Trinity, consult with a professor, browse in the library, perhaps spend an evening with the resident students with whom he was acquainted.

But if Douglas Hyde's steam-packet status—so different from that of English classmates dependent upon tide and weather and the varying moods of the Irish Sea—allowed him greater participation in Trinity life, it did not remove him from Roscommon. At home in Frenchpark, he continued to spend much of each day tending the trees, shrubs, and flower gardens around the glebe house; haying and cutting turf in season; visiting local cottages where he was always assured of a warm welcome, a new story, and a bit of local gossip; or fishing, boating, or shooting. Afternoons and evenings he still boxed with Francis O'Ruark, played cards with Johnny Lavin, talked Irish with Mrs. Connolly, and argued politics with Dockry.

In 1880, in both cottage and glebe house, Parnell was the main topic of almost every political discussion. He had been in the United States at the beginning of the year, making speeches, raising funds for the Land League, and holding meetings with those American Fenians whom he could persuade to accept his policies of parliamentary reform.

Forced to rush home when Parliament was unexpectedly dissolved, he won reelection but found himself at the head of a divided Irish party. At least a third were Home Rule moderates who deplored his use of parliamentary obstructionism and dissociated themselves from the Fenian-supported Land League. In Parliament, Parnell dueled with Gladstone over the question of compensation for victims of eviction; in the countryside he delivered speeches threatening to the status quo. On September 19, 1880, the implications of his speech to the tenant farmers of Ennis aroused hopes on the one hand and fears on the other in the entire divided population.

When a man makes a bid on a farm from which a family has been evicted, declared Parnell,

you must show him on the roadside when you meet him, you must show him in the streets of the town, you must show him at the shop counter, you must show him in the fair and the market place, and even in the place of worship, by leaving him severely alone—putting him into a kind of moral coventry—isolating him from his kind like the leper of old—you must show him your detestation of the crime he has committed.

Within days Parnell's "moral coventry" found a new name when his message was extended to include the case of Captain Boycott, a land agent for Lord Erne in county Mayo who had sent eviction notices to tenants demanding fair rents. For continuing to advocate these and similar measures, leaders of the Land League, including Parnell, were soon arrested and charged with seditious conspiracy, but their trial in January 1881 only publicized their cause, especially as witnesses called in their defense were former tenant farmers whose families had been forced by eviction into the workhouse in Castlebar, county Mayo.

In the Land War that followed, despite passage of a new and more draconian Coercion Act, Parnell and his followers used parliamentary obstructionism, legal challenges, and rent strikes in their continuing battle for reform. The government retaliated with suspensions, arrests, and armed support for eviction squads. Early in the struggle Michael Davitt, founder of the Land League and a convicted Fenian, had been released on probation; now he was returned to Portland Gaol. On October 12 Parnell joined the Land Leaguers and other followers who already had been sent to Kilmainham. Abroad, especially in North America, anti-British sentiment spread as the Ladies' Land League used graphic descriptions of tenant conditions to build a relief fund for those who had been evicted. At home, "Captain Moonlight" rode the countryside after dark, intimidating and terrorizing landlords and agents.

This was the situation in the late spring of 1882 when, having established a record as an outstanding student, especially in language and literature, Douglas persuaded his father to allow him to spend the final term of his second year in borrowed rooms at Trinity. Between 1880 and 1882, relying only on self-directed study at home, he had earned honors twice in German and once in French and had won prizes in both. More significant to his father, he also had been awarded the Bedell Scholarship for future Irish-language preachers. But the cost of this achievement had been a recurrence of his old trouble with his eyes. By April the soreness was so constant that it was a severe strain for him to attempt to keep up with his schedule of readings. Douglas proposed that he stay in town for the last term before the long summer vacation. Temporary accommodations were always available, he knew, in the rooms of students not currently in residence. The double advantage, he pointed out to his father, was that attending lectures would help relieve the burden on his eyes, while being closer to Fitzgerald, the eye specialist, would provide him with better medical supervision.

In these years when Hyde's Anglo-Irish persona was winning academic honors and awards, his Irish persona, now publicly identified as An Craoibhin Aoibhinn, was assuming a more active role in the Gaelic Union, the impertinent offshoot of the Society for the Preservation of the Irish Language (SPIL) which had been founded in 1880 by members of the SPIL who favored a more activist approach to language preservation. Although continuing his SPIL membership, he regularly attended Gaelic Union council meetings, frequently taking the chair. Essentially antiquarian in spirit and politically mainly Unionist, the SPIL had concentrated its efforts, which Hyde supported, on republishing rare Irish texts, promoting the availability of courses in Irish, and encouraging successful students to qualify as Irish teachers, thereby assuring the future of the language as an academic subject. Watching the rapidly receding boundaries of the endangered Gaeltachts, the pro-language nationalist founders of the Gaelic Union had concluded that such a program was not sufficient. Their plan, which Hyde also approved, called for more active promotion, cultivation, and expansion of the use of Irish as the only means by which to avoid complete loss of the living language.

It was to publicize the goals of the Gaelic Union that Hyde had written "Smaointe" (Thoughts), an awkward and wordy open letter to David Comyn which had been printed in the October 1880 issue of the *Irishman*. Labored and deadly dull, it presented Hyde's then simplistic views in the turgid prose of a pontificating twenty-year-old. More successful were Hyde's lyrical, fiery, and humorous poems that had appeared regularly in the *Irishman* and the *Shamrock*. Many were reprinted in the *Celtic Monthly,* the *Celtic Magazine,* the *Pilot,* the *Irish Echo,* and other American periodicals, often with English translations by Michael Cavanagh. Among those that excited patriotic readers on both sides of the Atlantic were a moving address to the Fenian rebel, O'Donovan Rossa, and "Come Boys to Camp, We'll Sprightly Tramp," a marching song with a rollicking meter and clearly revolutionary message. Predicting that soon there would be an outright call to arms, the speaker of "Come Boys to Camp" urges his readers to obtain a "Snider" or "repeater," coat the weapon with oil, lubricate the hammer, plug the bore, and bury it in a properly prepared hole in the ground against the fast approaching day when it would be needed, for "The talking line you must resign/And try 'The Good Old Way,' boys!"

At the beginning of May 1882 the no-win political conflict that had placed Parnell, the Irish party, and the Land League on one side and Gladstone, William E. Forster, chief secretary for Ireland, and the landlords on the other was settled by compromise: Parnell promised that the Land League would support a modification of the Land Act passed in 1881 and would try to control terrorism; the government promised that it would free Parnell, Michael Davitt, and other Land Leaguers and provide relief for tenants in arrears. Parnell was released from Kilmainham on May 2. Opposed to all compromise, concession, or commutation of sentences, Forster resigned. With a sense of relief Ireland awaited the arrival of the new chief secretary, Lord Frederick Cavendish, Gladstone's nephew by marriage. There was general agreement that Cavendish would better serve both Ireland and Gladstone than Forster, whose reliance on ever harsher and more rigorously enforced coercion laws had so outraged the tenant population as to result in two years of unprecedented violence in the Irish countryside.

On May 6, 1882, for the first time since his brief and unhappy enrollment in 1873 in a Dublin boys' school, Douglas again became a student among students, an Ascendancy-class Irishman in an Ascendancy institution. Also on May 6—the day on which Douglas arrived at Trinity—Dublin welcomed Lord Cavendish. That evening at sunset, as Cavendish strolled near the Viceregal Lodge in Phoenix Park with the permanent undersecretary, Thomas Burke, both were assassinated by a radical group that called themselves "the Invincibles." The target of the attack was the undersecretary, the man who had been charged with responsibility for implementing Forster's coercive policies. Lord Cavendish died attempting to help him. Unmoved by the fact that all Irish leaders, including Parnell, Charles Kickham, and John O'Leary, denounced the murders, anti-Irish crowds surged around Parnell's London hotel. In London and other cities they filled the streets, threatening Irish citizens. In Ireland, where all parties immediately perceived that the senseless attack could only result in a return to coercion on the one hand and violent resistance on the other, it was a good time for a young man who had published fiercely nationalistic poems to be discreet.

Finding accommodations at Trinity was even easier than Douglas had anticipated, for Cambreth Kane (a Frenchpark neighbor who later married Douglas's sister) was not then using his college rooms. At Trinity he already had a good friend in Mackey Wilson, brother of Christine. Stimulated by the cultural and intellectual atmosphere of residential college life, Douglas quickly plunged into the give-and-take of after-lecture discussions. In the easy atmosphere of hall and quadrangle he forged lasting ties with others, among them W. M. Crook, George Coffey, John R. Eyre, F. I. Gregg, Friedrich Lipmann, Charles H. Oldham, James Sheehan, and the Stockley brothers, names that began to appear in his diaries of 1882 and recurred often thereafter. Many of these Trinity friends belonged to the same college clubs and societies as Hyde. Many agreed more or less with what, filtered through his Anglo-Irish persona, he cautiously revealed to them of his intellectual and political outlook. His fascination with the language and culture of contemporary Gaeltacht Ireland, although unusual, did not strike them as radical, for Parnellism was the issue of the day and neither preserving nor reviving the Irish language was a plank in Parnell's political program. The question of just where the preservation or restoration of Irish did fit in the political spectrum was in fact confusing, since there were language revivalists in almost every movement, from those advocating physical force to backers of parliamentary reform. In general those who opposed language revival were reformers and revolutionaries concerned with diffusion of effort; conservatives and Unionists who believed, with the editor of Maria Edgeworth's *Castle Rackrent,* that to achieve peace between Ireland and England it was necessary for Ireland to lose its separate identity; pragmatic nationalists who regarded the Irish language as an anachronism that crippled Ireland's relations with the world; and others convinced that the dying language was a lost cause. Those who supported language revival were reformers and revolutionaries for whom Irish was a nationalist badge; conservatives and Unionists with scholarly and antiquarian interests; cultural nationalists who considered themselves pragmatists; and others convinced that the language could and should be saved.

Like Dockry, with whom Hyde had had many arguments on this subject, neither Parnell's lieutenants nor the agents of the British government assigned to keep a careful eye out for possible seditious activities considered language revivalists relevant to the tensions of 1880–1882. Parnell was the leader of the day; he neither spoke Irish nor advocated that it be taught to others: there was little indication that the plight of the language concerned him. At Trinity in 1882 there was, therefore, little harm in being regarded as a language revivalist (especially one associated with SPIL)—except perhaps to such an obstreperous, opinionated, and influential Trinity Fellow as John Pentland Mahaffy. A classical scholar, Mahaffy had introduced Oscar Wilde to Greece; he respected only Old Irish. In 1878 he had openly criticized SPIL's successful lobby in favor of teaching modern Irish and had vociferously protested its addition to the list of intermediate subjects for which teachers were paid result fees. For the moment his animus was without consequence, as apparently he was not yet aware of the connection between young Hyde of the Gaelic Union and young Hyde, son of the rector of Frenchpark. (In fact, it was he who had administered Hyde's entrance examination in German and had rated it as an honors performance.) Certainly in 1882 neither he nor anyone else on the Trinity faculty knew anything that would connect Hyde with the poems by An Craoibhin in Irish and English that advocated physical force.

In 1882 W. M. Crook was perhaps Hyde's only Trinity classmate who understood the depth of Douglas's interest in Irish. He remembered the dismay with which Hyde had heard of a bewildered German scholar who had come to Dublin to perfect his Irish but could find no one, not even at Trinity (much less at his hotel, a fact that astonished the poor German) who spoke anything but English. But Crook also recalled how impressed he had been by Douglas's broadly based scholarly interests in general. A classics man himself, he had not expected to find a student of modern literature, even one with honors, reading the *Iliad* not just for "the grammatical niceties of Greek" but for the "imagination, melody, and beauty" of its lines. One day he asked Hyde to name the other languages that he knew. Douglas ticked off French and German—languages he read for pleasure, as his diaries show, when he needed relief from subjects less to his liking—then added Latin, some

Italian, and a bit of Hebrew. Irish, he declared, was his favorite. He had learned to speak Irish, Hyde had said (stretching the truth to fit his wishful thinking, as he often did to everyone but himself), "almost as early" as English. It was, he confided, the language of his dreams. Years later other Trinity students recalled that the young man from Frenchpark who had joined them in 1882 had seemed amiable and attractive, interested in but not yet passionate about politics, and on the whole very much like themselves. They described him as tall and raven-haired, with a ready smile, a relaxed disposition, and gray eyes that sparkled with good humor and enthusiasm. Always among the liveliest participants in impromptu debates and late-night parties, he was also, they remembered, hardworking and serious, even if he did have what then seemed to them to be an eccentric interest in the language and life of Irish peasants.

As a boy in country Roscommon, Douglas had disliked groups, preferring the company of one or two or at most three companions. When visitors descended on the glebe house in awkward numbers, he and his dog would take to the fields. Trips with his aunts and visits to Drumkilla had armed him with the social skills and easy, friendly social manner he now demonstrated at Trinity. Something of these qualities had been evident during the summer holidays he had spent at Drumkilla, especially during the years 1876 to 1878 when he had learned to relax and enjoy his Anglo-Irish persona. Arthur was now dead. Oldfield had created for himself a different and remote life in the Royal Irish Constabulary. Douglas's beloved Hyde aunts—more friends than female relatives—were no longer present to monitor his behavior. For the first time in his life he was his own man, free to assess each situation and skilled at moderating his Irish and Anglo-Irish personae as the occasion required. Through his Trinity classmates he met interesting young women among whom he quickly became popular. To Oldfield he wrote that these young women of Dublin were as pretty and vivacious as the girls he had met in Frenchpark and Mohill, but more independent and better read. Among them was Frances Crofton, the "F.C." of Hyde's 1882–1890 diaries.

As June approached, Douglas did not look forward to returning to steam-packet status in Roscommon. On the evening of June 6, a month exactly from the day of his arrival and two days before the end of term, Douglas was enjoying an after-dinner glass of punch with Johnson, a fellow student, when the two decided to look up another student, Richards. In Richards's rooms they joined a happy crowd, singing and drinking. At first Douglas (who by all reports could scarcely carry a tune) sat sipping quietly, listening. But after he had drunk his share, he rose to his feet, and to the cheers and congratulations of all, offered a rendition in Irish of "Beannacht leat, beannacht leat, a chondae Mhuigh Eo" (Goodbye, goodbye, O county Mayo) which he followed with an encore in French, "Trinquons et toc" (Let us clink glasses, so!). After that he was not sure exactly what happened. Lawson, he recalled, threw out some sort of challenge concerning their respective drinking abilities. He vaguely remembered buying a bottle of claret for seven shillings and sixpence. "I shamed him properly," Douglas wrote triumphantly in his diary, adding, "I went to bed at about 1:30 in the morning, and when I woke up I had nothing on but my boots."

It was not until the early autumn of 1883, more than a full year after the end of his temporary term as a Trinity College resident, that Douglas persuaded his father to allow him to give up his steam-packet status entirely and take rooms of his own. Father and son had been more congenial than usual during the academic months of 1882–1883. The Reverend Hyde was immensely pleased with Douglas's academic record. To him, Douglas's work in Irish was preparatory to his completing divinity school and obtaining a living as rector in an Irish-speaking district. Douglas too felt proud of his academic achievement, although outwardly he assumed a cavalier manner, as reflected in his flippant choice of *Foghlam Gan Eolas* (Learning without knowledge) for the title of the bound volume of the examination papers that he had carefully saved. Ironically, it was the academic success celebrated by both father and son that became the focal point of their dissension. The more prizes, awards, and honors Douglas won, the more tensions were exacerbated, for these led to discussions about his future. The Reverend Arthur Hyde still insisted that Douglas regard his work at Trinity as preparation for a career in the church. Douglas was adamant: never, he declared, would he become a clergyman. Frustrated by Douglas's obstinacy, the Reverend Arthur Hyde threatened, bullied, and drank. Resentful and angry, Douglas wrote sneering, satiric anticlerical poems that railed against "peace-preaching humbugs" whose "slave's creed" advised, "Go cringe, hat in hand, to the Saxon."

Matters came to a head one showery day in the summer of 1883. Douglas had been to Boyle to leave the smaller of the two family carriages to be painted. When he returned home on horseback the Reverend Hyde greeted him with "a droning monologue" on the subject of a minister's life and work. Interrupting his father, Douglas declared that his conscience never would allow him to enter the ministry. His private reason, he explained in his diary, was that as a child he had heard and seen too much of ministerial hypocrisy. To his father he offered philosophic and ethical arguments. Furious, the Reverend Arthur Hyde unleashed an old threat: he would cut Douglas off without a farthing if he did not uphold the family tradition. Douglas countered with an old threat of his own: he would leave Ireland; he would seek a living in some other country; he would become a bohemian, more shame to the father who had left him with no alternative. It was a familiar and futile dialogue that neither seemed able to avoid.

On the evening of July 28, 1883, thoroughly tired from two days of bringing home turf, with the haying yet to be done in the week to come, Douglas retreated to his room to watch the still lingering light fade. It had been a beautiful day. Earlier he had had a drink with Seaghan na Pinghe and had taken down from Martin Brennan a story in Irish, "Monachar and Manachar," to add to his growing collection of Irish folktales. Opening his Craik, he dutifully read some fifty pages about English literature. But the continuing quarrel with his father rankled inside him. Taking out ink and paper, he began an essay entitled "Why I Do Not Want To Be a Minister in the Irish Protestant Church." It was late when he stopped writing and went to bed, his head still full of reasons. On August 9 father and son quarreled again, this time about belief in the Bible and the nature of angels. So heated was the exchange that both were shaken by their mutual vehemence. Neither was prepared to make a permanent break with the other. Having buried his eldest and alienated his second son, the Reverend Arthur Hyde could not risk estranging the third. Douglas was unwilling to cut himself off from mother, sister, aunts—or even from his father, who aroused in him such turbulent feelings, such a mixture of love and wrath and honor and shame. Yet neither could find a middle position.

Retreating to his room, Douglas began a new composition entitled "Reasons for Not Becoming a Clergyman in the Irish Protestant Episcopal Church (Late Disestablished)." The parenthetical cynicism of his title addressed aspects of his subject that from time to time he had unsuccessfully tried to broach: the church of his forefathers that his father wanted him to serve belonged to the past; the future of the disestablished church was still uncertain. Douglas's main objective, however, was not to argue about past or future but to state his own moral, ethical, and philosophical positions on the question of his becoming a clergyman. Choosing dialogue as his format, he argued his case through two characters: a "poor devil of a student not out of college yet" (an obvious surrogate for himself) and an abstract figure at first called "Christianity," then simply "a florid man draped in black." Between these two he placed Reason. Reason explains that the man in black has been consulted because the student, having no inclination to become "a minister rather than a soldier, lawyer, banker, doctor," is now "over twenty years of age and of no profession." The student defends his refusal on moral grounds: he has always felt, he says, the "utmost repugnance for all kinds of metaphysical and religious arguments." From his "earliest years" he has believed "the difference of creeds to be of so slight an importance as not to merit any consideration from a man whose trade it is not to expand them." Religion and politics are to him "the two great sources of strife and embittered feelings in the world, and the fruitful spring from which domestic quarrels and social splits occur." He has concluded that "religion divides men more than politics."

From arguments and assertions intended for presentation to the Reverend Hyde, Douglas shifted his focus to matters of internal dispute. The student accuses the man in black of instilling "all kinds of prejudices and absurdities" in his brain. Yet he vehemently dismisses the idea of conversion:

I believe that it is . . . nonsensical and impossible for a man to choose a religion for himself, but that all men should remain in that one in which they have happened to be born, as being probably the most consonant to the manners and ideas of that place. . . . I happen to have been born in the Protestant Episcopal Church of Ireland, disestablished (rightly as I think) in 1870 [*sic*], and I have no desire to change it, since my conscience tells me, or since I think it tells me, that I shall not be punished after death for having been born and brought up in the religion of my parents, even if it be an untrue one, since the fault was not mine.

He is equally opposed to the idea that he might convert others. His responsibility, he declares, is to examine for himself only whether he believes in the Old Testament, the New Testament, and the Thirty-nine Articles espoused by his particular denomination. He is not responsible, he avows, for imposing belief on anyone else. For himself he can say that he is as skeptical about souls being saved as souls being lost. Furthermore he rejects the right of "divines of all classes" to forbid "the reading of unorthodox books, as they call them, as a sin, and . . . the perusal of atheistic writings as a wickedness." "If a man were from his earliest days to circumscribe his reading . . . on religious subjects to those volumes only which relate to Christianity," the student declares, "he would soon by continual running in the same circle satisfy himself that nothing true or good existed outside."

Off and on through the few remaining weeks of summer Douglas continued to work on this composition. Writing and rewriting in both pen and pencil, he struck out entire pages, inserted explanatory words and phrases, scribbled revisions along margins and between lines, repeated himself, deleted repetitions, and reintroduced them. When he stopped he had filled nine copybooks—a total of 139 pages—with a vehement statement, part essay, part parable, part satire, shored up by authors he had long admired, especially Voltaire. Although "Reasons for Not Becoming a Clergyman" was never read by its targeted audience, the Reverend Hyde, it did strengthen Douglas's inquiry into his own felt truths concerning his philosophical and ethical positions.

At the beginning of October the Reverend Hyde capitulated: if Douglas could find an appropriate alternative to the ministry, he would consider approving it. Douglas's main interests were language and literature: like Voltaire's father the Reverend Arthur Hyde regarded these as but gentlemanly pleasures to be pursued during leisure hours, not the stuff of an honest profession. His recommendation was that Douglas consider the army. Douglas objected on the grounds that soldiering was an "ungodly and immoral profession" (an irony, given the call to violence so often sounded in his poetry). He in turn countered with medicine, a career he had proposed several times before. To his surprise and dismay, this time the Reverend Arthur Hyde assented, leaving Douglas with a dilemma: He knew he could never overcome his "secret aversion" to the clerical life. It had been embedded in childhood, he told himself, as a result of his father's "inexcusable conduct." Yet he did not want to study medicine either. "If I were sure that my health would not collapse under the strain," he told himself, "I would not hesitate a moment." He was, however, "practically sure" that the study of medicine would cause his death. "Hence my state of mind," he lamented in his diary, "which is so awful that I would not wish it on a dog."

The truth, as at one point "the man in black" suggested, was that at the age of twenty-three Douglas was not yet far removed from adolescence. He had no strong interest in medicine or in any other profession. He had in fact no wish to be anything but what he was—simply a student. He had not proposed medicine with either serious intent or with the expectation that his father would find it acceptable. In fact, he had anticipated rejection. Now faced with the unhappy prospect of being given what he said he wanted, he tried to present second thoughts based on his past illnesses and his weak eyes. He did, of course, suffer from eye infections, and in recent years he had had several bouts of pleurisy and other respiratory ailments, but it was surely an exaggeration for him to call himself frail or even to suggest, given his academic record, that his eyes would be a greater disability in medical school than in divinity or in any other academic program.

On the morning of October 6, 1883, a month before the beginning of the Michaelmas term, Douglas awoke in the glebe house feeling uneasy and unwell. The night before he had been drinking poteen. Taking up pen and paper, he described his circumstances and set for himself an ethical question: was it proper for him to countenance a trade forbidden by the government? His answer was quick: "the government not being a native or self-chosen one, its orders could not be allowed to be valid." In that case, he asked himself, what of the precept "Render unto Caesar the things that are Caesar's"? And what about St. Paul's advice to those living in Rome, "that one ought to endure the state he is in and not seek violently to alter it"? Fitting these ideas into a narrative that relied heavily on the content of both "Why I Do Not Want to Be a Minister in the Irish Protestant Church" and "Reasons for Not Becoming a Clergyman," Douglas produced a dream allegory of 194 bound handwritten pages that reveals more about his struggle with himself than his conflict with his father.

The new composition begins with Hyde's author persona suffering from a headache. He tries to get rid of it by going out fishing "upon a lake that was broad and lovely." There, however, the wriggling of a worm on his hook so troubles him that he removes it. He falls asleep in his boat and has "a remarkable dream" that leaves "rather a deep and vivid impression behind it" in which he sees himself walking with his Conscience and Reason. Conscience proposes that they all live together in his house; Reason offers to be the servant; Conscience suggests that the dreamer be the host. Two visitors to the house, a Jew and a Muhammadan, advise the dreamer that he ought to choose a religion. They are accompanied by a man in black, described by the dreamer as one who had "served my family so well" that not only were "both my grandfathers . . . in receipt of some £800 a year, thanks to him, during the greater part of their lives," but they were both assured "a comparative sinecure." Dreamer and man in black debate the relative merits of the clerical, medical, and military life but reach no conclusions.

The Jew, Muhammadan, and man in black leave; Mr. Nogod appears, introduces himself as the representative of atheism, and presents the dreamer with a number of books, among them Kant's *Critique of Pure Reason,* Hobbes's *Leviathan,* and Thomas Paine's *Rights of Man.* His advice is that the dreamer read the last book first because it is "lively" and will "lay a foundation." Before the dreamer has time to open it he receives a Chinese visitor and is interrupted by the delivery of notes from earlier visitors who ask for second interviews. Uneasy, he refuses the interviews. It would be best, he tells himself, to follow Mr. Nogod's advice and read the books he has been given before talking again with those who seek to convert him to their respective faiths. At that moment Mr. Nogod returns and, echoing almost to the word the student of "Reasons for Not Becoming a Clergyman," argues that religion is only another name for party. Religion and politics, he says, "are the two great sources of nearly all the quarrels social and domestic, the two great causes of all the strife and embittered feelings of the world, the two fruitful springs of pain and cruelty and heart-scalding all over this earth." Of the two, religion, he declares, does the most harm. For the dreamer, denial is difficult. "There is more or less truth in what you say," he concedes, although he suggests that the fault is "in the villainous nature of man rather than in the fact of his having religion or no religion." In the midst of this discussion a letter arrives for the dreamer from the "old family friend," the man in black:

I have a rather good position vacant just now if you care to accept it. As matters go, it is not bad in a monetary point of view, and payments are regular. There is a good house attached, and the farm . . . contains 30 English acres of good arable land. . . . P. S. I forgot to mention that the work is practically nil.

The dreamer's boat, which has drifted to the opposite shore of the lake, strikes a rock. The dreamer awakens to hear himself say, "I will think about it."

As the first day of Michaelmas term approached, wriggling like the worm on the hook of his own allegory, Douglas continued to declare himself irreversibly against a career in the church at the same time as the offer made by the man in black remained before him. In his diary he posed for himself questions that were both revealing and speculative: If he turned his back on a living so easily obtained, what else might he do? What was he prepared to do? A few days later his father drove him to the railroad station. They passed John French's Ratra, a handsome Georgian house overlooking the bogs where so often their guns had brought down numberless birds. They passed the road to Seamas Hart's house and garden. They passed the blue hills beckoning in the distance. Horse and carriage, father and son continued on, toward the spire of the cathedral at Ballaghaderreen and the train to Dublin. Saying nothing further about the matter to his father, Douglas decided that he would neither apply to the medical program nor drop out of divinity school. A major crisis had been averted, at least for a time. The next question was whether Mahaffy, who disapproved of Douglas's commitment to Irish, had succeeded in blocking his request for rooms in the college residence hall.

Back at Trinity, Douglas attended lectures on theology, apparently as the price of the residential status to which his father had agreed. "Oh, how my heart sank at hearing the same boring old phrases I had heard with loathing so often before," he complained to his diary following the first lecture on November 2. After the next lecture on November 6 he scribbled angrily, "I hated it, and hated the people who were with me." His new anathema was the changing character of the Irish church. Previously he had attacked its Ascendancy snobbishness. Now he deplored theology students who were "not refined or well bred." One consolation was that, despite opposition from Mahaffy, he had been assigned his own rooms, number 24, on the ground floor of the residence hall. The walls had just been repapered, and a new grate had been installed to replace one that had been on the verge of collapse. He added a "very nice" carpet, several cabinets, three or four agreeable pictures to hang on the walls, and an ample supply of refreshments. Then very carefully he unpacked the books he had brought with him from his personal library in Frenchpark. Among them were works in Irish, French, and German that he had read and reread since he was sixteen. Some—among them *The Ballad Poetry of Ireland*, a collection by Charles Gavan Duffy published in 1848—were prize books that he had been awarded between 1880 and 1882.

Resident status at Trinity offered Douglas happy distractions that he never had had to resist in Roscommon: teas, dinners, and dances to which he was regularly invited; twice-weekly lessons in which he learned (or "almost" learned) the cotillion; long walks with James Sheehan (later remembered by Hyde's daughter Una as a frequent visitor to Áras an Uachtaráin); afternoons and evenings with "F. C.," with whom for a long time he shared an emotional tie that seemed destined to end in marriage; meetings of college clubs and societies to which he had been admitted. In the Chess Club he was soon recognized as a formidable opponent. At Theological Society meetings he was hailed as a talented speaker. But it was the College Historical Society, or "Hist"— the most prestigious and influential of Trinity's student organizations and the one that, since its founding in 1770, traditionally attracted the brightest minds and strongest personalities—that set the tone of his student life. One of thirty-one students elected to membership in April 1883, he was deeply stirred by the fact that among those who had preceded him were such men as Edmund Burke, Wolfe Tone, and Robert Emmet. "Hist" alumni—renowned scholars, barristers, physicians, men of letters, and members of Parliament—returned frequently to speak at meetings. "Hist" debates taught him how audacity and eloquence could become elements of style. Throughout his college years Douglas's favorite annual event was the full-dress spring meeting and banquet at which "Hist" speakers, judged as much by their talent for humor as by their poise, laid on a mixture of serious speech and mischievous bombast. Long after he had completed the last of his Trinity degrees, throughout the different times of his life when he was often at odds with his alma mater over questions of policy, politics, and the Irish language, Hyde remained an active participant in "Hist" affairs. He served as the organization's president from 1932 until his death in 1949.

Typical of regular "Hist" sessions was the first that Douglas attended, in which he watched with admiration as one member, a man he did not know, played the devil's advocate with humor and skill and "stirred up a great row . . . with his fooling." The next meeting was addressed by William Lecky, the distinguished Unionist historian. Although still awed by his surroundings, Douglas ventured a comment from the gallery. Other comments at other meetings followed. He discovered that he was a witty and effective impromptu speaker. In 1884 he was elected to the prestigious position of auditor. He also began to take his turn at presenting papers.

Among the prepared topics on which Douglas Hyde spoke at "Hist" meetings during 1884–1885 were "The Classical Temper," "Celts and Teutons," and even, boldly, "Irish Rule in Ireland." At the March 1885 meeting of the Theological Society he addressed an unsympathetic audience on an even bolder topic, "The Attitude of the Reformed Church in Ireland." His thesis—that the clergy of the Irish church should express their approval of nationalism—was described in the *Dublin University Review,* a new journal founded in February by Charles Oldham, as having "evoked . . . many hostile criticisms." Douglas himself acknowledged that he had been supported only by his friends Stockley and Hackett; others had remained silent or had railed against him. Yet the *Review* also noted, "It is not often that an essay is read in College where clearly defined views are expressed in language so beautiful and simple." Years later, Crook recalled that invariably, on any Irish subject Hyde addressed, he could be expected to take the "extreme nationalist viewpoint." However, not all the controversial causes he embraced were Irish. On a postcard to Annette written in 1885, Hyde noted regretfully that, although it was one of his "pet" subjects, he had spoken "very badly" on another unpopular issue, "Female Emancipation."

From 1884 to 1887, Crook, Mackey Wilson, and Hyde frequently formed the affirmative team in "Hist" debates. Whatever their subject and whether or not their audience agreed with them, Douglas handled his part of each program with a rhetorical skill that to some degree he owed, he knew, to the cottage and kitchen and dinner and drawing-room debates of his boyhood in Frenchpark. For that he could credit his father, Johnny Lavin, and even Dockry. At the opening of the 116th debating session on November 11, 1885, Hyde was among the speakers chosen to take the affirmative on the question of whether the Church of England ought to be disestablished. Although his arguments were unpopular, his eloquence was unchallenged. In the oratorical competition of 1885 Hyde stood second of thirteen; in 1886 he was fourth out of eleven; in 1887 he won the silver medal for oratory.

Between 1883 and 1887 Hyde discovered the network of off-campus "clubs" (many, as Breandán Ó Conaire points out, more properly called "soirees") that were attended not only by Trinity College students but also by graduates of Trinity and by other Dubliners with political, intellectual, and cultural interests. One was the Discussion Club on York Street, meeting place of the Young Ireland Society, where papers on topics related to nationalism were read and discussed. At Young Ireland meetings Hyde and Yeats discovered their mutual interests; there too, as well as at the Contemporary Club, founded in 1885, Hyde and John O'Leary (the Fenian leader convicted in 1867, newly returned from imprisonment and exile) often clashed on the subject of Parnell and Home Rule, about which O'Leary was severely critical. In time the group that formed the nucleus of both the Young Ireland Society and the Contemporary Club (the latter met Saturday evenings in Charles Oldham's rooms across from the main gate of Trinity) expanded to include women, notably O'Leary's sister Ellen, Rose Kavanagh, Katharine Tynan, and the beautiful and sophisticated Maud Gonne. Even before Oldham established his Saturday Evening Club his rooms were a meeting place for T. W. Rolleston, George Coffey, Willie Stockley, W. B. Yeats, Fitzgerald (Hyde's eye specialist, perceived in a new role), and Hyde, who served as a kind of informal editorial staff to discuss with him how best to introduce the Irish national spirit into the *Dublin University Review*. For literary rather than political discussion, Hyde went to the Shakespeare and the Mosaic clubs. Sometimes the Mosaic Club's biweekly format was changed to allow for a playreading or even an amateur production, in which Hyde frequently was chosen for a leading part. Participation in all these groups expanded Hyde's social circle and increased his invitations to teas, dinners, evening lectures, and concerts. They also provided him, as Daly suggests, with a school of contemporary politics and literature.

Hyde's diary entries describing Saturday evening meetings of the Contemporary Club (written in a mixture of Irish and English punctuated by an occasional German phrase) note that about twenty men usually were present. Approximately half were, like Hyde, Trinity students; the other half, from Dublin's professional and intellectual community, included Fitzgerald, Hyde's eye specialist; George Sigerson, a medical doctor with an outstanding reputation in his own field who was also a notable literary figure, language revivalist, and nationalist; Alfred Webb, M.P.; and John O'Leary. Discussion ranged from the pros and cons of Parnell's parliamentary strategies and current educational schemes (including one that would have turned Trinity over to the Catholics) to the efficacy of English representative government and the relative merits of single- and double-chamber legislatures. Michael Davitt came on December 12 and was questioned on the current position of the Land League; O'Leary, who was almost always present, was the self-styled resident expert on almost every political question, but especially anything to do with Fenianism. In meetings of the Young Ireland Society, Yeats lionized O'Leary. At the Contemporary Club, Hyde found the old Fenian tiresome at best, exasperating at his worst. "I never came across so complete a Tory," Hyde wrote on December 20, 1885. "He did not think that the masses have a right to the franchise; it was not expedient he said, forgetting that he constituted himself the judge of expediency."

Despite his full round of extracurricular activities, Hyde's academic career continued to prosper, even though, as always, its direction was difficult to discern. In 1884, when he received his B.A. with honors, he was one of only three students to be awarded the vice-chancellor's gold medal. Still undecided about his future yet still maintaining that he would not enter the clergy, he continued in the divinity program, taking a first in his examinations in 1885. In 1886 he again won the vice-chancellor's medal, this time for a thousand-line poem on Deirdre. For the history medal awarded in June 1886, he wrote on Lord Cornwallis's blunders as viceroy of Ireland. By this time, as Crook observed, it was certain that Hyde was "too Irish for the church of an unsympathetic minority." In the fall of 1886 he transferred to law. The move—dictated not by aspiration but by necessity—provided both an escape from divinity and a reason for his continuing residence at Trinity. Serendipitously, his successes to this point having owed as much to passion as to prowess, it also provided him with practice in writing and speaking on subjects in which he had little interest. For his examination for the LL.B., awarded in 1887, he was required to state the principal rules regulating the descent of an estate in fee simple. For his next major hurdle he had to give an account of the law of entail, explain the succession to the Crown of England, and write a short historical sketch of canon law. Again he placed first; again he won the vice-chancellor's prize. With a sigh of relief and a quatrain—

> With, oh, such a wealth of distinctions
> And, oh, such a splitting of straw,
> He must be a patient poor devil
> Who gives himself up to the law—

in 1888 he was awarded the LL.D.

Although Hyde's harvest of medals and prizes suggests a single-minded devotion to the programs in which he enrolled, he maintained in addition all through his student days a self-directed parallel course of study in Irish culture, history, language, and literary and oral traditions from which he drew the information he needed for his published essays. The first of these essays was inspired by a treatise by Justin McCarthy on Irish language and literature published in August 1885 in the *Dublin University Review*. In it McCarthy argued that not only did the "splendid stories" of Ireland's legendary history rival those of the Romans and the Greeks but that Ireland's legendary heroes were "as noble as any to be found in western Europe."

Cuchulain is as fine a hero as Theseus; Queen Maeve is no less marvellous than Helen; the fate of the children of Tureen is as grim as the fortunes of Heraclidae. Nor must I forget that wonderful story of the adventures of Oisin in

the Land of Youth, a legend which . . . has not to my mind its superior among
all the legends of the earth. . . .

Calling on his countrymen to examine these neglected works from their
own imaginative tradition, McCarthy urged also that they acquaint
themselves with the language in which their ancient literature had been
preserved—a language that might have been theirs, he reminded them,
had history been different.

Two months later an essay by Hyde entitled "The Unpublished
Songs of Ireland" appeared in the October issue of the same review.
Readily acknowledging his debt to McCarthy, Hyde announced that
his different but related purpose was to draw attention to an overlooked
and "humbler field" of Irish tradition found in the songs and folktales
of the Irish peasantry. Writing with a sense of style and an idea of his
reader (neither previously evident in "Smaointe"), Hyde recalls the
question Wordsworth asked on hearing a Gaelic song in the sweet
mouth of a young girl: "Can no one tell me what she sings?" His essay,
he says disarmingly, will tell something of what she sings about—but
will also consider what songs are on the lips of her Irish sister in the
"Connacht Highlands." However, he cautions, his own experience has
been that the best songs ordinarily are sung not by a young girl standing
alone in a harvest field but by old men and old women huddled over
the smoke of a turf fire in a chimney corner. "You share a piece of twist
tobacco with the *ban a' tee*," Hyde explains, and "you can pretty easily
sound her as to her knowledge about the Fianna Eireann, and as to the
songs and 'bubberos' [spinning-wheel songs] which she used to sing
as a girl." Moreover, young girls grow shy at the approach of a stranger,
whereas an old woman "often . . . will feel rather flattered than otherwise at your noting down her verses." Thus he gracefully draws the
reader to the subject that is his main concern.

That Hyde's selection of verses obtained under these conditions was
derived from his own personal experience is evident from his extensive
use of examples from the notebooks he had been filling since boyhood,
at first with stories and poems told to him by Seamas Hart, then with
those from the mouths of others. Each verse or poem or song included
is presented within the context of a brief dramatic narrative that sets
the scene of its telling. Each is accompanied by a comparative analysis
of form and content that draws on Hyde's knowledge of nineteenth-
century poems from the oral tradition, bardic poems from centuries
past, and analogous writings in the languages and literatures of modern

Europe. His writing is seductive. Instead of scolding and preaching as in "Smaointe," he now suggests and persuades. His ending neither imposes a conclusion nor suggests an action but leaves the reader aligned with the forces of insight, reason, and virtue:

But alas! . . . as our language wanes and dies, the golden legends of the far-off centuries fade and pass away. No one sees their influence upon culture; no one sees their educational power; no one puts out a hand to arrest them ere they depart for ever.

The essay demonstrates not only how much Hyde had learned about writing since he struggled through "Smaointe" in 1880 but also how much he had developed intellectually. It introduces both the idea and the substance of what soon would be his first two full-length published books, *Leabhar Sgeulaigheachta* (A book of storytelling) and *Beside the Fire.*

Eight months later in June 1886, T. W. Rolleston, now editor of Charles Oldham's *Dublin University Review,* included in his "Notes of the Month" a few lines on a dinner that had been held in May to celebrate the centennial of the Royal Irish Academy. Congratulating the academy on its accomplishments of the past 100 years, he took the opportunity to question the aims of its language revivalists, including An Craoibhin.

Do they wish to make Irish the language of our conversation and our news-papers? Impossible, and wholly undesirable. Do they wish to make us a bilin-gual people in the sense that everybody should know two languages? But peasantry and artisans cannot be expected to know two languages except at the expense of both. Would they separate Ireland into an English-speaking country and an Irish-speaking country? But how seriously this would affect the free circulation of thought. . . . What is there left except to treat Irish as a classic, and leave it to the Universities? Sufficient endowments will secure their atten-tion to its interests.

As Hyde was one of the members of the *Review*'s informal editorial board and Rolleston was among his friends, and as the policy of the *Dublin University Review* was to stir up debate over different facets of nationalism, there is every chance that Rolleston's remarks and Hyde's reply—the latter announced in July and printed in August—had been planned. The time was right for such a discussion: in February, Parnell's position had been strengthened by the results of a new election which the Liberals had won by the slim majority of eighty-six (exactly the number of votes in the Irish party). Gladstone, who had promised

Home Rule, was again prime minister; Parnell held the balance of power. In April, Gladstone introduced his first Home Rule bill. In May the question seemed to be not whether there would be Home Rule in Ireland but when. Nationalists predicted that the bill would be passed by the end of summer. Meanwhile, as pressure for Home Rule was mounting, language revivalists were planning measures to take to the country on the occasion of its first independent election. They were most concerned with answering objections from anti-revivalists who, equally aware of the approaching moment, also had become increasingly vocal. As things turned out, within days of publication of Rolleston's "Notes," Home Rule was defeated. The country was in the midst of a general election when Hyde's reply, "A Plea for the Irish Language," was announced. By the time it was published the Tories were back in office. Yet the situation was not so upsetting as it might have been: the Liberals were no longer in charge, but the Tories could not take credit for either the defeat of the first Home Rule bill or the fall of Gladstone's government. Both had been the result of Whig opposition, some of it led by Lord Hartington, brother of the unfortunate Lord Frederick Cavendish. Parnell had come through the July election as popular as ever, with his strength intact. Lord Salisbury, leader of the Tories, had declared that he would concede nothing to the Irish but would in fact reduce if not eliminate Parnell's influence, but observers and proponents alike believed that it was only a matter of time before Parliament would find itself considering another Home Rule proposal.

Although predicated on such expectations, Hyde's essay was not merely topical but a reply to Rolleston's *cui bono* based on both philosophic and practical but not materialistic considerations. Within "a few short years," Hyde predicted, the dream of centuries would be fulfilled. With that hour approaching, the task of preserving the language had become more important than ever. For this reason there could be no question of leaving Irish to the universities. "We know what that means. We have seen our very numerous, very ancient and very interesting MSS handed over to the safe keeping of the colleges. . . . There they lie in their companies: 'No one wakes them, they are keeping/Royal state and semblance still.'" As these were manuscripts—the work of scholars, many of them Irish-speakers from infancy—that preserved the history, the traditions, the culture of the Irish people, they always must be accessible, Hyde insisted, to those to whom they rightfully belong.

Hyde's argument, however, was not for Irish by fiat. There could be no question, he declared, of an extreme in which Irish replaced English as the language of newspapers and clubs: "That is and ever shall be an impossibility." On the contrary, his prediction was that, almost certainly, social and commercial relations would make it necessary for "every man woman and child" in Ireland, even those in the Gaeltacht, to learn English sooner or later. But if English was to be not only maintained but fostered, so Irish too must have national support, for without it the Irish-speaking population would have little chance of surviving the heavy losses inflicted upon it—steadily for hundreds of years; precipitously, in their own late nineteenth century.

A reasonable plan for Irish, Hyde suggested, to avoid separating the people of Ireland from the stored memories and imagination of generations, would be for the government to foster a bilingual population in Irish-speaking areas on which future generations might draw "as from a fountain." Anticipating twentieth-century studies in language and psychology, he cited the importance to a cultural community of preserving the "stream of collected thought" shared by all, the traditions embedded in place-names, the characteristics of a language that shape a people's perceptions of themselves and their world. Those who have had no experience with the death of a national language, wrote Hyde, could have no conception of its impact on the thoughts and habits of a people.

Yet if the Irish people themselves resolved to let the Irish national language die, should it be kept alive through "twopenny-halfpenny bounties"? Hyde's answer was no. But had the Irish people ever had the opportunity to confront such a decision? Briefly recounting the history of Ireland, Hyde argued that Irish in Ireland had not been given either this or any other choice related to their cultural identity for more than 250 years. Only abroad, he avowed, had the Irish had the opportunity to promote the language of their ancestors: in New York City (he had the statistics from O'Neill Russell) it "has found a more congenial soil than in the streets of Dublin." That living Irish language, Hyde asserted, had to be given an equally fair chance in Ireland.

"A Plea for the Irish Language" took Hyde far beyond "Smaointe" if not yet as far as his 1892 speech, "The Necessity for De-Anglicising Ireland." As Daly points out, the very task of writing it forced him to come to terms with what hitherto had been contradictory ideas of his own about the nature of the Irish language and its contribution to the

Irish ethos. The result was the development of a perspective later to influence his work in the Gaelic League and his plans for a place for the language in Irish education.

Hyde was not in Dublin in August when "A Plea for the Irish Language" appeared in print. Early in July, accompanied by Mackey Wilson, he had gone to Scotland, to make an on-site assessment of the comparative status of Scots-Gaelic and Irish, a subject in which he had been interested for some years. In preparation for his trip he had read everything about the Scottish language movement that he could find and had seized every chance to engage Scots-Gaelic speakers in conversation. One day at Trinity, walking with his friend Crook, he had spotted a Highland piper on the cricket field. Crook recalled that the pipes were quickly laid aside while the two men, one in a kilt, the other in tweeds, engaged in an animated conversation incomprehensible to others.

Nothing Hyde had learned from his studies, however, had prepared him to find in Scotland such a vigorous and extensive commitment to the native language. It exceeded anything he ever had encountered at home. He noted that wherever Scots-Gaelic was spoken it was the language of everyone, not just the smallest of children and oldest of the elderly. Nor did anyone apologize for not using English. On the contrary, all seemed proud of their fluency in their native tongue and eager to help him engage them in conversation. There were problems: of vocabulary, because Irish and Scots-Gaelic often use different Gaelic roots for common concepts and items; of comprehension, because Hyde had not had sufficient ear training to catch correspondences between Scottish and Irish vowel sounds. Nevertheless, caught up in the positive spirit of the people, Hyde persisted in his attempts to understand and make himself understood. In the essays and lectures he later wrote about his experiences and observations, he credited the Scottish Presbyterian church with providing the environment in which Scots-Gaelic was thriving. The singing of Gaelic hymns and delivery of extemporaneous Gaelic prayers during church service were "a most powerful instrument," he said, "in cultivating the language."

Hyde and Wilson returned to Dublin on July 31. A few days later he was in Frenchpark, where he found his mother neither completely well nor seriously ill. For some years her recurrent asthma attacks had been steadily sapping her strength. She had rallied and failed, rallied and failed, in a predictable pattern. On August 23, as he was about to go off to the horse show, she suddenly collapsed. For two days she lay writhing and unconscious, struggling for breath. Annette was traveling on the Continent; his father was no help at all. On August 25 she died. She was only fifty-two. In his diary Hyde described her as a woman "as selfless and disinterested . . . as ever walked this earth." For the next six weeks he remained in Frenchpark, alone with his father, awaiting Annette's return. To avoid quarrels he kept himself busy looking after the house, supervising the servants, and studying. He made considerable progress on a project he had begun, on the literature of the Celts. Evenings he did not allow himself to be drawn into conversations that inevitably would end in disagreement. To break the silence his father read out loud to him from Lecky and *David Copperfield*. He listened wordlessly. Occasional visits with the Frenches of Ratra helped relieve the tension. He was greatly relieved when at last it was time for him to go back to Trinity and the fall term. At Christmas he dutifully but briefly returned home. The prospect of soon departing with Mackey Wilson for an extended tour of the south of France helped him endure the gloom.

Ever since his first visit abroad in 1878 Hyde had longed to return to the Continent, especially to France. Yet during his Trinity years his few trips outside Ireland had been limited mostly to England. To keep the French experience alive within him he had had to content himself with reading and rereading. For years Rousseau's *Confessions* and the *Maxims* of Rochefoucauld, both bought on the quays during his memorable first tour, had been among his favorite books. Steadily and purposefully, his progress recorded in his diary, he also had forged his way through the French classics, French philosophy, French political thought, and French history. These readings had developed the sophistication he needed for a greater appreciation of Voltaire. They had sharpened his appetite for ideas and had aroused new intellectual passions. One year the "great book" was *Emile*. Another year he copied into his commonplace books long passages from the works of George Sand. Molière so fascinated him that he filled page after page of his diary with a long critical commentary on the French playwright's entire dramatic canon. Studying Taine and Carlyle, he declared that never had he read "anything in which French good sense and clear eye were more conspicuous." When discussions among members of Young Ireland turned to new political and philosophical theories, especially those Continental in origin, Hyde listened intently. Paris, with which Maud Gonne, Yeats, and others seemed so familiar, was for him a City of Light in more than the usual sense. French was a language of new values. It often had served as a bridge between his Anglo-Irish and Irish-Gaelic personae.

In the spring of 1887, following the usual route from Dublin to Paris, via Holyhead, London, and Folkestone, Hyde and Wilson set out for France. Hyde regretted bypassing Brittany. Annette had assured him that he would find this Celtic province fascinating. In Paris his disappointment vanished as he and Wilson spent a few days sipping aperitifs in boulevard cafés, indulging themselves in fine French dinners, and making the rounds of the best-known Parisian cabarets. Then, marking sights along the way, they set out for the south, following a route that took them through Tours, Angoulême, and Orleans. Bordeaux impressed Hyde particularly: still quite unsophisticated, he had not anticipated there being so large a city outside Paris. He had thought that, like Ireland, France would have but one truly major urban center and the others would be essentially towns. To Wilson he remarked the contrasts in the countryside through which they traveled: the central plain rapidly giving way to heavily wooded hills; a mountain so broad and so high that the train passed through it instead of over or around it; the number of boats on the broad riverways. Wherever they went the punctuality of the French impressed him. He noted that even in the picturesque town of St. Jean de Luz at the edge of the Bay of Biscay where they stayed nearly a fortnight in the small and charming Hotel de France, morning coffee was brought promptly at nine, lunch was served promptly at twelve, and dinner was served promptly at six. It was a phenomenon that in some ways seemed more remarkable to him than the perpetual sunshine of southern France.

On his first Sunday morning in St. Jean de Luz, Hyde went to church. Up to this point his Parisian French had proved quite adequate for all occasions, but the sermon, he discovered, was delivered in Basque. He had not expected it to be so widely used. It interested him to learn that many farmworkers knew no French at all. The next Sunday he again went to church—this time, according to his information, to a service in French—but so strong was the Basque influence on the local dialect that again he could not understand the sermon. Fascinated by these new linguistic experiences, he longed to stay on and explore them, but his itinerary did not allow sufficient time. He and Wilson were expected in Biarritz, where there was a large British colony. There, in a round of lunches, teas, and tennis tournaments, Hyde forgot his curiosity, found new friends, flirted with young ladies who invited him to visit them in London, and otherwise allowed his Ascendancy persona free rein to enjoy itself for a full month.

On the trip home Hyde and Wilson again interrupted their journey in Paris. Again they sipped afternoon drinks in the cafés along the boulevards, dined in style, and made the midnight rounds of cabarets, but they also attended a play by *Dumas fils* at the Théâtre Française and a production of Gounod's *Faust* at the Opéra, went driving in the Bois de Boulogne, and visited Napoleon's tomb. On his last Sunday in France, Hyde attended the morning service at the Madeleine. The sermon, he noted happily in his diary, was in fully comprehensible Parisian French.

By the middle of May, Hyde was back in Frenchpark. In the small cemetery beside his father's church he erected a headstone of Sicilian marble to mark his mother's grave. She was the first of the family to be buried there. Arthur had been buried in Mohill; the Oldfield plot was in the Protestant cemetery in Castlerea, almost directly across the street from the house in which he was born. Through summer and early fall Hyde remained in Frenchpark, studying law, making uneven progress on assorted writing projects, performing glebe house chores, taking long walks alone and with Annette, visiting Big House neighbors who invited them both to luncheons, teas, and tennis parties, and fishing, boating, and swimming. On November 9 he returned to Dublin for the "Hist" awards ceremony, at which he received a silver medal for oratory and a gold medal for an essay on Celtic literature. He had arrived prepared to stay in Dublin for about a month to cram for his examinations for the LL.B. Since these examinations were no great worry to him, he made the rounds of his usual clubs, visited friends, and attended parties. As always he was vaguely troubled by a nagging concern about what he would do with the rest of his life, since law had no more appeal for him than the ministry, but in general his spirits were good.

On December 7, 1887—the last day of his LL.B. examinations— everything changed. Word reached him that Mackey Wilson was ill; that he was not expected to live; that he had died. Hyde had known him long before they entered Trinity. They had shared boyhood adventures and confidences. So warm was their friendship that Hyde's daughter Una remembered hearing Wilson's name when she was a child, although his death occurred nine years before she was born. Hyde's response to the tragic news was more intense than he himself had expected:

I was so shattered . . . that I cried like a child, and had to turn to the punch to calm myself. I drank half a pint and more, and smoked until my mouth was sore and raw. O God, I was miserable. I do not ever remember crying so much, even when my mother died. Then I began arguing with myself as to the cause of my sorrow . . . and this heart-searching left me worse than ever.

Mackey Wilson's funeral on December 21 at the Wilson home near Enfield was a small affair, with only close friends and relatives present. Wilson's body was laid to rest in the grave beside that of his younger brother. As soon as the formalities were over, Hyde went home to Frenchpark. Ten days later, in the end-of-year review he wrote in his diary, he scolded himself for having whiled away so much of 1887, amusing himself when he should have been settling down and earning his living. At the beginning of the new term in the new year he returned to Dublin, ostensibly to study for the LL.D., actually to continue work on two projects that consumed the greater part of his time and attention. One was his long essay in English on the development of Gaelic literature; the other, in Irish, an annotated edition of folktales from the oral tradition that he had obtained from the mouths of native storytellers. On April 30, 1888, Hyde was informed that he had received a first in his examination for the LL.D. Although the ceremonial conferring of his degree did not take place until December 19 (it cost him ten shillings for his hood and gown and £22—"dear enough," he writes—for his sheepskin), that last day of April in 1888 was in fact the last day of his college life.

Hyde's transition from Trinity student to Trinity graduate was barely noticeable. Someone had to stay with the Reverend Arthur Hyde, and Oldfield's duties rarely allowed him much time at home. In any case Oldfield's relationship with the rector was still strained. Douglas's works-in-progress also required much time in Dublin, where his day-time hours were spent in bookshops and libraries; evenings he made the rounds of his clubs (additions to the list included the Pan-Celtic Society, the Franco-German Society, and the Theosophical Society), presenting papers and participating in discussions, or attended dinners, theater performances, concerts, and lectures. Responsibility for keeping up the glebe house and grounds and looking after the Reverend Arthur Hyde was therefore unevenly shared by Annette and Douglas.

Between 1888 and 1890, Hyde's club activities revolved chiefly around Young Ireland, in which he had been active since 1884, and the new Pan-Celtic Society, founded on March 1, 1888. Membership in the Pan-Celtic was restricted to published authors, but as the amount of publication required was minimal, it was far from exclusive. The significance of the membership clause was mainly the focus it gave to meetings. For Yeats, who was also a member, and whose muse had become increasingly Irish since 1885, meetings were important. For him the Pan-Celtic offered opportunities to talk about native Irish traditions with people like Hyde, whose work he had followed with particular interest since the publication of "Unpublished Songs of Ireland."

The Hyde-Yeats relationship was complex from the start. Yeats was fascinated with Hyde's developing translation ethic, which subordinated literal meaning to the character of a language and found evidence in oral expression of linguistic influence on the mind and imagination of native speakers. Although Yeats himself knew little if any Irish, he recognized not only the soundness of Hyde's concepts but also the success of their application to Irish rhythms and diction. To Katharine Tynan and John Millington Synge he recommended the study of the Irish quality of Hyde's translations into English. For himself he found in them qualities that he adapted in the development of his own poetic voice. Yeats also recognized Hyde as a source of information for the articles on bardic poetry that he had agreed to write and as a potential contributor to the *Fairy and Folk Tales of the Irish Peasantry*, a small book scheduled for publication in late 1888. In a letter to Hyde written on July 11, Yeats described his search for "little books of fairy tales to be found in peasant cottages brown with turf smoke." Listing the categories he planned to use in his collection, he asked if Hyde would help. Hyde agreed; consultations followed; and four days later Yeats wrote again: "I will be thankful for any stories. The more the better—I have just discovered my book to be 60 or 70 pages short." Hyde obliged with three stories, among them one that Yeats later described as the "best tale" in the collection: his "style is perfect—so sincere and simple—so little literary," he confided to Katharine Tynan in a letter written in September. Meanwhile, early in August, Yeats had asked Hyde, "Will you be even more generous still and consent to look through my proofs so as to give me some short notes?" And on August 25 he wrote again to say that he was sending Hyde his first batch of proofs, so that Hyde might correct any mistakes Yeats had made in them.

Attracted to each other by certain common goals and values, Yeats and Hyde differed in their attitudes toward Irish Ireland and anglicized Ireland. Different also were their respective concepts of self. Richard Ellmann's insight into the dominating consciousness of Yeats's poetic self is underscored in the titles of his biographical-critical studies: *The*

Man and the Masks and *The Identity of Yeats.* Yeats understood that even a minor poet could be driven by a sense of poetic mission. What he did not understand was the apparent lack or subordination of it (he was never sure which) in a poet as talented as Hyde. In fact, when he first met Hyde, he did not recognize him as a poet or even as a member of the social class to which he mentally assigned all poets, by virtue of their profession. Recalling that encounter, Yeats wrote in 1922:

I have a memory of . . . a very dark young man, who filled me with surprise, partly because he had pushed a snuffbox towards me. . . . I had set him down as a peasant, and wondered what brought him to college, and to a Protestant college, but somebody explained that he belonged to some branch of the Hydes of Castle Hyde, and that he had a Protestant Rector for father. . . . He had already . . . considerable popularity as a Gaelic poet, mowers and reapers singing his songs from Donegal to Kerry. (*The Autobiography of William Butler Yeats*, 145–46)

Suspicious that Hyde never spoke his real thoughts, Yeats complained to his diaries of Hyde's "super affability," "diplomatizing," and tendency toward "evading as far as he could prominent positions and the familiarity of his fellows," which he attributed to a fear of "jealousy and detraction." Years afterward it still troubled Yeats that the tenant farmers and villagers whose sparse communities were to him but wide places on a country road, having "picked up, perhaps" a "habit of Gaelic criticism" from "the poets who took refuge among them after the ruin of the great Catholic families," sang Hyde's words without a clue to his true identity—and that (the story may be apocryphal) "an old rascal was kept in food and whiskey for a fortnight by some Connaught village under the belief that he was Craoibhin Aoibhin [*sic*]." For a poet to choose a pseudonym and therefore anonymity was for Yeats as incomprehensible as a poet's choosing to subordinate his talent to the creation of "a great popular movement," however important "its practical results." Bewildered by the course of Hyde's career, he came to mourn "the great poet who died in his youth."

For his part, Hyde admired Yeats's single-minded dedication to poetry, often demonstrated in his generosity not only to younger writers but to those of a slighter talent; he had no doubts about Yeats's abilities. But impatient with Yeats's ego, he often expressed his irritation with the "blather" with which Yeats monopolized the company of others. To Hyde it was an impediment to serious talk. Hyde was particularly irritated one afternoon when having come, out of affection, to see his friend and former Trinity professor Edward Dowden, he found Yeats there, trying to impress Dowden with his "blather." He also criticized Yeats's social climbing, his condescending behavior toward anyone he regarded as not his social equal, and his patronizing attitude toward Irish men and women whom he knew only collectively as "the peasantry."

Yeats and Hyde frequently saw each other at meetings of the Young Ireland Society and the Contemporary Club, where Yeats always deferred to John O'Leary. Impatient with the unshakable biases and inflexible attitudes of the old Fenian leader, Hyde preferred George Sigerson. Yeats was prickly and argumentative with John F. Taylor, a barrister, orator, and biographer of Irish subjects; to Hyde, Taylor was a silver-tongued "king among men." Both Yeats and Hyde were single-minded in their pursuit of the development of an idea. Hyde would spend hours tracking down elusive bits of information. Yeats would devote the same time to writing letters to able people like Hyde who could root out and present him with what he required. Hyde did not mind Yeats's steady stream of research requests, although they often took hours to fill, because he found the subjects intrinsically interesting. He was therefore merely amused to receive two letters from Yeats in December 1888, asking for help in finding "some ragged peasant ready to sell his rags cheap." A pencil sketch of what Yeats had in mind accompanied the request. The clothes were needed by the Royal Irish Academy, Yeats explained, for an artist by the name of Nash who had been commissioned to illustrate John Todhunter's *Tom Connolly and the Banshee*. Hyde obliged, and in February 1889, having received the "peasant rags," Yeats asked Hyde's advice on what should be sent to the "old fellow": "clothes, money, tobacco?" Never fully understanding Hyde's tongue-in-cheek replies but nevertheless thankful for his help, Yeats welcomed opportunities to do him a good deed in return. He praised Hyde's work to the editor of the Academy; he introduced him to David Garnett of Fisher Unwin; he urged young poets to read his essays and translations.

Both Hyde and Yeats were infatuated with the tall, beautiful, articulate, and cosmopolitan Maud Gonne, a self-acknowledged Irish revolutionary who was as much at home in Paris as in Dublin. Hyde declared in his diary that her presence in a room was a signal for all the men to gather around. Charles Oldham had introduced her to the Contemporary Club, until then an all-male preserve, without a word of protest from anyone. Hyde, who had met her earlier at George Sigerson's, declared her "the most dazzling woman I have ever seen."

Courtier-like, Yeats incorporated her into his mythologizing poetry that celebrated his devotion to her beauty. Hyde offered to teach her Irish, but their "tutoring sessions" ranged over such a number of topics that there was never time to try to discuss them in anything but English. Nevertheless, he continued to come to her flat on Nassau Street, convenient to the daily haunts of Pan-Celtics and Young Irelanders, first at the appointed weekly hour, then several times a day—sometimes when, musical-comedy style, other admirers were also swarming around her. Watching them all, Maud Gonne recalled in her autobiography, were two Special Branch men assigned to surveillance outside her building. "The tricks we used to play on those unfortunate sleuths," she wrote, "would fill a volume."

A less spectacular but more comfortable woman in Hyde's life during this period was Ellen O'Leary, coeditor with her brother, John O'Leary, of an important volume in the history of nineteenth- and twentieth-century Irish literature, *Poems and Ballads of Young Ireland*. Contributors to the book were the Young Irelanders of the 1880s; its contents followed the principles of the Young Irelanders of the 1840s, who had proclaimed that Irish poetry should be the servant of political nationalism. Ellen O'Leary was almost thirty years Hyde's senior. Their warm relationship was reminiscent of Hyde's boyhood affection for Anna White, his "Una Bán." On New Year's Day, 1889, he presented her with a brace of game birds that he had shot for her. In April he sent her his photograph and expressed his concern about her declining health. By summer she was too ill to have visitors, but when she could she answered his long letters, full of gossip and small talk. A few months later, all was over. Tuberculosis, that ghastly scourge of nineteenth-century Ireland, had again struck down someone he loved. Deeply shaken by her death, Hyde asked John O'Leary to return the letters he had written to her, promising on his part to return those she had written to him. Mourning Ellen, Hyde and O'Leary established their own friendship deeper than the differences of opinion that previously had divided them.

Meanwhile the initials "F.C." continued to weave through Hyde's diary. A close friend and frequent companion since their first meeting in the spring of 1882, Frances Crofton often walked with Hyde in the morning, lunched with him at noon, dined with him in the evening, and accompanied him to after-dinner lectures, concerts, and club meetings. At Hyde's insistence they sometimes talked of marriage. In 1886 she had deflected rather than refused him by saying that she simply had no intention of ever marrying. In one way her answer made it easier for him to continue their relationship, since his prospects and financial situation were not yet sufficient to permit him to make a formal proposal. In another it left him socially and emotionally in an odd state, neither attached nor committed.

In June of 1889—an important year for Hyde, as at last he had put his name to a major publication, *Leabhar Sgeulaigheachta* (A book of storytelling)—Hyde, Frances Crofton, and Hyde's sister Annette made a two-week trip to Paris. Hyde was then striving to secure a university teaching position somewhere in Ireland. Had he succeeded he might well have pushed his suit with Frances, but his prospects remained uncertain. The only offer he received was from his friend Willie Stockley, who was then teaching at the University of New Brunswick in Canada. What Stockley proposed was an interim professorship for Hyde that would suit them both. With Hyde to replace him, he explained, he could take a year's leave in 1890–1891. Hyde meanwhile would have the advantage of an academic base from which he might launch a search for a more permanent post. Hyde immediately realized that it was an attractive idea, especially as his second book, *Beside the Fire*—a collection of folktales translated by him into the English that Yeats had so admired—was scheduled for publication in December 1890. By June 1891 he would have two published books and a year's teaching experience behind him. The fact that he had been teaching English, French, and German would expand the kind of position for which he might apply. Stockley was right: there was little doubt that such a move would improve his credentials immeasurably.

7

To Canada

The purser on the Allan Line's *Polynesia* out of Liverpool, westbound for Quebec and Montreal, September 11, 1890, Captain R. G. Barrett, master, had "Dr. Douglas Hyde" on his list of saloon passengers. Hyde's destination was Montreal. He had paid eighteen guineas for his passage—"six too much," he complained to his sister, as he made his customary pre-trip reckoning of anticipated costs and money already expended. Easily singled out in the crowd of passengers boarding the ship, most of them more concerned about the whereabouts of their belongings than each other, Hyde was, at thirty, tall, dark-haired, broad-chested, and attractive, with eyes that sparkled with an intense intellectual curiosity and a demeanor that bespoke energy, enthusiasm, and a genuine liking for people. Fellow voyagers who became better acquainted with him during the crossing later remembered him as altogether a pleasant young man, courteous, well mannered, and well informed; an amusing conversationalist; an inveterate reader.

If Hyde seemed confident and self-contained to his traveling companions, he himself was filled with excitement to be aboard a ship on his way to Canada. Stockley's warnings that life in Fredericton might be dull after a decade in Dublin did not trouble him. Dull? With all of Canada and the United States to explore, in whatever time he would be free from his teaching duties? His only concern was his sister Annette. He worried that she might face a difficult time in the months ahead; he felt guilty about leaving her home alone to cope with his father's tantrums and recurring attacks of gout. They had agreed before his departure that they would stay in close touch. She would send him all the domestic news, personal and political; he in turn promised to provide her with a full picture of life in the New World. He hoped that in his absence his brother Oldfield would offer some support.

But all that was now behind him—the question was, what lay ahead? Stockley had told Hyde that in the few years that he had been in Canada he had taken the opportunity presented by the Christmas holidays to go to Boston, where John Boyle O'Reilly—one of the Fenians who had escaped from Australia to America in 1869—presided over a lively circle of old revolutionaries and young nationalists. He had suggested that Hyde do the same. It had been an interesting prospect: he and Boyle O'Reilly were acquainted by mail: several of Hyde's poems had been published, in the respectable company of work by T. W. Rolleston, Katharine Tynan, and W. B. Yeats, in the newspaper Boyle O'Reilly edited, the *Boston Pilot*. Boyle O'Reilly was, moreover, a staunch Parnellite. It was he who had presented the welcoming address when Parnell visited New York. But just weeks before Hyde's departure, word reached Ireland of Boyle O'Reilly's unexpected death at the age of forty-four. Hyde was dismayed by the loss yet sure that he would still be able to count on a warm welcome in Boston, if he chose to follow Stockley's advice. He was not yet certain that he would go to Boston. He knew that winters in Fredericton had not always been so dull as Stockley now professed. Until recently, in fact, Stockley had written enthusiastically of his Canadian life, enlivened as it was by a young Fredericton woman. But then Stockley had proposed, and the young woman had refused him. It had been such a blow that in order to recover he had decided to take the year's leave of absence from which Hyde was now profiting. Remembering his brother Oldfield's unhappy affair of the heart some twelve years before, Hyde was sympathetic. Oldfield had loved the girl dearly but had been without prospects, so the father of the girl had forbidden him to see her. Oldfield's disappointment had been bitter. He was still unmarried. It was only with difficulty that Hyde himself had avoided entangling alliances, following his rejection by Frances Crofton, for he was a man who greatly enjoyed the company of women. In Dublin even now there were eligible and attractive young ladies whom he counted among his closest friends. He had been fiercely attracted to more than a few. But without being settled in any profession, without adequate independent means of support, he could not risk losing either his heart or his head. Discreet notes in his diary suggest that only recently he had been in danger of losing both. That had been another good reason, he told himself, for accepting the invitation to Canada. If, as he hoped, the year's interim professorship led to a more permanent position in an Irish university—if not in Dublin then perhaps in one of the Queen's colleges established in 1845 in Belfast, Cork, and Galway—it would improve his future prospects. For now there was only the present and the coast of England fading behind him.

The *Polynesia* bucked mountainous seas and September gales of near hurricane force on the westward crossing. Again and again the call went out to batten down the hatches. For a time many of the other passengers were seasick. Watching through the windows of the passenger lounge as wave after wave rose and crashed against the ship, or reading or writing in the smoking room, Douglas rejoiced that he was not afflicted. When the weather improved and the others emerged from their cabins, he spent much of each day on deck, often in the company of two fellow passengers, Miss Ede and Miss Nicholls, watching the roll of the ocean, alert for signs of iceberg, whale, and porpoise, delighted with each sighting. Evenings he read, smoked, played quoits and cards, sang an Irish song at a shipboard concert, learned to drink "that most insidious but excellent drink," the cocktail—and enjoyed a shipboard flirtation with Miss Ede (the romance all from *her* side, he insisted). His drinking companions included a German ("generally drunk") who, finding that Hyde spoke German, "unbosomed himself" with "awful lies" and stories of slave-dealing in Constantinople; an elderly English general traveling with his daughter who set up his headquarters in the smoking room; and "a fool of a young conceited idiot" who became the good-natured butt of everyone's jokes. The consensus with which Hyde heartily agreed was that never had anyone struck a pleasanter crowd.

The *Polynesia* docked at Quebec on the twentieth of September and at Montreal on the twenty-second. Hyde had arranged to stay at the Windsor Hotel—the equal of the Metropole or the Grand, he assured Annette—with the Tayleurs, a "curious couple," brother and sister, who were friends of Maud Gonne. After some time at the railroad station, seeing off several of his new acquaintances, he joined others who were celebrating their safe arrival in Canada with cocktails. The next morning he himself set out on the 430-mile journey by rail through dense forests to Fredericton, seat of the Province of New Brunswick and home of its university.

Then as now, Fredericton lay on the banks of the St. John, at a point where the river, a half-mile broad, flowed in wide, sweeping turns toward the Bay of Fundy. By European standards it was a new city, but already the various architectural styles of its houses, which ranged from pre-1820 Georgian to Queen Anne Revival, gave it a sense of history. The town's dominant structure, the decorated Gothic Christ Church Cathedral, was the mother church for the Anglican diocese of Fredericton. In the center of town on Phoenix Square, built of red brick and granite, stood Fredericton's city hall. Its 115-foot tower housed a clock and bell; its second floor was called the Opera House. Nearby on neatly laid out streets were the shops Hyde visited almost daily: Chestnut's Apothecary, Hall's bookstore, and James Hawthorne's confectionary.

Hyde spent his first three weeks in Fredericton at the old officers' barracks on Queen Street. Built in 1825, it was an imposing reminder of the British military presence before Confederation. The location suited him for a number of reasons, not the least being that, as the Scott Act prohibiting the sale of alcohol was "rigorously enforced" in Fredericton, Colonel Maunsell (a Limerick man and a relative of Stockley's who had strong nationalist sympathies) had thoughtfully placed Hyde's name on the officers' mess list so that he could purchase an occasional glass of rye whiskey. At the edge of the city—easily reached on foot, as it was no great distance from the center—rose dense timberlands, "the endless Canadian woods" of his letters to Annette, that were virtually uninterrupted except by isolated small farms with wooden houses and checkerboard fields outlined by wooden snake fences. The forests of Ireland might have been just so dense and tall before they were cut down by the Elizabethans, the landscape as majestic. Along picturesque gravel roads that led out of town, timbered bridges spanned fast-running creeks and small rivers in which the tops of the tall trees were reflected.

The people of Fredericton were for the most part Protestants of English birth or background. French Canadian farmers, called "habitants," lived in outlying areas, where there was also a scanty but significant population of native Americans of the Milicete tribe. Other Milicetes lived in nearby settlements or in the forests. Taking his attitude, no doubt, from that of the townspeople with whom he soon became acquainted, Hyde ignored the Milicetes for the first several months of his stay. Not until late December did he make the fascinating discovery that they had a tenacious commitment to their separate language and culture and to an oral tradition through which they kept alive their native lore.

Before the first of October—the first day of Michaelmas term—Hyde moved from the officers' barracks to Willie Stockley's "nice and comfortable" rooms in the Arts building. There he could prepare his own breakfast and lunch and keep on hand some items appropriate for tea or a late evening snack. The prices of some of his purchases surprised him. In a letter to Annette he listed those that struck him as excessively high: 25¢ for marmalade, 15¢ for a piece of soap, $3.50 for 100 cartridges. Apples, however, were both cheap and good. For dinner he arranged to go every evening at six o'clock to the home of one of his colleagues who lived but a ten-minute walk from the university. This very satisfactory arrangement, he told Annette, cost him $1.75 a day. As after he had moved from the barracks the officers continued his membership in their mess, he often joined them evenings in the bar they called the Caserna, the only place in the city where he could get a proper nightcap.

In 1890 the University of New Brunswick had three buildings—Arts, the Jack Observatory, and the Neville homestead. The eighty-six students enrolled for the academic year were boarded in private houses in town. Although described as nondenominational, it offered elective denominational religious classes taught "by those whose proper province" it was "to give such instruction." There was a faculty of eight. The president was Thomas Harrison, a man Hyde both liked and admired, who in turn was both friendly and encouraging to him. In general Hyde did not find his fellow faculty members quite so congenial, but with Alexander William Duff, professor of mathematics and physics, he formed a close and lasting friendship. To Annette he wrote that Duff was "the only person around here who *thinks* and has a mind of his own; being educated in Edinburgh as he was, he is, like all Scotchmen, a real thinker and I can exchange thoughts with him." That Hyde felt inhibited about expressing some of his ideas in the company of other members of the faculty is evident from his repeated statements in his diary and in his letters to Annette that Duff was the only man with whom he could "exchange a thought freely."

By the tenth of October, Hyde was well settled in. He noted with pleasure that his name appeared on the faculty roster of the 1890–1891 calendar. His schedule required that he give three lectures a day, on French, German, and English literature, five days a week, between nine and one o'clock. His German classes, he reported to Annette, were made up chiefly of "ladies who know nothing." His second-year French classes were "ditto," although some of the ladies were "very pretty indeed, but not clever or in any way intellectual like the girls in the Mosaic Club, for example." His third- and fourth-year students in French and

English seemed brighter but nevertheless "troublesome" in terms of their lack of preparation. English was his largest class, because it was compulsory. His lectures were attended by upwards of fifty students. Consequently it was difficult to provide unprepared students with the special attention they needed. Responding to Hyde's complaints, James Sheehan, writing from Dublin, puckishly advised that Hyde forget trying to educate his women students and concentrate simply on amusing them. "Take them on shooting expeditions as a group," he said lightly, yet with a warning based on long acquaintance: "never *solus cum*."

New Brunswick skies were often blue at the beginning of October, very different from the high white overcast and dark scudding underclouds of Frenchpark. Hyde marveled at the frequent full days of sunshine, the absence of lashing rain, and the brightly colored fall leaves, so different from the gray skies and yellow and brown foliage of Ireland and England. Within a short time fall was over. A relentless cold crept stealthily across the land. In letters to Annette he expressed his astonishment at finding that by late October the birds had gone and the woods were silent. At night he watched the northern lights, vast flickering bands of forest-green, orange-red, and cloudy white that played across the Canadian sky. All through the fall and into the winter he spent his free hours at the end of almost every week fishing and shooting. Although he was often joined by other friends from town or barracks, his usual companion was Forester, an English officer who formerly had been a banker, "a good decent man . . . without much knowledge of literature," whose companionship Hyde enjoyed. At home during fall and winter Hyde often fished and shot the bogs and skated on Lough Gara with Annette. He now filled his letters to her with details of his New Brunswick experiences, plodding through swamps thick with alder and lignum vitae, breaking through bushes fifteen feet high, seeking elusive game. Dismissing the Canadian preference for hunting the ruffed grouse (to him, he said, it was no sport at all), he regarded snipe and woodcock as the greater challenge. His best bag, on "one of the pleasantest days of my life," he declared, was eleven birds, which he proudly displayed to his admiring friends. He encouraged Annette to go out shooting also, in the fields where they had learned their gunsmanship as children and often had hunted together, and he urged her to be sure that in general she was getting sufficient outdoor exercise: "Fresh air seems to be the great secret of health. No one here seems to get old. The bishop is 86, the chief justice 80, the judge, 75."

Hyde's principal concern, in the cold weather that now gripped New

Brunswick, was "to keep my blood in motion," he wrote, in temperatures to which he was not accustomed. His regimen included taking a cold bath each day; walking for at least an hour; protected from frostbite by a fur or sealskin cap; and skating. On the twenty-fifth of November the St. John River froze solid, and there was a whole week's "capital skating" before the first heavy snowfall. He regaled Annette with descriptions of the scene: "A lot of people went down through the thin ice the first day or two, some had miraculous escapes. I skated for miles up the river and it was delicious." A friend froze his ear. For Douglas the cold surpassed anything he had ever felt, the temperature falling to seventeen below zero at night and rarely rising above ten degrees below in the daytime. By early December, travel was possible only by sleigh since wheeled vehicles could not move in the eight inches of snow. To Annette he wrote, "It is rather exciting when a number of sleighs come tearing through the town, the bells jangling and the horses trotting madly." With his usual penchant for keeping records, Hyde noted in his diary that after early December the snow cover remained at between one and two feet, drifting to three or four, until nearly the middle of March, while temperatures remained below freezing nineteen days out of twenty. Snow fell on the average about once or twice a month, he observed, often changing to rain that melted the upper layer which then hardened to ice, forming a strong crust. Before February he recorded "three cold 'snaps' as they call them here" in which "the thermometer fell to 35 below zero." The winter of 1890–1891 was proving "exceptionally cold," he was told.

Between the start of the Michaelmas term and the beginning of the Christmas holiday, Hyde's weekdays were fully taken up by preparing for and presenting his lectures. At times these were interrupted by incidents of a curious kind that both startled and amused him. One morning a skunk wandered out of the forest that half-circled the school. As everyone watched from the windows it waddled across the quadrangle, directly toward the Arts Building, bringing all lectures to a halt. Another morning, to the consternation of some of his students, a "giant of a man" appeared in the hall in which Hyde was lecturing, held out a piece of paper containing a mysterious string of words, and insisted that Hyde explain them. In as many languages as he could muster, since the man's English seemed limited, Hyde tried to tell the man that he had no idea what the words on the paper said—or even in what language they were written. He could only explain which languages they were not. The man vanished, never to be seen again, but the incident surfaced years later in a similar scene involving a giant of a woman who pushed her way past porters to confront a group of Trinity professors in Hyde's satiric *Pleusgadh na Bulgóide, or The Bursting of the Bubble.*

Except for Sunday school in Roscommon, Hyde had had no prior teaching experience, so it was with enormous pleasure that he listened to President Harrison's assurances that all his classes liked him. It was important to him that his first job go well. But he also discovered that he enjoyed teaching and that in fact he had been quite well prepared for it by his presentations and debates in meetings of the College Historical Society at Trinity and by his stint on the Dublin amateur stage. When he realized how earnest his naive students were, his Pygmalion-like role no longer troubled but simply amused him. For Annette he compiled a list of the howlers he found in their written work: "Portieres," wrote one, "a street on which the aristocracy walked"; "A chignon" wrote another, "is a leg of mutton." An instruction to his English literature class to list some of Milton's archaisms garnered "arch-enemy" and "arch-fiend." Asked to comment on Abbot Sampson's linguistic accomplishments, one student offered, "He said little but kept up a great thinking." To the question, "What is the regular habit?" another replied, "an ordinary coat." One essay he received contained the statement that "Milton had studied the writings of Homer whose plays he much admired," because "he had an apithy for the stage." But they all were learning, Hyde assured Annette, even as he too was learning to be more tolerant of their inexperience. Early on he had written his sister that the college magazine, the *University Monthly,* was "a detestably edited clearly dull little affair," but when the students who published it, members of the Literary and Debating Society, elected him honorary president, he was sufficiently flattered to accept their invitation and even to contribute some poems and essays to future issues. His first contribution, a satiric poem, was published at his request under a pseudonym, because "any little thing creates a furor here." Expecting that there would be "great canvassing as to the author," he did his best, he declared, to "screen" himself "from knowledge." In December his name did appear under the title of a short story, "The Knight of the Trick," which he had translated from the Irish as he had taken it down "from the telling of an old peasant." The January number contained his translations of "The Judgment Day," a poem by Tadgh Gaolach Ó Suiliobhain, and "Eachtra Chloinne Lir" (The children of Lir). To Annette he sent copies of all three issues of the *University Monthly* in which his work appeared.

All through November and December Hyde impatiently awaited author's copies and newspaper notices of *Beside the Fire,* his collection of stories told in Irish that was scheduled to be published in London by David Nutt before the end of the year. It was almost Christmas when he finally received the issue of the *London Daily Express* that contained a very satisfactory lead review article, a full column and a half in length, but to his frustration books themselves did not arrive. He was of course eager to see a copy himself but he also wanted to give copies to the university and to friends. The book may have been available in Boston bookstores, but he could not be sure, as he had decided against following Stockley's advice on how to spend his holidays. Instead he set out on St. Stephen's Day in the company of two young Fredericton traders and three Milicete hunters for what was to be one of the memorable trips of his life—a shooting expedition in the Gaspereaux, a region some "forty to fifty miles from Fredericton where there were said to be lots of caribou."

On the first day of their journey, enthusiastically described by Hyde in both letters and diary, he and his companions were pulled forty-two miles in a large sleigh by a team of horses. With them they brought food and other necessities, a tent, and toboggans. So tricky were the rutted, icy drifts along the snow-covered roads that although they started at eight o'clock in the morning it was midnight before they reached their destination—the home of an old Irishman from Kilkenny who came out to greet them "stark naked without a screed on him." The next day, despite a snowstorm, they again set out early for the location deep in the woods where they made camp. There they remained for twelve days while the temperature remained at ten or fifteen degrees below zero. Yet, wrote Hyde,

in the woods where I was camped I never felt it cold. We pitched a beautiful tent and left about three inches of snow on the ground, then covered it thickly with spruce boughs, spread our blankets and skins, and slept as soundly and comfortably as if we were at home.

There was no question of roughing it, Hyde assured his sister, as they had brought "quantities of provisions" with them.

Unfortunately for the hunters, there was also no chance of getting a caribou, although plenty were sighted. The crust on the snow was too thick. Moreover, "rain had fallen and made the top of the snow like ice." Consequently, "the sounds of . . . snowshoes clattering on it and crackling could be heard a mile away." They were unable to creep up on the herd or otherwise get close enough to any of the animals to shoot. In the twenty-five to thirty miles that they snowshoed, however, hoping their luck would change, Hyde did bag a couple of partridge, a ruffed grouse, and three large porcupines "weighing 25 or 30 lbs. each."

In the evenings Hyde, the two traders, and the three Milicete hunters sat around their campfire smoking and telling stories. It was then that Hyde first heard Milicete tales, among them "The Story of Heb-a-da-hone." It was a true tribal tale, insisted the tellers, but as Hyde remarked in his notebook, in his opinion it had filtered into local native American lore from a Gaelic source, perhaps through one of the Irishmen or Scotsmen who worked for the Hudson Bay Company and who had taken a native American wife. The story was, he acknowledged, "clad in Indian or rather Canadian dress," by which he meant that descriptions of such activities as log cutting, traveling by sled, driving a team of horses, building a camp, and duck hunting reflected Indian life. Other features of plot, character, event, and narrative style were to him recognizably and indisputably Gaelic. During the twelve days of his trip Hyde heard and discussed with traders and guides other Milicete stories that also struck him as Irish and acquired "a couple of hundred" Milicete words—not enough, he regretted, "to reduce the language to any kind of grammar, or even to learn the conjugation of its verbs," but a sampling that at least gave him an idea of phonemic patterns. He would have stayed longer had he been able, but as the new term began on January 8, he had to return to Fredericton.

Back in Fredericton, Hyde discovered that two of his friends, Colonel Maunsell and a government surveyor, Edward Jack, were able to provide a fair amount of information about the Milicetes. From them he learned that Milicete stories were so well known in the Lake Superior region as to raise speculation that the tribe originally had come from there. Although the tribes had not clashed for a long time, he was told, an old feud between the Milicetes and the Micmacs was still smoldering. He heard that, once numerous in New Brunswick, the Milicetes had declined in number to fewer than seven hundred, yet the tribe had remained so fiercely protective of its language and cultural traditions that these were not only alive but in constant use. Both Maunsell and Jack agreed that the squaws represented the strongest force for the retention of the language. Many refused to speak English. Working men picked up English for use on their jobs, but at home and among themselves they spoke only their own language. In his notebook Hyde noted the analogy to Connacht, where the women kept Irish alive in the cabins while the men who went out to work learned English. In his letters to Annette he remarked other similarities: As in Ireland Irish-speakers learned English but the English living in Ireland did not learn Irish, so in New Brunswick the Milicetes learned English but no one of European stock in or around Fredericton seemed competent in the Milicete tongue. As in Ireland when the English-speaking government adopted an Irish place-name, it frequently blundered, so in New Brunswick the Milicete word for camping ground was erroneously used in a text in which the reference was to the St. John River. Between Ireland and New Brunswick there were also differences: the Irish regularly absorbed common English phrases and even English syntactical structures into their language, but listening to the Milicetes, Hyde "could never catch an English word being used amongst them when conversing with one another, unless occasionally, the name of a place." It impressed him particularly that they had their own words "even for such imported articles as guns and stoves and whiskey and never seemed to have to fall back on English words, as . . . people do when conversing in Welsh or Irish."

So fascinated was Hyde with the Milicetes that he set for himself the task of learning more about their stories, in order to compare them with Irish tales that he had collected and published in 1889 in *Leabhar Sgeulaigheachta* and most recently in *Beside the Fire*. The very strength and endurance of their language handicapped him, however, for most stories were circulated only in Milicete. Concentrating on "The Story of Heb-a-da-hone," otherwise known as "The Adventures of Closkarp and the Great Turtle," Hyde asked a Milicete whose father was French Canadian if he would recite it in English. The man agreed, although he told Hyde that he himself had never heard the story "except in Indian," and there were those who maintained that it could not be told properly in any other tongue. Hyde wanted to take notes as he listened, but he was concerned that his storyteller might be discomfited by the idea of having his words written down on paper. His solution was to seat himself behind a caribou skin. He regretted that he could not take fuller advantage of the cooperation of the Milicetes, who would have told him more stories had he but had a better grasp of their language. "I could not follow them," he wrote, "so lost something that promised to be very interesting. It is only one more proof that the folklorist must know the language of his victims if he is to draw any reliable harvest from them."

Two things apparently puzzled Hyde about "The Story of Heb-a-da-hone." One was the matter of the name of the central character. In the first part of the story he was called Heb-a-da-hone but in the last part he was given the name of Closkarp, a figure so "known and reverenced all along the St. John River" that there was at least "one place sacred to him" where the native Americans of the region flung "a bit of tobacco or some other small propitiatory offering" when they passed. Another was the matter of the story's origin. Hyde's first theory was that Milicete elements had been woven into the fabric of an essentially Irish or Gaelic story. But as he was unable to find a single identifiable Irish source that matched "The Story of Heb-a-da-hone," he concluded that the Gaelic elements he had recognized in it were prototypical rather than specific, very likely absorbed over a period of time from a number of sources rather than from one story taken whole from a single "story-telling Gael":

I imagine that some of the Milicetes travelling to the northwest to the Hudson Bay country on a hunting or furring expedition picked up this story and brought it back with them and that in process of time the national hero of the Milicete race, this Closkarp or Glus-cap, was made the hero of this tale too, by the natural enough infection or "association."

Within weeks of Hyde's return from his caribou hunting expedition he wrote an essay on Milicete folklore that appeared on April 12, 1891, in the *Providence Journal,* a publication that previously had printed other examples of his work.

Meanwhile, with holidays over and classes again in session, the Fredericton winter social season had become hectic. As Douglas Sealy notes in his summary of Hyde's New Brunswick diaries, there were dances and balls (despite the disapproval of "the confounded Puritans and Methodists"), card parties, dinners, teas, lectures, concerts, tennis in the drill shed at the barracks, moonlight sleigh rides, and snowshoe parties, all enlivened by flirtations. Early in the fall Miss Ede of the *Polynesia* had written and sent her photograph from Vancouver; at first Hyde had responded, even sending his photograph in return, but after a few weeks he had let the correspondence lapse, in part because his interest had been lukewarm at best, but mostly because he was enjoying the company of a good many agreeable young Fredericton women who, in contrast to women in Ireland, seemed remarkably independent and unchaperoned. Shortly after his arrival he had noted in a letter to Annette that Canadian women were "as far as society goes . . . quite emancipated." He was astonished, he told her, that one young woman, quite on her own, had invited him to come to see her. "You can go driving with a girl here, alone, or visit her, or I think go out walking with her (but of this last I am not sure) at nearly any hour." Although Hyde deplored their lack of intellectual interests (he complained that, unlike Annette, they knew nothing of Spencer's *First Principles*), he found New Brunswick women "very pretty, . . . lively, and talkative." To his Dublin friends as well as his sister he declared that they would create "quite a furor at home." With them, he avowed, he had "danced, talked, laughed and flirted more in a month" than "in six months in Dublin."

By the third of December, Hyde's letters suggested that he was concentrating his attentions particularly on one young woman, "an interesting oddity in her way" whom he referred to as "the Italienerin," but his diaries make clear that this was by no means to the exclusion of others. In January he wrote Annette that, after the holidays, in addition to the circles in which he continued to be in demand, he had "come on a new stratum of Fredericton society" that consisted of "half a dozen families who seem to mix chiefly with themselves." Like other Europeans accustomed to a more easily identified social stratification, he was struck by the ease with which he himself was accepted, on an intimate basis, in such groups. To Dublin friends and to his diary he reported dancing with pretty girls, squeezing their hands, feeling his own hand squeezed in return, and exchanging significant glances and photographs. So many pictures were pressed upon him, in fact, that he was obliged to sit for his own photograph in order to have a sufficient number of copies on hand to go around in return. Often he was out until three or four in the morning in subzero temperatures; rarely did he go to bed before one or two. At times he chided himself for having been carried away in a "vortex of dissipation."

By mid-February Hyde had found still another way to keep his blood in motion during the long cold New Brunswick winter. Out of the round of dances, parties, and teas there emerged a young woman whom he referred to in his diary as "the Fräulein." She was first mentioned in January 1891 after she and Douglas had spent several hours together, talking and reading. Better acquainted with books and far more intellectual than the other young women with whom he had flirted, she was also less coy. By early February their meetings had become longer and more frequent; by mid-February visits that had begun sedately, over a cup of tea or a book that they took turns reading to each other, were ending in ever more ardent embraces. Afraid that she was falling in love with him, Hyde sometimes scolded himself for treating her dishonestly, as he knew he was not in love with her. Sometimes he excused himself: if he could just get his old Dublin love out of his head, perhaps he would feel more deeply for the Fräulein. Sometimes he was callous and flippant: he could like her more, he was sure, if only her feet were smaller or her breath less unsweet. The affair intensified, with less resistance than ever on her part and less restraint on his, even as he continued his round of parties and lighthearted flirtations with others, berated himself for acting like a cad, and blamed the late Canadian spring for the state of his emotions, poured out in a poem as unpunctuated as the alternating melting and freezing ground cover of late March:

O dreary weary wintry snow
The dreary weary months go round
And thou art yet upon the ground
More white more bright and more profound
Will nothing make thee go

I dream of green the livelong night
Of wavy woods, of grassy wold
I wake and what must I behold
Ah Canada thy breath is cold
Thy face is cold and white

As always, Hyde's inner troubles were soon accompanied by vague complaints of developing illness. He felt fine after an innocent tussle with Miss Gregory or a playful party on snowshoes, squeezing Miss Fisher's fingers; his sick headaches and sore throats became most severe after his evenings with the Fräulein. It was nearly April before he acknowledged to himself that the hot encounters which were now stopping just short of a full sexual relationship were the cause of his weakness and exhaustion. On April 1 he felt quite ill after a late night in which he had come closer than ever to "going too far"—so ill, in fact, that he cancelled all other commitments that he made, refused invitations that he wanted to accept, and simply stayed in his rooms. There would have to be an end to the affair, Hyde told himself. It could go on no longer. His year in Canada was nearly over.

On the sixteenth of April after no mention of the Fräulein for nearly two weeks, Hyde accepted her invitation to afternoon tea but did not tempt himself by staying beyond teatime. On the seventeenth he noted that he was feeling better. On the twenty-fifth they went out walking together in the morning but he returned to his rooms after midday dinner with her and her family. On the sixth of May after an emotional

day in which he and the Fräulein had talked frankly to each other, he
trying to explain himself, she railing bitterly against her father, he felt
really well for the first time in months. He had taken a load off his heart,
he declared; "he had shown her clearly that he was only a man of the
wind." Yet one more dangerous encounter occurred on May 10, before
the end of the semester, during a walk that ended with Hyde feeling
frightened and unhappy, aware that she loved him, aware that he had
compromised himself, regretting his foolish behavior.

Hyde's on-and-off struggle to extricate himself from his affair with
the Fräulein had implications and temptations unrelated to his emotional and sexual turmoil. Her father was influential: she was said to
be rich. If he allowed the relationship to take its course, inevitably they
would marry and he would remain in Canada, no doubt in a post arranged by his father-in-law. In one diary entry he chided himself for
not being thankful to have won such a gentle, well-off girl; in another
he wondered if what he had heard was true, if in fact she did have substantial financial assets of her own. If she was as well-off as everyone
said, could he make his home in Fredericton? He was enjoying his
academic year—of this he had no doubt—but there were aspects of life
in the capital of New Brunswick (tactfully confided only to letters to
Annette, to his diary, and to his friends Alexander Duff and Colonel
Maunsell)—that troubled him.

Hyde's biggest objection to Fredericton was its "absolute want of
cultured and literary people." He longed for the long talks about books
and history and European travel that were so much a part of life at
home. He missed Annette, his friends, Frenchpark, Dublin. But he also
tried to present a balanced picture: He contrasted the generosity of the
Canadians, who seemed to look on hospitality to strangers as a duty,
with that of the Anglo-Irish "who live in sets and cliques and think only
of themselves." He enjoyed Fredericton's dinners and balls, sumptuous
by Irish standards, but could not get used to the idea that the only drink
served at them was ginger beer. It was pleasant to be in a "free country
where rank counts *absolutely nothing* and efficiency is everything"; unfortunately what it produced, in his opinion, was a "contented lot of
Philistines." At first it had seemed to him that the people of Fredericton
were deeply religious. To Annette he wrote, "I don't think the spirit
of Rationalism has touched them at all. They . . . have no thoughts on
unpleasant subjects of the soul but follow their good bishop and go to
church and sing, oh sing, hymns on all occasions possible. . . . It is quite
refreshing to be among them." After a few months it troubled him that

in Fredericton he never heard discussions of Huxley, Darwin, or Spencer. He suspected that most people had never heard of them. Still later, complaining of the way in which the president of the university, Tom Harrison, had censored an essay he had written, striking "passage after passage . . . lest it give offence somewhere," he concluded that most of the people were in fact not religious but only "grandmotherly stick-in-the-muds who cling to the outside husk, the dry form" while others made Fredericton "a very hot-bed of religious prejudices." Creeds, Hyde insisted, made absolutely no difference to him. "I have been living on terms of intimacy with Methodists, Presbyterians, Baptists and everyone but Catholics who are almost non-existent in the higher classes here, and I never know the difference," he wrote in his letters to Annette. "If a man is good and kind it is all you want—and for that matter all that God wants."

But if Hyde did not want to remain in Fredericton, what of some other place in North America? With a teaching record, the prospect of good references, and a growing reputation as a scholar, poet, and essayist, he felt more confident about obtaining a post. Earlier he had been approached about an appointment paying one thousand dollars a year at McGill University in Montreal. In April, O'Neill Russell wrote to tell him that a new university was being established in Chicago: if he applied for a post there, he might earn *three* thousand dollars a year. When his sister protested at the idea of his not returning home, he pointed out that, after all, "one must do something and one cannot very well spend the rest of one's life idling and starving." Yet knowing only too well the situation in which he had left her, he felt guilty at the thought of abandoning her. He tried to respond with sympathy to the continuing gnawing, nibbling problems that she faced. The old trouble with housemaids arose periodically, after each tirade by the Reverend Hyde against servants that he accused of being two-faced and backbiting. With genuine concern he urged her to play vigorous tennis with John French, to ride, and to break the "terrible monotony" of the glebe house with visits to neighbors. He encouraged her literary efforts. Warning that Canadian newspapers "are insufferably bad and do not pay," he promised to try to place a story in one of them and speculated that he might manage to get others into the American papers when he went to the States. In his letters to her he included passages in Irish, French, and German and encouraged her to keep up her language skills by doing the same. He repeatedly recommended new books for her to read and asked for her opinions on Spencer, Cellini, and Emerson. He appraised frankly for her confidential information what he considered to be negative aspects of the social and cultural structure of Fredericton and the university that he dared write to no other.

Throughout the year Annette had been responding to her brother's letters not only with details of household affairs and discussions of literature but also with news of Irish politics, particularly the rise and fall of Parnell, which both followed with similar concern, as the O'Shea divorce case proceeded through the courts. On this subject Hyde of course also received both information and comments from friends in Dublin. In a letter dated December 20, 1890, Charles Oldham had described the effect of the Parnell affair on the people he knew: "The dividing line runs through all one's acquaintances. . . . Everybody feels under a fierce unavoidable pressure *to take sides*." If he were in Ireland, Oldham had assured Hyde, he too would feel the pressure, and "like *all the purely national* elements among the Irish people," he would be for Parnell. "All purely national Ireland," Oldham avowed, was looking to Parnell "as the only hope of an independent party for Ireland in our generation." "He must win," declared Oldham, "if his health does not break down." The only Irish force against him, Oldham reported, was the power of the priests. December letters from James Sheehan were less sanguine. He suggested that "if Parnell had had the decency in the face of this strong feeling to retire," the whole thing would have blown over, "and he could marry Mrs. O'Shea all the time directing the party though not nominally leader." Hyde wrote to Annette:

I am greatly cut up over Parnell's business. I think I would support him if it were not for the clergy proclaiming against him. My sympathies were strongly aroused by his manifesto, but if the priests remain hostile to him I do not see what is to be done except to sacrifice him.

In Fredericton, Hyde discussed the situation with Fred St. John Bliss and Colonel Maunsell, both Parnell supporters. Often the three men spent long evening hours in the barracks over a glass of whiskey discussing alternate strategies that Parnell might follow. With others, mindful of the strong pro-English history of the city, the damage a pro-Parnell position could inflict on his aspirations, the power of rumor, the speed with which it can be inflated, and the nature of New Brunswick politics, he was cautious. A potential confrontation was avoided when a St. John newspaper published an article accusing him of having refused to drink the queen's health at a public dinner. He denied the charge and succeeded in convincing the Fredericton newspaper not to copy the item.

Observing a political campaign in New Brunswick in March 1891, Douglas declared himself appalled at the corruption. "The bribery is shameful," he wrote Annette, describing an incident in which, having learned of one man whose vote was purchased for fifteen dollars, he was assured that such spending was proper, for victory for the Liberals would mean free trade with the States and taxes on English goods. Even Hyde's own friend Captain Forester saw nothing wrong with can- vassing votes for his father-in-law ninety miles up the St. John River, bribing one hundred people and returning with the votes of sixty or seventy. The local newspaper condemned bribery and voters who took bribes—but in the same article it reproached those who failed to stand by their promises and voted on the "wrong" side. Meanwhile in Ireland, the price of a vote was being paid in a very different currency. When Annette's letters and clippings detailing Parnell's "great defeat at Sligo" reached Hyde in April, he could only say "I am sorry."

New Brunswick was greening early in May; the red buds of the maples were swelling, the birches beginning to leaf, when Douglas wrote Annette that following the end of the semester he was planning to spend two weeks in Boston, New York, and Niagara, and then sail home. "Have the tennis ground sown and well-rolled," he instructed, promising that he would stay close to home for most of the coming summer.

On the twentieth of May, to his students' applause, Hyde gave his last lecture at the University of New Brunswick and turned to the read- ing and marking of 130 examination papers. In his spring report to President Harrison he summed up his year's pedagogical achievement: "I beg to report that since the opening of the University in October I have delivered an average of fifteen lectures a week on English, French and German literature and have found all my classes made satisfactory progress." His task had not been easy, however, as half his freshmen studying French and all his freshmen studying German had proved "utterly ignorant" of these languages. With the latter, he said, the situ- ation had been so bad that he had been unable to do anything except work on grammar. On occasion, however, he had departed from the prescribed readings in the calendar to "intersperse the course with oc- casional lectures on topics of literary interest." Years later in a rem- iniscence prepared for the editor of the University of New Brunswick yearbook, Hyde, who never himself found any language less than fascinating, still recalled with exasperation the difficulty he had had with his first foreign language classes: "I used to divide the students into the Sheep and the Goats! i.e. Honours and Pass students," but "I liked them all very much."

The students liked Hyde, too. The Literary and Debating Society held a night meeting to which he "went unsuspiciously." There he found "the whole college, ladies and all," who presented him with pipes, stems, a case, and other items, then "crowded round . . . and shook hands and said good-bye most cordially." The Alumni Society invited him to their banquet where "healths were drunk in air or water until one o'clock, the chairman saying each time, 'now gentlemen I want you to fill up your glasses and drink,' which was adding insult to injury." To Annette he confided, "I have probably been the most popular professor amongst the students who was ever there! At least so people said. You see I have become Americanised sufficiently to blow my own trumpet." His commencement address drew tears from his women students. "Henceforth," he said, "you face life no longer as a body, but as units. Your May is before you still, but when the diplomas were handed to you I distinctly and with a feeling of sadness heard the clock strike the last hour of your April."

Unofficial farewell parties, with plenty of whiskey, followed, the last on May 31. He staggered home, he wrote in his diary, falling "200 times before I got into bed, where I lay without taking my coat or anything else off. It is years since I was as bad as that." Then finally, on the third of June, with all Fredericton good-byes said (including a tearful but not yet final good-bye from the "Fräulein"), Hyde boarded the train for Boston. He had been pleased with the cheap rail fare he had managed to obtain and the dollar-a-night room he had reserved at the Crawford House, he wrote to Annette, until he was charged two dollars for the transfer of his luggage from the Boston railroad station to his hotel. The flippant note hid deeper feelings. Until the end of his life, his grandsons remember, he always kept on display a photograph of himself in bearskin hat and fur coat, holding snowshoes, along with some items that had been made by the Milicetes. He continued his friendship with Alexander Duff by mail. And even after his departure the *University Monthly* printed items that he had submitted to the Literary and Debating Society. One, a fondly if wryly sentimental poem entitled "To Canada," published in 1892, was reprinted in a number of Canadian newspapers, both in New Brunswick and in other provinces.

The ravaging winter is over,
    The Wizard of Silence is fled,
And violets peep from their cover,
    And daisies are raising their head.
Earth blushes to life like a lover,
    And wakes in her emerald bed,
And she and the heavens above her
    In torrents of sunshine are wed,
Forgetting the swoon of the snow.

By the pole slope that Canada faces
    The ice giants hurtle and reel,
For her seven months winter she cases
    Her land in a casket of steel.
Yet I pine for her mighty embraces
    In the home of the moose and the seal,
And I pine for her beautiful places
    And sad is the feeling I feel
When snow flakes remind me of her.

8

A Different America— A Different Ireland

"Your May is before you still," Hyde had assured the am- bivalent graduating class of 1891 on May 28, as, torn between antici- pation and uncertainty, he and they prepared to part from one another and the University of New Brunswick. Few beside his sister Annette understood that it was the kind of assurance that he, too, needed on Wednesday morning, June 3, when having packed clothes, books, and memorabilia and made his last farewells but one, he was again torn be- tween anticipation and uncertainty as he boarded the 7:45 train for Bos- ton. It had been one thing to count the ways in which Canada had been good for him and to assert, as he had in letters written shortly before his departure, that he was not the same young man who nine months earlier, with no definite prospects, had gratefully seized Willie Stockley's suggestion of a temporary appointment. At that time—only weeks ago—daily anticipation of favorable news concerning the possibility of a university post in Toronto, Montreal, or Chicago had buoyed his spirits, increased his optimism, and given him a sense of control over his own destiny. The anticipated news, however, had not arrived. Fred- ericton would soon be behind him. Before him lay—what?

Even as Hyde's anxieties mounted with the increasing speed of the train that carried him out of Canada into Maine and through northeast New England, these were countered in some measure by the prospect of spending the next three weeks among the brash and volatile American Irish. In New Brunswick he had met few countrymen—almost none of his own class—and even fewer aside from his friends in the officers' barracks who shared his nationalist sympathies. Historically, Fredericton was Tory territory. Between 1776 and 1812 it had absorbed a number of American colonists, Irish and English (the census rarely distinguished between them), who had sided with the British. During the same period such cities as Boston, New York, and Charleston had developed a continuous Irish presence that, although chiefly Ascendancy in class and Protestant in religion, was not pro-British and in fact included a number of Irishmen whose opposition to English rule had made them persona non grata at home and patriots in the New Island.

The first major change in this Irish presence in the United States had occurred in the 1830s when, tuberculosis and cholera having become serious threats at home, a small but steady stream of families, extended families, and even neighbors from Irish villages had arrived in search of economic security and a healthier environment. Mostly Catholic and of modest means, thrifty, hardworking, and respectable, these new immigrants had proved to be such desirable citizens that communities had begun to compete for them, advertising incentives in American Irish newspapers for Irish families willing to settle in the inland states of the East and Midwest. A second major change had occurred in the late 1840s with the appearance of the earliest refugees from the Famine. Year by year, month by month, and day by day their numbers had multiplied with the arrival of "coffin" ships so packed with the penniless, homeless, unskilled, and illiterate that public perception of the "typical" Irish immigrant family had become the dockside tableau favored by artists, of a skeletal man standing beside an exhausted woman nursing an emaciated infant, her other half-clothed, half-starved children clinging to her knees. Yet, largely unnoticed by the public, the earlier pattern of emigration—of families of modest means and marketable skills and of unmarried males seeking opportunity, adventure, or a stake in the New World—had continued. Among them always were also the rebels and reformers whose participation in the various movements that marked late-eighteenth- and nineteenth-century British and Irish relations had placed them in jeopardy. Safe in the United States, in frequent communication with their counterparts in Paris, Canada, and other established places of refuge, they continued their efforts on the part of their countrymen, while in Ireland stories about them circulated at crossroads meetings, in tenant cottages, on the steps of city tenements, and in local pubs.

By the 1860s the profile of the American Irish was very different from that of the turn of the century. Except for those involved in the Irish nationalist cause, Anglo-Irish Protestants were generally neither distinguished nor distinguishable from their English-born neighbors. Others who had cut their cultural and emotional ties to the old country sought a similar assimilation. There was now, however, a visible and vocal majority—mostly Catholic and largely working-class, but consisting also of successful business and professional men—that considered themselves both Irish and American. The bulwark of Irish-American social, fraternal, and cultural societies, they openly expressed their resentment of British rule in Ireland; enthusiastically provided refuge for escaped patriots; encouraged anti-British activism; and funded Irish nationalist organizations.

It was in New York in 1858 that after a few tentative starts two Irish immigrants, John O'Mahony and Michael Doheny, both veterans of revolutionary and reform movements of 1848, had founded the Fenian Brotherhood. Its chief purpose was to support the militant Ireland-based Irish Republican Brotherhood, but it provided also the quixotic headquarters for impossible dreams that set up an Irish government in exile in Philadelphia and sent its "Fenian army" to bring Great Britian to its knees by invading Canada through sporadic "battles" mounted between 1866 and 1871. Named to evoke nationalist feelings through association with the Fianna of the ancient Celts, the Fenian Brotherhood was perhaps the best known of the Irish-American political and paramilitary organizations for some thirty years (it gradually was superseded by the Clan na Gael), during which time "Fenian" was a term applied specifically to the American-based Brotherhood and its counterpart in Ireland, the IRB, but also generically to any anti-British Irish attitudes, actions, agents, agencies, and goals. Thus John O'Leary was known as "the old Fenian" who had been jailed for his part in "the Fenian conspiracy" of the 1860s, but in the Frenchpark cottages of Hyde's boyhood and among the Canadians and Americans who proclaimed their "Fenian sympathies," "Fenian" was used in both the particular and the extended sense. Hyde, therefore, was going to Boston to see the "Fenian" editor of the *Pilot*, James Jeffrey Roche; in New York he hoped to encounter such "old Fenians"—veterans, like John O'Leary, of the 1860s—as the celebrated O'Donovan Rossa, the daring patriot of heroic tales circulated in Hyde's Connacht, to whom Hyde himself had addressed a poem published in Irish and English in the *Irishman* of April 1880:

I drink to the health of O'Donovan Rossa,
Where will I find his like at home or abroad,
Who would drive the people without arms or uniforms
Into the midst of the soldiers, the swords and the bayonets,
Who bought and kept the powder and the guns
Which he could not send to the poor defenceless people,
Who nevertheless urged our poor unarmed peasantry
To drive the Saxon soldiers away across the sea.

By the time the train from Fredericton reached Boston at 9:30 P.M. on June 3, 1891, Hyde had been traveling for almost fourteen hours, watching the changing landscape and reflecting on his changing life. These thoughts had reawakened the Irish persona which had had little more than an epistolary identity for almost nine months. Making his way to the Crawford House on Court Street in the center of the city, he settled himself in his rooms. Then, before going to bed, he sat quietly in the lounge, sipping whiskey and considering what the next few days would bring. Boston would prove to his liking he was sure. His name was already known to the Boston Irish community through its two newspapers, the *Pilot* and the *Irish Echo*. The *Echo,* edited by P. J. O'Daly, had begun publication in 1886 as the organ of the Boston Philo-Celtic Society. In its December 1887 issue Hyde had published a special message to its readers, written in Irish and signed "An Craoibhin Aoihbhinn," that had exhorted them to enroll in the semi-weekly Irish-language lessons offered by the society and to promote the *Echo*'s new "Irish Language Department." In January of 1888 the *Echo* had printed an English translation by Michael Cavanagh of one of his shorter poems. Entitled "Craoibhin Aoibhinn's Song" and ironically described by O'Daly as a typically Irish Christmas carol, it ended in characteristically Fenian rhetoric:

. . . though our hateful foemen,
Through tyrant force and guile
By English laws and "yeomen"
Should threaten us meanwhile
(The thought my heart doth lighten),
I think we yet shall see
Our country's future brighten—
The Saxon forced to flee.

In August 1888 the *Pilot,* the older and better-known of the two publications, also had printed one of his poems, for which he had received two pounds and a friendly note that John Boyle O'Reilly had written before his death. Remembering O'Reilly, Hyde promised himself that the very next day he would hunt up James Jeffrey Roche, O'Reilly's successor as editor of the *Pilot*.

On the morning of June 4 Douglas Hyde was warmly greeted by Roche who, delighted with his visit, was eager to show him about Boston and introduce him to other leaders of the Boston Irish community. They began with lunch at the St. Botolph Club, described by Hyde as a meeting place for "the elite of the cultured Bostonians," "a nice set of men, . . . unassuming, perfectly educated, quiet and for the most part wealthy, but somewhat lacking in wit and readiness." There they joined a group whose major business of the day focused on proposed plans for a statue of John Boyle O'Reilly. As they warmed to their subject, Hyde's mind was on other concerns. It really was not at all against his best interests, he had begun to realize, to return home rather than settle in North America. It was in fact, as he later confided to his diary, much better that he did return home, for certainly he could not leave Annette with full responsibility for the supervision and maintenance of the glebe house or the care of their aging father. As for his future, in Fredericton he had been accepted not simply for his Trinity or family connections but as a man of creditable accomplishments in his own right. On parting, the president had spoken in the most complimentary way of the fine reputation he had earned as teacher, author, and scholar. In ballrooms, drawing rooms, and dining rooms he had been regarded as an interesting and charming gentleman, a versatile conversationalist, a desirable guest at dinners, soirees, and teas. Describing to Annette the farewell parties that had been given in his honor, he had written modestly, "You see I am getting slightly over the shyness which . . . life among the bogs afflicted me with." He knew this was an understatement, for at the university he had discovered that he was as comfortable in the lecture hall as he had been on the Dublin amateur stage or among his peers in the "Hist." The role of professor suited him well, in fact. Students ranging from rather dull to very keen not only had liked him but had shown a satisfying improvement under his tutelage. He had developed, moreover, a successful classroom manner—a combination of banter, anecdote, gentle chiding, and entertaining digression that had held their attention and piqued their curiosity. His relations with most of his colleagues had not been close, but he had made no enemies, he was sure, and he had managed to get on capitally with the president. Surely, given all these facts plus his reputation as a writer and scholar— his work was now being read not only in England and Ireland but in

North America and on the Continent—there would be an academic post for him in Dublin, Cork, or Galway.

Day after day, during Hyde's short stay in Boston, Roche continued to serve as host, friend, and guide. One evening after the two men had dined together, they walked all around Back Bay, discussing a subject of importance to Roche, the status of the American Irish, in which Hyde also had become keenly interested. In his notebook Hyde recorded his opinion that Roche and O'Reilly, through the *Pilot,* had helped the Irish displace the "Puritans" and increase their own political power in Boston. On another evening Roche invited Hyde to accompany him to the home of his brother-in-law in a suburb "far out of town." After tea the three men sat talking, drinking beer, and smoking cigars until midnight. Curious about the American educational system, Hyde questioned them on the subject of the comparative costs of parochial and public school tuition. Their reply, he noted, had less to do with money than with what each described as a trend toward "un-Irishness" among the Boston Irish in particular and the American Irish in general. Corroborating their statements, a Boston bookseller with whom Hyde talked complained of the diminishing demand for Irish books. Hyde attributed the situation to the improved social and economic status of affluent Irish Americans. Other immigrant groups, he knew, were having similar experiences. Yet among the Irish poor, there seemed to be no shame in or wish to shed their national identity. Was this, he asked himself, thinking of the tenant poor in Ireland, because they were giving up other distinguishing characteristics?

One morning Hyde took the trolley to Cambridge where faculty and staff whom Fredericton friends had told him to look up showed him "all over that mass of luxury, Harvard College." In his notebook he recorded the institutional statistics that they provided: the student body numbered 2,100, the professors, 180; fees for the Arts course totaled $150; the cost of rooms was $120. He also outlined the curriculum, noting the physical development requirement and elective system, and observed that all the people he encountered on campus were very friendly. Some he knew by reputation from their work; he was both pleased and amused to discover that he, too, was known by reputation. In fact, on one occasion, having been introduced to a folklorist who was unaware that Douglas Hyde was An Craoibhin Aoibhinn, he had been proudly shown a new book that he was urged to examine: his own *Beside the Fire.*

During the weekend the Fräulein arrived. On Sunday morning Hyde escorted her to Trinity Church to hear a sermon by Phillips Brooks which he criticized as having been delivered "like a torrent for speed." They spent the afternoon at the home of a Miss Conway, where he became engrossed in a conversation with Louise Guiney, an American poet and essayist born in Boston of Irish parents who had visited Ireland and was a friend of Katharine Tynan. On Monday he and the Fräulein lunched at his hotel, then went to the new library and museum where he pronounced the pictures "worth nothing, all daubs." The obviously unsuccessful rendezvous ended before dinner "without tears on either side," leaving Hyde free to spend Tuesday with Louise Guiney, who had invited him to lunch. She was, he wrote to Annette, "one of the most fascinating creatures I ever met, a pleasant girl, full of talk and enthusiasm," although "a bit deaf." Of the Fräulein he said nothing but offered the general comment that Boston girls are pretty but have bad complexions ("owing to the changeable weather"), while Canadian women have "lovely" complexions—a last gallant remark, perhaps, regarding the woman to whom it could not be delivered directly without fear that his intention might be misunderstood.

On Tuesday evening, June 9, Hyde took the train to Fall River, where for four dollars he boarded "an enormous floating palace of a steamer" for the overnight journey to New York City. Arriving at seven o'clock in the morning, he booked into the Everett House in Union Square and immediately set about sightseeing, accompanied by a man from Ohio who was a guest at the same hotel. First they took a day steamer to the Statue of Liberty, which impressed him mostly by its size: "so large that 12 men could stand round the torch held in the right hand." Then they boarded the elevated railway for Central Park. Meanwhile Thomas O'Neill Russell, who had kept up his correspondence with Hyde during the entire Fredericton year and had been scouting out possible university appointments for him, waited impatiently at the Everett House with Pádraig Ó Beirn, another language activist. As soon as Hyde returned, Russell and Ó Beirn, eager to introduce him to members of the New York Irish community, whisked him off to the Manhattan quarters of the Gaelic Society just over half a mile to the north on Twenty-eighth Street. There they remained until midnight, Hyde cautiously drinking little on account of his fatigue.

Early the next morning, June 11, Russell was again at the Everett House, to breakfast with Hyde and take him back to the Gaelic Society. There—his search interrupted by Russell, who insisted on showing him off as though he were "a prize fighting cock"—Hyde looked in vain for O'Donovan Rossa and "another man" whom he did not identify but clearly had expected to meet. Of Russell's possessive behavior he complained to his diary, "This I don't like but can't help." Russell was "far too touchy" to address on the subject. Had he been less irritated, Hyde might have admitted that Russell was also far too helpful to alienate. Hyde did manage, however, to get away on his own for the evening, which he spent "very pleasantly with Pádraig [Ó Beirn], drinking and talking" until nearly midnight.

The next morning, June 12, Hyde breakfasted with two old Trinity friends, Carman and Gregg, then wandered downtown on his own to the foot of Manhattan to see the Brooklyn Bridge, which he sketched for Annette, and to look over the stock of several gun shops before returning as promised to the rooms of the Gaelic Society. There he passed the late afternoon and early evening sipping tea with Russell and joining others in a long and serious discussion of current affairs in Ireland. On June 13 Hyde at last had the chance to visit O'Donovan Rossa in his lodgings. After drinking and talking most of the morning, the two men went together to the office of the *Irish World* where, sitting close together around the desk of the Galway-born editor and founder, Patrick Ford, they continued to talk, mostly about the Irish language movement. It was a subject in which Ford, an ardent Land Leaguer, was not particularly interested. Hyde and O'Donovan Rossa tried to convince him of its strong political implications without success.

The morning's business over, Hyde planned to spend the afternoon at a baseball game in Harlem. However, with the temperature at ninety degrees in the shade, he soon left the ballpark to take refuge in the cooler lounge of the Gaelic Society. There discussion continued to focus on Irish politics. In the evening he and Russell dined together, after which they joined members of the society at a concert of Irish music by McGilvey's band at "Madison Hall" (Madison Square Garden)—"the biggest hall," Hyde declared, that he had ever been in. The next day was Sunday. Hyde, Russell, Gregg, and Carman lingered together over breakfast until half past twelve. Then, as the temperature was again over ninety in the shade, Russell and Ó Beirn suggested that Hyde go with them to a country house owned by the Gaelic Society on Long Island.

On Monday, to Hyde's dismay, the heat wave continued, interfering with many of his sightseeing plans. The thermometer now registered 113 degrees in the sun and 95 degrees in the shade—temperatures unheard of in Ireland. He had complimented himself on his ability to endure the winter cold of Fredericton; the summer heat of New York required a far more difficult adjustment. Yet with only ten days remaining before he sailed for Ireland, it was time to shop for the purchases he wanted to make before his departure and the trip to Niagara Falls that he had promised himself, even before he left Canada. Returning to one of the gun shops he had visited earlier, he bought a Colt revolver and bullets for twenty dollars. After checking the commitments he had on his calendar—a *feis* in his honor that evening, a speech on the state of the Irish language the evening after—he booked a three-day excursion to Niagara on June 17. His round-trip ticket, noted in his expense book, cost sixteen dollars.

The *feis* was a cheerful affair attended by about twenty people, all Irish speakers. A good supper accompanied by chilled wine and plenty of punch held them, despite the heat, through six speeches in Irish and as many more in English, all in praise of Hyde's work. The party went on until three in the morning, after which some six of the guests returned with Hyde for a nightcap at his hotel. On June 16 he awoke close to noon and sat on his bed, looking at the thermometer which had risen to 100 degrees in the shade, uncertain how much more he could endure. At just that moment a storm broke, bringing the relief for which everyone had been waiting, and assuring the success of the evening's Gaelic Society meeting at which he was scheduled to present a speech in Irish and English. The next day he journeyed by boat and train up the Hudson River to Buffalo and Niagara Falls.

Published in the *Gaelic American* for June 27, 1891, Hyde's speech of June 16 on the present state of the Irish language was not just the right thing at the right time but a preview of things to come. Identifying himself to his partly bilingual audience as no expert on his topic but only a late observer of a situation with which they were equally if not more familiar, he declared that the views he expressed were those he held personally, not as a spokesperson for any association concerned with the revival of the Irish language. Then dramatically balancing negative against positive, he established his facts: Irish was in "bad health" but not dead; it was not a patois nor the "poor, mean, limited language" described by those who for selfish and political reasons would have it destroyed but "a vast, varied, very opulent one" that "stands upon an equal footing with Greek, Latin, and Sanscrit"; it was the direct descendant and moreover the key to an "enormous mass of Irish literature, . . . lying at present in manuscript," which "has not only never been equalled but never been approached either in age, variety, or value by any vernacular language in Europe"; it was "the language of the

Bards and Brehons, of the Saints and sages," which must not be "kicked contemptuously aside" or allowed to crawl away, as it were, with a broken leg, to die like a hunted dog in a ditch, a vile and lingering death." Nevertheless, acknowledging the damage that had been done to Irish by well-meaning friends as well as enemies of Irish Ireland, Hyde assured his listeners that he recognized that he was "standing in a practical country amongst practical men" to whom he felt required to give "some adequate reason for continuing to keep alive the Irish language" and therefore "to state clearly" what he wished to see done.

His reasons, Hyde told his audience, were fourfold: it was not good for any race "to throw sentiment to the dogs"; for the Irish their language was the key to their "great national heritage"; language was one of the most effective means that could be used to bring a people together; a bilingual race was always and in every way "infinitely superior to a race that speaks only one language." Acknowledging that for the Irish in America much of what he had said about language applied to Catholicism—that indeed, for many, "Irish" and "Catholic" had become synonymous terms—Hyde questioned whether Catholicism alone could prove a satisfactory bond in the future, given the influx of other European Catholics even then in progress. Better to have also the advantages of bilingualism, he avowed, for "bilingual races" were "doubly men, and . . . double in sharpness and mental capacity."

Hyde next raised the question, at first quietly, of how the Irish language had been allowed to sink to its current sorry state. "It is a most disgraceful shame the way in which Irishmen are brought up," he then thundered, "ashamed of their language, institutions, and of everything Irish." Softly again he described a recent encounter with two young Irishmen. Asked where they were from, one had replied deprecatingly, "I come from a little village over there called Ireland." Hyde's voice rose again as he pointed to the self-deprecating but common practice of translating and anglicizing Irish names. Ashamed to bear the surnames of their saints and heroes, Hyde declared, there were Irish who adopted instead for themselves and their children such non-Irish names as "Stiggins or Hunk or Buggins." Nor had "one single word of warning or remonstrance" been raised "against this colossal cringing, either by the Irish press or by Irish public men." In the face of such facts the Irish of Ireland had good cause to be thankful to the Gaels of America, Hyde avowed, for without them the Irish language movement would not have achieved its present position.

But how now to proceed beyond the position—and, more important, not lose any ground that had been won? Again, Hyde was practical and reasonable. He saw only two possible ways of keeping up "the Irish spirit of the people and a due regard for the language of the past." One was to win Home Rule; the other was to "put the Irish language in all institutions and examinations upon the same footing or a little more favorable footing than French, Latin, and Greek, and to insist on having Irish-speaking functionaries and schoolmasters in Irish-speaking parts of the country." Lest he be misunderstood, however, he stated clearly that in no way was he suggesting that Irish should replace English:

I do not for a moment advocate making Irish the language of the country at large, or of the National Parliament. I do not want to be an impossible visionary or rabid partisan. What I wish to see is Irish established as a living language, for all time, among the million or half million who still speak it along the West coast, and to insure that the language will hold a favorable place in teaching institutions and government examinations.

In conclusion he outlined briefly a practical program through which he believed that the goals he had set forth might be accomplished.

Following publication of Hyde's complete speech in the *Gaelic American,* excerpts appeared in newspapers in Ireland. Among those who read with interest and later recalled what Hyde had said were John Mac-Neill, 24, at his desk in the Accountant General's Office in Dublin; John Dillon, 40, in Galway Prison; Lady Gregory, 39, in her home near Gort overlooking the Seven Woods of Coole; and W. B. Yeats, 26, in Dublin. Unaware of Hyde, hearing only, like Joyce's Stephen Dedalus, the quarrels over Parnell that were dividing families and estranging friends, were two others whose world would later be changed by the implications of Hyde's speech: Patrick Pearse, 12, soon to be enrolled in the Christian Brothers school on Westland Row in Dublin, and Eamon de Valera, 9, a National School boy living in Bruree, county Clare.

On Hyde's return from Niagara Falls, O'Neill Russell and Ó Beirn took him to the Irish school on the Bowery about which he had heard extraordinary reports. About thirty people were in attendance. All were speaking Irish; all had, it was clear, an immense interest in the language. When Hyde addressed them in Irish, they responded enthusiastically and with obvious understanding. He questioned Russell and Ó Beirn about the methods and materials that were used at the school, the cost of instruction, and the background of the people who were attracted to Irish classes. If such a school could flourish in New York, he asked himself, why not in Dublin, Galway, Limerick, or Cork?

On June 23, with but two days to finish all his business in New York, Hyde again went to visit O'Donovan Rossa. After a drink and a long talk, they set out for the top of the Herald Building, from which they had a view of the entire city, and then parted. Hyde's afternoon was spent at the British Consulate filling out forms and attempting to obtain the necessary approval concerning the shipment of his gun and his books. Shortly after six-thirty he arrived at the Gaelic Society where, he discovered, a feast had been prepared in his honor. After dinner there were speeches and dancing and drinking and talking far into the night. Most of the guests went home at about two-thirty in the morning. Six or seven remained behind, discussing Parnell, until six in the morning.

The news of the day was that on June 25 Parnell was to marry Kitty O'Shea. Details of the civil ceremony scheduled to take place at Steyning near Brighton had been published by the Irish-American newspapers. They had all given full coverage to the O'Shea divorce trial. Most had opposed Parnell. The *Irish World* had been particularly bitter in its invective. Yet reluctant to desert him, the American Irish were as divided as the Irish at home. Even so, few believed that Parnell could recover the political support needed for him to continue as head of the Irish party. At the same time, as some pointed out, if the Parnell era was over, what would take its place?

At noon on the twenty-fifth of June, Douglas Hyde boarded the *State of Nevada* bound for Moville and Londonderry, his portmanteau bulging with bottles of rye whiskey and other gifts from the Irish-American community. He stood at the stern of the ship as it eased past the tip of Manhattan under the eyes of the Statue of Liberty, then headed through the Narrows into New York's outer harbor toward the open Atlantic. Nine months had gone by since September 10, 1890, when, bound for Montreal, he had boarded the *Polynesia* in Liverpool. Political observers of the time had then been speculating not on whether but on when and how there would be Home Rule in the country that at the time they were calling "Parnell's Ireland." Expecting the year to be historic, Hyde had anticipated that he would return to an Ireland very different from the one he was leaving. But neither he nor anyone else had foreseen what that difference would be: an Ireland in which Home Rule had again slipped out of reach and Parnell was fighting for his political life. Once before, over an earlier incident, the Tories had almost succeeded in containing the man known to his party as "the Chief" and to the voters who supported him overwhelmingly as "Ireland's uncrowned king." But the attempt to discredit him publicly by implicating him in the Phoenix Park murders had only boosted his popularity when evidence presented to the Special Commission had proved that the incriminating letters on which charges were based were forgeries.

Small wonder that the divorce suit filed in December 1889 by Captain William O'Shea against his wife, Katherine, in which Parnell was named as co-respondent, was at first widely regarded as just another doomed anti-Parnell plot, designed "to recover in the Divorce Court," in the words of Winston Churchill, what had been "lost before the Special Commission." Even when the divorce was granted on November 17, 1890, there was little to suggest the trouble to come. Rallies on behalf of Parnell had drawn large crowds in Ireland, England, and America. On November 25 he had been unanimously reelected chairman of the Irish party. But after Gladstone called for Parnell's resignation on November 26 and the Catholic hierarchy followed with a similar message on December 3, the anti-Parnellites within the party had seized the initiative. The vote had gone against Parnell by a margin of almost two to one. For the next six months, as Parnell stumped the countryside, taking the issue to the voters, controversy had raged. The latest announcement that he would now marry Kitty O'Shea in a civil ceremony had again raised a clamor. From what Hyde had been hearing from the Irish in America who knew much more of the situation than he himself had been able to fathom in New Brunswick, Canada, it was unlikely that Parnell would be able to recover the support he needed to regain control of the party.

9

A Bridle for Proteus

Annette had driven the trap from the glebe house to Ballaghaderreen to meet Douglas at the station. He stepped down from the train into July sunshine and his sister's smile. Eager to maintain their mutual involvement in each other's life through their long separation of 1890–1891, they had kept up a thoughtful and detailed correspondence. Yet as always when they were face to face, there was still so much to say that their conversations flitted from subject to subject like butterflies in a meadow. They were, they agreed, the best of friends as well as members of the same family. The only other person with whom Hyde had ever shared a similar friendship was his father's youngest sister, Sisilla Hyde.

Some things, of course, had not been put in letters, because neither wanted to upset the other. Douglas was sure that Annette had refrained from telling him half or more of the trouble she had had with "Der Alte," the term he now used instead of "the Master" or "the Governor" to refer to his father. It was an indication of his changing relationship with the Reverend Hyde. Annette suspected that Douglas was far more disappointed than he acknowledged to return to Roscommon with no prospects of future employment. It would not be easy for him, she knew, to face Der Alte's questions on the subject. No matter: in his last letters from North America, Douglas had promised that he would not go off again for at least a few weeks. In the days to come there would be time enough to talk things over. For the moment the pressing problem was to get all his bags into the trap without breaking any of

the bottles of whiskey that had been given to him in New York or crushing the photograph he had brought home for her of himself in his
Canadian backwoods hunter's outfit. It was his favorite picture of himself, he said. Everything he was wearing or carrying, he assured her—fur
hat, fur coat, fur gloves, the snowshoes clutched under his arm—were
necessities for anyone planning to spend time outdoors in the fierce
Canadian winter.

But now it was July, and the sun was pleasantly warm rather than
unremittingly hot as it had been in New York. Small white clouds
propelled by a constant but gentle breeze rippled the shadows of the
landscape. It was a day for tennis. Annette assured him that, in accordance with the instructions he had given her in his letters, she had
attended to the spring rolling of the tennis court and had had his tennis
clothes washed and pressed. She also volunteered that her game was
perhaps now the equal of his, thanks to the hours that she had been
spending on the courts at Ratra. In any case he would have an opportunity to practice his skills against a variety of partners, for invitations
to rounds of social activities had come from Boyle, Frenchpark, and
Castlerea. Other mail, she knew—for she had stacked it there herself—
was also on his writing table. She could not help but wonder about
letters from Fredericton addressed in an unfamiliar feminine hand.
Which of the young women about whom he had written in his long,
descriptive letters could these be from? Of greater curiosity were the
other envelopes, for perhaps one of these might contain the news for
which they were both hoping, of the possibility of a university appointment in Ireland.

For the moment, however, Hyde's questions concerned the smaller
world of glebe house and village. There was no major work to be done
indoors, Annette assured him. Nor was there any reason for him to involve himself in seasonal chores. Connolly had everything in good
order; the prospect for a second hay crop was excellent. As for the
fortunes and misfortunes of glebe tenants and neighbors, there had been
the usual sicknesses and a few predictable deaths, but nothing much
different from other years. Annette was pleased that she could give him
so favorable a report. As the trap rolled up the drive to the glebe house,
with its avenue of trees and glimpses of ripening fruit behind the
orchard wall, Douglas's spirits could not have been higher. He was
genuinely glad to see the Reverend Hyde, who came to the door
to greet them, his limp rather more pronounced, but whether from
arthritis or gout Douglas could not tell. As father and son sat down

together indoors, Annette disappeared to give the *ancilla* (as the house-maid still was called in the Hyde household) instructions for the disposition of Douglas's boxes and bags.

To Douglas's relief his father did not quiz him about his prospects for the future but listened attentively to his description of Phillips Brooks's sermon in Trinity Church in Boston and the magnetic appeal of Thomas DeWitt Talmage who had packed some four thousand people into a church in Brooklyn on a hot Sunday morning. Later, while the Reverend Hyde was resting and Annette was occupied with household affairs, he went for an old-fashioned ramble, stopping as usual at some of the cottages he passed, then returned home to read his mail and look over the invitations Annette had mentioned. She was right: if the weather held, there surely would be great times during the next few weeks. The prospect pleased him, not only for himself but also because he still felt a little guilty about having left Annette solely responsible for their father and the glebe house for such a long time, with so little chance to get away on her own. Oldfields's visits apparently had been, as always, infrequent.

On July 14 Douglas and Annette went to a tennis party at Frenchpark House. The next day they had to choose between a dance in Boyle and tennis and dinner at Ratra; they decided to skip the dance. But two days later, on the first day of the annual Boyle tennis tournament, they left home early and stayed so long after the last game, dining and visiting, that they were not back at the glebe house until nearly midnight. The tournament continued on July 17, with both Annette and Douglas participating. After a few good games Annette and her partner, Mr. Fagan, lost to a Miss White and a Mr. Smith. On July 20 there was a cricket match at Frenchpark which drew a number of people, including many Hyde had not seen since his return home. The finals of the Boyle tennis tournament were on July 21. The weather was very wet. Despite heavy showers Hyde and his partner, a Miss Marsh, played their match but were soundly beaten. Hyde kept up a good face about it at dinner at the Hamiltons, but in his diary he rather ungallantly blamed his loss on his having drawn Miss Marsh, whose game was not up to his standards. The weather improved by July 27 in time for another cricket match—Castlerea against the garrison—at Frenchpark. Playing for Castlerea, Hyde fielded fairly well but was disappointed that he got in only one or two runs.

On Monday, August 3, despite a steady cold rain, Hyde set out for a five-day visit to Cork at the invitation of Charlotte Grace O'Brien.

Daughter of William Smith O'Brien (leader of the last battle of the rising of 1848, which had ended in Tipperary, in the widow McCormack's cabbage garden), Grace O'Brien had a modest reputation as a writer, having published a number of poems and a well-received novel. Hyde admired her not just for her writing but for her commitment to relief work among the poor, especially single women and young girls who for lack of any other means of support were forced to emigrate to America. Her home was Ard-an-óir in the Blackwater Valley near Foynes, the same area in which Hyde's ancestors had settled and built Castle Hyde. The journey by rail to Foynes was long and roundabout. It began with one train to Castlerea and another to Athlone and Athenry. There he was forced to endure a long delay before he could continue on through Gort, Ardrahan, Cratloe, and Ennis to Limerick, where he spent the night at the George Hotel. Tuesday morning, after several drinks with an old friend who by chance was also staying at the George, he proceeded by train to Foynes and by carriage to his destination.

As Miss O'Brien had become seriously hearing-impaired in recent years, Hyde talked with her, as he noted in his diary, "on my fingers." With her when he arrived was Lord Monteagle's sister. In the afternoon they were joined by Willie Stockley, not yet returned to New Brunswick, and a Miss Osbourne. On Wednesday, except for Lord Monteagle's sister, who had another engagement, the entire party went to Monteagle's home, Mount Trenchard, a mansion that Hyde found quite dazzling. On Thursday, having been invited to the estate of Sir Stephen de Vere for some shooting, Hyde took a boat to Foynes Island. A classicist and a poet with a lyrical talent as well as a fine sportsman, de Vere, second son of Sir Aubrey de Vere, was an agreeable companion. At the time of Hyde's visit he was close to completing an edition of his own translations of the odes of Horace, a task at which Hyde himself had tried his skill informally some years before.

Hyde's bag for the day was scarcely his best: a white rabbit, killed at forty yards, and a crow. Nevertheless, given host and scenery, he enjoyed himself immensely. When he returned to Mount Trenchard he discovered that the party had been increased by a Miss Knox. The entire week had been like that—agreeably relaxed and informal, with people coming and going as they wished, and much good conversation. On Friday, after walking a couple of miles or more through the spectacular countryside, Hyde dined with Lord Monteagle and his family. After dinner he had a long talk with Miss Butcher, Monteagle's wife's sister, who was both intelligent and independent—like Grace O'Brien, the kind of woman whose company he most enjoyed.

Back in Roscommon, with summer drawing to an end and with it the diversions that had kept him from dwelling on the bleakness of his prospects for the future, Hyde's spirits began to sag. Remembering the prizes and awards he had won at Trinity, the reviews his published work had received, and the respect with which he had been treated in Fredericton, Boston, and New York, it was difficult for him to accept the fact that he had had no offers at all, in Ireland or anywhere else, since he had returned home. The political news was unbearably depressing. With Tim Healy and other jackals after him, Parnell was losing one by-election after another. In September, to occupy himself profitably and take his mind off the current political situation, Hyde began the study of Anglo-Saxon, a subject certain to enhance his qualifications for a university post, should one become available. He also continued his own writing and translating—he was then at work on poems from the Irish to be published in *Love Songs of Connacht*—but he noted ruefully that successful as his publications had been, earning a literary reputation was not earning a living.

Hyde's best work was always that which he completed rapidly, during periods of inspiration. In the four days between the seventh and the eleventh of September he produced nine verse translations. These eventually appeared in *Love Songs of Connacht*, but while the manuscript was still in progress he allowed some to be published in the *Weekly Freeman*, where they attracted an enthusiastic response from readers. One of his translations of this period was "Ringleted youth of my love," the most popular poem in the collection and the one that has been reprinted most often. For all of his creative and scholarly labor, however, Hyde received no payment, only the *Freeman*'s promise that he could have the plates of everything they published without charge.

At the end of September Hyde was deeply saddened by the news that Parnell was seriously ill. By October 6, 1891, Parnell was dead, and half the nation was in mourning. From Parnell's home in Brighton his body was brought back to Ireland. Crowds of supporters met carriage, train, and boat at every point of transfer, despite weather as black as their mood. Thousands filed past his coffin as it lay in state in the City Hall in Dublin. A torchlight procession accompanied the hearse that took him to his grave in Glasnevin. Someone—probably Lord Wolseley, but the story has been attributed also to Arthur Balfour, among others—is reported to have said that the only crowds of which he ever was afraid were those that gathered to pay silent tribute to the man people called their "uncrowned king." The Parnell era was over, and with it all hope of Home Rule in the foreseeable future. But Hyde was certain that, like the phoenix that many had used as a symbol of the Irish nation, hope would rise again. Yet he could not prevent his thoughts from returning to his memories of how agreeable life had been in Canada, how well he had been treated in Boston and New York, how futile it seemed, at least for the present, to remain in Ireland.

It was with anticipation, therefore, of perhaps some interim improvement in his own particular situation that Hyde learned in December that O'Neill Russell's advance information had been correct: a formal announcement had been made of an opening in language and literature at the new University of Chicago. At the same time he received word of an opening at Queen's College in Belfast which called for the qualifications in history and English literature that he could provide. Setting aside the poems on which he had been working, Hyde concentrated on preparing a six-page summary of his academic record and other accomplishments to accompany letters of application to both Chicago and Belfast and on obtaining persuasive letters of recommendation.

Hyde's application to Belfast, addressed to the Earl of Zetland, was written by necessity in the formal and obsequious language of the day:

May it please your Excellency,

I have the honour to offer myself as a Candidate for the Professorship of History and English Literature now vacant in the Queens College, Belfast.

I beg to enclose a list of degrees and honours which I obtained in Trinity College, Dublin, both [sic] in English, Celtic, and Foreign Literature.

I am not ignorant of University teaching, having lectured during the year '90 '91 on English and Modern Literature in the State University of New Brunswick.

A presentation was made to me by the Students when leaving, and I enclose the testimonial of the President of the University.

Although I have chiefly worked at English and Modern Literature I am also fairly acquainted with the Greek and Latin Classics, with Anglo-Saxon, and with the Language and Literature of the Gaels of Scotland, and have some knowledge of Hebrew.

Praying that this Memorial may receive your Excellency's favourable consideration,

I have the honour to be your Excellency's most obedient servant.

Douglas Hyde, LL.D., M.R.I.A.

Among those who wrote cautiously to Chicago and Belfast on Hyde's behalf were George Salmon, Hyde's former professor in the divinity program, now the Provost, and Edward Dowden, professor of English literature at Trinity. Salmon endorsed Edward Dowden's letter as consistent with what he knew of Hyde and added that he himself considered the candidate "a good linguist, a man of minute and various reading, and a very diligent Student." He pointed to Hyde's record of publication as evidence that he had "not been idle since the termination of his college course" and drew attention to Hyde's experience as an interim professor of modern languages in New Brunswick.

Calling Hyde "one of our most brilliant and distinguished scholars of recent years," Dowden was no less laudatory. He enumerated Hyde's areas of expertise ("English, French, German, Italian, Celtic, History, Law, Literature, Theology") and noted that, "in all the wide range included by what these names imply," Hyde had "proved his ability and attainments." Like Salmon, Dowden pointed out that already Hyde's scholarship "had produced fruit in works . . . widely and favourably known to Celtic students." With this "abundance of learning," Dowden declared, "Dr. Hyde has retained his brightness and freshness of intellect and his geniality of temper; he has not lost touch with actual life and reality." Hyde would make, he avowed, "an admirable Professor" who "would augment his present roll of distinctions by works of scholarship which would do credit to the great Institution with which he would be connected."

Maxwell H. Close, treasurer of the Royal Irish Academy, did not send his letter directly to the provosts of Chicago or Belfast but addressed it to Hyde for inclusion with his applications. Close testified to his personal knowledge of Hyde's academic qualifications, his literary sensibility, and his attainments; he expressed his belief that Hyde would succeed particularly in the task of imparting to students the benefits of his intellectual capacity and cultured taste. He had the highest esteem, he declared, for Hyde's "power of acquiring Languages"—a "great advantage," he noted, "in dealing with the genius and individual character of the English."

Although everything else was put aside during the last month of 1891 as Hyde concentrated on presenting the best possible case for his appointment to both institutions, there was no further mention of these applications either in his diary or in the letters and papers that have survived to suggest the kind of acknowledgment or response, if any, that he received. What seems certain is that he was never seriously considered for either job, but there is no indication as to why. In later years Hyde often spoke bitterly of Mahaffy, whom he apparently suspected of continuing to undermine his efforts to secure a university position, but whether or not Mahaffy was implicated remains, in the absence of any other evidence, a matter of conjecture. Certainly Mahaffy did nothing to help Hyde's candidacy for these and other posts, and relations between them remained strained, with occasional eruptions, through the years. But the fact is that Salmon, Dowden, and Close were not much help either—perhaps because they could not be. Try as they might to emphasize the excellence of Hyde's academic background in modern history and literature, English and European, it was clear from Hyde's record of publication that his scholarship was limited to Celtic subjects, a factor that might have worked against him. Moreover, by 1891 the connection between Dr. Douglas Hyde, the public man, and An Craoibhin, the public persona of Hyde's private Irish self, was as well known to the Ascendancy as to Irish Ireland, although the extent of his Fenian connections and sympathies seems not to have been recognized outside nationalist circles, even by some who were closest to him. No one thought of Hyde as a danger, but to any alert university administrator, his dossier would have suggested that he could be an embarrassment and might be a nuisance.

New Year's Day, 1892, found Hyde again at work on the manuscript of *Love Songs of Connacht*. On February 11 in the library of the Royal Irish Academy he made the acquaintance of a young priest from county Meath who, like himself, had as a boy learned Irish from local native speakers. At Maynooth, Eugene O'Growney had spent his holidays mostly on Inismaan (the Aran Island later visited by John Millington Synge) but he had also made the rounds of other Gaeltachts, to get a good feel for spoken Irish wherever it survived in Ireland. Ordained in 1889, he had served for a while as curate of a small parish in Westmeath. He had contributed to the *Gaelic Journal* and *Irish Ecclesiastical Record*. In 1891 he had succeeded John Fleming as editor of the *Journal* and had been appointed professor of Irish at his alma mater. Hyde described O'Growney in his diary as "a young man with a large head and thick lips," "kindly and slow-speaking," who was "nice looking without being handsome or well-groomed." Their shared interests and experiences emerged in a long conversation that occupied most of their afternoon. Among the ideas on which they agreed was that the time had come—the country was ready—for a plan that would restore the Irish language to the people of Ireland. But it would have to be offered as an aspect of their culture that was theirs by choice; they would have to be assured that it would augment but not replace English; and they would have to be convinced that it would enhance rather than detract from Ireland's position in the world. These three concerns had been addressed by Hyde in "A Plea for the Irish Language" (1886), in his preface to *Beside the Fire* (1890), and in his speech on the present state of the Irish language (1891) that had been printed in full in the *Gaelic American*. These same concerns had informed an essay entitled "The National Language" that Eugene O'Growney had published in the *Irish Ecclesiastical Record* of November 1890.

As Hyde was scheduled to leave on the night boat for London, he could not continue his conversation as long as he liked with O'Growney, but he assured his new friend that he would look him up at Maynooth immediately upon his return. That evening, in one of his occasional bursts of hyperbole—piqued perhaps by his conviction that his own failure to obtain a post in an Irish university was the work of such men as Mahaffy and Atkinson—Hyde declared in his diary that O'Growney was "perhaps the only learned man in Ireland today who speaks Irish correctly." He also could not help but wonder: Had he himself been a Catholic graduate of Maynooth instead of a Protestant graduate of Trinity, would he now be in O'Growney's position? Had his *Leabhar Sgeulaigheachta* been about German tales, had his *Beside the Fire* been translated from the French, had his poems and essays celebrated the eloquence and independence of English yeomanry—had he assumed the accepted Anglo-Irish role of Englishman born in Ireland and written about almost anything but the Irish heritage, Irish language, and native traditions of his own country—would he have been more attractive to Cork or Queens or even Trinity?

In London, Hyde's sense of himself returned. He had an agreeable interview on the day of his arrival with David Nutt, publisher of *Beside the Fire*. The next day, quite by chance, his old friend W. M. Crook from Trinity College stopped him on the Strand and invited him to a meeting of a new Irish society that had been founded on a "wet and windy" night in December by W. P. Ryan, W. B. Yeats, T. W. Rolleston, D. J. O'Donoghue, J. G. O'Keefe, and John Todhunter—all well-known veterans of other short-lived Irish organizations. Various schemes and programs designed to promote the new society (the term "club" was rejected) had been discussed, Hyde learned, in a series of subsequent meetings which had resulted in the choice of a name, the "Irish Literary Society," and an agenda that included a missionary drive for an enlarged membership. The February 6, 1892, issue of the *Freeman's Journal* had published an article outlining the new society's aims: first, to resume the long-neglected work of Young Ireland, take up the unfinished schemes of 1842 and 1845, and voice the aspirations of 1792; second, to promote the publication of a series of books on Irish history, biography, poetry, and folklore and reprint old editions and valuable out-of-print books; third, to bring Irish books within easier reach of London readers and to improve the distribution of Irish books in Ireland. Among the difficulties encountered had been the counterproductive efforts of well-meaning members less interested in literature, the diluting effect of competing organizations that drew on the same membership pool in England and Ireland, and the skepticism of publishers. (One, quoted by W. P. Ryan in his account of the organization, had written, "I should be inclined to say that it would put another St. Patrick to the pin of his collar to convert the Irish people into a book-reading and book-buying nation".) To counter these difficulties, the organizers adopted the strategy of encouraging loyalty and involvement by assigning titles and tasks to as many different people as possible. At the February 13 meeting to which Crook had invited Hyde, twelve vice-presidents were chosen. Hyde's reputation as poet, scholar, and active participant in the language movement made him a desirable person for such a post. He was given two tasks. One was to translate a selection from the sagas sufficient to fill eight or nine volumes of a new Irish Saga series to be published by Fisher Unwin. The other was to write a guide to Gaelic literature for a second series, to be undertaken by a proposed subsidiary of the society tentatively called the Irish Publishing Company, of which Sir Charles Gavan Duffy (the Young Irelander of the forties, editor-founder of the *Nation,* and former prime minister of Australia) had agreed to serve as director.

On February 17, Yeats arranged a luncheon at which he introduced Hyde to David Garnett, the reader for Fisher Unwin who was interested in the idea of the Irish Saga series. Attentive, courteous, and grateful for Hyde's cooperation, Yeats insisted that in the evening Hyde visit his home in Bedford Park to meet Dr. Todhunter. With Todhunter, described in Hyde's diary as "a thin, distinguished looking man, of medium build, with finely chiselled features" whose wife's sister was a Dublin acquaintance, Hyde spent a pleasant few hours discussing folklore in general and Irish and Norse tales in particular. On the way back to his hotel he stopped at the National Liberal Club where he hoped he might have a cigar and a glass of punch with Crook. To his dismay Tim Healy was also at the club. Reluctant even to lay eyes on the man he regarded as the scoundrel who had brought down Parnell,

Hyde studiously avoided speaking to him. But nothing could spoil his elation at feeling himself involved in the future once again.

The following week Miss Butcher, whom Hyde had met at Lord Monteagle's, had arranged for him to stay at the home of her friends, the Protheros, in Cambridge. The Prothero home seemed to him to be constantly filled with a variety of interesting and talented people whom he would have been content to stay and talk with, but Miss Butcher insisted on taking him to meet Sir Edward Burne-Jones. Although no more than sixty, the English painter seemed at first to Hyde to be "an old, grey-haired man, kindly, child-like, with a faraway look in his eyes." Hyde was therefore astonished to discover not only Burne-Jones's extraordinary interest in Ireland and Irish literature but the extent of his Irish library. Both of Hyde's books and almost every other recent publication of Irish interest were on the shelves, as well as the complete works of the French Celticist, d'Arbois de Jubainville. Moreover, to Hyde's great enjoyment, Burne-Jones talked at length on the current status of Irish literary studies, a subject on which he was also astonishingly well informed.

A week later Hyde returned to Dublin. Within a few days he kept his promise to himself and O'Growney to pay a visit to Maynooth. After an excellent lunch accompanied by champagne during which the two men discussed a recent essay by John MacNeill on the role of the clergy in preserving the Irish language, they toured the campus. So impressed was Hyde that he made notes for his diary: Total enrollment, 500. Students attend three lectures each day and study for over five hours more. They cannot have fires or friends in their rooms, or smoke, or speak at meals or in the quadrangles. During each of the first three years they are required to take both O'Growney's class and a class in English literature. Hyde could not help but admire the results: all the students spoke Latin competently and seemed well schooled in Shakespeare, Milton, and Macaulay. He wondered what would happen if such a regimen were instituted in New Brunswick. He was particularly interested in O'Growney's estimate that about two hundred students (forty percent of current enrollment) had some knowledge of Irish.

Before returning to Frenchpark, Hyde called on another friend, the historian and novelist Standish James O'Grady. Several other people, including a man named O'Clery, were there before him. With plans for new publishing projects on Irish subjects fresh in his mind, Hyde listened thoughtfully to their conversation, which included a discussion of the Irish novels based on early history and mythology on which

O'Grady was then working. Mrs. O'Grady, who read Hyde's hand, said that among the hundreds of hands she had examined she had never seen one more interesting or more unusual. She took an ink impression of it and urged him to "have great courage and self-confidence" for he had it in himself "to do great things." He left at about two o'clock in the morning, with curlews crying over his head. Whether from the bottle of wine he had drunk or the words of Mrs. O'Grady or the talk of promising prospects (he was not sure which), he was, he acknowledged, "a little tipsy."

Back in Frenchpark, Hyde sat down to work on *Love Songs* but also began making a list for Garnett of the titles he would recommend including in the Irish Saga series. With June came the sad news that the Frenches were leaving Ratra. A neighbor for twenty-five years, John French had been for Hyde a direct link with Seamas Hart. As a small boy Hyde had often followed Hart over Ratra meadow and bog, asking interminable questions, receiving Hart's laconic answers. As he grew older he and Hart and John French often went shooting together, sometimes accompanied by Hyde's father and two brothers. Ratra had been the place that he had missed most—especially in fall and spring—when he was in Canada. During the entire time that he was away in Dublin, London, and North America, it had reassured him to know that the Frenches would cheer up Annette if she grew lonely and would invite her for tennis or tea. He himself, in fact, had always been glad to receive an invitation from Ratra when Annette was on holiday and he was the one who was staying alone with his father in the glebe house. The loss struck him particularly in the middle of summer when his Oldfield aunts and his sister went off to Killarney for several weeks. On the one hand, with so much to do, Hyde was glad that there was little to tempt him away from his writing desk. On the other hand, it was strange to be without the people and activities that had been so closely woven into the fabric of his Frenchpark life.

Meanwhile, in Dublin, W. B. Yeats, John O'Leary, Dr. George Sigerson, Maud Gonne, J. F. Taylor, Alice and Mary Furlong, and others had been meeting informally to discuss plans for an Ireland-based affiliate of the Irish Literary Society, to be called the National Literary Society. They named a provisional committee and organized a June meeting in the Rotunda, attended by Hyde, at which they issued a statement of purpose which read in part, "Every Irish movement of recent years has drawn a great portion of its power from the literary movement started by Davis, but that movement is over, and it is not possible to live for ever upon the past. A living Ireland must have a living literature." A slate of candidates for office was drawn up and distributed, officers were chosen, and at an August meeting Douglas Hyde was elected president.

Hyde knew that he had not been Yeats's first choice for the top leadership role of the new society. Yeats had made no secret of the fact that he preferred John O'Leary for his managerial skills, but he had recommended Hyde for one of the vice-presidencies because of his persuasive powers and his prominence in the growing Gaelic Revival. The membership, however, resisted Yeats's political maneuvering (even O'Leary complained of the tactics that had been used to support him) and opted for Hyde as president—"not for any merit" on his part, Hyde wrote to James Jeffrey Roche, but because he was "a good neutral figurehead." Yeats accepted the rebuff more or less gracefully until Duffy arrived, dismissed the statement read at the Rotunda, and substituted his own publication choices for the list of books and authors that had been drawn up in London. The first was to be an historical essay by Thomas Davis. To Yeats this meant creating a memorial to the Young Ireland of the forties at the expense of Young Ireland of the nineties in complete opposition to everything the National Literary Society had planned. However, since Duffy's plans were not contradictory to the prospectus of the Irish Literary Society that had been printed in the February 6, 1892, issue of the *Freeman's Journal,* they were not rejected out of hand. A bitter debate developed. O'Leary sided with Yeats; Taylor and Sigerson sided with Duffy. For months heated arguments broke out at every National Literary Society meeting, often lasting well into the night. Some nights the participants came close to blows. "I was in the chair," Hyde complained, "and I had a hopeless task of trying to keep order." Yeats had a different view of the situation. Perceiving himself as a young David battling the old Goliath, he wanted neither neutrality nor order—he wanted support. Later he wrote scathingly of how he had been bested by Taylor while "Dr. Hyde, 'most popular of men,' sat dreaming of his old white cockatoo in faraway Roscommon." In the end all arguments proved moot, for Duffy was not able to raise the money needed to fund the proposed publishing company; all that could be salvaged of the project were a few titles that were undertaken by Fisher Unwin at the recommendation of Garnett in consultation with Rolleston and Hyde. Among these—it looked like a compromise but more likely was based on what was then complete or nearly complete and readily available—were Davis's *Patriot Parlia-*

ment of 1689, the selection by Duffy that had begun the dissension, and Hyde's *Story of Early Gaelic Literature.*

In the fall of 1892—already overcommitted, with *Love Songs of Connacht* in its final stages and *The Story of Early Gaelic Literature* in progress—Hyde's third pressing task was to compose a presidential address to be delivered in Leinster House on Molesworth Street on November 25. Sponsored by the National Literary Society, the event was to be open by subscription to the public. There was really no time left for refereeing shouting matches and giving pep talks to individual men and women who had expressed an interest in knowing more about the society. There was no time either, to Hyde's regret, for the Dublin or Big House social life that ordinarily he enjoyed. Even shooting, usually his principal recreation of the season, had to be curtailed. Summer tennis and teas had provided the usual opportunities, but he allowed no flirtations to occupy him. The women mentioned in his diary or letter book were primarily old friends such as Frances Crofton and Maud Gonne or members of the London or the Dublin literary society. From time to time he received a note from the Fräulein in Canada.

In October the Oldfields gave a large party. Hyde could not excuse himself without offending them. He chatted agreeably with aunts, uncles, and cousins, exchanged personal news with people he had not seen for a time, and met a young Englishwoman, Lucy Cometina Kurtz, a new friend whom Annette had encountered the previous summer in Killarney. From then on until November 25, except for meetings, his time was spent almost exclusively in the library of the Royal Irish Academy or at home at his writing desk. Tickets for the National Literary Society event were going well at a shilling apiece, he had been told. Hyde was pleased. He felt that he had selected a good topic for the occasion. Dr. Sigerson's inaugural address, delivered in August, had been "On the Origin, Influence, and Environment of Irish Literature." Entertaining and informative, it had been an education for many people who had been unaware of the extent of their ignorance on the subject. Hyde had welcomed it as a good introduction to his own lecture, "On the Necessity for De-Anglicising the Irish People." Particular interest in his topic had been generated by notices and news items in the *United Ireland* and *Weekly Freeman* which suggested that in their twin presentations he and Sigerson were in fact setting the tone and establishing the level of discourse of the new Literary Society. A few correspondents from the press had expressed curiosity about the meaning of his title.

He had declined to go into detail, and now they stood ready, their pencils poised, to examine what he had to say.

Although Hyde had revised his address again and again, he was still not satisfied with it on the morning of November 25. In the academy library he sat writing and rewriting almost to the moment when he had to leave for Leinster House. There he immediately saw that the turnout was good. He had been told that over a hundred people had subscribed in advance. The press was present. So were a number of people whose reaction and response would be very important to him personally as well as to the society. The moment came for him to speak. He heard the sound of his own voice. It carried well in the hall, rolling into the far corners and spreading to the side walls without a hint of a resonant echo. One hour and twenty minutes later his voice stopped. It was over. No one had fallen asleep; no one had walked out. The applause was satisfying. He had done a good job, he told himself. Then, smiling and shaking hands, he prepared himself to hear the opinions of others.

W. P. Ryan called Hyde's address "sensational," a statement on which he elaborated positively two years later in his overview of the period, *The Irish Literary Revival*. W. B. Yeats reported that as the audience left the hall he heard someone say that it was "the most important utterance of its kind since '48." Reviews in the nationalist newspapers ranged from approving to enthusiastic. On December 3 the *United Ireland* carried an editorial in which the writer declared, "I have no hesitation in saying that it was one of the best, and, what is better, one of the most practical lectures on a National topic I have heard for a long time." Most of the other nationalist newspapers concurred. Many called for immediate publication. Even the usually hostile *Irish Times*— then very much a Castle paper—could find nothing more biting to print than the curiously ambivalent statement that nowhere else in the world would "an able, well-educated man" get away with saying the things that Hyde had said. The reviews had a healthy impact on public perception of the National Literary Society. Meetings to further its aims increased in different parts of the country; other cultural societies sought affiliation; and (largely through the efforts of Maud Gonne) the planned book distribution project was launched. Nor was Hyde's success attributable simply to his heady rhetoric. On the contrary, according to W. P. Ryan, Hyde's lecture had gone "to the heart of a national evil which was preying on Irish life like a cancer."

What Hyde meant by deanglicization, the idea that captured his listeners' imagination, was simple, subtle, and bold. Giuseppi Mazzini had said that the Irish ought to be content to belong to the United Kingdom, as they had lost their "notes of nationalism"—language and custom—and consequently no longer had an identity of their own. Hyde challenged the people of Ireland to prove that the Italian patriot was wrong. Item by item, he reviewed with them the evidence that appeared to support Mazzini's remark and established that nothing had been lost beyond recovery, that where the Irish "notes of nationalism" had been suppressed they survived beneath a veneer of anglicization that was easily removed. Nor did he advocate an immediate and wholesale stripping of this veneer from Irish life. On the contrary: it would be foolish, he declared, to give up the best of what Ireland had borrowed from England and made its own. The English language and English customs could live in harmony with the native tongue and native traditions, if that was what people wanted. But to have a choice, both English and Irish had to be openly and freely available to everybody, with no false value being attached to one or stigma to the other.

What had to end, Hyde avowed, was the self-destructive and contradictory simultaneous hating and aping of the English that had been going on for two hundred years and more. What had to stop was the self-defeating clamor to be recognized as a distinct nation even as the distinguishing characteristics of Irish nationality, language, and custom were being discarded. If an Irishman could become a good Englishman, he thundered, there would be no problem. But as hard as some tried, as often as others had been stripped of their Celtic characteristics, they had not been able to divest themselves of the mantle of the past. It was now time for both Unionists and nationalists to accept that mantle, to transform their dim consciousness of the shaping force of place and tradition into an active and potent feeling, and thus to increase their sense of self-respect and of honor.

To the question of how to proceed, Hyde had practical answers: by arresting the decay of the Irish language and rediscovering its honorable roots in antiquity so that native speakers might use it with pride; by linking past with present by employing traditional Irish personal and place names; by enjoying traditional Irish music and games; by preserving traditional Irish customs and habits of dress; by reading Irish and Anglo-Irish books. In conclusion he appealed to everyone, whatever his or her politics, whether unionist or nationalist, to help the Irish, "even at the risk of encouraging national aspirations," to become again what they once were: "one of the most original, artistic, literary, and charming peoples of Europe."

Practiced in the art of arousing an audience, Hyde made his points not once but several times, each time from a different perspective, thus reinforcing without repeating. He anticipated questions and objections; he provided anecdotal evidence; he appealed to emotion as well as intellect. Deanglicization would not be easy, he warned: it would require that his listeners examine themselves for the latent West-Britonism that some had allowed to settle inside themselves. He promised, however, that out of their efforts would come the reward of recovering their personal and national identity—first and most easily, perhaps, in their music, then in their customs and games, then in their history and literature, and finally in their minds and hearts.

What Hyde proposed offered something for everyone within a national context. It touched the common sensitive nerve concerned with belonging. It allowed even the most committed Irish Unionists, who traced their lineage through generations of English ancestors living in Ireland, to distinguish themselves from the English of England and explain their Irish roots through place rather than race. It provided a more acceptable alternative to Irish nationalists who hitherto had had to choose, both actually and metaphorically, between throwing rocks and hiding under them. It required no either/or commitment but suggested a range of individual nationalist behavior that could be as nonassertive as singing an Irish song or playing an Irish game or as assertive as immediate and thorough self-deanglicization. Because it was not coercive, it did not invite a coercive response.

The essential point of Hyde's address was that national identity was not something that had to be awaited through long and patient suffering or seized by violence but was available to every Irish man or woman who would simply deanglicize—that is, give up imitating the English. It was foolish, he declared, to express a hatred of the English and at the same time adopt English names, English customs, and English culture. It was equally foolish to reject a bilingual, bicultural solution when, as in the case of language, it might be necessary to employ English in certain contexts without there being any reason to use it in another. In discarding what was their own, he pointed out, the Irish had thrown away the best claim they had to the right to be recognized as a separate and equal nationality. To regain that claim, they now had to discard what they had not made their own and indeed what they did not want or need.

For Douglas Hyde, the radical and revolutionary doctrine of deanglicization, delivered at a time when for many people the alternatives appeared to be only acquiescence or violence, made his National Literary Society presidential address the most important speech of his career. He was immediately invited to talk on the same subject in Cork on January 23, 1893. Two weeks after the Cork lecture, on February 9, Hyde spoke to the literary society in Dublin about Irish books that had been published during the past year. A week later he presided at a lecture presented by Standish O'Grady. On February 28 he took the night ferry to London to attend a March 1 meeting of the Irish Literary Society. At the meeting he was introduced to Alfred Perceval Graves and Stopford Brooke. Brooke's lecture to the society, on the English language as a medium for the Irish people, interested Hyde particularly. He liked Brooke, who invited him and Rolleston to dinner and who turned out to be not only a good lecturer but an intelligent and amusing conversationalist. Unfortunately, Hyde's days were so full that they had no chance to meet again during this London trip, but they vowed that they would make a point of seeing each other in the future.

March 3 was filled with appointments with publishers; March 4, with a meeting of the council of the Irish Literary Society; March 5, with an afternoon lecture and dinner with the Todhunters; March 6, with an examination by a new eye specialist, a visit to the British Museum, and a dinner party at the home of Fisher Unwin. The next week had fewer meetings but more social engagements: lunches, dinners, theater; a visit to the British Museum and Parliament and to the Grafton Galleries to see an exhibition of Impressionist paintings; long talks with Lady Wilde, Francis Fahy, and John Redmond; and social calls on the Protheros, Miss Butcher, and others. On March 17 Hyde "drowned the shamrock" in champagne with Rolleston. On March 23 he returned to Dublin. By the end of the first week in April he was relieved to be again in Roscommon, enjoying the unhurried quiet of Frenchpark after months of frantic activity, and putting the finishing touches to the manuscript of *Love Songs of Connacht,* which was about to go to press. Already the days were longer, and there was a pleasant warmth to the sun that appeared between April showers. Annette had invited Lucy Kurtz for a visit. Hyde remembered meeting her in October at the Oldfields' party and hearing much about her from his sister and his aunts, but he had not seen her since.

Lucy Kurtz was tall and slim, with a mass of wavy hair, an oval face, high cheekbones, large and expressive eyes, a slender, acquiline nose, and full womanly lips. Annette had been particularly eager to introduce her to Douglas not only because she herself enjoyed Lucy's company but because she knew that he liked educated, clever, and independent women. Their Oldfield aunts also approved of her, which Annette took to be a good sign. Her brother Oldfield, unmarried and remote from his family, seemed cynical and lonely on the rare occasions when they met. She knew he had been disappointed in love as well as in other aspirations; she remembered his dismay in 1887 when he did not succeed in his application for an appointment as resident magistrate. Both she and her aunts agreed that little could be hoped from him. But for Douglas, who was charming and gregarious and who enjoyed the company of women, marriage to a compatible wife would be an advantage. Surely it would relieve their anxieties if he were married and settled in Ireland, for then perhaps there would be no more talk of his going back to America. A good marriage, they assured each other, might even help him secure the university position in Ireland that continued to elude him.

Annette had anticipated the situation correctly: Douglas and Lucy were immediately attracted to each other. At the end of Lucy's April visit Annette prevailed on her to return in May, before she went home to England. After their fortnight together in May, Lucy and Douglas began to exchange letters, usually in German. She was a witty and charming if sometimes saucy correspondent. "Mr. Know-it-all," she called him, when he insisted too much on his own ideas. Hyde's diary was neglected as he devoted his time to their increasingly frequent playful and teasing correspondence. The only entry he made in June, on the twenty-fifth, began exuberantly, "ANNETTE AND MISS KURTZ CAME HOME." During July there was again not a single entry in his diary until two days before the end of the month when he wrote:

I do not remember exactly what we did. . . . However, things took their course, between hope and despair, certainty and uncertainty, doubt and assurance, anxiety and confidence, but each day the net was closing about my neck until we decided firmly and finally that we were going to get married, and we were publicly engaged.

As the news spread, cousins, friends, and neighbors flooded the couple with invitations to luncheons, dinners, and teas. To Douglas's delight he was able to arrange a lease with John French that would allow them to live at Ratra, from the beginning of 1894, for fifty pounds a year. Eager to become a full partner in Douglas's life, on July 21 Lucy accompanied Hyde to Athenry, where they stayed with the Roches near Monivea and she enjoyed the company of the neighboring Dalys,

Frenches, and Blakes while he wrote stories and songs from the mouth of an old man and spoke Irish with him and with other local people. On July 29 Hyde and Lucy went to Dublin. There, between shopping for furniture, sitting for photographs, and more visits to friends and relatives, Hyde managed to spend the evening of July 30 with Sigerson and O'Neill Russell and attend the short afternoon meeting on July 31 in Martin Kelly's rooms at 9 Lower Sackville Street* at which, almost parenthetically, the Gaelic League was founded.

On August 1, Lucy sailed for England, and the furious letter writing resumed. Now their correspondence (usually beginning "Dear Muffin" and still almost entirely in German) was less playful, more serious. In one letter Lucy discreetly referred to Hyde's relationship with the Fräulein of Fredericton; in another she responded emotionally— "You must not go to Canada without me!"—to news that again Hyde was considering a position in North America. Hyde filled his letters to her with a complete account of all his activities. Interested in everything that involved him, even the Irish language (proudly she scattered the phrases he had taught her through her letters and assured him that he would be astonished when he saw how rapidly she would learn more), she responded with comments and questions and a full account of her own, including her latest successes in the investment market. She had been dabbling in stocks, she told him—initially to the horror of her brothers—for several years. But as her cautious and astute analyses had brought her a considerable return on her money (in addition to her other attributes, she clearly had a good head for business), they no longer said a word against it and indeed sometimes asked her advice.

Although someone had said that Lucy was "half Austrian, half West Indian," and Hyde had later repeated this description to John O'Leary, she was in fact, according to Diarmid Coffey, a descendant of "a distinguished Würtemberg family" that had settled for a time in Odessa before coming to England in 1815. Among the Kurtzes who had arrived in 1815 were Lucy's great-uncle, a distinguished research chemist, and her father, Charles Kurtz, who was then only a boy. Charles Kurtz had been educated at Trinity College, where he studied chemistry; he then had gone to work for his uncle, also as a research chemist. According to Coffey, Lucy's great-uncle and father had prudently invested the comfortable fortune they earned from their profession in works of

* Unofficially called O'Connell Street between 1882 and 1922; officially O'Connell Street since 1922.

art. Charles Kurtz had married a Miss Hill whose father was "an English West Indian planter of good family." When Kurtz died in 1880 (apparently preceded by his wife, as nothing is said of her having survived him) his art collection had been valued at £27,000. He had left four children, of whom Lucy was the only daughter and the youngest child. At the time when Lucy and Annette met in Killarney, Lucy already had inherited three thousand pounds from her father; still pending when she and Douglas married was a share of profits from property sold by the court that she would later receive. Eventually she became the beneficiary also of substantial amounts from the residual estates of her three brothers, Charles, Alexander, and Harold.

Hyde remained in Dublin, mostly on Gaelic League business, for a few days following Lucy's departure. The session on July 31 (so casually mentioned in his 1893 diary, so significant later in restrospect) had been the outcome of efforts, principally by John MacNeill, to bring together a number of men with new ideas about how and why the Irish language ought to be preserved. It was he who had sent out a printed letter on June 12 to a number of people, including Hyde, asking if they would attend a planning session for the development of an organization to "maintain and promote the use of Gaelic as a *spoken language in Ireland*." Hyde had responded immediately and affirmatively, in a letter that included specific recommendations drawn from his 1891 observations of the Irish language study groups he had visited in Boston and New York. The emphasis, he declared, must be on the spoken language: "There is no other way to revive Irish," he insisted, "than for a crowd of people to spread it." He preferred, he said, five people speaking Irish to ten people trying to read it.

Hyde and MacNeill met by prearrangement to introduce themselves to each other in the library of the Royal Irish Academy shortly before the July 31 session in Kelly's rooms. Hyde was impressed not only by MacNeill's Irish but also by the fact that while waiting for him MacNeill had been reading the Book of Leinster. The others they joined on Sackville Street were Martin Kelly, C. P. Bushe, J. M. Cogan, the Reverend William Hayden, S.J., P. J. Hogan, Patrick O'Brien, and T. O'Neill Russell. As president of the National Literary Society, Hyde volunteered to arrange time and space for future meetings in the society's quarters at 4 College Green. At the first of these, held on August 4, Hyde was elected president and J. H. Lloyd honorary treasurer. The first order of business, everyone agreed, was to enlarge the membership, so for a time they proposed to retain their Dublin base.

Nevertheless, all sessions were to be Irish-speaking, and to encourage conversations in Irish and otherwise emphasize that Irish was a *living* language, the organizers agreed on a format that would include free admission to readings and lectures in Irish at each weekly meeting. Even before Hyde left Dublin to return to Frenchpark, George Sigerson, David Comyn, and Michael Cusack had been added to the membership list. Their support was expected. More heartening to the organizers, in the weeks and months that followed, was that there were raw recruits as well. This was by no means insignificant in a city in which, as W. P. Ryan observed, new Irish societies rose and died "with perplexing regularity." Writing in the *Gaelic Journal* in August, John MacNeill attributed the instant success of the league to the fact that the idea had been in the air for a long time. He cited particularly the arguments that had been "put forward by Dr. Hyde in New York" just two years before. He emphasized that literature in Irish would be left in other hands— that the league would concentrate on spreading Irish as a spoken language.

Before leaving Dublin, Hyde made sure that everything was in order in both the league and the Literary Society. By mid-August he was in Roscommon, arranging his own affairs, enjoying the shooting season that he had missed during the previous year, and contemplating his future. He had taken care in July, when he had struck his bargain with John French, to guarantee his shooting privileges over the meadows and bogs familiar to him from the time he had learned to hold a gun. The July 20 agreement was drawn up to last, with renewals, until 1910. It gave Hyde exclusive rights to shoot certain bogs near Ratra. In return the tenants and "occupiers" promised to preserve the game on their land for him and to keep off all others. For these privileges he agreed to pay eight pounds immediately and three pounds each year for the next four years to twenty-five tenants, all but one of whom signed with an *X*.

Six weeks after his return to Frenchpark, Hyde was back in Dublin; on October 9 he sailed for Liverpool, where he was met by Lucy, who brought him to the home of the Caroes, the family of the Danish consul, with whom he was to spend the night. Hyde's diary for October 10, 1893, begins, "MY WEDDING DAY." A carriage arrived to take him to the church, then returned to pick up Lucy. The priest, a Mr. Winslow, married them "straight out of the book" despite Hyde's request that he omit certain parts of the Church of England ceremony. "I got my own back on him," he wrote in his diary, "when I signed my name in Irish in the register."

Douglas and Lucy spent their honeymoon in France, the country he loved best after Ireland. They went first to Paris where they visited Douglas's favorite places, the bookstalls on the Seine and the Bibliothèque Nationale, as well as the new Eiffel Tower, erected for the exposition of 1889. From Paris they traveled south by rail to the Riviera, in part along the route he had first seen with Mackey Wilson, to whom he dearly wished he could introduce his new bride. In Nice they visited Sir Charles Gavan Duffy who was hungry for political anecdotes about Ireland. Duffy had moved to France with his wife and three daughters in 1880, following his retirement as prime minister of Australia. From Nice they went on to Monaco for a few days and then began their return. On their way home they stopped in England to attend the London theater and visit Lucy's brothers.

By November 17 Lucy and Hyde were in Dublin, visiting Hyde's Oldfield aunts and again making the rounds of luncheons, teas, and dinners in their honor. On November 22 Hyde recited the Irish text of "Monachar and Manachar," a folktale he had translated for Yeats's *Fairy and Folk Tales of the Irish Peasantry,* at a meeting of the Gaelic League. The next day he and Yeats attended a meeting of the council of the National Literary Society. A paper he had promised to read to the Gaelic League on November 29 had to be cancelled on account of a cold, but he attended the meeting. Thus having taken care of his Dublin obligations, on December 1 Hyde bought a brougham for thirty-three pounds. On December 3 he and Lucy received a warm welcome in Roscommon. "WE CAME HOME," began his diary entry for December 3. At the first crossroads out of Ballaghaderreen hundreds of people were waiting to welcome them with music and cheers. Across the road an arch covered with ivy carried a green banner reading *"Fáilte"* (welcome) in large letters. Similar arches and crowds greeted them at other points along the way. At the road into Ratra, under another green arch, the crowd unharnessed the horse and themselves drew the brougham into the yard with "such shouting and hullabaloo you never heard." Douglas responded with half-barrels of porter, sent out to the crowds gathered at each arch, then went to the glebe house to see his father. The Reverend Arthur Hyde was not well. He had been spending most of his time in bed, Douglas was told. One hand was badly swollen, and he had a touch of eczema.

In December 1893, in his usual summary inserted in his diary at the end of each year, Hyde wrote, "The greatest thing I did in the past year indeed, the greatest thing I ever did in my life— was that I got married." For the moment it seemed, at least to his sister Annette and his Oldfield aunts, that this happily uxorious man would remain content at home, writing his books, perhaps eventually teaching in Dublin, where there were again rumors of a possible future appointment. What they had not reckoned with was the Gaelic League, now nearly six months old and growing, against all the conventional wisdom that had predicted its early demise. In March 1894, when an Irish Language Congress was held in the Mansion House in Dublin, under the presidency of Lord Mayor Valentine Dillon, more than half the addresses were delivered in Irish by Gaelic League members. In September 1894 the league's first annual report showed that membership had grown from the nine founders who had met in Dublin on July 31, 1893, to three hundred men and women scattered throughout the country—and that its budget came exclusively from members' dues. By the beginning of its second year the Gaelic League had branches in Dublin, Cork, Galway, Derry, and New Ross. By its third year it had seventeen branches in Ireland, four in England, and one in Scotland, while in the United States three Irish societies (in Chicago, Boston, and San Francisco) had all come under its umbrella. It was this continuing phenomenon that later led Yeats to write, in a poem addressed "Dear Craoibhin Aoibhin":

> You've dandled them and fed them from the book
> And know them to the bone; impart to us—
> We'll keep the secret—a new trick to please.
> Is there a bridle for this Proteus
> That turns and changes like his draughty seas?

10

The Happiest of Men

In January, 1894 Douglas Hyde was the happiest of men. He was married to a charming and intelligent young woman, a friend of his sister and a favorite of his aunts, who was interested in everything that interested him and whose personal income placed no strain on his own financial resources. Their home was Ratra, a bright and spacious Georgian house overlooking Lough Gara that he had loved as long as he could remember. From its windows he could see in the distance Rathcroghan, the Sligo mountains, and the steeple of St. Nathy's cathedral in Ballaghaderreen. The meadows and bogs that he surveyed were his to shoot; the neighboring cottages were those in which he had grown up, sitting by the fire, sipping poteen, listening to stories and gossip and song. His father was failing, but along with old age and infirmity had come a milder disposition that was almost gentle at times. Sitting beside his bed, talking about Trinity, cricket, well-known sermons by well-known clergymen, and the Cork relatives—the latter, vivid memories to his father, to himself scarcely more than names—Douglas often wondered if the stormy days of his youth had really happened or were just bad dreams, the result of eating too much beef or mixing wine and whiskey.

From the day of their return home in December the Hydes were flooded with mail. Much of it was social, consisting of invitations and good wishes to which Lucy in her charming way quickly directed her attention. As soon as she could she also set about arranging the furniture, working with the seamstress who was making new curtains and

193

cushions, writing long lists of items that were needed to stock kitchen, pantry, and cellar, and otherwise turning this house that Hyde had always loved into their home. His large and comfortable study was conducive to work. He soon had it arranged just the way he liked it, with a semiorganized clutter of books and papers piled on the floor around his desk, where he could easily reach them. There was no problem with the housekeeping staff, no series of *novae ancillae*. The Mahons and Morrisroes, an extended family of old friends whom he had known since he was a boy, lived just outside the gate or in the cluster of neat little houses with pretty gardens along the road. They had taken care of Ratra, house and gardens, inside and out, for almost as long, he imagined, as it had stood there.

Mail that could not be answered by Lucy included letters from publishers and reviewers, people seeking assistance or recommendations or proposing new projects, professional friends, and fellow scholars, plus memoranda and notices from the various organizations to which Hyde belonged. Among the new books received were his *Love Songs of Connacht* and *Contes Irlandais*. Both had been published in 1893, a year that had gone by in such haste that even now, looking back on it, Hyde was astonished that he had been able to accomplish anything at all. Before him was the evidence to the contrary: reviews of *Love Songs*; reports of business that had been transacted in accordance with resolutions that had passed at meetings he had attended; ongoing correspondence concerning work in progress. The earliest of the reviews he had in hand had appeared in the *Speaker* on July 13. It had been followed by reviews in the *Spectator* (August 12), the *Daily Chronicle* (August 21), the *Belfast Irish News* (August 28), the *Daily News* (September 1), *United Ireland* (September 2), the *Weekly Sun* (September 3), *Truth* (September 14), the *Star* (September 14), and *Literary World* (September 29). Others he had not yet received included some that had been published in America.

Earlier—last year, in fact—Hyde had received advance copies of *Love Songs* that he had sent to the usual list of friends and professional associates. *Contes Irlandais*, a handsome book in a gray-green wrapper, was one he had not previously seen. A French companion to (but not copy of) *Beside the Fire*, it contained Georges Dottin's translations of selected stories from *Leabhar Sgeulaigheachta*, printed together with the Irish on facing pages. A lecturer at Rennes and editor of the *Annales de Bretagne* who had been trained by the famous French Celticist d'Arbois de Jubainville, Dottin had first written to Hyde in 1889 or 1890, to compliment him on both the contents and methodology of his Irish "book of storytelling" and to propose a collaboration: he would, Dottin said, translate the stories of *Leabhar Sgeulaigheachta* into French for publication with the original Irish texts in successive issues of the *Annales,* if Hyde would check his French translations and read proofs of the Irish. The first fruit of this joint endeavor had appeared in Dottin's journal in 1892, the second in 1893. Meanwhile, Hyde himself had translated half the stories into English for *Beside the Fire,* a bilingual edition published by David Nutt in which Irish and English were printed on facing pages. (This was the book he had had so much trouble getting a copy of when he was in Canada.) Dottin, with his usual efficiency, had had his own copy sent to him in Rennes and—even before Hyde himself had seen *Beside the Fire*—had written to suggest to Hyde a similar French-and-Irish edition of the remaining *Leabhar Sgeulaigheachta* stories. This, then, was the handsome book in the green wrappers that Hyde had just received. Glancing through the French translations of his Irish texts, Hyde was again reminded of the affinity that so often in the past—first, when he was just a boy—he had perceived between French and Irish. As the Irish stories had slipped easily into French, so his collaboration with Dottin had ripened quickly into a warm friendship.

Little had Hyde realized when he first began working on *Leabhar Sgeulaigheachta* how much his "book of storytelling" would bring back to him. In its way it had some characteristics of the magical tales to be found between its covers. The publication of *Leabhar Sgeulaigheachta* had initiated his correspondence with a number of other scholars abroad, in addition to Dottin. In 1889 it had had an unusually good beginning sale for a book of its kind. Even now, five years after publication, it was still selling steadily, although of course not so well as the newer *Love Songs* or the bilingual *Beside the Fire.* He had the facts before him in his publishers' year-end statements for 1893. He knew, moreover, that there well could be an increase in its readership in the future, if the Gaelic League developed and prospered: O'Growney already had discussed with him his concern that, to maintain emphasis on *spoken* Irish, the league would need texts from the oral rather than the literary tradition for its beginning Irish classes. The Reverend Edmund Hogan (the latter's book *Distinguished Irishmen of the 16th Century* had just been announced) had written to him some years ago, before the founding of the league, about the suitability of *Leabhar Sgeulaigheachta* as a text for new students of Irish. It was a subject to discuss with

O'Growney, who had been in Scotland in July 1893 when the league was founded, but whose commitment to the revival of the Irish language was so well known that he had been appointed vice-president in absentia and was now working on exactly this question of appropriate texts.

The publishing project that required Hyde's attention at the moment, however, was *The Story of Early Gaelic Literature,* one of the few titles that had been salvaged from the Yeats-Duffy debacle that had ended with the decision to abandon the Irish Publishing Company proposed in 1892. The manuscript was now with Fisher Unwin; publication was scheduled for 1895. Also slated for publication by Fisher Unwin in 1895 was Hyde's translation *The Three Sorrows of Storytelling*: it was all that had come of the ambitious "Irish Saga series in seven or eight volumes" that he and Yeats had discussed with Garnett, Fisher Unwin's reader, at a long lunch in February 1892, when the Irish Literary Society had just been organized and everyone was optimistic about what it might accomplish.

Some of the mail Hyde had received concerned the London-based Irish Literary Society as well as the National Literary Society in Dublin and the Gaelic League. Many members of the London-based society, it seemed, reviewing the optimistic plans of 1892, were unhappy about its current lack of activity. There *were* problems: Duffy was still president, but he lived most of the year in Nice, and in any case he had become somewhat disaffected during the controversy over the Irish Publishing Company. T. W. Rolleston, who had been an efficient and active secretary, had moved to Dublin last summer to manage the Irish Industries Association. Rolleston had been succeeded by Alfred Perceval Graves in the post of acting secretary, but as so many council members were scattered far and wide (including Hyde himself, W. B. Yeats, and others, who were usually to be found in Ireland), Graves lacked a clear mandate to do anything of real significance on his own. Meanwhile the National Literary Society, which Hyde continued to serve as president, was apparently thriving, and he had had good news also of the first-year growth of the Gaelic League. Hyde believed that it would succeed, for as John MacNeill had said in his report of the league's first two meetings, the idea for a "more popular and practical" movement to revive Irish had "long been in the air." The emphasis on speaking Irish rather than simply talking about it, as had been the practice in the Society for the Preservation of the Irish Language and even to a certain extent in the Gaelic Union, had received a good response.

So had the focus on texts from the oral rather than the literary tradition. There had not been, as some feared, a dearth of qualified people willing to present a short recitation or reading in Irish which others attending might listen to and discuss. The format adopted on August 4, 1893, provided both ample time for such discussion and—more important, perhaps—a common subject that subtly prescribed, for the benefit of beginners, the limits of vocabulary needed. The long-range plan, toward which the organizers wanted to move as soon as it was feasible, was to establish a branch wherever there were enough people to carry on a similar program, with Dublin headquarters providing whatever help was needed.

What was popular and practical about the Gaelic League was not only its *modus operandi* but its decision to leave the preservation of the literary tradition to others and (following the course that Hyde, Mac-Neill, and O'Growney had been advocating) focus on the neglected and more seriously endangered state of the oral Irish tradition of native speakers. This was an aspect of revivalism with which Hyde had been consistently concerned even as a young member of the Society for the Preservation of the Irish Language, for in the Frenchpark of his boyhood he had witnessed firsthand the last days of a dying Gaeltacht in which each year the number of Irish speakers declined dramatically, and with them the number of stories, songs, and poems that were part of their heritage. Teaching Irish grammar to English speakers in Dublin and providing them with exercises that helped them speak Irish the way it was written in books was of little use in preserving the language; it did nothing at all to save the Gaeltacht or keep ordinary Irish people in touch with their ancient and honorable cultural heritage or provide them with the sense of a nation. Whatever well-meaning antiquarians and romantics might proclaim to each other, it could not compensate for the fact that in Irish-speaking districts, everything possible was being done to make native Irish speakers ashamed of their language, ashamed of the poverty and ignorance they were told that they brought on themselves and their children by continuing to use it, ashamed of belonging to an Irish nation. By encouraging the use of Irish among people of all classes, (*not* as a replacement for English, for as Hyde had said over and over again, this was obviously both impossible and undesirable for practical reasons), the Gaelic League hoped to reverse the trend that otherwise was sure to lead to extinction of the language within the next generation and with it all sense of a nation, all personal experience as a member of a uniquely Irish civilization.

It was the threat of this irreversible loss that Hyde had deplored privately in his diaries and publicly in speeches and essays ever since he himself realized what had gone from the world with the death of men like Seamas Hart. Its implications had led him first to collect and then to preserve through publication the endangered stories, songs, and poems of the Irish oral tradition. Even this, of course, was an expedient, as he had explained many times. In his notes to *Leabhar Sgeulaigheachta*, he had described in detail the problems of translating spoken language into the language of print. In his preface to *Beside the Fire* (1890), he had documented the ways in which "the waves of materialism and civilization combined" were destroying oral tradition. In his preface to *Love Songs of Connacht*, he had lamented the "unavoidable ignorance of the modern Irish idiom" among the educated Irish that had left the transmission and interpretation of Irish culture to native speakers, who were becoming fewer every day. As a result even the "great philologists and etymologists" were now prevented, he said, from having direct contact with the tradition.

What the Gaelic League proposed to do—what Hyde had advocated in many of his speeches and essays—was, first, to provide the kind of opportunity for instruction and practice in *spoken* Irish that would result in its more natural use outside the Gaeltacht; second, to involve the people of the Gaeltacht in this project; and finally, to pressure the government into improving the quality of education in the Gaeltacht by providing instruction in Irish for Irish-speaking children. The goals of other nineteenth-century societies had focused on the printed word. Whether or not these innovative ideas would work remained to be seen.

In the first few years as league president, Hyde's principal task was to travel to communities that sought to establish a branch, address its members, meet its committees, consult with its priests, teachers, and civil servants, and talk informally with everyone involved, especially the young men and women. It was also his responsibility to identify in each community a qualified teacher of Irish who would provide weekly instruction for a moderate set fee. If no such teacher was available, Hyde had the authority to arrange for a substitute, preferably from the Gaeltacht, to come once a week to give the necessary instruction. Eugene O'Growney already had begun work on lessons in Irish for use by league members. These were being published first in the *Weekly Freeman* (later, in the *Gaelic Journal*) and then in book form under the title *Simple Lessons in Irish*. The first books appeared in 1894, at about the same time as the doctors identified the cause of O'Growney's declining health as tuberculosis. In October he was sent by Maynooth to Arizona where it was hoped that the dry air and sunshine would help his recovery. He did not improve, nor was he happy in America. In September 1895, after receiving the second of two sad and discouraged letters from him, Hyde wrote asking O'Growney to come to Ratra, where he would be well looked after and would have a home as long as he wished. By then, however, the disease had gone too far to permit the long and tiring journey back to Ireland. Thus sentenced to exile, in 1896 O'Growney resigned his post at Maynooth. He tried also to resign his league vice-presidency, but the Coiste Gnótha (executive committee) refused. During the next three years league travelers to America made a point of going to see him if they possibly could. Although their reports were distressing, O'Growney did manage to continue writing occasional articles for the *Weekly Freeman*. He died in Los Angeles on October 18, 1899, leaving all rights to *Simple Lessons* to the league. For a number of years these books, continued by John MacNeill, provided the league with a handsome source of income. Grateful Irish Americans who knew how painful his exile had been raised a subscription to return O'Growney's body to Ireland. When he was reburied at Maynooth in 1901 a mourning Hyde, publicly overcome by private sorrow, kissed O'Growney's coffin and wiped tears from his eyes. Only the deaths of Seamas Hart in 1875 and Mackey Wilson in 1887 had affected him so strongly.

In the early months of 1894, however, no one considered the consequences of losing O'Growney; concern focused on the need to respond to rapidly growing public interest in the Gaelic League. Much of the responsibility fell upon Hyde as league president. Since she enjoyed traveling and did not like to be left home alone, Lucy at first accompanied him on some of his trips around the country. But she was now no longer particularly keen on the league. During their courtship, enthusiastic about Hyde's lectures and books, she had been interested in learning Irish. But at that time she had seen herself as a woman of independent intellect and opinion, the future wife of a scholar, moving within socially and intellectually sophisticated circles. Then she began to meet members of the Gaelic League who clearly did not belong to these circles. She had difficulty feeling comfortable among them. Their familiar manner disconcerted her. She could not get used to the way in which shopkeepers, civil servants, and country people spoke to Hyde, as if he were one of them. It astonished her that he did not mind at all. For herself, she chose to go to Dublin whenever he had to be away.

But soon such travel was no longer an option, for she was expecting their first child. Isolated and unhappy, she developed a dislike of Ratra, Frenchpark, the whole of Roscommon, and especially of the Gaelic League that she never got over as long as she lived. Delighted with the prospect of parenthood, Hyde attributed Lucy's low spirits to the discomfort of pregnancy. He assured himself that when the baby was born her spirits would improve and with it her attitude toward her surroundings. Meanwhile he promised her that he would again make inquiries about a possible university appointment in Dublin, Cork, Belfast, or Galway. Nothing developed, and after Nuala was born Lucy did indeed feel better, but she remained visibly discontented in Frenchpark. Occupied with his writing and his work on behalf of the league, cheered by the happy personality of his outgoing little daughter, Hyde did not realize how deep-rooted Lucy's feelings were.

On the eleventh of February, 1896, less than four weeks after his own thirty-sixth birthday, Hyde received word of the death of his brother Oldfield. Although they had not seen much of each other in recent years, Hyde was saddened by the news. He could not help but remember Oldfield's brilliant academic record, how easily he had excelled at sports, his gentle understanding when young Arthur lay dying in Drumkilla. Three brothers they had been, and now two were gone. Of his father's five children there remained only himself and Annette. Thinking of his own children—Lucy was pregnant again, the baby was expected in June—he wondered what it must be like for his father to grow old and feeble watching his children die before him, one by one.

In March 1896 Hyde received word of still another professorship at Trinity. Keeping his promise to Lucy, he applied. He had, in fact, high hopes of succeeding, for his publication record was now much stronger than it had been in 1891, and this time the appointment was not in modern European languages and literature but in Irish. George Salmon, who had provided one of Hyde's letters of recommendation in 1891, was still provost at Trinity; Hyde fully expected that Salmon would support his candidacy. To his astonishment, again his application was not given serious consideration. This time, however, he was not left wondering why. His appointment, he learned, had been opposed by both Salmon (whom he had, he thought, no reason to distrust) and Robert Atkinson, professor of languages. Although willing to concede Hyde's scholarly qualifications, Salmon based his opposition on the fact that Hyde's chief interests were known to be political rather than philological. He had no doubt, he said, that if Hyde were appointed, he would use his position to advance his nationalist views. Atkinson's criticism was cloaked in professionalism. He knew nothing whatever of Hyde's political position, he maintained, but the language Hyde spoke was simply "baboon Irish," not anything that could be taught in a classroom. Against them, to no avail, Hyde mounted a barrage of supporting opinion from outstanding Celticists and historians. The list included Edward Gwynn and William Lecky of Trinity, Kuno Meyer of Liverpool, Standish James O'Grady, and Georges Dottin and Joseph Loth, French scholars who had been trained in Paris by d'Arbois de Jubainville. Their letters were uniformly not merely approving but full of high praise. Evaluating Hyde's reputation in the international academic community, Meyer wrote that his appointment "would confer a great honor on Celtic research throughout the world." O'Grady declared that Hyde had the Irish language "practically and as a living tongue." When the appointment of James Murphy was announced in May, Hyde wrote wryly to Yeats: "They would not have me at any price and I fancy the worse the man was the better pleased they were, so that no attention could be drawn to Gaelic studies by him. Yet I had the most excellent letters from the great Gaelic scholars."

Stung by this rejection from what he called the "English fort in Ireland," Hyde understood at last why he had had no interested response from either the University of Chicago or Queens University in 1891. There was little doubt that Salmon had poisoned the waters before he had been given a chance. Yet he was doubly stung for the effect his defeat would have on Lucy, who, unable to conceive of Hyde's rejection, had been looking forward to a move to Dublin. At the same time Hyde could not help but be relieved that he would not have to give up Ratra. Nuala was a lovely, friendly, outgoing child. The new baby was approaching term. Soon, with the pregnancy over, Lucy would feel better. Surely it would be an advantage for the children to have a Frenchpark summer on the shores of Lough Gara.

Hyde's second daughter, Una, although quieter and shyer than her sister, was an agreeable, even-tempered child. Hyde could not have been happier. Lucy was pleased with the baby, but her disappointment with her husband's failure to secure the Trinity appointment was hard to conceal. Characteristically, Hyde himself did not dwell on the matter but concentrated on the league, on additional translation projects, and on his literary history of Ireland, the long-range project on which he had been working consistently (although at some times with more leisure than at others) for almost twenty years. Rearranging priorities after having spent so much fruitless time on the Trinity application, he revised the welcoming speech he usually presented at the ceremonies that opened new branches and wrote hundreds of letters to organizers, priests, friends, and academic associates in Ireland, England, America, and on the Continent. In May 1897 the Gaelic League's first countrywide festival was held in Dublin. The purpose of this *oireachtas* was to "stimulate public interest in the Irish language movement and to encourage the cultivation of modern Irish." It was both a popular and a public-relations success. Hyde awarded Gaelic League prizes to successful competitors in seven categories, including best poem, best essay, and best recitation in Irish.

Visiting the *oireachtas* with her family was young Mary Butler. Soon she joined Agnes O'Farrelly, Nellie O'Brien, Molly Kennedy, and the other Gaelic League women who for most of the term of his presidency provided Hyde with a strong and dependable source of friendship and support. Fifty years later, Mary Butler recalled her first impressions of the 37-year-old Hyde and the four-year-old Gaelic League:

I heard one of the officers of the Central Branch saying to Dr. Hyde, "I should like to introduce some new members to you." . . . In a moment we were shaking hands with the President of the Gaelic League while he was saying cordially, "Welcome to Irish Ireland." . . . Strange to say, he was not very Irish looking. He had straight jet black hair and a heavy black moustache. His complexion was sallow, and he had rather high cheek bones. The eyes were the only attractive feature in his face and they made one forget all the rest! Their colour seemed to change like his expression, according to his mood. They would blaze with anger when he spoke of Ireland's wrongs, or be tender when he pleaded for the saving of her soul; a moment later they would be twinkling mischievously as he poked fun at some "West British" affectation of country people. . . . He really seemed to possess some gift of drawing people and captivating them, whatever it was.

Not all those who joined the league were captivated by Hyde. Nor were they all revivalists or nationalists. The very success of the league, like that of the bicycle and the new European theater, meant that it had a faddish attraction for hundreds of young men and women drawn to it more for its collateral social activities than for its language classes. Some dropped out early; some got caught up in its activities and remained. There were also those who joined for serious reasons and left because of minor scraps, such as the one that divided supporters of *Fáinne an Lae* and supporters of *An Claidheamh Soluis,* when the league shifted its official allegiance from one newspaper to the other. And then

there were those who, from Pa Burke of Castlerea to the poet AE
(George Russell), simply could not master the language despite their
genuine enthusiasm for it. AE wrote to Hyde, "I think I will join the
Gaelic League and learn Irish in my old age. Why the blazes was I not
taught it in my childhood? I would like to fight in its battles and write
in Irish if I could learn." Pa Burke, looking back on the ninety-odd years
of his life from his customary vantage point, the bridge on Main Street
over the river Suck that had been built the year he was born, used to
reminisce about the day Douglas Hyde rode into town on his bicycle
and recruited members for a Castlerea branch of the Gaelic League.
Hyde was so cheerful, said Pa Burke, and he had such a lively look in
his eye, that all the young men thought the league would be great crack.
And it was, partly. But the other part was hard work of a kind that,
like Russell, Pa Burke could not do, so in the end, he declared, he left
it to the scholars.

Despite this flux and reflux the league continued to prosper beyond
anyone's hopes or expectations. By 1897 it was attacting attention
abroad as well as at home, partly as a result of its own achievements,
partly because of Hyde's scholarly reputation, especially in Celtic studies
circles. Links developed between the league and similar organizations
in Wales and Scotland. Fraternal delegations were exchanged with the
Welsh Eisteddfod and An Mod in Scotland. In France the prospect
of an Irish-led pan-Celtic movement appealed to Breton language revivalists who had modeled their own new organization, L'Union Re-
gionaliste Breton, on the Gaelic League. (An interesting irony is the
fact that there is evidence to suggest that the structure and goals of the
league had been loosely modeled on the Félibrige that Mistral had
founded in midcentury in Provence). In October 1898 Anatole Le Braz,
Dottin's colleague at Rennes and another of Hyde's correspondents,
was elected its director. Meanwhile the league's treasurer, Stephen
Barrett, had had letters from two young Breton nationalist students
who confirmed having received requested copies of O'Growney's *Simple
Lessons in Irish*. What they now needed, they explained, were an inexpen-
sive Irish dictionary and grammar and copies of the league's newspaper,
An Claidheamh Soluis. "Like yourselves in Ireland, we have great pains
and difficulties in the struggle for our land and our tongue," wrote
François Jaffrenou, who shortly after became editor of the weekly
Breton nationalist journal *Le Resistance*. The contribution of his co-
worker, François Vallee, was *La Langue bretonne en 40 leçons*, an adap-
tation of O'Growney's *Simple Lessons in Irish*.

International cooperation was the goal of the Pan-Celtic Association, whose major project in 1898–1899 was to plan a Pan-Celtic Congress to be held in Dublin in 1900. All organizations concerned about the future of any one of the Celtic languages were invited to send a representative. Douglas Hyde was urged particularly to attend. The situation, as he knew, was delicate: some members of the Pan-Celtic Association were old friends of such leaders of the Gaelic League as himself, MacNeill, and Patrick Pearse; others had enemies on the Coiste Gnótha. Proceeding with a caution that some say only invited the complications that followed, Hyde asked the Coiste Gnótha for permission to accept the invitation he had received, on the grounds that it was the province of the executive committee to name league delegates, not the privilege of the president to assume that he was one of them. Blown out of proportion, the question became a matter of debate which ended with the Coiste Gnótha refusing to dispatch any official representative but permitting Hyde's attendance if he would establish clearly that he was present only as a private person. Expressing an attitude that was to continue to plague the league and often cause divisions from within, the executive committee issued a statement that it "would be sorry that any of their members should give time or money to an enterprise that could not help the Irish language." Determined to avoid internal dissension, Hyde reluctantly refused the invitation to the 1900 Pan-Celtic Congress but privately maintained close scholarly relations with as many of the participants as he could.

For some time before he became embroiled in the controversy over the Pan-Celtic Congress, Hyde had been quietly searching for the work of a blind Connacht poet, Anthony Raftery, who died in 1835, leaving the story of his life and the fate of most of his compositions to the oral tradition. This research was partly a recreational activity, as it gave Hyde the opportunity to cycle the scenic roads of Galway in the area of Gort. There he learned that some of Raftery's work had been written down by Raftery's admirers. Often Hyde was put on the trail of a notebook said to contain a number of poems and songs only to have it end at the edge of the Atlantic, the notebook having sailed with its latest owner to America. Then in 1897 Hyde met Lady Isabella Augusta Gregory of Coole Park, who shared his interest in Raftery and successfully traced one of the notebooks to the home of a stonecutter not far from her estate near Gort. Meanwhile, Hyde's own sleuthing in the Royal Irish Academy library rewarded him with an unindexed and therefore previously unnoticed sheaf of poems. He and Lady Gregory obtained still other poems and songs viva voce from storytellers who included them in their repertoire and from ordinary people who enjoyed reciting and singing them. One result of their efforts was Hyde's *Songs Ascribed to Raftery* (1903), a bilingual edition of Raftery's compositions, with translations by Hyde, that included an account of Raftery's life. More important perhaps were the friendships, collaborations, and working relationships that developed as a result of Hyde's and Lady Gregory's search, with their far-reaching implications for both the Gaelic Revival and the Irish Literary Renaissance.

Lady Gregory of Coole Park was the widow of Sir William Gregory, a former colonial governor of Ceylon whom she had married when she was twenty-eight and he was sixty-three. Widowed at forty, she had during her short marriage lived a life of privilege and plenty in the highest circles of society, politics, and art. Although in appearance a rather plain and properly Victorian gentlewoman, as her recent biographer, Mary Lou Kohfeldt, reveals, Lady Gregory was in fact something of a bohemian well before she achieved world recognition as founding mother of the modern Irish theater, the "Presence" of the famous Green Room of Dublin's Abbey Theatre, a successful writer of short plays and significant books, and in many other respects, as Kohfeldt calls her, "the woman behind the Irish Renaissance." There had been at least one discreetly conducted yet wildly romantic love affair, with the poet Wilfred Scawen Blunt, during her short marriage; there would soon be another, with John Quinn. She was already Yeats's patroness, a reader well acquainted with Irish writing in English, and an admirer of Hyde's *Beside the Fire* and *Love Songs of Connacht* when they met. Her preference was clearly for masterful, charismatic, and energetic men. Her politics reflected the conservative convictions of her late husband, except when she was confronted directly by their implications, as often happened when she visited the tenants on her estate. When, as a young woman, she had listened to Gladstone's views on women's emancipation, and, more recently, when she had heard Balfour on the Irish Question, her conservatism had asserted itself. But she had come to accept if not approve the idea of Home Rule, and she embraced cultural nationalism wholeheartedly, having developed in her teens a rebellious taste for the poems of Young Ireland. Twice in the years before she met Hyde, on two different and widely separated occasions, she had tried to learn Irish and had given up. With Hyde to encourage and assist her and

O'Growney's *Simple Lessons* to guide her, she finally succeeded to the point of publishing her own English translations and adaptations of Irish literature.

Not since his courtship of Lucy had Hyde enjoyed such a correspondent as Lady Gregory. Her letters had the same sparkle, the same playful, teasing quality. "Now don't you think I deserve credit as a detective?" she wrote on October 23, 1897, describing how she had tracked down a shopkeeper who owned a manuscript in which Hyde had expressed an interest. Describing a visit to Spiddal, she told him how much she had regretted her ignorance of Irish when she had to enlist the help of two Irish-speaking schoolmasters to obtain stories for him. One of the schoolmasters had told her that he was assembling material for a collection of songs that he hoped to publish. She had sent him a copy of Hyde's *Love Songs of Connacht* to use as a model. To encourage her reading in Irish, Hyde sent her a copy of his recently published second volume of *An Sgeuluidhe Gaodhealach,* which contained five Irish stories—"very simple, and at the same time in good classical Galway Irish, so that if you are really thinking of learning to read the language you will probably find this as easy a stepping stone to it as you could have." He also promised to help find subscribers for the "Celtic theatre" that she and Yeats were trying to establish.

In late December 1898, at Lady Gregory's invitation, Hyde and Norma Borthwick (who was then tutoring Lady Gregory in Irish and giving classes to local people in Lady Gregory's Coole Park gatehouse every afternoon) presented an Irish-language Punch-and-Judy show at a Christmas party for workhouse children. Hyde triumphed in scenes in which he scolded the baby in Irish, for many of his young listeners had often heard the very same words used in the scoldings they themselves had received. In early January of 1899 Lady Gregory sent a brace of cock to Ratra, to which Hyde replied, "Your kindness pursues me even when out of sight and out of reach." On January 9 at the Kiltartan School, with Father Fahey, the Irish-speaking priest from Gort, in the chair, the Kiltartan branch of the Gaelic League held its first meeting. Hyde addressed the new branch in Irish and English in his capacity as league president. Although she listened carefully, Lady Gregory admitted that she had not been able to understand his Irish. However, when he said in English, "Let English go their road and let us go ours, and God forbid their road should ever be ours," she heard only too well and was in fact a bit shocked, as she had been assured that the league was nationalist but nonpolitical in its sympathies. If her response seemed naive, Hyde knew that it was also self-protective, as nationalist but nonpolitical was how she described her proposed Irish theater.

Hyde encouraged Lady Gregory to keep up her study of Irish, to avoid losing the progress she had made, even when she was in London for extended visits. His letters to her in the spring of 1899 were well punctuated with Gaelic words and phrases which (like Lucy, during their courtship) she then picked up and made use of in her letters to him. In an eight-page letter of January 1899, he sent her a long anecdote, completely in Irish, about a peasant woman who lay in fear on her deathbed lest her soul be taken in charge by an English-speaking priest. She understood what he was doing and why it was successful: getting through the amusing story had been a bit of a struggle, but this kind of learning was pleasure, not drudgery.

Wherever she went Lady Gregory became an ambassador for the Gaelic League. In London with W. B. Yeats in 1897 she wore the Gaelic League badge that she had received from O'Growney. Taking Hyde's advice she had brought *Simple Lessons* with her to work on in her spare moments, and she also had a copybook, inscribed "Agusta Gregore," her name in Irish, in which she faithfully wrote out her Irish exercises. When in 1899 the league's newspaper, *An Claidheamh Soluis,* began sniping at the Irish Literary Theatre for staging Irish drama written in English, Hyde wrote a stern note dated May 7 to John MacNeill, the paper's editor: "I beseech you please to say nothing in *Claidheamh* against the Literary Theatre. Many of our friends, especially Lady Gregory, are on the Executive Committee, so don't go against them. . . . They are not enemies to us. They are a half-way house." As proof of this statement he pointed out that they had also planned *Oisín* and *Pádraig* for the same time, in the same theater. MacNeill complied with Hyde's request, but it was not the last time Hyde had to act as arbitrator between adherents of the Irish Literary Renaissance and those committed to the Gaelic Revival. Belonging to both, seeing each as a support for the other, Hyde not only deplored but feared their rivalry. It was one reason why he had undertaken his long and serious study, nearly twenty years in work, of the literary history of Ireland. In this book he hoped to present evidence that all Ireland, city and country, Big House and cottage, Gael and Gall, had cause to identify itself with Irish culture and history.

A work of permanent value that would do most to establish Hyde's reputation as an outstanding scholar but that had proved most difficult for him to bring to a close, *A Literary History of Ireland* was published in 1899. As he reviewed the manuscript he was about to deliver to the publisher in April 1898, it seemed to him, as he complained to his friend Alice Milligan, that he was undermining all his long years of research and preparation in the haste with which he was now rushing toward publication. Confessing both his impatience and his ambivalence, he declared that on the one hand he hoped that he might finish putting the manuscript in final form by the end of the month, on the other hand he feared that fault would be found. In that case, he said, the book would just have to make up in volume what it lacked in quality. It was evident that Hyde was beginning to feel the burden of work and emotional strain that he had been carrying since his annus mirabilis, 1893.

Hyde need not have worried about the literary history. Within a year of publication over nineteen favorable reviews had appeared in French, English, Irish, and American newspapers and magazines. One of the earliest, in the *New Ireland Review* for July 1899, congratulated him on the "imperial manner" with which he had placed his work before the public, so that it could make its own judgment. His verse translations were praised as "uniformly excellent." Public judgment was swift: purchased, read, borrowed; quoted by hundreds of bank clerks, school-teachers, priests, nuns, and civil servants; hyperbolically described by Patrick Pearse and others as the equal in effect of *Uncle Tom's Cabin,* it was a book for its time. Its central thesis, adapted from d'Arbois de Jubainville, was (a) that cultural influence conquers, and (b) that the imposition of a language on a people obliterates both heritage and history, for it governs the very "form of thought during every instant . . . of existence." Hyde sent copies to O'Conor Don, Maud Gonne, members of the Young Ireland group that had met in Dublin in the 1880s, and a host of others who showered him with further words of praise for his achievement. A few close friends and neighbors recognized its personal stamp. They noted the names of ancestors of O'Conor Don scattered throughout as well as allusions to places near his boyhood home, as in: "There is never a camping-ground of Maeve's army on their march . . . from Rathcroghan in Roscommon to the plain of Mochruime in Louth, and never a skirmish fought by them that has not given its name to some plain, or camping-ground or ford." Later, in her published memoir, Maud Gonne recalled the *Literary History* as an "inspiration" that supplied "the intellectual background of revolt." Reviewed again after republication, it has been described in recent years as "still unsurpassed."

Although the period of its gestation began long before the founding of the Gaelic League, Hyde dedicated *A Literary History* to the organization that was for him "the only body in Ireland which appears to realize that Ireland has a past, has a history, has a literature, and the only body in Ireland which seeks to render the present a rational continuation of the past." The book itself he called "an attempt at a review of that literature which despite its present neglected position" is felt and known to be "a true possession of national importance."

The restrained tone and note of sadness evident in the dedication of *A Literary History* no doubt reflected Hyde's anger and frustration with another battle in which, during 1899, he and the league were engaged. This time the field was education. The government had raised no great objection to the league's program of evening classes that by 1899 had put O'Growney's *Simple Lessons* in the hands of roughly 40,000 members. But Hyde, MacNeill, and O'Growney had agreed that until access to Irish was guaranteed in the national schools, only a fraction of the population would have the opportunity to learn it—and meanwhile, with English still the medium of instruction and that instruction provided by teachers who spoke only English, education in the Gaeltacht was effectively no education at all for children who knew no language but Irish. "Hence it became," as Tomás Ó Fíaich noted in *The Gaelic League Idea*, "a primary objective of the League to ensure that the teaching of Irish would find a place in the normal educational system of the country, at both primary and secondary level, and if possible at university level as well."

There had been no progress with this problem at the intermediate level since 1878, when the Society for the Preservation of the Irish Language had successfully petitioned the Board of Intermediate Education to include "Celtic" as a subject (along with classical and modern languages) in which students could present themselves for examination. Although the decision itself had seemed a triumph at the time, "Celtic" was allotted fewer points than classical and modern languages, and fewer teachers of Irish were qualified to prepare students for examination. Ó Fíaich estimates that as a consequence rarely did more than five percent of students presenting themselves in any given year choose to be examined in Irish. The situation in primary schools was far worse. Although (again, largely thanks to SPIL) it had been established in 1879 that Irish could be taught as an extra subject outside of regular school hours, in practical terms so few schools offered this option that little more could be said for it than that Irish had been put on the books.

In 1899, in response to pressure from the league, the government named a royal commission to conduct an investigation and make recommendations for change.

To those who had been campaigning against Irish, chiefly on the grounds that enrollment figures proved that the public did not want such instruction and in any case the program clearly was not cost-effective, the appointment of a commission provided an opportunity to eliminate Irish from the curriculum. The assault was led by Hyde's old enemy, John Pentland Mahaffy, now professor of ancient history at Trinity. Mahaffy testified that teaching Irish was an impractical waste of time supported only by foolish sentimentalists and wild-eyed separatists anachronistically committed to repeal of the Act of Union. He concluded with a statement for which, Hyde surmised, Robert Atkinson had been his source: "I am told by a much better authority than any of them in Irish that it is almost impossible to get hold of a text in Irish which is not religious or which is not silly or indecent." Hyde counterattacked by sending press reports of Mahaffy's testimony to an imposing list of Celtic scholars in England and on the Continent, inviting their rebuttals. Disbelief and outrage were expressed by, among others, Owen Edwards and York Powell at Oxford; E. C. Stern and Ernst Windisch in Germany; Georges Dottin at Rennes, and Holger Pedersen in Copenhagen. From the University of Liverpool Kuno Meyer wrote that to refrain from teaching Irish to Irish youths who talk it as their mother tongue must be regarded as "a grotesque educational blunder." York Powell at Oxford concurred: "It is a good subject, a useful subject, and a subject that far from being discouraged, should be encouraged by any who really care for Education in the true sense in Ireland." Armed with these and similar carefully measured opinions from reputable scholars who all attested to the educational value of Irish, Hyde appeared before the commission, attacked Mahaffy's allegations, and questioned the qualifications of his unnamed expert. Thus drawn into the fray, Atkinson came before the committee, giving a new turn to Trinity's campaign with his assertion that Irish must be considered deficient as it lacked standardization of its spelling and grammar. He also renewed Mahaffy's charge that early Irish literature was indecent and that Hyde's collected folklore was "low" since "all folk-lore is at bottom abominable." The fracas spilled over onto the pages of the *Freeman's Journal* and the *Daily Express*. In the league's paper, *An Claidheamh Soluis,* Father Peter O'Leary wrote a series of articles in which he found Atkinson woefully ignorant of Irish grammar, particularly the verb *is* (to be). To Atkinson's embarrassment, excerpts from his earlier published works were used to counter his own testimony before the commission.

In the midst of the fray, Hyde confessed that he was afraid that Trinity's attack would "wipe out the language all together," but as the tide began to turn he wrote Lady Gregory in February 1899 that "the intermediate battle has been fought, and I think won." He was correct in his estimate, but at least two of his Trinity foes remained defiant in defeat. George Fitzgerald, professor of philosophy and a former commissioner of education, wrote Hyde: "I will use all my influence as in the past, to ensure that Irish as a spoken language shall die out as quickly as possible, for I consider the Gaelic League in their endeavor to preserve Irish as a spoken language are enemies of their country whose mischievous sentimentality should be denounced by all friends of Ireland." Mahaffy fired his last shot in an essay in the August 1899 number of the *Nineteenth Century* entitled "The Recent Fuss about the Irish Language," in which he attacked "genuine enthusiasts"; politicians and "political ladies" who want to humor the people to whom they refused Home Rule; professional Welsh nationalists; "misguided Prelates"; and "self-developed enthusiasts" who teach Irish because they hope to earn their living and achieve fame by leading the new movement. The opposition press also had its several diehards, notably *Irish Figaro,* which on April 21, 1900, declared that Irish was "worthless" and that the victory had gone to professors and students of Gaelic who were greedy for jobs and remuneration: "Away with sentiment and puerile nonsense," it advised, "and leave the mouthing of Irish to the Douglas Hydes and George Moores of the day or hour or minute."

With Irish secured in the curriculum by the Intermediate Education (Ireland) Amendment Act of 1900, the numbers of students presenting Irish at examinations more than trebled between 1899 and 1902. By 1908 roughly half the secondary school students of the country were taking Irish as an examination subject. Never again would Irish education be the same. The implications of the league's victory over the Trinity dons extended into other areas as well. Aided by the nationalist fervor ignited by celebrations commemorating the rising of 1798, the agitation of such nationalist newspapers as Griffith's *United Irishman* and Moran's *Leader,* and a widespread yearning for some cause that could heal the rift occasioned by the fall of Parnell, public opinion had mobilized behind the language. Victory had its effects on the league's lean treasury. From Patrick Ford in New York came a bank draft for

£300 in reader donations collected through his paper, the *Irish World,* to further the league's work. Hyde seized the day in a widely quoted speech in which he declared, "The cry of the next ten years must be 'nationalise Irish education.' If our education is national, our nationality is safe and sound, if it is un-national, nationality is lost." Few who listened to him doubted that his next goal—whatever it was—would be won. Usually cautious and mild-mannered, Edward Martyn wrote Hyde that he had worried lest he had been too "violent" in his own letter to the press regarding the education bill, but he had now decided that he believed in violence when dealing with the British government. "Unless we shake up our rulers, they never attend to us . . . the only argument with such people is fear."

With the literary history off his hands and Irish safely established in the schools, Hyde turned back to Raftery. Lady Gregory had identified the exact spot where he lay buried in a small cemetery near Craughwell; she also had located some additional poems. "What an extraordinary energetic scholar you are to find Raftery's grave and to lay hold of those manuscripts," Hyde wrote to her. He invited her to compose a preface for the collected songs of Raftery, now planned as the fifth volume of his continuing Songs of Connacht series, to appear after periodical publication in the *Weekly Freeman.* When she declined, he dedicated the book to her and described her contribution to the collection in the preface that he wrote himself. Another publishing task before him was the manuscript of *Ubhla de'n Chraoibh* (Apples from the branch), a collection of thirty-three of his own poems in Irish that had appeared in weekly newspapers. In the preface to these poems he wrote in Irish, "I would like better to make even one good verse in the language in which I am now writing, than to make a whole book of verse in English. For should any good be found in my English verses, it would not go to the credit of my mother Ireland but my stepmother, England." The year had ended well, even if the themes of his little book were emigration, exile, defeat, and death.

11

Plays and Players

Before her marriage to Sir William Gregory of Coole Park, Lady Gregory had been Augusta Persse and her home had been Roxborough, a neighboring estate. Another near neighbor was Edward Martyn of Tullira whose distant cousin was George Moore, an established literary figure well-known in Paris cafés and London salons. Moore's home was Moore Hall in county Mayo, but since 1873 he had spent little time there, living instead first in Paris, then in London, where he saw much of Martyn. By 1900 Moore's published work consisted of more than twenty separate books and a number of items that had appeared in fashionable English periodicals. He also had written, alone and with others, a number of plays and librettos. In 1895 a play on which he had collaborated with Mrs. Pearl Craigie, *Journey's End in Lovers' Meeting,* had been a success of the London theater season. Martyn, who also had written plays, none as yet produced, often talked to Moore about playwriting, showed him his works-in-progress, and even invited his suggestions. One evening in Moore's London flat, during a conversation about the Gaelic League, Martyn confessed that he wished he could write a play in Irish. As Martyn talked, Moore found himself increasingly fascinated by the possibilities of "a new language to enwomb new thought."

Two years later, on one of his frequent visits to Moore, Martyn was accompanied by Yeats. They had come together to show Moore a proposal for an Irish literary theater which Yeats had dictated and Lady Gregory had typed at Coole Park. Lady Gregory's typewriter had belonged to Sir Henry Layard, Sir William Gregory's closest friend; it had been given to her but a few months before on her forty-fifth birthday, March 15, 1897, by Sir Henry's widow, Enid. The proposal Martyn showed to Moore was but the first of many items that would have astonished the conservative Sir Henry, a staunch defender of everything English, had he seen the uses to which his old friend's wife had put his prized typing machine. It described a new Irish theater society that every spring would perform in Dublin "certain Celtic and Irish plays" chosen to appeal to "an uncorrupted and imaginative audience" capable of understanding that "Ireland was not the home of buffoonery and of easy sentiment . . . but the home of an ancient idealism." Following the example of the Gaelic League, the organizers appealed to all Irish people for support for a work which was "outside all the political questions" that might divide them. Signed by Yeats, Martyn, and Lady Gregory, it was intended to solicit the support of potential subscribers.

Moore ascertained, as he questioned Martyn and Yeats about their new Irish theater, that in its first year it would not yet "enwomb new thought in a new language," since none of the organizers could speak (let alone write) more than a couple of words of Irish. Yeats and Martyn assured him, however, that Irish plays would follow. Lady Gregory was discussing the subject with Douglas Hyde. Not two months earlier at the end of the summer Hyde had joined them at a "Celtic party" at Tullira. Meanwhile, they avowed, there were many other English-speaking Irish like themselves who would provide an audience for a language, a literature, and a theater that reflected their own distinctive voice. For Yeats this meant writing in English "with an indefinable Irish quality"; for Lady Gregory, bringing into such writing a consciousness of the Irish folk tradition; for Martyn, weaving together Irish past and present and viewing the particulars of Irish life from a broader European perspective. Moore responded especially to this last point. He had been trying to educate his ascetic and reclusive "dear Edward" in the ideas of Ibsen, Zola, and the like; in *The Heather Field* he thought he had seen a spark.

The Irish Literary Theatre was the formal name of what Hyde knew and already had subscribed to as Lady Gregory's "Celtic Theatre." He had promised to provide her with a list of people who might be interested in contributing to such a project. He also had been intrigued with her idea that the flair for drama and ear for dialogue that she had perceived in his poems, prose, and speeches might be used to produce a simple one-act play written in Irish. A series of such plays might serve one of the league's most important yet most difficult goals: to bring its members into closer contact with native Irish speakers of the Breac-Ghaeltacht, those areas bordering the Gaeltacht where a degree of bilingualism could be found among both English-speaking and Irish-speaking Irish. It also might provide English speakers with insights into aspects of true Gaeltacht life that their stereotypes obscured.

Lady Gregory's eagerness to involve Hyde in the Irish Literary Theatre stemmed in part from her conviction that Hyde had exactly the talent, skills, and knowledge that were needed to add an Irish-language component to its program, in part from the fact that she genuinely liked him. She could not say the same, she confessed, of her neighbor Edward Martyn. The truth is that although Lady Gregory might not have been fond of Martyn, he was more practical—more like herself—than she admitted. His visit to Moore in London, about two months after his Celtic party, had been undertaken for the specific purpose of drawing into the circle now consisting of himself, Yeats, and Lady Gregory a man who, like Hyde, could serve the proposed Irish Literary Theatre in ways that they could not. Both Yeats and Martyn had been involved in theater in only a marginal way. In 1894, at the Avenue Theater in London, Yeats's *Land of Heart's Desire* had been performed as a curtain raiser, first for Todhunter's *Comedy of Sighs* and then for Shaw's *Arms and the Man*. It had "roused no passions," Yeats readily admitted, but it had "pleased a sufficient minority" for it to be kept on stage throughout the period for which it had been booked. Of Martyn's plays, *The Heather Field,* although not yet produced, had been considered promising by Moore and others. Lady Gregory had had no previous involvement at all in the world of the theater, but she did have good contacts and she knew something about fund-raising. What was required, all agreed, was someone with practical professional theater experience—someone like Moore. By the time their visit was over, Martyn and Yeats had added another subscriber to their list and aroused Moore's skeptical if ambivalent curiosity—in the Gaelic League, as it turned out, as well as in the Irish Literary Theatre.

In the months that followed, the proposal dictated by Yeats, typed by Lady Gregory, and approved by Martyn became their blueprint for the future. Response to their circular letter soliciting subscriptions was prompt and encouraging, but not yet sufficient to support production. Encouraged by Moore's generally favorable reaction both to the idea of the theater and to his own projected part in it, Martyn underwrote a first season in which his *Heather Field* and Yeats's *Countess Cathleen* were offered. The week-long run in the Antient Concert Rooms in Dublin beginning May 8, 1899, was a success, despite problems in production (resolved by Moore) and public protests: Yeats's play was denounced as heretical by some members of the Catholic clergy and hierarchy because in it the countess of the title sells her soul to feed her starving people; Gaelic Leaguers objected to Irish theater produced entirely in English. The important thing was that crowds were at or near capacity all week and reviews reflected the general enthusiasm of the theatergoing public. T. P. Gill, editor of the *Daily Express,* gave a dinner in honor of the event to which, in addition to Lady Gregory, Martyn, and Yeats, were invited Douglas Hyde, George Moore, John O'Leary, T. W. Rolleston, J. F. Taylor, John Eglinton, William P. O'Brien, Max Beerbohm, and many others. The founders agreed that a second season scheduled to open on February 19, 1900, in Dublin's larger Gaiety Theatre was clearly indicated.

Hyde could not help but be impressed by these developments and a bit sorry that he had been unable to contribute anything to them. Remembering the success of the Irish play that he and Norma Borthwick had attended in the Donegal Gaeltacht in November and the Punch-and-Judy show that they had presented for the workhouse children of Gort in December, he recognized the potential value of theater in Irish. But the phenomenal growth of the Gaelic League was taking all and more of his time. What had started with a single branch in July 1893 and expanded to more than forty branches by the end of 1897 had tripled by the middle of 1899. It was difficult to keep up with just the task of officially commemorating the establishment of new branches, but in addition there were problems that required his attention. A rift was developing between the Coiste Gnótha (the executive committee in Dublin) and some of the larger branches that were insisting upon greater autonomy. There was continual squabbling among members of different Gaeltachts over whose dialect set the standard by which modern Irish might be judged. Publication of printed material for the use, information, and enjoyment of league members had roused related arguments over typeface and orthography. Stung by the testimony of Trinity scholars at the royal commission hearings—that Irish was not a language but an inferior patois lacking in uniformity and consistency—zealous educators were advocating conformity to the "correct" grammar and usage of printed texts, although the founding purpose of the league had been to dignify and promote the spoken word. It was one thing to put what had been said into print, as in the Gaelic League pamphlets: even now the one about to be issued drew on a speech Hyde had made concerning university education; others scheduled to follow contained the arguments that had been presented on behalf of the language by himself and others before the royal commission. It was another thing, Hyde believed, to make printed texts the authority for "correct" conversational Irish.

Lady Gregory continued to press Hyde on the subject of a little play in Irish—perhaps for the 1900 program. He continued to make his excuses: There was *Úbhla de'n Chraoibh*, the little book of poems to which he was now putting the finishing touches; there was the continuing task of editing and translating Raftery's songs and poems. There was also, although he said little about it, the matter of Lucy's chronic poor health. Remembering his own experiences with local doctors (including his uncle-by-marriage, Dr. Cuppaidge), Hyde was unwilling to accept their judgment that nothing was the matter with her. He had asked George Sigerson, an old friend and respected Dublin physician, a specialist in neurology, to examine her.

In August of 1900, six months after the Irish Literary Theatre scored its second success (albeit without a play in Irish), Lady Gregory invited Hyde and Lucy to spend a few days at Coole. She had ordered a headstone for Raftery's grave; she needed help in arranging a ceremony that would establish an annual *feis* in Raftery's honor; she wanted to discuss the Celtic sagas that she had agreed to retell in English for book publication. She also intended to talk again to Hyde about his contributing a play in Irish to the repertoire of the Irish Literary Theatre. There would be but a small house party, she had indicated, in response to Hyde's concern over Lucy, perhaps just the three of them and Willie Yeats. But Hyde knew that at Coole it was never possible to predict just how many would arrive in the morning or sit down together for an evening dinner or come and go unexpectedly in the middle of the afternoon. It was only possible to say that the conversation, whatever its source, would be interesting. The tablets and powders Sigerson had prescribed seemed to be having a good effect. He pressed Lucy to accompany him and was pleased when she agreed.

Early on August 26 the Hydes set out by train for the meeting at Craughwell and the visit to Coole Park. As their carriage reached the familiar road leading to the Coole estate, Douglas identified for Lucy the lanes he had cycled while collecting the poems of Raftery. Along the avenue the carriage passed under arching ilex trees reminiscent of the arching boughs draped with the banner reading "*Fáilte*" that had welcomed Hyde and Lucy over seven years ago, when they had arrived in Frenchpark to take up residence in Ratra. He told her of the Seven Woods with their phonetically spelled Irish names: Kyle Na No (*caoile na cnó*, "nut wood"), Shanwalla (*seanbhaile*, "old home"), Kyle Dortha (*caoile dorcha*, "dark wood"), Pairc Na Tarav (*pairc na tairbh*, "bull field"), Pairc na Carraig (*pairc na carraige*, "rock field"), Pairc Na Lee (*pairc na lao*, "calf field"), Inchy (*inis taoide*, "tidal island"). Then suddenly, as if it had appeared on cue, there was the house itself, its geometric lines contrasting with the curving drive, the arches of ilex, and the unpruned fullness of the beeches. Taking Lucy's hand, Hyde helped her from the carriage. Very elegant she was, as always, in her stylish hat and well-tailored traveling suit that emphasized her slender waist. Like Lady Gregory, Lucy favored black, but the cut and style of her clothing made clear that her choice was based on fashion in dress, not convention in mourning.

Lucy and Hyde found Coole both gracious and charming. Its spacious, airy rooms were fragrant with flowers from the splendid gardens of which Lady Gregory was justly proud. Willie Yeats was there before them. Tall, thin, and nervous with dark, unruly hair, a pale complexion, and an abstracted look in his eyes, he seemed acutely conscious of the fact that he was both resident poet and housepet. Lucy took an instant and permanent dislike to him, which he in his absentminded manner probably did not notice. In any case, as neither had any reason to be concerned with the other beyond polite nods of greeting or parting, her dislike of him hardly mattered. She preferred the small, plump, slightly imperious but unfailingly cordial Lady Gregory. Her house was pleasant; her servants were well-trained and attentive; and the guests who came and went during the next few days were friendly and agreeable. Hyde, immediately at home, plunged into discussions of Irish folklore, principally with Yeats, and of Irish saga, principally with Lady Gregory. When talk turned to matters that did not interest her, Lucy sat outdoors, reading a book, or excused herself and went to her room to lie down. She no longer entered into conversations with the same enthusiasm and self-confidence that had made her such a favorite with Hyde's sister Annette and his Oldfield aunts when they had met her in Killarney. It was better in any case that she not get involved. It was sometimes hard for her to repress the tinge of sarcasm that now often colored her remarks. She had come to resent these Irish members of literary and nationalist organizations who took so much of Douglas's time yet gave so little in return. She often complained to him that he had allowed himself to be exploited to the detriment of his professional career.

By August 27 Yeats and Hyde had narrowed their subject to one Irish folktale in particular, "Casadh an tSúgáin" (The twisting of the rope), which both admired but each interpreted differently. Yeats had incorporated references to its well-known story (of how the people of a Munster village tricked a Connacht poet bent on seducing a village woman) into his Red Hanrahan poems; Hyde had printed a version of it in verse in his *Love Songs of Connacht*. By August 28 Yeats had sketched a scenario based on their discussion. Taking Yeats's scribbled notes to his room, Hyde closeted himself for two days, forgoing shooting, conversation, walks by the lake, and other favorite pastimes to see what he could make of them. Late in the afternoon of August 29 he put the finishing touches to his manuscript. Then, so tired from this concentrated effort that he confessed to himself that he felt rather ill, he dressed and joined the others for dinner. A bottle of champagne provided by Lady Gregory to celebrate the event helped restore him in both body and spirit. On August 30 and 31, translating into English, Hyde began dictating his play to Lady Gregory, who had offered to make a clean copy of it on Sir Henry Layard's typewriter. That evening Martyn came to dinner and Hyde read him the translation of his play; Martyn was pleased with it. On August 31, Lady Gregory having finished her typing, Hyde returned to his room and wrote part of another play.

Hyde's simple one-act dramatization of the story "The Twisting of the Rope" combined Hyde's and Yeats's differing concepts of the folktale in a comedy first published in the October 1901 issue of *Samhain* and first produced—together with *Diarmuid and Gráinne*, a collaboration between Yeats and Moore—on October 21, 1901, in the Gaiety Theatre. *Diarmuid and Gráinne* was played by Benson's, a company of professional actors. Hyde played the part of Hanrahan in *Casadh an tSúgáin*. Other roles were performed by members of the Keating branch of the Gaelic League.

Hyde was happy with the results of this first playwriting effort. In his diary for October 21, 1901, he noted that the Keating branch actors had become so personally involved in making the play a success that they had supplied or made their own costumes. He himself, despite his usual frugality, paid four pounds to a man who supplied the scenery. When the curtain rose, he wrote, still filled with the excitement of the event, "we could see nothing, but went gaily through our piece without a trace of nervousness and the audience loved it. The house was packed to the doors, and they all said that they preferred 'Casadh an tSúgáin' to 'Diarmuid and Gráinne' Reviews were generally excellent. The nationalist papers were wildly enthusiastic. Writing in the *United Irishman* of October 26, 1901, Frank Fay declared the evening "a memorable one for Dublin and for Ireland." The Irish language had been heard on the stage of its "principal metropolitan theatre"; "A Nation Once Again," Thomas Davis's rousing lyric set to music, had been sung within its walls. In contrast, he wrote of *Diarmuid and Gráinne*, "the greatest triumph of the authors lies in their having written in English a play in which English actors are intolerable. . . . The stolid English temperament was . . . at variance with what we wanted." It was a message not lost on the organizers of the Irish Literary Theater, soon to be re-formed as the Irish National Dramatic Company and then the Irish National Theatre, who thereafter used only Irish actors. As for Hyde, he was of course delighted with these reviews but what particularly pleased him were the comments on his acting. It had been more than ten years since he had appeared on the stage of the Mosaic Club in *The Heir-at-Law* and *The Liar*. He had had good notices then. Now the *Freeman's Journal* saluted him as "a born actor . . . whose eloquent tenderness to Una threw into strong relief the fierce savagery and scorching contempt with which he turned on Seamus and his friends."

Hyde's *Casadh an tSúgáin* was an immediate popular success. It drew on the Irish tradition of paying extravagant respect to a poet; it echoed the people's fear of the poet at the bottom of that respect—the same fear later described by Tomás Ó Crohan in *The Islandman*: "He's a great poet, and maybe he'd make a rann on you that would stick to you forever, if you were to anger him." It invoked the memory of Finn, a popular hero of Irish folklore, with its description of Hanrahan as like "Ossian after the Fenians." In Hanrahan's derisive song about Munster people who "cannot even twist a sugaun," and Seamus's triumphant final line ("Where's Connacht now?"), it played up, to the amusement of its audiences, provincial rivalry and pride. Its artifact from the Gaelic past—the straw rope with which the Munster villagers tricked the Connacht poet—offered an ironic element lost on neither country nor town audiences. The linking of Una's name with that of Helen of Troy ("my fine Helen," Hanrahan calls her) and allusions to the elopement motif in the Ulster tale of Deirdre and Naoise presented Gaelic myth as the equal of that of the Greeks, a comparison Hyde never had failed to make even before he had heard Standish O'Grady's persuasive arguments on the subject.

In the years that followed, *Casadh an tSúgáin* was frequently presented by both professional and amateur players in the original Irish and in English translation. It was but the first of Hyde's plays, yet it had all the qualities that assured his success as a playwright: his delicate sense of the parameters of language; his ability, evident in childhood, to orchestrate language for maximum effect; its introduction at a time when thousands of leaguers who had progressed through O'Growney's *Simple Lessons* were eager for Irish plays that they could enjoy and that also could give them the sense that through language they were now truly in touch with their Irish culture. The simplicity of Hyde's plays also encouraged other aspiring playwrights to try their hand at writing skits and one-act plays and eventually full dramas in Irish. Amateur dramatic societies welcomed the chance to perform in such plays, which also became a popular feature of the annual *oireachtas*.

Meanwhile, noting the direction in which the cultural life of his native country appeared to be moving, George Moore, still living in England, began to take a greater interest in both the Irish Literary Theatre and the Gaelic League. In 1898, moving quickly to avert disaster, he had taken over as director of Martyn's *Heather Field*, then in rehearsal in London (together with Yeats's *Countess Cathleen*) for the Irish Literary Theatre's 1899 Dublin season. After the success of *The Heather Field* he had spent the summer of 1899 at Coole Park, working with Yeats on a much-needed revision of Martyn's *Tale of A Town*, scheduled for production in February 1900 in the Literary Theatre's second annual program. To Martyn's dismay, both Yeats and Moore had judged it hopeless in its present state. With Martyn's permission—he insisted only that his name not be used—it appeared as *The Bending of the Bough* by George Moore. By that time, outraged by the British army's conduct in the Boer Wars, Moore had decided to move to Dublin. He was still fascinated with the idea of a new language to enwomb new thought. Whether or not he could learn Irish himself (he had begun to have his doubts), he would, he avowed, continue to embrace Hyde's concept of a country enriched by its two languages. Giving up his flat in London, he installed himself in a charming house with a very large garden on Dublin's Ely Place, within easy walking distance of Stephen's Green and the Shelbourne Hotel.

Within months of the premiere of *Casadh an tSúgáin*, Hyde finished his second play in Irish, *An Tincéar agus an tSidheóg* (The tinker and the fairy), begun on August 31, 1900, when the excitement of having written his first play was too strong to allow him to concentrate on much else. Based on a folktale, it tells the story of a fairy queen condemned by a jealous rival to old age and death unless she could, in her last hour, persuade a man to kiss her. In a bold move, Moore proposed to turn his beautiful garden for one day into an outdoor theater for the premiere performance of *An Tincéar*. He would also, he said, host an elegant by-invitation-only reception for more than three hundred guests; review the English translation of the text; suggest substantive revisions on the basis of his reading of the English translation; and direct the production. The purpose of his plan (amusing to some, diabolical to others) was to force recognition of the Irish language by taking it out of the cottages, huts, and hovels of the Gaeltacht and making it the focus of a major event of the Dublin social season.

Delighted with Moore's plan as well as his purpose, Hyde at first looked forward to the event, set for May 19, 1902. It was arranged that Belinda Butler would translate the Irish script into English for Moore to read. Hyde, as agreed, began to rehearse the part of the Tinker; he was joined by Sinéad Ní Fhlannagáin (later the wife of Eamon de Valera) in the role of the Fairy. But as May approached, Hyde began to dread Moore's almost daily letters. At first these contained only suggestions for minor changes in the text and such queries as whether the meter should be preserved in the English translation and if the dialogue might not be lengthened: the sort of thing, Hyde told himself, that one might expect from a man who was first and foremost an experienced and successful writer whose particular interest for many years had been aesthetics. Hyde not only accepted much of Moore's advice but acknowledged that his opinions had merit. He only wished there could be fewer letters. Real difficulties arose when it became obvious that the two men differed in their concept of the Tinker and therefore on the content of the Tinker's final soliloquy. Of the final scene, Moore wrote, "He is abstract humanity, and you can make him say what you like regardless of individual limitations." Hyde was patient with Moore, but he understood his audience. What he needed, he knew, was not an abstraction but a flesh-and-blood tinker. Finally, just as Hyde was running out of patience, peace returned, for details of the reception diverted Moore's attention. *Tincéar* was performed as scheduled on May 19, 1902, in a much-publicized and highly successful by-invitation-only social event. Play and reception, author and director, were warmly praised. The Tinker and the Fairy were congratulated on their performances. Irish-language theater had come of age in Ireland.

In quick succession, from 1901 to 1905, Hyde wrote the series of plays that he had conceived as forming the core of a repertoire for Irish-language drama. Each was also available in English; many were printed in both Irish and English in current periodicals. *An Pósadh* (The marriage) was presented at the Connacht *feis* in Galway in August 1902, with Hyde in the role of Blind Raftery. The idea for it had come from a tale told to Lady Gregory, about how Raftery had come to a poor cottage where two young people were to be married, and how by his song and laughter he "had made a feast where no feast was." Like *Casadh an tSúgáin*, the play calls for a country setting (a cabin kitchen) and three main characters plus "the neighbors." *An Pósadh*, again like *Casadh an tSúgáin*, focuses on the traditional fame and power of the Gaelic poet, a rich source of story and history familiar in Ireland that owed nothing to English culture. Observing Hyde in the role of Raftery in a Rotunda production in February 1903, the inveterate Dublin theatergoer Joseph Holloway recalled that he "looked the part to the life" and enacted it "capitally," even to the "natural" way in which he ate a boiled egg. (Hyde credited the verisimilitude to the fact that he had gone on stage without having had a chance to eat dinner.)

In late August of 1902 Hyde was again in Coole Park. His diary entry in Irish for August 25, 1902, reads, "They shoved me into my room and I wrote a small play in three or four hours on Angus the Culdee." Entitled *An Naomh ar Iarraid* (The lost saint), it was published in the 1902 issue of *Samhain* and performed in early 1903. A first attempt to adapt for popular theater themes and characters from the Irish manuscript tradition, it drew upon Hyde's reading and research in ninth-century monastic Christianity, especially the legends that had been woven around the figure of Aongus Céile Dé (Oengus the Culdee). In Hyde's simple and stirring modern miracle play, a reworking of an incident from the saint's life as recorded in early Irish hagiography, the "holy saintly man" disguised as Cormacín (a "poor-looking, gray old man" who grinds meal and minds ovens) intercedes with God on behalf of a slow-witted student who has been kept at his desk because he was unable to recite correctly a verse from the saint's ancient *feilire*, or calendar. Admirably suited for performance by children, it adheres to a formula developed by Hyde especially for amateur productions: its simple setting is a country schoolroom, and the action is carried by three main characters (two adults and one child), yet the stage instructions provide the opportunity to include as many "other children" as there are players available. Encouraged by the ease with which *An Naomh* had almost written itself, Hyde decided that his next subject would be the Nativity; his source, a medieval miracle play. Although now it seemed that his muse resided in what had become "his room" at Coole, he could not begin it at once. Guests already were arriving for the *feis* at Raftery's grave that had been scheduled for August 31.

The *feis* was itself a theatrical production of sorts on which Lady Gregory, assisted by Hyde, had been working for two full years, although this fact was discreetly concealed on the handsome program that contained only the names of the local committee. It was, as it was designed to be, an Irish affair, complete with prizes for Irish singing, dancing, storytelling, and flute playing. Its stated purpose, printed near the top of the program, was "to perpetuate the memory of Raftery, the Connacht poet, and aid the revival of the Irish language." Added at the bottom was the hope that this "little Feis" might "do something to keep alive . . . the language of Patrick, Brendan, and Colman MacDuagh, of Brian Borumha, Owen Ruadh, and Sarsfield, and to drive from our homes the tongue of Henry VIII, Elizabeth, and Cromwell." In the crowd that gathered, in addition to Lady Gregory and Hyde (by now familiar figures in Craughwell), were W. B. Yeats, his brother, Jack B. Yeats, his father, John Butler Yeats, and a stranger—an American lawyer by the name of John Quinn who was making his first trip to Ireland and who was avidly interested in Irish writing, theater, and art. After the program at the graveside these guests of Lady Gregory returned with her to Coole, where Hyde read his play in Irish and John Quinn was invited to add his initials to those which other favorites of Lady Gregory had carved in the bark of the Coole Park beech tree. Eager to return to his playwriting, Hyde was not yet aware of the significance those initials would assume in the lives of everyone present, including himself.

Dráma Breithe Chríosta, Hyde's nativity play, was finished within the month that followed and published in the Christmas, 1902, double number of the *Weekly Freeman,* accompanied by a translation in English by Lady Gregory. There was trouble about it almost from the start. A 1904 performance scheduled for Christmas had to be cancelled when it became the subject of a resolution passed by priests in Kilkenny, criticizing some questionable passages that they perceived as causing possible confusion between superstition and dogma. Continually refused for six years thereafter, *Dráma Breithe Chríosta* finally had its premiere at the Abbey Theatre in January 1911, with Sara Allgood as the First Woman, Máire O'Neill as the Second Woman, and Máire Nic Shiubhlaigh as Mary. The Abbey sets were designed by Robert

Gregory, Lady Gregory's son. The production charmed both audiences and reviewers. Other productions followed. For almost a quarter of a century—until the offending passages were blacked out in a school edition of the play printed in 1935—no one took notice of the problem that had troubled the Kilkenny priests.

Hyde's next play, also written at Coole in 1902, was *Teach na mBocht* (The poorhouse), a short, appealing comedy which Lady Gregory translated as *The Poorhouse* and later reworked and expanded to produce *The Workhouse Ward*. It was followed in 1903 by a maverick in Hyde's canon, a sharply satirical bilingual play not unlike the later bilingual satires of Brian O'Nolan (especially those written under his pseudonyms, Myles na gCopaleen and Flann O'Brien). *An Pleusgadh na Bulgóide, or The Bursting of the Bubble* was clearly intended not for Hyde's usual audiences but for more sophisticated theatergoers familiar with the opposing sides in the continuing battle over education in Irish; its targets were easily identified by them as Mahaffy and Atkinson, the Trinity professors whom Hyde had correctly identified as prime enemies of the Irish language. "Bulgóide," in fact, as the "notes" to Hyde's Irish text point out, is suspiciously similar to "Trínóide," Irish for "Trinity," and two of the major characters of the play are called Magaffy and Hatkin. Moreover, in their dialogue with the lord lieutenant, Magaffy and Hatkin are given lines that only slightly exaggerate the charges made by their real-life counterparts in their 1899 testimony before the Intermediate Education Commissioners, of the implausibility of identifying Irish as a bona fide language and the vulgarity and obscenity of its literature. The play's Sean Bhean Bhocht, or Poor Old Woman (a traditional symbol of Irish Ireland), whose curse ("that the thing which in this world ye most loathe and dread shall instantly come upon you") forces all the Bulgóide professors to speak Irish, is not the old hag of Yeats's *Countess Cathleen* (who becomes a beautiful young queen when she wins the pure and devoted love of the young men of Ireland) but the fierce woman of "The Shan Van Vocht," a nineteenth-century ballad that commemorates the rising of 1798.

Hyde's next play, also written in 1903, was based on a folktale account of James II's escape from Ireland in a barrel. Although it was first published in the Christmas 1903 number of the *Weekly Freeman* and had since been reprinted in both Irish and English, there is no record that *Rí Séamus* (King James) was ever performed, perhaps because by then Dublin Castle had identified the league as a subversive organization and had begun to keep a file on its activities. Lady

Gregory's *The White Cockade,* however, a dramatization of the aftermath of the Battle of the Boyne and the cowardly flight of James II, first produced by the Abbey in 1905, contains a central comic scene clearly modeled on Hyde's *Rí Séamus* in which King James hides in a barrel from the Irish soldiers he has deserted.

In *An Cleamhnas* (The matchmaking), first published in two parts in December 1903 and January 1904, Hyde returned to the life of the Irish cottager, the subject of his first playwriting successes—but with a difference. Half-serious, half-comic, it takes a sharp, satiric look at the hard bargaining that goes on between a country father, Patrick Ó Malain, and his old crony, Peter Ó Gioblan, over a proposed match between Patrick's daughter, Kate, and Peter's son, young Peter. Kate's own wish, ignored by her father, is that she might marry Diarmuid, a young man who also has the approval of Máire, Kate's mother. Kate gets her wish, but only because of a transparent trick played by Máire that emphasizes how differently things turn out in real life. The same bitterness is evident in Hyde's last play written before 1905, *Máistín an Bhéarla* (The mastiff of the English language), in which the target is again the Irish educational establishment, this time at the primary-school level, represented by the cruel schoolmaster who beats Irish-speaking children, bullies their parents, and justifies his behavior as merely fulfilling government requirements. Unsuccessful as a play, this diatribe is evidence of how deeply bruised Hyde felt by other events, outside the theater, with which he had been coping between 1900 and 1905.

12

The Larger Stage

For Douglas Hyde, preoccupied with the new Irish theater, the success of his plays, and the growth of the Gaelic League, recognition that some things were going awry dawned slowly. Between 1893 and 1899 he had come to think of himself as the happiest of men. On January 17, 1900, when he turned forty, he was, in the opinion of those who knew him well, a practical, adaptable, resourceful, and optimistic leader. His best asset, as described by one acquaintance, was his "superb and adroit capacity for making the best of an opportunity." He might have been more wary of the twentieth century had flashes of lightning or claps of thunder instead of minor cracks and distant rumblings signaled that his life was about to change.

There had been, for example, the hearings before the Royal Commission on Intermediate Education in 1899. Everyone had thought that their purpose was to strengthen an 1878 ruling concerning instruction in Irish that was not being enforced. Then Mahaffy, attacking the small ground that had been won twenty-one years before by the Society for the Preservation of the Irish Language, had suddenly succeeded in changing the issue to whether there should be such a ruling at all. Momentarily caught off balance, complainant had unexpectedly become defendant, but Hyde had recovered quickly and marshaled such support from so many distinguished scholars that in the end the Intermediate Education (Ireland) Amendment Act of 1900 seemed to have put the Irish language in a better position than ever before.

Then, even as Hyde had incorporated this experience into the speeches he made, welcoming new branches into the League—even as he was editing for a Gaelic League pamphlet the arguments in favor of the language that he and his blue-ribbon referees had presented to the commission—there were distant rumblings. They came from restless leaguers who, agreeing with Hyde's estimate of the league's strength and accomplishments, challenged his continuing policy of nonconfrontation with British authorities. True, they said, nine men had met on July 31, 1893, in Martin Kelly's rooms at 9 Lower Sackville Street to found the Gaelic League, and current membership stood at between 10,000 and 12,000. Yes, even with only nine members the league had not defined itself narrowly but had sought to represent a cross section of Irish society, and now at the turn of the century its strength was its broad base of Catholics and Protestants, nationalists and Unionists, landlords and tenants, civil servants and schoolteachers, old and young, women and men, all working together. And yes, when these women and men looked at what they had accomplished in seven short years, what they saw, as Hyde proclaimed, was a network of organizers, traveling Irish teachers, strong local committees, and rank-and-file members who had by their own efforts set up classes in spoken Irish and Irish music, dancing, and sports. It was indeed the general membership, these leaguers confirmed, that had fostered the spread of literacy in Irish in both Irish-speaking and English-speaking areas. It was they who, working together, had established a publishing program that included a league newspaper, league texts to help them learn, improve their Irish, and teach their families and neighbors, and league pamphlets that countered the propaganda of their enemies and kept their members informed. Through local and regional *feiseanna* and through the annual *oireachtas* the league had brought to its members enjoyment and pride in being Irish and living an Irish life. If Hyde himself had said that all these things were so, why, these discontented leaguers asked, did he insist that they must continue to avoid confrontation with the British authorities?

Many leaguers could not understand why Hyde opposed the mail-in-Irish campaign. They deeply resented the ruling enforced by the British postal system in Ireland that all letters and packets must be addressed in English. Speaking from his lecture platform, Hyde had urged his fellow members of the league to keep alive their language and culture, to speak Irish among themselves at every opportunity, to sing Irish songs and tell Irish stories, and even to write to each other in Irish. But, they asked, must they then send their Irish letters to each other in envelopes addressed in English? If the Gaelic League could fight for education in Irish in the schools, why not, they asked, fight for the right to send letters and packets addressed in Irish through the Post Office?

For Hyde the answer was, as the old storytellers would say, *ní hansa*—not difficult to relate. The Intermediate Education (Ireland) Amendment Act had been worth the risks presented by the royal commission hearings. Victory had assured the Irish people that within the educational system Irish could grow and spread in response to popular demand. Whatever it had cost to wage the battle against the Trinity dons had been an investment in shaping the attitudes of the young and therefore the future of the Irish nation. He was not willing, however, to jeopardize the league's prospering position for any lesser cause, especially one that could be used against them to their detriment. To be sure, the mail-in-Irish campaign that restless leaguers were advocating (indeed, already had begun on their own) had raised an issue that some day would have to be confronted. But if the Post Office refused to handle letters and packets addressed in Irish and league members insisted that only Irish be used on league mail, the result would be a disruption of communications among league branches and a crippling of league efforts to raise much-needed funds.

Earnest leaguers eager for another victory could not understand such caution in the man who had been a founder of their organization and the author of its policy of deanglicization, especially as among themselves they were discovering new, young leaders who disagreed with him. They continued their mail-in-Irish campaign. It was the first serious challenge to Hyde's policies and leadership.

What Hyde understood, of course, but could not convince protesting leaguers to accept, was that by insisting on the right to address envelopes in Irish, they were touching a sensitive nerve that affected not just British government in Ireland but the entire British Empire. One of the strengths Hyde brought to his position as president of the league was that he had only to repress An Craoibhin and assume momentarily the persona of the son of the rector of Frenchpark to see how the Ascendancy viewed such matters. For decades, for example, as he knew well, the British postal system had prided itself on the speed and efficiency of its worldwide service. It was the primary channel of communication in the largest and most widely dispersed bureaucracy the world had ever known. It employed thousands of civil servants with titles such as postmaster, sub-postmaster, inspector, surveyor, surveyor's assistant, clerk, telegrapher, and sorter who obtained their jobs through a political patronage system that rewarded loyal citizens of country, colony, and distant outpost. It was an instrument of British policy through which the government provided support for factions and classes that it wanted to foster and denied it to those it wanted to weaken or render invisible. There was no doubt that a campaign to allow addressing in Irish would be seen by the Post Office as an overt threat to the entire system in all its ramifications. Bilingualism in Ireland was not British policy. Irish might be taught in schools—a postal clerk who knew Irish might be useful in an Irish-speaking area when a monolingual person needed assistance or the odd letter addressed in Irish slipped through the cracks— but it was not officially recognized for government use. If the Irish were to win the right to mail letters and packets addressed in Irish within Ireland, it would mean that they would be able to send such letters and packets through the entire British postal system. The Post Office would have to hire people competent in reading and writing Irish not just to assist an occasional customer but to sort and deliver mail. It would have to violate government policy, which did not recognize Irish as an official language.

Leaders of the mail-in-Irish campaign were not persuaded by Hyde's argument that because the league's policy of avoiding direct confrontation with British authorities had proved so successful in the past, it should not be abandoned in the future. Many openly resented his declarations on the subject. Underneath all, some quietly reminded others, An Craoibhin was, of course, not really one of them but the son of the Protestant rector of Frenchpark. He was, moreover, a kinsman of Lord de Freyne, whose treatment of the Frenchpark tenantry had become a public scandal. And in his youth he had been a protégé of Charles Owen O'Conor Don, the man descended from an ancient and honorable Celtic family who once had had the respect of his countrymen but now, in his opposition to land reform and tenant relief, revealed, they said bitterly, the soul of a landlord. It was not that they suspected Hyde's loyalty—they were confident that he was a committed nationalist (many said he was a sworn Fenian)—but all the same, they told each other, there was no mistaking the fact that he still had a lot of the country squire in him. How much further could they follow him, they asked themselves, if he continued to insist on avoiding open confrontation?

At home in his study at Ratra, Douglas Hyde was disturbed by the distrust and dissension that seemed to be increasing all around him. At the same time he was preoccupied with the implications of Lucy's persistent illnesses. Through the winter, spring, and summer of 1900 her condition had steadily declined. Her numerous symptoms, which had puzzled other doctors, had prompted Dr. Sigerson to prescribe a bewildering variety of remedies, including steaming, tincture of iodine, Vichy water, poultices of turpentine and mustard, a tonic, and a half-drop of belladonna every quarter hour until six or eight in the evening. What was to become of her, of him, of their children, and their home at Ratra, Hyde asked himself, if she continued in this semi-invalid state? He had been assured that there was no question of life or death. That, at least, was a comfort. But poor Lucy was so miserable most of the time. Where would he turn if Sigerson's prescriptions did not bring some relief? In December 1900 Hyde sent Lady Gregory a packet of his early work: "Irish songs I made, some of them twenty years ago, and printed in various places." With it was a wistful request that she, his trusted friend, keep these manuscripts for him until such time as he felt he could retrieve them, for he liked to think that he might rewrite and republish them some day.

Three months later, on Monday, March 25, 1901, the skirmishing of the mail-in-Irish leaguers expanded into what became a long and costly battle between the Post Office and the Gaelic League. The first shot was fired when Thomas O'Donnell, an Irish M.P., stood up in the House and asked why a circular had been issued to Post Office officials, directing them to regard all letters with Irish superscriptions as insufficiently addressed. O'Donnell, who previously had signed his name in Irish on the parliamentary roll and had attempted to give his maiden speech in Irish, had not long to wait for the government's reply. Austen Chamberlain, secretary of the treasury, later postmaster general, condescendingly explained that the authorities presumed that senders of such letters in Great Britain were able to write directions on their envelopes in English. It was to those patrons, he said, that the circular had referred. He conceded, however, that letters bearing addresses in Irish that were mailed from Irish-speaking districts would be delivered. Not satisfied, O'Donnell pressed the government with a second question: "Does the honorable gentleman know that there are thousands of Irishmen who prefer to write their letters in Irish?" Chamberlain replied that anyone might write in Irish if he pleased, but that the Post Office required that all addresses be written in English "by those who presumably know English."

Aware that O'Donnell's question probably signaled an intensification of the mail-in-Irish agitation which the Post Office had tried to ignore by treating it as a series of unrelated incidents, postal authorities issued instructions that henceforth all press reports on the controversy together with internal Post Office correspondence, directives, and memoranda be preserved and filed. In the London Post Office an anonymous civil servant was assigned responsibility for monitoring the daily British and Irish press, underlining or bracketing with blue pencil pertinent passages of all news items pertaining to the mail-in-Irish agitation, cutting out and pasting these items in bulky folders labeled "Correspondence Addressed in Erse," and filing these folders with others labeled "Irish Minutes." As Hyde had warned, no longer would any action of the Gaelic League go unnoticed or unrecorded. It was only a matter of time before a second order of surveillance was issued by Dublin Castle.

Meanwhile, in a written answer to O'Donnell's query (copies of which were dispatched to postmasters in Manchester, Sheffield, Nottingham, Bradford, and other cities with large Irish colonies), the postmaster general rejected "special arrangements for the translation of addresses in Irish into English, especially in the case of letters posted in England." Like Chamberlain, he offered a concession: that "in the event of a letter in Irish passing through an office where it can be deciphered, the address shall be translated into English and the letter sent on to its destination."

Even as this reply to O'Donnell was written and publicly distributed, it was underscored by the internal circulation of an unsigned memorandum based on the only facts that mattered to the Post Office: the number of people in Ireland who could write Irish and only Irish. Armed with statistics from the 1891 *Statesman's Yearbook* that established this figure at 40,000, the unnamed author declared that this was not a constituency whose demands justified changing rules that had earned the Post Office its name for economy and efficiency. Questioning whether special arrangements should be made for educated people who could just as well write in English, he recommended that letters addressed in Irish be treated as undeliverable and dealt with in the Returned Letters Office. This was, in the writer's opinion, the simple solution to the problem—the same solution, he noted, that was used in Germany where writers understood that letters addressed in Polish would be treated as undeliverable. As for the matter of requiring Post Office appointees to have a knowledge of Irish, it would so limit the field of choice, he believed, "as in some instances to raise a grave danger of leaving the Department without any candidate fit for appointment."

This unsigned memorandum established official Post Office policy for years to come.

The mail-in-Irish campaign continued. On October 13, 1901, Mr. J. MacNamee of Navan complained to the Post Office that the local postmaster had refused to cash a postal money order. Always quick to follow up complaints, the Post Office queried Navan. On October 18 the inspector reported that MacNamee had endorsed his postal order "with his signature written in Irish characters" and, on being asked, had refused to sign his name in English. Furthermore, MacNamee had stated that he was making a test case, that he intended to have the matter taken up by "the central executive of the Gaelic League," and that in his opinion postal officers should understand the Irish language. The Navan report concluded: "None of the officers at Navan are conversant with the Irish language." Not until December 23, 1901—and then only after prolonged consultation among the Post Office, the comptroller, and the accountant general—was it decided that MacNamee's order could be paid if the words "described as J. MacNamee" were added below his Irish signature.

The first Gaelic League "Language Week" was held in March 1902 in conjunction with a long procession commemorating St. Patrick's Day. Hyde, of course, was among the principal speakers. He was relieved that little was said about the mail-in-Irish campaign, which he still hoped to confine before it brought the trouble he had predicted. His main concern was the annual fund-raising drive set for this time of year and conducted largely through the mails. Sporadic complaints concerning the handling of letters and packets addressed in Irish continued to be received by the Post Office. All were handled routinely, with reference to the official policy statement drawn up in 1901. On Monday, November 6, 1902, an Irish M.P. by the name of Tully rose in the House to ask the postmaster-general whether, given complaints from the Gaelic League in London about nondelivery of letters and postcards addressed in Irish in Sligo, he would "consider the advisability of insisting on persons obtaining Post Office appointments in Ireland having some knowledge of the Irish language." Back came the unequivocal answer: "In my opinion there is no sufficient reason for requiring a knowledge of the Irish language from entrants into the Post Office service in Ireland." On Monday, December 1, 1902, the subject came up again when Patrick O'Brien, M.P., asked if the postmaster general would supply copies of an Irish dictionary to each post office to facilitate delivery of letters in Irish. Chamberlain's response was again immediate: "I do not think the circumstances are such as to justify the provision of Irish dictionaries at Post Offices."

By March 1903 Dublin Castle had begun to keep its own files on Douglas Hyde and other "key agitators" of the Gaelic League. Long clippings from the *Independent* and the *Weekly Freeman* containing passages from their speeches underlined in blue pencil were added to a file labeled "Irish News Cuttings." From September through November the Post Office was kept busy investigating the complaint of a leaguer from Galway, the Reverend A. J. Considine, concerning a postal money order that a clerk had refused to cash because the order was made out in some form of Irish that he could not understand. After investigation, the Galway Post Office reported to London that the Irish in Considine's order was unintelligible—and that he had admitted that his was a test case. On December 2, 1903, a postal service customer by the name of Hugh Graham complained in a letter written in Irish to the secretary of the Dublin Post Office that the postmistress of his branch would not release a registered letter posted to him in England after he had signed his name in Irish on the receipt. "Is it not proper, allowable and right for an Irishman to write down his name correctly in his own language?" asked Graham. During the same month Henry Morris, Gaelic League organizer in the Dundalk area, editor of the Gaelic department of the *Dundalk Democrat,* and Hyde's close friend (albeit one who disagreed with him on this matter), published some words of advice to leaguers engaged in the mail-in-Irish campaign. Their twin aims, he declared, should be recognition of Irish as a national language and the addition of Irish to the list of obligatory subjects required of all candidates for all departments of the postal service. To achieve these he recommended increased use of Irish, since Post Office policies were based on statistical evidence of language use: "Those . . . who can write the whole letter in Irish should do so, but those who cannot do that much should at least address the letter in Irish—and in Irish only—except in cases where great dispatch is necessary."

Pleased with their escalating provocation and unaware of the files that were being kept in the London and Dublin headquarters of the Post Office and in Dublin Castle, leaders of the mail-in-Irish campaign, now in its fourth year, did not fail to draw attention to the fact that it had not resulted in the kind of crushing retaliation predicted by Douglas Hyde. Even the sallies on the floor of Parliament had evoked not the outraged protest or condescending rebuke that might have been expected but only a matter-of-fact repetition of official policy. The British government had not mellowed; it was otherwise occupied. Cabinet minutes from August 1899 through 1903 reflect continuing concern over the conduct of the Boer War, the Boxer Rebellion, the negotiation of an agreement with the United States to create a transoceanic canal in central America, and the possibility of a Russo-Japanese war. When Parliament did turn its attention to Ireland, the debate was usually over the Land Purchase Acts and other legislation concerning the Land Question.

Throughout the years 1900 to 1905 the Land Question also concerned Douglas Hyde on a personal level. The de Freyne estate in Frenchpark had become a battleground as Lord de Freyne, irate over land reform, infuriated by tenants who were withholding their rents, enraged by the "interference" of the United Irish League in his disputes with these tenants, carried out draconian evictions that were fully and graphically reported in London, Dublin, and provincial newspapers. In 1904 the Congested Districts Board, with its authority to buy up and redistribute uneconomical holdings, moved against de Freyne. Although no doubt spurred by the evictions, the action of the Congested Districts Board was not necessarily punitive but merely part of a process of land reform that had started in 1870. Despite help offered through O'Conor Don by the Committee of Landlords, which saw the reform process as disastrous to Ireland's agricultural economy, de Freyne finally gave up and set a price at which he was willing to sell his tenanted and bog land. It was only a matter of a very short time, Hyde knew, before the Congested Districts Board would be pressing him to buy or leave Ratra. How could he even contemplate parting from these meadows and fields, the lake, those distant hills? Lucy was insisting that they must go.

Meanwhile, the Gaelic League was faced with a funding crisis. The situation could not be blamed entirely or even chiefly on the mail-in-Irish campaign, but it had not helped. Even Henry Morris had advised that urgent letters should be addressed in English, not Irish, but having committed themselves to the mail-in-Irish campaign, league fundraisers were addressing solicitations in Irish, with consequent incidents of nondelivery and delay. The biggest drain on the budget, however, as Hyde had written in October 1903 to his friend William Bulfin, Irish emigré to Argentina and publisher and editor of the Buenos Aires *Southern Cross*, was an increase in workload that required additional paid staff.

League membership had passed the 50,000 mark and was still growing. Full-time organizers were now needed to handle the paperwork involved in adding new branches in Ireland and affiliates abroad. The subsequent demand for new language books had resulted in larger and larger printing costs. Determined that all 1903 debts would be paid before the end of the league's fiscal year in February and the new collection in March, Hyde asked Bulfin if there was any possibility of obtaining a second contribution from the sources usually tapped by the *Southern Cross*. In a speech to a large audience in Dundalk in February 1904, Hyde proclaimed what he called "the Battle of Ireland." The underlying subject was the funding crisis—his point was that growth and achievement were costing more money than was being received—but his appeal stressed what the league had been accomplishing. The mail-in-Irish campaign was now frankly acknowledged to be one of the league's activities.

The fact was that, measured by the number of items addressed in Irish that were being processed by the Post Office, the mail-in-Irish campaign actually was succeeding. Official British Post Office policy had not changed; it remained the same, in fact, under three postmasters general (the Marquess of Londonderry, 1900–1902; Austen Chamberlain, 1902–1903; Lord Stanley, 1903–1905) and their secretaries (Sir George Murray, 1899–1903 and Sir H. Babington Smith, 1903–1910). Official communications consistently and publicly maintained that there was no reason why the workings of the British postal system should be jeopardized for the purpose of serving a handful of Irish monoglots. But the Post Office had not achieved its worldwide reputation for speed and efficiency without having had to make practical adjustments. In the case of Irish this meant that by early 1905, with the Dublin Post Office receiving over two hundred letters addressed in Irish daily, Charles Sanderson, the Dublin postmaster, had taken from their regular assignments four junior clerks and telegraphists with "an adequate knowledge of the language" and set them to work translating Irish addresses. In a letter to his superior, however, Sanderson expressed concern that these measures would not be sufficient if, as expected, he received a huge mailing addressed in Irish "by a particular organisation." The effect, he warned, could be costly and surely would cause delays.

The organization to which Sanderson was referring was of course the Gaelic League; the huge mailing that he was correctly anticipating was the annual "collection," which provided the greater part of the league's financial support. Hyde had emphasized to Patrick O'Daly, secretary of the league since 1901, that this year more than ever a successful collection was a vital need. Even as Sanderson wrote, O'Daly was halfway through the task of supervising the assembly of hundreds of packets containing announcements of Language Week and the fundraising kits to be used by canvassers in the local branches. By the first week of March, O'Daly's crew had addressed 600 parcels with the recipient's name and address in Irish. But if at times the Post Office might bend, it would not allow itself to be broken. On March 1 the Irish secretary of the Post Office wrote to his British counterpart in London: "It must of course be borne in mind that there is no necessity for these letters to be addressed in Gaelic. There is no pretense in Dublin at any rate that Gaelic is a common language. So far as necessity goes the letters might just as well be addressed in Greek or Hebrew."

Since parcels addressed in Irish had been accepted at the General Post Office earlier in the year, O'Daly was outraged when several hundred parcels were refused on the grounds that they were unacceptable for mailing and would have to be readdressed in English. O'Daly wired the Dublin postmaster on March 7: "250 parcels addressed in Irish refused last night are lying here. Will they be accepted today?" His reply came from London: "Parcels addressed in Irish cannot be accepted without English translation of addresses." Indignant, both O'Daly and Hyde refused to believe that the problem was caused by the addresses in Irish. The Post Office officials were fully aware of the purpose of the contents of the packets, Hyde declared. These officials also knew that if the collection was destroyed the league would be left virtually without the money it required for operating expenses for the coming year. For him there was no doubt: the sudden imposition of a work-to-rule order was made "with ill will and full knowledge." As the rule, however, was being applied only to bulk mailings, O'Daly sent out a call for Irish speakers to come to an emergency meeting. Two hundred responded. Each was given a packet and all went down to the main post office. "They took over the place entirely," O'Daly reported. "Each Irish speaker there offered his own packet to the officer inside. Each person did this one after the other, calmly and quietly in Irish. No more work was done in the Post Office while this was going on. It put a stop to the work that is the ordinary business for an hour, the place was so busy."

Realizing, however, that a prolonged impasse with the Post Office could destroy the 1905 collection and surely would raise costs (the rates for individual mailings were greater than those for bulk mailing), Hyde decided to try personal diplomacy. He immediately sought an interview with Lord Stanley, the postmaster general, in London. Using his best Ascendancy manners, Hyde was persuasive and persistent; cloaked in governmental invulnerability, Stanley was courteous and attentive. Stanley promised nothing.

Although his interview with Stanley came to little, Hyde was quick to seize the opportunity to generate public sympathy for the league. The motives to which he had ascribed the Post Office's refusal to handle the bulk mailing addressed in Irish already had made headlines in Dublin and London newspapers. In an interview with the *Irish Independent* of March 3, 1905 (duly cut and pasted in the Post Office file labeled "Correspondence Addressed in Erse"), Hyde struck back: "It is nothing short of a scandal that the Post Office authorities have not made Irish a subject of examination for Post Office officials considering the number of letters that pass through the post addressed in Irish. . . . I hope the authorities will soon discontinue their foolish opposition, which will serve no good purpose but to irritate the public."

On March 4 the *Freeman's Journal* printed a lengthy account of the battle between the Post Office and the league, stressing the capriciousness of the postal authorities who had, after initial refusal, reversed themselves and accepted six or seven packets, only to reverse themselves again and refuse on the next day over two hundred parcels that had been picked up by Post Office van. According to the writer of the article, the reversal had occurred when a minor official in the Dublin post office had been overruled by the Irish secretary who, in a memo to London sent on March 4, had complained that "the whole thing is an attempt to force the Department into having a Gaelic-speaking staff throughout the country, a matter as impracticable as useless and wasteful."

On March 6 the matter reached Parliament where Boland, an Irish M.P., asked if the Gaelic League parcels had been refused at the order of the postmaster general or without his knowledge. Pursuing the same line of questioning, John Redmond rose to inquire whether the postmaster general knew that the Gaelic League had been handicapped by this refusal, because the packets contained material about the annual collection. He also asked flatly if, now that the matter had been brought to his attention, the postmaster general could assure him that the parcels in dispute would be dispatched in due course.

By March 12, the day set for the Language Week procession, the conflict between the Gaelic League and the Post Office had attracted the attention of thousands. Since the government crackdown already had affected the annual collection, Hyde's strategy was to win at least a propaganda victory. He spoke openly before crowds and to newspaper reporters of the clash between the Post Office and the language movement. The result, reported the *Freeman's Journal*, was "one of the most imposing public demonstrations that . . . ever passed through the streets of Dublin." Editorializing on the situation on March 13, the *Freeman's Journal* continued:

No greater proof could have been given of the strength of the language movement. . . . There was hardly any element of Irish life that was not yesterday influentially represented. . . . The aggressive and bitter vendetta of the English Post Office Department against the movement gave the opportunity for a really most extraordinary and effective promulgation of public opinion.

Placards and bannerettes proclaimed, "No Surrender to the Post Office. Address all your parcels and letters in Irish." When the Irish-language section passed the General Post Office, the procession paused to render a rousing chorus of "A Nation Once Again." On the side of a tableau wagon someone had scribbled, at the bottom of a prominently displayed white banner bearing the familiar red insignia of the Post Office over the monogram of Edward VII, "We Don't Like Irish." On this same open wagon an Irishman ("in typical Gaelic costume," according to the *Freeman's Journal*) and a Post Office clerk played a perpetual Beckettian dumbshow. The Irishman picked up a parcel and offered it to the clerk at the counter, who looked at the parcel, shook his head, and handed it back to the Irishman, who immediately picked up another parcel and offered it to the clerk, who shook his head, and handed it back to the Irishman: "all most effective and excellent comedy at the expense of the Post Office," the *Freeman's Journal* reported.

The procession wound its way to Smithfield where Hyde shared the speaker's platform with the archbishop of Dublin. Standing before a shouting, cheering crowd, smiling and waving as he waited for a quiet moment to begin his speech, Hyde began slowly: "First—First—First, I want to tell you—First I want to tell you of—First I want to tell you of the wonderfully mean and miserable, petty and paltry attempt that was made to spoil our collection last week by the General Post Office." He paused. The crowd groaned loudly. He accused the Post Office of trying to break the spirit of the league. The crowd booed. He described his attempt to negotiate with Stanley:

I asked . . . to make Irish not, mind you, a compulsory subject at all, but an *optional* subject for entry into the Post Office. And what was their answer? They not only refused me, but they have made Irish *penal* in the Post Office. They will not be *allowed* to do it. There are only *seventeen* letters in the Irish alphabet, and there are only *three* of those that are not the same as in English, *and the Post Office people are not able to learn those three.*

Loud laughter was followed by more cheers. "This struggle was forced upon us by them and was none of our making or our seeking. It has been *forced* upon us. We have no desire whatever to quarrel with these people. It is they themselves who have brought the quarrel upon themselves." Amid laughter and applause the archbishop, following Hyde, announced that he himself would not have attended the Language Week celebration but for the Post Office refusal that had threatened to make the League's procession a failure. There was more laughter and cheering as everyone, looking around, saw nothing but crowds in every direction.

On March 13 the secretary of the Post Office for Ireland sent London his report accompanied by the account in the *Freeman's Journal* of the procession and rally. "It is to be regretted," he wrote, providing a fitting final line to the comedy, "that the action of the Department should be looked on as hostile to the League itself. What the promoters of the movement fail to understand is that a translation must be affixed to a parcel before dispatch and there is no reason why the additional work should be thrown on the Department."

Five days later the words of Henry Morris writing from Dundalk were more somber.

The Post Office has declared war against the Irish language and the Gaelic League. The Gaelic League could not refuse to accept this challenge. So now it behooves every Gaelic Leaguer to take a share in the battle. . . . Irish Ireland insists that Irish . . . being the national Language . . . be dealt with in the Post Office exactly on a par with English.

The public, Morris avowed, must force the Post Office to provide a bilingual staff. It must address all letters, cards, telegrams, and parcels in Irish until the Post Office is blocked and everywhere there is evidence of chaos and delay. Readers must complain in writing (preferably in Irish) to the secretary of the Post Office each time a delayed piece of mail is received. They must demand an explanation for the delay. (What Morris knew was that Post Office rules required a written response to every complaint, including those in Irish.) All these moves should be followed, concluded Morris, "for the express purpose of asserting our own right to use our own language in our own country. Dr. Hyde has sounded the tocsin . . . and every Irish Irelander should take a genuine part in the fray."

By April 2 the continuing pressure on the Post Office had begun to have its effect. The number of letters addressed in Irish that passed through the Dublin Post Office had climbed from 313 on March 20 to 600 on March 26. Within a single week over thirty hours had been spent translating a total of 2,498 items from Irish to English. In his 1905 report to London the Irish Secretary warned that the dispute had to be settled in some way, as the work of translation had become "formidable." Yet he did not know what to propose, for if anyone were specially assigned to translation as his regular duty, he had no doubt that the Gaelic Leaguers would consider that they had gained their case in principle and would press home their advantage by multiplying the number of letters addressed in Irish. The secretary assured his superior in London that "the general expression of feeling which reaches me is a hope that the Postmaster-General will not give way in the matter."

Believing that the time was right for such communication, on April 3 Hyde wrote two letters for delivery to Lord Stanley. The first was typed. He called it his "official letter." The second, a "private letter," was written in his own hand. In the five-page "official" letter, a combination of a carrot and stick, Hyde repeated the arguments he had made to Stanley in person but referred to the case of the packets addressed in Irish only once. He focused instead on acceptance of Irish as an optional subject for Post Office examinations. He argued that Irish already was accepted as either a compulsory or optional subject in many business, professional, and educational areas of Irish life. To facilitate the work of the Post Office, he offered to send Stanley copies of a directory compiled by the league of postal towns and stations in Ireland which gave on one side the "correct" Irish form and on the other "the corrupt or translated forms by which these places are known." He also offered Stanley a Gaelic League volume in press that showed the correct form of Irish surnames being widely adopted. "With these two volumes at its disposal," he declared, "the Post Office will experience little or no difficulty dealing with the new order of things." Hyde closed with the pointed reminder that 50,000 people had marched in the Language Week procession of March 12, forming a line witnessed by 200,000 people that wound through the streets for two miles—proof "that the whole country is solid behind Dublin in respectfully making this . . . reasonable request of the Post Office." "We feel confident," he concluded pointedly, "that it is only necessary to put these plain facts before you for your compliance."

In sharp contrast (*Dr. Jekyll and Mr. Hyde* was a story that Hyde found amusing) was the conciliatory tone of the handwritten "private letter," which expressed the hope that Lord Stanley, without any inconvenience to himself or to the working of the Post Office, might find it possible to comply with Hyde's "requests." "I beg of you," wrote Hyde, his sharply slanted writing bearing uphill, "not to treat this question from the narrow point of view of the Post Office, but from the standpoint of a statesman." If the Post Office rejected the league's demands, Hyde wrote,

I see with alarm the prospect of an agitation in Ireland which however it may end will at least have a certain effect . . . to still further alienate English public opinion from the English government, and to turn into opponents of the government a great portion of the Gaelic League who have up to this never touched politics in any way but have turned into a wholly laudable channel a very great deal of energy which would but for it have been used in a different direction.

Calling for use of "the oiled feather on both sides and a little give and take," Hyde warned Stanley that if the controversy were not stopped, it could prove "a very nasty business later on"—one that might even turn the Gaelic League into a channel Hyde himself was most anxious to avoid. Clearly separating the Jekyll-and-Hyde alternatives he had offered, Hyde closed with the reminder that his handwritten letter was private, his typed letter official.

What Hyde could not know, of course, was that his "official" letter had confirmed the suspicions of the secretary of the Post Office for Ireland that the real issue was not the matter of whether the Post Office henceforth would allow letters and packets to be addressed in Irish but how the Post Office henceforth would be staffed. Six weeks passed before Hyde received Stanley's official reply rejecting all his proposals: the requirement that parcels and registered letters addressed in Irish be accompanied by an English translation stood; the request to make Irish an optional subject for Post Office candidates was denied; the demand that Irish-speaking postmasters be appointed in Irish-speaking districts was rejected. Ignoring Hyde's veiled threats and other ploys, Stanley's personal reply of May 15, 1905, was no less adamant: "I am afraid," he wrote, that "you must take the views that I expressed in my official letter as being the line of conduct which I propose to take with regard

Douglas Hyde at twenty. (Courtesy Sealy collection)

Hyde's sister, Annette (later Mrs. John
Cambreth Kane). (Courtesy Sealy collection)

Hyde's father, the Reverend Arthur Hyde, Jr.
(Courtesy Sealy collection)

Dr. Douglas Hyde, Trinity scholar. (Courtesy Sealy collection)

Hyde in New Brunswick, Canada (1890–91).
(Courtesy Sealy collection)

Lucy Cometina Kurtz, shortly before her marriage
to Douglas Hyde in 1893. (Courtesy Sealy collection)

Douglas Hyde with sister, Annette, and wife Lucy, in his carriage in front of his county Roscommon residence, Ratra. (Courtesy Sealy collection)

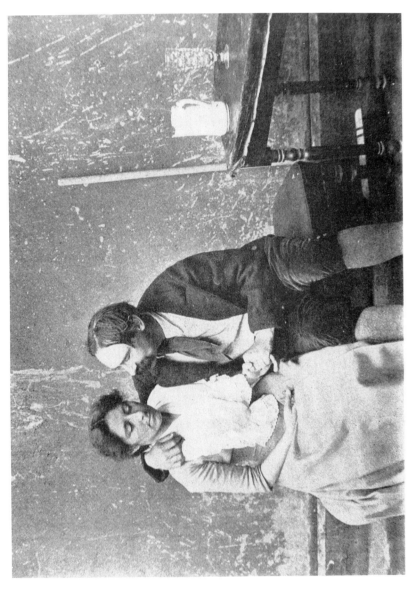

Douglas Hyde with Miss O'Kennedy, in "Casadh an tSúgáin" (The Twisting of the Rope). (Courtesy Colin Smythe, Ltd.)

Douglas Hyde with Miss O'Kennedy and Teig O'Donahue, in "Casadh an tSúgáin" (The Twisting of the Rope). (Courtesy Colin Smythe, Ltd.)

Douglas Hyde at Ratra, between daughters Una (left) and Nuala (right), with family dog. (Courtesy Sealy collection)

Douglas Hyde with pet cockatoo. (Courtesy Sealy collection)

Douglas Hyde, professor of Modern Irish, University College, Dublin.
(Courtesy Sealy collection)

Senator Douglas Hyde, 1937. (Courtesy the *Irish Press*)

Postcard photo of first president of Eire, 1938, with signature on reverse in Irish and English. (Courtesy Sealy collection)

Douglas Hyde addressing Dublin crowds in June 1938. (Courtesy the *Irish Press*)

Douglas Hyde with Eamon de Valera and Sinéad de Valera, June 1938.
(Courtesy the *Irish Press*)

Douglas Hyde on steps of Áras an Uachtaráin with John Cudahy, American minister to Ireland (left) and Douglas Corrigan (center), following Corrigan's "Wrong Way" flight to Ireland in July 1938. (Courtesy Sealy collection)

President Douglas Hyde with daughter Una and grandchildren, Christopher, Douglas, and Lucy Sealy. (Courtesy Sealy collection)

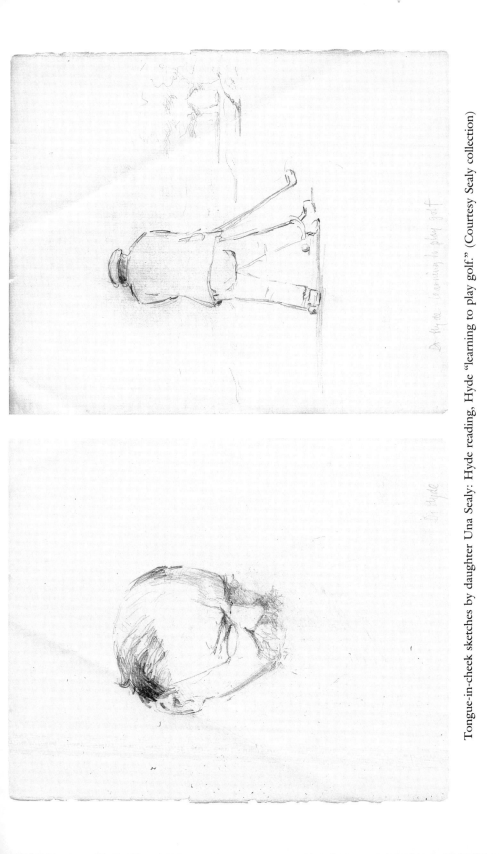

Tongue-in-cheek sketches by daughter Una Sealy: Hyde reading, Hyde "learning to play golf." (Courtesy Sealy collection)

Sean O'Sullivan drawing of Douglas Hyde, reproduced and distributed by
Irish Press, Christmas 1938. (Courtesy Sealy collection)

Douglas Hyde at work at his desk in Áras an Uachtaráin. (Courtesy Sealy collection)

Douglas Hyde with French minister, a few months after stroke suffered in 1940.
Hyde note, back of photo, reads "I am a whited sepulchre for underneath
my coat I have only a blanket!" (Courtesy the *Irish Times*)

Douglas Hyde chatting with P. L. Doyle, Lord Mayor of Dublin, July 1941.
(Courtesy Sealy collection)

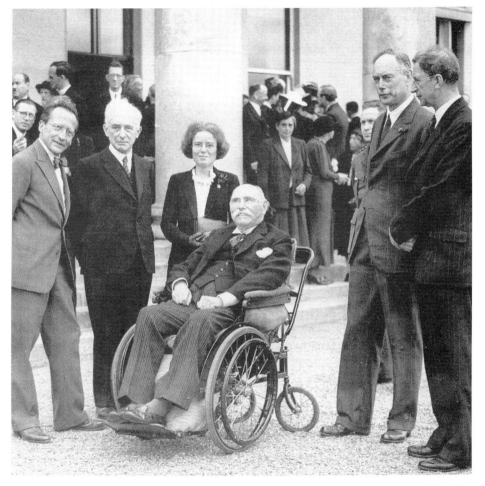

Douglas Hyde at reception marking 1943 opening of Dublin Institute for Advanced Studies. With him are Erwin Schrödinger, first director (far left), Eamon de Valera, (far right), and other scholars and dignitaries. (From the *Bulletin of the Department of Foreign Affairs* No. 1037 [May/June 1987]:14)

1944 portrait by Sean O'Sullivan. Confined to a wheelchair following his stroke, Hyde
sat for head and shoulders; his aide-de-camp, Eamon de Buitléar, served as model for the
standing figure—an arrangement that became a source of amusement between them.
(Courtesy Sealy collection)

Ratra, unroofed and derelict. (Courtesy the *Irish Times*)

Frenchpark church where the Reverend Arthur Hyde, Jr., was rector, 1867–1905, with graves of Douglas Hyde (foreground) and other family members.
(Courtesy the *Irish Times*)

Schoolboys at grave of Douglas Hyde. (Courtesy the *Irish Times*)

to this subject." Hyde's failure to move Stanley was a bitter pill, as he was sorely in need of a coup to counter continuing threats to his position within the league and worries about the league's financial situation. It had not been an easy spring, nor did it look as if summer would bring an improvement.

Scarcely the most important yet another one of the upsetting situations Hyde had had to face in the early months of 1905 involved accusations from Father Brennan of Killarney, a member of the Coiste Gnótha, or executive committee, that stemmed from the dismissal of a reporter named Kelly from the *Weekly Freeman* staff. Brennan alleged that Hyde, Agnes O'Farrelly, and Edward Martyn had carried on a campaign against Kelly on account of his failure to use Connacht Irish in his Irish-language columns and had succeeded finally in getting him fired. Stung by what he called "this horrid insinuation against my personal honor," Hyde repeatedly denied the charges against himself as well as O'Farrelly and Martyn, to no avail. Brennan persisted, creating tension at a time when Hyde could least spare the hours or energy to cope with it.

Then in early May there was another flare-up in Dublin in a continuing dispute over the right of owners to paint their names in Irish on their carts. Like the mail-in-Irish campaign, the crusade of the cart owners was a cause that all Hyde's instincts told him to avoid. When someone in the league had suggested that the statute prohibiting such signs should be challenged, Hyde specifically had ordered that the matter not become an issue for the law courts. To Hyde's dismay, Patrick Pearse, whom he regarded as a close friend and protégé, had ignored Hyde's pronouncement and had himself gone to court to plead on behalf of the "cart martyrs," providing the *Weekly Freeman,* which reported the May 19 trial, with ample material for a dramatic profile of the passionate young barrister. What was worse, Pearse lost the case, assuring a future escalation in demonstrations, charges, and trials, and the *Weekly Freeman* profile of Pearse was added to the files in Dublin Castle. Additional clippings were generated in May, when the *Cork Examiner* reported rumors of "revolutionary tendencies . . . in certain districts" in connection with league activities. There were rumors that the chief secretary had ordered the county inspectors of the Royal Irish Constabulary to keep a careful eye on branches in their districts.

Meanwhile another source of dissension came from Protestant members of the league, many of them Hyde's closest friends and earliest supporters, who had begun complaining of bias in the organization—

evident, they said, in attitudes toward the Craobh na gCuig Cuigi, or "branch of the five provinces," which some leaguers had dubbed the "branch of the five protestants," since it was this branch that most Protestants joined. Far worse was the news, as the spring of 1905 became summer and figures from Dublin showed the league barely able to meet its monthly expenses, that the depleted treasury might present Hyde with no choice but to reduce the corps of league organizers and teachers—a serious blow, as the league's next major objective, the founding of a new university in Ireland, stood little chance of achievement unless substantial funds materialized. At the very moment of swelling grass-roots interest it looked as if the work of the league might have to come to a halt unless a source of substantial new funding could be found. But the most difficult of Hyde's problems as summer became fall required decisions that affected his personal life and an embarrassing situation that involved John Quinn.

In December 1903, with the first indications that a threatening financial crisis could stall the league's progress, Hyde had sent out urgent cries for help to friends and affiliate organizations abroad. One of his appeals had been addressed to John Quinn. In the treasury, he had told Quinn, there were but two hundred pounds to carry the organization until March. Two thousand dollars voted for league support nearly two years before by the Ancient Order of Hibernians had never been sent; he had asked repeatedly when the league might expect this needed contribution, but the AOH president kept putting him off. Quinn responded at once with a $100 donation which, as it was lost in the mail, generated a continuing exchange of letters. In one of these Quinn suggested to Hyde that they meet during Quinn's next trip to Ireland and discuss the possibility of an American fund-raising tour. "Yeats has no doubt told you of his trip here and how badly you are needed to organize the country on behalf of the League," he wrote. Hyde and Quinn met in Dublin in October 1904. Quinn presented his plan, assured Hyde of success, and—extending his personal guarantee against any possibility that the tour could result in Hyde's personal loss—promised to organize the details.

Meanwhile, as soon as the Congested Districts Board had taken over the tenanted land of Frenchpark (which of course included Ratra), Lucy had begun to urge Douglas to sell their lease and move to Cork or Dublin. She was still a clever woman with a good business sense. She did not share Charles Owen O'Conor Don's commitment to preservation of local control or concern for the future of Ireland's agricultural economy; she did not have Douglas's sentimental attachment to Ratra. It was said that those who were selling to the CDB were getting prices well above market value. As for the prospect of a trip to America, it was not at all attractive to her. On the contrary, skeptical of John Quinn's assurances of success and anxious about leaving her daughters for eight months, she was adamantly opposed to it. For one thing, she worried what her role would be when Douglas was lionized and feted across a country that many English and Irish travelers of her acquaintance regarded as in large part a primitive wilderness. For another, she suspected Quinn (a handsome, wealthy bachelor ten years her husband's junior) of being something of a ladies' man; she had heard much whispering about the freedom of American women; and she remembered that there had been a "Fräulein" in Fredericton with whom Douglas had had something of a romantic attachment. Her opposition to the American tour became an obsession when in the spring Douglas received word that there was to be a vacancy in the university at Cork. Her disappointment at her husband's previous failures to win a university post had been as keen as his own. If he let this opportunity pass, there might never be another. Moreover, with a university position he could gracefully resign his presidency of the Gaelic League, which to her mind had brought him nothing but anxiety, infelicitous associations, and the disapproval of the kind of society that was their proper sphere.

Hyde could not really reassure Lucy on the matter of the American tour, as he himself was having reservations about it—mostly because of the possible university position, but also because he still had many correspondents in America, and from them and others he had been hearing disconcerting stories of feuds and animosities both within and between Irish-American groups. What would become of his lecture tour if, right at the start, in New York, he inadvertently offended an influential group with national connections or if anywhere in the country he was caught between competing societies? He wished he could discuss his concerns with Quinn, but how could he, when Quinn's letters were filled with enthusiastic reports of ever-increasing bookings and predictions of success? In February he thanked Quinn for a gift of rye whiskey and assured him that Lucy was looking forward to escaping the Irish winter. As for himself, he said that he had been doing what he could to spread the word of his upcoming tour: from the Reverend Peter Yorke of San Francisco he had received assurances that invitations from the universities in California would be forthcoming. He did not know quite how to say that at the same time his old Trinity friends, Stockley and Windle, were urging him to apply for the vacant chair in English literature at Queens College, Cork—or that he had solicited letters of recommendation from Stopford Brooke and others to support his application.

On March 31, in response to repeated requests, Hyde wrote to Quinn from England, enclosing, along with a letter describing large turnouts at successful meetings, a list of his books and other major publications and titles for the lectures he might give at American colleges. For himself he wrote a memorandum with the mocking title, "Self-Laudatory," in which he set down what he considered to be his outstanding achievements, beginning "I was without doubt the first person into whose head it ever came to deanglicise Ireland, or gave utterance to this idea. The Gaelic League is practically built upon my lecture to that effect in 1892." He continued: he was, he said, the first person to write a book in modern Irish; the first to collect folklore in Irish; the first to "collect the poetry of the people from their own mouths"; the first "to write a play in Irish and act in it myself"; the first to write a literary history of Ireland; the first to address a mass meeting in Irish; the first to ask the Irish to keep speaking Irish to their children, "in New York before ever the Gaelic League was started"; the first to say go to "the poor people, the Macs and O's and the priests, and if they are for letting the language die—then let it and be damned to them."

In a letter of April 30 Hyde revised his lecture topics on the advice of Seamas MacManus ("who knows the ropes," he assured Quinn). Formerly a Donegal schoolteacher, Hyde explained, MacManus had gone to the United States in 1899 and had found there a receptive audience for the stories he told of his own parish. Hyde also advised Quinn that Tomás Bán Ó Concannon (Thomas Concannon), a native speaker of Irish from the Aran Islands and a league organizer in Connacht, would accompany him as he toured rather than go on ahead as an advance man as Quinn had suggested, as he felt that in this way he might help Hyde "make a bigger impression." Concannon "wants to use glamour. What do you think of this?" wrote Hyde, obviously amused at the idea. Quinn's answer had he given it might not have been flattering. An advance man was needed, and if Hyde did not have glamour enough on his own, it was unlikely that Concannon would be able to help him. Quinn did not like amateurs interfering with his careful planning. For months he had been devoting two to six hours daily to the organization of Hyde's tour. His New York apartment had become an office for the project, with a special secretary hired to handle the heavy correspondence.

On June 22 Hyde cabled Quinn that the American trip was off. In the letter that followed he explained that he could not go because the Cork position would begin in October. "This is too good an offer to let go," he apologized, suggesting that instead he might be able to make a short trip in the spring of 1906, appearing only at events arranged by Irish-American groups and excluding the university lectures. He concluded plaintively, "Will you ever forgive me?" On June 28 he wrote again. The Cork position was in fact not yet assured, his letter implied, but still might be. However, his responsibilities as president of the league were overwhelming him: "My last post brought me five different requests to go to programs in various parts of the country." He also confessed his fear of being caught in the notorious power struggles of quarreling Irish-American organizations. He described conflicting statements in letters he had received from America. He had been visited at Ratra by the secretary of the New York Gaelic League who had impressed him favorably but against whom he had since received written warnings. He had canceled the tour, however, primarily on account of Lucy: "My wife's delight knows no bounds at escaping the American journey and I really think she could not have borne it. She had almost got into a state of nervous collapse thinking of it and she *would not* let me go by myself."

Quinn could not have been less than mystified and distressed by this curious and continuing sequence of contradictory letters so uncharacteristic of the man he thought he knew and of whom he had spoken highly to such people as Martin J. Keogh, an eminent jurist with cultivated tastes and a broad knowledge of history and literature whom Quinn had invited to chair the committee appointed to serve as Hyde's official hosts. He also had been placed in a difficult position, for months of work that had gone into scheduling lectures and rallies in over fifty cities now had to be unraveled.

On July 7 Quinn received still another letter from Hyde. Having at first indicated that he had been offered the Cork appointment, and then altered that statement to say that he was being seriously considered for it, he now wrote that in fact he had decided not to apply for it but would accept it if it was offered to him! As for withdrawing from the American tour, he blamed that decision on a crisis involving Ratra.

If he did not buy it, he would be evicted by the Congested Districts Board; he did not want to give it up but Lucy hated it and was "most anxious . . . to leave."

Obviously torn by aspects of his situation he had not revealed to Quinn, Hyde turned to Lady Gregory. In a private letter he confessed that he needed to find his way out of a "muddle." She knew something of the reasons why he was close to being overwhelmed by problems and responsibilities: she had heard that the Reverend Arthur Hyde had been failing; she assumed that as usual Lucy was not happy or not well; she knew of the internal dissension within the league, its shrinking treasury, and its problems with the Post Office; she had seen newspaper reports that the league was now under Castle surveillance; she suspected that there was more. Nor had Hyde's feelings of panic been improved by the fact that every day he was receiving a stream of reports from Pádraig O'Daly, Nellie O'Brien, and Agnes O'Farrelly—loyal members of his inner guard—about the league's latest internal controversies. Whatever transpired to change Hyde's mind has not been recorded, but on July 19, in an unexplained reversal as astonishing as his abrupt cancellation on June 22, he cabled Quinn that he was "available after all for November." In the letter that followed he explained that he had settled the Ratra matter and had persuaded himself that "preaching" to American universities would raise the prestige of the Gaelic League.

Some ten to twelve days later a smiling Hyde stepped off the train in Foynes to which he had come to attend the annual Shannon *feis*. There to greet him were friends who, like himself, were nationalists of Ascendancy stock. Most had learned their Irish from O'Growney's *Simple Lessons*. Among them were Alice Stopford Green, whose historical research had lately focused on Irish topics (only recently Hyde had written to her complaining of the difficulty he had been having finishing his lectures for America); Sir Horace Plunkett, son of Lord Dunsany, like the poet AE a pioneer in the Irish agricultural cooperative movement; Sir Roger Casement, who had just established, with Hyde's support, an Irish language school at Tawin Island near Galway; Lord Monteagle and his daughter, Mary Spring-Rice (she now called herself Máire Spring Rís); and Mary Elizabeth Massey of Killakee House, Rathfarnham, described by Desmond Macnamara as so "handsome fair-haired, beguiling and by inference, attractive and demanding" that she encountered no difficulty in spreading Irish culture among the Ascendancy by introducing Irish dancing at hunt balls and house parties.

Exactly how long Hyde may have known Mary Elizabeth Massey is not certain, but it appears that they had met some time before 1903, for on February 21 of that year, at the Dublin performance of Yeats's "The Pot of Broth," he had inscribed on her program a verse in Irish that plays on the first four lines of a sensuous lyric entitled "An Chúilfhionn" (The fair maiden), which Hyde had published in *Love Songs of Connacht*. Others had made less personal signed and unsigned contributions to the same program: Yeats, a couplet; Lady Gregory, a flourishing signature; F. A. Longworth, an eight-line verse on dancing; a reference to a jig class; some lines in Arabic; some sketches. Hyde's prose translation of the verse published in *Love Songs* reads:

> Mist of honey on day of frost over dark woods of oak, And love without concealment I have for thee, O fair skin of the white breasts. Thy form slender, thy mouth thin, and thy cooleen [tresses] twisted smooth. And O first love, forsake me not, and sure thou hast increased my disease.

On Mary Elizabeth Massey's program Hyde had altered the lines of the Irish verse. Translated, they read:

> Mist of honey on day of frost over dark woods of oak, And love without concealment I have for thee, that I may see you again, your bright eyes, your slender form, O fair skin of the white breasts, and your blue dress, a dark mist on me, O young woman of the yellow hair.

Unsigned but unmistakably in his own hand on another part of the same sheet Hyde had provided what Desmond Macnamara describes as a "somewhat bowdlerised and sentimentalised" translation:

> Like a honey mist on a day of frost o'er a grey wood of Desire of thee in the heart of me at thy gay mood woke, frock of blue, pointed shoe, and laughing rogue face. Have you found my heart, bound my heart, and left grief in its place?

Two years later at the Shannon *feis* of 1905 Hyde wrote in Mary Elizabeth Massey's autograph book an untranslated signed sequel to the 1903 lines. Beginning with a near repetition of the fourth line of the 1903 verse, it evokes the dark mist of the blue dress; continues with a description of the blue dress fluttering behind and around her; and ends with a lament that were it not for the worldly cares that have left him disheartened he would follow her to the ends of the earth. Gossip continued to link their names sporadically for some time thereafter.

At the beginning of August the Reverend Arthur Hyde, a semi-invalid for much of the time, began to fail noticeably. Dr. O'Farrell was

called. He diagnosed the elderly man's problem as "the natural complications of old age" and left some powders. Had the patient known, he
probably would have rejected the powders. In his Kilmactranny years
the rector had been a serious student of folk medicine, particularly
herbal cures. Folk medicine and the classics had been his favorite subjects of study. Above his bed, like dominoes in the dust, were his Latin
and Greek grammars, Lucian, Livy, and Horace. Some stood upright,
some leaned against others, some were laid flat. Among his books and
papers was the induction oath administered to him by his bishop in
1867: "to take real, actual and corporeal possession of the one rectory
of Tibohine in the Diocese of Elphin together with all singular tythes,
glebes, profits and appurtenances to the said and one rectory"; "to teach
and instruct, or cause to be taught and instructed in the English
Tongue . . . the children of said rectory." The oath's emphasis on rent
and profits and its charge that the children be instructed in the "English
Tongue" had always troubled Douglas. Still, Douglas's criticism of the
church had focused primarily on his father's interpretation of doctrinal
matters and beliefs, not on the church itself, which he continued to
attend.

Douglas reached up and removed from the shelf his father's *Commentary* on the first twenty psalms, written in October 1851. On its verso
pages were the prescribed Church of Ireland daily morning and evening
prayers. Its binding disintegrating, its pages discolored, the home-made
prayerbook was filled with the stern and self-righteous marginal glosses
the Reverend Arthur Hyde, Jr., had thundered at his flock over the
years. Alongside Psalm 4 the rector had written: "Do not the great bulk
of mankind go astray as soon as they are born, speaking lies so that
amongst domestics in families one seldom finds one whose honest lips
will speak the simple truth upon every occasion?" Douglas had read and
reread this passage written by his father in 1851. Did it help explain
the *"novae ancillae,"* the maids who had barely been taken on before
they fell under his father's suspicion? From verses in Psalm 12 that con-
demn those who beg instead of work and score flatterers and deceivers,
the Reverend Hyde had found corroboration for his view of the Irish
tenantry and had written in a marginal note, "This part of David's
description is painfully like the lower order of Irish Romanists."

His father stirred and Douglas heard his harsh breathing over the
sound of Annette's approaching steps. Annette had married Douglas's
old friend Cambreth Kane in 1902, but as she and Cam lived in the
Frenchpark glebe house, sister and brother still saw much of each other.

They sometimes took tea at their father's bedside. Douglas rose and replaced his father's prayerbook on the shelf with a glance at its last page, "The Office for the Burial of the Dead."

The obituary in the *Weekly Freeman* was succinct: It noted that both the Reverend Arthur Hyde, Jr., and his father before him had been Protestant rectors, that An Craoibhin himself had earned a bachelor of divinity in Trinity College, and that he had won in fact a theological exhibition before "Irish Ireland had claimed him" for its own.

On August 11 Hyde wrote again to remind Quinn that he wanted Concannon to be with him during the American tour. Describing the Aran Islander as "a born diplomat," Hyde assured Quinn that Concannon's "transparent honesty and simplicity" would win over everyone. Nothing more was said about either Hyde's own erratic behavior during the summer or Lucy's state of mind. Hyde was busy with his usual tasks as president of the league. He set up with Agnes O'Farrelly, Nellie O'Brien, Pádraig O'Daly, and Stephen Barrett procedures that would enable them to carry on in his absence. He wrote and revised his lectures for the American tour and completed work on *Religious Songs of Connacht,* scheduled for publication in 1906.

During this same month, after a period of printing mostly innuendoes, the newspapers again began carrying items concerning government surveillance of the league, its president, and some of its members. The *Irish News* reported that the Royal Irish Constabulary, the police force for all Ireland outside the Dublin metropolitan area, had been given instructions to look into the question of whether the Gaelic League was the peaceful educational organization that it professed to be or "a revolutionary party, meditating the overthrow of English supremacy in Ireland." In September the *Church of Ireland Gazette* attacked both Hyde and the league for activities inimical to the interests of Irish Protestants. Nellie O'Brien leaped to the defense with a strong rebuttal in a long letter to the *Gazette* printed on September 29: "We have no secrets in the Gaelic League," she declared, "whatever those may say who look on it as a dark and dangerous conspiracy." Stephen Gwynn proposed a public meeting on the topic, "Protestant Attitudes Toward the Gaelic League" to get all the accusations and counteraccusations out in the open once and for all. Patrick Pearse, Joseph Lloyd, O'Neill Russell, Stephen Gwynn, Nellie O'Brien, and Agnes O'Farrelly were among those who came prepared to speak. Hyde chaired the meeting, held in October. When it was over, Joseph Lloyd approached him again with the complaints and threats that had been marring their relationship for some time. He was a founder of the league, he insisted (he had been present at the second meeting of 1893, at which time he had been named honorary treasurer), and he was being mistreated by the Coiste Gnótha. If Hyde could not put an end to the mistreatment, he would quit and emigrate to Manitoba. Hyde began to look forward to his American tour. It would be good, he acknowledged to himself, to get away for a while.

Hyde's last messages, including a hurried note to Roger Casement, had been sent off; Lucy had reviewed last-minute instructions with housekeeper, nurse, and maid. On November 5, scarcely two months after the Reverend Arthur Hyde, Jr., had been buried in the graveyard of the Portahard Church where he had been rector for thirty-eight years, Douglas and Lucy exchanged tearful farewells with Una, Nuala, and nurse Jane. As the carriage passed through Ratra's gate and along the eight miles to Ballaghaderreen, Connollys, Lavins, Mahons, Morrisroes, and Dockrys (Hyde was pleased that the families of his old Frenchpark neighbors were staying on the land) raised their hands and caps and shouted messages of good health and good luck. There was a low mist over cropland and bogs; the previous night had been chilly. In town the brougham passed St. Nathy's, the neo–Gothic Revival Catholic cathedral whose spire was visible from Ratra. It continued past Dillon's shop to the railroad station where a crowd of Gaelic Leaguers from Mayo and Roscommon joined students from St. Nathy's College to send up a shout as the carriage came into view. Hyde waved to the young men and women he had coached in the spring of 1903 in response to their request for help in staging two of his Irish plays, *The Marriage* and *The Lost Saint*. There was scarcely time for the recitation of a poem in Irish to wish him success in America and for Hyde's response when, amid a round of cheers, the train pulled out.

13

With The Irish in America

Ireland's living symbol was now a big-headed, dark, big-mouthed man, loud-voiced, with a weighty moustache that gave a bend to his shoulders, and curtained off the big mouth completely; a man who was hilarious with everyone that seemed to matter, who was ever shouting out, with his right arm lifted so that its shadow seemed to stretch from one end of the land to the other; shouting in a strange tongue, Come and follow me, for behind me marches the only Ireland worth knowing.

Sean O'Casey, *Drums Under the Windows*

On Monday, November 6, 1905, the day of the Hydes' departure from Ratra to Dublin, the featured news items in the *Irish Times* (then the leading Ascendancy newspaper) were the massacre of Jews in Odessa, a banquet held in London to celebrate the conclusion of an Anglo-Japanese treaty, and an account of student demonstrations—headlined "The Disorders at the Royal University"—that had broken out in Dublin when "God Save the King" was played at a Royal Irish University convocation. Not mentioned was the fact that a reception at the Gresham Hotel on Sackville (O'Connell) Street and a giant torchlight procession, planned to bid farewell to Douglas Hyde on the eve of his departure for a lecture tour in America, were scheduled for 7:15 in the evening. Inside the Gresham, reporters for the *Evening Herald,* the *Irish Independent,* and the *Weekly Freeman* scribbled notes as Hyde responded to the well-wishers who took turns at the podium, among them representatives of the Dublin Corporation, the Trades Council, the students at Maynooth, the Gaelic Athletic Association, and, of course, the Gaelic League. The stories filed by the reporters later that evening described Hyde as a pale-complexioned man in his forty-fifth year (actually forty-sixth, as he had had his forty-fifth birthday in January), middle of height (group photographs show him as taller than average), dressed in dark blue serge, standing before the crowds in the glare of the gas lamps. They took note of his Gaelic League pin gleaming in his buttonhole; the gleaming silver streaks in his drooping, dark mustache; the same silver streaks in his thick, dark hair, worn a bit longer than fashion dictated; and his small but bright blue-gray eyes, set in his broad, bony, round forehead. They quoted his words of thanks to his assembled well-wishers and his assertion that the principle behind the Gaelic League was the resurrection of Ireland. "Our movement is founded on the bed-rock principle of nationality," he had proclaimed to the excited audience's cheers. The stories also included details of how the Hydes looked on their departure: he seated next to Lucy in the lord mayor's carriage, waving to the crowd from the depths of a greatcoat with collar and cuffs trimmed with the fur of Irish otters (a talisman from thirty devoted friends), a hard bowler hat upon his head; she in an outfit made exclusively of Irish lace and wool by Irish dressmakers. As the lord mayor's open coach bearing the Stars and Stripes front right, the Irish harp front left, drew away from the curb, the complementary colors of the two flags were illuminated by the flaring torches. At either side of the coach a file of marching hurlers shouldered their sticks as if they were rifles, to the cheers of dreaming men.

Preceded by an advance guard of hurlers and representatives from the different branches of the Gaelic League, carriages bearing the Hydes, the lord mayor, and the Coiste Gnótha headed a procession that wound its way from the Gresham on Sackville Street to Kingsbridge Station. Leaning forward in the coach, his bright eyes shining even more when they lingered momentarily on a familiar face, Hyde waved now right, now left, to those who lined the route. They were followed by the hurling and football leagues of the Gaelic Athletic Association, Trades Council executives, temperance bodies, boys' brigades, Friendly Societies, the Old Grand Union, and the Foresters. Separating the marching units were five Dublin bands.

Marching close beside Hyde's carriage that evening, wryly taking in the fine display, was a young laborer for the Great Northern Railway, twenty-five-year-old John Casey, better known to his friends in the Drumcondra branch of the Gaelic League in which he was learning Irish as Seán Ó Cathasaigh. Forty-one years later the playwright and prose writer Sean O'Casey would publish a semifictionalized account of the night that Dr. Douglas Hyde went off to America:

> The hurlers of Sean's club were chosen to be the bodyguard around the coach bearing him to Kingsbridge Station. . . . Sean, in full dress of the club's jersey, of hooped bands of alternate dark blue and dark green, walked beside the protestant Chief of the Gael, in the midst of thousands of flaming torches carried before and behind the carriage, followed by all the hurling and football clubs of the city and its suburbs. Horsemen headed the cavalcade, carrying the Stars and Stripes, the French Tricolour, and the green banner of popular Ireland. . . . Everywhere the drums beat again their lusty rolls, making the bright stars in the sky quiver, and bands blew Ireland's past into every ear, and called forth her history of the future. . . . On we all went slow along the mean-looking flanks of Anna Livia Plurabelle singing songs of Eireby by the dozen that would rouse up even the stone outside Dan Murphy's door.

Momentarily blocked by the Dublin Metropolitan Police from the station platform, hurlers and footballers, tactical experts in such situations, rushed and broke through the line.

> There was the big beaming face of Hyde, topped by the globular skull, with the bushy moustache like an abandoned bird's nest, filling up a carriage window, nodding, nodding to the excited crowd, while a band outside played *When shall the day break in Eirinn* with extreme dignity and unction.

Watching the spectacle along with O'Casey were Dubliners who wondered how it was that this country squire with his Ascendancy manners and his old-fashioned Roscommon Irish had such a grip on Dublin crowds. Yet a grip it was, according to the *Irish Independent,* not just in Dublin but all over Ireland. In the *Independent's* recent poll Hyde had been declared the fourth most popular man in the country, preceded only, in 1905, by John Redmond, Cardinal Logue, and Archbishop Walsh. The young laborer on the Great Northern Railway, wondering too, listened and remembered:

> "Look, there." He's waving a last farewell! The guard's green flag was waving, the engine gave a few steamy snorts, strained at the carriages, and began to slide out of the station through a storm of cheers. Hyde was high on Ireland's shoulders, and his carriage window framed the big head, the bunchy moustaches, the staring eyes, draining down the last drop of the mighty farewell and godspeed, till distance hid the crowd, and stilled the stormy sweltering roar of the gathered Gaels.

In the *Irish Times* for November 7, twenty lines at the bottom of a page in the middle section (next to the day's racing selections at English tracks and an announcement by the Post Office of a new form for postal orders) briefly noted what it clearly considered to be a nonevent that had ended when "a procession was formed outside, and Dr. and Mrs. Hyde were accompanied to Kingsbridge. Many of the processionists carried torches." The *Evening Herald* and *Weekly Freeman* were more generous with their space and attention. The *Irish Independent* carried an interview with Hyde in which he credited his June 1891 observation of Irish classes in America, sponsored by the Bowery branch of the New York Philo-Celtic Association, with having given him and through him MacNeill and others the idea of founding the Gaelic League. He was going back to America, he said, to carry the creed of the Gaelic League to Irish Americans, to let them know what they had started here at home. What Hyde did not explain fully was exactly what had started at home. That the *Times* should regard the public celebration of his departure as a nonevent; that the *Independent* should regard him as an ambassador from the Irish of the United Kingdom to the Irish of the United States; that the other newspapers should accurately depict the size and extent of his popular support: all this was in his favor. The correlative of Thomas Davis's proposition—"a nation without a language is a nation without a soul"—was implicit in the founding principles of the Gaelic League: to restore the soul of a nation it was necessary to recover its language. Whether the Gaelic League would be able to continue on its course would depend on how much support, for its spirit and its treasury, it could obtain from America. For the moment spirits were high—certainly there had been plenty of evidence of that in Dublin on the evening of November 6—but the treasury was nearly depleted.

Young O'Casey understood better than most Hyde's immediate purpose: he was to tell the Americans, of course, "of Ireland's honour, nobility, and undying devotion to her ancient language," but above all he was to "rake in the needful, argent and or, at all costs." That had been John Quinn's understanding as well. In a frank letter to Lady Gregory written from New York on October 27, 1905, he had stated his own reasons for arranging Hyde's tour: "I am after money for Hyde. Hyde and his work need money. I wouldn't have got Hyde to come out if I thought he couldn't get money and I don't hesitate to say so."

Whatever personal misgivings Hyde had had during the past ten months about the trip on which Quinn had so firmly insisted, on the eve of his sailing he kept them firmly under control. Yeats had assured him that he was doing the right thing by going—that it was important to Ireland to keep the friendship of Irish America, and important to Irish Americans to have a sense of the dignity and antiquity and continuity of their culture before all was lost in the melting pot. It was Yeats who had spoken of Hyde to his own audiences on his trip to America and had urged Quinn to bring him over. Wherever he went in America, Yeats had made a point of arousing interest in Hyde and the Gaelic League. The train chugged slowly out of the station, gradually picking up moderate speed; at each stop between Dublin and Cork people gathered to cheer him on his way. The journey that ordinarily took five hours stretched out for two days, with an overnight stop at Limerick Junction and trackside meetings on November 7 in Tipperary and Mallow where, addressing enthusiastic crowds, Hyde warned that it was "a hard and difficult task to build up a nation from the inside." It was also a hard and difficult task to get through Cork, where an immense crowd that included the Cork branch of the Irish Drapers' Association, as big or bigger than the one that had cheered him out of Dublin, had assembled at the station to form the procession that would escort him to City Hall. There, at the lord mayor's reception, the Reverend Father Augustine extolled Hyde as "our pride, our joy, our hope, our glory, and the uncrowned king of Ireland."

That night Hyde and Lucy stayed at the home of Willie Stockley, Hyde's old friend from Trinity, the man for whom he had served in 1890–1891 as interim professor of modern languages at the University of New Brunswick. Now on the faculty at Queens College, it was Stockley who had tried unsuccessfully to secure for Hyde the vacant chair in English. On the morning of Wednesday, November 8, Stockley accompanied the Hydes on the 9:50 mail train to Queenstown (now Cobh) for one last mass meeting on the dock before they boarded the tender that took them to the SS *Majestic,* where in a sitting room reserved for his use Hyde held a last informal reception.

As the tender bearing the last of his well-wishers edged from the liner's side to return to the quay, Hyde felt the throb of the *Majestic*'s engine through the planks of the deck. For better or worse the future of the language movement now lay in the hands of John Quinn and himself. It was curious, the partnerships that had evolved out of this work. Who would have thought that he, born in Castlerea, brought up in Kilmactranny and Frenchpark, educated at Trinity, would one day, for the sake of what he had learned as a boy in Roscommon cottages, be drawn into an alliance with the man he was now on his way to meet?

A prominent lawyer, son of Irish-Catholic parents, who had been brought up in Ohio, John Quinn, B. L. Reid's "Man from New York," was a sophisticated lover of literature and art, a hardheaded, anticlerical, narrow-minded, opinionated American, an admirer of efficiency, optimism, and pragmatism and a hater of brashness, boorishness, and low taste, who for a time, at least, excepted the Irish from his stereotypical prejudices because he had a soft spot in his heart for Ireland. His support of the populist Gaelic League was especially unlikely, as it was the beautiful, lofty Ireland in which Lady Gregory, Yeats, and Hyde made their lives to which Quinn on his first visit had responded in 1902. To the circle of literary and cultural nationalists that had then become his friends he was unfailingly patient, generous, and loyal. No doubt there still would have been an Irish Literary Renaissance without Quinn; with him it came more easily. An irony of history is that, although Quinn mistrusted extremists of either political persuasion and abhorred coercion and physical violence, it was his masterful organization of Douglas Hyde's United States tour in 1905–1906 that secured the funds critically needed for the league's survival—funds that thereby nurtured, sublimated the force that ten years later Quinn deplored. Had there been no fund-raising tour of America on behalf of the impoverished Gaelic League, no doubt there still would have been an insurrection. But when would it have occurred, who would have been its leaders, and what would have been its outcome?

Characteristically, Quinn had taken personal charge of arrangements for Hyde's arrival. In a letter to Lady Gregory, he explained why:

If I let it go it would be miserably bungled. . . . One Gaelic Leaguer here wanted Hyde to be met at the dock by the 69th Regiment (all Irish), by a band (all German, I suppose), and by a platoon of policemen (all Irish, of course). I had to kill that. Then another wanted a "ladies chorus" (all singing through their noses as they usually do) "just so his lecture wouldn't be so dry."

Nothing was either bungled or in bad taste when Quinn was in charge. For Hyde's arrival he had arranged a dignified reception. Absent from the dockside event were the enthusiasts ("nothing is more dangerous than enthusiasm," he assured Hyde). In their place he had assembled a small party of handpicked "representative Irishmen," by which Quinn meant men like Martin J. Keogh, justice of the New York state supreme court.

When Quinn was in charge, there was also never a moment wasted. The itinerary he had set for Hyde for the next seven months made that clear. It called for Hyde to crisscross the country as follows, with one or more lectures and fund-raisers in each location, depending on the proximity of colleges and universities and the popular audience potential, and with some locations marked for a second or third visit:

November: Boston; New Haven, Connecticut; Washington, D.C.; Hartford, Connecticut.

December: Boston again; Manchester, New Hampshire; Springfield, Massachusetts; Ansonia, Connecticut; Lowell, Massachusetts; Boston again; Waterbury, Connecticut; Providence, Rhode Island; Philadelphia; Worcester, Massachusetts; Lawrence, Massachusetts; Brooklyn; and New Haven, Connecticut.

January: Pittsburgh; Chicago; Milwaukee, Wisconsin; Chicago again; Cleveland and Columbus, Ohio; Indianapolis; Cincinnati; St. Louis, Missouri; South Bend, Indiana; Madison, Wisconsin; St. Paul and Minneapolis, Minnesota.

February: Omaha, Nebraska; San Francisco, Berkeley, San Jose, and Oakland, California.

March: Sacramento, Santa Barbara, Los Angeles, and Santa Clara, California; Portland, Oregon; Seattle, Washington.

April: Spokane, Washington; Butte and Anaconda, Montana; St. Paul again; Chicago again; Memphis, Tennessee; Louisville, Kentucky; Baltimore; Ithaca and Elmira, New York; and Scranton, Pennsylvania.

May: Buffalo, Niagara Falls, and Rochester, New York; Toronto, Canada; Washington, D.C.; Bridgeport, Connecticut; Paterson, New Jersey; New York.

Lucy, meanwhile, was to be entertained in the major cosmopolitan centers along Hyde's route.

From Wednesday, November 15, the day of his landing, until November 19, Hyde's days and nights were spent in the Manhattan Hotel with newsmen whom Quinn had thoroughly briefed in advance. The week before the *Majestic* docked, Quinn personally had visited the offices of the *Sun, World, Journal, Tribune,* and *Times* to arrange interviews, discuss pictures, and issue reports of Hyde's visit and its purpose. For those papers that could not (or would not) spare a reporter, he provided for distribution to news writers a printed "interview" that required only that they strike out the questions and put the answers in narrative form to have an item that would fill one-and-a-half newspaper columns. Wonderfully wise in the ways of publicity and the necessity for, as he said, "beating the drum," Quinn repeatedly reminded Hyde to talk up the program on which he would lecture on Sunday evening, November 26, in Carnegie Hall at every chance that he got. Other lectures were to precede it, but this, Quinn pointed out, was the first major fund-raising event on Hyde's schedule.

Hyde was nervous at first about talking with the American press: the reporters at home were all people he knew, who would write what they wanted whatever he said; the fact that he did not know what to expect of American reporters intimidated him. Quinn, however, was pleased with the results of Hyde's interviews. Although Hyde was not always sure that he was "beating the drum" appropriately, Quinn had been satisfied that he had an instinct for the right phrase at the right time when, in response to a potentially delicate question from a *New York Times* reporter on November 19, Hyde had explained:

We have worked a tremendous revolution in Ireland. It has no political significance yet. It is simply an intellectual fight at this stage. What it may lead to
can be conjectured. . . . The English government is doing everything possible
to suppress the movement. It wants a benighted Ireland.

It was true that Hyde quickly perceived the wisdom of Quinn's advice: with the American press, being accessible, amusing, intelligible, and wary yet quotable obviously paid off. Only once did he falter in those first few tense weeks, when after an exhausting day he fell into bed late at night, only to be awakened by an insistent newsman's continuous knocking on his door. His remarks to the reporter were, according to Maurice Leahy, "not in the nature of a benediction," with the result that the next day Quinn was faced with the necessity of having to correct a fictitious account of a forthcoming event which the offended reporter had submitted to his paper in place of the interview he had tried to obtain.

Hyde's first commitment before the fund-raiser in Carnegie Hall was a lecture at Harvard on Monday, November 20. Remembering the pleasant day in 1891 that he had spent on the Cambridge campus lo-cated close to metropolitan Boston, Hyde looked forward to being there again. For his topic he had selected "The Folk Tale in Ireland," described in his publicity notes as "founded on more than sixty tales taken directly from oral sources and never before collected." On the day of his lecture Hyde took the train from Grand Central Station in New

York to the Back Bay Station in Boston, where he was met by Fred Norris Robinson, a medievalist with Celtic interests with whom he shared a mutual regard. Hyde and Robinson had little time to talk on this occasion, as Hyde had only moments to spare for a quick bite and a change of clothes before he had to be delivered to the office of the dean of the college, who was to introduce him. Time was short, the dean was shy, and Hyde was full of nervous energy as together they started up the stairway to the lecture hall. "We stuck halfway up the stairs," Hyde wrote to Annette, "as we could not decide which of us was to go first nor . . . whether I was to be on his right hand or on his left hand, as though that made any matter. But," he added impishly, "they are much more formal in America."

Hyde's Harvard lecture drew about five hundred students and faculty. It was for him a reassuring experience. After all his months of worrying and rewriting, he discovered that he had hit just the right note. His audience not only listened attentively but laughed in all the right places. Robinson hosted a reception following the lecture at which Hyde took the opportunity to study the "matrimonial tastes," as he put it, of Harvard society. "As the ladies seem better looking than any I have yet seen," he noted in his diary, it "speaks highly in favor of Harvard culture." The next day, as he had mentioned to Robinson that he was very anxious to see the place from which the shot heard around the world had been fired, Robinson's brother was enlisted to provide a tour of Concord by motorcar. The statue of the Minuteman, he confessed to his diary, had the greatest effect on his imagination. He made a point of reading the rolls on stone monuments and working out how many of those who had fallen were Irish.

The Concord tour included a visit to the home of Ralph Waldo Emerson. There Hyde talked at length with Emerson's daughter and tried to imagine what it would be like to use Emerson's library, "a dark, dingy, square room, very puritanic in style, no ornaments and very little brightness of any kind to relieve it." He saw the Old Manse on Monument Street that had been Hawthorne's house and talked with Longfellow's daughter and the daughter of the Harvard ballad collector, Francis James Child. In the evening he was taken to meet the editors and writers of several Boston newspapers. At their request he wrote greetings in Irish to the Boston Irish community which were printed in facsimile in the next day's papers. There was so much to see and do in Boston and everyone was so congenial that Hyde hated to leave. Robinson cheered Hyde with the reminder that he was due back for a "great Boston meeting" at which Robinson himself was scheduled to introduce him on December 3.

After a day's rest in New York, on Thursday, November 23, Hyde went to New Haven to lecture at Yale. No one met him at the station—his train had arrived early—and for some moments he stood looking at the unfamiliar surroundings and feeling disconsolate. Then suddenly he found himself surrounded by a group of local Irish Americans who appeared with apologies and elaborate explanations of what had happened, delivered with much good-natured pushing and shoving and laughing. They took him at once to the university, where his Irish-American escort was overcome with awe to discover that Hyde was to be presented by President Hadley himself. It was a thing, these young Irish Americans said, that Hadley never did for any visitors. The topic Hyde had chosen for Yale was fortuitously "The Gaelic Movement: Its Origin, Importance, Philosophy, and Results." New Haven, he discovered, was the home of "a lot of fine old veterans . . . who had fought in the Civil War and then had become Fenians and gone to Ireland." Politically sophisticated and nostalgic, they provided him with the core of an ideal audience. Later, at the New Haven Irish Club, a Captain O'Brien regaled everyone with an account of how after weeks of filing through the bars of his window he had broken out of jail in Clonmel, in County Tipperary, just as he was going to be condemned to death or penal servitude.

New Haven was but one of many American cities in which Hyde encountered Fenians who had fought as officers in the American Civil War. He was acquainted as a result of his 1891 visit with the old Fenians of Boston and New York. As many had died, their numbers had been reduced. He knew or knew of others—with some he had exchanged correspondence—through Frenchpark connections. In Philadelphia he was startled to learn that one of his dinner partners, "an ascetic looking Episcopalian clergyman" with an English accent whom he was prepared to dislike, turned out to be a grandson of John Mitchel who hated England "as deeply as ever his grandfather" did. The clergyman had, moreover, family connections with the O'Conors of Clonalis House in Castlerea, through collateral relatives of their American cousin, Charles O'Conor of New York. Another guest at the same dinner was an ex-Fenian Catholic priest. In Milwaukee, Hyde met Jeremiah Quinn, a leader of that city's Irish Third Ward and a bitter anticleric because of the Church's attitudes toward Fenianism. All the way to California,

Hyde would continually cross and recross the Fenian trail that extended between Ireland and Australia, with the United States and Canada forming part of the bridge in between. Sometimes, as he sipped whiskey and talked far into the night of Fenian exploits and Fenian heroes, the years slipped away and he felt as if he were a boy again sitting with Seamus Hart, listening to the men from Mayo in a cottage in Frenchpark.

On Friday, November 24, accompanied by John Quinn, Hyde took the night train to Washington D.C., where Quinn had booked rooms for them at the Willard Hotel; Lucy remained in New York, shopping and dining with Quinn's friends and attending the theater. The next day Hyde made his first call on Theodore Roosevelt, then president of the United States. Hyde and Roosevelt liked each other immediately. He was invited to have lunch with the president and his family. "Roosevelt was delightful, perfectly genial, and very gracious," Hyde wrote in his diary. "There was no formality whatsoever about him." Like Jeremiah Curtin before him, Hyde discovered that Roosevelt had a strong interest in everything related to Ireland and an unexpectedly broad knowledge of Irish folklore and history. They talked of present conditions in Ireland, especially education. Hyde told him about the government's attempt to cut off result fees for the teaching of Irish. "Extraordinarily wrong and stupid," Roosevelt said, shaking his head. Assuring Hyde that he understood what the Gaelic League was trying to accomplish, he promised to appeal to monied Irish Americans to see if he could persuade them to endow chairs in Celtic literature in American universities. Relaxing and smoking together after lunch, they put problems aside and talked of Curtin (whom Roosevelt had known but Hyde had never met), of folklore, of Irish and Norse sagas, and of the great heroes of Irish literature. Roosevelt explained that he had been brought up by Irish nurses and that Cuchulain and Finn MacCool had been familiar and vivid figures to him before he ever saw their names in literature. His children, he said, had been brought up by Irish nurses, too. They parted reluctantly, with Roosevelt insisting that Hyde try to arrange a return to the White House before going back to Ireland.

So far Hyde had been in the United States for ten days and he had begun to feel a little foolish that he had allowed himself to be upset by talk of feuding and backbiting in the Irish-American community. Everyone he had met had been warm and generous, interested in talking with him, eager to be friends. It seemed to him, in fact, that he had encountered nothing in America to match the sniping and backbiting and feuding that he had left behind him in Ireland. The mail would catch up with him eventually, he was sure, but for the moment it was a pleasure not to receive the daily communications from the Coiste Gnótha with their chronology of petty problems or the clippings from newspapers that still showed a frustrating ignorance of the Gaelic League's goals and aspirations. There in the White House sat the president of the United States, that great and famous man, and *he* had an immediate and perfect understanding of why the league had been founded and what it was trying to accomplish. But Hyde had no time to think about these things as the train took him back to New York. It was Saturday, November 25, and on Sunday he would have his first big test of his ability as a fund-raiser in New York's famous Carnegie Hall. Quinn had told him just to relax and concentrate on delivering his lecture with his usual combination of humor and seriousness, a good mix. For his topic he had chosen, with some additions, his old warhorse on the necessity for the deanglicization of Ireland.

The Carnegie Hall lecture followed a pattern with which Hyde unfortunately was soon to become familiar as, in his travels across the country, he found himself in territory where the long knives of factionalism had been drawn between competing Irish-American groups. To his dismay he slowly discovered that the roots of this factionalism were in part much the same as they were in Ireland (parochialism, social and economic status, attitudes for or against language revival). In part they were peculiarly Irish American, in that attitudes differed depending on such factors as time of and reason for emigration. In general, he observed, a higher status was conferred on those whose families had been in the United States for one or more generations.

As Hyde described the situation that developed at Carnegie Hall, the first indication that all was not well came moments before the time announced for the program to begin. A man named Finn had arranged to buy the entire tier of boxes, thirty-one or thirty-two in number, and at the last moment he had canceled these reservations, apparently with the sinister intention of spoiling the event. He also returned 150 tickets, apparently for the same reason. Quinn was at the door within moments. The immediate task, he instructed the ushers, was to mask what had happened, and the only way to accomplish that was to fill the visibly empty boxes with those who arrived from that moment on, without regard for the original price of the tickets they were holding. Quinn himself stood at the door to make sure that this was done as expeditiously as possible. His quick thinking resulted in some grumbling, as it delayed the start of the program for half an hour, but it saved the day, although it could not recover the lost revenue represented by the returned tickets.

The chair of the program was Judge Keogh of the New York supreme court, the man Quinn had chosen also to chair the host committee. An eminent, much-respected, and much-loved figure in the city, especially in Irish-American circles, as a young man Keogh had been introduced to Charles O'Conor of New York—a man honored in his state, as he told Hyde, as the father of both the appellate court and the bar association. Keogh kept his introductory remarks to a minimum, then stepped aside to allow Bourke Cockran to make the opening speech. A popular political figure with a reputation for spellbinding oratory, Bourke Cockran would have the task, Quinn had explained, of warming up the audience. Bourke Cockran had promised to hold his remarks to fifteen minutes but he talked for over half an hour—a feat Hyde found both entertaining and remarkable, as he spoke not just convincingly but even "eloquently" upon a subject he "knew nothing about."

When Hyde finally rose to take his place at the podium, he saw that the delegations from each of the Irish-American clubs were seated separately, each beneath its own large identifying green banner. Small green pennants with words of greeting in Irish had been hung in rows around the perimeter of the auditorium. The most numerous and prominent were those that carried Thomas Davis's famous message to the Irish people: "A nation without a language is a nation without a soul." It was a stirring sight, all those people and all those banners and all those messages from Thomas Davis, but Hyde knew that it would be better if the banners, too, had been hung around the perimeter and the people were sitting together.

Hyde began his speech, he later confessed in his diary, "with fear and trembling." The success of his entire trip depended on whether what he had to say would fire the imagination and reach the hearts of the people before him. It was an entirely different experience from that of speaking to Irish men and women who were already committed to his cause or to lecturing about folklore or early Irish literature. For five minutes he spoke only in Irish, dumbfounding the majority of the audience who obviously thought that they were going to have to sit quietly and listen to an hour or more of sounds that were completely unintelligible to them, unable to leave because the purpose for which they had come was to raise money for the preservation of this language that they did not understand. When he switched to English there were audible sighs of relief and wild applause.

Although Hyde had said to himself that he would adapt his talk, as Quinn had advised, from his old speech on deanglicization, during the day he had reviewed his notes against the nature of the event and what he had learned of the composition of his audience. His conclusion had been that a presentation that required less specific knowledge of Irish history beyond the recent past but which would yield slogans and quotable lines would be more appropriate. Drawing on the rhetorical devices and oratorical style that had earned medals at Trinity, Hyde therefore began his revised speech by celebrating the sense of kinship that had brought him and his listeners together ("When I hear your voices, I feel as if I had only transported myself from one Ireland to another"), then introduced, strengthening his statements through contrast, the ideas they shared ("Twelve years ago we found our country becoming a province, no, not a province but a mean little outpost of England. Today we are making it a nation").

As minute by minute, in response to such statements, applause rose, filled the hall, and washed over him, Hyde knew that he had chosen correctly. He emphasized the bonds that joined the Irish in Ireland and America ("I look upon the moral support of the Irish in America to be the most valuable asset that the Gaelic League at home could have") and played on the idea of the word "bonds" to introduce the purpose of his speech ("I would sooner have the moral support of the Irish in America than a quarter of a million dollars poured into the Gaelic League tomorrow"). He then raised the significance of his appeal through a series of statements separated by dramatic pauses, reaching for a level of oratory appropriate to the sum he had mentioned. Beginning softly, he allowed his voice to grow louder as he approached his penultimate exclamation, then reduced it to end the first part of his lecture on almost a whisper:

I am here today to explain to you the life and death struggle upon which we are engaged in Ireland.

I see that the papers say that this is the last grand struggle of the Irish race to preserve their language.

Oh, ladies and gentlemen! It is ten times, it is a hundred times, it is a thousand times more far-reaching than that!

It is the last possible life and death struggle of the Irish race to preserve not their own language but their national identity.

The applause rose and swelled again and then died down as, now comfortable that his audience was with him, Hyde moved gradually from peroration to explanation (of the league's nonsectarian character, of how it embraced Catholic and Protestant), concentrating their attention. Quickening his pace and raising his voice, he reached again as if for the final high moment of his speech, then—once more reversing expectations—dropped his voice to normal level and intoned matter-of-factly:

We are the white dove of peace passing over the land and obliterating the old feuds and hatred and black bad blood of the country. . . .
We are no clique, we are no faction, we are no party.
We are above and beyond all politics, all parties, and all factions; offending nobody but the anti-Irishman.
We stand immovable on the rock of the doctrine of true Irish nationhood—an Ireland self-centered, self-sufficing, self-supporting, self-reliant; an Ireland speaking its own language, thinking its own thoughts, writing its own books, singing its own songs, playing its own games, weaving its own coats, wearing its own hats, and going for nothing outside the four shores of Ireland that can possibly be procured inside them.
The Gaelic League is founded not upon hatred of England but upon love of Ireland. Hatred is a negative passion; it is a powerful, a very powerful destroyer; but it is useless for building up. Love, on the other hand, can remove mountains and we have removed them.

It was over. He had spoken for ninety minutes, interrupted only by bursts of applause. Now there was more applause and cheers, they were on their feet, and somewhere in the audience some small group was singing "A Nation Once Again." Judge Keogh and Bourke Cockran were shaking his hand, and people were holding out their programs for his autograph.

His spirits lifted by the success of the New York meeting, on November 27 Hyde wrote to Pádraig O'Daly and Nellie O'Brien in Dublin, assuring them that the factionalism he had feared was indeed a factor of Irish-American life, but that he had developed a technique for staying above it. Two days later, in a letter to the Coiste Gnótha, he said that already he had made a start at building a financial reserve, but as he needed to be able to assure the Americans that it would not be frittered away, he wanted to establish that no more than £1,000 of it would be used for routine operating expenses in any one year. He knew he could not expect every meeting to yield the sum that had been collected in New York, but if he did half as well on a regular basis with occasional larger returns in places like Boston and Chicago, there should be no trouble, he believed, in not just reaching but exceeding the figure he and Quinn had set as a reasonable goal. The thing was to watch out for tactics such as those that had been used to nearly wreck this first performance. If it had not been for Quinn's quick action, anger and embarrassment on the part of those who were the real target of the intended sabotage would have distracted his audience from his speech in particular and the purpose of the program in general.

It was in this mood that Hyde set out for Hartford. The crowd was large and responsive, but at the end of the program there was no collection. Somehow, someone had overlooked this important detail. Distressed local organizers drove him around the city the next day, stopping at the offices of successful Irish Americans—most of them in the wholesale liquor, paper, or insurance business—where Hyde could introduce himself, explain his mission, and request a donation. No one even pretended that the results of this approach could begin to match what he might have had if a collection had been taken at the end of his lecture, but no one thought he would leave Hartford with net proceeds of only a little more than a hundred dollars. Hyde made a mental note to remind Concannon, who had been serving as his advance man, to check before each event about arrangements for the collection. Months later Hyde's suspicion that the Hartford problem had been not oversight but sabotage was confirmed by a letter of apology from one of the Hartford organizers. There had been a last-minute falling out between Irish-speaking and non-Irish-speaking groups in the city, he explained. He had thought he had things patched up, but on the day of the program tempers had flared and some people had walked out, with the result that all his hard work of nearly two years had been nullified. Hyde could not help but feel sorry for this well-meaning, honest but frustrated man.

Although the Boston meeting was successful, it was threatened by a different set of problems. The city had been well prepared by the newspapers for the December 3 event. The influential archdiocesan weekly, the *Pilot,* had given prominent space to Hyde's visit to the White House. Under "Entertainment" the *Boston Post* for Saturday, December 2, carried a large advertisement for Hyde's speech next to another advertisement for Maggie Cline ("the Irish Queen"), and "ten other big acts" that were to follow Hyde in the Boston Theater. The Philo-Celtic Society of Boston had announced that it would sponsor a reception.

On Saturday, with Lucy accompanying him, Hyde left New York

by an early train in order to reach Boston in time for a luncheon in his honor to be hosted by acting mayor Whelton on behalf of the city of Boston. En route Hyde received a telegram instructing him to leave the train at the Back Bay station where he would be escorted to the Hotel Lenox and introduced there to the acting mayor and a number of leading educators and newspaper editors. All seemed to be going well and Hyde was about to sit down to luncheon with the acting mayor and other guests when he was called to the telephone. The caller was Concannon, who insisted that Hyde make clear to Whelton that his presence was to be regarded as the visit of one friend to another and not an official event. His acceptance of Whelton's invitation, although innocent, already had caused a split in the Boston Gaelic League, which was divided, Concannon explained, on the question of which candidate to support in the coming mayoralty elections. Taking the acting mayor aside, Hyde tactfully told him that he understood that there was a mayoralty campaign in progress and hoped that the luncheon would not be construed by anyone as an indication that he was involving himself in Boston politics. Whelton laughed at the suggestion and assured him that no politicians, just a few educators, had been invited, but Hyde was so wary of the situation that he could not give his luncheon address the concentration it required. The next day Hyde discovered that another welcoming committee accompanied by Concannon and headed by John F. Fitzgerald (grandfather of John Fitzgerald Kennedy, and a leading candidate in the mayoralty race) had been waiting for him at Boston's other railroad station. Moreover, Matthew Cummings, president of the Ancient Order of Hibernians and the chair of the committee that had planned Hyde's visit, was upset at not having been invited to the Hotel Lenox luncheon.

Meanwhile, stories began to circulate about an erroneous newspaper announcement that had given the wrong time and place of Hyde's lecture. Rumor had it that this was no honest error but the work of the United Irish League. It was contested by a second rumor that the first rumor had been planted to embarrass the United Irish League. Although both rumors added to Hyde's discomfort, neither had any other effect, nor did the erroneous announcement apparently discourage attendance, for despite pouring rain the Boston Theater was four-fifths full when the moment came to begin the program. Moreover, as the figures seated together on the stage indicated, the politicians had managed to reach a détente, at least for the duration of Hyde's visit. With them were officials of the organizing committee and other prominent persons, including Professors Fred Norris Robinson (who, as promised, introduced Hyde), George Lyman Kittredge, and Leo Wiener of Harvard; high-ranking dignitaries of the Catholic church in Boston; and various local officials. Thomas Concannon was also there, identified on the program by a title he had newly bestowed upon himself: chief organizer of the Gaelic League in Ireland.

The event began inauspiciously with the long and painful reading of a pedestrian poem entitled "The Language of the Gael" and Robinson's polite but not exciting introduction. There had been no Bourke Cockran warm-up, Hyde realized, with a certain amount of trepidation, as he took his place at the podium. As in New York, he began speaking in Gaelic to a partly delighted but mostly bewildered audience, then switched within a few minutes (to a roar of laughter and much applause) to English. This time he did focus on the necessity for deanglicization, denouncing "that devouring demon" that has "swallowed up our language, our music, our songs, our dances, and our pastimes." "Back, demon, back! You shall swallow no more," he cried melodramatically, acting the part as if he were performing at the Mosaic in Dublin, gratified by his Boston audience's appropriate cheers and whistles and catcalls. Then, pausing somberly, he introduced his sober topic: As a result of imitation the people of Ireland have "ceased to be Irish without becoming English." An Irish identity is essential if Ireland is to become "a new nation on the map of Europe." The idea of reviving Irish is no longer a dream; it is already a reality. In Ireland, "a dozen years ago Irish was taught in only six schools. Today it is taught in 3,000 schools. . . . 250,000 Irishmen are learning to read and write Irish." The Gaelic League is "a popular democratic movement" with a modest budget. "On this we are trying to save Ireland." Despite its limited funds, it already has accomplished much. "We brought together for the first time Protestant and Catholic, priest and parson, landlord and tenant. If we have the support of the Irish in America, we are bound to win."

Similar to the speech he had delivered in 1892 as president of the Irish Literary Society yet modified for American audiences, the text that Hyde used in Boston became a basic item in his repertoire. It became the one that he employed most frequently during his entire fund-raising campaign, with small changes to incorporate local or current references or to infuse the text with more energy or more constraint, as the occasion required.

The Boston program received excellent press coverage that was picked up and repeated in other newspapers across the country as well as in Ireland. The *Boston Evening Transcript* ran a full column on the entertainment page under the headline "The Revival of Gaelic"; it was fairly handled. But the real public relations advantage was the *Boston Globe*'s front-page story under the two-column headline "Dr. Hyde Tells of Erin's Last Fight," followed below by "Preservation of Her Identity at Stake." The text, which began on page one with the announcement that $1,000 had been subscribed in twenty minutes and continued on page three with a full transcript of Hyde's speech, ended with the announcement that the *Globe* had opened a subscription list to which it, the *Boston Post,* the *Boston Herald,* and the *Republic* each had donated $100. Page three also carried a two-column picture of Hyde. Under the heading "Big Fund for Hyde" the *Post* gave the address to which contributions might be sent, noted the "tremendous ovation" Hyde's speech had received, and said that "wild enthusiasm" had characterized the entire program.

Although Hyde's complaints about the Boston program had focused on the embarrassing position in which he had been placed by the competing local politicians, John Quinn's concern was the amount of money raised. It was substantial; it should have been more, he declared. Assuring smooth relations and arranging efficient methods of fund-raising were both responsibilities that had been assigned to Concannon. Immediately upon meeting him Quinn had felt, as he wrote to Martin Keogh, that Concannon was the wrong man for the job. "He is a child of nature and a child of nature is not the man to organize meetings in this country or to get people to give money." Any Irish-American millionaire would give money to Hyde if he asked for it but would "size up a man like Concannon in ten minutes and wouldn't give him a cent. . . . Money is what we want, we need a man who can touch the hearts of plutocrats."

In Quinn's objections to Concannon he had an ally in Lucy, whose different criticisms focused on the self-aggrandizing interviews the self-appointed Gaelic League's chief organizer gave to the newspapers. She addressed her complaints to Agnes O'Farrelly in Dublin: "We have in plain language brought out the *wrong man*—but for Concannon's blunders and conceit and selfishness Dr. Hyde would have got by now *thousands of dollars*." Moreover, influential men had told her that Concannon "was *giving a bad impression of the Gaelic League*." She was especially indignant at the report that he had been telling people that he himself was going to "remodel the Gaelic League in Ireland . . . on new and modern lines." And he had not yet provided an account of his expenses but had been buying expensive presents for "his girl."

Both Quinn and Lucy believed that Concannon should not be allowed to proceed to California, but Quinn felt restrained as Hyde had specifically requested that Concannon be put in charge of arrangements. Nor would Hyde listen to Lucy, who finally out of exasperation sent her observations to Agnes, with instructions that she use her own discretion about how to bring them to the attention of O'Daly or Barrett, the league's secretary and treasurer. Agnes went instead to John MacNeill, Hyde's close friend and co-worker, and the vice-president of the league. Her recommendation was that MacNeill call a special meeting of the Coiste Gnótha to discuss Lucy's general observations and to recall Concannon if he did not promptly give an account of his expenses. MacNeill agreed to demand from Concannon, by cable, an immediate accounting, and to write a letter to Hyde suggesting that Concannon's services might be better employed in Ireland, but he refused to snatch Concannon from Hyde's staff with only Lucy's testimony against him. To Agnes, MacNeill confided that a good part of the problem could well be that Concannon had "made himself obnoxious" to Lucy. Others before him had felt the scorn of her disfavor and the sharpness of her tongue.

With no one willing to dismiss Concannon or change his assignment, he remained on the fund-raising tour, to the dismay of both Quinn and Lucy, who fumed in New York while Hyde and Concannon left on a three-week tour of New England and the Northeast. When they returned, there remained only two more commitments in the New York area before the Hydes and Concannon began their journey westward. Lucy again asked Hyde if Concannon had drawn up an account of his expenses; Quinn again reviewed receipts and found them short of what he expected. To Lucy's question Hyde responded by urging her to tell him all about how she had been enjoying herself with the Keoghs and her other new friends in New York who had taken charge of her during his absence. To Quinn he insisted that animosities among Irish-American societies were to blame. In Lowell, after a small turnout had left him with a meager collection, a man had volunteered the information that it was the fault of the local organizer, the chief of police; had matters been left in the hands of the Irish societies, the program would have been more successful. In Philadelphia, where Hyde personally solicited a contribution from the archbishop and received but a token sum, he was told that behind the scenes an intense campaign against the Gaelic League had been waged on behalf of the United Irish League, who feared a loss in their subscriptions. And also in Philadelphia, Hyde reported, if it had not been for the Clan na Gael, which stepped in with a contribution of $1,500 supplemented by an additional $500 from one of its leading members, Joseph McGarrity, expenses might have been greater than contributions, for again as in New York there had been a last-minute return of a large block of reserved tickets.

There seemed to be nothing either Quinn or Lucy could do about Concannon, who already had headed toward the Midwest as advance man when on January 4 the Hydes boarded the train for Pittsburgh, their interim stop en route to Chicago. Lucy had received assurances of sumptuous accommodations and invitations to luncheons, dinners, concerts, theater performances, parties, and sightseeing and shopping trips during the three weeks she would spend in Chicago. Hyde's schedule included trips out of the city to Milwaukee, where Jeremiah Curtin had grown up; to Minneapolis and St. Paul; to Cleveland, Columbus, and Cincinnati; to South Bend and Indianapolis; and to St. Louis, Missouri.

All through the Midwest Hyde encountered women and men whom he had known in Ireland or who were relatives of people he knew in Ireland. Usually these encounters were joyous, but at least one was upsetting. After his lecture at Butler College in Indianapolis, Hyde had turned to shake hands with committee members and their guests who had been seated on the platform. Suddenly he found himself in front of "the notorious Lenchechaun," a scoundrel with a vicious temper who had fled from Ireland after disfiguring his landlady (who was also very likely his mistress) by biting off her nose. (Lenchechaun's full story recently has been told by James Carney in *The Playboy and the Yellow Lady*). Discovered living in Indianapolis, Lenchechaun was charged and would have been extradited had he not aroused the sympathy of Indianapolis Irish Americans with his claims that the crimes he was said to have committed were but the actions of a poor tenant trying to save himself from the landowner who had mistreated him. On the one hand Hyde wholeheartedly approved of Irish unity in America when it came to protecting Irish patriots and righting genuine injustice; in this case he regretted that the object on which so much trouble had been wasted was not a worthier one. Caught among the crowd on the platform with no alternative but to join in the general handshaking, Lenchechaun had tried to keep his head down "in a rather shame-faced way," but Hyde had recognized him. "I have heard talk about you," Hyde said icily, turning away. Other aspects of Hyde's Indianapolis visit more than compensated for this unpleasant encounter. In his diary he described an old-fashioned Irish evening in which everyone told ghost stories of the kind he used to hear from Seamas Hart. One afternoon he visited the Hoosier poet, James Whitcomb Riley, bringing him a "splendid floral harp of roses and lilies of the valley, about four feet high," in return for a large bouquet of roses sent by Riley that he had found in his hotel room when he arrived.

From Indianapolis, Hyde went to Cincinnati, where the weather was warm and pleasant, but as soon as he reached St. Louis, he encountered winter. The further north he traveled, the lower the temperature dropped. Standing in train stations, braving icy winds, freezing rain, and snow at temperatures that rivaled those he remembered from New Brunswick, Hyde thought wryly of a note he had sent to Quinn the preceding February, when plans for his tour were in the making. Lucy, he had said, was "looking foward" to America as an "escape from an Irish winter"! In Milwaukee a cold wind blew continuously off the freezing waters of Lake Michigan, but the warmth of the greeting he received from the Ancient Order of Hibernians, the Norwegian governor, and the general population more than made up for the continuing chill. Madison weather was worse. Finishing his January 30 evening lecture on folklore at the University of Wisconsin, he and his host, A. C. L. Brown, a former student of Fred Norris Robinson and a specialist in Celtic elements in Arthurian literature, went to Brown's rooms where a convivial group smoked and sipped whiskey and talked late into the night. At one o'clock in the morning—too late to get a cab—Hyde and Brown started out on foot for the railroad station, usually a simple walk of a mile or two. On this night, however, they had not taken more than a dozen steps before they found themselves in the teeth of a snow-filled howling gale. Since Brown did not seem to be intimidated by the weather, Hyde assumed that there was nothing unusual about it for Madison, although he wished that he had brought with him the fur hat he had worn in New Brunswick. When they reached the station he had to wait a half hour, his teeth chattering, for the 2:15 A.M. train to St. Paul. For some days afterward he had a severe earache that left him partially deaf in one ear. Later he discovered that he had walked through one of the worst midwestern blizzards of recent years.

Despite the weather the Hydes enjoyed Chicago, which Lucy described in a postcard to Nuala and Una as "a fine city with pleasant buildings," "only 50 years old" with "streets thirty miles long" and "no indians now." There they were lavishly entertained by well-to-do Irish-American bankers and businessmen, political figures, celebrities, and literary figures; Hyde was invited to talk at the University of Chicago. As they prepared to leave they assured the friends they had made—among them, Chicago's "Mr. Dooley"—that they would return in April.

Days were already longer and the birds had begun to return to the lakefront when, at seven-thirty in the evening, February 6, the Hydes boarded their train. By eleven o'clock the next morning they were in Omaha—a visual shock, as they had not seen the gradual change in the countryside through which they had passed overnight and therefore were not prepared for the sweeping flatness of the northern midwest. To Nuala and Una, Lucy sent a picture postcard: "This is a castle of an American millionaire. Would you like one? Jane will tell you what an American millionaire is. These fine homes have no gardens worth speaking of, which is a pity."

In Omaha, Hyde continued to encounter fluent Irish speakers (including the bishop of Omaha, a Dr. Scannell from Cork) and Roscommon neighbors (such as Father Stritch, who now lived in Omaha, but was a native of Ballaghaderreen). It was not at all difficult to have such chance meetings there, he discovered, as more than one-sixth of the city's population of 150,000 was either Irish-born or of Irish extraction. Often in Omaha, as in other parts of the United States, he found among the native-born Irish and their American-born children and even grandchildren books or manuscripts in the Irish language which they preserved but could not read. The future fate of these items concerned him greatly, as he began to mention in his speeches in the hope that the owners might take steps to make sure that these endangered relics of their past would be preserved.

On February 11 the Hydes were again on a train, now headed in full daylight across the Great Plains and through the Rocky Mountains toward the coast of the Pacific Ocean. Concannon, to Lucy's great relief, had gone on ahead to spend a few days with his brother in California. Hyde divided his time between looking out the train window and translating canto 5 of Dante's *Inferno* from Italian into Irish, for a priest he had met at Notre Dame. He felt awed by the immensity of America, the enormous farms, each one stretched over what seemed to Hyde to be all the land and more of an Irish county, and the wild and barren scenery. Sometimes, seeing a solitary figure near a farmhouse, he thought of the people they had met most recently in the Midwest, many of them Irish women married to German husbands or Irish men married to German wives. It struck him that, given the cultural values he felt that they shared, this might be a better combination than English and Irish. Idly, enjoying the leisure, he let his mind wander, not caring how long it might take to reach the crowds, the reporters, the photographers, and the well-wishers in San Francisco. They had left Ireland more than three months ago—ninety-six days ago to be exact—and he had spent few of them resting. He had arrived in the Midwest with a bad cold that he had never quite shaken. His ear—the one he had exposed to a Wisconsin blizzard—still bothered him from time to time. He was nodding, almost asleep, when the train stopped in Ogden, Utah, and two reporters for the San Francisco newspapers boarded to interview him. His first reaction was dismay that he quickly tried to mask. His second reaction was astonished pleasure, for one reporter was Edward F. Cahill, a Trinity man, and the other was J. T. Smith, a fluent Irish speaker. They had a fine, companionable time together, and the next day readers of the San Franciso *Examiner* awoke to find Douglas Hyde looking out at them from a four-column story on the front page of their newspaper.

San Francisco captured the hearts of both Lucy and Hyde. They arrived in the evening in time to see the Ferry Building and City Hall dome outlined in lights above the sparkling Pacific. Accompanied by Father Yorke and Frank Sullivan, members of the organizing committee, they were introduced to photographers who snapped them "in all the moods and tenses" and were then brought to the St. Francis Hotel where they could look out at the famous trolleys. On February 12 Hyde spoke in San Francisco. On February 14, after an informal session with the organizing committee, they were taken in a Mercedes to the Cliff House to view the sea lions, after which Hyde lectured in Berkeley. Fascinated by San Francisco, Hyde was eager to explore every corner of it, but between head cold and fatigue, he had begun to lose his voice. On Saturday, February 17, he remained in his room the entire day, steaming his throat over jugs of hot water in order to be able to address the major program set for Sunday at the Tivoli Opera House. All the boxes, he was told, had been sold in advance, bringing in $1,400 immediately, without counting the income anticipated from the stalls.

The crowd at the Tivoli was the most enthusiastic Hyde had yet encountered. He stepped up to the podium following Father Yorke's introduction, eyes sparkling, hands behind his back, bowing to a cheering, clapping, fully packed house. For an hour and a half (his vocal cords fortunately did not betray him) he alternately roared and whispered in an embellished version of what he had come to call "the Speech." Hitting all the notes that had aroused audiences of the past three months—"the devouring demon of anglicization" whose "foul and gluttonous jaws have swallowed everything that was hereditary, natural, instinctive, ancient, intellectual, and noble"; the lateness of the hour; the desperate need for Irish men and women to plant their feet firmly and say, "Back, demon, Back! Not one more mouthful of the heritage of Irish nationhood shall you swallow again forever"—he urged his lively audience not to let the abundant wealth of the Irish in America be lost in abundant indifference. He pleaded with them not just to save the dying Irish race but to help it develop upon Irish lines in a healthy future. Frank Sullivan was so moved by Hyde's performance that at its conclusion he himself pledged $1,200 on the spot. Others joined in the fever of the moment. The next evening Hyde found himself at the head table of "the greatest banquet ever given to a private person on the coast or indeed I believe to anyone else in California." Even Lucy was impressed and pleased—especially as there was no sign of Concannon.

Neither Quinn nor Lucy had given up on getting rid of Concannon. Although they were not otherwise fond of each other they exchanged letters about him through which they vented their anger and frustration. Lucy complained that he still had not provided an account of his expenses. Quinn was still dissatisfied with the discrepancy between what he had anticipated and what he was told had been collected. To Quinn, Concannon was "a fumbling, procrastinating, and conceited ass." To Lucy he was a "rat," an "eel," a "viper." If Quinn tired of this correspondence before Lucy, it was no doubt only partly because of the pressure of other matters, as he said, but also because Lucy had expanded the subject to include Quinn's conduct of his personal life, including his smoking, of which she did not approve.

Concannon presumably was still with his brother. Lucy enjoyed his absence and dreaded his return. Also absent in California were the jealousies and grievances within and among local societies on which Hyde blamed past fund-raising troubles and disappointments. After San Jose on February 26, Oakland on February 28, and Santa Barbara on March 8, the next major program was scheduled for Los Angeles on March 10. With sufficient time to rest between commitments, the Hydes were delighted when William J. Robinson, a goldminer from the north of Ireland, offered to drive them around to give them a better acquaintance with the countryside. The weather was ideal, the scenery spectacular. On March 9 Laurence Brannick, who had escorted Father O'Growney's coffin from California to Maynooth in 1901, brought them to Los Angeles, where Lucy watched with pleasure as Hyde was feted at the Alexandria Hotel, extolled in the *Los Angeles Times,* and rewarded with a substantial collection for "the Speech."

In the California sunshine of Los Angeles and San Francisco Lucy did not even mind the questions of reporters, which until then she had been reluctant to oblige, but talked easily about herself and her two children. She showed the reporters pictures of both Nuala and Una; she told them that she had sent the girls more than two hundred post-cards of America; she even gave an interview in which she stoutly defended the role that Irish women were playing in the Gaelic League. "The great advantage of the League," she said, was that it gave to women "as much scope for their activity as men." It was in this respect, she declared, with the poise and self-assurance of the Lucy whom Hyde had courted, that it differed from other organizations run by men, in which women have little representation. Within the league women were "fellow-workers." "Cut off women," she asserted, "and the League would not survive." One by one, she ticked off the names of the women who were most active in the league, noting their responsibilities and contributions. The only one she did not mention was Nellie O'Brien, perhaps because she was beginning to resent the pleasure with which Hyde seemed to receive Nellie's frequent long and friendly letters.

On the evening of March 26 Father Yorke, the Sullivans, and others who had been their daily companions accompanied the Hydes across the bay to their waiting train. On the Oakland ferry Hyde turned for a last look at the receding pier. Taking off his hat he waved and shouted a farewell that encompassed not only his friends but the entire city. "San Francisco, I shall never see you again."

Nothing before or after San Francisco could match it for enthusiasm, hospitality, and contributions. Its spell, although muted, seemed to continue, for all went well in Portland and Seattle, although collections were again not what had been expected. In the copper-mining city of Butte, a different world in which the emphasis was clearly on the struggle for survival, Hyde persuaded a hundred hopeful Irish Americans to form a branch of the Gaelic League, then sat down to read a waiting packet of Nellie O'Brien's letters, thinking that Ireland seemed very far away. With Lucy he visited Anaconda, where they spent the day touring the mines and where Hyde was horrified to watch a cloud of arsenic pour out of a smokestack 300 feet high and, carried by the breeze, settle on the distant farmland. During the next few days they visited the impoverished villages of local tribes of the largest population of native Americans they had encountered and talked with a young Irishman who explained the economy of the state. "Montana is completely owned, almost body and soul, by the Standard Oil Company and other kindred corporations," Hyde wrote in his diary. "They have succeeded in pre-empting every source of wealth that is worth anything—all the mines, the timber upon a thousand hills, the sources of all the water power, and even all the good valley land, and of course they own the newspapers." He had come to Butte to ask for help in relieving the oppression of a people thousands of miles away. They had contributed to his cause. And who was there to help them? The people understood their plight, he was assured by several of the Irish Americans with whom he spoke. In fact, if it had not been for the election of Roosevelt, from whom they expected some help, some might have been brought to the point of revolution. But could Theodore Roosevelt really help, asked Hyde. The young men shrugged.

At the beginning of April, while Hyde was still in Butte, he received a letter from John Quinn, who was now thoroughly fed up with Concannon. Not half of what Concannon had guaranteed had been sent in, he declared. "I am done with him," he told Hyde. He must be kept out of Baltimore, Washington, and Buffalo, for it would be "money thrown away" for him to go there. On April 9 Hyde at last conceded. He cabled the league, saying that he looked upon his tour as practically finished and therefore had released Concannon, who would sail in three weeks' time (Concannon had asked for those three weeks for himself). He wrote to Concannon, giving him leave to go whenever he chose.

From Butte, the Hydes retraced their route through St. Paul and Chicago. On April 19 they were in Memphis when they awoke to news that their beautiful and generous San Francisco had been nearly destroyed. "We were unspeakably horrified . . . ," Hyde wrote in his diary, trying hard not to see in his mind's eye its ground gaping, its buildings overthrown. Some of the money he had raised in San Francisco had to be used to pay expenses. The small fees he received from his college lectures were supposed to be his own money; it had been John Quinn's idea to arrange these for that purpose, as a way to compensate Hyde for the eight months that he was devoting to the campaign. The rest was for the league. Calculating what these figures came to, Hyde estimated that he could safely return $5,000 for the relief of the people of

San Francisco without danger of dipping into league funds or using them for expenses. He arranged with John Quinn for the money to be sent. Quinn telegraphed the money to Father Yorke who mercifully had not been among the dead and injured.

Memphis was a shock to both Lucy and Hyde, who now had been traveling in the United States for five months. Their hotel, the best in the city, was "unutterably dirty and slovenly," Hyde complained in his diary. Everything was in "ramshackle condition." The hotel elevator "always stopped three feet short of our floor, and to scale up from the lift to our landing was a feat" which required "considerable athletic prowess." They were taken to the horse races by the mayor, "a nice old man of the name of Malone" who, to Hyde's amusement, seemed to have stepped out of a novel. "He had the slow drawl and the objection to sounding an 'r' and talked about his family and the aristocracy and his estates in Ireland two hundred years ago." He said that his family had been in Virginia for two hundred years before settling in Tennessee. They were, he declared, "the old aristocracy befo' the wah, suh." Aside from their host, Father Larkin, and another man named Walsh, Hyde's impression was that there were not many Irish in Memphis. Nevertheless they had a good turnout in the theater for his lecture, and before they left, Father Larkin took Hyde to see the cotton bales packed and tightened by hydraulic pressure on the "great sheet of water" that was the Mississippi River.

By Saturday, April 21, the Hydes were on their way from Louisville to Baltimore. Delighted with the return of spring, Hyde captured the scenery in his diary:

The white blossoms of the dog trees brightened the woods and forests on both sides of the railway, and the pink patches made by the Judas trees, as they are called, were beyond anything lovely. The Judas tree appears to have no leaves, but is thickly covered with pink blossoms. Judas is said to have hung himself on one of these trees, hence the name. They are numerous all over the South, but apparently not in the North. Toward evening we struck the Allegheny Mountains, a series of lovely ridges with a beautiful river running through them. All night long these ridges were lit up by brilliant flashes of summer lightning which kept playing on the hills and river for hours.

In Baltimore, Hyde spoke to a packed theater "decorated for the meeting with what appeared to be Irish words in large Irish letters: GINN FINN GINN FINN AMAIN FAILICE 7 GLAINCE." (Obviously intended was *Sinn Féin Sinn Féin amhain fáilte agus sláinte*: "Sinn Féin [the name of Arthur Griffith's new nationalist organization, literally "ourselves"] only Sinn Féin, welcome and health.") It was nicely done, anyway, thought Hyde, and since it was a decoration that so few could read, it made no difference. But perhaps there would come a time when it would.

At six o'clock in the evening on April 23 the Hydes were back in New York, at John Quinn's apartment. Quinn was not looking well; in the four months since they had left New York he had lost his only brother. He was thirty-six; he came from a close family; his father had died in 1897; his mother and two of his four sisters in 1902. Yet he had not for a moment put aside or ignored in this latest grief anything that had to be done on Hyde's behalf. Just three days before their return he had written a long letter to Lady Gregory about the difficulties with which he had had to cope, not through any fault of Hyde's, but on account of the "stubborn and blundering Concannon" and the "bad tempers and petty jealousies" of a small but intensely irritating number of people in the Irish-American organizations on which he had relied. If it had not been for others, "broadminded, patriotic and generous Irishmen," the tour would have failed. He had nothing but admiration for Hyde and for the way he had managed to hold up in situations that would have discouraged many another. He noted particularly Hyde's capacity for getting along with everyone, including some whom Quinn frankly admitted that he himself could not abide. It was for Hyde that he had worked Saturdays and Sundays as well as weekdays for many months.

The Hydes were back, but the work was not yet over. There were still commitments in and around New York and as far north as Toronto that had to be kept. At nine the next morning Hyde was on his way to Cornell University. Quinn accompanied him on the ferry to Hoboken where he boarded the train to Ithaca. He was met at the station by a Trinity man, a Professor McMahon, who put him up in his own house. His evening lecture, the first of two, was about the philosophy of the Gaelic movement. The next morning was pure pleasure, devoted to examining the Cornell Dante collection (about eight thousand volumes, he estimated) and a "splendid Petrarch and Icelandic collection as well." In the afternoon he lectured on Irish poetry; by evening he was in Elmira for a banquet that lasted until almost two o'clock in the morning.

The students at the Elmira Ladies' College, where Hyde was to lecture on April 26, excelled, he was told, in athletics. In the morning he talked to them for about a half hour and made them laugh. In the evening he was to address a much larger audience—about twelve hundred, he estimated, that included the students of the ladies' college, who arrived in their caps and gowns. Unaware that no more than a fifth of those he was addressing had any Irish background or connections, Hyde had decided to give them "the Speech." Part way through, when he began to realize that he was not getting the reactions he expected, he "switched around a little," but not before the editor of the Elmira *Telegraph* had noticed his error, for which he afterward took Hyde to task. Had this happened four or five months earlier, Hyde would have been devastated. As it was he was grateful that his listeners received what he had to say as well as they did.

From Elmira, Hyde went to Scranton, accompanied by a Father Hurst, an "old friend . . . who had been in Ratra some years ago" and who had lived for a time in Swinford, in Mayo. He would have enjoyed talking during the journey but he was so tired he could hardly keep his eyes open, and eventually he fell asleep on the train. Another of his hosts in Scranton was a Casey from a village near Coolavin, the home of The MacDermot very near to Ballaghaderreen. The mayor, the bishop, and another crowd of 1,200 turned out to hear his evening lecture. In the morning he was on his way back to New York, grateful that he had two weeks to rest before the next major fund-raising event, in Buffalo on May 13.

Hyde spent most of his time on the train from Scranton to New York just looking out the window. It was April 28. There was not yet much foliage, but the willows, he noticed, were putting on their green and the red buds of the hard maple had started to sprout, giving the trees a reddish-yellow rather than green appearance. Taking note of the difference between Irish and American trees, he observed that in an American wood just beginning to green there were "all kinds of shades, a whitish green, dull green, dark green, but very little vivid green." He thought the green of the drooping willows "the prettiest thing in the landscape." Soon it would be time for him to return to Ireland. He wondered again, as so often before, what his life would have been like if in 1891 he had remained in North America.

By one o'clock Hyde was in New York, at Quinn's office. Although it was Saturday, Quinn was, as usual, working with other members of the host committee. A letter had come for Hyde from Father Yorke, assuring him that all his friends were safe but the city was destroyed, and they were now rebuilding. Over lunch Hyde raised the question of sending an additional $5,000 for the relief of "the San Francisco suf-

ferers." The committee members gave their permission, and Quinn telegraphed the money to Father Yorke. A few days later, catching up on
his correspondence, Hyde wrote to Yorke, offering to send another
$5,000 for earthquake relief from the money he had collected in San
Francisco if it were needed. He assured Yorke that he took full responsibility for returning money which he felt under the present circumstances was needed more by San Francisco than by the league. He
also felt confident that there was "not a single person in Ireland" who
would not back him up in making such a contribution. Hyde asked
Yorke if he should not also return to the Sullivans the $1,700 they had
given to the league as they might now be in need of it. "All the pleasure
has been taken out of my trip to America by this frightful accident,"
he declared. "My heart is really broken over what has happened to you."

After dinner on April 28 Hyde went alone to an evening performance
of one of his plays, *An Pósadh* (The Marriage) at the Lexington Opera
House. He spoke in Irish at the end of the performance. "Idle generally
today," he wrote in his diary on April 29. It was the first notation of
its kind since well before he had left Ratra. It was Sunday: he and
Quinn took a long walk along the river, looking at the French and
American battleships; he was overjoyed at the prospect of being just
a visitor to America for a few days, with no fund-raising events to worry
about. The local committee that had arranged his lecture in Philadelphia
had invited him and Lucy to return and really see the city, a prospect
that pleased Lucy. On Monday morning they took the train to Philadelphia for a four-day visit that included a tour of all the historic sites
and buildings, a banquet attended by forty people who had been to
his lecture in December, and a night playing twenty-one with three
Catholic priests, Father Coghlan, Father O'Donnell, and Father Mac-
Laughlin, who had become his friends.

On May 4 Hyde returned with Lucy to New York, lunched with
Quinn, and caught a train to Poughkeepsie, where he lectured on Irish
poetry at Vassar College. After his lecture there was a reception followed by a "curious ceremony" with Celtic overtones in which students
dressed in "fantastic costumes" to represent Juno and other deities "had
limelights thrown upon them and chanted weird songs and college
ditties." The next evening, again back in New York, Hyde spoke at a
review of the Irish Volunteers at the Grand Central Palace. He had
reservations about participating in such a meeting, especially as the Volunteers were Clan na Gael men, but as all proceeds of this meeting were
to go for the relief of the sufferers in San Francisco, he could not bring

himself to refuse. On May 8 he found himself in very different company, at dinner at Delmonico's with Judge Keogh, with whom he attended the quarterly meeting of the Friendly Sons of St. Patrick—the only society, Hyde noted, that many of the wealthiest and most successful Irish Americans would join, having been disaffected by the "perpetual disputes and unsavoury bickerings" that went on in others. On May 9 Hyde, Quinn, and Lucy were joined at dinner by the Janviers, a couple from still another circle, supporters of the Félibrige, the organization founded by Mistral to help preserve the language of Provençal. On the last day of what he and Lucy had been calling their holiday, they went to the Hippodrome, laughed at the trained seals, and enjoyed the ballet.

On Saturday morning, May 12, the Hydes left for Buffalo. From the moment they got off the train at 7:10 P.M. they were surrounded by people: members of the local host committee, local dignitaries, members of Irish-American societies, and a steady stream of reporters. "Back, back, demon, back," Hyde wished he could say, but instead he again did his best to be accessible, amusing, intelligible, and wary yet quotable. On May 13, the day of the program, it poured rain, but a good crowd (about twelve hundred people) turned up anyway, and the collection was satisfying. On Monday, Hyde took Lucy to Niagara Falls, which he had first seen fifteen years ago, and then delivered a lecture at Niagara College entitled "The Last Three Centuries of Irish Literature." On Tuesday, Hyde went alone, by invitation, to meet a Mr. Sweeney, the kind of man who in Dublin might be called a character, a dry-goods merchant from county Antrim who had given $100 at the Sunday night event. "It is not easy to get money out of me," he told Hyde. "If you didn't strike me right you wouldn't have got it."

Hyde and Lucy started for Rochester at one o'clock on May 16 via the Empire State Express. Hyde knew that it had the reputation of being one of the fastest trains in the world; still, he was astonished when they made the sixty-nine-mile journey in seventy minutes. In the afternoon he and Lucy were given an automobile tour of the Genessee Valley. Hyde's lecture in the evening was followed by a banquet complete with champagne and cigars. Although Hyde enjoyed himself, he could not forget that his next lecture was in Toronto, where he feared the attack of the Orange newspapers. All turned out well, however. "I . . . turned their flank," he noted in his diary, "by making common cause with the Scotch, saying that this was a movement of the Scotch Highlanders as much as one of our own, and that it was monstrous of the University of Toronto not to have a chair of Gaelic for the men who practically made Canada and made Toronto." The ploy worked, to Hyde's delight. "This astute move took the wind out of the other people's sails and brought in all the Scotch audience." Even the Toronto newspapers were friendly, to the astonishment of the Toronto Irish community. Hyde returned to New York covered with glory.

After a short respite in New York, Lucy again accompanied Hyde to his next destination, Washington, D.C. They arrived on Sunday, May 20, well before his scheduled lecture. For the first time he failed to draw a big audience. Only about four hundred people attended—partly, he noted in his diary, on account of the heat, partly on account of the lateness of the season. But what the crowd lacked in number it made up for in prestige, for the Speaker of the House, "Uncle Joe Cannon," was in one of the boxes, and "others of authority and position" were present. Hyde spoke at a terrible disadvantage, as during dinner he had been struck by a severe pain in his back that kept him from drawing a long breath or even moving his arms. Nevertheless, the show went on. There was, however, "one passage where, under ordinary circumstances," Hyde would have had to stoop down "by way of picking a piece of mud off the street." He cut it out, knowing that he was "absolutely unable" to bend forward. It was a dismaying disability, for it continued, and the next day Hyde had his second luncheon date with President Roosevelt. He "hobbled up" to the White House and was rewarded with the opportunity to discuss an article which the president had just written on Irish and Norse saga. Hyde was astonished that the president of the United States could find time for such activities, but Roosevelt explained that as he knew his recent letter about railway rates would be "attacked and abused all over the country, . . . to take his mind off it he sat down and wrote his article." To their daughters Lucy sent postcards of the White House on which she wrote, "May 23, 1906. Pappy had lunch with the president in this building."

His back having improved, Hyde divided his time during the next four days between lectures and lunches at Catholic University and sightseeing with Lucy in Washington, a city he much admired for its beauty. His one criticism was the Library of Congress, "a forest of lovely marble pillars . . . spoiled by the tawdry coloring and silly paintings upon the walls." Catholic University he found particularly impressive, on account of the freewheeling conversations he was able to have with its faculty, "the most broadminded" that he "had yet met." A chance meeting at the Smithsonian gave him the opportunity to renew his friendship with Mooney, a man whose company he had enjoyed in New Brunswick.

In Hyde's opinion Mooney knew "more about Indian rites and ceremonies than anyone living perhaps."

The next two weeks in New York were a flurry of activity as the
Hydes prepared to return home. Hyde had agreed to write an article
for Scribner's entitled "Scenes from the Ancient History of Ireland,"
to accompany a series of pictures. There were still two commitments
to keep, one in Bridgeport, Connecticut, the other in Paterson, New
Jersey, both within easy traveling distance. Hollenbeck, a "phonog-
rapher" who had developed a "complete apparatus" for learning French,
German, and Spanish on his phonograph, had asked Hyde to "speak
an Irish record" into one of his cylinders. He also had to see a publisher
by the name of Wessel who had received copies of *The Religious Songs
of Connacht* from Fisher Unwin for sale in the United States. Robinson,
the mining engineer from California, showed up suddenly, invited
Hyde to dinner, drove him back to Quinn's apartment, insisted on
coming in, and "remained talking and reciting poetry" (which the disgusted Quinn called doggerel) until 1:30 one morning. There were also
lunches and dinners and evening parties and excursions, as almost
everyone whom the Hydes had met in New York wanted to entertain
them before they left.

Eager to have a quiet dinner to themselves before they parted,
Quinn, Hyde, and Lucy went to Tappan's Hotel in Sheepshead Bay
on Sunday, June 10. Afterward they went to the home of Quinn's
friend, Ada Smith, from whose balcony they could watch the lights go
on at Coney Island. As the sky darkened, the amusement park lit up
like fairyland and became a blaze of light, while in the opposite direction
sheet lightning and fork lightning played over Sandy Hook. Lucy sent
a last postcard to her daughters: "This is called a skyscraper because it
nearly touches the skies. Keep it for me."

On June 15 Quinn put the Hydes aboard the *Celtic*. With their luggage, they had five boxes of gifts, many from Quinn himself. Among
the souvenirs they brought home were a rattlesnake skin, arrowheads,
and the skin of an Alaskan polar bear purchased in Spokane for sixty
dollars. As the *Celtic* steamed eastward, taking a course two hundred
miles outside the usual Atlantic shipping lanes to avoid icebergs, Hyde
sat in their cabin, trying out his newly acquired typewriter and rereading
letters from Nellie O'Brien, Agnes O'Farrelly, and Pádraig O'Daly, to try
to concentrate his attention on what lay ahead. Twice daily he strolled
the first-class deck of the White Star liner, pausing occasionally at the
stern in the long June twilight to lean on the massive bleached and

holystoned teak rails, his eyes fixed on the churning ship's wake stretching westward, reaching back toward the New Island. He thought of the name the reporter from the *Gaelic American* had put on him, "The Man in the Gap" who would reconcile, he said, opposing Irish factions. He wished he could be equal to that task, but he knew it was beyond him. He had not even managed to explain to Quinn that the reason he could not sack Concannon was that Concannon was the man who so often, on his trips back and forth between his brother in California and his mother on Aran, had broken his trip to be a carrier of messages to and from Eugene O'Growney, dying first in the Arizona desert and then in Los Angeles. Quinn was a strong man: he would understand the feeling but deplore the sentimentality.

On balance—as it was not for a newspaper reporter to assign him his tasks, but himself alone—he had done most of what he had come for. The money he had raised for the Gaelic League was not as much as Quinn had hoped but more than enough to keep the budget going for a good few years. The people whose support he had won were another kind of treasure that both he and the Gaelic League could store away against—against what? That was the question he now had to ponder.

14

Triumphs and Troubles

In the middle of an ocean, approximately equidistant from points of departure and arrival, the mind rests and the inner eye is able to look back and ahead with a clarity of vision rarely achieved in any other place. In mid-June, 1906, the middle of the Atlantic was sufficiently calm to provide travelers dozing in deck chairs with a particularly good perspective. Although soon after the Hydes had boarded the *Celtic* the mock-serious British captain had warned, shaking his head, "Dr. Hyde, if you pronounce the name of our ship with a hard *C* you shall have a hard sea on this crossing," he had been wrong. Many times in the four days since leaving New York, Hyde had mischievously invoked the ship's name—always in the presence of the captain, always with a hard *C*—but the ocean had remained subdued, mirroring the mood of the reclining passengers. Cradled in his own customary deck chair, with Lucy in hers, dozing beside him, Hyde spent hours on end ostensibly reading but actually reflecting on past and future.

Viewed retrospectively from the middle of the Atlantic, the states of America were united for Hyde in a kaleidoscope of images juxtaposed not by place or time but by association: red-bricked Boston contrasted with gray New York, both with sand-hued Chicago and (his heart still stopped whenever he thought of it) sparkling San Francisco. In Pittsburgh, usually a study of gray and black, the rays of the setting sun so colored the smoke from the steel mills that all seemed engulfed in one great flame. In the pale, cold light of early morning the rugged mountains and valleys of Montana appeared from the windows of Butte and Anaconda to be devoid of a blade of grass, a tree, a scrap of plant life, so devastating were the effects of the arsenic-laden emissions spewed out by its smelters. Brockton, Massachusetts, was, like Butte, an industrial town, but it was a major boot-manufacturing center, and as the boot business was booming, people were cheerful and content. Nothing of Brockton's cheer, however, was attributable to bottled spirits; it was a prohibition town. When Hyde discovered that no drink could be had to smarten him up for his lecture there, his resourceful host had with some difficulty procured from a drugstore a small bottle of whiskey "for medicinal purposes" that Hyde then had to imbibe unconvivially in his bedroom.

Aboard the *Celtic* in mid-June Hyde needed only a laprobe to be comfortable in his deck chair. Winter already had set in when he visited Brockton. Manchester, New Hampshire, was in the grip of hard frost by early December, a fact that would have come as a surprise to him had it not been for the year that he had spent in New Brunswick. The cities and towns of all northern New England, in fact, were peaceful and picturesque under their winter blanket of snow. At the same time on the opposite coast in places like Santa Barbara, American millionaires and millionairesses strolled beneath palm trees along walks overlooking a beautiful sunlit bay. Most of Southern California, Hyde concluded, had no visible means of existence but seemed to live upon the reputation of its climate.

People as well as places were fixed in Hyde's consciousness. For genuine friendship no place surpassed San Francisco, but Philadelphia certainly had lived up to its reputation as the City of Brotherly Love, and the predominantly German population of Cincinnati had given Hyde such a wonderfully Irish welcome that he had responded, to their amusement and pleasure, with a speech of appreciation in German. In Los Angeles the Celtic Club, whose members were Irish, Scottish, and Welsh, had bestowed on him an honorary membership. It was the only club in America, as far as Hyde knew, that brought these three branches of the Celts together. Maud Gonne, the Hinksons, Rose Kavanagh—all the Pan-Celts in Dublin—would be interested to hear of its success, although it would not be approved at all by some members of the Coiste Gnótha.

Just before the Celtic Club dinner Hyde had been taken by Dr. Jones, a Welshman, to another American refuge for millionaires, Pasadena, so that he could call on Michael Cudahy, the meat-packer from Chicago, and talk for a while with Cudahy and his wife. The Cudahy family were among the richest of the Irish in America, Hyde had been told; they had come out of Callan in county Kilkenny about the time of the Famine. To Thomas Curtin, Quinn's personal secretary, Hyde had given an account of the ability this family displayed in avoiding him. They had dodged him in Milwaukee, in St. Louis, and in Chicago. But Archbishop Riordan had seated Michael Cudahy beside Hyde at a big dinner in San Francisco, and impressed, Hyde believed, not by what he had said but by the enthusiasm of the archbishop, Michael Cudahy had given the Sacramento committee a check for $500 on the spot. Hyde's impression was that Cudahy was strong, thoughtful, and matter-of-fact. He had heard others refer to him as the "brain carrier" of the Cudahy family. It was an odd expression but in substance, Hyde thought, it probably was true.

In the east Hyde had visited another millionaire, Andrew Carnegie. Judge Keogh, who accompanied him, had arranged the introduction in the hope that Carnegie might be interested in the work of the Gaelic League. They were kept waiting for a long time, but when he finally appeared, Carnegie was apologetic and cordial. Hyde recalled him as very small, an ugly little man with gray hair and an immense ego, as revealed in the stories he told about himself, yet very human. He was clearly unimpressed with what Hyde had to say about the goals of the league until Hyde mentioned Horace Plunkett's approval of it, at which point Carnegie suddenly became attentive. After their talk he escorted Hyde and Keogh to the door in the most friendly manner and asked Hyde to visit him again when he came back from the West. Then in January, just before his lecture in St. Paul, Hyde was handed a note signed "Frederic Stewart" offering the Gaelic League $25,000 for which, the note said, Carnegie had agreed to serve as trustee. As "Frederic Stewart" was also the name that had been left by a man who had been waiting for him before his lecture, Hyde lingered after the program, talking and shaking hands, expecting that he would turn up again. No one named Stewart approached him, no one had heard of him, and his name was not in the local directory. If it was true that Stewart was indeed representing Carnegie, something yet might come of it, Hyde thought hopefully. It never did.

America, Hyde discovered, was like Ireland in that to be a great character one did not need great wealth. There was, for example, John D. O'Brien of St. Paul, the only man Hyde ever had met who shot wild ducks with a bow. He had been brought up among the Indians on an island in one of the big lakes and he spoke Chippewa fluently. He was known for miles around. In Manchester, New Hampshire, the bishop was a hail-fellow-well-met by the name of Delaney who wore a billycock hat and smoked a big cigar. The locals, even the Catholics, never addressed him as "My Lord" but only as "Bishop," and nobody dropped on one knee or kissed his ring or anything like that. Hyde had met him through two other extraordinary Irishmen, characters themselves. One was a wonderful old fellow by the name of O'Dowd, an avid collector and reader of Irish books who knew all about the language movement at home and everything that was going on in every parish in Ireland better than those who lived there. The other, O Multhain, or Mullin, was a fine Irish speaker from Sligo with a good memory for Irish songs. In Waterbury, Connecticut, at a banquet organized by a man named Luddy, a counterpart of O'Dowd, the master of the feast had been Moriarity, the most jovial undertaker Hyde had ever met.

Moriarity would have fit nicely into the evening Quinn had arranged in New York at the Players Club. The guests Quinn had assembled included Paul Elmer More, editor of the *Evening Post*; Arthur Brisbane, editor of the *Evening Journal*; Munroe, a Tolstoian; J. I. C. Clarke, editor of the *Sunday Herald*; Witter Bynner of *McClure's Magazine*; Richard Watson Gilder of the *Century*; Malone, the old actor; and Van Thorne, a former student of Hyde's from the University of New Brunswick. There were no speeches, but much talking. Everybody had to tell stories. Clarke recited his "Kelly and Burke and Shea." They had gone on nonstop, smoking cigars and drinking highballs, until three o'clock in the morning. Quinn later had told Father Yorke that Hyde "had outdone himself as a story-teller" at that affair. That evening he had told stories just for pleasure, but there were other times when both his storytelling and his playwriting talents had saved the day. One such incident had occurred in January in Cincinnati, when a magazine called *Men and Women* set up an interview to be printed around St. Patrick's Day. The editor arrived with a stenographer, but he was unable to ask any questions because he did not know what to ask. The stenographer could not help—she was a young German girl. So Hyde had interviewed himself, asking himself questions on behalf of the editor, and answering them in his own voice, as the editor listened and the amused stenographer wrote everything down.

Four days out of New York. Reporters of course would be at the dock when he arrived in Queenstown, full of questions about his seven-month tour of America. What would they want to know? How much money he had come home with, for one thing; what he had thought of America, for another. He began to compile for them a list of American superlatives: the best cold punch was served by the president of the University of California; the queerest things were the sea lions on the rocks near the Cliff House in San Francisco; San Francisco also had the most beautiful views and had arranged for him the most sumptuous banquet; Father Peter Yorke was the finest speaker he had heard; Frank Sullivan had been (except for Quinn, of course) his best host; San Francisco had the best hurling team he had seen outside of Ireland; Bishop Conaty of Los Angeles, who had taken the reins of the four-horse team that drew their carriage from Santa Cruz to the redwood forests was the best driver he ever had met; the nicest and most homelike hotel in America was the Touraine in Boston; he had left his best nightshirt in Waterbury, Connecticut, where the people had the best manners. The most beautiful woman he had seen in America was the supple and graceful Sarah Bernhardt, who had performed in New York in *La Femme de Claude* on December 16. No one else could hold a candle to her, although in general (at least one reporter was sure to ask) American women were very pretty, somewhat pretty, and not very pretty, much as they were at home. The worst thing in America? Unutterably bad country roads, just mud tracks, not much better in many towns. His worst fear: that his voice would give out. Many times, of course, he had spoken in theaters and opera houses where the acoustics were good. But many more times he had had to roar to his audiences in halls that had all the acoustical features of a drafty barn, and since January he had suffered a series of colds and sore throats.

Five days out of New York. Bertie Windle, now president of the University of Cork, had written on April 12 to invite Hyde and Lucy to stay with him when they arrived. Windle also had warned Hyde that a vicious attack on the league had recently appeared in the *National Review*. It was, said Windle, both "diabolically clever and . . . diabolically untruthful." It lumped together the Gaelic Athletic Association, the Gaelic League, and other organizations. John Quinn had complimented Hyde on his deft handling of competing Irish-American organizations. Quinn had no idea, Hyde thought, how much practice he had had at home. Of greater interest was Windle's progress on his attempts to "slowly and cautiously" work Irish into the college curriculum against the opposition of the church. Hyde needed to be kept informed on such matters as he had recently been named to a newly appointed commission to study the question of whether a new college should be added to Trinity to meet the growing demand for university-level education in Ireland. It was a question that was certain to divide the people of all thirty-two counties on issues of curriculum, religion, and language.

Six days out of New York a marconigram—probably the first in the Irish language to be received at sea—was handed to Hyde. It was from the Skibbereen branch of the Gaelic League. It said: "Thousands of welcomes home to you, An Chraoibhin Aoibhin! Behold the country on fire welcoming you." The country on fire—an Irish metaphor in Skibbereen, it was a very real prospect to the old Fenians, the AOH, and the Clan na Gael in America who shouted "Up the Revolution!" and sang "A Nation Once Again" with moist eyes. But if it came to physical force—the ill-equipped, untrained Irish against the mighty United Kingdom—the revolution would be over before the Americans reached Cork, if they came at all. At home some maintained, and they could be right, "The farther from the battlefield, the greater the patriot." For that matter, how many at home would risk their own lives in such a foredoomed gesture? Hyde was convinced that before there could be a revolution—with or without physical force—the Irish had to feel that they were indeed a nation. Rich and poor, city and county, Catholic and Protestant, east and west, north and south, whether their roots were deep in Ireland or had but recently been transplanted into its limey soil, on that one matter at least all had to be agreed. Language and culture and a commitment to Irish manufacture were the bonding agents that could make a people of a population. Deanglicization was the prescription. When the Irish had that accomplished, they could decide, with or without the Americans, what to do next.

One thing that would have to be considered eventually was the form of government a new Irish nation should adopt. Hyde had been asked about that in America. Would Ireland follow the English or the American system? It was not a question he could answer. What were the factors, he asked, turning the question back to his questioners. What were the advantages and disadvantages that should be weighed? Privately, Hyde had doubts that the American-style bicameral legislature would work in Ireland. He noted that in most states in America the legislature met only once every two years, and then only for about two months. It was for him proof positive of American practicality and distrust of mere talk. In the United States people were always doing something, making money, he noted; they did not have the same tendency to engage in endless debate. The Irish would never be satisfied with a two-month legislative session every two years.

The current political struggle, however, was not about representative government—that day was not yet at hand—but about university education. Like everything else, it would not be settled without endless debate. In the end, Hyde suspected, there would be no new college at Trinity but a new institution. At the moment the choices available to students were only Trinity College, still very much a Protestant Ascendancy enclave; the three Queen's Colleges, Cork, Galway, and Belfast, established in 1845; and the old Catholic University established in 1854, called University College, Dublin since 1882. Hyde hoped that what might emerge from commission discussions would be a recommendation for a new nonsectarian national institution in which Irish would be taught as an academic subject. As for its goals, the philosophy of one of the American public universities he had visited—the University of Wisconsin—had intrigued him. Its president, Charles R. Van Hise, had told Hyde during his trip to Madison that this university produced for the state many times what the state spent on it. Its success, Van Hise said, was in his opinion attributable to the fact that he had always tried to make the university as democratic as possible and to foster personally meaningful connections between it and the citizens of the state. He gave as an example the contribution the university had made to Wisconsin farming. By teaching modern scientific methods to the farmers of tomorrow and providing the scientific environment necessary for invention and development, the university had enormously improved agriculture throughout the state. As a consequence it had earned the gratitude of the whole population. It was a splendid example, Hyde thought, of how a national university ought to function.

Seven days out of New York another message was received. It was from O'Daly, who reported that arrangements had been made for a public reception in Dublin on Sunday evening, June 24. Could Hyde be there? With the greatest of pleasure, Hyde replied; but for most of the next twenty-four hours he had serious doubts, as dense fog and heavy rain slowed the *Celtic* almost to a halt. Then suddenly the rain stopped, the fog cleared, and bright sunshine bathed hill and harbor of Queenstown: they were home. The tender from the landing station was approaching, threading its way past sailing schooners loaded with grain toward Roches Point and the ocean liner. At the same time, steaming into the harbor from the southwest was an armored cruiser and eight destroyers fresh from maneuvers; they weighed anchor beside all the other ominously visible warships and submarines of the British

Imperial Fleet, just a fraction of the whole, for which Queenstown was a home port.

Aboard the tender which had come out to take Cork-bound passengers to the landing station before the *Celtic* steamed off to Liverpool were the first of many welcoming committees. Hyde could hear the musicians long before he could make out the faces. Formal presentation of greetings and addresses began as soon as he stepped into the tender; they did not cease until the tender docked at the landing station at ten minutes before seven o'clock. The date was June 24, 1906. It had been 227 days since Hyde and Lucy had last set foot on Irish soil. On the train into Cork City and the first of many elaborate receptions that would continue on for days, there were more musicians and welcoming speeches.

Asked by reporters what he expected would be the principal result of his American visit, Hyde replied that what already had been achieved and surely would continue in the future was American understanding of the Gaelic League and what it stood for: nationality in the highest sense of that word, above creed and politics; an intellectual movement that sought to perpetuate the best characteristics of the race. With that understanding, he declared, he was confident that American sympathy and support would continue. Tangible evidence of what he said was, he assured them, in his pocket, in the form of a check for over ten thousand pounds and an audited account showing what had been collected, how much had been used for expenses, and what remained, free and clear, to be used by the league in installments of no more than two thousand pounds per year to assure its maximum benefit. That sum, and the goodwill to which it testified, had been collected, Hyde said, during more than nineteen thousand miles of land travel in the course of which he had made seventy-eight separate railway trips, many of them double journeys. He had spoken five nights a week to audiences large and small depending on the size of the locality, for American support could be found everywhere, in the smallest towns and largest cities. The total number of people that he had addressed could not have been less than eighty thousand. Clearly they had been generous. Had the league not returned the money collected in San Francisco for relief of the victims of the earthquake the figure on the check in his pocket would have been considerably greater. And in addition to contributions for the league, he had also a small check from a private donor for the fledgling School of Irish Learning in Dublin. Established in 1903 under the directorship of the distinguished German Celticist Kuno Meyer with the help of Alice Stopford Green, the school had caught the particular attention of university scholars, as Hyde hoped it would, for one of his dreams was to create a facility that would bring Celticists from all over the world to study, conduct their research, confer, and write their books and papers in Dublin.

To questions about how he had organized such a campaign, Hyde gave fullest credit to John Quinn above all, to Judge Martin J. Keogh and the members of his host committees in New York, and to Father Peter Yorke of San Francisco. Their effective publicizing of his tour had been evident everywhere, in public meetings and private conversations with American citizens—farmers, merchants, businessmen, doctors, lawyers, editors, and priests and bishops of the Catholic church, the professors and presidents of the universities, the president of the United States. Once the Americans were apprised of his visit and its purpose, the organizing was done by the people themselves. How had he been received by the bishops? With the greatest warmth and generosity, Hyde could say honestly, reeling off their names. And by the universities? The answer was the same. That was as much as Hyde wanted to discuss with reporters. He declined to be questioned on his appointment to the Trinity College commission; he refused to be drawn into a discussion of what had been publicly said about him in the House of Commons. His deft handling gave them plenty to print yet placed him firmly in charge. This skill, too, he knew, he owed to John Quinn.

The processions and celebrations that greeted Hyde's return were even larger and more elaborate than those that had marked his departure. They began as soon as he stepped off the train in Cork; they continued the next day in Dublin. In separate ceremonies he was made Freeman of Cork, of Kilkenny, and of Dublin. Lucy returned to Ratra and a reunion with the children—Nuala was now twelve and Una had just had her tenth birthday—but it was a number of days before Hyde himself could go home, as in addition to being feted he had people to see and work to do in the Dublin office of the league, and even then other welcoming ceremonies and invitations to speak took him away to different parts of the country several days out of every week.

Meanwhile, awaiting Hyde's attention on his desk in Frenchpark were books, examination papers, reports, bills, and hundreds of letters that would each require an acknowledgment or answer. Most of the correspondents were familiar: William Kennedy, a Dublin journalist

now in London who had accompanied the Hyde entourage to Queenstown last October, congratulated him on the success of the American
tour and thanked him for his "unfailing courtesy and kindness." Charles
O'Conor, son of Charles Owen O'Conor Don (there was no mistaking
the O'Conor hand) appreciated Hyde's public mention of his dying
father's support of the language movement, especially his father's role
in the work of the Society for the Preservation of the Irish Language.
Alice Stopford Green, friend and formidable ally since 1900, who had
put aside her writing of *The Making of Ireland and Its Undoing* in the
months of his American tour to write letters to the press in praise of
the league's work, had encouraging news of Kuno Meyer's progress.
Meyer himself, at that moment in Hungary, sent greetings and congratulations on Hyde's safe return. And there was a card, signed simply
"Gráinne," which read:

> O welcome back my fairy king!
>   Your faith has moved the mountain.
> You struck dry rock and lo! the spring!
>   The rushing Gaelic fountain!

In this same stack of mail Hyde found a letter and a check for $2,000,
sent by the president of the Ancient Order of Hibernians in America,
"in appreciation of the Gaelic League's campaign to revive and reestab-
lish the language." Curious that it should arrive now. It had been a
query to Quinn about this promised contribution that had led to discussions about fund-raising and ultimately to the trip from which Hyde
had just returned.

In a corner of Hyde's study stood his newly acquired typewriter, a
parting gift from John Quinn in New York. He had tried to master its
complexities on his return voyage, and in time he was sure he would,
but for the moment it was faster and more efficient for him simply to
hunch over his desk, pen in hand, and push either Irish or English words
uphill in his small, slanted writing, as the occasion demanded. His first
letter was to Quinn to tell him of the check from the AOH and describe
his Dublin reception: "The whole of O'Connell Street was packed from
side to side, and from the Rotunda to below Nelson's Pillar, with one
solid mass of people, and they all with one accord cheered for John
Quinn, as well they might. I left nobody under any doubt as to whom
the American success was due." A second, which Quinn had insisted
on, was to a Dublin investment house for advice on where best to place

the six hundred pounds he had earned from his thirty-one lectures at American colleges and universities, his own small financial compensation for his seven months' work.

Many problems Hyde had left behind when he started out on his tour of America awaited his return, unresolved. Chief among them was the government program that awarded small fees to teachers who provided instruction in Irish (eighty half-hour lessons or forty lessons of one hour each) as a supplement to the regular curriculum. The program had made an impact in many parts of the country with the ironic exception of the west. Hyde had expressed his concern in an October 1903 letter to Colonel Maurice Moore, George Moore's brother: "The tide is rising everywhere except in the Irish-speaking districts themselves." Like George, Maurice was a strong supporter of the league; unlike George, he had learned the language. Hyde had given him, as an example, the situation in Mayo where school managers, usually priests, had refused to cooperate: "They don't believe in our movement and hence they won't do anything." He had told Moore that if the managers continued their refusal he would apply pressure directly to their bishops. On the eve of Hyde's departure for America, the situation had worsened, as Hyde had explained to Roosevelt, for James Bryce, the newly appointed chief secretary for Ireland, had cut back the Irish fees. Hyde had taken the bad news directly to his American Irish audiences. In a speech reported in the *New York Times* of November 19, 1905, he had told a rally of how hard the league had worked to increase the fees from less than one thousand pounds a year to a still inadequate twelve thousand pounds, and now that had been taken from them.

On his return to Ireland, Hyde discovered that the funds for teaching Irish had been used to appoint assistant schoolmistresses. Remuneration for Irish teachers had been cut so severely that Hyde calculated that they would earn only slightly more than three pounds for an entire year's teaching of sixty pupils. He sent letters of protest to Sir Anthony McDonnell, undersecretary for Ireland, as well as to Bryce. Reminding Hyde that he had been "almost the only English politician" who had "ever expressed sympathy with the movement," Bryce regretted that he could do nothing as he was powerless; he "had no education officials under him." Nevertheless he expressed his continuing wish that he might do "his very best" for the league. Hyde instituted a plan for pressuring the government for restoration of the Irish fees; it continued all through the winter and early spring of 1907. The league urged members to write to Parliament. Hyde called on Colonel Maurice Moore to lobby through letters of protest sent to the *Weekly Freeman*. The government did not budge. Early in March 1907, Bryce having been appointed ambassador to the United States, Hyde told Moore that he intended to take the matter directly to Augustine Birrell, the new chief secretary. "If he won't help us, wrote Hyde, secure for the moment in the power of his position, he would "denounce him at a public meeting." Within the month, in a subsequent letter to Moore, he renewed his pledge not to let Birrell alone but to "press and press him till the thing is done." Hyde also wrote personally to John Redmond, head of the Irish party in Parliament, and to Stephen Gwynn, M.P. from Galway, urging that they, too, intervene with the government to restore the lost fees. Finally, on March 24 he was able to send Nellie O'Brien good news from Gwynn in London. Characteristically, he gave all the credit to others; it was the sheer weight of resolutions, telegrams, and letters from all over the country that had been generated by the league, he said, that had had their effect. Hyde's philosophy of organizational behavior was to work behind the scenes as much as possible. His reward came from success achieved by allowing others to enjoy a sense of accomplishment. "It is all right. It was a battle. If the fees had not been returned I was prepared to go to any length, even to denounce Bryce to the American Irish." For a while at least Hyde knew that his American trip had given him another kind of capital on which he could draw. Like pounds, it could be lost all at once if he invested it unwisely; unlike pounds, it would not accumulate interest but would slowly diminish if it was left unused.

Hyde's most vexing problem at this time was to find ways to use his limited capital effectively while still trying to work through the league's unwieldy, top-heavy, forty-five-member executive committee. For several years it had been evident that the Coiste Gnótha's size and composition was a handicap, especially as the egos of some members led them to challenge everything that was presented and the egos of others prompted long-winded speechifying. The analogy with money held: the bad drove out the good. The problem was not only that when the wrangling and the speechmaking began, serious and competent members left; there were also those who accepted subcommittee assignments because they wanted to be in charge of something and then attended erratically, forcing postponement of discussion and decision on substantive issues. This was exactly the kind of behavior that Hyde feared might occur in a national government if Ireland adopted an American-style bicameral legislature. It had driven many good people out of active participation in league affairs.

Frustrating as these shortcomings were, Hyde decided, to the dismay of O'Daly, Barrett, and O'Farrelly, to withdraw plans to recommend revisions in the league's constitution. The league, he said, was too vulnerable to risk reorganization at this point. To others this sounded strange, but Hyde knew that although the position in which he found himself in 1906–1907 as a result of the success of his American tour had brought him increased support, it also had increased petty jealousies and evoked charges of high-handedness whenever he so much as ventured an opinion different from that of others. On the Coiste Gnótha the majority was still pretty much behind him, but Father Brennan kept renewing his charges of manipulation in the case of the writer dismissed by the *Weekly Freeman*; Father Dinneen had joined in the attack; he was accused by others of regional favoritism; and still others were suspicious of his continuing relationship with members of the Pan-Celtic Society. There was also the matter of the large branches, ever insistent upon greater autonomy. Revising the constitution might well provide them an opportunity to diminish rather than strengthen the executive committee. Despite all the hoopla that impressed those looking at the league from the outside, the view from within revealed too many stress points, in his opinion, to risk opening the question of the league's basic structure to general debate. Better wait, he cautioned, for a more propitious moment. O'Daly, Barrett, and O'Farrelly accepted Hyde's decision. Outside his inner circle of support his failure to act in the face of widespread dissatisfaction with the Coiste Gnótha was perceived by some as weakness, by others as ambivalence, nor were these perceptions limited to his detractors.

There was no doubt that the trouble in the branches was serious and that the Coiste Gnótha was doing little or nothing about it. The evidence predated Hyde's American tour. As early as 1903 he had begun to receive complaints of branch meetings that were unpunctual, starting as much as a half hour or more after announced times; of Irish courses disrupted by the late addition of new members that necessitated starting again from the beginning, to the disgust of those who were eager and ready to progress; of poor scheduling of language and dancing classes, which often resulted in members having to choose between one or the other; of incompetent teachers, insufficient textbooks, and dismay at the difficulty of the third volume of O'Growney's texts (prepared by

John MacNeil after O'Growney's death). From Fionan MacColuim he had but recently received word that, far from having abated, these problems had increased. Now, in 1906, Hyde received a highly critical report from E. O. Cameron, a Scottish observer of language revival who had recently completed a tour of traditional Irish-speaking areas.

Cameron's most disturbing observation recalled Hyde's own comparative study of Scottish and Irish native speakers undertaken in 1887 when he and Mackey Wilson had toured the Gaelic-speaking districts of Scotland. At that time he had been struck by the pride, so different from the embarrassment of Irish speakers, with which the Highland Scots used their native language. Cameron's report was even darker; he spoke how lack of pride infected teachers, leaving them with no enthusiasm for what they taught and how they then passed on this infection to their students. In such a climate conscientious supporters of the language lacked the courage, Cameron said, to confront the open hostility toward the language exhibited by school inspectors, preferring to write ineffectual anonymous letters to the press rather than risk confrontation by complaining directly to the national board. Cameron also declared that he had found more oppostion to the language among school managers of the Gaeltacht—all Catholic priests—than among "offensive and alien Protestants." He was puzzled, he wrote, by "these renegade Gaels" who were "acting against the declared resolution of the Roman Catholic hierarchy of Ireland."

Of all Cameron's criticisms, the problem of clerical antagonism toward the language was the most delicate. In a letter to his friend James Owen Hannay (the novelist George Birmingham) written July 11, 1906, less than a month after his return from America, Hyde had argued that the support of the Catholic clergy was indispensable to the league's success.

Our game is a waiting game. Keep on the work, leaven the masses, and above all so long as there is any principle of growth in the League let it grow, avoiding *at all hazards* any clash with the priests or the church. They are, and will be for the next 50 years (unless a strong Home Rule Bill is passed) the dominating factor in Irish life. They are always on the spot, they have the women behind them, they can do almost what they like. Make them think the League is theirs and do nothing to frighten them off.

In a second letter to Hannay, written November 3, 1906, Hyde repeated and strengthened his argument, explaining, "I'm awfully afraid of frightening the clergy off. We'll never revive the Irish language if

we do. We must keep them by hook or crook for 6 or 7 years more."
What Hyde also recognized was that it was easy to blame trouble on
a single cause, more difficult to understand that many factors were involved in the problems that beset the league in 1906–1907. Not the
least was the league's new popular appeal, the inevitable result of the
favorable publicity that had attended Hyde's return. It added a substantial number of less disciplined, less committed members that would have
to be absorbed into the whole. The same sort of thing had happened
to other movements as they gained strength and popularity. Hyde's
analysis of the situation, based in large part on his study of previous
Irish nationalist movements, especially those rooted in revival, explains
his insistence on remaining patient and avoiding public conflict at all
costs. Without the language as its base, the league had no identity to
distinguish it from any other pronationalist group, and there was now
a spectrum. The British technique of divide and conquer could easily
destroy them all. With language as its *raison d'être* the league had been
able to rise above internecine conflicts, biding its time as it fostered
emotional rather than political ties to the idea of a nation.

Meanwhile, explanations were not solutions, and something had to
be done about the trouble in the branches or the league would begin
to lose both its members and its unique character. Teachers who did
not meet league standards could be transferred, threatened with suspen-
sion, or sacked. Volunteers who engaged in petty squabbles could be
maneuvered out of leadership positions. But to discipline or censure a
priest, on whose support the league had to count at the branch level,
was virtually impossible. Fortunately such priests, although all too visible as well as audible, were in the minority. Allied with Hyde in coun-
tering their influence were such distinguished clergy as the indefatigable
Dr. Michael O'Hickey of Maynooth, elected vice-president of the league
in 1903, the irrepressible Father Peadar O'Leary, and hundreds of
parish priests devoted to the language. Nor did it hurt that in America
he had a platoon of Catholic bishops and archbishops solidly behind
him. There was nothing to do but watch and wait.

Meanwhile there was "damp Ratra," which Lucy disliked and held
responsible for all her illnesses. Before their departure for America she
had been pressing Hyde to sell to the Congested Districts Board.
Within days of their return she renewed her campaign. For months she
had enjoyed the best of American society, fine restaurants, theater,
opera, and the company of cultured, intelligent, and educated men and
women—perquisites of upper-class life to which she had been born and

had been accustomed at the time of her marriage. To be sentenced again to years in Roscommon was more than she could bear. By January 1907 Hyde had capitulated. To Nellie O'Brien he wrote that he was again planning to give up Ratra "for some place that will be dry, on the east coast, perhaps near Dublin." Nothing immediate was done; in November when Hyde developed a virulent case of pneumonia, nothing could be done. He was incapacitated for months. For a time there was doubt that he would survive. But by January 1908, although still gravely ill, he seemed to be slowly recovering.

On January 31, urged on by Agnes O'Farrelly, twenty of Hyde's closest league associates, including Father O'Leary, Patrick Pearse, and John MacNeill, signed a circular letter to the league branches proposing that Ratra be purchased and presented to An Craoibhin and asking for contributions to meet the estimated cost of one thousand pounds. The letter reminded their fellow leaguers that "overexertion" on the American trip had "told very severely on his constitution," and that his health unfortunately was even yet "not at all in a satisfactory condition." Subscriptions came in from priests and nuns, members of Parliament, fellow scholars, and hundreds more. On August 4, 1908, at an event kept private at Hyde's request, a small committee headed by MacNeill presented Douglas Hyde with the freehold to Ratra. Deeply touched by their affection and by the prospect of remaining on the land and among the people who had nurtured him, Hyde accepted their gift with sincerest thanks. Lucy could only watch the door to Dublin closing gently but firmly before her.

During Hyde's long illness of 1907–1908, as rumors circulated that he might never return to his leadership post, factions both in the league and outside began to position themselves to make a bid for control whenever word came that the expected vacancy was about to occur. To many aspiring politicians, secular and clerical, the organization had become a glittering prize. Its 550 branches and related infrastructure permeated every sector of Irish life including the Ascendancy. It had a propaganda machine that included a well-edited newspaper. American support had enhanced its prestige. Hyde's strategy was to concentrate on numbers and play for time, meanwhile avoiding confrontation with the British authorities, as he steadily drew in everyone he could—republicans, moderates, fence sitters, and even those who (like Lady Gregory) regarded themselves as anti-Home Rule, pro-Union. Let others posture, shake their fists, and shout. The threat of extremist action from other sources gave him far more leverage with the British than any threat that he would then dare to make. One of his earliest lessons in Irish history had taught him that physical force used prematurely led only to sacrificial martyrdom. Its time might come. For the moment there was the matter of the new university.

Hyde's campaign for the new university was three-pronged. The first task was to eliminate any chance of the commissioners reporting in favor of a second college to be established within Trinity. The second was to back a proposal for a new university in the Dublin area that would be controlled neither directly nor indirectly by either the Church of Ireland or the Catholic church (although he had no illusions that at the start student enrollment would divide along these lines). The third was to establish Irish as an essential subject for matriculation. To achieve his first objective, Hyde carefully prepared a brief for the use of one or more selected witnesses. Testimony should stress, he wrote, why the witness would not want to send his own children to Trinity even if the ban of the Catholic bishops on such enrollment were to be lifted. Second, the witness should object to the bias built into Trinity faculty appointments, sizarships, and prizes in Irish by virtue of the fact that support for these came from sources committed to assisting Church of Ireland ministers to proselytize among Irish Catholics in Irish-speaking areas. Further, testimony should note the absence of instruction in such subjects as the history and culture of Celtic Ireland. It was possible, he declared, to use as evidence the ignorance of Ireland and the Irish that could be found in Trinity's own publications: "Crucify their tardily published unutterably ill-spelt catalogue," he advised. "Look it up in the Library and you'll see some *howlers* . . . that would make a schoolboy laugh." It also might be effective, Hyde suggested, to draw attention to the absence of Irish manuscripts on view in the library ("Is it because they don't wish people to know that such a thing exists?") and the presence of Queen Elizabeth's head, "an emblem of spoliation and conquest," on Trinity's medals. Finally, Hyde said, a witness before the commissioners might ask if it was true that the man who "went out of his way to identify Robert Emmet and get him hung" was a provost of Trinity.

Coolly prefaced to this brief was Hyde's statement that its purpose was to establish that even among upper-class Protestants Trinity College's attitude toward Irish culture and history was an embarrassment and an anachronism. Evident also in the intensity of his opposition and the scale of his vituperation were years of bitterness and disappointment over the way in which Mahaffy and Atkinson, the prime targets of his attack, had frustrated his academic aspirations. He had had one sweet victory over them in 1899. Now the stakes were higher, there was more to be gained and lost, influence and power were for once on his side, and his side was the side of justice and virtue. Ordinarily Hyde was passionate but not vengeful. If he threw himself into this particular fight with more than his usual ardor, who could blame him? The opportunity was irresistible.

The hearings ended. The commissioners recommended a new university, separate from Trinity. The Irish Universities Bill enacted by Parliament in 1908 established a National University of Ireland, to be comprised of three constituent colleges. One was University College, Dublin, the successor to Catholic University, which until then had been run by the Jesuits; the other two were the Queen's Colleges of Cork and Galway. Queen's College, Belfast, remained separate and independent. The degree-granting function of the Royal University was to be taken over by the new government-supported National University. The bill also gave to the senate of the National University, to which Hyde and John MacNeill were named, full responsibility for designing its curriculum. It was only a matter of time—both were determined to win—before the Irish language would be listed as a subject required for matriculation, on a par with Latin and English. Excited and optimistic, looking forward to this third and last phase of his campaign, Hyde wrote Quinn that the new university would "bring young men of Ireland together." In every country in which university students gathered, he proclaimed, they were "always in the forefront for liberty."

In the winter of 1908 a giant meeting on required Irish in the curriculum of the National University was held in the Rotunda. "There will be a fight," Hyde promised the cheering crowd, although it was not yet clear who would win. No one was opposed to the teaching of Irish—everyone was for it. The bishops and their supporters favored Irish as an optional rather than required subject. To the league and its supporters optional status was marginal status. In an Irish university, they insisted, the Irish language must have the same status as Latin and English. To Hyde's dismay his friend Windle sided publicly with the bishops, despite everything he had said and done privately to promote the teaching of the language. Windle's problem, which he had tried to explain to Hyde, was that as president of University College, Cork, he could not publicly oppose the bishops without detriment to himself, his position, and his college. Deploring Windle's attempts to have both a public and a behind-the-scenes solution, Hyde clearly forgot (it would not be the last time) his own analogous position in his battle with the Post Office, still far from over.

Hyde's chief opponent in the senate debate over the place of Irish in the university curriculum was Father Delaney, rector of University College, who opened his attack by challenging the necessity for making the "uneducated language of the peasant" a test for a university education. For Hyde it was 1899 and Mahaffy and Atkinson all over again. He and his lieutenants went into action. He had more than a partner in MacNeill, a formidable ally who disliked face-to-face confrontation but wielded a mighty pen. He also had the league. MacNeill prepared an eloquent argument supported by all the evidence Hyde had collected in his winning battle of 1899 and more. Published in pamphlet form under the title *Irish in the National University*, it was distributed all over Ireland, largely through the branches of the league.

Hyde also had the support of many important church figures, including Cardinal Logue, a native speaker from Donegal and former professor of Irish at Maynooth College; the archbishop of Dublin; and Dr. Michael O'Hickey, Eugene O'Growney's successor in the chair of Irish at Maynooth, vice-president of the league from 1899 to 1903, and a veteran of the 1899 debate. O'Hickey entered the fray with the same gusto that he had demonstrated first in the battle to save Irish in intermediate education and subsequently in other battles, among them some on which he and Father Dinneen were divided in the Coiste Gnótha. Lashing out in scathing terms against all opponents of required Irish, including his own superior, Dr. Mannix, then president of Maynooth, he was first reprimanded by the ecclesiastical authorities, then given a chance to apologize which he refused to take, and finally removed from his chair at the college, an action which he immediately appealed to Rome. The public joined the debate with letters to the newspapers. Some writers within the league urged Hyde to take stronger steps to impress on all 550 branches the urgency of uniting behind the university question. One writer from the north advised Hyde that although leaders in Donegal and Derry were "alive to the crisis" and everything was being done to "rouse the branches," more information was needed. He urged Hyde to write a long article for the very next number of *An Claidheamh Soluis* to explain to the entire membership the complex fee and university questions, both "confusing to the ordinary Gaelic Leaguer." He also added, in one of many such expressions of concern that Hyde was to hear in that year following his long and nearly fatal illness of 1907–1908, that he was "not to fret" because "the great heart of the Gaelic League is . . . with the right side; only those who gave lip-devotion are turning aside."

In early 1909 Hyde drew into the campaign a powerful ally, the Irish Nationalist party. At its February convention it took up the language issue. Siding with the bishops, John Dillon argued the motion in favor, dismissing the idea that to be Irish the National University must require Irish. Misjudging his audience, for whom the issue was not logical but emotional, not pedagogical but patriotic, Dillon pointed out that requiring Latin would not make a university Latin any more than requiring arithmetic would make it an arithmetic university. The audience was not persuaded. John Redmond then called on Hyde to speak on behalf of the motion. O'Daly's circular letters, MacNeill's pamphlet, O'Hickey's speeches, and the efforts of Fionan MacColuim and other head organizers had prepared his case. He had only to repeat the arguments with his usual oratorical skill and wait for the tumultuous applause. The question carried. Months of careful planning, hard campaigning, and meticulous teamwork had paid off.

There were, however, serpents in the garden. Vague rumors had been reaching Hyde for some time—as early as spring of 1908, in fact, when he was recovering from his near-fatal bout with pneumonia—that clerical dissidents in the Coiste Gnótha were planning to nudge him out of office and replace him with "a clerical Gaelic League with a bishop at its head." As the strongest opposition to required Irish was coming from the bishops and as Father Dinneen, who was close to them, was Hyde's chief opponent on the executive committee, these rumors had a certain credibility. By March of 1908 there had been more specific charges. An angry Agnes O'Farrelly had called Hyde's attention to articles by Father Patrick S. Dinneen in D. P. Moran's *Leader*: they revived the old charge of 1905 concerning the dismissal of the columnist named Kelly from the *Weekly Freeman*. Broyden had let it be known at the time that it was his dissatisfaction with Kelly's performance and not any deputation led by Hyde that had resulted in the columnist's dismissal. Everyone thought that that had settled the matter, but here it was again.

It was Agnes O'Farrelly's belief that the Kelly case had been revived by D. P. Moran and Father Dinneen in 1908 as part of a conspiracy to discredit Hyde so that Dinneen himself might succeed to the presidency of the league. To destroy this "sinister design," a product of the "jealousy and ambition of meaner minds," she insisted that Hyde obtain, once and for all, a public statement from Broyden on the subject. She also pressed Hyde to confront the lean and hungry Dinneen with his ulterior ambitious motives. Dinneen was playing, she insisted, a "desperate game." If he and Moran did not succeed on the Kelly/ *Freeman* charge, "they would trump up another." Hyde accordingly wrote Broyden asking him to set the record straight. When it finally came, Agnes O'Farrelly dismissed Broyden's statement as "half-hearted" but she did not recommend further action. By then she had assured herself that Hyde had nothing to worry about. The leaders of the cabal, she declared, had "overreached themselves this time." All honest leaguers, she believed, were "sick of them." Quoting an Ulster proverb, she warned, "If you wrestle with a sweep, if he does not throw you, he'll sully you."

Hyde was puzzled that the Coiste Gnótha had not put a stop to Dinneen's trouble making. Agnes O'Farrelly's explanation was not reassuring: the executive committee, she maintained, was afraid to stir up controversy that would injure the annual collection and give ammunition to unnamed "others" who were causing added problems with their objections to the special fees paid by the government to Irish teachers in the schools. Disgusted with the pettiness of it all, Hyde spilled his feelings into a letter to Lady Gregory: he was confronted, he told her, with "alarms and excursions" and "lots of spite." Dinneen, he declared, was at the botton of it all: "his ingenuity in breeding strife is diabolical." Other letters on the same subject went to the Reverend James Hannay in Westport and Colonel Maurice Moore at Moore Hall, whose own perspectives were based in part on the fact that they saw things not from Dublin but from Mayo. Hannay had a ready solution: "Get rid of Dinneen." With him, the league was "in danger of going under," he warned; "it looks powerful but it is helpless," he declared. His recommendation was to apply the gardener's solution to the problem of tangled vines: cut back to half a dozen branches in Dublin and perhaps two in the rest of the country and then wait and watch the league grow healthy again. For some time he had been displeased with aspects of the organization's wild and unchecked growth, especially as it related to attitudes toward Protestants other than Hyde within the predominantly Catholic Gaelic League.

Moore, however, who had been hearing reports of the trouble that was brewing within the Coiste Gnótha, agreed with Hyde that the situation was too complicated to yield to Hannay's gardening techniques. Sinn Féin was now supporting the Dinneen party. Moreover, Agnes O'Farrelly had reported from Dublin that Sinn Féiners were spreading rumors that Hyde was making secret visits to the Castle, behind the league's back, to strike a bargain with the chief secretary, Augustine Birrell. She urged Hyde to repudiate the insinuation quickly, either at the league's annual congress, the *ard-fheis,* or before:

I hate telling you these sorts of things and worrying you but it is better you should know them. You must not be over-sensitive. You cannot escape criticism in public life. . . . Give one rousing speech and give the lie direct to these people and also explain the university question. You would have the ear of the public speaking in English in a way you cannot speaking in Irish and we could get you a good report in the *Freeman.* It would turn the tide.

Hyde's response was to urge Moore to come to the *ard-fheis,* bringing all the delegates he could. He now understood, he told the colonel, that "they were never more wanted, for the malcontents will make this their final or rather their supreme effort to smash the League." He also alerted John Quinn, who suggested to John Devoy, publisher of the New York *Gaelic American,* that the paper come out against Dinneen, on the grounds of his being "a crank, a fault-finder and a meddler." At the *ard-fheis* the crisis passed after a "hell of a row" with Dinneen, Hyde reported to Quinn. Dinneen and his group had been "able and absolutely unscrupulous," but Hyde's supporters had been "too strong for them." Hyde's other good news for Quinn was that both he and MacNeill had been appointed to the faculty of the new university at annual salaries of £600. Quinn responded positively to Hyde's personal good fortune but cautioned him against expecting too much from his public campaign for required Irish, given the position of the bishops. Quinn's strong anticlerical sentiment made him skeptical about chances for success. "If you don't get compulsory Irish at once, take it in two or three years," he advised. "The Church is still supreme in Ireland," he warned. "So long as the bishops are sure of hell at their backs to threaten the Irish with, reason, patriotism, nationalism and idealism will all plead in vain." Nor was it likely that Hyde could obtain support against them from America, where the United Irish League and Ancient Order of Hibernians were strongly probishop. Quinn reckoned in any case that ninety percent of the American Irish population regarded the introduction of the Irish language "as a monstrous anachronism." He cautioned Hyde to be ready to compromise. The Gaelic League was at risk, he warned; if it dissolved, "Ireland without the Gaelic League would be like *Hamlet* without Hamlet."

In August, Pádraig O'Daly sent a circular letter to all county councils, presenting the league position on the subject of Irish in the university curriculum. What the league espoused was not compulsion or coercion, his letter explained, but a policy necessary to preserve Irish language, history, culture—everything. From his office throughout the fall the stream of broadsides, circular letters, and pamphlets continued. A letter headed "Ireland or West Briton—What Distinguished Men Say" offered quotations from Colonel Maurice Moore, Agnes O'Farrelly, Dr. O'Hickey, monsignors, priests, and canons. Moore's statement was unequivocal: "We want and we are determined to get a university for Irishmen above all things and for the Irish language; if the new university is not that, it is not for us, it is for foreigners." Reports from league branches indicated that O'Daly's campaign literature was getting through to the people and was making converts to the language cause. But it was always necessary to be vigilant, Hyde knew, and indeed one morning he awoke to discover in the Irish newspapers a long letter from Cardinal Moran of Australia to John Redmond, charging that the "Celtic League promoters" were hostile to Redmond's Parliamentary party. Hyde responded at once with a publicly printed letter to Redmond reiterating the nonpartisan position in the league's constitution and begging him to ignore the cardinal's "vague, untrue and mischievous charges." In a separately communicated private note, friendly in tone, Hyde wished Redmond good luck in his grouse shooting; reminded Redmond of the league's thousands of members who were also members of the Parliamentary party; and issued an invitation no politician could ignore, to address the great procession on behalf of the language, scheduled to be held in Dublin in September. "The meeting I am sure will be very large and representative," Hyde noted, adding as an apparent afterthought the fact that twenty-three of the county councils would be represented at the demonstration.

O'Daly had done his work superbly. The procession in support of required Irish, a nearly endless line of floats, placards, and thousands of children, most of them from Christian Brothers schools, took three hours to pass a given point before it came to Sackville (O'Connell) Street where scores of platforms were erected so that the huge crowd could be reached by the speakers. Prominently seated in full view of the crowd, sharing the limelight with dignitaries and dedicated leaguers, were members of county councils. Under the rules establishing the National University, the councils not only controlled scholarship monies but were empowered to attach conditions to these grants. Some county councils already had announced that unless Irish was required, scholarship grants would go only to students who chose to attend Trinity College, and the new university would lose both funds and enrollment.

The massive turnout at the September procession, the Parliamentary party's endorsement, and the councils' messages had their intended effect on the new university's senate. Speeches made in sessions and in interviews with reporters all indicated that sentiment was overwhelmingly in favor of required Irish. Nevertheless, as the debates continued, Hyde and his cohorts grew increasingly uneasy about the outcome, for every week without a final vote was a week in which the tide could change against them. They did not dare relax. Continuing to turn out pamphlets, circular letters, and broadsides, only O'Daly seemed confident. His mind was already on the future and the next task that might be undertaken after the expected affirmative vote. Writing to a friend in Killorglin on April 4, 1910, he set forth a list of points in favor of required Irish history that made clear the way in which the new university was expected to serve the Irish cause:

Most of us want to produce in Ireland a race of spirited Nationalists who'd go as far as Mitchel or Wolfe Tone if the opportunity offered. It may not be politic to talk of this openly in discussing the terms of the university curriculum as this would frighten the Bishops altogether but we should never lose sight of it ourselves. We can never hope to have a real live national agitation in the country unless the spirit of freedom animates our people.

Hyde was included in the "we" for whom O'Daly spoke. "In the forefront for liberty" were the women and men who had joined him in increasing numbers since 1893. Until now their only national university had been the Gaelic League.

On June 18, 1910, the front page of John Devoy's New York *Gaelic American* carried a three-column story under the banner headline, "Splendid Victory for Essential Irish." Hyde's resolution that would make Irish mandatory by 1913 had passed the senate's Board of Studies. The paper hailed it as "the most significant achievement in the history of the Gaelic League" and a victory that "had the moral support of the whole country." The full senate vote followed on June 23. Hyde cabled the news to Quinn who responded by cable on June 25: "Heartiest congratulations on tremendous personal victory." Even Lucy was pleased. To her, Hyde's victory was evidence of his strength in his new position at the university. At last she had what she wanted: a professorial appointment for her husband, a town house at One Earlsfort Place for herself and her children. Ratra was still home. It was where they would continue to spend summers and holidays. But from now on she would be able to look forward to enjoying the day-to-day life of the city, for which she had yearned so long.

15

The Rocky Road
to Revolution

At the moment of personal victory Hyde felt as if he had driven a team of powerful and unruly horses across a finish line. Whether the carriage could hold together, whether he could hold the reins through another contest, was a matter of grave doubt. He himself was still convinced that he had found, through the "nonpolitical" emphasis on national being in the Gaelic League and its policy of deanglicization, a way of separating Ireland from England in the most effective way possible. Once that task was accomplished—once Ireland felt and thought and moved like a nation—there was every chance, he still believed, that the continuing pressure for Home Rule would be irresistible, and that Ireland would be able to achieve legislative independence on its own terms without the use of physical force. But the pressure for physical force was itself becoming irresistible, and he did not know how long he could hold out against it. It was not, as some charged, that he was opposed to the use of arms; there was a time in his life when he, too, had thought that the freedom of the nation could never be achieved through any other means. It might yet be so. What he had hoped, still hoped, to avoid was another blood sacrifice that would leave the country once more with its young men dead, in prison, or in exile; its people demoralized; and its future hostage to still another draconian Coercion Act.

For some time the question of just how far he could take the Gaelic League along the road to nationhood had been before him. So many things had been a matter of persuasion rather than control. Everyone now talked in code: Was the league still nonpolitical? (That meant opposed to physical force.) Had it been, was it being politicized? (Inclining toward physical force.) Which of the people around him were political or nonpolitical? (For or against physical force.) How long would he himself maintain a nonpolitical stance? As a boy he and his brothers used to race a sailboat in Roscommon. Remembering those days, he had often thought of the league as a sleek and sturdy craft pointed into the wind, his trembling hand on the rudder, his unblinking eye fixed on the sail, in his heart the fear that the end of a ship was wreckage. If now he had changed his metaphor, it was because circumstances had changed.

What were those unruly horses that now threatened to destroy the league? For one thing there was the movement founded and promoted by Arthur Griffith. On Hyde's return from America in June 1906 the Thurles branch of the Gaelic Athletic Association had hailed him as Ireland's "uncrowned king"—but had taken the opportunity also to affirm their allegiance to Sinn Féin. Since 1906 the movement's influence on the league, the GAA, and other organizations had remained philosophically strong but politically diffuse. Mary Colum was later to describe the Dublin of the first decade of the twentieth century as a "Swiftian town" in which Sinn Féin was the champion of "Swiftian ideas." Hyde himself had regarded those ideas as positive in sentiment and potentially useful in "spurring . . . lazy, incompetent, useless parliamentarians into some kind of activity." Often he had been warned, however, by John Quinn and others, that among Sinn Féiners there were those who regarded the league as an organization sufficiently close to their own ideas as to warrant attempts to pull it further in their direction. Hyde and his supporters had resisted these attempts not because they disagreed with Sinn Féin but because a boycott of English goods and services was a political statement bordering on physical resistance that would be swiftly punished by the British, leaving its perpetrators languishing in British jails. His friend James Hannay had advised Hyde that there were natural limits to such resistance: "I take the Sinn Féin position to be the natural and inevitable development of the league principles," he had said, repeating words Hyde had heard from others. "They couldn't lead to anything else." Hannay saw Hyde with but two alternatives: to become a great Irish leader or to lapse "into the position of a John Dillon." Whichever way Hyde turned, he had predicted, "the movement you started will go on, whether you lead it or take the part of poor Frankenstein who created a monster he could not control."

A more recent faction within the league were the Larkinites. When the Liverpool labor leader, "Big Jim" Larkin, founder of the Irish Transport and General Workers' Union, had arrived on the Dublin scene in 1908, many leaguers, especially the poorer workers and those attracted by Larkin's socialist theories, had joined his movement. Again, Larkin's ideas were sufficiently compatible with Hyde's own philosophical ideals as to create no serious conflict. Yet the Larkinites worried Hyde more than the Sinn Féiners because their hostility toward people of wealth and position threatened to divide the country along socioeconomic lines. At the same time Hyde himself could not help but admire the "tall, black-haired, powerfully built man with a great resounding voice" when he assured enthusiastic crowds that "no power on earth could prevent Irish from being taught to their children if that was what was wanted."

And then there were the young men, intense and impatient, like Hyde's close friend Patrick Pearse. One of Hyde's ablest lieutenants, Pearse had resigned the editorship of *An Claidheamh Soluis* in October 1909 to devote himself, he said, full-time to St. Edna's School. But Hyde knew that he had been chafing under Hyde's insistence upon achieving nationhood through "nonpolitical" methods which had become too slow and uncertain for Pearse. Of Larkin, Pearse declared that he was "at least *doing something*; he was making history." Hyde had countered with evidence that the league, too, had been making history, but without anyone being jailed or shot for it. It was not, Hyde knew, what Pearse and other young men wanted to hear, and he worried about the consequences of their impatience.

For the moment, however, the overriding problem was money. The last of the $55,000 that had been donated during his 1905–1906 tour of America was all but spent. Without funds nothing, active or passive, could be ventured or gained. Someone had to go back to America to seek support for another five-year plan. Fionan MacColuim was a loyal, hardworking, and efficient organizer. In August 1910 Hyde proposed that MacColuim and Father Michael Flanagan, a priest from Elphin and member of the Coiste Gnótha, be sent on a second money-raising tour. Plans were made to pay their expenses for approximately two years. Briefing MacColuim on how to get along with American reporters, Hyde had advised him not to distribute prepared statements but to anticipate questions and make himself available for interviews. As he had then decided not to go in August to the Celtic Congress being held in Brussels (any mention of the subject led to the usual row with Lucy about the time he gave to league activities), he spent the month instead preparing the ground for his envoys, who were scheduled to arrive in New York in October. He drew from league files for MacColuim's use his list of contributors to his 1905–1906 campaign and sat down to compose what he privately called a "new American manifesto" (the actual title was "The Gaelic League in Ireland to the Irish People in America") to be distributed through Irish-American organizations in advance of their arrival. He alerted O'Daly to expect from him a circular letter to the Americans and asked him to speed it on its way.

Hyde began his American manifesto by assuring contributors that their donations of 1905–1906 had been well spent. It was their funds, he declared, that had made possible the campaign that had resulted in establishing Irish as a required subject in the National University. Without them Irish Ireland would not now be at "the climax and highest point" to which "it had yet risen." The truly Irish National University that had been blueprinted by this achievement would revolutionize "the entire intellectual outlook of Ireland." Until the founding of the Gaelic League, that outlook had been "imitation-English." Henceforth, thanks to American generosity and concern, it would be genuinely Irish. A fair and honest statement, it lacked the urgency of a specific attainable goal. There was little in it to stimulate the imagination, stir the heart—or open the pocketbook.

Fionan MacColuim arrived in New York on October 1, 1910. He set up an office on Madison Avenue and issued an appeal signed by members of the same committee that had backed Hyde in 1905–1906, including John Quinn. Quinn had agreed to allow the use of his name and even to pledge $250 to the new drive on condition that he not be asked for active assistance. Hyde did what he could to direct and advise MacColuim through letters and cables from Ireland. In December he mailed Christmas cards and a personal request for donations to 750 American supporters of his 1905–1906 tour.

From the start, however, things did not go well for MacColuim and Flanagan. Hyde's manifesto did not evoke the expected response. MacColuim was overwhelmed by America's immense size and the difficulties he foresaw in trying to cover it with only two men. The campaign of 1905–1906 had had distinct advantages. Hyde had arrived in the United States as a man of some achievement, with a name already known to most of the people he approached for funds. Many of them had been reading his revolutionary poetry and prose in Irish-American newspapers for a quarter century. They had welcomed him as a founder of the Gaelic League, its president since 1893, and the author of its policy of deanglicization. The rich regarded him as urbane, well-educated, well-connected, charming. To the general population he was jolly, irreverent, unaffected, friendly. Neither MacColuim nor Flanagan had a reputation like Hyde's on which to draw, nor did they have his *savoir faire*. Hardworking, dependable, intelligent men who relaxed with a glass, a dance, a song, a story, they worked for the Gaelic League because they had a deep respect and love for Gaelic Ireland. Added to their difficulties, as MacColuim complained to Hyde, were the political uncertainties and "rotten financial condition" of the United States at the beginning of the second decade of the twentieth century.

By October 1911 it was evident that results of the MacColuim-Flanagan fund-raising tour would be at best mixed. To Hyde, MacColuim expressed hope that the outlook might change after the election of a new American president, but the next United States presidential election was still a year away. When the totals were calculated at the beginning of December, it turned out that between October 1910 and December 1911, MacColuim and Flanagan had grossed only slightly more than $14,000–$41,000 less than Hyde had netted in seven months in 1905–1906. Moreover, meetings planned for the spring of 1912 in Philadelphia, Chicago, St. Paul, and Minneapolis had had to be canceled, so there was a serious question about how much more there was to come.

Hyde had foreseen the possibility of just such a situation when, several months earlier, Shane Leslie, a self-appointed, self-financed Celtic ambassador, had come to him with the offer that he would "roam America" on behalf of the league, pleading for dollars. Hyde accepted: he was at that point ready to enlist help from almost any quarter, even a Cambridge dandy from county Monaghan who wore a saffron kilt. "Cuchullain-og," as Leslie was known in Dublin (the ironic reference was to the hero of the *Táin Bó Cuailnge*, ancient Ireland's national epic), had startled and amused county Monaghan in 1906 with a campaign to spread the wearing of the kilt throughout Ireland. In that same year he had joined the Gaelic League. In 1911, with Hyde's blessing, he sailed for America to join the collection campaign.

Leslie was not received warmly by Hyde's American friends, least of all by John Quinn. He was, to be sure, a bit of a character, as Hyde had acknowledged—an amateur Irish Irelander. But recalling Quinn's 1905–1906 complaints of Concannon's "peasant" mentality and behavior, Hyde believed that Leslie actually might be more successful in obtaining contributions from rich Americans. He had, after all, qualities Concannon lacked that Quinn had declared essential, including an aristocratic cachet and, through the Churchills, good family connections. As for his eccentricities, Americans, Hyde thought, might find them simply amusing.

John Quinn was an American who was definitely not amused. In letters to Hyde and Lady Gregory (she was then in America with the touring company of the Abbey) John Quinn wrote scathingly of Leslie's ridiculous appearance and preposterous behavior. He was certain, he declared, that Leslie would have no success raising funds for the league; he suspected that many Irish Americans would find him embarrassing. Quinn himself was embarrassed by some of the things that Leslie had said to American audiences and newspaper reporters. He suggested strongly that Hyde attempt to make amends. In response to Quinn's criticism, Hyde instructed Leslie on how to handle himself with the press. Leslie readily admitted that he had found reporters intimidating. "They are out for fun and misrepresentation as surely as I am out for dollars," Leslie complained. Hyde also supplied Leslie with points to make for the "practical people" who liked to know how their money was spent and advised him to visit and thank personally the Americans identified by MacColuim and Flanagan as their largest contributors. This was a task he could not leave to MacColuim—not after MacColuim had treated American audiences to his one-man song-dance-and-story show (mostly in Irish, which few understood) that reduced to laughter those whom it was supposed to move to tears. He therefore wrote encouragingly, expressing solicitous concern for Leslie's constantly sore throat, assuring him that he well remembered his own. What he hoped was that Leslie's good-natured charm and ready smile might induce some of the wealthier contributors to become permanent subscribers to the league.

As Quinn had predicted, Leslie's Gaeilgeoir (Gaelic-enthusiast) style was counterproductive. His timing, moreover, through no fault of his own, was unfortunate. In New York, where he had hoped to have his best audiences, news coverage of his appeal on behalf of the league and interviews to which he had given particular attention were crowded out by newspaper accounts of the December 1911 *Playboy* riots. Picked up by the national press, the *Playboy* protests were reported in other cities as well. Fearing their effect, Leslie postponed meetings in Chicago, Philadelphia, and San Francisco. "I will get you the money, Creveen, never fear, but at the cost of a sick heart," he declared melodramatically. "*The Playboy* has proved a sickening piece of bad luck for me."

The Playboy was even worse luck for Douglas Hyde, whose response to the riots was soon revealed as one of the most serious missteps of his career. It was he himself who, by his indiscretion, did the most damage to the league's campaign, brought his own judgment into serious question, nearly alienated Lady Gregory, and so infuriated John Quinn that their frequent, friendly correspondence cooled significantly.

In New York the traveling company of Lady Gregory's Abbey Theatre was appearing nightly in Synge's *Playboy of the Western World.* According to some newspapers, every evening the crowds were howling down the actors, interrupting their performance; outraged members of the audience were proclaiming that the play was an insult to Ireland, to Irish family life, and to Irish womanhood. According to Quinn, however, *Playboy* had as many supporters as detractors, and not all the newspaper coverage was bad by any estimation. Supporting his opinion was the fact that on December 3 the *New York Times* printed a long interview with Lady Gregory conducted backstage at the Maxine Elliott Theater. In the course of this interview, as she often did, Lady Gregory paid generous tribute to Hyde and the league for reviving the language and thus "sending writers back to the life of the country itself." John Devoy, publisher of the *Gaelic American* and chief conduit of American funds, interpreted Lady Gregory's statement to mean that the Gaelic League endorsed *Playboy* in particular and the Abbey Theatre in general. He threatened to abandon the Gaelic League unless Hyde published an immediate and official denial that the plays of the Abbey Theatre had been inspired in any way by the Gaelic League. In a panic, Father Flanagan sent Hyde an urgent request for a cable dissociating the league from the Abbey. "I am convinced," wrote Flanagan, in a letter explaining his sense of the situation, that unless such a cable is sent, "the Gaelic League must begin all over again in America and look for new friends in a most unpromising field."

Meanwhile Hyde, who had received similar threats from Clan na Gael, already had cabled Devoy not once but twice (the first cable, Devoy complained, was not strong enough). At the time these cables were sent Hyde knew nothing of Lady Gregory's interview, for it had not yet been published. By the time they arrived, however, they seemed to come in response to the furor over Lady Gregory's statement. That he had repudiated the Abbey Theatre was bad enough. That he appeared to have repudiated also Lady Gregory added insult to injury. "Furious and disgusted" with Hyde, as he privately told Lady Gregory, John Quinn maintained a tight-lipped silence, knowing that almost anything said or written even confidentially could, if leaked indiscreetly, only make matters worse. Lady Gregory's concern was less for the effect of the blow on the reputation of the Abbey than for the feelings of the Abbey players who, faced with Irish-American invective across the footlights and the league's betrayal at home, were thoroughly demoralized. To Hyde she wrote only, "Oh, Craoibhin, what are these wounds with which we are wounded in the house of our friends?" His lame response—that he never intended to harm the Abbey but had felt forced to send the damaging cables because of the threats he had received from New York—did little to make amends. Nor did his cables reverse the already disappointing shortfall in contributions to the league's faltering fund-raising drive of 1910–1912.

Hyde could do nothing for the time being but hope that eventually his relations with Lady Gregory, Yeats, and all the others whose efforts centered on the Abbey could be repaired. He was not yet aware of just how seriously his foolish move had damaged his friendship with Quinn, for apparently he did not know that Quinn and Lady Gregory were then engaged in a passionate love affair. He realized that he had to do something to avert financial disaster for the league, but for the moment he did not know where to turn. Meanwhile, in addition to his new duties at University College, Dublin, where at long last, as professor of Modern Irish, he had the position he so long had been denied, demanding his attention were major changes in England that had implications for the future of Ireland and therefore the Gaelic League.

For several years the solidly entrenched Liberal government that had come to power in 1906 had been feuding with the House of Lords, which had the power to veto any bill passed by Parliament. In 1909 the Lords' veto of the budget precipitated a crisis that resulted in two parliamentary elections in 1910, neither of which produced the majority needed by the prime minister, Lord Asquith, to conduct the business of government. Asquith's problem was complicated by the fact that if he did not maintain the program for which Liberals had voted, he faced certain defeat from rising Tory strength; if he did follow the agenda promised the voters, he faced a veto in Lords. His solution to the dilemma was to propose a bill that would remove the threat of a Lords veto. Called the Parliament Act, it provided for an act of Parliament to become law despite a veto from Lords if it passed Commons three times without revision. The only problem was that to secure passage of such a bill Asquith needed additional support. He turned to John Redmond for help, placing the Irish party for the first time since 1886 in a position to bargain for Home Rule. After several false starts the critical measure concerning the Lords' veto was passed in 1911; as Asquith had promised, a third and ultimately successful Home Rule Bill was introduced in 1912.

This was the moment for which Hyde had been waiting. He could now unleash his "political" feelings by degrees, to stir public opinion in favor of the bill. He began slowly, gradually strengthening his statements in favor of physical force as the bill progressed through the parliamentary process. In June of 1911 he had participated in a debate with Pearse at St. Edna's College on methods of achieving nationhood. Pearse had told the boys of St. Edna's that if Home Rule came as expected within the next few years, they would have a part in directing Irish affairs. If Home Rule did not come, he had declared ominously, they would have to use force to attain independence. Hyde did not contradict Pearse but cautioned against impatience, as Home Rule now seemed assured. The sword must not be used unless there was no alternative, he warned, and even then, only if they could muster the strength necessary to assure victory. By May of 1912 he had moved closer to Pearse's position. In a speech at Mullingar, Hyde roared to an enthusiastic crowd, "You will be living in a fool's paradise if you keep waiting for the spirit of imperialism to fuel the office of patriotism and to fire you with *pride of race and country* and *energy of action*." In November 1912, in Castlebar, he proclaimed, "The breath of freedom is in the air. The man without love of race and pride of country is a poor specimen." During the same month, referring to the September signing, in Belfast Cathedral, of the "Solemn League and Covenant" to defeat Home Rule and to the establishment by Sir Edward Carson and others of the "Provisional Government of Ulster," he told the Gaelic Society of Trinity College that Ireland suffered "no religious hatred now except in one province only." For the moment he took no public notice of a simultaneous third threat from the Carsonites, the raising of a private Ulster army, the Ulster Volunteers.

Between December 1911 and December 1912 the league's budget crisis grew steadily worse. There was now work to be done and the spirit with which to do it, but no funds. In a personal plea to Judge Keogh in New York, written January 26, 1913, and printed and dispatched to other key Irish-American figures, Hyde described plans to

increase the number of traveling league teachers from 100 to 300, set
$100,000 as the sum needed, and avowed that he would raise $3 in
Ireland for every $1 sent from America. The $5,000 Keogh had sent
him in June 1912, he explained, had been spent in part for salaries
($360 per year) for fifty teachers of Irish in the poorer parts of the coun-
try, especially the Irish-speaking districts of the west where each teacher
covered 100 square miles on bicycle to reach the schools and branches
of the league. These teachers, he told Keogh, using the militaristic
analogies he always applied to the work of the league, were "the soldiers
of the Irish Revival Movement."

John Quinn was among those to whom Hyde sent a copy of his letter
to Keogh. The answer he received was not what he had anticipated but
the blunt and angry words Quinn had not written in December 1911.
Quinn had withheld comment on Hyde's part in the *Playboy* affair, he
explained, because his trio of envoys was still seeking funds in America.
But now he told Hyde that he had no stomach for Irish matters since
the "filth and lies of the Playboy episode." Making no direct reference
to Hyde's part except by implication, he wrote, "I never saw a man
stoop to such meanness as Devoy did. . . . The whole episode was piti-
ful and nauseating." The Gaelic League, he declared, had been hurt by
attacking the Abbey, for the company had had "the sympathy of cultivated people in this town." "It mystified some people here, was not
understood by others, and gave the ordinary man the impression that
the Gaelic League was on the side of the rioters."

Between 1912 and 1913, while the Home Rule bill continued to
pick up support throughout Ireland and Hyde tried to restore the flag-
ging fortunes of the Gaelic League, labor trouble was brewing in Dublin and preparations for armed defense against violence threatened by
the Ulster Volunteers were becoming increasingly visible. Meanwhile
Arthur Griffith made a concentrated attack on Hyde in the form of a
personal letter published in *Sinn Féin* in early July. Point by point, Hyde
defended his record in a lengthy letter to Griffith which appeared in
Sinn Féin on July 26, 1913. For a time it silenced Griffith, but Hyde
had no illusion that his rebuttal would be either final or lasting. Certainly, bitternesses and dissension still characterized the Coiste Gnótha.
The Kelly/*Freeman* controversy had gradually died down only to be
replaced by new rumors and charges. In another 1913 crisis Hyde was
assailed for the league's failure to protest the printing of Insurance
Stamps (under the National Insurance Act of 1911) in English rather
than Irish. At that point he decided that he had had enough. In a long

speech to the Coiste Gnótha sent to all branches, he blamed the incident on the fact that his heart was no longer in his work. His conclusion sent shock waves through the entire organization: "I therefore now leave this chair which I have occupied for twenty years and put myself under the protection of the Coiste Gnótha and the country. Goodbye." He was returned to the chair by acclamation, but he suspected that it would not be long before he would have to take the step again, the next time perhaps for good. The league, he confided to close friends, had begun to lose its charm for him when it became powerful and therefore worth capturing and exploiting. There were those, "notoriously Griffith," who had "set about to do" just that.

In August 1913 labor problems erupted in a sequence of violence and vicious retaliation that nearly paralyzed working Dublin through fall and winter and into the early spring of 1914. The violence led to the development of an Irish Transport and General Workers' Union "army" consisting of squads of workmen armed with hurling sticks assigned to protect members attending strike meetings; these squads became the basis of the Citizen Army. In November 1913, in response to growing threats from the Ulster Volunteers, a meeting held in the Rotunda resulted in the formation of the Irish Volunteers under the leadership of John MacNeill. Word spread of new recruits joining the Irish Republican Brotherhood. By the spring of 1914 military drills had become a regular feature of Irish life, reported and photographed for the newspapers, and often reviewed by Hyde and other public figures. Speaking in March 1914 at two such events at Lanesborough and Longford, Hyde proclaimed,

Our duty is to be prepared to take the field as one man against any enemy tyrant or oppressor from whatever quarter of the globe he may appear. A country which is not prepared to make some sacrifice for its freedom at a moment like this is unworthy of that freedom—and mark my words, will never attain it.

Addressing Volunteers at Bray and Balbriggan on July 5, Hyde hailed "a wonderful national awakening, a marvelous resurgence of nationality." "I make bold," he declared, "to say that the way of the Volunteers has been made easier by the doctrines preached by the Gaelic League." Even if "the still small voice of culture is silenced amid the clash of arms and din of warlike preparations, it will assert itself later on. It cannot be silenced." On July 12 Hyde reviewed 4,000 Volunteers at Castlebellingham. On July 30, addressing Volunteers at drill on the Earl of Kenmare's demesne in the company of the kilted Lord

Ashbourne, Hyde avowed, "We will put the guns in the hands of our soldiers, please God, and when they fire the noise will be felt from the hills of Ireland and the seashores." In early August, addressing a meeting of the Gaelic League in Killarney, he argued that if Ulster Volunteers were permitted to drill with arms, so should the same permission be given to the Irish Volunteers. No one mentioned England. Anticipating smooth passage of the Home Rule Bill, no one seemed to think there was any reason why they should. The problem, if any, everyone agreed, would come from Ulster. When the Great War broke out in August 1914 and Redmond in September pledged the service of the Irish Volunteers wherever England might need them, Sinn Féiners and Gaelic Leaguers committed to physical force against Britain split with the Redmondites.

Hyde had been correct in anticipating, in 1913, that he would soon have no choice but to offer his resignation again, but he scarcely could have predicted the reasons. What changed everything for Hyde and those with whom he had worked since 1893 was no petty sniping from within but the guns of August 1914. The final stages in the process of peaceful attainment of legislative independence, so long awaited, so recently assured, were postponed indefinitely—most thought forever—by Britain's involvement in the conflict that became World War I. Angry and frustrated at having their nationhood snatched from them on the eve of victory, many refused to accept the British pronouncement. "England's disadvantage is Ireland's opportunity," they cried, urging a call to arms. Others, especially those who had suffered through the fall of Parnell, were simply too dispirited to protest. Certain that the war would not last more than a few months, Hyde tried to hold the center by preaching patience on the one hand, preparedness on the other, and reminding all of the folly of futile and fatal action.

Meanwhile there was, as always, another league crisis over money. In 1914–1915 a second deputation had been sent off to America in the hope of obtaining sufficient funds to cover operating expenses for a year or two. Diarmuid Lynch, a Gaelic Leaguer from county Cork who had previously been president of the Gaelic League in New York State, and Thomas Ashe, a native of Dingle, had gone to New York in February 1914. They in turn had been followed by Fionan MacColuim, Nellie O'Brien, and Eithne O'Kelly, who had had the fresh idea of using a traveling exhibition to promote Irish industries and art. Again, the effort proved disappointing. Total league expenses for March 1, 1914, to January 31, 1915, had run to £3,600, while receipts for the same period had been only £3,400. As the cost of sending the delegation had come to over £600, a £1,000 advance from American sources had barely prevented a league deficit. The Irish products delegation, which had exhibited in many of the cities Hyde had visited in 1905–1906, reported gross contributions of £1,500.

In the spring of 1915 Hyde called Nellie O'Brien and Fionan Mac-Coluim home from America. He warned them that the league needed careful steering at present, especially as it seemed likely that O'Daly might resign from his post as secretary. Quickly arranging passage, they prepared a last appeal to the American Irish for St. Patrick's Day, 1915. Their message: "$300 will keep one man on the wheel for a year, circulating and teaching Irish language and history and Irish songs and dances." Awaiting their return in the middle of the deteriorating world situation during that unhappy spring, Hyde received a pathetic call for help from Julius Pokorny, a German Celticist. Pokorny had not known that his maternal grandfather was Jewish. An anti-Semitic purge had resulted in his suspension from the university. There was disturbing news also about Kuno Meyer, who had founded the School of Irish Learning in Dublin in 1903 and had been the first editor of its journal, *Eriu*. Since the outbreak of the war he had become publicly and vehemently pro-German, creating an uproar that led both Dublin and Cork to rescind the Freedom of the City awarded him in 1911 and 1912. Hardest to bear were the daily casualty lists that announced the deaths of sons of many of Hyde's Connacht friends, boys Hyde remembered as children playing in the endless summer twilight beneath the trees that lined the long avenues leading to their gracious homes. As they grew older sometimes he had joined them in informal cricket games when they were home on their holidays from Trinity, Oxford, and Cambridge. Now in the spring of 1915, one by one they paid their final dues, loyal members of a vanishing class. To John Quinn, Hyde wrote:

Nearly everyone I know in the army has been killed. Poor young Lord de Freyne and his brother were shot the same day and buried in one grave. The MacDermot of Coolavin, my nearest neighbor, has had his eldest son shot dead in the Dardanelles. All the gentry have suffered. *Noblesse oblige*. They have behaved magnificently.

From Georges Dottin at the University of Rennes, Hyde received news that there, too, sons of scholar-friends had been summoned to the killing fields of the western front.

In the months leading up to the league's *ard-fheis* in August 1915,

Hyde tried to check the separatists with speeches that pleaded with them to eschew violence until the time was right and to avoid any armed confrontation with the formidable British military machine until they were better prepared. He offered no apologies for the fact that, despite his own increasingly political rhetoric, he continued to insist that the league remain nonpolitical. Challenged to "go political" with the league, he argued eloquently that most branches were run by officers and secretaries, National School teachers, and customs and excise officers—Irish women and men filled with national feeling who were precluded from taking any part in political activity. For them the league provided an acceptable outlet for their energies.

On St. Patrick's Day, 1915, Moore and Hyde addressed a crowd of over three thousand people in Dundalk's Market Square. Moore, who had retired to the sidelines until he received Hyde's summons, told the crowd that he had come back to the league only to find it "deserted by its bravest and best." The Galway branch was "withered, killed by these wise young men, these know-alls of Irish politics, who have reduced to impotency and almost bankruptcy, the Gaelic League." In mid-May the *Weekly Freeman* reported that Hyde had spoken in Wexford before "an enormous concourse of people." "To be a nation," he told them, "they should have the marks of a nation." Reasserting his belief in the place of the Gaelic League, he declared that it "stands for no party, but for all Ireland."

Self-evident to anyone intimately acquainted with league affairs was what Hyde did not explain: that the league's nonpolitical stance had won and held the support of hundreds of younger clergy and their bishops while successfully warding off such clerical imperialists as Father Patrick Dinneen; that by keeping national politics out of the league he had secured the support of Redmond and his Parliamentary party at a critical juncture during the fight to establish mandatory Irish in the university; that he had written endless letters, mediated quarrels without number, smiled when he was seething inside, and balanced, juggled, temporized, and conciliated to the point of exhaustion. Nor were his struggles over.

Pearse Beasley was among those who did not agree. On June 12, 1915, he published "The Gaelic League—Wanted, a Policy" in which he insisted that the league must stop "marking time." Hyde did not mind: the issue had been debated again and again. He stood on his record of twenty-two years. But did he want to continue the debate? Was it indeed worth arguing, with Home Rule assured as soon as the war was over? Did he want to try to hold together the existing coalition of disparate factions until then? Did he want to face again the prospect of bringing back the league from the brink of bankruptcy? He was halfway to his fifty-sixth birthday. He felt old and tired. Ever since the league was considered newsworthy, letters criticizing him had appeared regularly in the Dublin press. Just a few days before, he had been attacked in the *Irish Times* for being "a dreamer, a man who lives and moves in a world that is not the real world." It would be strange to pick up the paper and not be able to find out what he had been doing wrong. The prospect had an unmistakable appeal.

A few weeks before Hyde went to Dundalk for the *ard-fheis* of 1915, he made his decision. He would resign the presidency rather than preside over a league in which he could not believe. He would not resign his membership, of course; that was not necessary. But as it now appeared that those who wanted activist planks in the league's program were in the majority, they could have the chair. On August 1, in a much-publicized ceremony in Glasnevin Cemetery, O'Donovan Rossa, that fierce Fenian celebrated in the Irish poems of the young Hyde, was eulogized by Patrick Pearse. Rossa, whom Hyde had visited in New York, first in 1891 and again in 1905–1906, had died in America after a long illness. His body had been brought to Ireland for burial. As Ruth Dudley Edwards, Pearse's biographer, explains, the funeral, attended by hundreds of thousands, was calculated by its organizers to arouse the passions of activist Ireland. Instructing Pearse on the content of his oration, Thomas Clarke had told him, "Make it as hot as hell, throw all discretion to the winds." Pearse responded with a panegyric that left the crowds sobbing and cheering. Its peroration—

They think they have pacified Ireland. They think that they have pacified half of us and intimidated the other half. They think that they have foreseen everything, think that they have provided against everything; but the fools, the fools, the fools!—they have left us our Fenian dead, and while Ireland holds these graves, Ireland unfree shall never be at peace—

echoed all the way to Dundalk where the twenty-second *ard-fheis* of the Gaelic League was about to begin.

Fairly certain that he would be returning on the afternoon train, Hyde packed only a light bag in preparation for the meeting. He too had prepared a script. He already had told Colonel Moore that if the votes favored an activist motion, he would gather up his papers, vacate the chair, and walk out of the *ard-fheis*. After the usual housecleaning motions had passed and minor disputes had been settled, the resolution for which Hyde had been waiting was read. It came in the form of a motion from Pádraig Ó Maille; it called for adding to the league's objectives that of working to free Ireland from foreign rule. This was the one Hyde could not accept, not because he did not want Ireland free from foreign rule but because such a motion made the Gaelic League a political party. He began to collect his papers. Colonel Moore, hoping to avoid the inevitable, suggested substituting the single word "free" for "free from foreign rule." From the chair Hyde countered that the statement remained political. It was as he thought: Ó Maille's resolution passed by a large majority. Next on the agenda were elections to the Coiste Gnótha. Hyde wrote a note addressed to Pádraig O'Daly, to be read out the next day when the time came for choosing a president, declining the honor of reelection on the grounds of health.

On August 2, 1915, with Hyde's chair already empty before them, O'Daly read Hyde's letter of resignation. At first there was silence, then after some minutes, an all-around murmur. No proposal of any kind was advanced. The meeting was adjourned for two hours. When the meeting again came to order, the question of the presidency was raised. Several resolutions thanking Hyde for his service were read into the record. John MacNeill took the chair. He advised keeping the presidency vacant on the chance that Hyde might be persuaded to return if the league provided him with a private secretary. Pádraig O'Daly submitted his resignation. Sean T. O'Kelly was elected to O'Daly's post. For a number of days accounts of the Dundalk meeting passed from branch to branch, with everyone adding something about what someone had said or how someone had looked when Hyde's resignation was read. Even Hyde's enemies recognized that they were witnessing the end of an era.

As for Hyde himself, he wrote in his diary, "I got my baggage from the hotel without anyone noticing it, got into the hotel bus, and . . . to the train and was soon on my way to Dublin with a lighter heart than I had known for years."

16

The Terrible Beauty

In the eight months following his resignation from the presidency of the Gaelic League, Douglas Hyde maintained a discreet distance from all but his closest league friends. Faithful others, still hoping that he would return to active participation on the Coiste Gnótha if not to the presidency, dropped him notes from time to time to keep him informed on league activities. He scanned their letters dutifully, grateful for the devotion and appreciation that had prompted them, and tried to avoid reading between the lines. Sometimes he felt frustrated and angry that after so many years of struggle he had not been able to hold on for what was surely, he thought, the last mile. Then, remembering how the goal had been moved each time he thought he was closing the gap, he was again overwhelmed with the sense of futility that had led to his resignation. The fact was that his present life had its own rewards. Teaching was a genuine pleasure. And it was immensely satisfying to have time for the writing and research projects that in the past he had repeatedly postponed and delayed. On two projects in particular he had been making steady progress at last. One was a catalog of the books and manuscripts in the Sir John Gilbert collection, on which he had been working intermittently since 1901 with D. J. O'Donoghue, the librarian at University College, Dublin. The other was a translation for the Irish Texts Society of "The Conquests of Charlemagne," a Middle Irish account of a French saga found in the fifteenth-century Book of Lismore. Lucy seemed happier, too, with her Dublin town house and daily activities. The girls were well settled at school.

To his neighbors on Earlsfort Place, Hyde had become a familiar cheerful figure, cycling along "on his two round feet" in a gray knicker-bocker suit and green stockings on this errand or that or on his way to the college or the academy. In the warm April sunshine of Easter Monday (April 24), 1916, he cycled off through the south center of the city, thinking the afternoon sun might have had more warmth in it—thinking, too, of those friendly notes, some with printed enclosures, that kept him better informed than he cared to be. Around and around like the wheels of his bicycle went the words in his mind, saying things he knew but did not want to know, not wanting to know how he knew, about plans for the "advanced political section" of the league and the Volunteers to implicate themselves in some attempted insurrectionary work. It was no secret—almost everyone in Dublin, almost everyone in Ireland, certainly everyone in Dublin Castle was expecting something to happen. Of one thing he was sure: whatever it was would be con-nected with the Volunteer battalions, smartly done up and drilling with make-believe guns on the demesne of one Big House and another, that he had spent so many of his sunny Sunday afternoons reviewing from 1913 through 1915. The Volunteers had organized and armed (albeit inadequately, as the wooden guns indicated) to protect themselves from the Carsonites. Even members of Parliament had acknowledged the necessity for this defense, especially after the resignations at the Curragh in 1914, which had told everyone just where the army would be if Ul-ster Volunteers attacked Dublin, and the gunrunning episodes right under the bows of British battleships at Larne, which said as much for the protection of the navy. Defense certainly was required, for even after Asquith had assured Carson that the government would never coerce Ulster into accepting Home Rule (that had happened on Septem-ber 15, the very day that George V had signed the Home Rule Bill into law), the northern leader continued to declare that his mission was the destruction of any attempt to institute legislative independence any-where in Ireland. But no one believed that the drills and meetings and colorful reviews were merely preparations for defense, what with all the slogans proclaiming "Ireland's opportunity" that every schoolboy could recite. Neither, however, did they understand, those men who ordered the drilling, scheduled the meetings, and wrote the slogans, that when it came, the insurrection would be put down (please God, with no great loss of life) and the flower of another generation would go off to British prisons and into foreign exile. If John O'Leary were still alive, that would be what he would tell them, but they would not listen to O'Leary any more than they would listen to Hyde, for they would not listen to history.

A few years ago Cathal Brugha, who manufactured candles, had come to talk to Hyde about "Ireland's Opportunity," and he in turn had tried to talk to Cathal Brugha about patience and the promise of Home Rule at the end of the war. But as Brugha had pointed out, Asquith already had broken his 1912 promise of Home Rule for all Ireland and Carson already had received assurances of partition (the work of two Celts, Churchill and Lloyd George). Only a fool or a dreamer, he said, would believe in such British promises, which had no more substance behind them than those of Hyde's own Fairy talking to his Tinker. So Hyde had given up on patience and promise and had tried to talk to Brugha about history. They had parted sadly, warm friends, each sorrowing over the intransigence of the other.

As he cycled through Dublin on that Easter Monday afternoon, past University College, along Harcourt Street, past the Royal College of Surgeons, Stephen's Green, the Shelbourne Hotel, along Kildare Street, past Trinity College, and back to his home at One Earlsfort Place, listening carefully to everything he heard, did Hyde know that there would be great need for candles that day? Two years later, in an unpublished account of Easter, 1916, based on his diaries, Hyde wrote, "I never suspected for a moment that there would be such a rebellion as we had in Easter Week, 1916, or such violent fighting, or that they would have stood their ground so well." Was it the event itself or the force of it that he did not expect?

Noon, Easter Monday, April 24, 1916

At midday in Dublin approximately one hundred and fifty members of the Irish Citizen Army and the Irish Volunteers, some in uniform, many in their Sunday suits, all armed with a variety of weapons, left Liberty Hall under the command of James Connolly and Patrick Pearse, marched to the General Post Office on Sackville (O'Connell) Street, and on orders from their commanders, charged the building. They took prisoner a small unarmed detachment of British soldiers, then raised two Irish flags over the roof, fortified the windows, and barricaded the doors. When all was in order Pearse reappeared on the steps of the post office and read "The Proclamation of the Irish Republic" to a small crowd. Calling out to all Irishmen and Irishwomen, "in the name of God and of the dead generations from which she receives her old tradition of nationhood," he declared that Ireland now "summons her children to her flag and strikes for her freedom."

"We declare," he continued,

the right of the people of Ireland to the ownership of Ireland, and to the unfettered control of Irish destinies, to be sovereign and indefensible. The long usurpation of that right by a foreign people and government has not extinguished the right, nor can it ever be extinguished except by the destruction of the Irish people. In every generation the Irish people have asserted their right to national freedom and arms. Standing on that fundamental right and again asserting it in arms in the face of the world, we hereby proclaim the Irish Republic as a Sovereign Independent State and we pledge our lives and the lives of our comrades-in-arms to the cause of its freedom, of its welfare, and of its exaltation among the nations.

In the absence of a duly elected representative government, Pearse asserted that "the Provisional Government, hereby constituted, will administer the civil and military affairs of the Republic in trust for the people." Affixed to the printed copies of the proclamation that were distributed on behalf of the provisional government were the signatures of Thomas J. Clarke, Sean MacDermott, Thomas MacDonagh, Patrick Pearse, Eamon Ceannt, James Connolly, and Joseph Plunkett.

Shortly after 1:00 P.M. a troop of lancers charged down Sackville Street at a gallop with drawn sabres. Rifle fire from the post office killed three lancers and fatally wounded a fourth. The remainder wheeled and retreated quickly in the direction of the Rotunda. In the absence of police, widespread looting began of shops on Sackville Street by residents of the nearby slums. Reports brought to Pearse and Connolly in the post office by dispatch riders claimed that Dublin Castle had been taken and that Volunteer and Citizen Army units were in place at preselected strategic vantage points including St. Stephen's Green, the South Dublin Union, Jacob's Biscuit Factory, Boland's Mill, and the Four Courts.

Hyde's account:

Having cycled to Stephen's Green to see the pictures sent in for Miss Dease's competition, Hyde went on to Nassau Street to buy cigarettes but—it being a holiday—found the shops closed. It was a beautiful day—very warm. Bicycling back along Stephen's Green, as he turned out of Dawson Street he was startled by a loud burst from what sounded like the tire of a motorcar in front of the Shelbourne Hotel, then another burst, and then another. He said to himself, "There must be great mortality among tyres today." Minutes later, passing the Shelbourne, he saw the large gate of Stephen's Green shut, and thought it curious that the park would be closed on Easter Monday. He then spotted armed men in the park and watched two of them dig holes, wondering to himself, "Are these fools thinking to hide anything?" Later he discovered that the men were digging defense trenches. He had, he said, "not the slightest idea that there was anything really serious in the air, not even when in the garden half an hour afterward, I heard a furious outbreak of firing." What he had taken to be Volunteer target practice turned out to have been a fire fight between British soldiers and Volunteers at the Portobello Bridge. He worried about his daughters, Nuala and Una, who had gone for a walk, but like others strolling around Dublin in the warm sunshine of that Easter Monday afternoon, they returned unharmed and apparently unaware that anything had happened. Together all three walked over to the area around the Portobello Bridge, where they saw that severe damage had been done to a public house. Its windows had been shot out; ransacked goods lay on the street. From the direction of Stephen's Green they heard intermittent gunfire. From the Green, Hyde later learned, Citizen Army rebels under Commandant Michael Mallin and the Countess Markiewicz had been exchanging fire with soldiers atop the Shelbourne Hotel. "This night," he wrote in his diary before going to bed, "so far as I could make out, except for continual firing in the Green and round it, everything was quiet in this quarter of the city."

Tuesday, April 25
   Pearse's and Connolly's headquarters force in the post office heard sounds of machine-gun fire from south of the city, indicating British troop activity. Rumors flew. Pearse issued an optimistic communiqué. The British cleared the area around Dublin Castle. At Stephen's Green units of the Citizen Army withdrew to the Royal College of Surgeons. Martial law was declared. Pearse drafted and read a second proclamation to the people of Dublin. In the evening sniper fire increased and fires burned on Sackville (O'Connell) Street. British troops in the city now numbered 6,500. Artillery for shelling occupied buildings was brought into the city from Athlone.

Hyde's account:
   Having awakened early, before the rest of the household, Hyde had walked down Earlsfort Terrace to the corner of Stephen's Green, feeling "perfectly certain" that it had been evacuated during the night, for it appeared to him to be a place impossible to defend for any length of

time, as all the trenches and other cover for snipers could be searched by machine guns and rifle fire from the tops of surrounding buildings. To his surprise Hyde found that it had not been evacuated but in fact had been the scene of a sharp fire fight between marksmen from both sides, none of whom he could see. As he walked back up Earlsfort Terrace he stopped to chat with two women friends. A staccato of machine-gun fire interrupted their conversation. Bullets struck a window and rain pipe eight feet over their heads. The shots, he theorized, had come not from immediately behind them but from the roof of Oliver Gogarty's house next to the Shelbourne Hotel where British soldiers had set up their guns. It was a "criminally careless" act on the part of the military, he thought angrily, to shoot down a street that was empty except for three civilians.

After lunch Hyde strolled out again with Nuala and Una. From one passerby on the street he learned that among the first orders issued from the post office, headquarters of the Rising, was that an official baker be appointed to supply the new Irish Republic with bread. Another passerby told them that the Rising had been ordered over the head of John MacNeill and against his direct orders. MacNeill, the man said, having learned of the plan for a rising on Easter Sunday, had issued a counterorder cancelling all Volunteer parades planned for that day. The O'Rahilly and Bulmer Hobson had sided with MacNeill. On the basis of this and other conversations Hyde surmised that Pearse, Connolly, and Plunkett might have refused to cancel the Rising because they had been notified of a secret order smuggled out of the Castle for wholesale arrests of Volunteers and the imposition of what amounted to martial law in Dublin.

MacNeill had sent a copy of this secret order to Hyde on April 19. That same evening Hyde had dined with Stopford, brother of Alice Stopford Green, and Sir Matthew Nathan, under secretary for Ireland. He had shown the document to Stopford, who doubted its authenticity, but neither man mentioned it to Nathan. Hyde at first had shared Stopford's view that the document was a forgery but he had changed his mind when he considered that the Castle might have been alerted to the possibility of a coup. Hyde suspected that the more hotheaded among the leaders had called out the Volunteers on their own account by an order which purported to come from headquarters.

Wednesday, April 26

The British armed fishery vessel, the Helga, *shelled Liberty Hall from the Liffey Basin. Two infantry brigades arrived at Kingstown Harbor and began to march on Dublin. Sir John Maxwell was assigned to command British operations. The British conducted house-to-house searches while infantry and two eighteen-pound artillery pieces were moved closer to cordon off the central city. The pacifist writer and beloved Dublin character Francis Sheehy-Skeffington was executed without trial at Portobello Barracks. Incendiary rounds fired into Sackville (O'Connell) Street, apparently from Trinity College, caused an outbreak of fires. Scores of Sherwood Foresters lay dead and wounded as nine Volunteers from de Valera's command at Boland's Mill held up their advance guard for nine hours.*

Hyde's account:

In the morning Hyde and his two daughters set out to check on Nellie O'Brien. As they passed Stephen's Green they saw a dead horse on the street near the Shelbourne Hotel. The windows of the hotel were shattered by bullets; its hall and vestibule were barricaded with mattresses. They walked past the deserted Kildare Street Club to Nellie O'Brien's flat, where they found her calm but her housekeeper in a state of great excitement. They had been going through a much worse time than the residents of Earlsfort Terrace, as fighting had been going on all night with tremendous fusillades in the direction of Westland Row. The roof of Trinity College was full of men who apparently had been firing up Dame Street. Hyde was told afterward that they were men of the officers' training corps, with some Canadians and others. Nellie had been able to see them shooting quite plainly. Great cannon firing also had been heard; subsequent reports gave the target as Liberty Hall. Some people said that a gunboat had bombarded it from the basin of the river, others that eighteen-pounders planted in Tara Street had fired on it from there. The structure had not been demolished, all agreed, but it had been riddled and shattered with thousands of bullets and many shells.

Lucy's anxiety for Nellie's safety prompted a second trip by the Hydes that same day to persuade Nellie to return with them to Earlsfort Place. Lucy had shown "wonderful courage," Hyde said, as they passed Stephen's Green amid sounds of gunfire on all sides. On the way they met Sarah Purser, the artist, who was also out walking. When told of their mission to rescue Nellie O'Brien, she "sniffed and said 'That's always the way with the granddaughter of heroes.'"

With as many of Nellie's belongings as they could carry in their arms, the Hydes returned with Nellie to One Earlsfort Place. En route they paused to watch an English regiment weighed down with enormous field packs marching into the city from Kingstown, looking exhausted from the heat. People in the terrace and road waved handkerchiefs wildly and ran down with jugs of water and oranges and other refreshments. Disdaining mere water, some of the men threw it away, but when a poor woman in a shawl (drunk herself, Hyde thought) produced a bottle of something else, it was "highly appreciated and finished in a jiffy."

Thursday, April 2
British reinforcements continued to arrive, tightening the cordon around the city's center. The post office, taking its first direct hit from artillery, was machine-gunned. Fires on Sackville Street spread closer to the post office. Volunteer outposts around Sackville (O'Connell) Street had to be abandoned as heat from the fires became unbearable. James Connolly was wounded while attempting to establish an outpost outside the post office. Inside, Pearse, Clarke, and MacDermott, who had assumed command of military operations, were joined by The O'Rahilly. A bulletin written by Pearse on Wednesday was released. It claimed that republican lines were intact and asked citizens to build street barricades to hold up the British advance. Pearse also reported (inaccurately) that "large areas in the West, South and South-East" were now in arms for the Irish Republic.

Hyde's account:
Except for "a miserable edition" of the *Irish Times* which contained little more than a terse government announcement of the Rising, a Wednesday issue that contained Lord Wimbourne's proclamation of martial law, and a report that the provinces were quiet, there had been no reliable news for three days. All mention of the tumultuous scenes in Dublin was omitted from the paper, as was any news of the English armies on the western front.

The Hydes accompanied Nellie O'Brien on yet another risky trip to her flat to rescue more of her belongings. On the way back to the Hydes' they passed dead horses in the streets and observed a few women and officers in mufti peering cautiously from the windows on the Kildare Street side of the Shelbourne Hotel. A passerby reported that three Volunteers in a house near Haddington and Northumberland roads had killed twenty-five soldiers and then escaped dressed in womens' clothing. On Harcourt Street they encountered a belligerent dentist who demanded of Hyde, "How much are you responsible for this?" Hyde asked him, "How much are you?" The dentist muttered something about putting a bayonet into Hyde. "Your forceps, you mean," Hyde thought but restrained himself from saying. The dentist then threatened something to the effect of changing the professors of the National University "mighty quick." Hyde felt very sorry later when he learned that the dentist had one son at the university whom he had thrown out of the house because of his Sinn Féin sympathies and another son whom he had pressured to enlist in the British army. The son at the university was fighting with the Volunteers; the other son, an officer, had been shot in Flanders (ironically, along with a son of Count Plunkett). Hyde attributed the dentist's attack on him to the fact that, with John MacNeill a professor and MacDonagh an assistant lecturer at the National University, he must have confounded university teaching with Sinn Féin propaganda. His sympathy for the unfortunate man increased when he heard that two days later he lost his father also, killed in the street by a stray bullet.

Hyde was astonished by the number of soldiers and quantity of matériel pouring into Dublin. He estimated one contingent at two thousand, including cavalry, foot soldiers, and equipment, and wondered how many other columns had entered the city from other directions: the government evidently was taking no chances. On the street he obtained more information about the widespread looting and learned that Sheehy-Skeffington had been shot, not for fighting, of course (it was well known that he was a pacifist), but for posting notices about the formation of a citizens' committee to stop the looting. "It was most characteristic of him to be moving about and busying himself in public at such a time," Hyde wrote, remembering reports that "the military would hear nothing from him, would not look at his proclamation, but gave him half an hour to get a priest," an offer which he refused. "They offered him his choice whether he would be shot with his eyes bandaged or open. He tore open his shirt and on his breast were tattooed the words *Votes for Women,* and he bade them shoot him on that spot." The officer responsible for the shooting, Hyde was told, was to be tried for it. (Hyde did not know at the time what later became Dublin gossip: that the officer was a kinsman of Elizabeth Bowen, and that her father, a barrister, had declined to involve himself in the man's defense.)

Among the day's news items that Hyde picked up on the street and passed on to others were rumors that the post office garrison was holding twenty hostages; that pictures of the leaders of the Rising had been issued to British soldiers; that the soldiers had been instructed to shoot these men on sight; that the British officers expected the revolt to be over by week's end; and that those same officers had been astounded by the bravery and marksmanship of the Volunteers.

Back at the Hydes', the wife of Richard Irvine Best (Celtic scholar and assistant director of the National Library) stopped in to have tea with them. She told them that her husband had brought out Thomas Lyster, director of the National Library, to see the fighting at Haddington Road and had left him sitting on the lock gate of the canal, moralizing upon Cornwallis and the war of American freedom. Only a day or two before, Lyster had gone to Hyde's neighbors, the Coffeys, and apologized to Mrs. Coffey for having said to her that the Irish were cowards. He assured her that he could never again think such a thing— that it was really extraordinary that a couple of thousand men armed only with rifles should try to hold off an empire. Mrs. Best also reported that spent bullets were falling all around Sarah Purser's house on the Grand Canal and that her servants had offered her the bullets as souvenirs.

Thursday evening the Hydes had other visitors: Diarmid Coffey and his mother, who lived nearby. In her own diary of the Rising, Mrs. Coffey wrote, "We often go into the Hydes in the evening. They are a cheer, taking such a wise and sympathetic view." Through it all her husband, George Coffey, the archaeologist, lay gravely ill. Diarmid Coffey had that day gone out to try and find a doctor to attend him. After they left, Hyde noted that "the night was lurid with flames and hideous with firing."

Friday, April 28

Pearse ordered the evacuation of women from the post office and prepared a statement to be read to his soldiers: "I am satisfied that we have saved Ireland's honour." By midafternoon the upper stories of the post office were ablaze from shell fire. The O'Rahilly was killed while leading a sortie down Moore Street. By evening the post office fire was out of control. Pearse, Connolly, and Clarke were the last to evacuate the building for a small house on Moore Street.

Hyde's account:

Fine weather continued. Sitting in the garden, Nuala and Una heard bullets overhead. Hyde could not hear the whistle of them in the air, but he did hear them striking slates on houses. Hyde, his daughters, and Nellie O'Brien walked to Leeson Park to inquire after a relative of Nellie's who had been shot in the shoulder on Monday in Stephen's

Green. On their return at 4:30 in the afternoon they heard a burst of fire from Harcourt Street Bridge. Hyde learned later that five men and two women had been killed, apparently by British soldiers. That evening at about 8:30 he heard a "desperate outburst" of firing which seemed to come from the direction of the College of Surgeons, "the principal storm centre in this part of the city." He noted the effectiveness of the Volunteer sniper fire from the top floors and roofs of nearby houses:

The single shots which are going on in our neighbourhood all day and half the night appear to come from semi-detached or corner houses, or houses of a commanding height in the surrounding street. The Volunteers appear to quietly walk in and take possession of any building they want. They confine the family below, and then get on the roof or fire from the top windows.

That night more smoke and flames could be seen in the sky in the direction of O'Connell Street. The smell of burning was coming in through all the windows.

Saturday, April 29

Pearse proposed a negotiated surrender. Nurse Elizabeth O'Farrell was sent out from the Moore Street house under a white flag and was escorted to a British commander who told her that surrender must be unconditional. At 3:45 P.M. Pearse signed a general surrender order in the presence of General Maxwell. The order was later cosigned by James Connolly and Thomas MacDonagh. Orders were carried to other Volunteer and Citizen Army positions in the city.

Hyde's account:

Heavy firing could now be heard in Hyde's section of the city. In the street he learned that the Volunteer unit at Jacob's Factory was still intact and that the Volunteers there were able to slip in and out according to assigned shifts, exchanging bandoliers and rifles as they took turns going home to catch up on some sleep. There had been, he was told, heavy fighting at the Four Courts. A rumor that had swept through Dublin since Tuesday, that Sir Roger Casement had been captured off the south coast of Ireland and returned to England as a prisoner, had been corroborated. At six that evening Hyde was told by a driver for the Red Cross that the Volunteers had surrendered and that the Rising would soon be over except for desultory sniping that might continue for several days. He sent two men out to get provisions for the family, but bread, flour, oatmeal, and Indian meal were all unobtainable. At night Hyde observed only small conflagrations. Noting that the firing had nearly died down, he concluded that reports that the end was approaching were accurate.

Sunday, April 30

The remaining forces of the provisional government surrendered. Of all the major strategic sites occupied and held by the Volunteers and Citizen Army, only the post office had been lost to British military action. Exhausted and dejected, the captives were herded into the Rotunda gardens under cloudy skies. Soon it began to rain.

Hyde's account:

The morning was fairly quiet. Nuala and Una went to nearby St. Matthias Church where the sermon was punctuated by nearby shooting. Food remained short; Hyde was told of long lines of famished Dubliners waiting for bread outside a bakery at Ballsbridge. New outbreaks of firing occurred, this time from railway carriages at the Harcourt Street Bridge where a train had been stalled since Tuesday. Volunteers shot from carriage windows and were answered with fire from troops at Charlemont Bridge. In the street Hyde met Father Sherwin, who had been attending the wounded and dying since Monday. He stopped for a while in Hyde's garden, where he reported that the Citizen Army unit in the College of Surgeons, which had been fighting with such skill that it had dominated Stephen's Green since Monday, had surrendered at 2:00 P.M. According to Sherwin a good many of its members were women "who shot as well as the men." He praised "the courage and resourcefulness and intelligence of the Volunteers, many of whom were very young."

The priest's account of the looting was both grim and humorous. People were carrying off, he said, the most incongruous articles. He had seen one old woman staggering along under a huge box of soap. Just beside a British military outpost, unable to carry it any longer, she had put it down and sat on it. After a while, "with great aplomb" she raised it again on her back and walked right past the soldiers, who said she looked dirty enough to want it all.

Accurate news was still sparse and uncertain. That night, as he consulted the sky and listened for gunfire, Hyde was under the impression that the units at Jacob's Biscuit and Boland's were still holding out, but he noted that the sky was no longer bright with the glare of fires.

Monday, May 1

The rain continued. Many of the prisoners, including the leaders of the Rising, were taken to Kilmainham Gaol. The courts-martial began.

Hyde's account:

Following a quiet morning Hyde heard tremendous firing at about noon from the Leeson Street Bridge. He was told that the British soldiers were firing indiscriminately up and down every street. He supposed that they were clearing the way for an army contingent that came by later, in a long parade of wagons carrying tents and other cumbersome items, cavalry scouts, motor scouts, and a bicycle corps. Malone, a man who worked for the Hydes and who also was a driver for the Red Cross, brought news of the utter devastation on O'Connell Street. "When you turned around the Bank of Ireland and looked ahead of you," he said, "you would not know where you were. You might be in some foreign city in France or Germany." The only familiar landmark was Nelson's Pillar. Later in the day Hyde heard that the men of Jacob's Factory had surrendered, although their flag had been flying until six o'clock Sunday evening. "They have surrendered in Boland's also," he wrote in his diary, "and that definitely breaks the back of the revolt." Nobody could say with any certainty just how many prisoners were taken. No one had any other official information, either. Everyone had a selection of unconfirmed reports, rumors, and possible facts. The presence of police on the streets for the first time since Easter Monday prompted raillery among some of the citizenry. There was much speculation on the whereabouts of Countess Constance Markiewicz. One rumor had it that she had surrendered on George Street, a bayonet at her chest; another that she was taken prisoner at the College of Surgeons. All stories agreed that, dressed in men's clothing and with a feather in her hat, she had kissed her revolver before surrendering it.

The street-fighting skills of the young Volunteers was a source of considerable comment. Hyde noted that, although many were hardly more than raw recruits, they had learned to harass the British troops by taking cover in protected positions, firing, and then moving quickly to other sites. "Most comical," said Hyde, was the sight of civilians flying down the road when shots were fired. He had watched one group of five men jump in unison when shots landed near them, then wheel and run to the far end of the street. Diarmid Coffey, he added wryly, had such respect for the curfew under martial law that he chose not to walk the fifty yards from his own house to come to the Hydes' for dinner for fear that he might be shot.

Tuesday, May 2
The courts-martial continued.

Hyde's account:
Wild rumors were circulating in the absence of official news: that British soldiers had thrown the corpses of Volunteers into the Liffey; that Galway had been cleared of the Sinn Féiners by artillery fire. There were also stories, some amusing, some heartwarming, about the ability, honesty, and restraint of the Volunteers: that for several days one group had occupied a pub on Leeson Street but had drunk only one bottle of lemonade; that many had attempted to stop the looting; that even the British said that they were excellent shots.

After lunch Hyde and his family walked to Westmoreland Street where for the first time they could see for themselves the ruins that stretched down Sackville (O'Connell) Street to Nelson's Pillar. Not one window in Trinity College, Hyde noted, had been broken. At Nellie O'Brien's flat in College Park Chambers they were horrified to find that machine-gun fire had ripped through her rooms. They congratulated themselves for having insisted that she stay with them. There was word at last of John MacNeill: he was under military arrest in his own house. MacNeill had stated, Hyde was told, that he had nothing to do with the uprising, that it had gone forward against his advice and wishes, but that he accepted responsibility for it and wished to share the fate of his companions.

Shortages of food still plagued the city. The Hydes had begun to despair of getting milk. Officially, they were told, the Rising was over, but they continued to hear distant thunder from heavy guns.

II

The judges of the courts-martial completed their work quickly. Fifteen of the leaders were sentenced to die according to a published schedule. Thomas J. Clarke, Thomas MacDonagh, and Patrick Pearse were executed on May 3; Edward Daly, Michael Hanrahan, William Pearse, and Joseph Mary Plunkett on May 4; John MacBride on May 5; Eamon Ceannt (Kent), Cornelius Colbert, Sean J. Heuston, and Michael Mallin on May 8; James Connolly and Sean MacDermott on

May 12. Had Eamon de Valera's death sentence not been commuted to life imprisonment, there would have been one more.

For Hyde as for almost everyone else in Ireland, what passed for official news was spotty and suspect, especially as sounds of shooting continued for days after official word that the Rising had ended. The streets were full of rumors. Most concerned the systematic and thorough looting that had gone on under the heaviest fire, particularly in the poorer areas of the city, by British soldiers supposedly looking for arms. The headquarters of the Gaelic League had not escaped. Fortunately, Stephen Barrett, the treasurer, had removed £100 from the office the night before it was ransacked. The soldiers found only loose coins and stamps in a desk drawer.

During a May 5 house-to-house search for weapons, a team of two soldiers and two detectives had come to Hyde's door. He had been required to give up a valuable gun and gun case plus several other items for which he was not given a receipt. On May 12 he and Lucy dressed in their best clothes and drove to Dublin Castle in Hyde's Ford touring car (a prized possession purchased in Dublin just two years earlier). Everyone in Dublin had stories of confiscated items that had disappeared without record into the pockets of British soldiers. Consequently, although everyone had been assured that at a designated time all items would be returned by Dublin Castle, Hyde did not have much hope of ever seeing his gun and gun case again. In the Castle yard he met a man he knew, a resident magistrate from Drogheda, who advised him to see a Colonel Johnson. After being kept waiting for Colonel Johnson, Hyde asked for Commissioner Quinn. As Quinn was out, Hyde asked for Superintendent Dunne, who disclaimed any knowledge of anything confiscated by any military officer. At that moment a man in Dunne's office volunteered to take Hyde to the appropriate department.

"Do you know me?" he asked as soon as they were in the hall.

"I think I know your face," Hyde said cautiously.

"Well," said the man, "I'm Mrs. Hanley's brother."

As Mrs. Hanley was a Frenchpark neighbor, Hyde knew that he was in safe hands.

"I'll get your gun for you if it is to be had at all," Mrs. Hanley's brother assured Hyde, taking him to a room in which three officers were sitting around a table.

The officer in charge, however, gave little hope that, especially without a receipt, anything might be reclaimed. "You're the twentieth person in with us already today. We are inundated with complaints about watches and everything."

Hyde explained that the gun and gun case were not his but belonged to the brother of Lady Wright. As this information brought exclamations of concern from the officers, Hyde confided only to his diary the fact that he had "omitted to mention that the poor chap whose gun it was had died many years previously." The advice he received from the officers took him back to square one: he must see Colonel Johnson. Fortunately, Mrs. Hanley's brother had other ideas. Escorting Hyde to still another department, he stood in the doorway, saluted smartly, and announced that Dr. Douglas Hyde had come to look for his gun.

"Oh," said a jolly-looking little man, "I know him."

Then, putting his hand behind his chair, he produced gun case, revolver, sword bayonet, and a box of ammunition which he insisted on bringing out himself and placing in Hyde's Ford "in the friendliest and most amiable manner."

III

It was over. Hyde's image of the Rising was not, after all, one of candles burning in memory of the dead. It was the memory of the green, white, and orange-yellow flag hoisted over University College to the cry, "Up the Republic." To Lady Gregory he later declared, "That cry and that flag have taken possession of the imagination and I don't think it will ever be got out of it."

17

In and Out of Public Life

The facts had been confirmed: John MacNeill had indeed stated when he was arrested that although he had opposed the insurrection of April 24 he accepted responsibility for what had happened and wished to share the fate of the others who had been arrested. Fortunately the judges did not accept his request. On May 24 MacNeill was given a life sentence in Dartmoor Prison. Cautiously his friends began discussing how they might gather support for an appeal. It was clear that the British policy of swift and harsh punishment had been purposely chosen as a deterrent to others contemplating rebellion. The government did not swerve from its resolve even in the face of shocked and outraged protests from all over the world. The Casement trial was still pending, the evidence against him too strong for observers to expect anything but another highly publicized execution, for he had been involved in attempts to obtain German arms for the Volunteers and he had been seized on the coast of Kerry, on Banna strand, after having made the trip from Germany in a German submarine. His defenders insisted that he had returned to Ireland for the purpose of urging his confederates to cancel plans for the Rising; his accusers declared that he had been caught in the midst of a botched attempt to smuggle arms. It was not a good time, Hyde and other friends agreed, to draw attention to MacNeill. Hyde therefore concentrated for the moment on making sure that MacNeill was adequately fed and reasonably comfortable and that he had books and papers with which to occupy himself.

Meanwhile, the academic term over, Lucy was making arrangements for their return to Ratra for the summer holidays. Hyde gathered up what he needed to continue work on the Gilbert catalog and the translation of "The Conquests of Charlemagne." Before he left Earlsfort Place he had a talk with Diarmid Coffey, son of his friend and neighbor George Coffey. Diarmid had proposed that he write a biography of Hyde. Upon reviewing young Coffey's background, Hyde had consented. He was an Irish speaker. He had taken part in the Kilcoole gun-running of July 1914. In 1914–1915 he had served as secretary to the inspector general of the Irish Volunteers. He therefore could be counted on, Hyde thought, to appreciate Hyde's commitment to the language and to understand his unwillingness to narrow the membership of the Gaelic League to those committed to physical force. Hyde promised to provide him with letters and documents and to make himself available also whenever he was needed for interviews.

Six weeks later, settled at Ratra, Hyde began circulating a statement on MacNeill's behalf. On July 22 he wrote to Shane Leslie in America. MacNeill, he declared, had been the victim of a miscarriage of justice. He never had contemplated armed rebellion; in fact, had he not countermanded the orders of others, the insurrection would have been more extensive: "the fire would have spread all over the north and west." Hyde enclosed a copy of a petition, "to be signed only by a dozen scholars of eminence," which he asked Leslie not to publicize as "nothing could be more injudicious than a monster or public petition." He made similar requests of trusted friends in Ireland.

On August 3 Roger Casement was hanged in London, in Pentonville Gaol. He died in the tradition of Irish martyrs, calmly and with dignity, following an eloquent speech from the dock. Petitions seeking clemency had been ignored. Many had come from abroad. Public indignation increased. Unable to save Casement, men like John Quinn of New York, who had actively sought his release, were quick to respond to petitions for MacNeill. Hyde redoubled his efforts on MacNeill's behalf.

On September 5 Nuala Hyde suffered a hemorrhage. The diagnosis was tuberculosis; the prognosis was poor; the progress of the disease was rapid and devastating. Lucy and Hyde watched helplessly as day after day their once vivacious and beautiful daughter fought for breath. For Hyde all the horror of his boyhood when he had watched for months the suffering of his brother Arthur returned. Mercifully, Nuala's struggle was not so long. By September 30—at the age of twenty-two— she was dead. In notes to friends Hyde spoke understandingly of Lucy's great sorrow. What he did not speak of was his own. Poised, articulate, and gregarious, Nuala had been the daughter most like himself. To Quinn he wrote of how attractive and popular she had been. He had thought that one day he would give her to some young man who would escort her from the altar. Instead, escorted in the Irish tradition by twenty-four unmarried young men, her coffin was carried out of the little church in Portahard and into the graveyard where his father and mother already lay buried.

Hyde had written Shane Leslie that he had obtained all the names he needed on his Irish petition on behalf of John MacNeill. Rumor had it that Lord Wimbourne would be sympathetic. Hyde intended to make the presentation himself. He urged that an American petition, differently phrased, be sent at once. He knew that John Quinn would sign it; he asked if Shane Leslie had identified others. To MacNeill's family Hyde emphasized the importance of encouraging him, as a condition of his release, to agree to refrain from politics for the duration of the war. The petitions were submitted but MacNeill remained in Dartmoor. "What a dreadful year this has been, both public and private," Hyde wrote to Lady Gregory in December 1916. "Ireland seems in a hopeless muddle. So does everything, the Gaelic League included." To Quinn he wrote that the league, "which should be reaping golden harvests in the bankruptcy of politics, has been steered on the rocks by fools." As for Home Rule, it appeared as "dead as a herring." The general outlook was "as bleak as could be."

In April 1917 Hyde cautiously considered applying for amnesty for MacNeill but restrained himself to avoid the risks of raising the issue so close to the anniversary of the Rising. In June, however, the matter resolved itself. British prime minister David Lloyd George called for an Irish convention that would meet in Dublin to discuss the future of Ireland. Organizations representing all aspects of Irish political, social, religious, and economic life were invited to nominate delegates. To encourage participation, Irish prisoners in England were freed on June 16. Hyde relayed the good news of MacNeill's release to John Quinn. The struggle, he noted, was not yet over. Because MacNeill had been convicted on felony charges, he had been stripped of his university chair and deprived of his right to a lifetime reappointment. As for the Irish convention, Hyde's doubts that it would produce any significant agreement proved valid. Talks began on July 25, 1917, with Sir Horace Plunkett in the chair. Although delegates convened monthly through the fall and winter of 1917 and early spring of 1918, nothing was accomplished. It was the same spring in which John Redmond died and

John Dillon was chosen to succeed him as leader of the Home Rule party. How far they had come, thought Hyde, from Charles Stewart Parnell. The good news was that MacNeill was returned to his university chair in May, 1918.

Meanwhile, in the fall of 1917, Coffey's biography of Hyde was published. A brief and compact study, it reflected Coffey's own zeal for the revival of Irish and his uncritical admiration for his subject but included little discussion of complex issues and events. When the reviews appeared, Hyde read them avidly, then clipped and laid them into his personal copy. He was amused by one review that called his work as president of the Gaelic League "service to Ireland . . . [yet] perilous work, almost as dangerous to the reputation as the feeding of tigers is to life." Another over which he chortled appeared on February 22, 1918, in the pages of his old antagonist, the *Church of Ireland Gazette*. It asserted that all idealist movements in Ireland were doomed to capture and wreck by political extremists and that the Gaelic League, no longer a revivifying and reconciling force in Irish life, was now dead and damned beyond all recovery. Never had the *Gazette* considered him an idealist, never had it called the league "a revivifying and reconciling force in Irish life" during his presidency! It was good to be appreciated, he noted wryly, even in retrospect. Publication of the book brought him a flurry of letters from former acquaintances with whom he had lost touch. Lucy was happy with the sketch of herself and her family background. It was for her a small pleasure that momentarily lifted the depression from which she continued to suffer following Nuala's death.

In July 1918 the point of agreement that had escaped the Irish delegates to Lloyd George's convention emerged in Ireland's response to a conscription act that would have sent able-bodied Irishmen between eighteen and fifty to fight in France. A fire storm of public outrage united the country. Even the North joined the rest of Ireland in opposing the measure. Dillon and his party walked out of Parliament. De Valera—who had succeeded Arthur Griffith as president of Sinn Féin—charged that the British government had declared war on the Irish nation. Hyde published a three-part multiple-verse poem that drew on the satiric talent of his youth and added the sophistication of maturity. The first part, entitled "Almost Any *O* or *Mac* to Almost Any Englishman," contained such stanzas as:

> They held our homes by naked force
> By naked force they sucked our soil,

They seized our riches at their source,
They spun not, neither did they toil.
Our landmarks and our ancient signs
They rooted up with all things good;
They slew our priests before our shrines;
—We drew their water, hewed their wood.

Changing voices swiftly and dramatically, the second part, "Almost Any Englishman's Answer," makes a patronizing offer of redemption:

Now for your sake—more than ours—
We're giving you this chance
Come out against the Central Powers
And bleed with us in France.
By dying with us you will let
The whole world see we're Christians yet,
That you forgive and we forget.

Part three anticipates the response of the British press to Irish indignation:

But if you don't, and will not change
Nor answer freedom's call,
We're going to teach you something strange
You will not like at all;
What do you say to a firing squad
And a grave beneath a prison sod,
For that is what you'll get, by God.

What the British had got by their ineptitude, Hyde observed in an unpublished memoir written in 1918, was Sinn Féin. Analyzing the changing political scene from the sidelines, Hyde grudgingly admitted to himself that the nonpolitical strategy on which he had insisted probably had run its course. Yet he was not sure that things had turned out badly for the language movement. There was no longer a chance that the language would be the unifying factor in the history of modern Ireland, but at least it had rendered the movement homogeneous. In a letter to John Quinn he predicted Sinn Féin's victory in the elections of December 1918.

Hyde's political speculations were cut short in December by a sudden illness that struck the usually robust Una a day after, apparently perfectly well, she had been playing golf with him. Hyde and Lucy immediately feared the worst: that they would now lose their only surviving daughter to tuberculosis. To their relief the doctor's diagnosis was scarlatina (scarlet fever) and Hyde's next worry was that he himself could come down with the disease. An entry in Una's diary describes his morbid fear of contagion. For the family archives she made a pencil sketch of him holding a handkerchief to his nose and looking the picture of terror. Confined to the hospital, she appealed to him to send her writing materials. The next day she was amused to receive a large envelope, carefully sealed (she could not imagine why), containing paper, envelopes, and stamps, but no pencil.

Relieved that Una's illness was not life-threatening, Hyde again turned his attention to politics. To John Quinn he wrote that now would be the time for Sinn Féin to consolidate their strength if their best men (including de Valera) were not in prison. What he did not anticipate was that even without those in jail or in hiding Sinn Féin candidates who had won election to Parliament would make a bold move. First, of course, as agreed, they refused to take their seats in Parliament. Second, meeting in Dublin on January 19, 1919, they declared themselves to be members of Dáil Éireann, the parliament of the sovereign Republic of Ireland. Affirming that all rights of private party were subordinate to the public right and welfare, they set up the process through which local courts were established throughout the country. Meanwhile, also throughout the country, Volunteers who styled themselves the Irish Republican Army instituted a series of attacks on the Royal Irish Constabulary. The Dáil accepted them in their new role. The British answer, predictably, was to step up their policies of intimidation. The Anglo-Irish war, although never formally declared, had begun.

For the citizens of the new republic represented by the Dáil and defended by the IRA, things were not easy. In March, Hyde complained to Quinn that the country was under fierce oppression from a government that "rams men into jail with savage sentences for small crimes like wearing uniforms or making speeches." He estimated that the jails held nearly seven hundred political prisoners and he urged Quinn to do what he could in America to keep up the agitation for a free Ireland. By September conditions were even worse. Law and order, Hyde reported, had broken down completely; the Gaelic League had been suppressed; more people than ever were being sentenced to jail; within the jails hunger strikers protested the summary judgment, long sentences, and filthy, crowded conditions that they were forced to endure; the Black and Tans—British irregulars who took their name from uniforms

that were part Royal Irish Constabulary, part regular army—were loose
upon the land. On April 16, 1920, Hyde and Una bicycled to Mountjoy
Prison to join the demonstrators sympathetic to the hunger strikers.
Describing the scene to Lady Gregory, Hyde wrote that on their return
home he had postponed a dinner for invited guests. "How could we
eat," he asked, "and the prisoners starving?" Lady Gregory had her own
hands full, heading a committee that included Hyde, Katharine Tynan,
Stephen Gwynn, AE, W. B. Yeats, George Bernard Shaw, and other
distinguished writers and artists that were attempting to recover for Ireland the valuable paintings that had belonged to her nephew, Hugh
Lane. They had publicized the issue throughout the world. They had
appealed directly to Lloyd George.

In July 1921 a truce was declared between the two sides in the un-
declared war. An Irish delegation went to London to negotiate a treaty.
Under threat that the war would be resumed—an eventuality not acceptable to most of the Irish population, whatever their political sympathies—in December the Irish delegates reluctantly accepted the terms
offered by the British. At issue was British insistence on the retention
of the six counties of the province of Northern Ireland, separated from
the twenty-six counties by the act of Partition in 1920. The British Parliament immediately ratified the treaty. In the Dáil pro-treaty forces led
by Arthur Griffith and Michael Collins were almost evenly opposed by
anti-treaty forces led by Eamon de Valera and Cathal Brugha. So sensitive was the issue that the Dáil conducted its debate in secret sessions.
Nevertheless, almost everyone in Ireland seemed to have some information about them. Hyde wrote Quinn that, from what he had heard, he
believed that the treaty would pass by a small majority: "We seem
to have really hammered out a measure of real freedom. . . . So far as
I can see, we have got almost everything we want. . . . I think we got
the very most we could . . . without war, and war is too awful to contemplate again." In January 1922, as Hyde had predicted, the treaty
was narrowly accepted. War with England was over. The Irish Free
State, no one's idea of perfection but at least a workable entity, was
established. Bitter wrangling over the treaty continued, mainly on the
matter of Partition. Within six months another war was ravaging the
countryside, this time a civil war between Free State forces and republicans. Cathal Brugha was killed in a fire fight in July; Michael Collins
was ambushed in August; Erskine Childers, Sr., was executed in
November. Hundreds of others died before the fighting ended in the

spring of 1923; as the reprisals continued, dozens more—among them Kevin O'Higgins—died in the next several years for their real or supposed actions between 1922 and 1923.

Through Hyde's correspondence of this period runs a strong indication that he had hoped to be appointed to the new Free State Senate. That Yeats won a seat and he did not was a crushing disappointment. Pleased with the selection of Yeats, John Quinn was shocked that Hyde had not been similarly honored. He wrote to Yeats, Russell, and Lady Gregory, pressing them to do something on Hyde's behalf. In her journal for February 18, 1923, Lady Gregory noted that Hyde must have changed his mind, for he had told her that he was glad that he did not have a Senate seat. She added that he believed that he had been passed over because he had written to William Cosgrave, first president of the Executive Council of the Irish Free State, asking a reprieve for Childers.

The fact is that despite what he had said to Lady Gregory, Hyde never got over having been ignored by the Free State majority in the Dáil, as some of his writings reveal. In August 1923, for example, he published a long article entitled "The Irish Language Movement: Some Reminiscences" in England, in the *Manchester Guardian Commercial,* and in the United States, in John Devoy's *Gaelic American.* In it Hyde claimed that the Gaelic League was the spiritual father of Sinn Féin, and that Sinn Féin's progeny were the Volunteers who had forced the English into the treaty negotiations. "The Dáil," he said, "is the child of the Volunteers, and thus it descends directly from the Gaelic League, whose traditions it inherits." He praised the Dáil for establishing the importance of Irish at its first meeting and decreeing that Irish was the official language of the nation, thus affirming the status of the Gaelic tongue. Tactfully phrased to draw attention not to himself but to all the others whose efforts he related to the league, the article silently raised the all-important question: what of the man who had been one of the nine original founders of the league, who had led the organization to greatness, who had obtained for it world recognition, and who had nurtured within its protective environment the young men—some of them scarcely more than boys when they joined the league—who had become leaders of the Irish nation?

The idea for this article may well have originated in a letter from John Quinn dated January 5, 1923. The purpose of Quinn's letter had been to thank Hyde for the volume of *Connacht Half-Ranns* that Hyde had dedicated to him: "I accept the dedication with pleasure as a mark of our sincere and unbroken friendship," Quinn wrote, erasing the memory of 1911. In a postscript he declared that Hyde deserved membership in the Free State Senate because he had worked "for nationalist Ireland before the de Valeras and some of the others were out of their knickerbockers. You and I know that if it had not been for the Gaelic League there would have been no Sinn Féin. And with no Sinn Féin there would be no Free State today." Everyone after Hyde, he concluded, had built on the foundation of nationalist sentiment of "which you were the direct creator."

In March 1924, after tea with Hyde, Lady Gregory made another note in her journal: "He has kept quite out of politics and just does his university work." But in April, Lucy confided to her that Douglas was still deeply hurt at having been passed over for the Senate. Lady Gregory assured Lucy that she had missed no opportunity of pressing his claim to office. Privately she acknowledged that she was not quite sure whether Lucy had been speaking for herself or for Hyde. Lucy had always been ambivalent about Hyde's work on behalf of Irish Ireland. On the one hand, she had often expressed her disdain for the league and most of the people in it; on the other, she had been vociferous in her indignation that Hyde was not more appreciated, not better rewarded, not more justly recognized, for what he had done. Nevertheless, Lady Gregory again raised the question with Yeats, arguing that Hyde should be added to the Senate as a representative of literature, "the intellectual side"; that he deserved appointment on the basis of the achievement evident in his *Literary History* and *Love Songs of Connacht*; and that given the fact that his name was honored in France and in America, such an appointment would redound to the credit of the Senate itself. "Yeats was I think convinced," she wrote in her journal.

On July 28, 1924, John Quinn died in New York. For Hyde, whose American tour in 1905–1906 had been the product of Quinn's blazing energy and will, who kept Augustus John's sketch of Quinn on the mantlepiece in his Dublin drawing room, and whose Christmases for years had been enriched by Quinn's gifts of apples, rye, books, and cigars, the passing of this special friend marked the end of an era.

On February 4, 1925, Sir Hutcheson Poe resigned from the Free State Senate. Hyde's name was placed before the body. He was unanimously co-opted. Soon it was like old times: whenever he picked up the newspaper he looked first to see who had made sport of him in sketch or doggerel. He did not mind—he knew that all who step upon the political stage make themselves fair game to journalists and cartoonists. He was particularly amused by "The Celebrity Zoo" (1925), which promised readers a visit to a zoological garden, different from the one in Phoenix Park, "where rare and precious creatures are on view." Included were visits to "the Elite, the Dáil, the Senate and Society." One of its illustrations depicted Hyde with jet-black bushy brows, mustache, and hair, his large bony skull attached to a walrus body lying on a rock. The caption is in verse:

> Look at the lovely Walrus in its lair
> Hyde-ing its beauty under stacks of hair,
> As you may know, it never wastes a minute . . .
> Nor neither does its copy in the Sinate,
> It shows its love for Music to its flock
> By singing Gaelic on its lonely rock.

Despite his eagerness to serve in the Senate, Hyde was uncharacteristically quiet. He spoke from the floor only twice: once to pay tribute in Irish on the occasion of the death of his old friend Dr. George Sigerson; once in English on behalf of government assistance for the Celtic Congress held in Dublin in 1925. He was present and voting on ten of the eighteen motions called up in the Senate between February and June, 1925. Nevertheless, even before his term as a co-opted member expired, Hyde had decided to run for another term in the national election set for September 17, 1925. Contrary to Coffey's assertion that Hyde "made no effort to secure votes," he waged a vigorous campaign by mail and through paid advertising. He sought and received a promise of support from George Russell. He wrote to veteran Gaelic League supporters asking their help. He contributed twenty pounds toward the printing and distribution of advertisements for himself and fellow candidates that ran in major Dublin and Cork newspapers in July 1925. He paid another ten pounds toward publication of an illustrated campaign book. He spent ten pounds circularizing all Connacht members of the Dáil on the virtues of his candidacy. He sought and received the endorsement of the Cumman-na-nGaedheal party in Connacht. Senator Liam O'Briain, professor of Romance languages, University College, Galway, responded to Hyde's request for assistance in August by organizing an advertising campaign on behalf of the five Connacht candidates who lived in the province. Hyde and his fellow senators each contributed eight pounds to pay for leaflets that encouraged Connacht voters to vote for Connacht candidates. He paid for his own insertions in all the western county papers plus *The Teacher's World* and contributed to the cost of 50,000 handbills and 5,000 posters printed for distribution at churches and other places in Dublin on the Sunday before the election. His message to the voters was brief: "Douglas Hyde (An Craoibhin) respectfully asks for your votes, if you are satisfied that he has done useful work for Ireland during his lifetime . . . During the 22 years that he was President of the Gaelic League he never left a letter unanswered." P. M. O'Griffin, a staunch supporter, offered Hyde the use of his car while he was campaigning in Kerry. Two days before the election he assured Hyde that he was doing very well in Kerry and that although the Gaelic League's reputation was not strong in the country (hard evidence of its decline that shocked Hyde despite all he knew), "your reputation was made long ago."

On September 9 the *Manchester Guardian* estimated the eligible voters for the Senate election to be in excess of one-and-a-third million. It noted, however, that the republicans had boycotted the election and that of the seventy-six candidates, only Hyde and four or five others were known by name to the vast majority of voters. But the *Guardian* also reported that the liquor interests were running scared because of rumors that the government was planning a drastic cut in the number of pubs, and on September 11 the *Irish Times* published a letter from the secretary of the Irish Association for Prevention of Intemperance identifying Douglas Hyde as one of the candidates who had responded affirmatively to a questionnaire on temperance reform. Meanwhile, on September 9, the Catholic Truth Society attacked Hyde in the *Derry Journal* for having voted on June 11 for a divorce motion sponsored by Senator James Douglas. The motion was described as "an artful attempt to introduce divorce to the Saorstat [Free State]" and "a deadly blow at sacred Catholic principle." The writer warned that Catholic voters would not forget this item in Hyde's voting record.

As Hyde's supporters already had alerted him to the charge made by the Catholic Truth Society, he had tried to diminish the damage in a letter to the *Irish Independent* printed on September 9:

I hear from different sources that false statements are being circulated to the effect that I used my influence as senator in the interest of divorce. This is not true. I am utterly opposed to it. I did not join in the debate, but if I had, I would have spoken with all my power against allowing divorce into the Free State.

However, the *Independent* for September 10 repeated the charge against Hyde in a reader's letter that argued that since he had voted for the Douglas motion, "which was a recognition of the state's right to grant divorce and an attempt, which many people regarded as insidious, to allow divorce legislation to be introduced in the Dáil and Senate," he had in fact used his influence as senator in the interest of divorce. Hyde countered with a curious letter in the *Independent* of September 11 which stated that he had voted for the Douglas motion because "it was one way of rendering divorce in the Saorstat impossible. . . . There are more ways of killing a cat than by drowning." It was "not likely," he argued, "that the writer of two volumes of the *Religious Songs of Connacht* would be in favor of divorce. He is not, and never was."

Hyde's opponents had the last word in the *Independent* of September 12 in which F. O'Reilly challenged Hyde to state publicly that if elected to the Senate he would vote on matters involving the moral law "in accordance with the principles laid down by the Catholic Church." The damage was done. Fixed in the mind of the voters was the image of Hyde as a prodivorce candidate.

Election results printed in the *Irish Times* for September 21 with only three counties unreported showed that Hyde had failed to make the list of twenty-five candidates who had received over 4,000 first-preference votes. He had in fact only 1,360. By September 27 the completed count showed Hyde with a total of only 1,710 first-preference votes countrywide, finishing forty-ninth in a field of seventy-five candidates. In the *Observer* for September 27 Stephen Gwynn speculated on the reasons for Hyde's defeat. No man in Ireland seeking reelection was better known than Hyde; he was, moreover, unquestionably the most distinguished of those before the electorate. Fifteen years before, he had been the most personally popular man in the country. Inexplicably, the top first-preference vote had gone to a man no one had ever heard of, Thomas Toal, a member of the Monaghan County Council who always agreed with the bishops and whose candidacy had the support of the local bishop as well as that of Mr. Blyth, the finance minister. Gwynn dismissed the impact of Hyde's controversial vote for the Douglas motion. He attributed Hyde's defeat to popular resentment against the Gaelic League and its former president, the chief proponents of compulsory Irish in the schools. That was a new blow, after years of immense popular support for both the league and language revival.

Fortunately Hyde did have a less fickle constituency. At University College, Dublin, he had established for himself a pleasant niche with students and colleagues who enjoyed and appreciated him. From 1925 until his retirement in 1932 his university work—teaching, scholarship, and writing—became the principal focus of his efforts. It was a pleasant life, the kind Hyde might have pursued had Mahaffy and others not closed the doors of academe to him in 1891, when he had already shown his promise in these areas. From 1909 when he was appointed to University College through 1915 when he resigned from the Gaelic League, he had been too busy with league business to enjoy it. From 1915 to 1925 there had been the Rising, Nuala's death, MacNeill's imprisonment, the Anglo-Irish war, the establishment of the Free State, the civil war, and the Senate, all occupying large portions of his time and energies. And now? Not many men, he knew, had the opportunity to travel the road not taken. He accepted his good fortune gratefully.

It was well that Hyde had such a positive perspective, for at each turning, as Yeats would have explained, although one appears to stand again at the same point, the cycle is different. There had been many turnings between 1891 when Hyde completed his year of teaching at the University of New Brunswick and 1909 when he was appointed to University College, Dublin. As a result—as many of his students and colleagues understood—he was something of a maverick in the profession. By and large, Hyde's students were happy with his maverick qualities. His colleagues, however, were not always sure how they felt about either his methods or his results.

One of Hyde's students in 1917 had been Austin Clarke, the poet, novelist, and playwright. Clarke recalled Hyde's classroom:

On the first morning of our first term, he spoke of the aims and ideals of the language revival. We were all equal, all united in the Gaelic movement. There was no vulgar competition, no showing-off, no twopence-halfpenny looking down on twopence. Those plain words changed me in a few seconds. The hands of our lost despised centuries were laid on me.

Henry Comerford, who had enrolled in a first-year Irish class of over seventy students in 1924–25, remembered Hyde as a tall man, slightly stooped, casually dressed, who would enter the lecture hall with a muffler wound around his neck, "a laugh on his lips," and a "lovely manner" that employed yarns and jokes to lighten the burden of learning. One snowy winter day when, at the entrance to the university, two lines of students were pelting each other and passersby with snowballs, Comerford watched with amusement as Hyde tied a white handkerchief signifying truce to the top of his umbrella and marched between the ranks. The students "gave him a hearty cheer and safe passage." In Hyde's love for the language Comerford perceived "a driving force behind his enthusiasm . . . the desire not to let a beautiful expressive language die off the face of the earth; something like the urge a conservationist has not to let something fine and natural perish."

Impelled by that desire, Hyde joined An Seabhac (Pádraig Ó Siochfhradha) in establishing the Irish Folklore Society and founded and became first editor of *Lia Fáil* (Stone of destiny), a philological journal devoted to Irish language and literature. But the lure of teaching (or was it his old love of acting?) always brought him back to the classroom where, as his students observed, "a very happy, lively man, he would sing any verses he came on in the text that he was reading"; "squeeze up his eyes with fun and merriment, . . . trying to remember some verse, or limerick or episode . . . to strengthen the point under discussion"; "wander away from the point and make it all the more interesting by his wanderings, teaching all the while"; "lecture in tweeds and muffler from behind a walrus mustache, annotating his comments with jokes and anecdotes"; and in general "succeed in making everything look easy and interesting by his style of teaching." His last words to every class were always "Labhair i nGaeilge i gconaí le gach duine atá toilteanach Gaeilge a labhairt leat" (Always speak Irish with everyone willing to speak Irish with you). When Hyde retired, the students of his last term, sitting in what had been his lecture hall, chanted, "We want Dougie. We want Dougie" while they awaited his successor.

Some students admitted being uneasy in a classroom where there was so much laughing; could they really laugh and learn at the same time? Some colleagues could not accept the idea either. They also questioned Hyde's standards. Their goal was to teach *correct* Irish. His goal was to teach fluency—to provide students with an ability to use Irish as a living language and to postpone concern about the niceties of grammar to a later time. Myles Dillon, a distinguished Celticist in his own right, was one of Hyde's strongest admirers and also severest critics. On the one hand, "he was something of an enigma," Dillon declared, "a man of sanguine temperament . . . extremely cultivated," "a fire bringer who had a great gift of oratory and a dream that the Irish language would . . . link . . . people of different politics and background . . . an artist who set people on fire." That he was a popular teacher there was no doubt: his courses were always well enrolled. On the other hand, Dillon disapproved of Hyde's "keep them laughing" style of teaching; his selection of texts designed to introduce students to the major dialects of Irish, regardless of their intrinsic value; his "lack of strong belief" in grammatical accuracy (which Dillon condescendingly attributed to Hyde's lack of a scholarly or scientific knowledge of Irish and the fact that he had not spent a term in the Gaeltacht but taken his language from local Irish speakers in his neighborhood). Above all, Dillon was infuriated by Hyde's lack of high seriousness: "I remember being in the library working on a study related to the Irish course on a lovely sunny day, deeply immersed in the subject along with a senior colleague, when Hyde put his head in, golf clubs in hand, uttered a quotation from 'The Lotus Eaters,' slammed the door and rambled off to a game of golf."

Gerard Murphy, a colleague at University College, had a similar if less judgmental view: "Inside the college" Hyde was known,

not as the public speaker capable of inspiring enthusiasm in crowds, but as the genial professor beloved by all, though frowned upon by some of his colleagues for not exacting the severest standard of learning or accuracy from those who presented themselves for degrees. "We must not be purists," he would say, when it was pointed out that a student mixed his dialects and was careless about the rules of aspiration and eclipsis in particular and grammar in general. "Keep them amused," was his advice to a young assistant anxious to receive guidance in how to conduct his classes.

In 1929 Hyde was elected to the Council of the Royal Irish Academy and to the presidency of the Celtic Congress held at Glasgow University; in 1931 he was elected to the Irish Academy of Letters; in that same year he was chosen president of the Trinity College Historical Society (the club in which he had learned to twist the lion's tale during his undergraduate years). Twisting the lion's tale once again, Hyde replied to the "Hist":

If you cannot get anyone better, and the Society thinks that I would make a good president, I need not say I would esteem the honor highly, and will do my best to make as good a one as I can, though I know I will be a very poor successor of statesmen and men of affairs like Ashbourne, Ross, and Glenavy.

When Hyde retired from University College in 1932, former students from University College joined associates from the Gaelic League and other chapters of Hyde's life to rally support for a public acknowledgment of his service to the language. One of the first to come forward was Colm Ó Lochlainn, publisher of the Three Candles Press, who wrote to the *Irish Press* on December 21, 1933, "To those who were boys in my time his name is as a shining sword." He "must not be allowed to depart Dublin without honour," Ó Lochlainn declared, "for here surely was a prophet."

Departing Dublin meant, of course, that Hyde was returning to Ratra. For him it was not a difficult move: Roscommon, rather than

Dublin always had been home; he had never been away from it long. There were still perch to be caught in Lough Gara and grouse to shoot on the Ratra bogs. There would be time now to putter among the fruit trees and shrubs. For him the only sad news came in May from Coole of the Swans, the Seven Woods, and the Autograph Tree: his loyal friend Augusta Gregory was dead. For Lucy, however, the prospect of returning to full-time residence at Ratra after nearly a quarter of a century of city life was itself a matter for considerable dismay. It had been one thing to face the dampness and cold only during Christmas holidays ever since the move to Dublin in 1909, but she dreaded the thought of spending the entire winter there. Besides, such a move meant seeing less of Una, who had married James Sealy, and Una's two boys, now two and four years old. Nevertheless, the move was made.

Hyde's settled routine after the return to Ratra included reading, transcribing, and translating manuscripts, collecting folktales, corresponding with the French Celticists Dottin and Vendryes, and producing a steady flow of reviews and essays for *Lia Fáil,* the journal of Irish studies that he had founded at University College, Dublin, and *Béaloideas,* the journal of the Irish Folklore Society. Welcome interruptions from his scholarly projects were the visits he received from both old friends and from young men and women who sought his endorsement for civil service and teaching posts. Occasionally, during their holidays, young seminarians from Maynooth would drop by. Afternoon strolls provided opportunities for a visit to neighbors, for pleasant encounters with children whom he would encourage to speak a few words of Irish, and chats with their fathers and mothers about weather and crops. A favorite diversion was the walk to Lough Gara where he kept his fishing boat and where one of the Maxwell brothers would row him to a choice spot to fish for perch. In the fall, he shot the bogs. One day, walking across what seemed to be firm ground, he suddenly found himself standing in a small underground room—a poteen still—staring at two men who were staring back at him. Quickly recovering, the men offered him a sample of their product in an eggshell, then made him a gift of a small bottle which he secured by twisting wisps of bog cotton into a stopper.

Frequent visitors to Ratra knew that Hyde enjoyed long hours of talk on any subject but one: politics. Invariably if a political topic was introduced, Hyde changed the subject to crops or ghost stories or almost anything else that might evoke discussion. Peter Morrisroe, Hyde's chauffeur and handyman, recalled that Hyde's knowledge of saints, holy days, monastic sites, and local folklore was encyclopedic, but that creed for its own sake was a subject that was alien, even abhorrent to him. Morrisroe described Hyde as "an ecumenicist long before we heard anything about ecumenicism and when it was just a strange word hidden away in the recesses of the dictionary . . . and in this he was fifty years ahead of his time."

It was Peter Morrisroe who kept the Ford in running order and who occasionally drove Douglas to Dublin for a day's work in the manuscript room of the Royal Irish Academy or to accept an invitation from old friends or colleagues. One such event was the annual St. Patrick's Day party given by the Gaelic Language Club at University College, to which officers and past presidents were always invited. Since Agnes O'Farrelly and Hyde were often together, the students enjoyed speculating about the nature of their friendship. Had they once been sweethearts? They were fascinated also by O'Farrelly's various costumes. On one occasion she wore what she identified as the traditional Christmas dress of a Celtic woman, complete with a headdress that looked to the students like the cap of a cleaning woman. One student, startled by her appearance, uttered an oath that left everyone silent with embarrassment. Hyde and O'Farrelly, smiling broadly, walked on. It was just such behavior that had made them favorites with their students.

In June 1934 Hyde scribbled in pencil a twenty-four-page draft of a keynote speech that he had been invited to present at the International Celtic Congress to be held in Dublin from July 9 through July 12. Peter Morrisroe drove him up from Roscommon on a fine summer's day; Una (Agnes) O'Farrelly came down from her Donegal cottage to join him. Among others present were Eamon de Valera, head of the Free State government, who had pledged his backing for a permanent research institute where all the Celtic languages might be studied; and delegates from Brittany, Scotland, Wales, and the Isle of Man. Surrounded by former Gaelic League campaigners and old friends, including Maud Gonne MacBride, Hyde welcomed those attending "in the name of Ireland" and presented a program for preserving and propagating Irish that revealed that he was as committed to the language and as practical about saving it as ever. Among the recent government decisions that he spoke of approvingly was one to have Irish-speaking *gardai* in Irish-speaking areas. He argued also for subsidies for Irish-speaking families and praised Thomas O'Crohan's *Islandman* as the best book of its kind he had ever read. He also chided Robert O'Flaherty, the American filmmaker, for presenting English-speaking Aran Islanders in *Man of*

Aran and declared himself gratified by the rising interest among American academics in "everything concerned with us—history, archaeology and language." There was no doubt among those present that Douglas Hyde retired was still Douglas Hyde at work.

In the summer of 1937, Ben Greenwald, a graduate student at Columbia University, arrived in Ireland with a letter of introduction to Hyde from John Gerig, professor of Celtic studies. After meetings in Dublin with Hyde's former colleagues at University College, Robert Macalister and John MacNeill, Greenwald set out for Roscommon to spend a few days at Ratra improving his conversational Irish. Near Frenchpark Greenwald encountered Hyde on the Ballaghaderreen road, leaning over the engine of his disabled Ford. Hyde's appearance belied his seventy-seven years. Greenwald took careful note of Hyde's appearance: straight body dominated by a "massive head which George Moore had so uncharitably compared with that of a walrus. A broad face. Gray, sparkling eyes. A prominent hunk of nose. And *the* moustache! His trade-mark. Once jet, now silver, it drooped on either side of a smiling mouth." Despite the midday heat Hyde wore a baggy gray tweed shooting suit and muffler and heavy woolen golf stockings. Together they urged a response from the Ford and proceeded on to Ratra.

Throughout his stay in Frenchpark, young Greenwald worked alongside Hyde in Hyde's study, with its autographed photo of Theodore Roosevelt on the wall and Hyde's scholar's tools, books and manuscripts, closely packed on the shelves and piled on the floor. They chatted in Irish (Hyde offering frequent English translations for Greenwald's benefit) with interruptions for a Jameson's for Greenwald and poteen, "fresh from Paddy Maxwell's shebeen on an island in Lough Gara," for his host. "I used to enjoy this," Hyde said as he drank, "when the English collected the spirits tax. But now—I don't know. It seems *really* illegal—and he closed his twinkling eyes and kept on drinking." On a long twilight evening they were again sitting in the study when, something having caught Hyde's eye through the open window, he rushed out into the hall cluttered with fishing rods, guns, mackintoshes, and walking sticks, and returned with a gun. "With great aplomb," Greenwald reported, "he raised it to his shoulder and fired. 'Got him!' he shouted with glee. He had killed the rabbit that had been raiding his garden and depriving him of fresh lettuce."

Lucy Hyde, bedridden during the day, appeared at dinner. Greenwald, who had heard her referred to in Dublin as "a foreign woman," found her a "frail creature, slight and wrinkled, but ever the gracious hostess—cosmopolitan, assured, thoughtful," with a shy humor that occasionally turned acid, particularly when the conversation at the table turned to Irish. After dinner the two men strolled in the garden, Hyde speaking Irish.

Several months after his return to New York, Greenwald received the Irish manuscript of "How Swineford Got Its Name," one of the last stories Hyde had received from an eighty-year-old Mayo informant, Thomas Casey of Kiltimagh. The tale was written, Hyde explained, in nearly the same language he had learned when he was young. It was published in 1939 in Hyde's *Sgéalta Thomais Uí Chathasaigh* (Mayo stories told by Thomas Casey), the thirty-sixth volume of the Irish Texts Society series which Hyde had inaugurated in 1899. It was just one of many projects that occupied him during the years of his so-called retirement, strengthening his already distinguished place in the international scholarly community. In addition to Dottin and Vendryes, his regular correspondents included such other Celticists as Joseph Loth in France; Fred Norris Robinson, A. C. L. Brown, and Roger Sherman Loomis in the United States; and Rudolph Thurneyesen in Germany. He also kept in touch by letter with those old countrymen still alive from whom he had gathered, distilled, and preserved the folklore they held in their long memories. From an Irish immigrant to America, Eoin O'Cahill of Pentwater, Michigan, Hyde received Irish stories in a new genre, about heroes and villains of the American West whose character and deeds had been adapted from the Finn cycle of early Irish literature. Hyde kept in touch, too, with a wide circle of Irish friends, sending letters regularly to, among others, Sinéad and Eamon de Valera, Robin Flower, Alfred Perceval Graves, Eleanor Hull, Lennox Robinson, members of the family of O'Conor Don, Richard Irvine Best, Una (Agnes) O'Farrelly, the Yeats sisters, Shane Leslie, Willie Stockley, Stephen Gwynn, Walter Starkie, Jack B. Yeats, W. B. Yeats, and Oliver St. John Gogarty. To young Greenwald it seemed an enviable life.

18

The Road to Áras
an Uachtaráin

In this poor, misty month that's gone
They have, unto the Uachtarán

Appointed, in a manner very
Polite and prompt, a Secretary.

But who the Uachtarán *will be*
Is still eluding you and me.
                        Dublin Opinion
                        (December, 1937)

On November 10, 1937, Irish newspapers carried the announcement that Michael McDunphy, assistant secretary to the Executive Council of the Irish Free State, had been chosen to fill the newly created position of secretary to the president of Ireland. The first official to be appointed under the new Constitution, he would bring to this post, declared the *Irish Times,* not only the "zeal and ability" he had demonstrated in previous sensitive posts but his gift for languages, his firsthand knowledge of the Irish countryside, and his Continental contacts: personal qualities with which already he had served Ireland well. On the question of just exactly whom he would serve, Dublin journalists were more irreverent, especially as weeks of gossip and speculation failed to elicit any further announcement. The Constitution, to be sure, did not become official until December 29, the date established for

McDunphy to move to his newly appointed position. Even after that the government had 180 days—plenty of time to nominate candidates and hold an election—before it had to inaugurate a first president. But as the man chosen for the job was expected to maintain political strengths at home and foster diplomatic prospects abroad, government silence on the subject became a target of satire and a matter of curiosity and concern.

Concern increased when newspaper commentators began to speculate on the kind of office the president would occupy, given what many regarded as the vagueness of his duties and the limited extent of his discretionary powers under the new Constitution. For the most part they agreed that the man elected would be obliged to act routinely on the advice of the government. But certain functions required only that he consult the Advisory Council of State. What if he differed with the government and dominated the Advisory Council? The Constitution also obliged the president to sign bills not earlier than five or later than seven days after they had been presented to him. Could he manipulate these time limitations to the advantage of a bill he favored or the detriment of one he disapproved? What of his right to refuse to sign certain classes of bills or to refer them to the supreme court? Most important, what of his power to summon or dissolve the national parliament? Could this duty of a president be used to create a dictatorship? Many critics of the Constitution focused on this point, but some (mainly those still wary of de Valera) feared the opposite danger: that a weak and easily manipulated president might defer too much to the *taoiseach* (prime minister), allowing him too many potentially dictatorial powers.

For a people assuming full control over their destiny for the first time in almost eight hundred years, a new, untried Constitution inevitably raised questions about how fully the hard-won right to self-government was protected by a system of checks and balances. The candidate elected would do much to shape the answers. But who were the candidates— what was the field of choice?

In December 1937 *Dublin Opinion* honed its political wit on preparations for the new government, especially as these related to party alignments, personal ambitions, and popular rumor. As a seasonal variant on its usual doggerel it entertained its readers with a proposed "Christmas Celebrity Smoking Concert," featuring such program numbers as "I Know Where I'm Going" (to be sung by de Valera), followed by "The Vacant Chair" and "As I Sit Here" (by Michael McDunphy), "What are the Wild Waves Saying?" (by Thomas J. Kiernan, director of broadcasting), "If You're Irish, Come into the Parlour" (by Tomas Ó Deirg, minister for education, a returned Volunteer who had been deported after the Easter Rising), "There's Someone in the Orchard" (by the comptroller and auditor general), and "After the Thin Man," billed as "A Play produced by Candidates for the New Senate, with Mr. De Valera in the title role." The vacant presidency was targeted also in an "Imaginary Interview with the Secretary to the Uachtarán" as it might have been conducted by a *Dublin Opinion* reporter:

> "You desire to see his Excell—I mean to say, An t-Uachtarán?" said Mr. McDunphy.
> "But he hasn't been appointed yet—has he?" said I.
> "No," said Mr. McDunphy. "I'm only practising."
> "I tell you what," said I. "I'll help you to practise. . . . Let's suppose I'm a distinguished foreign visitor from, say Griqualand West. . . . Er. . . . do I get a . . . er . . . drink . . . glass of wine or anything?"
> "Well, no," said Mr. McDunphy; "at least, I don't think so. I'm nearly sure he'll be a teetotaler. . . ."

A candidate who did not drink? For readers wondering if this could be an insider tip, it raised doubts about one rumored candidacy and increased speculations about another.

> "I suppose I should just keep you going with a nice pleasant, general line of conversation until An t-Uachtarán signifies that he is ready to receive you."
> "Well," I said, "perhaps we needn't bother to rehearse that. . . . By the way, if it isn't a rude question, how do those letters come to be addressed to the Uachtarán already?"
> "I wrote them myself," said Mr. McDunphy, simply, "It's practise . . . Take this one . . . I signed it Mrs. McRafferty, Pallas, Co. Longford. It's asking An t-Uachtarán to get her second eldest a job as a postman . . . I'm replying immediately to say that the representations in her letter have received careful consideration but that An t-Uachtarán regrets that the matter must be left in the hands of the Department of Posts and Telegraphs. . . ."

Was this another tip? Had *Dublin Opinion* determined that the government choice would be a team player? If so, who were the members of the new team?

> "It'll flatter her to have what she wrote referred to as 'representations,'—and that'll keep her fairly contented."
> (. . . *A ring was heard, and Mr. McDunphy picked up the telephone.*)
> "Yes . . . Yes, Mr. De Valera . . . No, I'm afraid An t-Uachtarán cannot see you to-day . . . Perhaps if you made an appointment for to-morrow?"

Now here was news: Had that been de Valera himself telephoning McDunphy? Was the nominee not only chosen but already (unofficially, of course) at work? Some presidency watchers had been assuring others that McDunphy's appointment was evidence that, behind the scenes, a presidential candidate was in fact participating in some decisions. Was *Dublin Opinion* guessing, or did it really know something?

"That wasn't a real ring, was it?" said I.

"No," said Mr. McDunphy, "the messenger does it outside with a bicycle bell."

"Isn't it funny," I said, "that they didn't wait for the Uachtarán to appoint his own Secretary himself."

As the secretary made no reply, the "interviewer" broached the subject more directly.

"He can't be getting all the powers the newspapers were making out. Suppose he doesn't like you when he sees you? . . . Don't tell me you know who he is going to be!! . . . Or that somebody else knows?"

"I have no information," said Mr. McDunphy.

Few people in Ireland believed this statement, but it remained McDunphy's standard reply to all reporters, real or imaginary, during the next three-and-a-half months. There was also skepticism abroad. Both Franklin D. Roosevelt and Neville Chamberlain, the British prime minister, knew better than to underestimate Eamon de Valera. It would not be characteristic of him to leave such a choice to either chance or a committee of the Dáil. As for the newspapers, if Michael McDunphy could not or would not identify the president-to-be, there was no shortage of other front-page news. Guaranteed to attract readers throughout the English-speaking world was the developing melodrama of a British king willing to give up his throne for a beautiful American divorcée and suspenseful accounts of rising dictatorships in Germany and Italy. Meanwhile, while the Irish enjoyed the game of speculation, it was best for others not to try to play, for in 1937 Ireland was virtually unknown territory to foreign experts who used to get their information on Irish affairs from British information officers and had not yet tapped into their Irish equivalent. A case in point was Roosevelt's traveling emissary, Josephus Daniels, a former secretary of the navy (therefore Roosevelt's old boss), now United States ambassador to Mexico. Holidaying abroad in the summer of 1937, Daniels was asked by FDR to stop in Ireland to confer with de Valera and FDR's new minister to the Irish Free State, John Cudahy, Irish-American scion of a Milwaukee meat-packing family and nephew of the man Douglas Hyde had met in California in 1906. Convinced that 1932–1937 political and structural changes in the government of Ireland were insignificant and that, on the whole, events in Europe were remote from the concerns of the United States, Daniels dismissed de Valera in a report dated August 20 as a man so preoccupied with such strictly internal affairs as his north-south border dispute that he could not pay attention to the more immediate matter of cooperating with the United States on plans for a memorial in Cobh to men of the United States Navy who had aided British destroyers based in that port during World War I. Nor did Daniels perceive any significance in the election of a president who would have, in his opinion, "about as much power as the President of France, leaving the control of the country to the Prime Minister." The most serious consequence of this election, as far as Daniels could foresee, was that John Cudahy might have to give up his newly rented home with its handsome grounds called Phoenix Park because rumor had it that "the President will live in the house now occupied by the American Minister."

More astute and much better informed despite the short time he had been in his new post, Cudahy knew that Daniels was wrong on all points, including what he thought he had heard about the house the president of Ireland was to occupy. He continued to keep his ear to the ground and report what he heard to Roosevelt as, one by one, names of possible candidates for the presidency were discussed and dropped in Dublin pubs and drawing rooms.

By the third week of April 1938, the news was out, in Ireland and abroad: the unanimous choice of all parties and factions was Dr. Douglas Hyde. His name had come up before, in June 1937, when he had received the prestigious Gregory Medal. Reaction in Ireland was overwhelmingly favorable, a signal to Irish political leaders that they had read the mood of the country correctly. The news was also well received across the Atlantic. "Douglas Hyde Slated to Head New Irish State," proclaimed the *New York Herald Tribune*. Even in England, Douglas Hyde was regarded as a sensible choice, although most British newspapers studiously avoided treating the announcement as world news and many did not cover it at all. In Celtic areas where the progress of Ireland's struggle for independence had been watched with interest, the event received more attention.

In Ireland, private reactions mirrored public statements. For many among Hyde's still large and loyal following there was no doubt but that the choice was right. Others expressed their agreement with Hyde's vision of Ireland's future or noted his contribution to the making of modern Ireland in the past. Fifty years later, on the anniversary of Hyde's nomination and inauguration, reaction remained the same: "Who else was there?" was the question still asked. At the same time there was diversity in the opinions that contributed to the consensus. Some welcomed Hyde's candidacy as an important step toward reconciling diverse political factions. Some described it as a necessary political reality, a "sop" to the Protestant minority of the twenty-six counties in response to concern about the future of Irish Protestants under a Constitution that on the one hand assured separation of church and state and on the other mandated Catholic attitudes and values in family life and education. A number of close observers of the situation disputed as naive the public statement of the papal nuncio, that "the choosing of a Protestant President was a very clever move on the part of Mr. De Valera and should have a moderating influence on the whole country as well as please the Protestant pro-British element of Northern Ireland"; they agreed more readily with John MacVeagh, secretary of the American legation, that Hyde's nomination was a "fine gesture of good will toward the minority religious groups."

Analyzing the implications for Ireland's future, the American minister, John Cudahy, focused with greater perspicacity not on religious issues but on questions the newspapers had been raising. "In the opinion of this Legation, the nomination of Dr. Hyde is equivalent to an election," reported Cudahy, noting that the only other candidate being considered, Alderman Alfred ("Alfie") Byrne, T.D., the flamboyant lord mayor of Dublin, had withdrawn. Hyde's candidacy, Cudahy believed, reflected the conception of the office held by the framers of Ireland's new Constitution: "one of permanence, a symbol of Ireland, one of dignity and representation far removed from the tumult and hurly-burly of political strife." In the office as well as the man he saw a "curious analogy to the constitutional conception of the monarchy in England." Dismissing the idea that the Constitution offered any potential for presidential abuse, he noted that both executive and plenary powers granted in the document were "rendered impotent by subsequent enactments."

The chief critic of Hyde's nomination was Hyde himself. Irish newspapers quoted him as saying, "If my acceptance will be of any use to the country, I will gladly accept. My one objection is the fact that I am so old." Cynics suggested that this was the reason why he had been selected: an old man brought out of retirement would pose no threat to de Valera. The cover of the May 1938 issue of *Dublin Opinion* featured a bright-eyed An Craoibhín Aoibhinn in Edwardian plus fours seated on a branch labeled "Presidency." Inside, in a satiric dialogue entitled "The Special Committee Selects An Agreed President" (by-line, "As Imagined by our Grangegorman Correspondent"), name after name is brought up and objected to by one party or the other, until a Fianna Fáil representative proposes Hyde as the only name on which they are likely to agree. A member of the opposition supports the nomination, because,

"Well, for one thing, his selection would certainly dispose of the possible menace of the Uachtarán becoming a dictator. . . . I can't quite imagine the old gentleman marching into Leinster House at the head of his troops."

In a page of cartoons and quips, Hyde's age and walrus mustache (a feature of his appearance with which caricaturists had a field day) were again easy targets for the lampooners:

From all accounts, Dr. Douglas Hyde is such a quiet old gentleman that we may soon be wishing for the brave old days when we had Domhnall Ua Buachalla dashing around all over the place.

The ironic reference was to Donald Buckley, a veteran of Easter 1916 and a republican who had fought in the Four Courts in 1922, who had been appointed "chief steward" in 1932 to replace the governor-general, James MacNeill, with the understanding that, far from "dashing around all over the place," he would do nothing at all in any official capacity.

Dublin Opinion also reserved some of its swipes for the Special Committee: "After all the Hide-and-Seek, it became just Seek-and-Hyde!" There was even grudging good humor in one cartoon, depicting Hyde in toga and sandals surrounded by committee members, and captioned "The New Senator Who Took His Job Seriously."

Despite all the jibes and jokes, many observers regarded Hyde's nomination as another personal victory for de Valera. John Cudahy noted that in their conversations on the subject de Valera often had emphasized to him "the importance of language in the survival of nationalism" and had told him that while of course he could not predict the outcome of the election (a qualifier Cudahy accepted with tongue in cheek), "he would not consent to any candidate who did not speak Irish fluently and . . . insist upon the importance of the Irish language movement." De Valera was, Cudahy asserted confidently, "entirely satisfied with the selection of Dr. Hyde." Nor was this satisfaction based only on Hyde's commitment to the Irish language. In 1916 the two had differed strongly, to be sure, on how nationhood might be secured for Ireland, but de Valera never had forgotten or repudiated Hyde's vision of that nationhood, nor the extent to which his own concept of an independent, united Ireland had been molded when in 1908 as a young teacher of mathematics, he had first come under the influence of An Craoibhin and the Gaelic League.

In supporting Hyde for the office of president, de Valera honored, to be sure, his old mentor, old leader, old friend. But he also assured himself that, as together he and Hyde had shared a dream, together they might forge a reality. Others, of course, also had shared this dream—it had united advocates of physical force and cultural nationalism, coercion and persuasion, revolution and reform, throughout the nineteenth and early twentieth centuries; it had stirred alike the hearts of pro-treaty and anti-treaty Ireland. Hyde's particular importance to the astute de Valera was exactly the quality about which some members of his party complained: he owed no political debts, he carried no political obligations. The appointment of Michael McDunphy, a man well known to de Valera and trusted and respected by him, had been part of the same plan. Events of the next seven years proved to de Valera that in both choices he had been right.

A full twelve years had passed since de Valera had set the course he was following in 1938. Having abandoned his boycott of the Free State government in 1926, in 1927 he had submitted to the formality of taking the oath of allegiance to the Crown required of Free State officials and legislators and had assumed his elected seat in the Free State parliament. All but a handful of his republican colleagues had joined him in this new tactic, designed to erode if not erase provisions of the Treaty of 1921 and the subsequent Irish Free State (Constitution) Act of 1922 that they found most repugnant. In their new role of political party they had assumed a new and apt name: Fianna Fáil, "soldiers of destiny." By 1932 they had secured a majority in the Dáil, and Eamon de Valera was named president of the executive Council of the Irish Free State government.

Immediately upon assuming office, de Valera predictably had taken legislative steps to abolish the oath of allegiance to the Crown and had notified Westminster that henceforth Ireland would pay no further annuities against loans dating from the Land Purchase Acts of the late nineteenth and early twentieth century. Seven months later, having forced the retirement of the governor general, James MacNeill, he virtually eliminated the position MacNeill had held by retitling it "chief steward" and installing in it Donald Buckley (Domhnall Ua Buachalla), who neither moved into the Viceregal Lodge in which other governors general had continued the Crown's symbolic presence in Ireland nor engaged in any other official act.

The British did not take issue with de Valera over his abolition of the oath or even his revision of the position of the governor general, but they did retaliate for nonpayment of the annuities by placing special duties on Irish imports into Britain. De Valera countered with a protective tariff system of his own, designed to foster the growth of new industries in the Free State as well as to reduce Irish dependence on goods of English manufacture. The fact that the British found it necessary, in 1935, to scale down the "economic war," as the tax and tariff battle was called, was both a political and public relations victory for de Valera. In England it had been popularly believed that the Irish would not be able to hold out against British economic sanctions. In Ireland, however, there were many who feared that de Valera's policies might again give the British an excuse for military intervention. De Valera himself, having had dismissed as "hypothetical" (Cudahy took this answer to mean yes) his question of whether the British would respond with force if the twenty-six counties seceded, otherwise moved cautiously during his first four years in office. Then in 1936 he and his supporters once again perceived that "England's disadvantage was Ireland's opportunity." A four-man commission was established to study the Free State Constitution. In 1937—with the British economy still convalescent following the Great Depression, the British public upset over the abdication crisis, and British ministers warily watching the Spanish civil war and the spread of fascism in Europe—de Valera introduced to the Dáil proposals for a new constitution that was, in effect, a declaration of independence.

Approved by the *oireachtas* on June 14, 1937, and ratified by a plebescite held seventeen days later, on July 1, 1937 (the same day as the general election in which de Valera won, as everyone had expected, an overwhelming victory), the new Constitution became the legal instrument of Irish government as of December 29, 1937. In addition to establishing the position of president for which Hyde had been nominated, the bilingual English-and-Irish text presented to the people declared Ireland (not the Irish Free State, a term that was silently abandoned) a "sovereign, independent and democratic state" hence-forth to be known as Éire. It applied this name, moreover, to all Ireland, not simply to the twenty-six counties; it dropped all references to governor general or Crown; it established a bicameral legislature consisting of a Dáil, or Chamber of Deputies, presided over by a *taoiseach,* or prime minister, plus a Seanad, or Senate; and it firmly established Irish as the "first official language" of Ireland, even though most of its citizens were fluent only in its second. The purpose of this clause was closely linked to the goals of the Gaelic League: to emphasize the history and heritage that linked the people of Ireland, distinguishing them from the English whose stamp, despite policies of deanglicization, they still bore, and thus emphasize their nationhood. Although a small and committed minority hailed it on the one hand as evidence that Ireland would become truly Irish-speaking (as today's Israel is truly Hebrew-speaking) and a small and fearful minority on the other hand vowed to fight such a movement, most Irish people understood and observed the clause as a symbolic rather than a practical imperative.

In the elections that followed, de Valera's party easily controlled the Dáil; the foregone conclusion was that he would serve as Ireland's first *taoiseach,* a fact regarded as positive by most political observers because it assured a smooth transition of government operations. Again Westminster offered no challenge, no doubt because it was clear that Ireland would not for the moment press its claim to the six counties. For many in England references to "external association" in the new Constitution were assumed to mean that Ireland intended to remain within the British Commonwealth. The truth was that any objection might have placed Neville Chamberlain (not a forceful leader or political savant in anyone's estimation) on shaky ground, for under a 1931 statute every British dominion had the right to alter its constitution, and England already had recognized Northern Ireland's exercise of this right, thereby accepting the statute as applicable to both Northern Ireland and the Irish Free State. In any case, of greater concern to Britain was the continuing economic war and its consequences.

Throughout the fall and winter of 1937–1938, while Dublin speculated on the composition of its new government, in dispatches and personal letters Roosevelt, his ministers, and his advisers debated how they should respond to Irish requests for American mediation of economic negotiations between Britain and Ireland. In December, as rumors of a stalemate increased, John Cudahy, a strong advocate of mediation, welcomed the news that Joseph P. Kennedy probably would succeed

Judge Robert W. Bingham as American ambassador to London. "At this time of the pending trade treaty his selection . . . is nothing less than an inspiration," Cudahy wrote to Roosevelt, describing Kennedy as one of few Americans "not susceptible to the subtle brand of British flattery." A month later, talks having been suspended, Cudahy's letters became more insistent: Roosevelt himself should intercede, he declared, warning that "if [this] opportunity of settling the Anglo-Irish hostility of seven centuries is lost, no other real opportunity will be presented during this generation." For the United States the advantage of a settlement, Cudahy argued, would be its harmonizing effect on American public opinion. The advantage for Britain would be the measure of security a friendly Ireland would afford, for no British defense scheme could ignore the Irish coast. The issue on which discussions were deadlocked was, of course, Partition. De Valera's position, Cudahy explained, was clear and unequivocal: He was not opposed to the North retaining its own parliament in Belfast provided it sent representatives to a general Irish parliament in Dublin. Without some British initiative in this matter, there would be no tolerance of British military forces on Irish soil. Cudahy's advice to Roosevelt was that he express interest in a settlement to Sir Ronald Lindsay, British ambassador to the United States, and urge Chamberlain to persuade Lord Craigavon, the Ulster party leader, that England's defense was at stake.

The extent to which developments in Ireland were being watched carefully in Washington is evident from the fact that, despite the warm and friendly tone of Roosevelt's reply to Cudahy, the text of his letter was in fact prepared by the United States secretary of state, Cordell Hull. While agreeing that any improvement in Anglo-Irish relations would be a gain "from every point of view," this letter questioned whether United States intervention would be wise or would accomplish the effect "we had in mind." It proposed instead that England might be "led voluntarily" to the kind of action Cudahy advocated, perhaps after reviewing its own national defense needs. In any case, progress toward a solution would be "healthier" if slower and if based on England's own self-interest rather than on representations from a "third power." Meanwhile, encouraged by Cudahy, de Valera himself had approached Roosevelt, in language strongly reminiscent of Cudahy's own appeals:

Another great opportunity for finally ending the quarrel of centuries between Ireland and Britain presents itself. The one remaining obstacle to be overcome is that of the partition of Ireland. . . . Reconciliation would affect every country where the two races dwell together, knitting their national strength and presenting to the world a block of democratic peoples interested in the preservation of Peace. . . . If present negotiations fail, relations will be worsened.

Delivery of this message asking Roosevelt to use his personal influence to avoid a breakdown was entrusted not to diplomatic channels but to an old friend and former comrade-in-arms, Frank Gallagher, deputy director of Radio Éireann, the man whom de Valera had chosen to be first editor of his republican daily newspaper, the *Irish Press*. Confronted at home with an isolationist lobby strongly supported in Congress and a State Department that had warned against too close association with Chamberlain, Roosevelt reaffirmed his inability to act either officially or through diplomatic channels but promised that through Kennedy, his newly appointed ambassador to Great Britain, he would send a personal message to Chamberlain, urging reconciliation. Again, the respectful and sympathetic tone of Roosevelt's letter—"My dear President De Valera," he wrote, using the Irish leader's official title of "president of the Executive Council of the Irish Free State," and concluding with "As an old friend, I send you my warm regards"—contrasted with the evasiveness of his message.

It was no secret, of course, that in the spring of 1938 a threatened Britain would not have been able to stand alone against German forces, nor was Chamberlain able to negotiate from strength with Mussolini. A week after Roosevelt replied to de Valera, Cudahy sent home his report that Mussolini's "violent dislike" of Sir Anthony Eden, "common knowledge in diplomatic circles," was the story behind press reports of a British cabinet crisis. A condition Mussolini had placed on negotiations, wrote Cudahy, was that Eden be removed as foreign secretary. Rumor had it that in any case Eden was about to resign, for Chamberlain had directed foreign affairs ever since becoming prime minister, and Eden, who had had a free rein under Baldwin, had been placed in a difficult position. Their differences of opinion with regard to Mussolini were symptomatic: Insisting that Great Britain could not risk war, Chamberlain was willing to take Mussolini's good faith at face value. Pointing to previously breached agreements, Eden wanted to hold out for assurances. Cudahy agreed with Churchill, that what Chamberlain was preparing was "a meeting with Mussolini on his [Mussolini's] own terms." Such a policy, in his opinion, could be "fatal in encouraging the dangerous adventures of both Mussolini and Hitler." Awareness of this situation was reflected in the communications exchanged by Roosevelt, Cudahy, and de Valera on the subject of British-Irish eco-

nomic negotiations. The difference was that Cudahy and de Valera
shared a conviction that desperate need of American help would force
Britain to respond to United States pressure for an Anglo-Irish settlement; Roosevelt, warned by his State Department that the Chamberlain
government could fall at any time and unwilling, in any case, to be
forced into a war in Europe if direct involvement could be avoided,
would not accept the bargain implicit in such pressure.

Suddenly, in April 1938—the same month in which Hyde was nominated for the presidency—the economic war ended. The compromise
agreement drew mixed reactions among political observers. Some hailed
it as another political victory for de Valera: he had, they said, persuaded the British to reduce punitive tariffs against Irish products without capitulating on the matter of the annuities; he also had forced
them to relinquish the three ports within the twenty-six counties—
Cobh, Berehaven, and Lough Swilly— still held under the Treaty of
1921. Others hailed it as a political victory for Chamberlain: *he,* they
said, had refused to reduce British tariffs on Irish products until Ireland had agreed to pay, as final settlement against the annuities, the sum
of ten million pounds. Thus he had forced Ireland to acknowledge the
legitimacy of a debt it had sought to erase. Besides, they maintained,
the reduction of import duties had been mutual: Ireland, too, now
had to abandon its protective tariffs, to the detriment of its developing industies. As for Partition, the border remained; the Irish had won
nothing.

It was on the matter of the tariff that, in 1938, de Valera was vulnerable at home. Quipped the May issue of *Dublin Opinion*:

We didn't want Dev to bring home the bacon.
We wanted him to send out the beef.

So the battery of cameras which met Mr. De Valera
in London fired the last shot in the Economic War.

Mr. De Valera went over on the "Munster"
for the signing of the Agreement. Irreconcileable
critics will say that he went back on the Ulster.

And now all we have to do is to sit back and
listen to the disagreement about the Agreement.

A captioned cartoon depicting an angry golfer tearing up the green
succinctly revealed the source of Irish dissatisfaction: "Easy on there,
easy on! Even if you *are* a businessman hit by the Trade Agreement!"
The public paid less attention to Britain's promise to withdraw from

the Irish ports, a clause that shortly was to have greater consequences for the young nation about to take its final major step toward full independence.

Hyde's correspondence of 1932–1938 indicates that he was carefully watching political and economic developments. During this period he corresponded frequently with his old friend Sinéad de Valera who had played the Fairy to his Tinker in 1901, but it does not appear (although letters may have been lost or destroyed) that he had extensive correspondence with de Valera himself. Circumstantial evidence and other documentation, however, leave little doubt that the two men were regularly in touch and had in fact collaborated on the scenario that developed.

There were, for example, Hyde's two major publications in 1937. After having concentrated for ten years on scholarly editing, folklore, literary, historical, and linguistic studies, and translating from the Irish, suddenly he dusted off, reviewed, revised, and saw through the press *Mo Thuras go h-Americe* (My voyage to America), his account of his 1905–1906 lecture tour, and *Mise agus An Connradh* (Myself and the league), his diary of his years as president of the Gaelic League. Published in 1937 (therefore prepared for publication beginning at least a year or two earlier), neither of these books has the objectivity of a backward look; both present Hyde as a strong, wise, and effective leader and ambassador. Hyde registered no surprise, made no statements, and issued no disclaimers when in June 1937 newspapers listed his name among those of possible candidates for the presidency. Although he readily agreed in 1938 to serve in the Senate (by March 31 the fact of his co-option was well established), he did not campaign for election but was returned to the Dáil through an avenue that did not involve him in a political contest—a wise move requiring cooperation and advance planning for a potential presidential candidate. Although received but "ten minutes ago," the telegram from de Valera offering this appointment had rated only offhand reference in a letter to Horace Reynolds interrupted by its arrival; he had taken time, he said, to wire his affirmative reply. Hyde's suggestion that he might be "too old" for public office had come not from the private Hyde but from the public figure, who was aware that the question would be raised and that the best way to head off criticism was to bring it up himself. In 1938 Diarmid Coffey published *Douglas Hyde: President of Ireland* (a revision of his *Douglas Hyde: An Craoibhín Aoibhinn,* published in 1917); like *Mo Thuras go h-Americe* and *Mise agus An Connradh,* it had to have been in preparation before Hyde's nomination. All three of these books are of the kind produced to rouse public interest in a political figure or otherwise further public relations.

During 1937–1938 the people, such as Reynolds, with whom Hyde frequently communicated were for the most part those with whom he had carried on a voluminous correspondence for years: friends, former associates from his many and varied careers, scholars and writers in Ireland and abroad, former students. As always, he answered his mail promptly and was especially courteous and helpful to correspondents with whom he was not acquainted. Although Hyde now resided full-time in Frenchpark rather than dividing his time between Frenchpark and Dublin, the pattern of his life was business-as-usual. No one who knew him regarded him as slowing down or otherwise diminishing his daily activities, physical or mental. Yet no one foresaw that, having retired from the university, he was about to embark on a new and very different career. Even Lucy apparently had no idea of what was in store until, by letter and telegram, congratulatory messages began to pour into the post-office-cum-shop in the center of Frenchpark village, to be carried by bicycle the three miles out the Ballaghaderreen road to Ratra. Waiting for the news to break, conferring frequently with Lucy's physician, Dr. Kilgallen of Boyle, certainly Hyde must have wondered what Lucy's reaction would be. Often and bitterly she had expressed her feeling that he had given so much of himself to an ungrateful Irish people. Now that he was about to receive a signal honor, a signal opportunity to represent Irish Ireland on the world stage, beyond anything he could have enjoyed (or in fact did enjoy) as poet, playwright, teacher, scholar, and leader of a great national movement, would she be pleased?

Included in the first flood of congratulations that arrived in response to news of Hyde's nomination was a poem in Irish dated April 28, 1938, from Hyde's old Gaelic League friend "Torna" (Tadhg Ó Donnchadha), who had edited *Iris Leabhar na Gaedhildge* (The Gaelic journal) from 1902 to 1909 and who frequently commemorated events important to Irish Ireland in verse. The same post brought a letter from General Eoin O'Duffy, a controversial figure who had sided with the pro-treaty forces in 1921 and been rewarded with the post of commissioner of An Garda Síochána (Irish national police) in 1922. Dismissed by de Valera in 1933, he had then become head of the National Guard, or Blueshirts, a political-military organization that adopted a blue flag and fascist-style salute. When it was banned by the government, it had gone through several name changes but retained the same identifying characteristics, while O'Duffy had joined the new political party, Fine

Gael. In 1936 he had organized an Irish brigade to fight under General Franco in the Spanish civil war, despite the Irish government's policy of neutrality.

Having been quiet for about a year, in 1938 O'Duffy obviously was seeking a new public role. "Leader of the Irish Brigade to Spain, I greet you," his letter began. Then reminding Hyde of the position he had held in the Garda Síochána, he outlined the efforts he had made on behalf of the language in the new police force and noted the zest with which, in his youth, he had competed in *feiseanna* throughout the country. In his native county Monaghan, he had served as president of the local branch of the Gaelic League; in the Volunteers he had held every rank, from private to chief of staff. Hyde discouraged him, satisfied that with de Valera and the Fianna Fáil in control, there was little chance for O'Duffy to find a new perch from which to launch himself in a new enterprise.

Although almost surely the most flamboyant, O'Duffy was by no means the only favor seeker to use Hyde's nomination as an opportunity to promote himself. As *Dublin Opinion* had predicted, letters came not only from political hopefuls and candidates for civil service posts but from their mothers. Other letter writers sought Hyde's intercession in a variety of personal situations, some involving the government and some not. These were the kinds of letters that for hundreds of years tenants had addressed to the Big House landlord or to the resident heir to a title or to the M. P. or to the Crown itself. They reflected the continuing uncertainty among de Valera's "plain people of Ireland" about the exact nature of their twentieth-century nation and its leaders. To some observers, this uncertainty suggested a national ambivalence about relinquishing all links with royalty and depending entirely on elected officials.

Thanking well-wishing petitioners for their expressions of support, Hyde's letters apologized for his inability to influence government appointments for their benefit, circumvent the legal process on their behalf, settle their disputes with their neighbors, support their pension appeals, cut the red tape of which they complained, or otherwise assist them in bypassing the bureaucracy. A few of the people of Frenchpark were chagrined to discover that Hyde's election would not bring a bonanza to the area, nor even improve employment prospects for local people.

The election was held, but no one doubted the outcome. At 11:20 A.M. on May 4, 1938, in a simple ceremony conducted in Irish in the boardroom of the Department of Agriculture, Government Buildings, Hyde was formally declared elected to the office of the Presidency of Ireland. From then until his inauguration, Hyde's waking hours were filled with conferences, briefing sessions, planning sessions, introductions, and consultations, all in preparation for the day that he would take office. By his side each day were the people assigned to assist, advise, and guide him, a team carefully chosen to meet specific qualifications on which he and de Valera had agreed.

Early in May 1938, shortly after the election ceremony, the president's team, as they came to think of themselves, met in Roscommon. First Lieutenant Basil Peterson of the Irish air corps and Captain Eamon de Buitléar of the Defense Command motored to Frenchpark in an army car to meet their seventy-seven-year-old chief. Their assignment was to serve as Hyde's military aides. With Michael McDunphy, who had accompanied them, they were to develop and brief him on the protocol of his and the country's new office. As *taoiseach,* de Valera headed the government, a political entity. On Hyde, his aides and advisers, lay responsibility for determining and establishing the image of the new nation that they would soon be called upon to project officially before the other nations of the world. The rhetoric of Irish nationhood demanded that it be regarded as an old Ireland restored to its proper place—a nation once again—but the sovereign state of Ireland in 1938 bore little political resemblance to the aristocratic order of high kings, provincial kings, and local chieftains that had ruled the land and its people from ca. 600 B.C. through the twelfth century. Ceremony and precedent were the materials with which Hyde and his aides were to regenerate the old and give patina to the new.

Introduced by McDunphy, Hyde greeted Peterson and de Buitléar in Irish at the door of Ratra. Perceiving Peterson's discomfort, he quickly switched to English, tactfully noting as he led the three men on a brief tour of the grounds, that his wife had no Irish. Outdoors he chatted amiably about shrubs and flowers, about how little or much he had paid many years ago for seedlings that were now mature trees— about anything but the business at hand, to give the young officers time to get accustomed to his manner and personality and to recover from the nervousness they unsuccessfully tried to hide on this first meeting. Although Hyde's informality did put Peterson at ease, in 1938 army uniform—boots, breeches, and green tunic with high choke collar—he continued to perspire in the unseasonably warm May sunshine. It was again with relief, therefore, that he welcomed Hyde's suggestion that they return to the coolness of the house to meet Mrs. Hyde—a "frail woman with a waspish tongue" who seemed to Peterson to be "in no way pleased that her husband had been plucked out of his quiet retirement" to become president of Ireland. Over sherry, the talk turned to military procedures, especially those used on ceremonial occasions in which, as president, Hyde would be involved. The small party then went in to lunch. "We never saw Mrs. Hyde again," Peterson declared in a reminiscence published forty-two years later. "She refused to leave home and go to the Park. Some six months later she died."

Of the two aides assigned to Hyde in 1938, Eamon de Buitléar was the one who was to remain close to him and his family throughout Hyde's presidential career and indeed to the end of his life. A member of the Irish Republican Army before 1922, de Buitléar had served continuously in the Free State Army since its establishment. He had joined the Gaelic League at the age of sixteen; in league classes he had quickly demonstrated an affinity for the Irish language, which his instructor encouraged by introducing him to phonetics. Papers recommending his appointment to the staff of the new president described him as fluent in both written and spoken Irish, thus well able to carry out the bilingual responsibilities of his assignment. Hyde had stipulated that to the extent that it was consistent with obtaining qualified men and women, those appointed to his staff should be Irish-speaking. Taller than Hyde, slim and well-built, he was a handsome, smart-looking officer with high cheekbones and a thin, shapely nose. His attractive young wife, Máire, was also an Irish speaker and former member of the Gaelic League. Irish was the language they spoke at home, to each other and their young children.

Basil Peterson's knowledge of Irish was, by contrast, minimal, but as he quickly recognized, his appointment was essential for another reason: he was a Protestant. De Buitléar's Roman Catholic religion barred him from accompanying Hyde to the ten o'clock inauguration-day Church of Ireland worship service at St. Patrick's Cathedral scheduled to precede the oath-taking ceremony in St. Patrick's Hall, Dublin Castle. This task was therefore assigned to Peterson, who also was asked (with the logic of the military—his duties in the air corps had been to plot aircraft traffic lanes) to plan the route of the processions that would bring Hyde through the Phoenix Park gates, across the Liffey, and in and out the narrow, twisting streets of the oldest part of Dublin to the cathedral. The starting point was to be the Viceregal Lodge, henceforth to be known as Áras an Uachtaráin, or the President's Mansion.

(Josephus Daniels had been wrong about which residence in Phoenix Park had been chosen. Far from having to give up his own newly rented home, formerly the home of the chief secretary, John Cudahy became Hyde's nearest Park neighbor.)

Peterson accepted his assignment without a word, but with many misgivings. Only once before in his life had he ever been to the historic cathedral where in the eighteenth century Jonathan Swift, now buried within its walls, had been dean. He had little familiarity with the congested areas around it beyond the fact that the valley of the Poddle (the river that once flowed there had been reduced years before to a polluted underground trickle) was home to entire families crammed into squat, one-story houses, cramped flats above or behind small shops and public houses, partitioned living quarters in once-gracious three-story residences, and newer flats built by the Iveagh Trust. In the course of a day's business thousands more crowded into streets that must have escaped the notice of the eighteenth-century Wide Streets Commission, for scarcely wider than the medieval alleys and lanes from which they had developed, they paralleled, diverged, crossed, and rejoined one another without discernible logic, still following original routes traceable on old maps. Not only was he obliged to find his way through this maze to St. Patrick's Cathedral, Peterson learned, sitting in Hyde's home in Ratra, but when the worship service ended it became his responsibility to establish a smooth progression for the procession to nearby Dublin Castle, for the formal inauguration ceremony, then back to Áras an Uachtaráin for picture taking. Later he had to make another journey through the same streets to return with Hyde to Dublin Castle where the evening reception was to be held. And all this on a Saturday! There was no use trying to explain that air-traffic control was different from land-traffic control. No one in the army would listen. In addition to maneuvering through cars and crowds, he was to draw up plans that would not conflict with whatever security measures the Garda adopted for the occasion. With glazed eyes and moist forehead he sat in Hyde's drawing room in Ratra, looking out on the fields beyond, trying to visualize the maze around St. Patrick's Cathedral.

In the weeks following their first meeting at Ratra, Hyde listened closely to Peterson and de Buitléar as they briefed him on inauguration-day arrangements and instructed him in those matters of military ceremony in which he would take part. Beginning with his inauguration, such rituals as the salute to the flag and inspection of the honor guard would be, they reminded him, a regular feature of his official public appearances. He was no stranger to pomp, of course. Son of a Church of Ireland clergyman who often had assisted at services conducted by his father in the little church in Frenchpark, member of Trinity College's venerable "Hist," and frequent participant for nearly a quarter of a century in academic processions and other solemn rituals of university life, the seventy-seven-year-old Hyde was an experienced actor on the world's stage. Drama, he knew, was an integral part of life. It brought people together; it underscored values; it celebrated the fulfillment of dreams.

On the morning of Saturday, June 25, Hyde was ready when Peterson arrived to escort him. It was a bright day, warm but not sultry, as he stepped out the door with his daughter, Una Sealy, on his arm. She was lovely as always, with her round face and bright eyes so like his own. He was formally dressed, of course, with the dignity required by the occasion; but with his old sense of theater, admiring Peterson's new sky-blue Irish air corps dress uniform with its trimmings of scarlet and gold, its gold wings, its black cloak with scarlet lining, and its Austrian cap, he could not help but think what a fine figure he himself would cut if in such a costume he could walk into the morning's history. As their limousine moved along the route to St. Patrick's Cathedral, Peterson kept a careful eye on map and watch while Hyde and his daughter chatted, for the complicated plan required that Mrs. Sealy be delivered to a side door a quarter of an hour before Dr. Hyde arrived at the main entrance. As the car slowed near the back of the cathedral, a *garda* assigned to security duty eyed it suspiciously. With the seconds ticking, Peterson tried to explain quickly the arrangements that had been made and the necessity for adhering to them, but not having been informed of any exceptions to orders, the *garda* refused to allow the car to stop at the curb to allow Una to dismount. "For him," Peterson realized, "we were in the wrong place at the wrong time," nor could he be cajoled or bullied. Just as Peterson's watch signaled that if he did not escort Mrs. Sealy to her entrance within moments and drive around the cathedral to deliver Hyde to the main door, carefully coordinated plans would go awry, an inspector appeared, "dealt with the situation, whisked Mrs. Sealy away," and allowed the presidential car to proceed, to his great relief.

An ancient Danish structure rebuilt by the Normans in 1191 and repaired by the English between 1618 and 1671, St. Patrick's Cathedral again had been in a state of collapse when the Guinness family had undertaken a restoration in the mid-nineteenth century. At the main door of the cathedral, Hyde and Peterson were greeted by Dr. Gregg, Jonathan Swift's twentieth-century successor, who was also the Church of Ireland archbishop of Dublin. As they entered they could see that nave and transept were filled even though (as Peterson noted) certain "official representation [i.e., Catholic members of the government] was missing." Discreetly watching them, unnoticed by others, was a small boy, Liam Proud, who had stolen quietly from his seat in a front pew to peek through the door when he heard the jingling bridles of Hyde's cavalry escort approaching. Returning to his seat, he watched the procession form and make its way slowly down the center aisle to the strains of "Be Thou My Vision, O Lord of My Heart," performed by the cathedral's organist and choir. First came the archbishop, gloriously accoutred, followed by Hyde, holding his top hat over his chest. But when the archbishop stopped abruptly, Hyde, who had been looking to right and left out of the corners of his eyes with a small smile playing about his mouth, had continued forward, to young Liam's amusement: "I distinctly saw [the hat] . . . momentarily telescope under the impact. It was almost too much for a small boy, but I managed to divert my mirth into a fit of coughing."

Few others noticed the momentary shuffle, and the procession moved on without further incident to the front of the long, gray church. There the president-elect was seated in the pew formerly reserved for the viceroy, the other dignitaries around him. All through the cathedral were familiar faces. The simple worship service, much of it conducted in Irish, was for Basil Peterson "an emotional occasion." It "made me feel," he later avowed, "that at last the Irish had come into their own." First the congregation joined in the Lord's Prayer; it was followed by Psalm 121, with its antiphony, "Christ be with me, Christ within me," and its familiar text, "I will lift up mine eyes. . . ." After the lesson (Matthew 5:1–12) the congregation joined the choir in singing the Te Deum Laudamus. Then came the creed, prayers for Ireland, prayers for the president of Ireland and Christian citizenship, and finally the closing prayer, "God be in my head, and in my understanding." For Hyde, too, it was an emotional occasion, as words and music evoked echoes of the small church in Frenchpark in which, as a child, he used to listen to the familiar voice of his father speaking in an unfamiliar tone reserved for public occasions; the larger church in Mohill, where his grandfather had conducted Sunday service; the different churches of Dublin that he used to attend during his Trinity years. Like distant music, these other voices murmured in his memory. Past merged with present and present returned to dominate the past as the archbishop pronounced the benediction and the procession re-formed: first the choir moved slowly and solemnly down the aisle, followed by Hyde accompanied by Peterson, then the clergy, as the congregation stood respectfully silent, commemorating this poignant, penultimate moment of Ireland's history. Peterson later recalled that there was another second of confusion as the choir turned left and he and Hyde began to follow, no one having instructed them to do otherwise. "Suddenly I felt a jab in my back, and a voice hissed 'Straight on, straight on.' I redirected Dr. Hyde and finally we again reached the main door where the assembled clergy bade us farewell." Outside, a crowd of Dubliners— "outspoken," in Peterson's recollection, with opinions of his colorful uniform that were "less than kind"—had gathered to ogle, to cheer, to witness, to report, to remember for children and grandchildren, what had happened and who had passed, "so close, I could almost reach out and touch him," as Hyde, smiling and nodding, walked along a colonnade of saluting *gardaí* to his waiting car.

Accompanied by its cavalry escort, the motorcade moved slowly to Dublin Castle, formerly the fortified seat of British authority in Ireland. A formidable structure begun by the Normans, it had been modified during the reign of George III. Through its doors until 1922 viceregal lords and attendant bureaucrats had admitted only Ascendancy Irish, loyal to the Crown, to participate in the pomp and pageantry symbolic of their surrogate power. A few short blocks away stood that other British stronghold in Dublin, Hyde's alma mater, Trinity College. A quarter century before, he had lampooned both castle and university in his satirical play *The Bursting of the Bubble*. As a boy Sean O'Casey had watched processions enter and leave Dublin Castle's massive gates. Now other children mingled in crowds gathered to stare at diplomatic representatives from the countries of the world who had come to pay their respects to an Irish head of state. If they were fortunate, they caught a glimpse of the president-elect himself, the grandfatherly man with the walrus mustache and the twinkling eyes whom the newspapers called "Dr. Douglas Hyde," but who was known affectionately to generations of University College students as "Dougie" and to Irish-speaking circles as "An Craoibhín."

At precisely 12:45 P.M., according to a United States State Department report filed by John MacVeagh, the car carrying Hyde and his two aides entered the Upper Castle Yard, which was the oldest part of the structure and, in the medieval plan, corresponded with the court of the original castle. Not much more than a quarter century before, among those passing through this same yard had been the British civil servants who used to cut from the daily papers the blue-penciled items about Hyde and his Gaelic League that they pasted into the large scrapbooks in which they kept track of the activities of persons and organizations considered a threat to British law and order in Ireland. On this serene and bright June day, an honor guard of Irish infantrymen snapped to attention before the man about to become the symbol of Irish law and order in Ireland, their own commander in chief. Escorted by his aides, Hyde moved into St. Patrick's Hall, cleaned and redecorated in haste for the occasion by employees of the Office of Public Works. Ancient banners of the knights of St. Patrick hung from the walls; ladies' frocks and hats blossomed like summer flowers among the grays and blacks of formal coats and trousers. Still resplendent in his blue uniform trimmed in gold and scarlet, which he obviously enjoyed wearing, Peterson remarked how "the place shone with colour." "The only drab people there," he remarked, "were the politicians and our President-to-be."

Scarcely a half century had passed since George Moore, brother of Hyde's friend Maurice, had described St. Patrick's Hall in his own satiric passages directed against Dublin Castle and its British inhabitants in a novel called *A Drama in Muslin*. Now Moore was five years in his grave; thirty-six years had passed since Hyde's *An Tincéar agus an tSidheóg* had been performed in Moore's garden; a quarter century since—despairing that either the Irish Literary Renaissance or the Gaelic Revival could achieve its goals—Moore had lampooned their leaders as well, including Hyde, in *Hail and Farewell*. Now, joined by Chief Justice Sullivan, Hyde and his aides moved through the hall toward a platform where Eamon de Valera stood with his ministers. Above in a small gallery the No. 1 Army band stood ready to play not "God Save the King" but "A Soldier's Song," now the national anthem but formerly the marching tune of the Irish Volunteers, as veterans among the crowd were quick to remember. Peadar Kearney, another member of the Gaelic League, had written the words in 1907; Patrick Heeney had put them to music; Bulmer Hobson, a founding member of the Volunteers, had published it in his Irish Republican Brotherhood newspaper, *Irish Freedom*. Like Hyde and MacNeill, Hobson had opposed the Rising in which de Valera and Sean T. O'Kelly had fought. Hobson and O'Kelly also were in the hall, as Hyde, among a crowd of well-wishers, continued toward the platform.

From his vantage point in the block of seats reserved for diplomatic representatives to Éire, John MacVeagh, as secretary of the American legation, carefully noted details for his June 27 report to Washington, to which he added his own sometimes inaccurate observations. Apparently unaware, for example, that the man given a prominent seat on the platform was not, as he thought, "the last Governor-General of the Irish Free State," but Donald Buckley, the chief steward with whom de Valera had replaced, in person and in title, James MacNeill in 1932, MacVeagh joined his diplomatic colleagues in perceiving Buckley's presence as a gesture of goodwill on which they later commented favorably. In fact, at the time, not only was James MacNeill in London where he died in December 1938, but (a detail the American failed to note) there was no British representative among the diplomats with whom MacVeagh was seated.

The ceremony began with a fanfare of trumpets to announce the arrival of the president-elect; Hyde then took his seat with de Valera on his left and the chief justice on his right. On a table before Hyde lay the Declaration set forth in the Constitution. He leaned forward and signed the document, then rose as the chief justice administered the oath of office in Irish. Another fanfare of trumpets echoed through the hall as the chief justice presented Douglas Hyde with the Great Seal. De Valera, speaking for the government and the nation, addressed Hyde formally. Hyde's formal reply was distinctly heard in the ceremonial silence. The entire event took only fifteen minutes. As the band, to Peterson's obvious delight, "did its best to bring down the rafters with the National Anthem," Hyde, the chief justice, and Eamon de Valera, together with Hyde's aides, moved slowly from the hall for the concluding portion of the inauguration program in which, outside, as Peterson proudly remembered, "we, as military men, came into our own": "The guard of honour came to attention and then presented arms. The Presidential salute was played, the troops sloped arms and we followed the President as he inspected the guard of honour." Once more there was a moment of suspense after Hyde, having moved up and down the ranks of Ireland's first Irish-speaking battalion, stood ready for the officer in charge of the cavalry escort to dismiss his troop. The poor fellow had forgotten the Irish phrase necessary to request Hyde's permission to give the order, according to one of the soldiers present, and had to have a junior officer make the request for him and relay Hyde's reply.

From the Cork Hill gates of the Castle the president's car made its way past the Commercial Buildings and Daly's Club House, dignified eighteenth-century landmarks, down Dame Street and College Green, to Westmoreland Street, a creation of the Wide Streets Commissioners, to the Liffey. Crowds lined the sidewalks and spilled over into the road-ways, waving and cheering the old man who had become their head of state. Hyde's car moved slowly, as he waved and smiled in return, then stopped before the General Post Office. There it paused briefly for a moment of silence, the more dramatic in contrast to the cheers and shouts that had filled the air a moment before, to honor those who had lost their lives in the Rising of Easter, 1916, to make just such a day as this possible. Then, the cheering renewed, Hyde's car moved on again, past the Gresham Hotel where in 1905, as he left for America, other crowds had formed a torchlight parade to escort him to the rail-road station; past Nelson's Pillar; past the Rotunda where he had so often spoken; from Parnell Square on to North Frederick Street and Berkeley Road and the North Circular Road. As the procession of cars left the center of town, the crowds began to thin, but outside of schools the numbers increased again, this time with children whose eagerness to see and be seen by their first president moved Hyde deeply. MacVeagh's report to Washington made a particular point of the large and enthusiastic crowds and the "amazement and pleasure" expressed by the officer in charge of the cavalry "at the warmth of the reception given the president as he drove through the city." MacVeagh himself had been impressed by the number of clergy of various denominations who had been present in St. Patrick's Hall and the friendliness with which they had greeted one another, a fact also apparent to the news-paper reporters, he noted the following day.

Once more the presidential car passed through the gates of Phoenix Park to the President's Mansion, over which the presidential standard now flew. After the cars had paused to let off their passengers by twos and threes, the dignitaries who had participated in the motorcade moved to the south portico where they had been asked to assemble for official picture-taking. As flashbulbs popped, Douglas Hyde, now *an t-uachtarán,* president of Ireland, stood flanked by the *taoiseach,* the chief justice, government ministers, members of the Council of State, and distinguished visitors. His aides stood at either end of the large group. Among them certainly there were some who had been guests before in this same mansion, perhaps before 1932 when it had served as the home of the governor-general of the Irish Free State (appointed by the king on the advice of the Executive Council of the Free State government), perhaps before 1922 when it was still the Viceregal

Lodge. Many more no doubt had never entered its gracious hall, had never looked south toward Dublin from its great windows, had never dreamed that one day they would pass through its doors proudly, without thought of arson or destruction, admiring its beauty, knowing it was their own.

Built in the early eighteenth century as a hunting lodge, for a while the residence of the park ranger, shortly before 1800 the Italianate mansion had become the summer home of the British viceroy, who soon demanded additions and improvements appropriate for a place that would house the monarch on occasions when the Royal Presence visited Ireland. Some of these alterations were made in 1787. Michael Stapleton, a Dublin plasterer, probably designed and executed its famous Aesop's fables ceilings. In 1807 a Doric portico was added to the north front of the building. An Ionic portico was added to the south entrance in 1815–1816, at the same time as the wings that give the whole its classical balance. In 1840 Decimus Burton, whose name is associated with the building of the Royal Botanic Gardens of Regents Park, was commissioned to design the formal gardens on the south slope of the hill from which the Dublin mountains may be seen in the distance. Victoria had slept in one of the elegant second-floor bedrooms on her royal visits. Through over a hundred years of successive lords lieutenant, in all the rooms of the mansion servants had bustled to and fro, attending titled and knighted lords and ladies. From the large center reception room, the dining room at the east end, the sitting room to the west, each with great windows open to the south, the tinkling of crystal, the clatter of serving dishes, the laughter of ladies over afternoon tea, and the murmur of British statesmen had carried down the long, wide connecting hall. Both Timothy Healy, first governor general of the Irish Free State, and James MacNeill, his successor, had occupied the lodge following the departure of the last lord lieutenant in 1922. From 1932 to 1938, under the stewardship of Donald Buckley, the house had been but minimally maintained. Despite a flurry of activity to make it livable in time for inauguration day, the newspapers noted that it was but sparsely furnished on Hyde's first official day in residence, with few chandeliers, and fewer other lighting fixtures of quality. The restoration process, in fact, was to continue through his entire presidency and beyond, to his alternate amusement and dismay.

The picture-taking over, Hyde—who had been in the public eye and mostly on his feet from early morning—rested after lunch while McDunphy and the two aides opened and sorted a stream of congratulatory letters and telegrams from the four provinces of Ireland and abroad. According to Peterson, at one stage in the process, which occupied the better part of the afternoon,

there appeared a thick white envelope with the British royal arms embossed on it. Scarcely had we seen it than it was whisked away from our rude soldierly eyes and so I never learned what it contained, but I wondered a lot.

At the time we were still, in British eyes, a British dominion, so that the King could hardly address the President as an equal. The puzzle remains but maybe the document will turn up one day in State papers. [So far it has not.]

Still ahead, after the afternoon's chores had been completed, was an evening reception in the Castle, to which the diplomatic corps, the papal nuncio, ministers of state, members of the government, and a large number of men and women representing various Irish industrial, professional, cultural, and social groups had been invited. It was held in the former viceregal throne room, which had been restored and appropriately redecorated for the purposes which henceforth it would serve. The viceregal throne had been newly upholstered in St. Patrick's blue with a gold harp embroidered on the upright part of the chair.

At precisely ten o'clock, as planned, the president—now in evening dress—made his way up the stairway. Peterson, chronicler of all the day's near-disasters, later recalled that he helped avert still another, as he spotted a garter that had come undone and was in danger of tripping Ireland's first president. The garter refastened, the presidential party continued up the stairway and to the presidential chair. Smiling and waving to the assembled guests, Hyde seated himself and prepared to receive the long queue of well-wishers. First came the diplomats and dignitaries, in the order that had been established by McDunphy, whose talent for protocol, although resented by those who yearned nostalgically for the informality of former days, assured the success of each new presidential occasion for which it was required. The first-ranking guests having been seated, others were free to come forward in random order. The line seemed endless, the time allotted for it stretching into the night, as Hyde—rejecting the usual perfunctory handshake—made a point of spending a few moments in conversation with each person. Suddenly, just as Peterson himself spotted what he patronizingly described as "a number of tanned western faces looking somewhat incongruous in not-too-well-fitting evening dress," Hyde, forgetting all protocol, jumped to his feet to greet in their native Irish his old friends from the west, faithful since early Gaelic League days, who, patting backs and shaking hands, encircled the visibly moved president. In the excitement of the moment he was utterly unaware that when he stood, everyone else who had been seated rose too—and there they remained, on their feet, patiently waiting for him to seat himself again. Peterson felt a jab in his ribs. Behind him stood an official from the Department of External Affairs who muttered, "For God's sake, get the old bastard to sit down. The Papal Nuncio's got corns."

The marvel of the occasion for young men like Peterson was Hyde, his capacity for extracting maximum personal pleasure from each moment, his delight in the occasion, his indefatigability. Those closest to him wondered the most, for they knew that behind the ready smile and twinkling eye there was genuine worry over Lucy, who—unwell and unwilling to even try the trip to Dublin—had remained in Frenchpark. Meanwhile Annette and Una, on whom ordinarily Hyde counted for help in caring for Lucy and in keeping her company when he was away, had come with him, to assist McDunphy and other members of the presidential staff and otherwise take turns serving as the president's hostess in the absence of his wife. The truth was that nothing could diminish this momentous day for Douglas Hyde or dampen the emotions that accompanied it. Two days later, in his "Message to the Nation," printed in all the Dublin papers on June 28, 1938, Hyde tried to share his feelings with the Irish people, in the formal language required in his first presidential address:

The President has been deeply moved by the manifestations of cordiality and enthusiasm which greeted him on all sides on the day of his installation in office, both during the procession after the ceremony in Dublin Castle and on the other occasions when he passed through the streets of the capital. He feels that this generous attitude on the part of the people, which is reflected also in the numerous messages he has received from all parts of the world is a symbol of the deep-seated loyalty of the Irish people of all creeds and classes to their beloved country and of their earnest desire to cooperate with him and with each other in the furtherance of its interests.

The last lines were closest to the sentiments he was able to express more easily in personal letters to individuals: that on other than state occasions, he might always be able to move freely among the people of Ireland, in a "bond of equality with them." A favorite memento of the day was a cartoonist's version of his swearing-in ceremony, which he clipped and saved from the June 1938 issue of *Dublin Opinion*: The caption reads, "History Defeats Itself. Ghost of Cromwell . . . at Dublin Castle." "And 'e's from Connaught!" exclaims the glowering ghoul of the Protector, lurking in the shadows behind the walrus-mustached new president.

19

The Presidency

Ceremonies over, almost immediately Hyde and his staff, joined by Annette, settled down to work in Áras an Uachtaráin. To Hyde's relief and pleasure, Annette had agreed to stay on with him, to help Michael McDunphy look after his personal and social affairs and to serve as the president's hostess. Struggling with the series of undefined illnesses that continued to plague her, Lucy remained at home. It was ironic that she who once wanted so desperately to sell Ratra and leave Roscommon, preferably for Dublin, now wished only to be left alone there. It was ironic too that after years of deploring Ireland's failure to reward Hyde's service to the nation, she could not be present to see him honored. But Dr. Kilgallen, Lucy's physician, not only had approved Lucy's decision to remain in Frenchpark but had advised that she was much too nervous and easily upset to be moved to Dublin and certainly was not well enough to cope with the public life of a president's wife. There was nothing to do but accept the situation. Ratra was well staffed; the Mahons and Morrisroes were in charge; Annette and Una took turns going down to the country, although as the wife of a judge and the mother of four children Una had her own full share of responsibilities; Hyde went home to Frenchpark as often as he could. Lucy did not seem more than usually unhappy.

Given the amount of work that needed to be done at Áras an Uachtaráin to reverse the years of neglect, it was probably just as well that Lucy was not there to share its management with Michael McDunphy. If she were well, it is unlikely that she would have taken kindly to having such private matters become a governmental and therefore public concern. As for the social duties of a president's wife, Lucy would not have enjoyed these either. Among the qualities that Hyde had admired when first they met were the forthright way in which she expressed herself and the strength and sharpness of her mind. She would not have found attractive a situation in which she was obliged to entertain strangers and could not express her opinions frankly. It was one of the things that she had found troublesome about her 1905–1906 trip to America.

Annette was by nature more gregarious, more diplomatic, and less perturbed by the fact that public appointment to high office carried with it public involvement in private life. She was also better attuned to her brother's ideas, no doubt because it was he in fact who had had the most significant influence on her education. Whenever he went abroad when she was a girl, he had brought home for her books in different languages. He used to write letters to her in Irish, French, German, and Italian and had encouraged her to alternate the languages in which she replied. He had recommended books for her to read and then urged her to discuss them with him. Brother and sister were compatible in other ways as well. Unlike Lucy, who even before her sad chronology of debilitating illnesses never had been enthusiastic about outdoor life, they both loved activities—walking, riding, tennis, shooting, boating, swimming, skating—almost anything that took them outdoors. Annette had been married to Hyde's friend Cam Kane. They had never had children. Cam was dead; there was nothing to keep her from staying at Áras an Uachtaráin as long as she pleased, and she seemed to enjoy the prospect.

Watching Annette at the inauguration, Una was awed by the way in which "Auntie" could meet and chat with strangers. Her talent for putting others at ease never failed to elicit Una's admiration. Most astonishing of all to Una, who acknowledged frankly that she herself was far less outgoing, was that while she was willing to endure for her father's sake the lunches and teas to which she was invited, Annette genuinely enjoyed them. Una got on well with Captain de Buitléar, who was unfailingly kind and supportive, but she was just as happy to leave to Annette the tasks that required working with Mr. McDunphy, for she was certain that she could not possibly match his expectations of her father's daughter.

The most important member of the presidential team at Áras an Uachtaráin was Michael McDunphy. Solemn and highly principled to those who encountered him on his job, to family, friends, and close associates he was a warm and thoughtful person with a passion for the out-of-doors and a fondness for storytelling. Together McDunphy and Eamon de Buitléar were a superbly efficient pair. Their immediate and pressing problem, as inauguration day became a memory, was to decide what to do with the boxes and tea chests full of books and papers that had arrived by army lorry from Frenchpark—and how to allocate time between the unending stream of letters from well-wishers and favor seekers that daily poured into Áras an Uachtaráin and the daily visitors admitted on official business and by courtesy. For both, establishing a good working relationship from the start was a matter of highest priority. Hyde agreed: his years in the Gaelic League had taught him that his own success depended on the competence and goodwill of his staff.

At forty-seven Michael McDunphy was a tall, spare Dubliner who had devoted himself to government service. He had been twenty-one at the time of his first appointment in 1912; six years later, in 1918, he had been dismissed for refusing to take the oath of allegiance to the Crown. In 1922 he had become the first assistant secretary to the Free State government, a position in which he continued until 1937, although he was called to the bar in 1928. In 1937 he had been a member of the committee of four appointed to examine and revise the preliminary draft of the new Constitution. After its enactment he was named secretary to the president and clerk to the Council of State; he was also generally regarded as an expert on questions of letter and intent related to the Constitution. His wide-ranging personal interests included military history, the agricultural cooperative movement, aviation, and walking tours. One of his proudest possessions was a certificate dated 1928 for the first plane ever registered in Ireland.

Assessing the personalities of the men who would be involved in the new government, the *Irish Digest* had pointed out shortly before the inauguration that McDunphy's political background, like Hyde's, was nonpartisan. Whether he was working with Cosgrave or de Valera, his loyalties were always to concepts, not people. Those who knew him well said that it was not at all uncommon to see him walking, alone and thoughtful, along the narrow roads of the Wicklow hills and Dublin mountains. In the city his usual mode of transportation was his bicycle. Warm and happy within his family, he made no attempt to cultivate as friends the large circle of men and women with whom he came in daily contact, as liaison between Áras an Uachtaráin and the government. He was by nature and inclination what on the surface might have seemed the antithesis of Douglas Hyde: a very private person. What they both understood after a short time together was that they were both essentially private men with very different styles.

Within a few days of the inauguration, at Hyde's invitation, the president and his secretary sat down together for a working lunch at the Gresham Hotel. Hyde's opening gambit in the game of getting to know one another, although not immediately perceived as such by McDunphy, was a clear signal of his respect. As McDunphy later recalled:

Scarcely were we seated than he asked me what were the powers of the President of Ireland. It was not a question to be answered briefly amid the din of a public restaurant and to a man who had no previous interest or experience in politics, but I did my best to the detriment of the meal. I told him that apart from the ceremonial duties involving no authority the powers and duties conferred on him by the Constitution were to be exercised by him on the advice of the Government, although there were a limited few which he could exercise on his absolute discretion, and I told him what they were.

Hyde was in fact neither as naive nor as removed from the center of political discussion as McDunphy thought; he had closely followed the discussions of the new Constitution and talked with friends about its provisions, and he had agreed to stand for the presidency only after understanding what his contribution would be. What McDunphy's answers to Hyde's question revealed was McDunphy's concept of how they ought to work together. Comparing the powers of the presidency to those of a referee on a football field, McDunphy declared that "there were rules by which the game should be played and the referee should not interfere unless he saw an infringement of those rules." From that day forward, whenever he was briefed—even three years later when a stroke for a time confined him to bed—Hyde would ask McDunphy, in Irish or English, with a twinkle in his eye, "Do you think I should get out the whistle?"

Not all days ended so pleasantly. During their early weeks together, until they became accustomed to Hyde's foibles and working methods, both McDunphy and de Buitléar had moments of frustration. Both men prided themselves on their efficiency, their organizational concepts, their ability to set up systems and adhere to them. Hyde was not accustomed to teamwork. Ordinarily no one touched his books and papers but himself. McDunphy and de Buitléar sorted and shelved; in search of particular documents or quotations or facts, Hyde rearranged items to suit himself—in stacks, on the floor, or under the table at which he was writing, or in the chair in which he planned to settle down to read.

McDunphy's time schedules were carefully arranged so that the most important business of the day could be allotted the appropriate number of minutes necessary to its completion. These had to be rearranged to comply with Hyde's arbitrary decisions concerning which letters he would answer himself, by hand, and which could be answered on his behalf. Eventually, largely as a result of McDunphy's quiet determination, a routine was established.

Every morning after breakfast Hyde, de Buitléar, and McDunphy would confer. Papers sent by the government to the president for his signature were the first order of business. These were discussed thoroughly before being returned. The day's mail, already opened by McDunphy, would be presented next, often with replies already composed in response to routine requests for an interview with or a photograph of the president or to simple queries that did not require more than a few words. If Hyde approved (as he did almost without exception), these letters were signed and set aside for mailing. The remainder of the morning mail usually contained other letters that could be acknowledged almost as quickly: personal notes from fellow scholars and friends in all parts of the world accompanying copies of their latest books and articles or clippings in which they thought Hyde might be interested. Often Hyde would dash off handwritten replies on the spot. Some items that were purely personal or particularly amusing were saved to be shared later in the morning with Annette. One such was the businesslike message delivered from the secretary of the Board of Public Works to the secretary to the president on July 26, 1938, to inform Hyde of a perquisite of which he had been unaware: "The Office of Public Works has authorized killing some of the bucks in Phoenix Park. Enclosed find warrants entitling the President to the venison of three animals." Letters from America, from friends, and from strangers were set aside to be answered at another hour when Hyde would be alone in his study. Some, such as those written from the Dingle in the heavy black but highly readable lettering of an Seabhac (Pádraig Ó Siochfhradha), were easily identified and singled out for immediate attention. Among the letters from America there were often versions of the following, dated August 20, 1938, from Mrs. Dempsey of Milford, Massachusetts:

Dr. Douglas Hyde President of Eire you may think this letter inquisitive but I am thinking that you are of my Grandmother's people as I no [sic] that name was in my family years ago and as I thought you resembled my Uncle Maurice Walsh as I saw your picture in the paper and was proud you were made

President of Eire. Grandmother came in the Great Western ship and had a son born on board. I would love to see Ireland some time but I don't think I will unless I go with Corrigan as they had a time in Boston for him.

Douglas "Wrong Way" Corrigan and the story of his wrong-way flight across the Atlantic were familiar to the small staff of Áras an Uachtaráin. They all remembered the day the handsome young American pilot had left Dublin. It was McDunphy the aviation enthusiast who had learned that Corrigan's frail monoplane was to be dismantled and trucked to the Dublin docks before six o'clock in the evening, for shipment home on an outboard freighter. The day's schedule was quickly abandoned as McDunphy, Hyde, and de Buitléar rushed to Baldonnel Aerodrome outside Dublin to satisfy Hyde's great curiosity about the man and his plane. The elderly Hyde and the young American aviator were each fascinated by the other. The next day's schedule was also rearranged when it was discovered that Corrigan could visit Áras an Uachtaráin, where he was such a favorite that everyone from the gardener to Hyde himself wanted to be photographed with him.

Other letters were encapsulated tragedies. Mrs. Mahon of Fairymount, county Roscommon—a crossroads village not far from Frenchpark—sent a plea to the new president asking his help to get her son out of the British army. His father had been taken ill and was given only a week to live. "I will be put out of my place," she lamented, without a man of the family to work their small holding. Hyde was powerless to provide the help she requested, although he well understood her plight. With the landlords had gone the threat of eviction, but old women who outlived their husbands and lost their sons faced a new threat: an impoverished widowhood in the county home, formerly the workhouse, if they could find no one to hoe the potatoes, cut the turf, milk the cow, and mend the thatch. In the old days they would have had children to look after them. But now, strong young sons had little choice. With no future at home but that which could be wrested from a rock-strewn patch, their only hope of a decent living was what they could find on a construction site in Scotland or in a hotel in America. Emigration left no one at home to look after elderly parents.

After the correspondence of the day had been attended to in a way that satisfied both McDunphy and Hyde and the latter also had conferred with Annette about matters with which she was concerned, there was lunch, usually with one or more invited guests. Afternoons generally were reserved for receiving visitors from home and abroad, in accordance with a policy on which Hyde insisted: that no reasonable request for an interview be refused. This often created problems for McDunphy, whose task it was to arrange Hyde's days so that he also had time for a rest; for the scholarly reading and writing in which, like Theodore Roosevelt, he continued to be engaged; and for writing out by hand, in his usual fashion, the "heads" of an address he was to present, as part of his presidential duties. But once a visitor captured Hyde's attention, it was hard for McDunphy to bring the interview to a close. One day McDunphy had arranged a long lunch with an attractive American woman journalist. When time came for her to leave, she rose appropriately, prepared to end her visit on time, but Hyde insisted that she remain and continue their conversation. For McDunphy the rest of the afternoon was havoc. Returning to his office, he muttered grimly to de Buitléar, "He simply can't do this! It's not right!" "He *is* doing it," de Buitléar pointed out quietly, "and there is nothing we can do about it."

McDunphy had also to cope with Hyde's unscheduled interviews. On a number of occasions, de Buitléar recalled, McDunphy would come into Hyde's study to find him neither working on the speech he had sat down to compose nor having the rest that Annette had prescribed but sharing a wee drop with Luke Nangle, the gardener. It was a chill November day, Hyde pointed out; he had asked Luke to come in for only a moment to warm himself and have a sip of the national drink. Other visitors also recalled arriving at Áras an Uachtaráin on a wet day and being solicitously offered a sip from the small bottle Hyde kept in his study—"for patriotic reasons," he would explain, his eyes opening wide, as if in surprise that anyone might regard the scene differently. When McDunphy attempted to remonstrate with him, Hyde struck a mock-serious pose and complained that he was "but a prisoner" in Áras an Uachtaráin.

Only once, in the recollection of Eamon de Buitléar, did sparks ever really fly between Hyde and McDunphy: in spring 1939, Hyde had arranged a reception at Áras an Uachtaráin for a number of members of the Gaelic League, most of them Hyde's former associates and old friends. It was not until the event was half over that Hyde realized that not everyone invited had accepted—in fact, some of the refusals, he learned, had been insulting if not hostile. These McDunphy had withheld from the ritual review of the daily mail on the day they had been received. Hyde insisted that henceforth all letters addressed to him be opened before him. He was equally adamant that some of his visitors were to be admitted whenever they came, whatever the schedule. These included his old friend, the still beautiful Maud Gonne; the O'Conors of Clonalis; several former Trinity classmates; and Ó Siochfhradha, better known as An Seabhac ("the hawk"), cofounder with Hyde of the Irish Folklore Society, and a frequent and very welcome caller. Their conversations, like their correspondence, covered many subjects besides the current status of folklore collecting, in which Hyde remained actively interested. It was in Áras an Uachtaráin, in fact, that together Hyde and An Seabhac looked over the proofs of Hyde's last contribution to the series of books published by the Irish Texts Society: volume 36, *Sgéalta Thomais Ui Chathasaigh* (1939).

Frank MacDermot, at this time of his life Dublin correspondent for the *Sunday Times,* also visited from time to time. Youngest son of The MacDermot of Coolavin and a cousin therefore to O'Conor Don, MacDermot had campaigned for Home Rule in two Westminster elections before the establishment of the Irish Free State. In 1932 he had won a seat in the Dáil as an independent; he was widely recognized as a founding member of the National Centre party and its successor, the United Irish party, neither of which ever had grown to main-party status. He therefore had continued to sit in the Dáil as an independent until, like Hyde, he was co-opted for service in the Senate by de Valera in early 1938. The two men had much in common besides their Connacht background and political careers. MacDermot was also a writer. In 1939 he published a biography of Wolfe Tone. Josephine O'Conor, a daughter of O'Conor Don who worked for a time in MacDermot's office, also used to drop in, as did her sisters, especially Molly, later wife of Sir William Tealing, and the identical twins, Gertrude and Eva, who later married Maurice Staunton and Rupert Nash, respectively. With the twins, Hyde always played a little game: if they came together, it was the question of which was which; if one came alone, which one was she. For years the twins had teased him, each claiming to be the other, until he had found what he thought was a foolproof way of telling them apart: he would pretend to drop something accidentally, then watch as they bent to pick it up, knowing that Eva was right-handed, Gertrude was left-handed. But his confidence was short-lived, for the twins soon discovered his method and foiled him by deliberately using the opposite hand.

In addition to managing time so that Hyde could count on finding relaxed and private moments in what was otherwise a very public life, McDunphy arranged Hyde's schedule of presidential visits, state banquets, public addresses, and public appearances as well as monthly dinners with the Council of State. Meetings with de Valera were outside his control. The Chief, typically, would arrive very late in the evening, often around midnight. To outsiders who did not know of these regular sessions at Áras an Uachtaráin it seemed as if there was little connection between government offices and the president's home in Phoenix Park.

During the first months that Hyde was in office, always and ever there were newsmen, both reporters and photographers. Given Hyde's open-door policy, McDunphy was concerned about how much of Hyde's time was taken up by them. He was annoyed especially by the photographers who seemed to pop up from bushes and out of closets in their insistence on providing the public with "photo essays" of the real Douglas Hyde. "Just one more of the president in his study" (or on the south portico with his sister, or in McDunphy's office, or in conference with his secretary and aide-de-camp), they would say. Particularly time-consuming was a visit from the *Weekly Illustrated*'s journalist and photographer in early October 1938: Their assignment was to create a photo-essay that would depict a day in the life of the president, from morning to night. There were shots of Hyde "resting" (on a day in which they gave him no rest, thought McDunphy), stretched out full-length in his rough Irish tweeds on a sofa, holding a copy of *Silva Gaedelica*; Hyde "working" (on a day on which he did almost nothing except pose for pictures) at his desk; of Hyde dining with McDunphy and de Buitléar (the soup was cold by the time they were told that the cameras were ready to catch them eating). In the end Hyde turned the tables on the photographers: he insisted that Miss Dowling, the house-keeper, be brought out to pose with him on the gravel walk. "She is most valuable . . . You must take her," he had said. Then not only Miss Dowling but Luke Nangle was placed in front of the cameras. Then other members of the household staff. When almost every possible combination of Áras an Uacharáin employees and residents had been immortalized on film, McDunphy—who hours before had accepted the fact that little else would be accomplished that day—noted that one was still missing. Picking up the press camera, he snapped the cameraman standing between Hyde and de Buitléar.

Most photograph sessions were more formal. Following luncheons with archbishops, ministers, ambassadors, and other notables, the cam-eramen—familiar faces from the *Irish Times, Irish Press, Irish Independent,* and Keystone Press Agency, less familiar faces from provincial newspapers and newspapers abroad—gathered. On July 8, 1938, they recorded the visit of Roosevelt's ambassador to Great Britain, the flamboyant Joseph P. Kennedy, accompanied by his handsome eldest son, Joseph P. Kennedy, Jr. Hyde told the boy about his experiences in Boston in the winter of 1905, when he had met young Kennedy's maternal grandfather, John F. Fitzgerald, better known as "Honey Fitz," who was then waging his campaign for election to the office of mayor. John Cudahy, the American minister to Ireland, also was present at the luncheon. Hyde amused Cudahy with an account of his visit to Cudahy's uncle's home in California in 1906. Hyde regarded Cudahy as a decent fellow, very much on Ireland's side in the matter of the North—a man whose clear eye, common sense, and warm heart were an asset to Ireland as well as to the United States. More important to Hyde was the fact that Cudahy and de Valera got on well together, for it meant that the American minister could be helpful in confirming the analysis of Irish-American politics that Hyde had tried to impress upon de Valera. De Valera tended to think of Irish Americans as a monolithic group, single-minded in their dedication to Ireland's independence and their opposition to the continuing British presence in the North, therefore a reliable source of votes and money in support of the "Irish cause." What Hyde and Cudahy both knew was that Irish-American attitudes toward Ireland could better be described as a spectrum. They were aware, furthermore, that even groups that conformed to de Valera's stereotype were divided not only on the question of how the goal of an independent, united, thirty-two county republic might be achieved (this, after all, was a problem in Ireland as well) but also by petty power struggles, unsettled scores, personality conflicts, regional misunderstandings, private ambitions, and class and religious prejudice. Hyde was therefore delighted to have such a man as Cudahy in the American minister's residence in Phoenix Park.

McDunphy's personal souvenir of this luncheon was an interesting handwriting portrait of those present: a sheet of presidential stationery, labeled *"Lunch to the American Ambassador to Great Britian, 8.7.38"* in McDunphy's hand, on which each of the diners had signed his name. Hyde's signature—"Dubhglas de h-íde," written in large, clear letters without Hyde's characteristic uphill slant—heads the list, with McDunphy's addition in parentheses, "President of Ireland." Beneath it, the flourishing letters leaning sharply to the right, sprawled across two full lines, is "Joseph P. Kennedy/Ambassador to G. B." Next in order is the equally flourishing but perpendicular two-line signature of his colleague, "John Cudahy/American Minister," to which McDunphy added in parenthesis, "to Ireland." Beneath, in a simple and neat clear hand very different from his father's, is the signature of Kennedy's eldest son, "Joseph P. Kennedy, Jr." Next, in smaller letters, widely spaced yet difficult to read because of their idiosyncratic form, is the name and title of the papal nuncio, J. Paschal Robinson, preceded by a modest cross. Beneath is the erect, firm, and boldly black signature, as angular as a seismographic chart, of John MacVeagh: to it McDunphy had added "Secretary to the American Legation." Last is McDunphy's own signature, the "D" as sharply peaked as the mountains he loved to climb, complete with his own title, "Secretary to the President."

By early fall the presidential team was working expertly, dispatching papers with admirable speed, keeping appointments on schedule. Messages of congratulations and condolence, inspirational pieces for schoolchildren, greetings to the annual Congress of the Irish Red Cross, messages from the president of Ireland to various ministers of state: more than a match for the steady influx of communications received at Áras an Uachtaráin every morning was the steady daily outflow of letters, telegrams, and memoranda. All but the most routine were first drafted by Hyde in his own hand; all but the purely personal were typed in duplicate, the copies to be filed in accordance with procedures that had been established by McDunphy. They were doing what Hyde thought was the important work of the presidency: they were creating a public image of a nation. All went smoothly through the balance of 1938 with but two exceptions. Both were exceedingly distressing to Hyde.

The first incident came as a shock to both Hyde and de Valera. Routinely, Hyde had received an invitation to attend an international soccer match, to be held in Dublin on November 13, 1938. Routinely, he had accepted. Suddenly what had been anticipated as an enjoyable occasion, a welcome diversion from the usual daily schedule, became an ugly incident. Hyde was reminded that the Gaelic Athletic Association, of which he had long been a patron, expressly prohibited any support, by any member, of "foreign" games (i.e., games non-Irish in origin). By attending the international event, Hyde was told, he had violated this long-standing ban. Expulsion from the Gaelic Athletic Association was the penalty he would have to pay.

Founded in 1884 by Michael Cusack, a close friend and long-time associate whose death in 1906 at the comparatively young age of fifty-nine had been a blow to Hyde, the Gaelic Athletic Association (GAA) had been successful not only in reviving native games but in attracting to them, as players and supporters, Irish men and women from all the provinces of Ireland, regardless of religion, political sympathies, or social position. Long before he had made his famous speech on the subject, the GAA had in fact taken a giant step toward the deanglicization for which Hyde had called in 1892. When the Gaelic League was founded in 1893, Cusack, predictably, had been an early and enthusiastic member. The GAA quarterly journal, devoted to all aspects of native culture, had welcomed contributions from Hyde and other Gaelic Leaguers. An Seabhac, Erskine Childers, and Daniel Corkery had been among its authors. The lyrics of the GAA anthem, the "Marching Song of the Gaelic Athletes," had in fact been composed by Hyde. Despite these harmonious connections the members who had lodged the formal complaint against Hyde insisted that there could be no exception to the rules—Hyde's name must be struck from the list of GAA patrons. The matter went to the executive council of the organization, which supported the complaint despite protests from a number of district branches and opposition from de Valera. The expulsion was formally announced.

Eamon de Valera was furious when he received word of the executive council's action, but Hyde, although deeply wounded, argued against any public response. On his orders no statement was issued from the office of president. De Valera also acquiesced by keeping silent, but he did not forget. Biding his time, he waited until Hyde had retired from the presidency before bringing up the matter again, as a matter of principle, without involving personalities. His position was that no single organization had any right either to approve or bar the presence of the president of Ireland at any public function. This was a matter strictly between the president and the government. Yet the wound did not heal, at least not in Hyde's lifetime, so strong were the emotions involved. In August 1984 the contending voices were stilled at last when, in celebration of the GAA centennial, the Roscommon branch of the GAA held a ceremony at Hyde's graveside and affixed a plaque to the entrance of the small cemetery behind the Portahard church in Frenchpark to commemorate Hyde's friendship with Michael Cusack and his early contributions to the organization.

The second distressing incident was not unexpected but affected Hyde even more deeply. Lucy's health, for many years uncertain, had been declining steadily throughout the fall. Hyde wrote to her regularly, sent gifts of pâté, German newspapers, and other such items that he knew would appeal to her, welcomed what little he could find of good cheer in her letters to him, and was in constant touch with her physician,

Dr. Kilgallen. He had taken pains to find an understanding and dependable nurse to stay with her, and when he himself could not visit, he relied on his surrogates, Annette and Una, to go down to Roscommon whenever they could and to report to him on her condition upon their return to Dublin. In late November he was upset to hear that the nurse had resigned, leaving the maid, Kate, burdened with full responsibility for Lucy in addition to her regular duties. It was not easy to replace the nurse, nor was there any assurance that a new nurse would remain longer than the last, for Frenchpark was isolated and Lucy was not an easy patient. Moreover, the medication regularly prescribed for Lucy—the regimen had been begun many years before, partly on the advice of George Sigerson, when less was known of the dangers—contained ingredients such as belladonna that often left her weak and lethargic, in need of frequent assistance. The exact nature of her illness apparently was difficult to determine. In later years, in response to inquiries, Dr. Kilgallen spoke vaguely of "moral neurosis," by which he seemed to mean a form of neurasthenia. What was certain is that by the fall of 1938 there was little in Lucy's behavior or appearance that would recall the quick, intelligent, well-educated, self-assured, and assertive young woman Douglas Hyde had courted forty-six years earlier, except perhaps her continuing interest in German literature and culture. Those close to Hyde knew that her illness had been costly in financial as well as emotional terms. The newspaper might suggest that, with his salary of £15,000—a sum they obviously regarded as munificent—Douglas Hyde was a wealthy man. But in fact one of his aides was surprised at what he described as the starkness of Ratra, and spoke of one room in which the walls were covered in old newspapers, observations that suggested to him a miserly nature until he realized what sums were being spent by Hyde on medical attention for his wife and on the staff necessary to care for her.

Early in December came word from Roscommon that Lucy's physical condition was deteriorating rapidly; Hyde was advised to plan a trip earlier than Christmas, which he had planned to spend at Ratra. Quickly he and McDunphy reviewed his schedule to determine what could be postponed, what had to be done. One thing he could not put off was his radio speech to America, to be broadcast on December 22. While keeping in daily touch with Dr. Kilgallen and the faithful Kate, he prepared and revised his handwritten draft. "My friends, my very dear friends of America whom I have never forgotten and never can forget, . . ." it began in English, "I give you my warmest greetings in the Irish language which is the language of my heart." Continuing in English, after his Irish greeting, he wrote of his gratitude for the reception he had received in more than fifty American cities during the fall, winter, and spring of 1905–1906, "when I was only a humble worker in the cause for the restoration of our own language." The goal set those long years ago had been reached, he reported; his plea for funds for the Gaelic League to which the American Irish had responded so warmly had made the difference. Irish, he declared, "although not widely spoken yet, is recognised by our Constitution to be the national language of Ireland." Its literature is "being unfolded in all its beauty to all the people. . . . A sound beginning has been made." Yet, he reminded them, the dream remained short of full realization: "Ireland has independent statehood, though not . . . for the whole of our national territory." He concluded as he had begun, in Irish: "Beannacht Dé orraibh go léir, agus go dtugaidh Dia Nodlaig shona dhibh, agus bliadhan nua fe shean agus fe mhaise." (Blessings on you all, and may God give you a happy Christmas and a prosperous New Year.)

On December 22, Hyde gave his address as planned. When the engineers signaled that the broadcast was over, he rose and walked out with his aide-de-camp into the gathering darkness. There his car waited, the small tricolor above the presidential plaque on its roof barely visible. A detachment of local *gardaí* saluted, and the car began its journey west across the Shannon, into Connacht, on to Frenchpark, to Ratra and Lucy's bedside. Nine days later Lucy died.

As if the reality of words set down in ink could etch the reality of his widowhood on his conscious mind, within the next days and weeks Hyde often scribbled phrases on scraps of paper to remind himself of the routine tasks that had to be taken care of as a result of Lucy's death. First, of course, was the announcement for the newspapers, drafted and revised and reviewed with McDunphy, who then made sure it was properly distributed:

Hyde, December 31, 1938, at her residence Ratra, Lucy Cometina, beloved wife of Douglas Hyde, LL.D., daughter of the late Charles Kurtz of Coed-y-Celyn House. The President wishes that the funeral should be private and that no flowers should be sent.

Next came the matter of arrangements. "Burial, local," wrote Hyde, on one scrap of paper. Then "where—Portahard," "who notified—Canon Furlong," and, in response to information he had requested which then required a choice, "coffin—what price?" It was not, of course, Hyde's first experience with the death of someone close to him, nor even the first in which responsibility for arrangements had fallen on his shoulders. Indeed, with McDunphy and de Buitléar at his side, willing and capable of relieving him of the necessity of coping with mundane details, there was actually little for him to do, once decisions were made. His father's death in 1905; Nuala's death in 1916; these had been harder. And when Cam Kane died in 1932, leaving Annette a widow, he had come forward to perform the brotherly services through which he was able to communicate his affection for both Cam and Annette—his closest friends, really—in ways more effective than mere words. But Lucy: the feelings engendered by this last parting were much more complex than any he had experienced before. In October 1893 Lucy and Hyde had been married. Three months earlier Hyde, MacNeill, and others had joined in founding the Gaelic League. She had not then seemed unsympathetic to his interests and hopes for the future of the language. Together, they had brought two children into the world. Together, they had buried one of them. At what point had she discovered that she could not share his dream? He could not give it up, of course—it was too much a part of him, the part that in many ways had made him a son of Seamas Hart. He had not known when he married how fully the cloak of the Countess Cathleen would envelop him. He had not realized how much Lucy would resent his commitment. In the 1938 revision of his biography, Diarmid Coffey had written:

Mrs. Hyde has always been the greatest strength and stay to her husband. She was never a Gael; her contribution to Hyde's success was that of the cool critic who helped him to come to the right judgment in time of crisis. It is no exaggeration to say that without her help he could not have survived the strain of his years of struggle.

But in America she had blurted out to an interviewer, "I didn't marry a man, I married a cause," and at the dinner table, when Hyde tried to speak Irish with the children or referred to a place he had visited by its Irish name, she would mock the sounds of the language, purposely mangling them for comic effect when she repeated what he said. Yet she was always solicitous of him, of his health, of his energies, of his position. She was furious when he did not receive the attention or respect she thought he had earned; when she felt that arrangements for his talks had been badly handled; when his efforts were not acclaimed or publicized. Everyone who ever had worked closely with him had received her letters, full of concern for her husband, urging that he not be permitted to overexert himself, strain his voice in too many successive lectures, fail to take the daily rest he needed, to avoid the colds and sore throats that always plagued him. And in the end, thanks to her care, he was robust—she was the one who failed. Characteristically, what was deepest and most personal for Hyde was least expressed. As always he used the façade of the public man to shield his private self.

In the weeks following Lucy's death, 106 letters, some enclosing cards or press cuttings, were sent from Áras an Uachtaráin to people who had known her. They went into every province of Ireland and to far corners of the world. One recipient was Mrs. Fitzwilliam Hyde, in Berkshire; another, Lieutenant Anthony Hyde, serving the Royal Dragoon Guards in Palestine; still another, Ben Greenwald, the Columbia University graduate student who, during his extended visit to Ratra in the summer of 1937, had been kind to her. Letters were sent also to such old friends as Sinéad de Valera and Maud Gonne; to Lady Stafford King-Harman of Rockingham Park and other members of Lucy's Anglo-Irish social circle in Roscommon; to Willie Stockley, still living in Cork; and to O'Conor Don and other Clonalis House O'Conors, wintering at the Hotel d'Angleterre in Nice, where the Hydes had spent a portion of their honeymoon.

On a cold and cheerless day in January 1939 Douglas Hyde signed his name to a document authorizing payment of one pound to Lucy's gravediggers and eighteen pounds for her coffin. She now lay next to her daughter Nuala in the little Church of Ireland graveyard in Frenchpark, near her mother-in-law who had died in 1885, her father-in-law who had died in 1905, and Annette's husband, John Cambreth Kane, who had died in 1932. If Hyde wondered as he wrote how long it would be before he himself would join them, he gave no sign of such thoughts but concentrated on the work still to be done. Another speech to America had been scheduled; it was important. The occasion was the opening of the New York World's Fair, the first international exposition at which Ireland would have its own pavilion, under its own flag. Its purpose, like that of his speech of December 22, would be to make friends. The war drums were again beating louder, as they had in 1914. The nations of the Western world were choosing up sides again. Ireland was again in the role of innocent bystander, vulnerable and defenseless in the conflict that—it was now being said openly—probably no longer could be avoided. As in 1914 England was again exerting pressures that, now that Ireland was no longer under British rule, were even more unacceptable than they had been a quarter of a century earlier. Given

British refusal to consider steps that might lead eventually to the reunification of Ireland, de Valera refused absolutely to concede to demands
for British military use of Irish ports, especially as such use of these ports
inevitably would draw fire on Ireland.

Back in his study in Phoenix Park, Hyde sat at his writing table near
the great windows open to the south and west and began drafting what
he wanted to say to the American people. De Valera had asked Hyde
if he could strike the proper note to persuade them to keep British
troops out of Ireland and British ships out of its harbors. Hyde wondered: would the United States support Irish neutrality?

Death again diminished Hyde's personal world on the twenty-eighth
of January when Ireland received word of the passing of its first Nobel
Prize winner, W. B. Yeats. Time and circumstances had taken them
along different paths, but once they had shared a dream, and they had
both lived to see some of their dreams come true. De Valera, too, was
a dreamer of dreams—and, also like Yeats, a skillful manager of women
and men and a practical politician. It was practical for him to rely on
Hyde to speak to the American people of old friendships and former
support while he himself remained firm on questions of British military
use of Irish ports, Irish neutrality, and Northern Ireland. Hyde was a
symbol of de Valera's continuing commitment to Irish Ireland. Hyde
could keep the home fires burning while de Valera negotiated abroad.
De Valera was the Big Fellow, the Chief, the one who made the rest
of the world sit up and take notice. Hyde was the grandfatherly An
Craoibhin who, unable to contain his curiosity, stepped down from the
reviewing stand in College Green to peek down Dame Street, which
had begun to pulse with sounds of approaching martial brass and drum,
on St. Patrick's Day, 1939. Years later it was this image of the president
that endured in the heart of a small boy, present on that occasion, who
had himself inched forward impatiently for the same reason.

Behind the scenes in this last spring before war enveloped Europe,
John Cudahy's firm support for de Valera's tactics began to weaken.
War clouds had grown more threatening since Hitler's *Anschluss* in Austria in March and the Munich Pact of September 1938. On February 9,
1939, Cudahy had warned Roosevelt that the only hope of "staying
the aggressive tactics of Mussolini and Hitler" was by "confronting
them with the reality that the U.S." would support Great Britain and
France "by material means." When within weeks of sending this letter
he learned that de Valera had accepted an invitation from Roosevelt to
visit Washington in May, Cudahy was concerned. Writing scathingly

of "the crushing failure" of Chamberlain's policies regarding all Europe and the British government's refusal to admit its failures in Ireland, he told Roosevelt that he had tried to impress on de Valera the importance of not talking too much about Partition and unity with Northern Ireland during his upcoming American tour—to caution him that any attack on England would be detrimental to the Irish cause. On April 27 de Valera cabled Washington his regrets that he would have to postpone his transatlantic trip. His official explanation to the Dáil was that "certain grave offenses" of the previous day had "changed the situation." In diplomatic circles it was generally believed that this was a broad reference to Great Britain's announcement that conscription would include Northern Ireland. As likely a reason was de Valera's view that the trip could accomplish nothing for him if as both Cudahy and Hyde had warned, he could not seize the opportunity to attract Irish-American public opinion to his cause. In Áras an Uachtaráin, Hyde and Frank MacDermot reviewed Ireland's position between Scylla and Charybdis. It was a major topic of discussion also between Hyde and de Valera, on the latter's evening visits to the Park. A year earlier it had seemed even to Cudahy that the threat of war would force England into a conciliatory position favorable to those committed to a united Ireland. Pressure from America had been essential to their hopes. But the United States was now as then unwilling to take any stand that might in any way encourage the dictators in Europe; the psychological moment appeared lost.

On the same day that de Valera announced his postponement of his American trip, Hyde hosted an official dinner at Áras an Uachtaráin for his old friends and associates in the Gaelic League. The guest of honor was John MacNeill, another of the league's founders, and the man who had taken over the presidency of the league following Hyde's resignation in 1915. Even before, as vice-president (as Hyde had declared in *Mise agus An Conradh* and in his unpublished memoir of 1918), MacNeill had worked unstintingly on behalf of the language and the organization. A first-rate historian specializing in early Ireland, like Hyde, MacNeill had been tapped for service on the faculty of University College, Dublin; there the two men again had been colleagues. And although MacNeill had headed the Volunteers before the Rising, he had shared Hyde's unwillingness to resort to force in 1916, knowing as Hyde did the odds against its resulting in anything but tragedy for Ireland; he had tried therefore to forestall the Rising by countermanding, too late, Pearse's orders. The 1939 dinner brought together those who had fought and those who had opposed fighting in 1916 and again in 1922. A reminder of the bitterness that had separated the two sides on both those occasions was the absence of some who never had been reconciled to Hyde's or MacNeill's position and who had now become disappointed in and disillusioned with de Valera for not having achieved the goal for which they had twice risked their lives. In their impatience with Hyde, MacNeill, and de Valera, they were now joined by other young militants who were applying old pressures to the new constitutional government.

Despite the rising tensions, summer brought opportunities for Hyde to return to Ratra to fish on Lough Gara as he had fished every single summer of his life from the time his family moved from Kilmactranny to Frenchpark in 1867. De Buitléar accompanied him. Lucy's will had been probated on March 21; all her worldly goods, all her carefully managed investments, had been left to Hyde, for his use during his lifetime, in trust for Una. No longer did the enormous expenses of her care and medical treatment strain his resources, yet Ratra remained, in the opinion of his aide-de-camp, a sparsely furnished place unsuited to the president's position. Nor did de Buitléar approve of the careless way in which there were always books and papers scattered about. It was very different indeed from his own cozy and attractive though much more modest home. Thinking to give it the kind of cheerful order to which he himself was accustomed (and which he therefore could not help but associate with a well-managed household), one evening after the president had gone to bed the young officer set about arranging the books and putting the papers into neat piles. In the morning he was astonished to hear a roar of anger from the sitting room where, the night before, Hyde had been reading and making notes. Red-faced and raging, completely the opposite of the mild-mannered, jocular, easygoing old gentleman de Buitléar thought he knew, Hyde had scattered the neat piles of paper and tossed down the books that had been shelved, in a futile attempt to locate an item for which he had been searching. Never again, he told his aide, must anyone have the temerity to disturb his work. Contrary to what the young man might have thought, he declared through quivering mustaches, every piece of paper, every single volume on desk, chair, table, or floor had been given its place for a specific purpose. Only if the house were on fire could there be any exception to his rule. Although often tempted, de Buitléar never forgot, and eventually he got used to the president's unconsciousness of his surroundings and conscious disorder.

On one of their summer fishing expeditions to Ratra, de Buitléar glimpsed still another side of Hyde about which he had heard a certain amount of gossip. Early in the morning, as usual, they picked up their rods and strolled down the road—a cart path, actually—to the Maxwell cottage at the edge of the lake where Hyde kept his boat. The Maxwell brothers helped shove them out through the reeds into the silvery, shallow water. A warm sun rose; with them they had Carrie Mahon's good brown bread and butter and a couple of bottles of stout. One after the other the bottles were emptied as the sun rose high over the lake and then began its descent. The fish were not biting—Hyde had predicted as much when he realized that the day would be fine—and after a while de Buitléar, who had lost interest in the dim prospect of a catch, began amusing himself by tossing two bottles in the air and shooting at them with his service pistol. A gruff sound made him turn; he was astonished by the look of disapproval on the older man's face. Thinking that it was the noise to which Hyde objected, de Buitléar put away his pistol. In the quiet waters of the lake the bottles bobbed astern for the next hour or so until the two men decided to bring the boat in. "Shouldn't you get those bottles?" Hyde asked in Irish, in a tone that left no doubt about the expected answer. "There's money on them, you know."

Lucy often was indignant at any suggestion that Hyde was ungenerous, but stories about his "nearness" (as Frenchpark neighbors used the term, with a conspiratorial wink and toss of the head) are firmly fixed in local lore. One farmer recounts how, when he was "no more than a gossoon" he and his friends had knocked on Hyde's door one day, dressed in worn-out clothing and carrying a broken concertina someone had discarded, hoping for a few coins. Holding up a half-crown, a munificent sum to the boys, Hyde asked if they knew a certain tune. Excitedly they all chorused "Yes!" "If you will play it for me on that squeeze box there," Hyde said, grinning mischievously and pointing to the instrument which clearly could not produce a note, "here's two-and-six for you." Another man, a pensioner in 1971, recalled Hyde's hiring himself and his friend to clean up leaves one autumn. It was a cold day, he remembered, and they had been working long and hard when Hyde emerged from his house with a bottle of stout in each hand. "I don't drink at all," the friend had said, according to the storyteller, who had been eying the two bottles, he admitted, thinking they both would be his. "You're a good man," Hyde said to the workman who had refused the stout. Then, handing over just one bottle to his partner, he returned to the house with the other.

Others (many long retired, some now dead, since they recorded their memories) have added their recollections that Hyde had the Anglo-Irish landlord's habit of "paying half"—that is, reducing any bill presented by fifty percent, with promise of the balance (never fully forthcoming) the next time, when again only one-half of the sum due would be paid. The men and women who worked for the Hydes in Ratra dispute such tales, putting them down to jealousy, greed, and the Irish penchant for deflation, or blaming the newspapers for raising exaggerated expectations by making so much of Hyde's presidential salary of £15,000—a small fortune to the modest people of Roscommon in 1938–1945. All agree that whatever the truth of such stories, Hyde was generally well liked by his Roscommon neighbors, for he never put on airs or tried to be anything but what he was: the son of an Anglo-Irish clergyman. What criticism there is of his behavior toward the local people of Roscommon or the small farmers of the west comes, curiously, not from them at all, but from Hyde's more affluent contemporaries. "He never really was one of the country people, for all his talking Irish," said one man; "there was always a lot of the squireen about him, especially in the way he talked and dressed." For this he was in fact respected, declared a woman who had known Hyde as a friend of her parents, who both had been active in the Gaelic League.

He didn't embarrass people by trying to be more Irish than the Irish or wearing a kilt or chattering away in the Irish language to anyone he happened to meet driving cows along the road, as if everyone who looked after a couple of cows was just out of the bogs or down from the mountains. He loved the language, surely, and he wanted others to love it, too. But he was a very courteous and intelligent man; he'd never have such poor manners as to make someone feel bad for not having any Irish.

Such an attitude, however—adopted not as a result of personal conviction but out of overdiligence—was sometimes perceived in members of Hyde's staff after he became president. De Buitléar had a story that he told on himself, about a trip back from Galway one day, passing through Ballyhaunis. Noticing a teenage boy who was lounging against a gate, studying the presidential car with great interest, Hyde ordered the driver to stop, rolled down his window, and spoke in Irish. Back came a gibberish parody of what the president had just said. Indignant at what he regarded as disrespect, de Buitléar jumped from the car and demanded the boy's name. Back in Dublin, he complained to a *garda* official, who had the boy brought into the Ballyhaunis garda station for questioning. The report sent to Áras an Uachtaráin stated that the boy had meant no disrespect but only was having a bit of fun with the old gentleman. He had no idea that the man in the car was the president of Ireland. The interviewing officer added his own comments, that he knew the boy well and was sure he had intended no harm. De Buitléar was abashed, feeling that he had made himself and perhaps Hyde as well look foolish by making so much of the incident. By then he knew that Hyde not only could take such joking about Irish but was not above making a few jokes himself. Often, de Buitléar recalled, Hyde would say to him, "What is it that you call this country I am president of?" and then try to mimic de Buitléar's pronunciation of "Éire" which, according to his aide, Hyde could never say quite right, the slender *r* always proving too difficult for him. In later years, when they had come to know each other better, de Buitléar sometimes used to initiate the routine, in which he would ask the question and Hyde would give the answer, waving his hand in mock submission when his aide shook his head to signify that his slender *r* was still not correct. Hyde was in fact never a stickler for correctness, de Buitléar declared. As much Irish as anyone had was all he would expect; his delight in whatever few phrases a body could speak was what encouraged those around him who were not native speakers to try harder.

By late August 1939 the short Irish summer was visibly over: in the country oak trees were yellowing, and the vines that crept up the walls of great stone houses and twined around the trunks of large trees had turned a rich burgundy. On the last day of the month Hyde was in Galway to receive the Freedom of the City, an honor "exceeding all others," he declared, in a speech prepared in his own hand on Áras an Uachtaráin stationery, because Galway was for him "the most Gaelic city of Ireland." It was, moreover, a wonderful city that had undergone amazing growth and change in twenty years. Although it was a city he always had known well, because of its proximity to his native Roscommon, he had scarcely recognized it, he admitted, on a recent visit to the Taibhdhearc, Ireland's national Irish-language theater, so many new large houses had been built and there were so many new streets everywhere. That the city had flourished as it became more Irish was Hyde's important message. There were those who had said it could not happen—that an Irish-speaking Ireland would suffer economically and Irish-speaking children would be isolated from the rest of the Western world. Here, he told the lord mayor and members of the Galway Corporation, was evidence that such predictions were false. Galway had proved that it could take its place among the cities of the world without giving up its Irishness. In it he saw united the Ireland of past and future. Every true Irish man and woman in Ireland would continue to support and strengthen their language, Hyde avowed, until perhaps one day "only Irish will be spoken in every shop; every house, every street in this great city."

If in retrospect Hyde's sentiments seem exaggerated, rooted more in wishful thinking than in fact, in August of 1939 a city at the edge of Ireland's largest Gaeltacht that was indeed growing in economic strength and population was certainly a symbol of hope for supporters of Irish Ireland. Europe had begun to recover from the worst world-wide depression in history; the fortunes of western Ireland had begun to reverse after centuries of decline. With continued peace and increasing prosperity, prospects of a brighter future for Connacht seemed assured, for despite the general feeling that war in Europe almost certainly could not be avoided, de Valera was determined that, however close the conflict, Ireland would remain neutral. Other countries of the continent could bankrupt themselves in territorial struggles and senseless destruction. Ireland now free, its ports its own to control, would concentrate on its own development, on the education of its own people, on the building—after centuries of domination and exploitation—of itself as a modern nation. Dispatches from American and British consular officers described de Valera as a dreamer and dismissed Hyde as a powerless old man. The world was smaller than it had been twenty-five years ago, when the First World War raged in Europe without touching Ireland's shores; in the coming conflagration, they believed, neutrality would be out of the question.

On September 1, 1939, Hitler invaded Poland. At eleven o'clock that night Hyde was awakened in Galway. A telephone call from Dublin brought him the news and advised that he immediately return to Dublin. There was as yet no emergency—no need of speeding through the night along the narrow, twisting roads of Connacht, across midland bog and plain, until the looming Dublin mountains signaled that he would soon be within the gates of Phoenix Park once more. Nevertheless, it was best that he begin the journey the next day and keep in touch with the government should things change more rapidly than anticipated. In many respects on his return east Hyde traveled from future hope to present reality. Along the route he and his aide stopped at Costello's in Tuam, as was their custom when they were in that part of the country. Years ago, when he was collecting Connacht folktales, it had become one of Hyde's favorite stopping places. A bottle was produced, there was a round of drinks to accompany a round of talk, and the presidential car pushed on toward Frenchpark, so its occupants might spend the night at Ratra. By the time Hyde reached Dublin on the afternoon of September 3—for their lunch Annette Kane had prepared sandwiches of herring skins—the speech he made in Galway was might-have-been. England had declared war on Germany. Again as in 1914, just as he seemed on the verge of seeing his dreams realized, he was defeated by history. The truth of what was happening and what the implications would be for Ireland did not strike him immediately—indeed, not for some months, as events continued to unfold along lines he had not anticipated. But with the invasion of Poland and declarations of war came shortages of materials needed for Ireland's continuing development. At this time of expansion and growth in the west, such an interruption, which continued throughout the war, meant a steady diminution of prospects for an Irish Ireland. Hope and commitment diminished with them, as hard times returned not just to the west but to the entire country. By winter slow and sporadic shipments from Britain had reduced fuel stocks to critical levels; Hyde ordered that coal stored for use at Áras an Uachtaráin be distributed among the people of Dublin, and that turf be brought in from the bogs to heat the president's house in Phoenix Park. Hyde, Cudahy, and de Valera all agreed: it would be a long war; things would get a lot worse before they got better.

Throughout the fall, in letters to Roosevelt, Cudahy warned that de Valera's determination to remain neutral had to be taken seriously. Those who hoped for cooperation between Britain and Ireland could take no comfort, he said, from the fact that newspapers represented the Chief as assailed at home on all sides, the nationalists accusing him of being in Chamberlain's vest pocket and the Unionists denouncing his neutrality policy as treacherously pro-German. De Valera remained in charge, declared Cudahy, and adamant. He warned, furthermore, that any unilateral moves by the British admiralty toward conducting naval operations from the Irish ports returned to Ireland under the provisions of the 1937 agreement would engender nothing but implacable hostility among the Irish. His advice to Roosevelt—Cudahy saw the issues as economic rather than idealistic—was to keep the United States aloof from the British-Irish controversy and, if possible, remain neutral with regard to the war. He himself had tried to convince de Valera to preside over the upcoming meeting of the League of Nations, in hopes that some resolution of British-Irish tensions could be worked out in that international forum. De Valera had refused. Bitter and cynical about the league's influence and goals, certain that the meeting for which Cudahy had such high hopes would come to nothing, he had stated publicly that he would not even attend in person but would send a civil servant to represent Ireland.

War in Europe had no effect, however, on many routine aspects of Hyde's life. That letters from favor seekers continued to trickle into Áras an Uachtaráin, for example, sometimes gave the news from Europe a curiously unreal quality. In November there was a long letter from a Big House in Ballymoe, a small village within five miles of Castlerea: Would the president immediately take steps to stop the transfer of a "great sportsman of a sergeant at Ballintobber [sic]" who "has a great terrier for finding the foxes," asked Hyde's correspondent, further explaining that the *garda* in question was "a topper at the foxes" himself, as was his dog, and it would be "the devil's loss here" were he transferred to county Clare. For his 1939 "Christmas card"—actually a small illustrated book—Hyde sent his translation of *Deirdre*, which had won the vice-chancellor's prize at Trinity, to a long list of friends and associates. Acknowledging the gift, W. M. Crook, a former Trinity classmate, chided Hyde for having missed the last meeting of the College Historical Society, to which he had always been so faithful. At the same time, aware that only an illness could have kept Hyde away, Crook closed with the admonition, "You are very necessary to Ireland, so you must take care of yourself." In January, following receipt of an announcement that Hyde had been elected president of "the Hist," Crook wrote again:

Trinity was always slow to recognize your distinction. I always resented their narrow unwillingness to offer you the Irish chair in the University. Better later than never. They have repented. . . . At your age you are really a marvel, the reward of a well spent life, a life of much achievement in many spheres—and crowned at the end with great recognition.

From abroad also there were thank-you letters for *Deirdre* and for the good wishes from Hyde that the little book brought: other friends, former students, Gaelic League comrades from the old days, and fellow scholars were equally pleased to be remembered, and they marveled each in turn that with all the responsibilities of public office—and at his age— he still took time for the old courtesies that had characterized his personal relationships throughout his life. His mail did not consist only of compliments and congratulations, however. Predictably he received letters also from political opponents, mostly men and women who regarded de Valera as too powerful and his regime as a betrayal of nationalist ideals. Their target was the *taoiseach*, but the president also received a swipe of their satiric brush, because de Valera, it was said, had chosen him. There were also antilanguage people who regarded the Gaelic League as an anachronism and prolanguage people who read its populist programs, addressed in English, as hypocrisy. They, too, wrote letters to Áras an Uachtaráin, for they perceived the league as still controlled by Hyde, but more often they expressed their complaints in public, through broadsheets and similar publications.

One anti-Hyde pamphlet printed in early 1940, entitled *Imaginary Happenings*, was distributed by the Irish Book Society, 8 Upper O'Connell Street. In an essay entitled "Imaginary Manifesto from the Gaelic League," it announced:

We are issuing this Manifesto in English because we want to reach everybody, even the 257 people who do not yet understand Irish, in spite of the success that has attended our efforts both in the Old Gaelic League and the New. . . . This remarkable success has been achieved by keeping Republican politics and mad talk about separation from the British Empire out of our deliberations. . . . We are criticised for remaining silent and inactive when Gaelic Leaguers who are Republicans were imprisoned for their separatist activities, and even when they were at death's door in a hunger strike for justice. . . . but we must above all things be cautious, careful, prudent, diplomatic, non-sectarian, non-political and non-Republican, even to an extent that may at times appear to be non-National. And since we joined up with Co-Co, as the new Gaelic League is called, we have to be extra careful because there are salaries, jobs and pensions at stake—the Hire Culture, as it were. We must march behind Mr. De Valera and his Government in public, no matter how heartily we may curse them in private.

Another essay, entitled "Political Bombshell! Dr. Hyde Refuses to Sign A Bill," was more direct in its attack on Hyde, through the old technique of the imaginary interview. The occasion for the interview, according to the prefatory statement, was his "point-blank" rejection of legislation,

passed by a majority of the minority present in Leinster House on February 20 . . . [that] seeks to make it a crime to think for more than 32 seconds at a time about the restoration of the Republic of Ireland; every other conceivable form of offense being already provided for in the other Coercion Acts.

The "interviewer," the reader is told, caught "His Excellency" at the back entrance of the "Viceregal Lodge" (such terms were employed by disaffected nationalists to communicate their conviction that de Valera and Hyde had sold out to the British) as he was slipping out with his caddy, McDunphy, for "a quiet game of golf" on his private course. "The President of Ireland (less six counties) Hyde" (as the writer labels his subject) defended his decision by declaring it, in an imaginary quote, "'consistent with every action of my public life for the last forty years.'" Moreover, he continued,

I have discovered from a perusal of the splendid stories written about me during the past couple of years by Roddy the Rover and other scrupulously honest historians and humorists, that I have always been a hillsider, an out-and-outer, an extremist, a separatist, a hater of the British Crown and all the devilish things it represents in this country.

Furthermore, it would be "courting disaster" he said, to put his name on yet another of the

infernal British coercion laws against which my new found biographers say I have been swearing all my life . . . and whatever I may want to do in the courting line, it isn't that. Besides, we have enough coercion in force already to wipe out the last trace of Irish republicanism and we haven't been able to wipe out even the first trace of it.

Glaring at his caddy, "who was making signs to him to go easy," the imaginary Hyde then said,

Where would I be only for the Republic? In a moment of aberration and because, as Mr. De Valera would say, I denounced the Rising of 1916 as a criminal business, and told the British Government how I detested the action of Pearse and the rest of them, but it was Easter Week that got me the fine, easy enjoyable job I have today—not forgetting the *Irish Times,* of course, which first suggested my name for the Presidency. I have my job, I'm well paid for doing nothing, I'll probably get a pension like my predecessors here and why should I bite the hand that has fed me?

To suggest that the president of Ireland was no different in philosophy or political affiliation from the British lords lieutenant who formerly lived in the Park, even to the point of being eligible for the same kind of British pension, was a particularly hard slap at the government. Following other allusions to his "'cushy job'" and the "'lashings and leavings of everything and the salary of a prince,'" imaginary Hyde concluded the interview with a final sly suggestion of enlightened self-interest: "'Douglas knows just how much coercion is good for him, and he's as fond of his skin as the next guy. Do you get me?'" Then, "dignified as ever he bowed to your representative, gave McDunphy a prod with the putter, and proceeded to tee."

Libelous as such as article might seem to readers accustomed to today's strict laws, for Hyde it was simply another item to add to his scrapbook of verbal and graphic attacks in the same genre, albeit from radically different viewpoints, of which so often he had been the target during his many years in public life. Nor was it likely that a man who had been the subject of George Moore's satiric pen would be stung by such far less sophisticated journalistic needling: as satire, *Imaginary Happenings* suffered even in comparison with Hyde's own forays in the same field. Nevertheless, the imaginary interview of 1940 did address a particular set of issues that could not be regarded as less than ironic.

Thirty-five years earlier Hyde had published *The Bursting of the Bubble,* his savage attack on Trinity College, the lord lieutenant, the social circle that gathered at the Viceregal Lodge, and other facets of the British Establishment in Ireland. In his prime he often had been denounced for his anti-British attitudes and treated with pained condescension in the pages of the *Irish Times.* Now *he* was the Man in the Park; now *he* represented the Establishment to those regarded as hot-headed radicals; now *he* was perceived as the darling of the staid and respectable *Irish Times!* The truth behind the accusations was that the Gaelic League had gone its own way since 1915, when Hyde resigned as its president. Although he had never dropped his membership and he had always maintained a close friendship with those who had succeeded him, he never had led the league again; contrary to the impression communicated in *Imaginary Happenings,* he had not even been a guiding spirit behind the scenes in recent years. To be sure, he had continued to side with those who advocated promotion of the language through persuasion rather than coercion; for this reason he had been against excluding anyone interested in Irish, no matter how limited in comprehension or conversational ability. This attitude dismayed those within the league who maintained that the time for amateurism was long past, that the major task facing Gaelic Revivalists was the establishment of standards by which grammar and vocabulary might be taught and fluency in conversational and written use might be judged, in order that Irish might be studied on the same basis as French, German, English, and other modern languages. The embarrassing statistics on the poor success rate of Irish-language classes provided further ammunition for anti-revivalists already armed with figures on declining language use.

As for 1916, Hyde, like MacNeill, had indeed opposed the Rising, but not in the manner nor for the reasons suggested in *Imaginary Happenings*. For him the time had not been right, support had not been sufficiently strong, nonviolent alternatives had almost succeeded and could yet succeed. But above all he had feared exactly what had occurred: that Ireland would lose too many of its brightest and most talented young leaders and thinkers and writers; that the country he had struggled to unify would only be further divided. His long-range goals always had been independence for a united Ireland. If out of that Easter week sacrifice of twenty-four years ago had come a new nation, it was a nation still divided—politically and philosophically as well as geographically. By what means would those who now sneered at what he stood for and what he had accomplished achieve what was still beyond their grasp? More violence? A greater and more bitter divisiveness? These were questions that concerned him.

Yet there were points to these attacks that could not be ignored, even though Hyde's presidential powers did not extend into areas that enabled him to address them directly. Was the government stifling justified opposition? Had refusal to engage in dialogue with nationalists as impatient in 1939 and 1940 as de Valera himself had been in 1916 left them no alternative but separatist activities and hunger strikes? As there had been toadies and sycophants around the Castle and Viceregal Lodge, concerned with nothing more idealistic than the protection of their positions and the chance for personal advancement, was there now a "Hire Culture" that exacted loyalty to the government as the price of jobs, salaries, and pensions? Had Sean O'Casey been correct in suggesting that the new Irish government elected by the people was as unresponsive to their needs and wishes and desires and dreams as the old British government had been? Were the people right in turning to the president, through such avenues as *Imaginary Happenings,* to challenge him to provide—if indeed he had no power—at least the protection or assistance of his influence?

Closely monitoring these winds of Irish public opinion, a new neighbor had come to the Park in February. His name was David Gray; he replaced John Cudahy who for the past year had been chafing in his position on the sidelines of the European conflict. Cudahy's sincerest wish, he had been writing to Roosevelt, was to be transferred to Europe where he could better use his expertise to analyze events as they occurred, instead of conducting postmortems when finally the news reached him in Ireland. Where he was, Cudahy was convinced, he could do nothing. He was certain that de Valera could not be moved from his determination to maintain neutrality without some concessions on the border issue, nor would Chamberlain ever be able to screw up his courage sufficiently to confront Sir James Craig and his crowd in the North with the necessity of bringing de Valera around. Cudahy also was not at all convinced that England would emerge victorious in the conflict that now fully engaged it. In Europe, he told Roosevelt, he could keep a closer eye on developments and advise the president of the best moment to negotiate with Germany, if such negotiations appeared inevitable, or increase assistance to France and England. Roosevelt obliged Cudahy with a transfer, but clearly he did not agree that the Irish post had diminished in importance. Nor did the man whom he selected as the next United States representative to Ireland.

David Gray was an intimate member of the Roosevelt family circle. His wife, the former Maude Waterbury, was Eleanor Roosevelt's favorite aunt. Gray had had no previous diplomatic experience when he was appointed to the Irish post six months after his seventieth birthday. From 1893, the year after his graduation from Harvard, until 1899 he had worked as a journalist for Rochester and Buffalo newspapers; in 1899, although he was admitted to the bar, he had turned his efforts primarily toward a more creative kind of writing. During the next forty years he had produced plays, articles, and at least one novel. Since money never had been a problem, he had been able to cultivate his talent without worrying about whether it would pay the grocery bill. His wife also was independently wealthy. The circles in which they moved were educated, sophisticated, privileged. They were accustomed to life close to the seats of power and influence. What did not seem to occur to them was that such a position was in itself a source of power. They took for granted and simply assumed, somewhat disingenuously, that it was right. Lack of actual diplomatic experience or career training in diplomacy therefore did not worry David Gray when the rumor that Roosevelt intended to name him American minister to Ireland became fact. The telegram Gray sent to Roosevelt on February 7, 1940, nine days before the post was officially his, was indicative of the self-assurance, poise, and sense of humor he would bring to the position:

David Gray to FDR: Congratulations on excellent appointment to Ireland.

Aff

The Appointee

Throughout his seven years in Ireland, Gray's communications to Roosevelt were characterized by the same breezy, informal, irreverent style. Beneath their entertaining wit they contained a frankness of opinion and observation uncharacteristic of diplomatic reports. To the State Department, Gray sent briefer, more formal, and less informative communications.

David Gray came to Ireland with the obvious assumption that Douglas Hyde did not count. Although he paid the *pro forma* call on the president of Ireland to deliver his credentials, it was clearly with no expectation that he would be returning frequently to Áras an Uachtaráin or that it was at all necessary for him to cultivate the good opinion of the man who held the office and lived in the mansion. His attitude toward Hyde in his earliest letters from Ireland was a mixture of condescension and indulgence. Although he was but ten years Hyde's junior, his lack of regard was based in part on his transparent opinion that Hyde was a spent force, a bit of nostalgia, a formerly charismatic leader, now over-the-hill, who had outlived his followers. He might have received this impression from a State Department or Home Office assessment based on Hyde's disastrous 1925 senatorial campaign. More likely—Gray was not a man who relied on official files—it was a conclusion he had jumped to on his own. In any case he was certain that de Valera was his man; the Chief was the quarry he had been sent over to track down and put on a leash. To get to him he had to avoid McDunphy (Gray referred to him only as "Hyde's Secretary," as if his proper sphere were behind a typewriter or at the pencil sharpener), a nuisance who did not know his place. Bristling, Gray described to Roosevelt how, first on the twenty-second of March and then on the fifth of May, McDunphy had had the temerity to lecture both him and Vinton Chapin, secretary to the American legation, on the history of Irish neutrality and the futility of American attempts to force a change. Had Gray understood that the secretary to the president was a government official appointed by de Valera, not Hyde, with responsibilities for liaison between Áras an Uachtaráin and Leinster House, he might have regarded McDunphy as more useful and therefore more interesting. Had he realized that Hyde had a well-defined role as a member of de Valera's working team, he might have changed his own strategy. As it was, until mid-April, he spent a certain amount of time going around in circles, for when he had thought up a reason to ask for an appointment with de Valera, he was often referred to Hyde. And when he went to see Hyde, McDunphy sat him down to tea with Mrs. Kane.

On April 12 Ireland awoke to the news that during the night the president had suffered "a slight indisposition." Rumors spread through the country that Douglas Hyde was dead. On April 19 Gray wrote to Roosevelt:

In confidence we have been told that the President, Douglas Hyde, has had a stroke. He will probably make a partial recovery, but it is feared he is through. . . . I at once wrote him a note and sent flowers, and in a few days will write him that you have heard of his slight indisposition with regret and wish to convey your best wishes for his quick and complete recovery.

Gray added a note about McDunphy (whose name he consistently misspelled "McDumphy"): "We had tea yesterday with [Hyde's] sister and his secretary who insists that he is secretary to the *Presidency* and not to Douglas Hyde." Persistently misinterpreting relationships important for him to understand, he took it as "a little friction between the Government and the Vice Regal Lodge," as if the British still governed Ireland and Hyde were the governor general. All would be well, however, he assured Roosevelt, for his wife, Maude, had "made a smash [sic] both upon Mrs. Kane, the sister, and also on the Secretary, McDumphy." Roosevelt's temperate response was a letter to Gray expressing sympathy for Hyde, "a fine and scholarly old gentleman." "If you get a chance," he continued, "tell him how deeply I regret his indisposition and express the hope that some day he and I will have a chance to meet each other."

The "scholarly old gentleman" whom Roosevelt never met, although Hyde outlived him by four years, had suffered in fact only a moderate stroke. For the moment his right hand, arm, and leg were paralyzed. His speech, however, was unaffected, and to the relief of those closest to him his mind remained clear and sharp. Most important, he was determined to conquer his disabilities. For the time being he was confined to bed, with his sister Annette and Nurse Kathleen Fitzsimons from Virginia, in county Cavan, looking after him. His morning conferences with McDunphy were moved to his bedside. The number of items to be disposed of were held to a necessary minimum. All appointments were cancelled while his doctors, family members, and close associates did what they could to ease his frustrations. What bothered him most, because he was reminded of it each morning when he met with McDunphy, was his inability to scrawl more than an undecipherable semblance of his signature. Propped up in bed, he employed exercise and manipulation to regain control of the muscles of his hand and fingers.

By mid-June, Hyde was able to sign his name in Irish ("Dubhglas de hÍde"), his pen name ("An Craoibhin"), and his title ("President of Ireland"). Gradually his hours in bed were alternated with intervals in a wheelchair, pushed by either a second aide-de-camp, Lieutenant Thomas Manning of Ballyferriter, who had joined the president's staff on June 19, 1939, or his sister Annette, or McDunphy. With a plaid rug covering his legs, his tweed cap or black homburg on his head, and his muffler around his neck, once again he became a familiar figure on the grounds of Áras an Uachtaráin. Down the garden path he was wheeled, to the lake where swans and cygnets swam up to seize the scraps he brought, or to the greenhouses for a chat with Luke Nangle, the gardener, or to his study where on his desk official papers lay awaiting his scrutiny or signature. On the mantelpiece of his study stood photographs of his daughters, Nuala and Una. Beside them was an autographed portrait of the twenty-sixth president of the United States, Theodore Roosevelt, who had twice entertained him at the White House during his American tour of 1905–1906 and who had written and spoken publicly of his appreciation of Irish literature.

Hyde's disadvantage was David Gray's opportunity. With Hyde indisposed, de Valera stopped playing cat-and-mouse with Gray and even invited him to informal gatherings attended by Sean T. O'Kelly, Frank Aiken, Sean McEntee, and others who had been in jail with the *taoiseach* in the aftermath of the 1916 Rising. Gray was astonished at the easy way these men joked about May 7, the night before de Valera was to be tried. All those who had come to trial before him had been executed. He described their recollections in letters dated April 14 and 15 addressed to Roosevelt:

They told Dev that he was a goner and cut buttons off his coat as souvenirs. O'Kelly got his fountain pen. To brighten the evening they held a mock trial, . . . charging him with being a pretender to the Islands of Something or Other (some rocks down the bay) and finally condemned him to be shot.

To Roosevelt he commented, unaware of how significantly his observation was linked to what McDunphy had been trying to tell him, "You can't beat people like that. This companionship explains why there have been no cabinet changes. . . ."

A few weeks later, concerned about rumors that the Germans were loading 40,000 men on transports in Norway, Gray assured Roosevelt that unless the Germans were crazy these transports were destined for Ireland, not England. Deeply worried that an undefended Ireland with unmined coastal waters was ripe for a Nazi invasion, he wrote, "It is heartbreaking when so much depends on making this island impregnable" that "petty jealousies and hates" should make a United States stand impossible. De Valera mystified him. At one point, he had assured Gray that he fully expected tremendous air attacks, "not by hundreds of planes but by thousands." At another he had insisted that the only solution was for the North to join Éire in neutrality until both were invaded. At still another he had confided to Gray his conviction that "the freedom of Éire depends on the British fleet." Meanwhile, Gray confided to Roosevelt, he had it on good authority, from a source close to James Dillon, that de Valera had given Dillon, "very secretly," assurances that if a German invasion against Ireland actually began, Britain would provide immediate aid. For himself and Maude he assured Roosevelt, he was not worried. "I did what I have been putting off for two weeks, that is, examine the wine cellar as an air-raid shelter. We could retire there with a corkscrew and be very brave."

De Valera, of course, did not need to be warned of a possible invasion, by Gray or anyone else. The Irish government was well aware of the danger. In the meadows of Phoenix Park railway ties had been set on end in the ground, to a height of about four feet, to prevent gliders from landing. Every day, the rattle of machine-gun practice could be heard, interspersed with the sound of anti-aircraft guns. Nor were these preparations without cause. On August 26, 1940, several Wexford villages had been bombed by the Luftwaffe—by mistake, it was said; three young women had been killed. At Áras an Uachtaráin there was great concern for the safety of Douglas Hyde. The existing air-raid shelter was judged unsuitable, yet doctors had declared that in his state of health he should not be moved outside Áras unless it was absolutely necessary. Procedures issued by the Irish Defense Command called for stretchers to be available inside Áras for removing the president to other quarters while awaiting an ambulance, but they strongly urged that construction of a comfortable underground shelter be considered.

To David Gray, it was inconceivable that de Valera should be preparing for a German military invasion without doing the one thing most likely to save unarmed Ireland from disaster. Still hoping to find somewhere some aspect of the situation that would make sense to him, he consulted Senator Frank MacDermot of the MacDermots of Coolavin, currently an Irish correspondent for the London *Sunday Times*—and an old friend of Douglas Hyde. In such a man Gray hoped to find some understanding of the implications for Ireland of a recent agreement between England and the United States which would exchange overage destroyers for naval base privileges. MacDermot's response was to note that the Irish were having difficulty comprehending how this was, in Gray's words, "a first step toward an understanding of the democracies in cooperative defense against the Dictators."

Several months later Gray wrote Roosevelt that he had come to the conclusion that you either trust de Valera or you do not—but he was not sure which was the better choice. The Irish, he said, "are living in a world of unreality." Using Roosevelt's home in Hyde Park, New York, as an analogy, he complained that with only two exceptions "the whole government is of the timber of the Dutchess County Board of Supervisors." For all his frustration, however, Gray was beginning to understand something of the undercurrents of Irish politics at last. To Eleanor Roosevelt he wrote, "The politician in Ireland who has the custody of the Lion's Tail is the one who wields power." De Valera had the tail, he assumed, because he was honest and sympathetic to the underdog and concerned with the interests of the underprivileged. His government, he declared, was truly New Deal. "I like him very much though I deeply despair of coping with him. He has it over me like a tent."

It was now fall. The shooting season had begun. Although immensely improved, Hyde was still confined to a wheelchair. The doctors' judgment was harsh: he would not regain the use of his legs. Not since as a boy he had first raised a shotgun on the bogs of Roscommon had he missed a shooting season. Even in New Brunswick he had contrived to go hunting in the fall. The doctors were firm: there could be no shooting for him ever again. Hyde turned away, bowed his head, and wept. Several days later he was himself again. He had come to terms with his condition, more or less; in any case, he had no intention of inflicting his disappointment on everyone else; it was already late September; it was time to think about other things. In his old familiar upward-slanting hand Hyde drafted a message of congratulations for Cardinal McRory, primate of Ireland, on the occasion of his jubilee. In mid-October, having considered and rejected several other possibilities, he had described in writing his ingenious idea for a trophy to be awarded at the Punchestown races. Hyde's design employed the two great horses of Cuchulain, driven by his charioteer, Laeg. It required that the action of the horses, their heads, necks and forelegs, communicate the idea of speed. Cuchulain would be shown standing in his chariot, his spear poised; Laeg would be managing the steeds. It was also time to begin work on his annual Christmas publication—a small book that each year he sent to friends and associates. For Christmas, 1940, he had chosen *The Children of Lir*. He sent a copy to David Gray, for which he was thanked warmly.

In a letter to a friend written in January 1941, Annette described how Hyde had taken great pleasure and interest in revising his translation for what he called his "Christmas card." She reported that he was getting on well, except for a cold that had kept him indoors lately. "He is wonderfully patient, never complains or says a word of self pity, and we are very cheerful together. He gets through a fair amount of official work." What she did not mention was that, although less frequently than before, de Valera had resumed his off-hours visits to Áras an Uachtaráin. One topic they discussed were the serious shortages of food, fuel, and clothing in Ireland. In May, Roosevelt offered to sell or lease to de Valera two ships to bring food to the Irish population; for money to buy the food Roosevelt pledged a half-million dollars from his relief fund. With a carrot in one hand and a whip in the other, the Allies were determined to end Ireland's neutrality.

One evening in June the residents of the Park were startled to hear airplanes overhead, followed by firing from anti-aircraft guns. Quipped David Gray, Hyde's closest neighbor, "We get the benefit of any little war that is going on." In December, Pearl Harbor brought the United States into the worldwide conflict. It was the move the European Allies had been waiting for. America's direct involvement, they expected, would at last win de Valera's cooperation. But de Valera remained firm. When Menzies of Australia warned that de Valera's fixed ideas would not be removed by either aloofness or force, Roosevelt's patience began to fray. "People are frankly getting pretty fed up with my old friend Dev," he warned Gray. More overtures were made but nothing changed.

Gray's exasperation is evident in the immoderate letter he wrote to Roosevelt in November 1943:

Your friend Mr. DeValera is continuing to ignore those little events of history which in spite of him keep occurring. He is in fact too busy attending meetings celebrating the revival of the Gaelic language to give his attention to such matters. It is fifty years since Douglas Hyde, the Protestant Anglo-Irish squire from the west, founded the Gaelic League. He now has his reward in being the paralysed, dummy President of a country which would have seen Britain overrun by Hitler . . . without lifting a finger to prevent it. . . . If I go nuts, can you blame me?

In anticipation of the fiftieth anniversary of the league, the Irish and English newspapers had been running photo essays on Hyde. It was evident that neither age nor infirmity had turned Hyde into the "dummy president of Éire." During the year he had made speeches and presented awards on behalf of the Red Cross, the Boy Scouts, and other organizations. In commemoration of the fiftieth anniversary of the Gaelic League the Post Office had struck two stamps bearing his image. Visitors had been appearing by the score at the presidential residence, seeking his signature on these stamps. In characteristic good humor, over the usual protests from McDunphy, Hyde obliged.

That Hyde was in no sense a "dummy president" is evident also in a document that describes a delicate parliamentary dilemma that confronted him in May 1944. The drama—which presented Eamon de Valera with the first serious threat to his position since he became *taoiseach* in 1938—began a few minutes after nine o'clock in the evening. The government had been defeated by a small majority on the second stage of a controversial transport bill. De Valera had two choices: resign or call a general election. Hyde as president had the responsibility for determining which would be best for the country. De Valera had the right to place his opinions before Hyde. It was McDunphy's job to outline the constitutional choices and answer questions. Notified of the situation at his home in Clontarf, on a night when his own car was already in use and Hyde's chauffeur had the evening off, McDunphy set out on his bicycle against a strong headwind for the six-mile uphill journey to Áras an Uachtaráin. When he arrived, de Valera was already there, talking to Hyde. McDunphy waited in his office until Hyde called for him to join them. De Valera quickly outlined the situation as he had described it to Hyde. When he finished speaking, Hyde, propped up in bed, silently looked from one man to another. Catching Hyde's eye, McDunphy suggested to de Valera that it might be important as a constitutional precedent and matter of historical record for the president to be free from any suggestion of embarrassment or influence in making his decision. Hyde nodded. De Valera left the room. Hyde and McDunphy discussed the situation. A general election would be bad for the country. But the only alternative was for de Valera to resign, leaving it to the Dáil to name a new *taoiseach*. Reviewing the current membership of the Dáil, Hyde speculated on the possible consequences of such a move and concluded that, given the fact that no single party or combination of parties could secure the nomination, a general election was the only choice. De Valera was invited to return. He concurred in the decision. The entire discussion had taken almost two hours. When in 1950, in a letter to the *Irish Times,* a reader raised the question of exactly how this matter had been disposed of, the record was there to show that no political crisis had occurred. Both the Constitution and the men responsible for making it work had functioned smoothly. There was talk of Hyde remaining in office for a second term. Hyde declined, in part because he would turn eighty-five in 1945, in part because he believed that it would be best for the country for someone else to have a role in shaping the presidency.

This decision having been made, Hyde began to make an agenda for the time remaining before his departure from office. One of the things he wanted to do was to make some sort of significant gift to the nation. After several discussions with family and friends he decided upon a collection of busts, paintings, photographs, and engravings that would form a portrait gallery of famous figures in Irish history. McDunphy researched the possibilities; Hyde made the choices. Together they wrote the letters and made the telephone calls necessary to obtain what they sought. McDunphy supervised the arrangement of items—over two hundred of them—in a second-floor gallery at Áras an Uachtaráin. The exhibit was planned to open on the eve of Hyde's departure from office.

A second task involved choosing appropriate gifts for the personal and official staff of Áras an Uachtaráin. There were also letters to send, memoirs to write, personal possessions to dispose of, and portrait and photo sessions for which he had agreed to sit. Eamon de Buitléar, his first aide-de-camp, had been recalled for army duties in March 1941. Thomas Manning would be leaving the president's staff on Hyde's last day in office, June 25, 1945. Michael McDunphy remained at Áras an Uachtaráin as secretary to the new president, Sean T. O'Kelly. Nurse Fitzsimons went with Hyde to Little Ratra, a smaller residence in the Park that was being readied for him.

20

Death and Dispersal

The decision to move Ireland's first former president into the lodge in Phoenix Park that was the home of the lord lieutenant's private secretary was made by de Valera and McDunphy some weeks before Hyde was to leave office in June 1945. Designated "Little Ratra," the lodge that stood near the Blackhorse Avenue gate to the Park was Douglas Hyde's last residence. There, under the care of Nurse Fitzsimons (Hyde called her "the dark little one"), who had been at his side since his stroke in April 1940, comfortable in a favorite old tweed jacket, he received regular visits from Annette, Una, Michael McDunphy, and Dr. Boxwell and occasional visits from his closest old friends, including Eamon de Valera. Although now free of the staff that had constantly surrounded him, anticipating his needs and reminding him of his responsibilities for seven years, he missed the small pleasures of daily life at the Áras: feeding the swans in the park pond; circling the Áras, followed by a friendly pheasant who so trusted him that sometimes it even would follow him through the door of the mansion; chatting with Luke Nangle, the gardener; feeling the unobtrusive presence of genial Tom Manning, his Irish-speaking aide-de-camp from west Kerry; anticipating the special dishes prepared by his "most important person," as he always called her, Miss Dowling; making notes for his Saturday evening talks—part business, part pleasure—with Eamon de Valera; even being scolded for his frequent evasions of routine by the meticulous Michael McDunphy. One of his last acts as president had been to present McDunphy, who had arranged his daily schedule for seven years, with a plaster copy of the original casting of a bust of himself by Seamus Murphy and the original manuscript of one of his Trinity College prize essays, "The Organization of Philanthropy."

In spring 1947, Douglas told Annette and Una that he had decided to make a gift to the Gaelic League of "Big Ratra," the Frenchpark house that he had leased from John French when he and Lucy were married, which had been purchased for him by friends and associates in the league after his return from America in 1906. Except for Lucy, his family had been happy there. It was the house in which Nuala and Una had been born, the house to which he and Lucy had returned when he retired from University College. After Lucy's death on December 31, 1938, he had seen little of it except for brief visits during the August shooting seasons of 1938 and 1939. After his stroke in the spring of 1940 travel had become difficult, and his activities had been necessarily restricted. Confined as he was to a wheelchair, if he went there now he would not be able to inspect the fruit trees he had set out so long ago or stroll from Ratra to the glebe house to wind the clocks for Annette. The Morrisroes and Mahons kept an eye on the place and dusted and aired it regularly, but the jumble of guns, fishing rods, Wellingtons, umbrellas, and overcoats in the hall, noted by Hyde's American visitor, Ben Greenwald, in the summer of 1937, remained as they were. Gone from Hyde's study, however, were the hundreds of books, manuscripts, papers, letters, and press clippings that were his scholar's workshop. They had been moved to the Áras shortly after Lucy's death and then to the Secretary's Lodge when he finished his presidential term. There they were all accessible to him, for he had only to give Nurse Fitzsimons shelf and volume number for any book that he wished to consult, and she fetched it for him.

Thought was not deed: the decision to transfer Ratra to the league was easy; accomplishment was another thing. Not until May 1949 was Annette able to tell Hyde that the transfer that he had signed two years before, finally, after inordinate bureaucratic delay, had been approved by the land registry. She also had to give Douglas the first of a series of disappointing reports about his gift. The Dublin lawyer had written that "every scheme" he had "tried to work out for utilising the house for Irish language purposes" unfortunately had "turned out to be impracticable." Despite strong feeling among many of the people of Frenchpark that Ratra should be preserved, if not as a language study center perhaps as a convent school or hospital, house and land were sold and the proceeds, not the place, presented to the Gaelic League.

At one point the message that Annette had received from the lawyer indicated that the Roscommon county manager had thoughts about taking over Ratra as a "preventorium for young children threatened with tuberculosis." It would be a very good use for the place, Hyde had said, and would result in the Gaelic League getting more for it. In 1949, however, the roof and windows were removed, shrubs and trees were cut down, and the hollow shell was left open to the elements. The property passed through several hands after its sale by the league's agent, the parish priest in Frenchpark. By 1972 the walls had been leveled; the broken stone had been used for fill under a new creamery in Ballaghaderreen; the land itself was let for pasturage.

At "Little Ratra" it was Annette, who had always helped McDunphy with Hyde's personal mail, who took charge of his entire correspondence. Letters still came from every part of the globe. Some were from a new generation of Irish abroad who, determined to preserve their heritage, sent anecdotes, folktales, and poetry in Irish. Some, from scholars as distant as Queensland, Australia, expressed appreciation for Hyde's help in resolving a research problem or for his generosity in writing a foreword to a book. Gathered for their summer colloquium at 64 Merrion Square in July 1948, faculty and fellows of the School for Celtic Studies sent salutations and "blessings on the Craoibhin." Among the signatures affixed were those of famous twentieth-century Celtic scholars—Michael O'Brien, Osborne Bergin, Gerard Murphy, Cecille O'Rahilly, David Greene, James Carney, Brian O'Cuiv, Máire MacEntee—but also those of women and men just beginning their work or newly established in it. Notes, queries, articles and reviews from a new generation of French Celticists arrived frequently and were acknowledged and responded to in accordance with Hyde's instructions. Before each Christmas, working from the lists Hyde had maintained for years, Annette mailed scores of cards which brought greetings in return from such old friends as Sinéad de Valera, who addressed him in Irish as "friend of my heart."

Tended by Annette and Nurse Fitzsimons, visited by Una, his grandchildren, de Valera, McDunphy, and those old friends who were not dead or dying, Hyde lived quietly—for the first time in his life perhaps—for four years. Generally well, although troubled like most bedridden people with a variety of skin ailments, he sustained his good nature. In a later interview with Sean O'Luing, Nurse Fitzsimons remembered Hyde as simple and kindly, always smiling, a man of the people. Even when he had no choice but to summon her to his bedside in the early hours of the morning, to ask her to relieve the torment of his itching shoulders, he was, she said, always gentlemanly, apologetic and appreciative. He died quickly and peacefully, as if he had simply gone to sleep, at ten o'clock in the evening, July 12, 1949.

In July 1941, Hyde had made a will, noting special bequests to David and Ann Morrisroe of Ratra, Frenchpark; to the Irish Society for the Protection of Birds; to the Gaelic League and An Fáinne; and to Aileen Crofton, Kiltee House, Wellington Bridge, county Wexford. In a change from the instructions contained in his first will of July 1929, he asked that his Irish manuscripts be given to University College, Galway, instead of University College, Dublin. All remaining cash and worldly goods—he asked that the latter be sold—he left to Una.

Word of Douglas Hyde's death created the need for the new Irish nation to introduce a new tradition, a ceremonial mourning for a former head of state. Telegrams and cables, notes of condolence, official messages of sympathy from Europe and North America, and personal notes from all over the world from women and men whose lives he had touched poured into Little Ratra. First to pay his respects in person, within twenty-four hours after the news had been published, was Hyde's successor, President Sean T. O'Kelly. With McDunphy's help Annette set up a register for mourners to sign. At Trinity College, the college flag was lowered to half mast and the chief steward was instructed to drape the college mace in black crepe. The day following Hyde's death the Dublin press carried tributes and appreciations. Daniel Corkery declared that Douglas Hyde had restored Ireland's sense of nationhood. An Seabhac credited him with having pioneered a methodology for collecting Irish folklore. To Robert Farren, Hyde had awakened students and scholars in all branches of Irish letters "to be native, continuous, rooting, branching and fruitful." Agnes O'Farrelly saw Hyde's life as a panorama: poet, dramatist, folklorist, and "leader of a lowly cause," "a slave descendant of lofty and cultured traditions, making common cause with his Catholic fellow-countrymen, particularly the submerged of the race."

Douglas Hyde's last journey through the streets of Dublin began at 8:30 A.M. on Thursday, July 14, when his flag-covered coffin with a military escort was carried out of Little Ratra, out of Phoenix Park, to O'Connell Street, by way of the North Circular Road, past the Gresham Hotel. For half a minute the procession paused in silence before the General Post Office, symbol of sacrifice and nationalism. Then the hearse and its escort moved slowly up Dame Street and Lord Edward

Street to Patrick Street and to St. Patrick's Cathedral for a brief service
conducted by the archbishop of Dublin and the dean of the cathedral.
Official mourners from the nation's political and educational establishment huddled in an alley near the cathedral—unable, in an era before
official ecumenicism, to attend the service for Hyde, most ecumenical
of men. Critical of behavior that emphasized division rather than unity
at this time when, to him, Ireland was more than ever in need of unifi-
cation, Austin Clarke captured them in a tableau in the poem in which
he paid tribute to Hyde, "The Burial of an Irish President":

> Professors of cap and gown,
> Costello, his cabinet
> In Government cars, hiding
> Around the corner, ready
> Tall hat in hand.

The benediction in Irish having been pronounced by Archbishop
Barton, the coffin was borne out of the cathedral by eight military
policemen wearing black arm bands. Before them, in solemn parade,
were the clergy, the choir, and a bearer carrying the Trinity College
mace draped in black crepe. The coffin was placed in the hearse. The
hearse moved slowly, followed by long black cars containing diplomats,
politicians, the judiciary, and representatives of cultural and religious
groups. Behind them walked members of other groups and the general
public. Along O'Connell Street stood schoolteachers, schoolchildren,
members of the civil service, office workers, artisans and shopkeepers,
students from colleges and universities, priests and nuns. Some fell in
behind the soldiers carrying reversed arms, the hearse, the official cars.
The "Dead March" from *Saul,* played by the No. 1 Army band echoed
down the processional. As the funeral approached Phoenix Park, a
twenty-one-gun salute was fired by army artillery near the base of the
Wellington Monument. A mist began to fall. At the end of Conyngham
Road the army and police formed ranks to salute the hearse which, followed by an army lorry filled with flowers, slowly turned west, carrying
Hyde on his last journey to Frenchpark. In the next car were Hyde's
sister, Annette; his daughter, Una Sealy; his two grandsons, Christopher and Douglas; Nurse Fitzsimons; and Commandant Eamon de
Buitléar. Behind them rode the president, then Eamon de Valera,
Michael McDunphy, and representatives of the Gaelic League. As the
funeral motorcade passed through towns, from Mullingar to Longford

and Carrick-on-Shannon and Boyle, honor guards stood ready for their last salute to the nation's first president. At Rathdown near Longford, schoolteachers and their children stood at attention as the procession passed. The motorcade grew longer as it crossed into county Roscommon. In Frenchpark the entire population of the village lined the road as they had eleven years ago on May 15, 1938, when they celebrated Hyde's election to the presidency.

Outside the church at Portahard a large crowd awaiting the coffin included Catholic clergy, all friends of Hyde, many of whom had worked with him in the early years of the Gaelic League; Molly O'Conor, wife of William Teeling, M.P., representing her brother Charles O'Conor Don, S.J.; Lady de Freyne, Lord de Freyne, Major Pakenham-Mahon, Madame MacDermot, The MacDermot, and friends and neighbors beyond number. After the Office of Committal the coffin was carried to the far corner of the Hyde plot in the small adjoining graveyard. At Annette's request the military-police escort did not fire the traditional rifle salute over the grave lined with moss and flowers from the de Freyne gardens. Una dropped a small flowering branch, *an craoibhín aoibhinn,* on the lowered coffin. Douglas Hyde's journey had ended.

Next came the dispersal. In the weeks following, Commandant de Buitléar, at Annette's request, worked at Little Ratra, sorting out Hyde's books, many dating from his student years at Trinity. Announcements were published that a public auction of books, furniture, pictures, silver, and plate would be held at Little Ratra beginning October 10 and continuing daily until everything was sold. On October 11 in the drawing room of Little Ratra, Hyde's personal library, carefully and lovingly acquired over a period of more than eighty years, went to new owners. Included were the complete works of Shakespeare, Scott, Shelley, Wordsworth, and Spenser; dozens of prize books won by Hyde, resplendent in their rich morocco bindings, impressed with the gold arms of Trinity; dozens of Irish-language dictionaries, grammars, and texts, many annotated in Hyde's own hand; autographed copies of books that had been presented to Hyde by such authors as Lady Gregory, W. B. Yeats, Synge, Patrick Pearse, and George Moore; and much more. Auctioneer Eric Maguire withdrew Hyde's Greek New Testament printed in 1602 when it failed to meet the reserve price. Everything else went under the hammer. Hyde's correspondence and papers, accumulated over many decades—including some belonging to

his presidency—were similarly disposed of. Items remaining were removed for storage to McKee Barracks. There they gradually decreased
in number until 1970, when those that had not disappeared or dis-
integrated were rescued. Most of these are now preserved in the Manuscript Collection of the National Library of Ireland.

Sources Consulted

I. Works written, edited, translated by Douglas Hyde

A. BOOKS AND PAMPHLETS

A Literary History of Ireland. London: T. Fisher Unwin, 1899. Reprint (Introduction by Brian Ó Cuiv) London: Benn, 1967.

A University Scandal. Dublin: Eblana Press, 1899.

Abhráin atá Leagtha ar an Reachtúire, or *Songs Ascribed to Raftery.* Dublin: Gill & Son, 1903. Reprint Shannon: Irish University Press, 1973.

Abhráin Diadha Chúige Connacht, or *Religious Songs of Connacht.* 2 vols. London: T. Fisher Unwin, 1906. Reprint Shannon: Irish University Press, 1972.

Abhráin Grádh Chúige Connacht, or *Love Songs of Connacht.* Dublin: Gill, and London: T. Fisher Unwin, 1893. Reprint New York: Barnes & Noble, 1969.

An Bhliadhain (The year). Dublin: Three Candles, 1944.

An Sgeuluidhe Gaedhealach (Irish stories). London: David Nutt and Dublin: Gill & Son, 1901.

An Tarbh Breac (The speckled bull). Easy Irish Texts, 2. Dublin: Gill & Son, 1905.

Beside the Fire. London: David Nutt, 1890. Reprint Dublin: Irish Academic Press, 1978.

With D. J. O'Donoghue. *Catalogue of the Books and Manuscripts Comprising the Library of the Late Sir John T. Gilbert.* Dublin: Browne & Nolan, 1918.

The Children of Lir. Dublin: Talbot Press, 1940.

The Children of Tuireann. Dublin: Talbot Press, 1941.

The Conquests of Charlemagne. See *Gabhaltais Shearluis Mhóir.*

Contes Gaeliques (Irish stories). Trans. Georges Dottin. Bibliothèque Celtique. Paris: Editions Jean Picollec, 1980.

Contes Irlandais (Irish stories). Preface and translation by Georges Dottin. Rennes: Plihon & Hervé, and Paris: H. Welter, 1901.

Deirdre. Dublin: Talbot Press, 1939.

Filidheacht Gaedhealach (The art of Irish poetry). Dublin: Gill & Son, 1902.

Five Irish Stories. Dublin: Gill & Son, 1896.

Four Irish Stories. Dublin: Gill & Son, 1898.

Gabhaltais Shearluis Mhóir (The conquests of Charlemagne). London: Irish Texts Society, 1917.

Giolla An Fhiugha, or *The Lad of the Ferule; Eachtra Cloinne Rígh na n-Loruaidhe,* or *Adventures of the Children of the King of Norway.* London: David Nutt, 1899.

The Irish Language and Irish Intermediate Education: Dr. Hyde's Evidence. Gaelic League Pamphlets No. 13. Dublin: Gaelic League, 1901.

The Irish Language and Irish Intermediate Education: Dr. Hyde's Reply to Dr. Atkinson. Gaelic League Pamphlets No. 16. Dublin: Gaelic League, 1901.

Irish Poetry. MacTernan Prize Essays, 2. Dublin: Society for the Preservation of the Irish Language/M. H. Gill, 1902.

The Last Three Centuries of Gaelic Literature. London: Irish Literary Society, 1894.

Leabhar Sgeulaigheachta (A book of storytelling). Dublin: Gill, 1889.

Legends of Saints and Sinners. Dublin: Talbot Press, 1915.

Love Songs of Connacht. See *Abhráin Grádh Chúige Connacht.*

Mise agus An Connradh (Myself and the league). Dublin: Stationery Office, 1937.

Mo Thuras go h-Americe (My voyage to America). Dublin: Stationery Office, 1937.

Ocht Sgéalta ó Coillte Mághach (Eight stories from Kiltimagh). Dublin: Irish Folklore Society, 1936.

The Religious Songs of Connacht. See *Abhráin Diadha Chúige Connacht.*

Selected Plays of Douglas Hyde. Introduction by Gareth W. Dunleavy and Janet E. Dunleavy. Translations by Lady Gregory. Gerrard's Cross: Colin Smythe, 1990.

Sgéalta Thomais Ui Chathasaigh (Mayo stories told by Thomas Casey). Dublin: Educational Company, 1939.

Sgéaluidhe Fíor na Seachtmhaine (The week's genuine storyteller). Dublin: Gill & Son, 1909.

Songs Ascribed to Raftery. See *Abhráin atá Leagtha ar an Reachtúire.*

The Songs of Connacht, I–III. Ed. Breandán Ó Conaire. Dublin: Irish Academic Press, 1985.

Songs of St. Columcille. Dublin: Talbot Press, 1941.

The Story of Early Gaelic Literature. London: T. Fisher Unwin, 1895. Reprint 1920.

Taibhse An Chrainn (The spectre of the cross). Easy Irish Texts 1. Dublin: Cahill, 1915.

Úbhla de'n Chraoibh (Apples from the branch). Dublin: Gill & Son, 1900.

B. ITEMS IN BOOKS AND PERIODICALS

"The Adventures of Léithin." *Celtic Review* 10 (1914–1916):116–43.

"An Agallamh Beag." *Lia Fáil* 1 (1924):79–107.

"Beann agus Bunnan." *Lia Fáil* 1 (1927):183–84.

"The Book of the O'Conor Don." *Eriú* 7 (1916):78–99.

"Deux notes du manuscrit irlandais de Rennes." *Revue Celtique* 16 (1895):420.

"Differences Between the Gael and the Gall." In *Voices from the Hills: A Memento of the Gaelic Rally.* Glasgow, 1927.

"Eachtra na gConnachtach." *Lia Fáil* 1 (1927):153–60.

"A Few Rhymed Proverbs (with translations)." *Celtic Review* 1 (1904):18.

"Gaelic Folk Songs." In *Language, Lore and Lyrics,* trans. and ed. Breandán Ó Conaire. Dublin: Irish Academic Press, 1986.

"The Gaelic Revival." In *Language, Lore and Lyrics,* trans. and ed. Breandán Ó Conaire. Dublin: Irish Academic Press, 1986.

"The Great Work of the Gaelic League." In *Language, Lore and Lyrics,* trans. and ed. Breandán Ó Conaire. Dublin: Irish Academic Press, 1986.

"An Irish Folk-Ballad." *Eriú* 2 (1905):77–81.

"Irish Folk-lore." In *Language, Lore and Lyrics,* trans. and ed. Breandán Ó Conaire. Dublin: Irish Academic Press, 1986.

"Irish Folk Songs." *Providence Sunday Journal,* 16 February 1890.

"An Irish Funeral Oration over Owen O'Neill of the House of Clanaboy." *Ulster Journal of Archaeology* 3 (1897):258–71; 4 (1897):50–55.

"The Irish Language." In *Language, Lore and Lyrics,* trans. and ed. Breandán Ó Conaire. Dublin: Irish Academic Press, 1986.

"Leabhar an Domhnallaigh." *Gaelic Journal* (1904):667–68, 694.

"Letter from Dr. Douglas Hyde." *An Smaointeoir* 1, 1 (1919):10.

"From the Little Branch to the New Island." *Dublin Magazine* 13, 4 (1938):9–29.

"The Necessity for De-Anglicising Ireland." In *Language, Lore and Lyrics,* trans. and ed. Breandán Ó Conaire. Dublin: Irish Academic Press, 1986.

"The New National University in Ireland and the Irish Language." *The Celtic Review* 5 (1909):319–26.

"Ocht Sgéalta ó Choillte Maghach." *Études Celtiques* 2 (1937):142.

"On Some Indian Folk-lore." In *Langauge, Lore and Lyrics,* trans. and ed. Breandán Ó Conaire. Dublin: Irish Academic Press, 1986.

"On the Terminations -*áiste,* -*iste,* etc. in Substantives." *Gadelica* 1 (1912–1913):79–82.

"Oscar au fléau, légende ossianique." *Revue Celtique* 13 (1892):417–25.

"A Plea for the Irish Language." In *Language, Lore and Lyrics,* trans. and ed. Breandán Ó Conaire. Dublin: Irish Academic Press, 1986.

Preface to *The Irish Poems of Alfred Perceval Graves*. 2 vols. Dublin: Maunsel, and London: T. Fisher Unwin, 1908.

"The Reeves Manuscript of the *Agallah na Senorach*." *Revue Celtique* 38 (1920–1921):289–95.

"Sean Ráidhte i bhfoirm leath-rann." *An Reult* 1, 1 (1920):12–18.

"Seilg Mhór Sliabh Luachra." *Miscellany Presented to Kuno Meyer*, ed. Osborn Bergin and Carl Marstrander. Halle: Niemeyer, 1912.

"Smaointe Bhrón." *Dublin University Review* (August 1885):58–59.

"Smaointe: Thoughts." In *Language, Lore and Lyrics*, trans. and ed. Breandán Ó Conaire. Dublin: Irish Academic Press, 1986.

"Some Words on Irish Folk-lore." In *Language, Lore and Lyrics*, trans. and ed. Breandán Ó Conaire. Dublin: Irish Academic Press, 1986.

"Some Words about Unpublished Literature." In *Language, Lore and Lyrics*, trans. and ed. Breandán Ó Conaire. Dublin: Irish Academic Press, 1986.

"Sparling's Irish Minstrelsy." *Irish Monthly* (March 1888):175–79.

"A Story in Gaelic—An Adventure in Nebraska." *Irish Rosary* (January 1901):78–80.

"The Unpublished Songs of Ireland." In *Language Lore and Lyrics*, trans. and ed. Breandán Ó Conaire. Dublin: Irish Academic Press, 1986.

"The Well of 'D' Yerree-in-Dowan." *Irish Homestead* (December 1898):4–6.

II. General

A. BOOKS AND PAMPHLETS

Adams, Hazard. *Lady Gregory*. Lewisburgh, Pa: Bucknell University Press, 1973.

Annual Report of the Gaelic League and Proceedings of Ard-Fheis. Dublin: Gaelic League, 1904, 1905, 1908, 1912, 1913.

An Seabhac [Pádraig Ó Siochfhradha]. *Seanín no Eachtra Mic Mí-Rialta*. Pictures by Una Hyde. Dublin: Maunsel & Roberts, 1922.

Barrett, S. J., ed. *Proceedings of the Third Oireachtas . . . 7 June 1899*. Dublin: Gaelic League, 1900.

Beckett, J. C. *The Anglo-Irish Tradition*. Ithaca, N.Y.: Cornell University Press, 1976.

Boyd, Ernest. *Ireland's Literary Renaissance*. Dublin and London: Maunsel, 1916. Rev. ed., New York: Knopf, 1922.

Bromage, Mary C. *Churchill and Ireland*. Notre Dame: University of Notre Dame Press, 1964.

Brown, Malcolm. *The Politics of Irish Literature from Thomas Davis to W. B. Yeats*. Seattle: University of Washington Press, 1972.

Canfield, Curtis. *Plays of the Irish Renaissance 1880–1930*. New York: I. Washburn, 1929. Reprint 1938.

Casey, Daniel J., and Rhodes, Robert E., eds. *Views of the Irish Peasantry 1800–1916*. Hamden, Conn.: Shoestring Press, 1977.

Clarke, Austin. *Twice Round the Black Church*. London: Routledge & Kegan Paul, 1962.

Coffey, Diarmid. *Douglas Hyde*. Irishmen of Today. Dublin and London: Maunsel, 1917.

———. *Douglas Hyde, President of Ireland*. Dublin and Cork: Talbot Press, 1938.

Coffey, Thomas. *Agony at Easter*. New York: Macmillan, 1969.

Colum, Mary. *Life and the Dream*. Garden City, N.Y.: Doubleday, 1947.

Corkery, Daniel. *The Philosophy of the Gaelic League*. Dublin: Gaelic League, 1948.

———. *What's This About the Gaelic League?* Dublin: Gaelic League, 1942.

Cousins, James H., and Margaret E. *We Two Together*. Madras: Ganesh, 1950.

Coxhead, Elizabeth. *Lady Gregory: A Literary Portrait*. London: Secker and Warburg, 1961.

Curtis, Lewis Perry. *Apes and Angels*. Washington: Smithsonian Institution Press, 1971.

Dagg, T. S. C. *[Trinity] College Historical Society, A History (1770–1920)*. Dublin, n.d.

Daly, Dominic. *The Young Douglas Hyde*. Dublin: Irish University Press, 1974.

De Burca, Marcus. *The GAA: A History*. Dublin: Gaelic Athletic Association, 1980.

Digby, Margaret. *Horace Plunkett, An Anglo-American Irishman*. Oxford: Blackwell, 1949.

Dorson, Richard. *The British Folklorists, A History*. London: Routledge & Kegan Paul, 1968.

Doyle, David Noel, and Owen Dudley Edwards, eds. *America and Ireland 1776–1976: The American Identity and the Irish Connection*. Westport, Conn.: Greenwood Press, 1980.

Dublin Opinion. Dublin: December 1937.

Duffy, Sir Charles Gavin. *Young Ireland: A Fragment of Irish History*. 1840–1850. New York: Appleton, 1881.

Dunleavy, Gareth W. *Douglas Hyde*. Irish Writers Series. Lewisburgh, Pa.: Bucknell University Press, 1974.

Dunleavy, Gareth W., and Janet E. *The O'Conor Papers*. Madison: University of Wisconsin Press, 1977.

Dunleavy, Janet E. *George Moore: The Artist's Vision, the Storyteller's Art*. Lewisburgh, Pa.: Bucknell University Press, 1973.

Edwards, R. D. *Patrick Pearse: The Triumph of Failure*. London: Victor Gollancz, 1977.

Ellis-Fermor, Una. *The Irish Dramatic Movement*. 2d ed. London: Methuen, 1954.

Féilire na Gaedhilge. Dublin: Gaelic League, 1904.

Finneran, R. J., Harper, G. M., and Wm. Murphy. *Letters to W. B. Yeats*. London: Macmillan, 1977.

Flower, Robin. *The Irish Tradition*. London: Oxford University Press, 1947.

Gonne, Maud. *A Servant of the Queen*. Dublin: Golden Eagle Books, 1950.

Greene, David. *Writing in Irish Today*. Cork: Mercier, 1972.

Gregory, Isabella Augusta (Lady), ed. *Ideals in Ireland*. London: At the Unicorn, 1901.

———. *Poets and Dreamers: Studies and Translations from the Irish*. Port Washington, N.Y.: Kennikat Press, 1967.

———. *Our Irish Theatre*. New York: Capricorn Books, 1970.

Hobson, Bulmer. *Saorstat Eireann-Irish Free State Official Handbook*. Dublin: Talbot Press, 1932.

Hogan, Robert, and Michael J. O'Neill. *Joseph Holloway's Irish Theatre*. Carbondale: Southern Illinois University Press, 1967.

Hone, Joseph. *The Life of George Moore*. New York: Macmillan, 1936.

Howarth, Herbert. *The Irish Writers, 1880–1940*. London: Rockliff, 1958.

Hurley, Michael, S.J., ed. *Irish Anglicanism, 1869–1969*. Dublin: Allen Figgis, 1970.

Imeachta An Oireachtais. Dublin: The Gaelic League, 1897, 1902, 1903, 1905.

Kain, Richard M. *Dublin in the Age of William Butler Yeats and James Joyce*. Norman: University of Oklahoma Press, 1962.

Kilberd, Declan. *Synge and the Irish Language*. Totowa: Rowman and Littlefield, 1979.

Kohfeldt, Mary Lou. *Lady Gregory, The Woman Behind the Irish Literary Renaissance*. New York: Atheneum, 1985.

Jackson, T. A. *Ireland Her Own*. London: Lawrence and Wishart, 1976.

Leabhar Cuimhne, 1893–1943. Dublin: The Gaelic League, 1943.

Letters Containing Information Related to the Antiquities of the County of Roscommon During the Progress of the Ordnance Survey in 1837. I. Bray, 1928.

Lyons, F. S. L. *Culture and Anarchy in Ireland, 1890–1939*. Oxford: Clarendon Press, 1979.

———. *John Dillon*. Chicago: University of Chicago Press, 1968.

———. *Charles Stewart Parnell*. London: Collins, 1977.

McCarthy, Justin, ed. *Irish Literature*. 10 vols. Chicago: DeBowen-Elliott, 1904.

McDunphy, Michael. *The President of Ireland: His Powers, Functions and Duties*. Dublin: Browne & Nolan, 1945.

MacLysaght, Edward. *Changing Times, Ireland Since 1898*. Gerrards Cross: Colin Smythe, 1978.

Macnie, J. *The Celebrity Zoo (First Visit)*. Dublin: Browne and Nolan, 1925.

Maher, Helen. *Roscommon Authors*. Roscommon: Roscommon County Library, 1978.

Marieton, Paul. *Un Felibre Irelandais, W. C. Bonaparte-Wyse*. Lyon, 1882.

Martin, F. X., and Byrne, F. J. eds. *The Scholar Revolutionary*. New York: Barnes and Noble, 1973.

Maxwell, D. E. S. *A Critical History of Modern Irish Drama, 1891–1980*. Cambridge and New York: Cambridge University Press, 1984.

Meenan, James, ed. *Centenary History of the Literary and Historical Society of University College Dublin, 1855–1955*. Tralee, 1955.

Moody, T. W. *The Fenian Movement*. Cork: Mercier, 1968.

Ní Mhuiriosa, Máirín. *Réamh-Chonraitheoirí*. Dublin: Clódhanna Teoranta, 1968.

Nowlan, Kevin, ed. *The Making of 1916*. Dublin: Stationery Office, 1969.

O'Broin, Leon. *Fenian Fever: An Anglo-American Dilemma.* London: Chatto and Windus, 1971.

O'Casey, Sean. *Drums Under the Windows.* New York: Macmillan, 1960.

O'Connor, Ulick. *All the Olympians.* New York: Atheneum, 1984.

O'Conor-Eccles, Charlotte. *Simple Advice to Be Followed by All Who Desire the Good of Ireland, and Especially by Gaelic Leaguers.* Dublin: An Cló-Chumann, n.d.

Ó Cuiv, Brian. *A View of the Irish Language.* Dublin: Stationery Office, 1969.

———. *Irish Dialects and Irish-Speaking Districts.* Dublin: Dublin Institute for Advanced Studies, 1971.

O'Donoghue, D. J. *The Humor of Ireland.* London: Walter Scott, 1894.

O'Driscoll, Robert, ed. *Theatre and Nationalism in Twentieth-Century Ireland.* Toronto and Buffalo: University of Toronto Press, 1971.

Ó Droighneáin, Muiris. *Taighde i gComhair Stair Litridheachta.* Dublin: Stationery Office, 1936.

O'Faolain, Sean. *Vive Moi.* Boston: Little Brown, 1963.

O'Growney, Eugene. *Simple Lessons in Irish.* Gaelic League Series I. Dublin: Gaelic League, 1894.

O'Hegarty, P. S. *A History of Ireland Under the Union, 1801–1922.* London: Methuen, 1932. Reprint New York: Kraus, 1969.

Ó Lochlainn, Colm. *Irish Men of Learning.* Dublin: Three Candles, 1947.

Ó Muimhneachain, Aindrias. *An Claidheamh Soluis.* Dublin: Gaelic League, 1955.

O'Rahilly, Thomas. *Irish Dialects Past and Present.* Dublin, 1932. Reprint Dublin Institute for Advanced Studies, 1976.

Ó Tuama, Seán, ed. *The Gaelic League Idea.* Cork and Dublin: Mercier Press, 1972.

Pearse, Padraic. *The Letters of P. H. Pearse,* ed. Séamas Ó Buachalla. Gerrards Cross: Colin Smythe, 1980.

Plunkett, Horace. *Ireland in the New Century.* London: J. Murray, 1905.

Reid, B. L. *The Man from New York: John Quinn and His Friends.* New York: Oxford University Press, 1968.

Report of the Gaelic League for Two Years Ending September 30, 1896. Dublin: Doyle, 1896.

Reynolds, Horace. *A Providence Episode in the Irish Literary Renaissance.* Providence, R.I.: The Study Hill Club, 1929.

Robertson, Angus. *Children of the Fore-World.* London and Glasgow: Gowans and Gray, 1933.

Robinson, H. *Britain's Post Office.* Oxford: Oxford University Press, 1953.

[Russell, George.] *Letters from AE,* ed. Alan Denson. London, New York, Toronto: Abelard-Schuman, 1961.

Ryan, Desmond. *The Rising.* 3d ed. Dublin: Golden Eagle Books, 1957.

———. *The Sword of Light.* London: Arthur Barker, 1939.

Ryan, W. P. *The Irish Literary Revival.* London, 1894. Reprint New York: Lemma, 1970.

Saddlemyer, Ann, and Smythe, Colin, eds. *Lady Gregory, Fifty Years After.* Irish Literary Studies 13. Gerrards Cross: Colin Smythe, 1987.

Shannon, Elizabeth. *Up in the Park.* New York: Atheneum, 1983.

Sigerson, George. *Bards of the Gael and Gall*. Preface by Douglas Hyde. London: T. Fisher Unwin, 1897.

Smythe, Colin. *A Guide to Coole Park*. 2d rev. ed. Gerrards Cross: Colin Smythe, 1983.

Stanford, W. B., and R. B. McDowell. *Mahaffy: A Biography of an Anglo-Irishman*. London: Routledge & Kegan Paul, 1971.

Stephens, James. *Arthur Griffith*. Dublin: Wilson, Hartnell, 1922.

———. *The Insurrection in Dublin*. Dublin and London: Maunsel, 1916.

Stopford Green, Alice. *The Making of Ireland and Its Undoing, 1200–1600*. London, 1908. Reprint Freeport, N.Y.: Books for Libraries Press, 1972.

Thom's Almanac and Official Directory. Dublin, 1860.

Thompson, W. I. *The Imagination of an Insurrection*. New York: Oxford University Press, 1967.

Thornton, Weldon. *Allusions in Ulysses*. Chapel Hill: University of North Carolina Press, 1968.

[Trinity] College Historical Society Record Book, 1882–1883.

Ward, Alan J. *The Easter Rising: Revolution and Irish Nationalism*. Arlington Heights, Ill.: AMH Publishing Company, 1980.

Ward, Margaret. *Unmanageable Revolutionaries, Women and Irish Nationalism*. London and Dingle: Brandon Book Publishers, 1983.

Webb, D. A., ed. *Of One Company: Biographical Studies of Famous Trinity Men*. Dublin: Icarus, 1951.

Weld, Isaac. *Statistical Survey of the County of Roscommon*. Dublin: R. Graisberry, 1832.

Weygandt, Cornelius. *Irish Plays and Playwrights*. Boston: Houghton Mifflin, 1913.

Williams, J. E. Caerwyn, and Ní Mhuiriosa Máirín. *Tradisiún Liteartha na nGael*. Dublin: An Clóchomhar Tta, 1979.

Yeats, W. B. *The Autobiography of W. B. Yeats*. New York: Macmillan, 1969.

———. *The Collected Letters of W. B. Yeats 1865–1895*. Vol. I, ed. John Kelly. Oxford: Clarendon Press, 1986.

———. *Irish Fairy and Folktales of the Irish Peasantry*. London: Walter Scott, 1907.

———. *The Letters of W. B. Yeats*. ed. Allan Wade. New York: Macmillan, 1955.

B. ESSAYS AND ARTICLES IN BOOKS, PERIODICALS, NEWSPAPERS

Bairead, Ciaran. "Cisteoir Chonnradh na Gaedhilge 1896–1921." *Feasta* 9, 2 (1956):8–11.

———. "Seosamh Laoide." *Feasta* 9, 3 (1956):17–18.

Bairead, Sighle. "Stiophan Bairead." *Feasta* 20, 6 (1967):5–8.

"Bás an Dochtúra Dubhglas de híde." *Parliamentary Debates,* Dáil Éireann 117, 6 (13 July 1949):736.

"Bás an Dochtúra Dubhglas de híde." *Parliamentary Debates,* Seanad Éireann 36, 12 (13 July 1949):1481.

Bergin, Osborn J. "Dr. Hyde on Irish Poetry." *The Leader* (May 1903):151–52.

Botheroyd, Paul F. "Just Who's in Hyde's Bag?" *Éire- Ireland* 16, 2 (1981): 149–50.

Butler, Mary E. L. "An Al Fresco Irish Play in Dublin." *The Gael* (July 1902): 229–31.

———. "Some Intimate Memories of Douglas Hyde." *Scéala Éireann,* 1 November 1946.

Callan, Patrick. "D. P. Moran, Founder Editor of *The Leader.*" *Capuchin Annual 1977,* pp. 274–87.

Cary, E. L. "Dr. Douglas Hyde, A Gaelic Poet and Dreamer." *Lamp* 28 (1904).

Clery, Arthur F. "The Gaelic League, 1893–1919." *Studies* 8 (1919):398–408.

Cohn, Alan M. "Douglas Hyde in *Ulysses.*" *English Studies* 43 (August 1962): 1–2.

Crook, W. M. "Douglas Hyde, An Old Friend" *New Ireland* 9 (3 October 1903):5–6.

———. "Éire's First President." *Spectator,* 6 May 1938.

Dalsimer, Adele. "Players in the Western World: The Abbey Theatre's American Tours." *Éire-Ireland* 16, 4 (1981):75–93.

Daly, Dominic. "The Young Douglas Hyde." *Studia Hibernica* 10 (1970): 108–35.

———. "Printiseacht An Chraoibhín í Litroicht na Gaeilge." *Éigse: A Journal of Irish Studies* 8, Part 1 (1955):18–20.

Dottin, Georges. "*Abhráin Ghrádha Chúige Chonnacht* par Douglas Hyde." *Annales de Bretagne* 9 (1894):447.

———. "*The Story of Early Gaelic Literature* par Douglas Hyde." *Annales de Bretagne* 10 (1895):471.

Duff, A. Wilmer. "Douglas Hyde in Canada." *Toronto Saturday Night,* 8 October 1938.

Dunleavy, Gareth W. "The Birthplace of Douglas Hyde." *Éire-Ireland* 9 (1974):28–31.

———. "Hyde's Crusade for the Language and the Case of the Embarrassing Packets." *Studies* 73 (Spring 1984):12–25.

———. "The Pattern of Three Threads: The Hyde-Gregory Friendship." In *Lady Gregory, Fifty Years After,* ed. Ann Saddlemyer and Colin Smythe. Gerrards Cross: Colin Smythe, 1987.

Dunleavy, Gareth W., and Janet E. "Editor Moore to Playwright Hyde: On the Making of *The Tinker and the Fairy.*" *Irish University Review* 3 (Spring 1973):17–30.

Dunleavy, Janet E. Introduction to *Castle Richmond* by Anthony Trollope. New York: Arno Press, 1981.

———. "Trollope and Ireland." In *Trollope Centenary Essays,* ed. John Halperin. London and New York: Macmillan, 1982.

Dunleavy, Janet E., and Gareth W. "Jeremiah Curtin's Working Methods: The Evidence from the Manuscripts." *Éigse: A Journal of Irish Studies* 18, Part 1 (1980):67–86.

French, R. B. D. "J. O. Hannay and the Gaelic League." *Hermathena* 102 (1966):26–52.

"The Gaelic League." *Irisleabhar na Gaedhilge* (The Gaelic Journal) 4, 44 (1893):226–28.

"Gaelic League Remembers Its Founder." *Roscommon Herald,* 26 July 1968.

Glandon, Virginia E. "The Irish Press and Revolutionary Nationalism." *Éire-Ireland* 16, 1 (1981):21–33.

Greene, David. "The Irish Language Movement." In *Irish Anglicanism 1869–1969,* ed. Michael Hurley, S.J. Dublin: Allen Figgis, 1970.

———. "Robert Atkinson and Irish Studies." *Hermathena* 102 (1966):6–15.

Greenwald, Ben. "A Memoir of Douglas Hyde." *Irish Literary Supplement* 1, 2 (1982):1, 28–30.

Henchy, Patrick. "The Origin of *The Workhouse Ward.*" In *The Irish Book,* Dublin, 1959.

Hull, Eleanor. "Mr. Bergin on Dr. Hyde." *The Leader* 23 (May 1903):202–203.

Kavanagh, Peter. "The History of Gaelic Drama." *The Bell* 14, 1 (1947):56–61.

Keleher, Julia. "Douglas Hyde and the Irish Renaissance." *New Mexico Quarterly* 8 (November 1938):219–27.

Kilberd, Declan. "J. M. Synge: A Faker of Peasant Speech?" *Review of English Studies* 30 (1979):59–63.

Lennon, Michael J. "Douglas Hyde." *The Bell* 16, 6 (March 1951):46–54.

———. "Douglas Hyde." *The Bell* 17, 1, Part 2 (April 1951):41–52.

Loth, Joseph. "Georges Dottin." *Revue Celtique* 45 (1928):435–39.

McCartney, Donal. "Hyde, D. P. Moran and Irish Ireland." In *Leaders and Men of the Easter Rising,* ed. F. X. Martin. Ithaca, N.Y.: Cornell University Press, 1967.

MacCourie, Fionán. "The Gaelic League and the Work of Douglas Hyde." *The Brisbane Catholic Leader,* 26 March 1936.

McMahon, Sean. "Art and Life Blended: Douglas Hyde and the Literary Revival." *Éire-Ireland* 14 (Fall, 1979):112–25.

MacNeill, Eoin. "The Inauguration of President Hyde in Dublin." *The Ireland-American Review* 1, 1 (1938):128–30.

Madden, Regina. "Douglas Hyde, Savior of Gaelic Ireland." *Catholic World* 147.

Mahaffy, John P. "The Recent Fuss about the Irish Language." *The Nineteenth Century* 270 (August 1899):213–22.

Mercier, Vivian. "Douglas Hyde's Share in 'The Unicorn from the Stars.'" *Modern Drama* 7 (1965):463–65.

Meyer, Kuno. "The Monk and His Pet Cat." In *Selections from Ancient Irish Poetry Translated by Kuno Meyer.* London: Constable, 1911.

Morris, Henry. "Gaelic League Notes." *Dundalk Democrat,* 18 March 1905.

Munro, M.N. "*Love Songs of Connacht.*" *Celtic Review* 1 (1904):85.

———. "*Religious Songs of Connacht,* 1–6." *Celtic Review* 2 (1905):381.

———. "*Religious Songs of Connacht,* 7–8." *Celtic Review* 4 (1907):280.

Murphy, Daniel J. "Dear John Quinn." In *Lady Gregory, Fifty Years After,* ed. Ann Saddlemyer and Colin Smythe. Gerrards Cross: Colin Smythe, 1987.

Murphy, Gerard. "Douglas Hyde, 1860–1949." *Studies* 38 (1949):275–81.

———. "Celtic Studies in the University and the College." In *Struggle With Fortune*, ed. Michael Tierney. Dublin: Browne & Nolan, 1954.

Murphy, Maureen. "Lady Gregory and the Gaelic League." In *Lady Gregory, Fifty Years After*, ed. Ann Saddlemyer and Colin Smythe. Gerrards Cross: Colin Smythe, 1987.

Ní Mhuiriosa, Máirín, "Fear Óg ar Lorg na Gaeilge." *Feasta* 23, 4 (1970):5–10.

Ó Cleirigh, Pádraig. "Tomás Bán Ua Concheanainn." *Feasta* 23, 8 (1970): 7–11.

Ó Conaire, Breandán. "Daithi Ó Coimin 's Bunu Irishleabhar na Gaeilge." *Comhar* 39, 5 (1980):21–26.

Ó Fiach, Tomás. "The Great Controversy." In *The Gaelic League Idea*, ed. Sean Ó Tuama.

Ó Lochlainn, Colm. "The Literary Achievement of Douglas Hyde, President of Ireland." *The British Annual of Literature* 1. London, 1938.

Ó'Luing, Sean. "Douglas Hyde and the Gaelic League." *Studies* 62 (Summer 1973):123–38.

Peterson, Basil. "Aiding the President." *Irish Times*, 1 July 1980.

———. "All the President's Men." *Irish Times*, 2 July 1980.

"Political Bombshell!" *Imaginary Happenings*. Dublin: The Irish Book Bureau, 1940.

Power, Victor. "Eugene O'Growney, Arizona, the Catholic University of America, and the Irish Language Revival." *Éire-Ireland* (Summer 1987): 131–52.

Proud, Liam. "Inauguration Day." *Irish Times*, 16 July 1980.

Sealy, Douglas Hyde. "Douglas Hyde in New Brunswick 1890–1891." In *The Untold Story: The Irish in Canada*, ed. Robert J. O'Driscoll and Lorna Reynolds. Toronto: Celtic Arts of Canada, 1988.

Snoddy, Oliver. "Yeats and Irish in the Theatre." *Éire-Ireland* 4, 1 (1969): 39–45.

Stewart, Herbert L. "Douglas Hyde, The First President of Eire." *Dalhousie Review* 18 (1939):181–84.

Thuente, Mary H. "Lady Gregory and 'The Book of the People.'" *Éire-Ireland* 15, 1 (1980):86–99.

Vendryes, J. "*Abhráin Ghrádha Chúige Chonnacht.*" *Revue Celtique* 49 (1932):280.

———. "Douglas Hyde." *Études Celtiques*, 5 (1949–51):414–17.

———. "*Gabhaltais Shearluis Mhóir.*" *Revue Celtique* 38 (1920–21):351–54.

———. "*Legends of Saints and Sinners.*" *Revue Celtique* 37 (1917–19):381–83.

Welch, Robert. "Douglas Hyde and His Translations of Gaelic Verse." *Studies* 64 (1975):243–57.

"We Visit the President of Ireland." *Weekly Illustrated*, 15 October 1938.

Weygandt, Cornelius. "Dr. Douglas Hyde and His Songs of Connacht." *Tuesdays at Ten*. Philadelphia, 1928.

"What Dr. Hyde Told Bostonians of Ireland's Future in Harvard Lecture on Gaelic Letters." *Boston Sunday Post*, 24 April 1938.

C. BIBLIOGRAPHIES

Best, R. I. *Bibliography of Irish Philology and of Printed Irish Literature*. Dublin: National Library of Ireland, 1913.

————. *Bibliography of Irish Philology and Manuscript Literature, 1913–1941*. Dublin, 1942. Reprint Dublin: Dublin Institute of Advanced Studies, 1969.

De Bhaldraithe, Tomás. "Aguisín le Clár Saothair An Chraoibhín." *Galvia* 4 (1957):18–24.

O'Hegarty, P. S. "A Bibliography of Dr. Douglas Hyde." *The Dublin Magazine*, January-March 1939:57–66; April-June 1939:72–78.

D. MISCELLANEOUS

Catalogue of the Library of Dr. Douglas Hyde, decd. For auction on 10th October, 1949, and the following day. Dublin: Eric Maguire, 1949.

E. NEWSPAPERS AND JOURNALS

An Claideamh Soluis
An Lae
Belfast News Letter
Boston Globe
Boston Post
Boston Transcript
Catholic Leader
Church of Ireland Gazette
Cork Examiner
Daily Mail
Derry Journal
Donahue's
Dublin Evening Mail
Dublin University Review
Dundalk Democrat
Evening Herald
Evening Telegraph
Freeman's Journal
The Gael
Gaelic American
Gaelic Journal
Gaelic Union
The Irish-American
Irish Independent
The Irishman
Irish Press
Irish Times
Irish World
London Times

Manchester Guardian
The Nation
New Ireland
New York Times
North American Review
The Observer
Pall Mall Gazette
Pan-Celtic Quarterly
Providence Journal
Roscommon Herald
San Francisco Examiner
San Francisco Leader
The Shamrock
Sinn Fein
Weekly Freeman

III. Rare and unpublished materials

A. PRIVATELY HELD COLLECTIONS

Anonymous collections
Dunleavy collection
Aidan Heavey collection
McDunphy Papers
Ciaran MacGlinchey collection
Tadgh MacGlinchey collection
Henry Morris Papers
O'Conor Papers, Clonalis House
Sean Ó Luing collection
Sealy collection
Colin Smythe collection

B. ARCHIVES, INSTITUTIONS, AND STATE PAPERS

Boston College Library Irish Collection
Boston Public Library Special Collections
British Library
Archives of the British Postal Records Office
British Public Records Office
Franklin Delano Roosevelt Memorial Library
Harvard University Houghton Library
Harvard University Widener Library
National Library of Ireland

New York Public Library Berg Collection: Lady Gregory Papers
New York Public Library Special Collections: John Quinn Papers
Trinity College Dublin Library, Special Collections
United States National Archives: State Department Files
University College Dublin, Archives of the Irish Folklore Commission and Department of Folklore
University College Galway, Hardiman Library, Special Collections
University of New Brunswick, Harriet Irving Library Archives and Special Collections

C. UNPUBLISHED DOCTORAL DISSERTATIONS

Walczyk, Nancy Madden. "Eoin Ó Cathal: Exile in Tir na n-Óg." Ph.D. dissertation, University of Wisconsin-Milwaukee, 1983.

D. TAPES

Radio-Teilifís Éireann: Douglas Hyde items; interviews conducted by James Fahy.
Southern Illinois University Library: Eoin O'Mahony collection.

Index

Designer: U.C. Press Staff
Compositor: Prestige Typography
Text: 10/13 Galliard
Display: Galliard
Printer: Edwards Bros., Inc.
Binder: Edwards Bros., Inc.